STUDY GUIDE

with Practice Problems

STUDY GUIDE

with Practice Problems

for use with

microeconomics

Austan Goolsbee

The University of Chicago Booth School of Business

Steven Levitt

The University of Chicago

Chad Syverson

The University of Chicago Booth School of Business

Constantin Ogloblin

Georgia Southern University

With calculus content provided by
Anita Alves Pena

Colorado State University

WORTH PUBLISHERS

A Macmillan Higher Education Company

Study Guide with Practice Problems
by Constantin Ogloblin
for use with
Goolsbee/Levitt/Syverson: *Microeconomics*

© 2013 Worth Publishers

Printed in the United States of America

ISBN 13: 978-1-4292-6724-3
ISBN 10: 1-4292-6724-0

First Printing

Worth Publishers
41 Madison Avenue
New York, NY 10010
www.wortheconomics.com

Contents

Contents for Solutions

Preface

This **Study Guide** with Practice Problems is designed for use with ***Microeconomics*** by **Austan Goolsbee, Steven Levitt, and Chad Syverson.** Drawing from features in the text, this Study Guide is intended to help you master the core concepts of the course and provides numerous worked-out problems and practice problems to help you better prepare for quizzes and exams. It is our hope that this Study Guide will enhance your experience with the text and help you succeed in your intermediate microeconomics course.

To be more useful for all students, regardless of the degree to which your course integrates calculus, this Study Guide includes calculus material tied to the book's in-text and online mathematical appendices. This content is easily identified by the calculus icon used in the text: ∂.

Chapter 1 provides a walkthrough on how to use the features of this guide, but for handy reference here are the components of each chapter:

Summary of Main Concepts
In each chapter you will find a summary of main concepts for each section of the text. This will help you review the main concepts and definitions introduced in the corresponding text chapter.

Make the Grade
The Make the Grade sections in the Study Guide are similar to the Make the Grade boxes in the text. In these sections you will find more hints and suggestions about how to approach questions on quizzes and exams that you might find difficult, and how to avoid common pitfalls when answering those questions.

Figure It Out Worked-out Problems
In each Study Guide chapter, you will find several worked-out problems, which are similar to the Figure It Out problems in the text. These problems are typical of the problems you will encounter in your quizzes and exams. Each Figure It Out explains, step-by-step, how to solve a problem using the tools you have learned in the text chapter.

Practice Problems
This last section of each Study Guide chapter offers a set of problems that allows you to practice applying the tools you've learned for different situations and scenarios. Going through these problems should prepare you well for solving problems on tests. Practice as much as you can. Detailed solutions for all practice problems are included at the back of this book. But you should look at the suggested solutions only after you've done your best to solve the problem on your own.

In preparing this book, I would like to thank the authors for writing such an outstanding textbook. Many thanks also to Anita Alves Pena, Colorado State University, for adapting much of this material for calculus, and to Erik Zemjlic, Kent State University, for thoroughly accuracy checking this content. I would also like to thank Lukia Kliossis, Edgar Bonilla, and Stacey Alexander at Worth Publishers for their efforts in developing and producing this Study Guide.

Constantin Ogloblin
Georgia Southern University

Adventures in Microeconomics (including the Math Review Appendix and Notes on How to Gain the Most from This Guide)

1.1 Microeconomics (and What It Can Teach about Rosa and Lauren)

Summary of main concepts and relationships

You'll find a summary of main concepts and relationships in each chapter of the Study Guide. This will help you review the main concepts and definitions introduced in the corresponding chapter of the text. There are only few concepts in this introductory Study Guide chapter, but they are important to keep in mind.

Microeconomics

The branch of economics that studies the specific choices made by consumers and producers.

Theories and models

Explanations of how things work that help us understand and predict how and why economic entities (consumers, producers, industries, governments, etc.) behave as they do. To lay out and explain their theories and to build models, economists use the tools of graphs and mathematics. And they gather empirical data (i.e., data from the real world) to test their theories and predictions of their models.

Ceteris paribus

Latin phrase that means "all else is equal." Holding everything else unchanged when analyzing the effect of a particular factor on economic behavior is a very important and powerful method in economics.

1.2 This Book (and How Rosa and Lauren Would See It)

Empirical

Using data analysis and experiments to explore phenomena. Microeconomics has recently evolved into a more empirical discipline.

Make the Grade

This section of the Study Guide is similar to the Make the Grade boxes in the text. Here, you will find more hints and suggestions about how to approach questions on quizzes and exams that you might find difficult and how to avoid common pitfalls when answering those questions. The following is some advice that should be useful for the whole course.

The importance of holding everything else equal (the ceteris paribus principle)

When building economic models, economists usually make simplifying assumptions to make their models simpler and easier to analyze. One very important principle that you should use throughout the course is called *ceteris paribus*, which means "all else is equal." For example, suppose you want to see how the price of a laptop computer influences the quantity of laptop computers people want to buy. To see this effect, you need to hold constant everything else that may influence consumers' demand for laptop computers: their income, their preferences for laptop computers, the prices of related goods (such as desktop computers and electronic tablets), etc. This allows you to focus on the factor in question, i.e., the price of a laptop computer, and eliminate the influence of other factors on the quantity of laptop computers demanded. When solving problems on the tests, always be sure to use this *ceteris paribus* principle: analyze the effect of one factor at a time, holding everything else unchanged.

Following the *ceteris paribus* principle also means that you should not overcomplicate the problem you are given by considering various hypothetical situations or events beyond the scenario and facts provided. In the preceding example, if the problem does not say anything about whether a new, more powerful computer processor is introduced, or a major producer of laptops goes out of business, or a new operating system makes a better use of the touch-screen interface, then you should not worry about these possibilities at all. The problem you are given assumes these and other possible events that may influence the demand for laptops are unchanged, and so should you.

Finally, keep in mind that the "all else equal" assumption also means that when we talk about a particular good, we assume that all the characteristics of the good remain constant. In the example above, when we say "a laptop computer," we mean a laptop with certain characteristics and of certain quality, so we can't say that the price of a laptop computer rises because laptops become more powerful or their screen resolution improves. Such changes in characteristics and features are, in fact, changes in the laptop computer itself, and by allowing something other than the price of a laptop to change, we would violate the "all else equal" assumption.

Figure It Out

In each Study Guide chapter you will find several worked out problems, similar to those in the text. They are called Figure It Outs. These problems are typical of the problems you will encounter in your quizzes and exams. Each Figure It Out explains, step-by-step, how to solve a problem, using the tools you've learned in the chapter. The Figure It Out problems that follow illustrate some basic math and calculus concepts frequently used in economics. These concepts are covered in the Math Review Appendix in the text.

Math Review Appendix figure it out 1

A line has an intercept of 5. Suppose that as x increases by 6, y increases by 3.
a. What is the slope of the line?
b. Write the line in slope-intercept form.
c. Graph the line on a Cartesian plane.

Solution

a. The slope of a line is calculated as the change in y divided by the change in x: $\frac{\Delta y}{\Delta x} = \frac{3}{6} = 0.5$.

b. The slope-intercept form of a line can be expressed as $y = mx + b$, where m is the slope and b is the intercept. The slope-intercept form corresponding to $m = 0.5$ and $b = 5$ therefore is: $y = 0.5x + 5$.

c. Because the equation is in slope-intercept form, we already know that the intercept along the y-axis is at point $(0, 5)$. (Another way to solve for this is to plug $x = 0$ into the equation for the line. Note that when $x = 0$, $y = 0.5(0) + 5 = 5$.) We therefore know that we have a positively sloped line starting on the y-axis at $y = 5$. Furthermore, we know that the slope is such that as we add one unit of x, we get 0.5 units of y. Next, we can illustrate this line in the x–y plane. Notice that when $x = 0$, $y = 5$. When $x = 1$, $y = 0.5(1) + 5 = 5.5$, and when $x = 2$, $y = 0.5(2) + 5 = 6$, and so on.

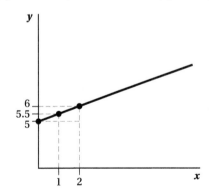

∂ Math Review Appendix figure it out 2

Suppose that a function of one variable can be written: $y = 500x - 5x^2$.
a. What is the first derivative of this function?
b. Optimize the function, and use the second derivative to determine whether this point is a maximum or a minimum.

Solution

a. The first derivative of this function is: $\dfrac{df(x)}{dx} = \dfrac{d(500x - 5x^2)}{dx} = 500 - 5(2)x^{2-1} = 500 - 10x$.

b. To determine the optimum, first solve for the first-order condition by setting the first derivative equal to 0 and solve for x. In this case,

$$500 - 10x = 0$$

$$x = 50$$

To tell if this is a maximum or a minimum, we take the second derivative and compare this to zero:

$$\frac{d^2 f(x)}{dx^2} = \frac{d(500 - 10x)}{dx} = -10 < 0$$

Because $\dfrac{d^2 f(x)}{dx^2} < 0$, we see that this is a maximum.

∂ Math Review Appendix figure it out 3

Line B and curve U on the following graph show two different relationships between variable x and variable y.

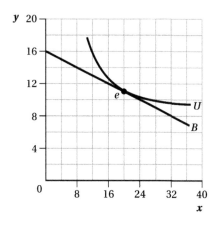

a. What is the slope of line B?
b. Is the relationship between x and y represented by line B negative or positive? Explain.
c. What is the slope of curve U at point e?
d. Is the relationship between x and y represented by curve U negative or positive? Explain.
e. Write the slope-intercept equation for line B.
f. Given your equation for line B, if x increases by 3 units, by how much will y change?

Solution

a. See the following graph. The slope of a line can be calculated as "rise over run," that is, the change in the variable measured on the vertical axis (y) divided by the change in the variable measured on the horizontal axis (x). We can pick any two points on the line and calculate the rise over the run between these points. For example, between point a and point c, the rise is $8 - 14 = -6$ (it is negative because y decreases when we move from point a to point c). And the run is $32 - 8 = 24$. Thus, the slope of the line is

$$\frac{\text{Rise}}{\text{Run}} = \frac{-6}{24} = -0.25$$

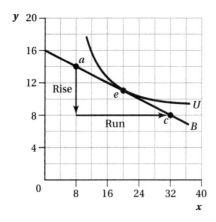

b. Since the slope of the line is negative, the relationship between x and y is negative, which means an increase in x results in a decrease in y. A negative relationship is also evident from the fact that the line is downward-sloping.

c. The slope of a curve at a point is equal to the slope of the line tangent to the curve at this point. Since line B is tangent to curve U at point e, the slope of the curve at this point is the same as the slope of line B, that is, -0.25.

d. Unlike line B, the slope of curve U is not constant. However, the curve is always downward sloping (i.e., has a negative slope). This means the relationship between x and y represented by curve U is negative.

e. The slope-intercept equation for a line is expressed as follows:

$$y = mx + b$$

where m is the slope and b is the vertical (y) intercept. As calculated in (a), the slope of the line is $m = -0.25$. And as the graph shows, the vertical intercept is $b = 16$. Thus, the equation for the line is

$$y = -0.25x + 16$$

f. The slope of the line (-0.25) shows that when x increases by one unit, y decreases by 0.25 units. Therefore, when x increases by 3 units, y decreases by $0.25 \times 3 = 0.75$ units.

Practice Problems

The last section in each chapter of the Study Guide offers you a set of problems to practice applying the tools you've learned to different situations and scenarios. This should prepare you well for solving problems on the tests. Practice as much as you can. Detailed solutions for all practice problems are included at the back of this Study Guide. But you should look at the suggested solutions only after you've done your best to solve the problem on your own.

To learn the intricacies of the microeconomic theories and models, you should be comfortable with basic tools of graphs and mathematics. It is often easier to express and understand economic ideas using graphs and mathematical symbols and not just words. The following practice problems reflect the content of the text's Math Review Appendix and will help you refresh your math background relevant to the concepts and techniques that will be useful in your study of microeconomics. Section 1 reviews basic algebra concepts; section 2 covers calculus that can be applied in intermediate microeconomics. Other chapters of the Study Guide include both algebra and calculus problems. Calculus problems will be marked with ∂.

Section 1: Math concepts and basic skills
Problem 1

The line that describes the relationship between an input variable x and the output variable y has a slope of 2 and an intercept of 8.
a. Write the equation for the line (in the slope-intercept form).
b. Graph the line on a Cartesian plane.
c. Is the relationship between x and y negative or positive? Explain.
d. If x increases by one unit, by how much does y change?

Problem 2

The line that describes the relationship between variable x and variable y has a slope of -0.5 and an intercept of 20.
a. Write the equation for the line (in the slope-intercept form).
b. Is the relationship between x and y negative or positive? Explain.
c. If $y = 0$, what is x?
d. Graph the line on a Cartesian plane.

Problem 3

The line on the following graph shows the relationship between variable x and variable y.

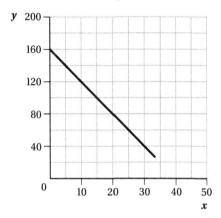

a. What is the slope of the line?
b. Write the slope-intercept equation for the line.
c. If x increases by 5 units, by how much will y change?

Problem 4

Curve U on the following graph shows the relationship between variable x and variable y.

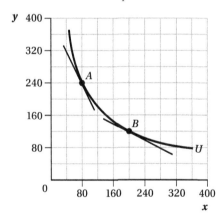

a. What is the slope of the curve at point A?
b. What is the slope of the curve at point B?
c. Suppose $x = 200$. If x increases by one unit, by how much will y change?

Problem 5

Solve the following equation for x:

$$64 = 4x - 20$$

Problem 6

Solve the following equation for P:

$$126 - 2P = -24 + 3P$$

Problem 7

Solve the following system of equations for P, Q^D, and Q^S:

$$Q^D = 75 - 0.5P$$
$$Q^S = -25 + 2P$$
$$Q^D = Q^S$$

Problem 8

Consider the following equation:

$$Q = 16K^{0.5}$$

where Q is the quantity of output produced by a firm and K is the amount of capital used. How much capital does the firm need to produce 80 units of output?

Problem 9

Calculate the shaded area on the following graph.

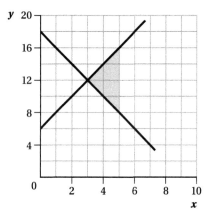

Problem 10

Calculate the shaded areas A, B, and C on the following graph.

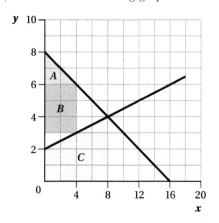

∂ Section 2: Calculus Review

Problem 11

Determine the *first* derivatives of the following functions of one variable:
a. $f(x) = 400x$
b. $f(x) = x^2 + 50x$
c. $f(x) = x^3 - 2x^2 + 3x - 4$
d. $f(x) = 2,000$

Problem 12

Determine the *second* derivatives of the following functions of one variable:
a. $f(x) = 400x$
b. $f(x) = x^2 + 50x$
c. $f(x) = x^3 - 2x^2 + 3x - 4$
d. $f(x) = 2,000$

Problem 13

Determine for which values of x the following functions of one variable are concave and for which values of x they are convex. If a function is never concave or convex, state so. If a function is always either concave or convex, state so.
a. $f(x) = 400x$
b. $f(x) = x^2 + 50x$
c. $f(x) = x^3 - 2x^2 + 3x - 4$
d. $f(x) = 2,000$

Problem 14

Determine the *first* partial derivatives *with respect to x* of the following functions of two variables:
a. $f(x,y) = 400x + 300y$
b. $f(x,y) = x^2y + 50xy$
c. $f(x,y) = x^3y^3 - 2xy^2 + 3x - 4y + 10$
d. $f(x,y) = 2,000$

Problem 15

Determine the *second* partial derivatives *with respect to x* of the following functions of two variables:
a. $f(x,y) = 400x + 300y$
b. $f(x,y) = x^2y + 50xy$
c. $f(x,y) = x^3y^3 - 2xy^2 + 3x - 4y + 10$
d. $f(x,y) = 2,000$

Problem 16

Determine the *first* partial derivatives *with respect to y* of the following functions of two variables:
a. $f(x,y) = 400x + 300y$
b. $f(x,y) = x^2y + 50xy$
c. $f(x,y) = x^3y^3 - 2xy^2 + 3x - 4y + 10$
d. $f(x,y) = 2,000$

Problem 17

Determine the *second* partial derivatives *with respect to y* of the following functions of two variables:
a. $f(x,y) = 400x + 300y$
b. $f(x,y) = x^2y + 50xy$
c. $f(x,y) = x^3y^3 - 2xy^2 + 3x - 4y + 10$
d. $f(x,y) = 2,000$

Problem 18

Totally differentiate the following multivariable function: $f(x,y) = x^3y^3 - 2xy^2 + 3x - 4y + 10$. (Hint: Review the Partial Derivatives section of the Math Review Appendix in your book and then think about how you can re-use some of the parts that you solved for above in the other Practice Problems.)

Supply and Demand

2.1 Markets and Models

The four key assumptions underlying the supply and demand model

1. We focus on supply and demand in a single market.
2. All goods sold in the market are identical (homogeneous).
3. All goods sold in the market sell for the same price, and all sellers and buyers have the same information about prices, the quality of goods being sold, and so on.
4. There are many producers and consumers in the market, so no particular consumer or producer has a noticeable impact on anything that occurs in the market, particularly on the price level.

Supply

The combined amount of a good that all producers in a market are willing to sell.

Demand

The combined amount of a good that all consumers are willing to buy.

Commodities

Products traded in markets in which consumers view different varieties of the good as essentially interchangeable.

2.2 Demand

Factors that influence demand
- Price
- The number of consumers
- Consumer income or wealth
- Consumer tastes
- Prices of related goods (substitutes and complements)

Substitute

A good that can be used in place of another good.

For these types of goods, there is a positive relationship between quantity demanded of the good in question and the price of the substitute (the other, related good). The partial derivative of quantity demanded with respect to price of a substitute good is positive: $\frac{\partial Q^D}{\partial P_s} > 0$.

Complement

A good that is purchased and used in combination with another good.

For these types of goods, there is a negative relationship between quantity demanded of the good in question and the price of the complement (the other, related good). The partial derivative of quantity demanded with respect to price of a complement good is negative: $\frac{\partial Q^D}{\partial P_c} < 0$.

Demand curve

The relationship between the quantity of a good that consumers demand and the good's price, holding all other factors constant. Demand curves typically slope downward, which means that all else equal, the lower the price of a good, the more of it consumers will be willing to buy.

The Law of Demand states that as prices increase, quantity demanded decreases, and vice versa. Mathematically, this means that the partial derivative of the demand function with respect to price is negative. Recall that derivatives from calculus are a way to calculate slopes. (This is reviewed in the math appendix to your textbook.) Stated mathematically, the Law of Demand written in terms of calculus can be expressed as: $\dfrac{\partial Q^D}{\partial P} < 0$, since this is another way to write that the demand curve slopes downward.

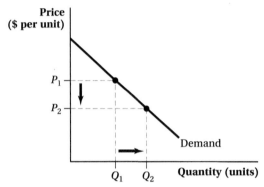

Mathematical representation of the demand curve

A demand curve can also be represented mathematically by an equation. For example:

$$Q = 40 - 10P$$

Where Q is the quantity of the good demanded and P is the price per unit. This equation implies that every \$1 increase in price leads to a 10-unit decline in the quantity demanded.

Demand curve equations are sometimes written in the form of the price as a function of quantity. This is called an **inverse demand curve.** For example, for the preceding demand equation, the inverse demand curve is

$$P = 4 - 0.1Q$$

It can be derived from the demand equation by solving it for P:

$$Q = 40 - 10P$$
$$10P = 40 - Q$$
$$P = 4 - 0.1Q$$

In this inverse demand equation, $P = \$4$ is the vertical intercept of the demand curve (as shown on the following graph), so the inverse demand curve makes clear that no consumer will be willing to buy the good at a price \$4 per unit or higher. This price level is called the **demand choke price.**

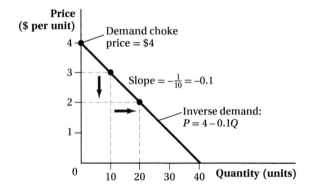

Changes in quantity demanded vs. changes in demand

A change in quantity demanded is a movement *along* the demand curve that occurs as a result of a change in the good's price. On the following graph, the rise in price from P_1 to P_2 causes a decrease in quantity demanded along the demand curve from Q_1 to Q_2.

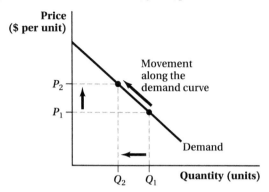

A change in demand is a *shift* of the entire demand curve caused by a change in a determinant of demand other than the good's own price. For example, on the following graph, a decrease in consumer income shifts the demand curve leftward, from D_1 to D_2, so the quantity of the good demanded decreases at each given price.

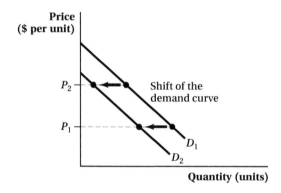

An "expanded" demand curve includes non-price factors that influence quantity demanded (e.g., income, prices of substitute or complementary goods, etc.); therefore, it captures relationships with the variables that shift demand. Rather than writing the demand relationship as quantity as a function of price alone (i.e., $Q^D = f(P)$), we can write an expanded demand relationship as quantity as function of price and other factors (e.g., $Q^D = g(P, I, P_s, P_c)$ where P again represents price of the good, I represents income, P_s represents the price of a substitute, and P_c represents the price of a complement).

make the grade

Verify your solutions to avoid math errors

It is easy to make math mistakes when solving economic equations. To avoid such errors, always verify whether the equation holds after solving it. For example, suppose you are asked to solve for the market equilibrium, given the following supply and demand curves:

$$Q^D = 50 - 4P$$
$$Q^S = -10 + P$$

To find the equilibrium price, you equate the quantity supplied and the quantity demanded and solve the equation for P:

$$Q^D = Q^S$$
$$50 - 4P = -10 + P$$
$$5P = 60$$
$$P = 12$$

Then, you find the equilibrium quantity by plugging the equilibrium price you've found into either the demand or the supply equation. For example:

$$Q^D = 50 - 4 \times 12 = 2$$

To verify you solution, you should also substitute the equilibrium price into the other equation:

$$Q^S = -10 + 12 = 2$$

Since the result is the same, you know that your solution is correct. But if you did not get the same answer, you would know that you made a math error because the quantity demanded must equal the quantity supplied in equilibrium.

2.3 Supply

Factors that influence supply

- Price
- Suppliers' costs of production, which depend on input prices and production technology
- The number of sellers
- Sellers' outside options: alternate markets and alternate goods

Supply curve

The relationship between the quantity supplied of a good and the good's price, holding all other factors constant. Supply curves typically slope upward, which means that all else equal, the higher the price of a good, the more of it sellers will be willing to supply.

The Law of Supply states that as prices increase, quantity supplied increases, and vice versa. Mathematically, using calculus, this means that: $\dfrac{\partial Q^S}{\partial P} > 0.$

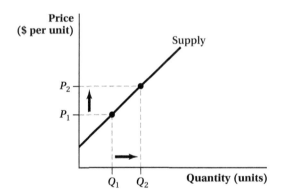

Mathematical representation of the supply curve

A supply curve can also be represented mathematically by an equation. For example:

$$Q = -20 + 20P$$

Where Q is the quantity of the good supplied and P is the price per unit. This equation implies that every $1 increase in price leads to a 20-unit increase in the quantity supplied.

Supply curve equations can also be written in the form of the price as a function of quantity. This is called an **inverse supply curve.** For example, for the preceding supply equation, the inverse supply curve is

$$P = 1 + 0.05Q$$

In this inverse supply equation, $P = \$1$ is the vertical intercept of the supply curve (as shown on the following graph), so the inverse supply curve makes clear that no supplier will be willing to sell the good at a price of $1 or lower. This price level is called the **supply choke price.**

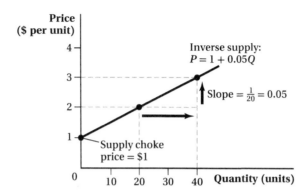

Changes in quantity supplied vs. changes in supply

A change in quantity supplied is a movement *along* the supply curve that occurs as a result of a change in the good's price. On the following graph, the rise in price from P_1 to P_2 causes an increase in quantity supplied along the supply curve from Q_1 to Q_2.

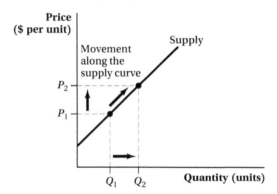

A change in supply is a shift of the entire supply curve caused by a change in a determinant of supply other than the good's price. For example, on the following graph, lower input prices shift the supply curve rightward, from S_1 to S_2, so the quantity of the good supplied increases at each given price.

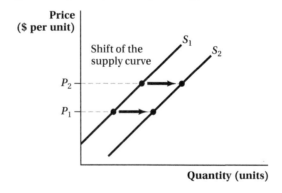

∂ An "expanded" supply curve includes non-price factors that influence quantity supplied (e.g., prices of inputs to the production process). Rather than writing the supply relationship as quantity as a function of price alone (i.e., $Q^S = f(P)$), we can write an expanded supply relationship as quantity as function of price and other factors (e.g., $Q^D = g(P, P_i)$, where P again represents price of the good, I represents income, and P_i represents the price of an input to the production process).

2.4 Market Equilibrium

Market equilibrium

The point at which the quantity demanded by consumers (Q_D) exactly equals the quantity supplied by producers (Q_S).

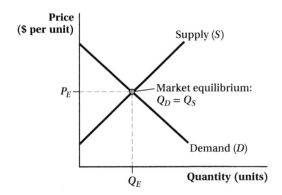

Excess supply (surplus)

The amount by which quantity supplied (Q_S) exceeds quantity demanded (Q_D) when market price (P_M) is higher than the equilibrium price (P_E).

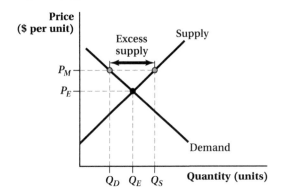

Excess demand (shortage)

The amount by which quantity demanded (Q_D) exceeds quantity supplied (Q_S) when market price (P_M) is lower than the equilibrium price (P_E).

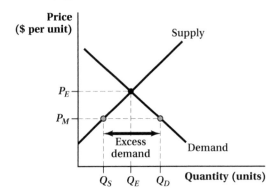

Changes in equilibrium resulted from demand or supply shifts

Curve that shifts	Direction of shift	Impact on equilibrium	
		Price	Quantity
Demand curve	Rightward (increase in demand)	↑	→
	Leftward (decrease in demand)	↓	←
Supply curve	Rightward (increase in supply)	↓	→
	Leftward (decrease in supply)	↑	←

Distinguish shifts of the demand and supply curves from movements along the curves

Consider the following example. Suppose you are trying to predict what will happen to the equilibrium price and quantity in the market for frozen yogurt if the supply of frozen yogurt increases due to a lower price of milk. You reason as follows: "An increase in supply will cause the equilibrium price to fall. A lower price will lead to an increase in demand, which will cause the price to rise. Thus, the effect of the increased supply on the equilibrium price is uncertain." Can you see the mistake in this analysis? Your first statement is correct: an increase in supply will surely cause the equilibrium price to fall. But the next statement is erroneous. A lower price does not cause an increase in demand. That is, the demand curve does *not* shift. Rather, a lower price causes an increase in the quantity demanded, as the market moves along the demand curve until it reaches the new equilibrium, where the price is lower (see the following graph).

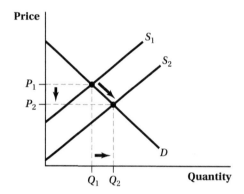

Don't rely on memorization, use of the supply and demand diagram

Although reviewing tables that summarize the effects of changes in supply and demand (such as the preceding table or Table 2.2 in the text) can be useful, relying on your memory when answering exam questions about these effects is not the best way to get the right answers. Instead, sketch a supply and demand diagram. This will allow you to clearly see the effects of a change in supply, demand, or both. First, label your graph's axes and draw a typical (downward-sloping) demand curve and a typical (upward-sloping) supply curve. Mark the initial equilibrium. Next, follow the advice in the text (p. 37) to determine which curve shifts and in which direction. Shift this curve on your graph (i.e., draw the shifted curve). Find and mark the new equilibrium. Now, compare the new equilibrium price with the initial equilibrium price and the new equilibrium quantity with the initial equilibrium quantity, and make conclusions about the directions in which the equilibrium price and the equilibrium quantity have changed.

2.4 figure it out 1

Suppose that the market demand and supply curves for corn are represented by the following equations:

$$Q^D = 600 - 60P$$
$$Q^S = -30 + 30P$$

where Q^D is the quantity demanded (in millions of bushels), Q^S is the quantity supplied, and P is the price (in dollars per bushel). Suppose the current market price of corn is $5 per bushel.
a. What is the quantity of corn demanded? Quantity supplied? Quantity bought?
b. Describe the situation in the market. Is there excess demand or excess supply? How large is it?
c. What do you expect to happen to the market price of corn? The quantity of corn bought?
∂ d. Use calculus to show that the Law of Demand holds.
e. Use calculus to show that the Law of Supply holds.

Solution

a. The quantity demanded at the current price is $Q^D = 600 - 60 \times 5 = 300$ million bushels. The quantity supplied is $Q^S = -30 + 30 \times 5 = 120$ million bushels. Although the buyers are willing to purchase 300 thousand bushels, they can only buy 120 million bushels, since the sellers are not willing to sell more at the current price. Thus, the quantity of corn actually bought is 120 million bushels.
b. Since the quantity demanded exceeds the quantity supplied, the situation in the market can be characterized as a shortage (excess demand). The shortage is $Q^D - Q^S = 300 - 120 = 180$ million bushels.
c. Buyers who cannot find corn because of the shortage will bid up the price, and sellers will be able to raise their prices until the shortage is eliminated and the market is in equilibrium. We can solve for the market equilibrium price as follows:

$$Q^D = Q^S$$
$$600 - 60P = -30 + 30P$$
$$90P = 630$$
$$P = 7$$

At this price, $Q^D = 600 - 60 \times 7 = 180$, and $Q^S = -30 + 30 \times 7 = 180$. That is, the price will rise from $5 to $7, and the quantity of corn bought will increase from 120 million bushels to 180 million bushels.
∂ d. Using the derivative of a constant and power rules of derivatives (see the math appendix to your book to review if necessary), $\frac{\partial Q^D}{\partial P} = 0 - 60(1)P^{1-1} = -60P^0 = -60$. Since this is less than zero, the Law of Demand holds.
e. Using the derivative of a constant and power rules of derivatives, $\frac{\partial Q^S}{\partial P} = 0 - 30(1)P^{1-1} = 30P^0 = 30 > 0$. Since this is more than zero, the Law of Supply holds.

2.4 figure it out 2

Suppose that the demand and supply curves for ethanol in the United States are represented by the following equations:

$$Q^D = 1,600 - 320P$$
$$Q^S = -800 + 640P$$

where Q^D is the quantity demanded (in millions of gallons per month), Q^S is the quantity supplied, and P is the price (in dollars per gallon).
a. Suppose that the market for ethanol is in equilibrium. What is the current price of ethanol? The quantity of ethanol sold?
b. Suppose that a severe drought in the Midwest raises the price of corn, the main ingredient used in ethanol production. As a result, producers reduce the quantity of ethanol supplied by 480 million gallons per month at every price. At the current price, how much ethanol is sold? How large is the shortage of ethanol?

c. After the market has adjusted to the new conditions, what will be the equilibrium price and quantity of ethanol?

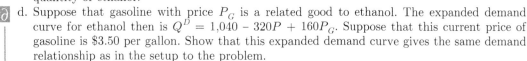

d. Suppose that gasoline with price P_G is a related good to ethanol. The expanded demand curve for ethanol then is $Q^D = 1,040 - 320P + 160P_G$. Suppose that this current price of gasoline is $3.50 per gallon. Show that this expanded demand curve gives the same demand relationship as in the setup to the problem.

e. Use calculus to determine whether gasoline is complementary or a substitute for ethanol.

Solution

a. To solve for the equilibrium price, we equate the quantity demanded and quantity supplied:

$$Q^D = Q^S_1$$
$$1,600 - 320P = -800 + 640P$$
$$960P = 2,400$$
$$P = 2.5$$

To solve for the equilibrium quantity, we substitute the equilibrium price into either the demand equation or the supply equation:

$$Q^D = 1,600 - 320 \times 2.5 = 800$$
$$Q^S_1 = -800 + 640 \times 2.5 = 800$$

Thus the equilibrium price is $2.50 per gallon, and the equilibrium quantity is 800 million gallons per month.

b. As the quantity of ethanol supplied falls by 480 million gallons at every price, the supply curve shifts leftward by this distance. Thus, the quantity supplied at $2.50 is $800 - 480 = 320$ million gallons. Although the quantity demanded remains at 800 million gallons, ethanol producers are not willing to sell more than 320 million gallons at the current price. Thus, the actual quantity sold is 320 million gallons. The shortage of ethanol is the difference between the quantity demanded and quantity supplied: $800 - 320 = 480$ million gallons.

c. Given that the quantity of ethanol supplied falls by 480 million gallons at every price, we know that the supply curve shifts leftward by this distance. Algebraically, we derive the new supply curve by subtracting 480 million gallons from the original supply equation. Thus, the new supply curve is:

$$Q^S_2 = Q^S_1 - 480$$
$$Q^S_2 = -800 + 640P - 480$$
$$Q^S_2 = -1,280 + 640P$$

To solve for the new equilibrium price, we equate:

$$Q^D = Q^S_2$$
$$1,600 - 320P = -1,280 + 640P$$
$$960P = 2,880$$
$$P = 3$$

To solve for the equilibrium quantity, we substitute the equilibrium price into either the demand equation or the supply equation:

$$Q^D = 1,600 - 320 \times 3 = 640$$
$$Q^S_2 = -1,280 + 640 \times 3 = 640$$

Thus, the new equilibrium price is $3 per gallon, and the new equilibrium quantity is 640 million gallons per month. As we would expect, the equilibrium price rises and the equilibrium quantity falls as a result of decreased supply.

d. Substituting $P_G = 3.5$ into the expanded demand curve, we can see that $Q^D = 1,040 - 320P + 160(3.5) = 1,600 - 320P$. This is the demand curve as given in the problem's setup.

e. Since the partial derivative of quantity demanded with respect to the price of gasoline $\frac{\partial Q^D}{\partial P_G} = 0 - 0 + 160(1)P_G^{1-1} = 160P_G^0 = 160 > 0$, gasoline is a substitute for ethanol.

2.4 figure it out 3

Consider the effects of the following two events on the market for soy milk (assuming that soy milk is a normal good):

(1) A severe drought decreases soybean production and drives soybean prices higher.

(2) Consumer income decreases a result of an economic recession.

a. Draw a supply and demand diagram to illustrate the impact of these events on the market (on the same diagram).

b. Predict what will happen to the equilibrium price and quantity of soy milk as a result of these events. Explain your prediction.

Solution

a. On the following diagram, the initial equilibrium is at the point of intersection of the demand curve, D_1 and the supply curve, S_1. Soybeans are an input in the production of soymilk. Therefore, when the price of soybeans rises, producing soy milk becomes more costly, so the supply of soy milk decreases, that is, the supply curve shifts leftward. The decline in consumer income reduces the demand for soy milk (since it's a normal good), so the demand curve also shifts leftward. The new equilibrium is at the point where the new demand curve (D_2) intersects the new supply curve (S_2).

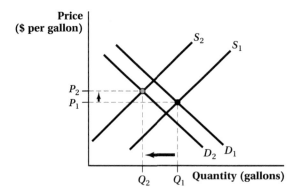

b. Both a leftward shift of the demand curve and a leftward shift of the supply curve lead to a decrease in the equilibrium quantity. Therefore, we can unambiguously predict that the equilibrium quantity of soy milk will decrease. A leftward shift of the supply curve leads to a higher equilibrium price, while a leftward shift in the demand curve leads to a lower equilibrium price. Therefore, unless we know the magnitudes of each of these effects, we cannot unambiguously predict the direction in which the equilibrium price will change. On the preceding diagram, the effect of the decreased supply (i.e., the impact of the drought) on the price is greater than the effect of the decreased demand (i.e., the impact of the lower consumer income); therefore, the equilibrium price rises. But if the decreased consumer income, not the drought, was the dominant factor, that is, the demand shift had a greater impact on the price than the supply shift did, the equilibrium price could fall, as shown on the following diagram.

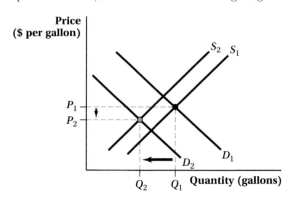

2.4 figure it out 4

Suppose you've noticed that the price of an average notebook computer has fallen, while the quantity of notebooks sold has not changed. You know that technological advances in the computer industry have made notebooks less costly to produce. Given this knowledge and your preceding observation, what conclusions can you draw about the behavior of the supply and demand in the market for notebook computers? Draw a supply and demand diagram to illustrate your answer.

Solution

On the following diagram, the initial equilibrium is at the point of intersection of the demand curve, D_1, and the supply curve, S_1. The decreased costs of production must have increased the supply of notebook computers, shifting the supply curve rightward and lowering the equilibrium price. But a rightward shift of the supply curve alone would also lead to a greater equilibrium quantity. The only cause that could keep the quantity from rising is a simultaneous leftward shift in the demand curve. Thus, we can conclude that the demand for notebook computers has decreased (perhaps because more and cheaper substitutes for notebook computers—such as tablets and all-in-one desktops—have become available). As shown on the diagram, a rightward shift of the supply curve (from S_1 to S_2) and a simultaneous leftward shift in the demand curve (from D_1 to D_2) have resulted in a new equilibrium, where the price is lower but the quantity has not changed.

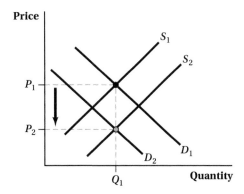

2.5 Elasticity

Elasticity

The ratio of the percentage change in one value to the percentage change in another.

Price elasticity of demand

The percentage change in quantity demanded resulting from a 1% change in price.

$$E^D = \frac{\%\Delta Q^D}{\%\Delta P}$$

where E^D is the price elasticity of demand, $\%\Delta Q^D$ is the percentage change in quantity demanded, and $\%\Delta P$ is the percentage change in price.

Recall that another way to write this formula (shown in the textbook) is $E^D = \frac{\Delta Q^D}{\Delta P} \frac{P}{Q^D}$. In terms of partial derivatives from calculus, the price elasticity of demand can be written mathematically, using calculus, as: $E^D = \frac{\partial Q^D}{\partial P} \frac{P}{Q^D}$.

Price elasticity of supply

The percentage change in quantity supplied resulting from a 1% change in price.

$$E^S = \frac{\%\Delta Q^S}{\%\Delta P}$$

where E^S is the price elasticity of supply, $\%\Delta Q^S$ is the percentage change in quantity supplied, and $\%\Delta P$ is the percentage change in price.

∂ Recall that another way to write this formula (shown in the textbook) is $E^S = \dfrac{\Delta Q^S}{\Delta P}\dfrac{P}{Q^S}$. In terms of partial derivatives from calculus, the price elasticity of supply can be written mathematically, using calculus, as: $E^S = \dfrac{\partial Q^S}{\partial P}\dfrac{P}{Q^S}$.

Terms for elasticities by magnitude

- *Elastic*: a price elasticity with an absolute value greater than 1.
- *Inelastic*: a price elasticity with an absolute value less than 1.
- *Unit elastic*: a price elasticity with an absolute value equal to 1.
- *Perfectly inelastic*: a price elasticity that is equal to zero; there is no change in quantity demanded or supplied for any change in price.
- *Perfectly elastic*: a price elasticity that is infinite; any change in price leads to an infinite change in quantity demanded or supplied.

Elasticity of a linear demand curve

$$E^D = \frac{1}{slope} \times \frac{P}{Q^D}$$

Where E^D is the price elasticity of demand, *slope* is the slope of the demand curve, Q^D is the quantity demanded, and P is the price.

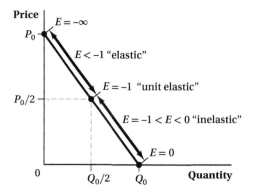

∂ The slope of a linear demand curve is constant. The preceding elasticity equation, however, can be used even when the slope is not a constant. Specifically, the *slope* in this equation can be written with calculus as: $\dfrac{\partial P}{\partial Q^D}$.

Elasticity of a linear supply curve

$$E^S = \frac{1}{slope} \times \frac{P}{Q^S}$$

where E^S is the price elasticity of supply, *slope* is the slope of the supply curve, Q^S is the quantity supplied, and P is the price. $\dfrac{P}{Q}$ falls as we move up the supply curve (as reflected in the decrease of the slopes of the rays from the points on the supply curve to the origin), so the elasticity of supply decreases.

∂ The *slope* in the preceding equation can be written, using calculus, as: $\dfrac{\partial P}{\partial Q^S}$, and this formula holds for both linear and nonlinear cases like the analogous partial derivative does, as previously mentioned, for the demand side.

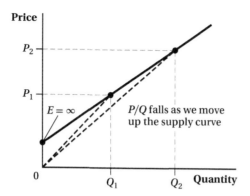

Perfectly inelastic demand/supply curves

When a demand or supply curve is vertical, its slope is infinite and it is perfectly inelastic. Any change in price will result in a 0% change in quantity demanded or supplied.

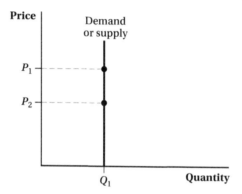

Perfectly elastic demand/supply curves

When a demand or supply curve is horizontal, its slope is zero and it is perfectly elastic. Any change in price will result in an infinitely large change in quantity demanded or supplied.

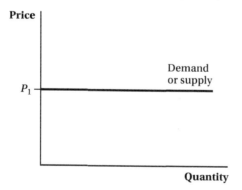

Expenditures and revenue along a linear demand curve

$$\text{Total expenditure} = \text{Total revenue} = P \times Q$$

At point C, price and expenditures are zero. Between points C and B, the demand curve is inelastic, and expenditures are increasing with the increase in price along the demand curve. Point B is the maximum expenditures point; at B, the demand curve is unit elastic, and expenditures are neither rising nor falling. Between points B and A, the demand curve is elastic, and expenditures are decreasing with the increase in price.

Expressed with calculus, this means that for inelastic demand, $\frac{dR(P)}{dP} > 0$, where $R(P)$ represents total expenditure as a function of price or likewise total revenue as a function of price. Similarly, for elastic demand, $\frac{dR(P)}{dP} < 0$. Finally, for unit elastic demand (when the price elasticity of demand is exactly 1 in absolute value), $\frac{dR(P)}{dP} = 0$.

Income elasticity of demand

The percentage change in quantity demanded, resulting from a 1% change in consumer income.

$$E_I^D = \frac{\%\Delta Q^D}{\%\Delta I}$$

Where E_I^D is the income elasticity of demand, $\%\Delta Q^D$ is the percentage change in quantity demanded, and $\%\Delta I$ is the percentage change in income.

Recall that another way to write this formula is $E_I^D = \frac{\Delta Q^D}{\Delta I}\frac{I}{Q^D}$. In terms of partial derivatives from calculus, the income elasticity of demand can be written: $E_I^D = \frac{\partial Q^D}{\partial I}\frac{I}{Q^D}$.

Inferior good

A good for which quantity demanded decreases when income rises, that is, the income elasticity of demand is negative.

For these types of goods, there is a negative relationship between quantity demanded and income. The partial derivative of quantity demanded with respect to income is negative: $\frac{\partial Q^D}{\partial I} < 0$.

Normal good

A good for which quantity demanded rises when income rises, that is, the income elasticity of demand is positive.

For these types of goods, there is a positive relationship between quantity demanded and income. The partial derivative of quantity demanded with respect to income is positive: $\frac{\partial Q^D}{\partial I} > 0$.

Luxury good

A good with an income elasticity greater than 1.

Cross-price elasticity of demand

The percentage change in the quantity demanded of one good, resulting from a 1% change in the price of another good.

$$E_{XY}^D = \frac{\%\Delta Q_X^D}{\%\Delta P_Y}$$

Where E_{XY}^D is the elasticity of demand for good X with respect to the price of good Y, $\%\Delta Q_X^D$ is the percentage change in the quantity demanded of good X, and $\%\Delta P_Y$ is the percentage change in the price of good Y.

Recall that another way to write this formula is: $E^D_{XY} = \dfrac{\Delta Q^D_X}{\Delta P_Y} \dfrac{P_Y}{Q^D_X}$. In terms of partial derivatives from calculus, the cross-price elasticity of demand can be written: $E^D_{XY} = \dfrac{\partial Q^D_X}{\partial P_Y} \dfrac{P_Y}{Q^D_X}$.

If the cross-price elasticity of demand between two goods is positive, these goods are substitutes. If it is negative, the goods are complements.

2.5 figure it out 1

Suppose the demand for movie tickets in a small town is described by the following equation:

$$Q = 800 - 50P$$

where Q is the quantity of tickets demanded per day, and P is the average price of a ticket.
a. What is the price elasticity of demand for movie tickets when the price is $8 per ticket? At this point, is the demand price elastic?
b. What is the price elasticity of demand for movie tickets when the price is $5 per ticket? At this point, is the demand price elastic?
c. Without further calculations, can you tell whether the demand for movie tickets is elastic or inelastic when the price is $10?
d. Use calculus to recalculate the price elasticity of demand for movie tickets when the price is $8 per ticket, and confirm that your answer is the same as in part (a).
e. Use calculus to calculate the price elasticity of demand for movie tickets when the price is $10 per ticket.

Solution

a. The price elasticity of demand can be calculated as

$$E = \frac{\Delta Q}{\Delta P} \times \frac{P}{Q} = \frac{1}{slope} \times \frac{P}{Q}$$

To easily see the slope of the demand curve, we rearrange the equation in terms of P, that is, find the inverse demand curve:

$$Q = 800 - 50P$$
$$50P = 800 - Q$$
$$P = 16 - 0.02Q$$

Now we can see that the slope of the demand curve is −0.02: every time Q rises by 1, P falls by 0.02. Then, the inverse of the slope of the demand curve $\left(\dfrac{1}{slope}\right)$ is $\dfrac{1}{(-0.02)} = -50$. Note that it equals the coefficient of P in the original demand equation. To calculate the elasticity, we also need to know the quantity of tickets demanded at $8. To find it, we plug $8 into the demand equation:

$$Q = 800 - 50 \times 8 = 400$$

Now we can compute the elasticity:

$$E = -50 \times \left(\frac{8}{400}\right) = -1$$

Thus, the demand at this point is unit elastic.
b. When the price is $5, the quantity demanded is

$$Q = 800 - 50 \times 5 = 550$$

Using the elasticity formula, we get

$$E = -50 \times \left(\frac{5}{550}\right) = -0.455$$

Since $|-0.455| < 1$, the demand at this point is inelastic.

c. From (a) we know that the demand is unit elastic at $P = \$8$. We also know that the price elasticity of demand increases as we move up and to the left along a linear demand curve (since $\dfrac{P}{Q}$ increases, while the slope of the curve remains constant). Thus, at prices higher than \$8, the elasticity must be greater than 1 (by the absolute value). To verify that the demand is price elastic at $P = \$10$, we can calculate the elasticity at this point. When $P = \$10$,

$$Q = 800 - 50 \times 10 = 300$$

and

$$E = -50 \times \left(\frac{10}{300}\right) = -1.67$$

Since $|-1.67| > 1$, the demand is in fact price elastic at $P = \$10$.

d. Using the derivative of a constant and power rules of derivatives, $\dfrac{\partial Q^D}{\partial P} = 0 - 50(1)P^{1-1} = -50P^0 = -50$. The price elasticity of demand is $E^D = \dfrac{\partial Q^D}{\partial P}\dfrac{P}{Q^D} = -50\dfrac{8}{400} = -1$. This is the same as in part (a).

e. At a price of \$10, quantity is $800 - 50(10) = 300$. The price elasticity of demand at this price is $E^D = \dfrac{\partial Q^D}{\partial P}\dfrac{P}{Q^D} = -50\dfrac{10}{300} \approx -1.67$.

∂ 2.5 figure it out 2

Suppose that the inverse demand curve for carne asada burritos in a local restaurant can be expressed as $P = 13 - 0.5Q^{0.5}$ where price is in dollars and quantity is in numbers of burritos. What is the price elasticity of demand at a quantity of 49?

Solution

Note that this is a nonlinear demand curve since quantity Q is raised to a power other than one and therefore the relationship between price and quantity is nonlinear. Calculus provides a way to calculate the price elasticity of demand for this equation at a given quantity. First, note that for a quantity of 49 burritos, $P = 13 - 0.5(49)^{0.5} = 13 - 0.5(7) = 9.5$; therefore, a burrito costs \$9.50. The price elasticity of demand formula written in terms of calculus is: $E^D = \dfrac{\partial Q^D}{\partial P}\dfrac{P}{Q^D}$.

One way to solve the problem then would be to rearrange the inverse demand curve in order to find the standard form of the demand curve. Then, we could take the partial derivative with respect to price and substitute it (and the relevant price and quantity) into the equation as given. Another way to solve for the price elasticity of demand, however, is to use the inverse demand curve directly. Specifically, we can write the price elasticity of demand formula as $E^D = \dfrac{1}{\dfrac{\partial P}{\partial Q^D}}\dfrac{P}{Q^D}$. Using the inverse demand curve equation as given, we can see that $\dfrac{\partial P}{\partial Q^D} = 0 - 0.5(0.5)Q^{0.5-1} = -0.25Q^{-0.5}$. At a quantity of 49 burritos, this value is $-0.25(49)^{-0.5} \approx -0.036$. Making the appropriate substitutions, we find that $E^D \approx \dfrac{1}{-0.036}\dfrac{9.5}{49} \approx -5.39$. Since this is greater than one in absolute value, we now know that burritos are price elastic.

Practice Problems

Problem 1

Predict how each of the following events will affect the market for gasoline in the United States. For each event, indicate which curve is affected and whether it will shift rightward or leftward. Explain your answers.

a. The price of crude oil rises.

b. The prices of alternative motor fuels fall.

c. Workers at oil refineries organize a union and negotiate higher wages.

d. People become more conscious of the fact that burning gasoline pollutes the environment and contributes to the global climate change.

e. Auto producers develop more fuel-efficient cars.

f. Car prices fall.

Problem 2

Suppose the demand for organic milk in a city is described by the following equation:

$$Q^D = -20 - 10P + 20P_C + 2I$$

where Q^D is the quantity of organic milk demanded (in thousands of gallons), P is the price of organic milk (in dollars), P_C is the price of conventional milk (in dollars), and I is the average consumer income (in thousands of dollars per year).

a. Draw the demand curve for organic milk when the price of conventional milk is $3 per gallon and the consumer income is $30 thousand per year. What is the quantity of organic milk demanded when the price of organic milk is $6 per gallon?

b. Given the preceding demand equation, are conventional milk and organic milk substitutes or complements? Is organic milk a normal or an inferior good? Explain your answers.

c. Suppose the price of conventional milk falls from $3 to $2.50, and consumer income falls from $30 thousand to $25 thousand. Illustrate the effects of these changes using the graph you drew in (a). After these changes, what is the quantity of organic milk demanded when the price of organic milk is $6 per gallon?

d. Given the demand curve in (a), what is the price elasticity of demand when the price of organic milk is $5 per gallon?

 e. Use calculus to calculate the income elasticity of demand when the price of organic milk is $6 per gallon, the price of conventional milk is $3 per gallon, and the consumer income is $30 thousand per year.

f. Use calculus to calculate the cross-price elasticity of demand under the same price and income assumptions as in part (e).

g. Is conventional milk a substitute or a complement for organic milk? Is organic milk a normal or an inferior good? Answer these questions, using a partial derivative, and confirm that the answers are the same as in part (b).

Problem 3

Suppose that the demand and supply curves for wheat in the United States are represented by the following equations:

$$Q^D = 900 - 100P$$
$$Q^S = -600 + 200P$$

where Q^D is the quantity demanded (in millions of bushels), Q^S is the quantity supplied, and P is the price of wheat (in dollars). Suppose the current market price of wheat is $6 per bushel.

a. What is the quantity of wheat demanded? Quantity supplied? Quantity sold?

b. Describe the situation in the market. Is there excess demand or excess supply? How large is the shortage or surplus?

c. What do you expect to happen to the market price of wheat? The quantity of wheat sold?

d. What is the equilibrium price of wheat? The equilibrium quantity of wheat?

 e. Use calculus to show that the Law of Demand holds.

f. Use calculus to show that the Law of Supply holds.

Problem 4

Suppose that the demand and supply curves for pizza in a college town when the school is in session are as follows:

$$Q^D = 2,100 - 140P$$
$$Q^S = -420 + 140P$$

where Q^D is the quantity of pizza demanded, Q^S is the quantity supplied, and P is the price of pizza.

a. Suppose that the market for pizza is in equilibrium. What is the current price of pizza? The quantity of pizza sold?

b. When the school is not in session, the quantity of pizza demanded is 420 less at every price. In this situation, what is the equilibrium price of pizza? The equilibrium quantity of pizza?

c. What is the price elasticity of supply of pizza when the school is in session and the market is in equilibrium?

d. Use calculus to calculate this elasticity again, and confirm that you come to the same answer as in part (c).

e. Use calculus to calculate the price elasticity of demand when the school is in session and the market is in equilibrium.

Problem 5

Consider the effects of the following two events on the market for orange juice:

(1) A new study published in an influential journal shows that drinking orange juice reduces the risk of heart disease and diabetes for people who eat an unhealthy diet. This finding is heavily advertised on television.

(2) The weather conditions in central Florida (where almost all U.S. orange juice is produced) become less favorable for growing oranges.

a. Draw a supply and demand diagram to illustrate the impact of these events on the market (on the same diagram).

b. Predict what will happen to the equilibrium price and quantity of orange juice as a result of these events. Explain your prediction.

Problem 6

Suppose the demand for ice cream is described by the following equation:

$$Q = 3,000 - 250P$$

where Q is the quantity of ice cream demanded (in gallons), and P is the price of ice cream (in dollars per gallon).

a. What is the price elasticity of demand for ice cream when the price is \$3 per gallon? At this point, is the demand price elastic?

b. What is the price elasticity of demand for ice cream when the price is \$10 per gallon? At this point, is the demand price elastic?

c. At what price is the demand for ice cream unit elastic? Explain your answer.

 d. At what price and quantity is total expenditure maximized?

Problem 7

Suppose the demand and supply for paper towels are described by the following equations:

$$Q^D = 70 - 20P$$
$$Q^S = -80 + 80P$$

where Q^D is the quantity of paper towels demanded (in thousands of rolls), Q^S is the quantity supplied, and P is the price of paper towels (dollars per roll).

a. Derive and graph the inverse supply and inverse demand curves.

b. What are the equilibrium price and equilibrium quantity in this market?

c. Now suppose that the inverse supply curve shifts upward by \$1.25 at each given quantity. Derive and graph the new inverse supply curve. Does this shift of the inverse supply curve reflect an increase or a decrease in supply? What could cause this change in supply?

d. After the change in supply, what are the market equilibrium price and quantity?

 e. Suppose that the extended supply curve for paper towels can be expressed as $Q^S = -77 + 80P - 6P_C$, where P_C is the price of cellulose fibers (i.e., paper). If the price of paper is \$0.50, show that this expanded supply curve gives the same supply relationship as in the problem's setup.

f. Use calculus to determine whether quantity supplied of paper towels increases or decreases as the price of paper increases.

g. Suppose that the price of paper decreases to \$0.40. What is the new equation for the supply of paper towels? In which direction has the supply curve shifted?

h. What will be the new equilibrium price and quantity of paper towels after the price decrease of paper?

Problem 8

Suppose that the price elasticity of demand for Hewlett-Packard (HP) computers is –1.6, and the cross-price elasticity of demand for HP computers with respect to the price of Dell computers is 0.8. If the price of Dell computers falls by 10%, what would have to happen to the price of HP computers to exactly offset the rise in the price of Dell computers and leave the quantity of HP computers demanded unchanged?

Problem 9

Consider the market for housing in two cities, City A and City B. In both cities population grew at about the same rate. City A, however, experienced a relatively small increase in the equilibrium price with a relatively large change in the equilibrium quantity of housing. City B, in contrast, experienced a relatively large increase in price and little change in quantity. How can this be? Draw a supply and demand diagram for each city to explain and illustrate your answer. Assume that factors other than population growth that could possibly influence demand or supply remained unchanged.

Problem 10

Suppose that in the world market for crude oil, the price elasticity of demand is –0.11, the income elasticity of demand is 0.4, and the price elasticity of supply is 0.21. If the world income grows by 16% over the next five years, what will be the percentage change in the price of oil over this period?

Problem 11

Suppose that the inverse supply curve for shampoo can be expressed as $P = -190 + 0.5Q^2$, where price is expressed in dollars and quantity in thousands of bottles sold. What is the price elasticity of supply when 20,000 bottles are sold?

Using Supply and Demand to Analyze Markets

3

3.1 Consumer and Producer Surplus: Who Benefits in a Market?

Consumer surplus

The difference between the amount consumers would be willing to pay for a good or service and the amount they actually have to pay.

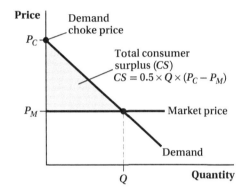

∂ Since this is an area, it can be calculated using either geometry or calculus.

Demand choke price

The price at which quantity demanded is reduced to zero (see the graph above).

Producer surplus

The difference between the price at which producers are willing to sell their good or service and the price they actually receive.

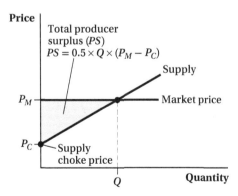

∂ Since this is an area, it can be calculated using either geometry or calculus.

Supply choke price

The price at which quantity supplied equals zero (see the preceding graph).

make the grade

Hints that will help you deal with problems involving consumer surplus, producer surplus, government policies, and deadweight loss

- The easiest way to find consumer surplus, producer surplus, deadweight loss, and the effects of various government policies is to graph the supply and demand curves, find the relevant prices and quantities, and use geometry to calculate the areas of interest.
- Consumer surplus is the area below the demand curve and above the price. Producer surplus is the area above the supply curve and below the price. Make sure that you look at the relevant price, relevant curve, and its relevant part. The following two examples illustrate this point.

Example 1. The following graph shows the effects of a tax imposed on buyers. With no tax, D and S are the demand and supply curves, and P_E and Q_E are the equilibrium price and quantity. In this situation, the relevant demand curve is D, and the relevant price is P_E, so the consumer surplus is the area below the demand curve D and above the price P_E (area $A + B$). For the producer surplus, the relevant supply curve is S, and the relevant price is P_E, so the producer surplus is the area above the supply curve and below the price P_E (area $E + F$).

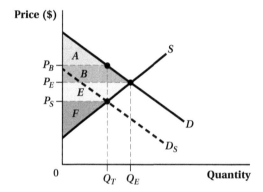

With the tax, although the demand curve faced by sellers is D_S, the buyers' demand curve is still D. The price buyers pay is P_B, and the quantity sold is Q_T. Thus, the consumer surplus is the area below the demand curve D and above the price P_B (area A). For the producer surplus, the relevant supply curve is S, and the relevant price is P_S. Thus, the producer surplus is the area above the supply curve and below the price P_S (area F).

Example 2. The following graph shows the effects of a price ceiling. With no price ceiling, the consumer surplus is the area below the demand curve (D) and above the equilibrium price P_E (area $A + B + C$). And the producer surplus is the area above the supply curve (S) and below the equilibrium price P_E (area $E + F + G$).

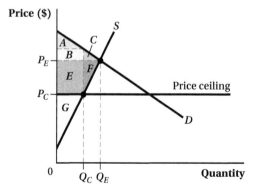

With the price ceiling, the consumer surplus is below the same demand curve (D), but it is now above the price P_C, since this is the price that consumers pay, and only up to the quantity Q_C, since this is the quantity consumers buy. This consumer surplus is represented by area $A + B + E$. The producer surplus is now the area below the price P_C (the price that producers receive) and above the supply curve up to the quantity sold, Q_C (area G).

- A deadweight loss occurs whenever the quantity consumed is different from the free-market equilibrium quantity. (This may not be the case if externalities are present, but for now we assume that there are no externalities. You'll learn more about externalities in Chapter 16.) The deadweight loss is a loss in consumer surplus, producer surplus, or both.
- Since in most cases consumer surplus, producer surplus, and deadweight loss take the shape of a triangle, it is useful to remember and feel confident with the formula for the area of a triangle:

$$\text{Area of triangle} = 0.5 \times \text{Base} \times \text{Height}$$

It is also useful to check your geometric calculations by doing them in an alternative way. For example, the following graph illustrates the effect of a tax imposed on sellers. With no tax, the consumer surplus is area $A + B + C$, calculated as

$$CS = 0.5 \times 220 \times (\$33.30 - \$30.00) = \$363$$

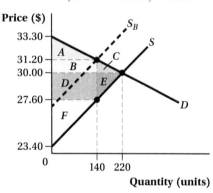

With the tax, the consumer surplus is area A, calculated as

$$CS_T = 0.5 \times 140 \times (\$33.30 - \$31.20) = \$147$$

Thus, the tax decreases consumer surplus by $\$363 - \$147 = \$216$. Now let's check this result. The decrease in consumer surplus is represented by area $B + C$. You can calculate it by adding the area of rectangle B and the area of triangle C:

$$\text{Area } B = (\$31.20 - \$30.00) \times 140 = \$168$$
$$\text{Area } C = 0.5 \times (\$31.20 - \$30.00) \times (220 - 140) = \$48$$
$$\Delta CS = \text{Area } (B + C) = \$168 + \$48 = \$216$$

which confirms your first result.

You can also calculate area $B + C$ as the area of a trapezoid, using the following formula:

$$\text{Area of trapezoid} = 0.5 \times \text{Sum of parallel sides} \times \text{Height}$$

That is,

$$\Delta CS = 0.5 \times (220 + 140) \times (\$31.20 - \$30.00) = \$216$$

Further, suppose you calculate the deadweight loss resulting from the tax (area $C + E$) as follows:

$$\text{DWL} = 0.5 \times (\$31.20 - \$27.60) \times (220 - 140) = \$144$$

Let's verify this result. First, we calculate the total surplus with no tax (area $A + B + C + D + E + F$) as follows:

$$TS = 0.5 \times 220 \times (\$33.30 - \$23.40) = \$1,089$$

Then, we calculate the total surplus (the sum of consumer, producer, and government surpluses) with the tax (area $A + B + D + F$), using the trapezoid formula:

$$TS_T = 0.5 \times [(33.30 - 23.40) + (31.20 - 27.60)] \times 140 = \$945$$

Thus,

$$\text{DWL} = \$1{,}089 - \$945 = \$144$$

confirming your first result.

∂ We also can solve for consumer surplus, producer surplus, and deadweight loss areas in microeconomics by using calculus. Specifically, consumer surplus at the equilibrium can be written:

$$CS = \int_0^{Q_e} \big(P(Q_D)\big) - P_e)dQ$$

where Q_e and P_e are the equilibrium quantity and price, respectively, and $P(Q_D)$ is the inverse demand curve. Recall that the inverse demand curve is a demand curve written in the form of price (P) as a function of quantity demanded (Q_D). We can derive producer surplus, using integral calculus by solving:

$$PS = \int_0^{Q_e} \big(P_e - P(Q_S)\big)dQ$$

where Q_e and P_e are the equilibrium quantity and price, respectively, and $P(Q_S)$ is the inverse supply curve. Recall that the inverse supply curve is a supply curve written in the form of price (P) as a function of quantity supplied (Q_S). Consumer and producer surplus for quantities and prices other than the intersection of the demand and supply curves can be calculated analogously by substituting the appropriate values for Q_e and P_e.

Deadweight loss measures the lost surplus (from both consumers and producers) when prices and/or quantities deviate from the equilibrium as often is the case under various types of government interventions. Deadweight loss, then, is an area that can be calculated, using calculus as:

$$\text{DWL} = \int_{Q_a}^{Q_e} \big(P(Q_D) - P(Q_S)\big)dQ$$

where Q_a denotes actual quantity, Q_e is again the quantity that would occur in a free-market equilibrium, and $P(Q_D)$ and $P(Q_S)$ are inverse demand and supply, respectively.

3.1 figure it out 1

Suppose the demand and supply curves for spring water are given by

$$Q^D = 120 - 40P$$
$$Q^S = -60 + 80P$$

where Q^D is the quantity of spring water demanded (in thousands of bottles), Q^S is the quantity supplied, and P is the price of spring water (in dollars per bottle).

a. Find the equilibrium price and quantity of spring water.

b. Calculate the consumer and producer surplus at the equilibrium price.

∂ c. Calculate the consumer and producer surplus at the equilibrium price using calculus and confirm that answer is the same as in part (b).

Solution

a. Equilibrium occurs where $Q^D = Q^S$. Therefore, we can solve for equilibrium by equating the demand and supply curves:

$$Q^D = Q^S$$
$$120 - 40P = -60 + 80P$$
$$120P = 180$$
$$P = 1.5$$

To find the equilibrium quantity, we substitute the equilibrium price into either the demand equation or the supply equation:

$$Q^D = 120 - 40 \times 1.5 = 60$$
$$Q^S = -60 + 80 \times 1.5 = 60$$

Thus the equilibrium price is $1.50 per bottle, and the equilibrium quantity is 60,000 bottles.

b. The easiest way to find consumer and producer surplus is to use a graph. First, we need to graph the demand and supply curves. Since both curves are straight lines, we only need to identify two points for each curve. The first point, common for the two curves, is the equilibrium, where $P = 1.50$, and $Q^D = Q^S = 60$. The second point on each curve that can be easily identified (and is useful for our further calculations) is the choke price for demand and supply. To find these points, we set Q^D and Q^S equal to zero and solve for P:

$$Q^D = 120 - 40P$$
$$0 = 120 - 40P$$
$$40P = 120$$
$$P = 3$$
$$Q^S = -60 + 80P$$
$$0 = -60 + 80P$$
$$80P = 60$$
$$P = 0.75$$

Thus, the demand choke price is $3.00, and the supply choke price is $0.75. Now we can use these points to graph the demand and supply curves (see the following graph). Consumer surplus is the triangular area below the demand curve and above the price (area A). It can be calculated as

$$CS = 0.5 \times 60{,}000 \times (\$3 - \$1.50) = \$45{,}000$$

Producer surplus is the triangular area above the supply curve and below the price (area B). It can be calculated as

$$PS = 0.5 \times 60{,}000 \times (\$1.50 - \$0.75) = \$22{,}500$$

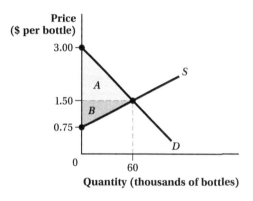

c. Since the consumer and producer surplus formulas using calculus require substituting in the inverse demand and supply curves, we first solve for these. We can rearrange the standard demand and supply curves to get, respectively, the inverse demand and supply relationships.

$$Q^D = 120 - 40P$$
$$40P = 120 - Q^D$$
$$P = 3 - 0.025Q^D$$

and

$$Q^S = 80P - 60$$
$$80P = 60 + Q^S$$
$$P = 0.75 + 0.0125Q^S$$

Using the integral equations for consumer and producer surplus and substituting the inverse demand and supply equations and the equilibrium quantity and price, we can see that:

$$CS = \int_0^{60} \big((3 - 0.025Q) - 1.5)\big)dQ = \int_0^{60}(1.5 - 0.025Q)dQ = \int_0^{60} 1.5dQ - \int_0^{60} 0.025QdQ$$

$$= [1.5Q]_0^{60} - \left[\frac{0.025Q^2}{2}\right]_0^{60}$$

$$= [1.5(60) - 1.5(0)] - \left[\frac{0.025(60)^2}{2} - \frac{0.025(0)^2}{2}\right]$$

$$= (90 - 0) - (45 - 0) = 45.$$ Since quantity is measured in thousands, this is the same $45,000 as shown in the preceding equation.

$$PS = \int_0^{60}\big(1.5 - (0.75 + 0.0125Q)\big)dQ = \int_0^{60}(0.75 - 0.0125Q)dQ = \int_0^{60} 0.75dQ - \int_0^{60} 0.0125QdQ$$

$$= [0.75Q]_0^{60} - \left[\frac{0.0125Q^2}{2}\right]_0^{60}$$

$$= [0.75(60) - 0.75(0)] - \left[\frac{0.0125(60)^2}{2} - \frac{0.0125(0)^2}{2}\right]$$

$$= (45 - 0) - (22.5 - 0) = 22.5$$

This is the same $22,500 identified in the preceding equation.

3.1 figure it out 2

Suppose the demand and supply curves for tomato juice are given by

$$Q^D = 52.5 - 10P$$
$$Q^S = -60 + 40P$$

where Q^D is the quantity of tomato juice demanded (in millions of gallons), Q^S is the quantity supplied, and P is the price of tomato juice (in dollars per gallon). Suppose a new study reveals that the health benefits of tomato juice are greater than they were previously thought to be. As a result, the quantity of tomato juice demanded increases by 12.5 million gallons at each given price.

a. What happens to consumer surplus as a result of this change?
b. What happens to producer surplus as a result of this change?

Solution

a. The easiest way to find consumer surplus and see how it changes in response to a change in demand is to use a graph. First, we graph the original demand and supply curves. Since both curves are straight lines, for each curve, we only need to identify two points. The first point, common for the two curves, is the market equilibrium. We can solve for the equilibrium price by equating the demand and supply curves:

$$Q^D = Q^S$$
$$52.5 - 10P = -60 + 40P$$
$$50P = 112.5$$
$$P = 2.25$$

To solve for the equilibrium quantity, we substitute the equilibrium price into either the demand equation or the supply equation:

$$Q^D = 52.5 - 10 \times 2.25 = 30$$
$$Q^S = -60 + 40 \times 2.25 = 30$$

Thus, the original equilibrium price is $2.25, and the original equilibrium quantity is 30 million gallons.

The second point on each curve that can be easily identified (and is useful for our further calculations) is the choke price for demand and supply. To find these points, we set Q^D and Q^S equal to zero and solve for P:

$$Q^D = 52.5 - 10P$$
$$0 = 52.5 - 10P$$
$$10P = 52.5$$
$$P = 5.25$$
$$Q^S = -60 + 40P$$
$$0 = -60 + 40P$$
$$40P = 60$$
$$P = 1.5$$

Thus, the demand choke price is $5.25 and the supply choke price is $1.50. Now we can use these points to graph the demand and supply curves (D and S on the following graph). The consumer surplus is the triangular area $A + B$ below the demand curve D and above the initial equilibrium price. It can be calculated as

$$CS = 0.5 \times 30 \text{ million} \times (\$5.25 - \$2.25) = \$45 \text{ million}$$

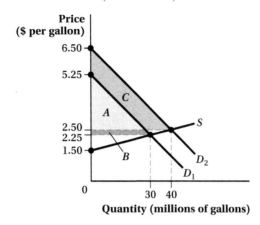

Now we need to find the new demand curve. Quantity demanded increases by 12.5 million gallons at each price, so we add 12.5 to the demand equation:

$$Q_2^D = 52.5 - 10P + 12.5$$
$$Q_2^D = 65 - 10P$$

To solve for the new equilibrium price, we equate Q_2^D and Q^S:

$$65 - 10P = -60 + 40P$$
$$50P = 125$$
$$P = 2.5$$

To find the new equilibrium quantity, we substitute the new equilibrium price into either the new demand equation or the supply equation:

$$Q_2^D = 65 - 10 \times 2.50 = 40$$
$$Q^S = -60 + 40 \times 2.5 = 40$$

Thus, the new equilibrium price is $2.50, and the new equilibrium quantity is 40 million gallons. To find the new choke price for demand, we set Q_2^D equal to zero and solve for P:

$$Q_2^D = 65 - 10P$$
$$0 = 65 - 10P$$
$$10P = 65$$
$$P = 6.5$$

Now we can draw the new demand curve (D_2 on the preceding graph). After the increase in demand, the consumer surplus is the triangular area $A + C$ below the demand curve D_2 and above the new equilibrium price. It can be calculated as

$$CS_{\text{new}} = 0.5 \times 40 \text{ million} \times (\$6.50 - \$2.50) = \$80 \text{ million}$$

As we can see, consumer surplus increases by $80 million – $45 million = $35 million as a result of increased demand. It decreases by area B because of the higher price, but this decrease is more than offset by the increase in consumer surplus due to the greater quantity of tomato juice consumed (area C).

b. The producer surplus is initially the triangular area F above the supply curve S and below the initial equilibrium price (see the following graph). It can be calculated as

$$PS = 0.5 \times 30 \text{ million} \times (\$2.25 - \$1.50) = \$11.25 \text{ million}$$

With the increased demand, the producer surplus is the triangular area $F + G$ above the supply curve S and below the new equilibrium price. It can be calculated as

$$PS_{\text{new}} = 0.5 \times 40 \text{ million} \times (\$2.50 - \$1.50) = \$20 \text{ million}$$

Producer surplus increases by $20 million – $11.25 million = $8.75 million (area G), which results from both a higher price and a greater quantity of tomato juice sold.

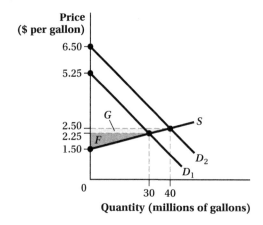

∂ 3.1 figure it out 3

Suppose that the demand curve for a new release DVD is given by $P = 50 - 0.05Q^2$ and supply is $P = 20 + 0.01Q^2$, where price is in dollars and quantity is in thousands of DVDs.
a. Find the equilibrium price and quantity.
b. Calculate the consumer and producer surplus at the equilibrium price.

Solution

a. The equilibrium condition is: $50 - 0.05Q^2 = 20 + 0.01Q^2$.

$$0.06Q^2 = 30$$
$$Q^2 = 500$$
$$Q \approx 22.36$$
$$P - 50 - 0.05(22.36)^2 \approx 25$$

The price of this DVD therefore is $25 and approximately 22,360 are sold.

b.

$$CS = \int_0^{22.36}\big((50 - 0.05Q^2) - 25\big)dQ = \int_0^{22.36}(25 - 0.05Q^2)dQ = [25Q]_0^{22.36} - \left[\frac{0.05Q^3}{3}\right]_0^{22.36}$$

$$= [25(22.36) - 25(0)] - \left[\frac{0.05(22.36)^3}{3} - \frac{0.05(0)^3}{3}\right] = (559 - 0) - (186.32 - 0) = 372.68$$

$$PS = \int_0^{22.36}\big(25 - (20 + 0.01Q^2)\big)dQ = \int_0^{22.36}(5 - 0.01Q^2)dQ = [5Q]_0^{22.36} - \left[\frac{0.01Q^3}{3}\right]_0^{22.36}$$

$$= [5(22.36) - 5(0)] - \left[\frac{0.01(22.36)^3}{3} - \frac{0.01(0)^3}{3}\right] = (111.8 - 0) - (37.26 - 0) = 74.54$$

The consumer and producer surpluses are $372,680 and $74,540, respectively.

3.2 Price Regulations

Transfer

Surplus that moves from producer to consumer, or vice versa, as a result of a price regulation.

Deadweight loss (DWL)

The reduction in total surplus that occurs as a result of a market inefficiency.

∂ Since this is a surplus measure and hence an area, it can be calculated using either geometry or calculus.

Price ceiling

A price regulation that sets the highest price that can be paid legally for a good or service.

Binding price ceiling

A price ceiling set at a level below equilibrium price. A binding price ceiling creates a persistent shortage in the market ($Q_D > Q_S$).

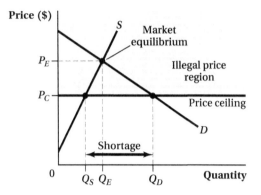

Nonbinding price ceiling

A price ceiling that is set at a level above equilibrium price and therefore has no effect on the market.

Price floor (or price support)

A price regulation that sets the lowest price that can be paid legally for a good or service.

Binding price floor

A price floor set at a level above equilibrium price. A binding price floor creates a persistent surplus in the market ($Q_S > Q_D$).

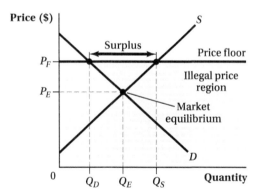

Nonbinding price floor

A price floor set at a level below equilibrium price.

3.2 figure it out 1

Consider the market for rental housing in a college town. Suppose the demand and supply curves for one-bedroom apartments are given by the following equations:

$$Q^D = 3,400 - 5P$$
$$Q^S = -100 + 1.25P$$

where Q^D is the quantity of apartments demanded, Q^S is the quantity supplied, and P is the rent charged for a typical apartment (in dollars per month). Suppose that with the intent to lower the cost of housing, the city council passes a regulation that says no landlord can charge more than $400 per month.

a. With no rent regulation, what is the equilibrium rent and the equilibrium quantity of apartments rented?
b. With the rent regulation, how many apartments are rented? At what price? Is the rent ceiling binding?
c. How does the rent ceiling affect consumer surplus? Producer surplus?
d. What is the deadweight loss resulting from the rent ceiling?
e. Use calculus to recalculate deadweight loss from the rent ceiling and confirm that your answer is the same as in part (d).

Solution

a. We solve for the equilibrium rent by equating Q^D and Q^S:

$$3{,}400 - 5P = -100 + 1.25P$$
$$6.25P = 3{,}500$$
$$P = 560$$

To solve for the equilibrium quantity of apartments rented, we substitute the equilibrium rent into either the demand equation or the supply equation:

$$Q^D = 3{,}400 - 5 \times 560 = 600$$
$$Q^S = -100 + 1.25 \times 560 = 600$$

Thus, the equilibrium rent is \$560 per month, and the equilibrium quantity of apartments rented is 600.

b. The rent ceiling is below the equilibrium rent, so it is binding. Since landlords cannot charge the equilibrium rent, they will charge the highest rent legally possible: \$400 per month. At this level of rent,

$$Q^D = 3{,}400 - 5 \times 400 = 1{,}400$$
$$Q^S = -100 + 1.25 \times 400 = 400$$

Thus, at \$400, consumers want to rent 1,400 apartments, but landlords offer only 400 apartments, so only 400 apartments are actually rented. That is, the rent ceiling creates a shortage of 1,000 apartments.

c. To find the consumer and producer surpluses and see how they change in response to the rent regulation, we graph the demand and supply curves, using the equilibrium point and the choke prices for demand and supply. To find the choke prices, we set Q^D and Q^S equal to zero and solve for P:

$$Q^D = 3{,}400 - 5P$$
$$0 = 3{,}400 - 5P$$
$$5P = 3{,}400$$
$$P = 680$$
$$Q^S = -100 + 1.25P$$
$$0 = -100 + 1.25P$$
$$1.25P = 100$$
$$P = 80$$

Thus, the demand choke price is \$680 and the supply choke price is \$80. We use these points to graph the demand and supply curves (D and S on the following graph). With no price ceiling, the consumer surplus is the triangular area $A + B + C$ below the demand curve and above the equilibrium price. This area is

$$CS = 0.5 \times 600 \times (\$680 - \$560) = \$36{,}000$$

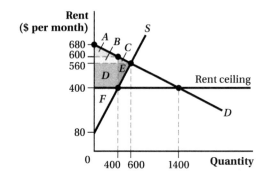

With the rent ceiling, the consumer surplus is the area above the ceiling and below the demand curve, up to the quantity rented (area $A + B + D$). An easy way to calculate the value of this surplus is to add the area of triangle A to the area of rectangle $B + D$. To find these areas, we need to know the price at which the quantity of apartments demanded is 400. To find this price, we solve the following equation:

$$Q^D = 400$$
$$3{,}400 - 5P = 400$$
$$5P = 3{,}000$$
$$P = 600$$

Now we can calculate the area of triangle A:

$$A = 0.5 \times 400 \times (\$680 - \$600) = \$16{,}000$$

and the area of rectangle $B + D$:

$$B + D = 400 \times (\$600 - \$400) = \$80{,}000$$

So the total consumer surplus with the price ceiling is

$$CS_{\text{new}} = A + B + D = \$16{,}000 + \$80{,}000 = \$96{,}000$$

Thus, the consumer surplus increases by $\$96{,}000 - \$36{,}000 = \$60{,}000$.
With no price ceiling, the producer surplus is the triangular area $D + E + F$ below the equilibrium price and above the supply curve. This area is

$$PS = 0.5 \times 600 \times (\$560 - \$80) = \$144{,}000$$

With the price ceiling, the producer surplus reduces to area F below the price ceiling and above the supply curve, up to the quantity rented:

$$PS_{\text{new}} = 0.5 \times 400 \times (\$400 - \$80) = \$64{,}000$$

Thus, the producer surplus decreases by $\$144{,}000 - \$64{,}000 = \$80{,}000$.

d. The consumer surplus represented by area C and the producer surplus represented by area E have disappeared because of the price ceiling. Since no one receives these surpluses anymore, this is a deadweight loss. The triangular area $C + E$ can be calculated as

$$DWL = 0.5 \times (\$600 - \$400) \times (600 - 400) = \$20{,}000$$

The deadweight loss can also be calculated as the difference between the total surplus that consumers and producers could get when the market is in equilibrium and the total surplus they receive with the price ceiling. In the free-market equilibrium, the total surplus is

$$TS = CS + PS = \$36{,}000 + \$144{,}000 = \$180{,}000$$

And with the price ceiling, the total surplus is

$$TS_{\text{new}} = CS_{\text{new}} + PS_{\text{new}} = \$96{,}000 + \$64{,}000 = \$160{,}000$$

So the deadweight loss is

$$DWL = \$180{,}000 - \$160{,}000 = \$20{,}000$$

e. Since the consumer and producer surplus formulas using calculus require substituting in the inverse demand and supply curves, we first solve for these. We can rearrange the demand and supply relationships to get the inverse demand and supply relationships, respectively.

$$Q^D = 3{,}400 - 5P$$
$$5P = 3{,}400 - Q^D$$
$$P = 680 - 0.2Q^D$$

and

$$Q^S = 1.25P - 100$$
$$1.25P = 100 + Q^S$$
$$P = 80 + 0.8Q^S$$

Recall that deadweight loss is the area between the demand and supply curves over the range of the difference between the old and new quantities.

$$DWL = \int_{400}^{600}\big((680 - 0.2Q) - (80 + 0.8Q)\big)dQ = \int_{400}^{600}(600 - Q)dQ = \int_{400}^{600}600\,dQ - \int_{400}^{600}Q\,dQ$$

$$= [600Q]_{400}^{600} - \left[\frac{Q^2}{2}\right]_{400}^{600}$$

$$= [600(600) - 600(400)] - \left[\frac{(600)^2}{2} - \frac{(400)^2}{2}\right]$$

$$= (360,000 - 240,000) - (180,000 - 80,000) = 20,000$$

This is the same $20,000 as previously calculated.

3.3 Quantity Regulations
Quota

A regulation that sets the quantity of a good or service provided.

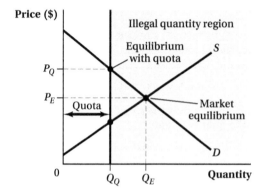

Crowding out

A reduction in private economic activity created by greater government presence in a market.

3.4 Taxes
Effect of a tax

If a tax is imposed on sellers, the supply curve shifts upward by the amount of per-unit tax.

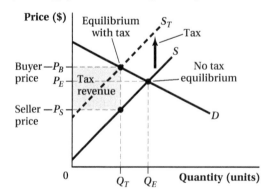

If a tax imposed on buyers, the demand curve shifts downward by the amount of per-unit tax.

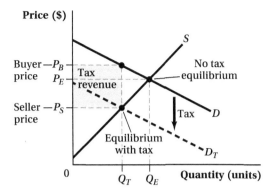

Tax incidence

Who actually pays a tax. On the following graph, the tax incidence that falls on buyers is $A = (P_B - P_E) \times Q_T$. And the tax incidence that falls on sellers is $B = (P_E - P_S) \times Q_T$. The incidence of a tax does not depend on whether buyers or sellers are legally bound to pay it.

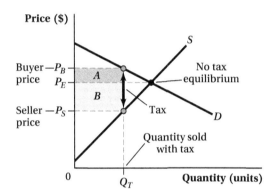

3.4 figure it out 1

Suppose that the demand and supply curves in a local market for pizza are represented by the following equations:

$$Q^D = 111 - 10P$$
$$Q^S = -39 + 5P$$

where Q^D is the quantity of pizza demanded (in thousands), Q^S is the quantity supplied, and P is the price of a pizza (in dollars per pizza). Suppose a tax of $1.20 per pizza is imposed on pizza sellers.

a. How does the tax affect the quantity of pizza sold? The price that buyers pay for pizza? The price that sellers receive?
b. How does the tax affect consumer surplus? Producer surplus?
c. What is the deadweight loss resulting from the tax?

Solution

a. With no tax, the equilibrium price of pizza is found by equating Q^D and Q^S:

$$111 - 10P = -39 + 5P$$
$$15P = 150$$
$$P = 10$$

To solve for the equilibrium quantity, we substitute the equilibrium price into either the demand or the supply equation:

$$Q^D = 111 - 10 \times 10 = 11$$
$$Q^S = -39 + 5 \times 10 = 11$$

Thus, with no tax, the price is $10 per pizza, and the quantity of pizza sold is 11,000.

Since the tax is imposed on sellers, they view it as an additional cost of $1.20 per each pizza sold. This causes them to charge $1.20 more per pizza at any given quantity sold. Therefore, in response to the tax, the supply curve shifts up by the amount of the tax ($1.20). In other words, for the sellers to get a certain price for their pizza after paying the tax, buyers have to pay $1.20 more per pizza. Thus, the price paid by buyers is the price received by sellers plus the tax:

$$P_B = P_S + 1.20$$

To solve for the quantity and prices with the tax, we substitute this expression into our supply and demand equations:

$$111 - 10P_B = -39 + 5P_S$$
$$111 - 10 \times (P_S + 1.20) = -39 + 5P_S$$
$$111 - 10P_S - 12 = -39 + 5P_S$$
$$15P_S = 138$$
$$P_S = 9.2$$

Thus, the price that sellers receive is $9.20 per pizza. Then, the price that buyers pay is

$$P_B = \$9.20 + \$1.20 = \$10.40$$

To solve for the equilibrium quantity with the tax, we substitute the buyer price into the demand equation or the seller price into the supply equation:

$$Q^D = 111 - 10 \times 10.4 = 7$$
$$Q^S = -39 + 5 \times 9.2 = 7$$

Thus, the tax decreases the quantity of pizza sold from 11,000 to 7,000.

b. To find the consumer and producer surpluses and see how the tax changes them, we graph the demand and supply curve, using the equilibrium points and the choke prices for demand and supply. To find the choke prices with no tax, we set Q_D and Q_S equal to zero and solve for P:

$$Q^D = 111 - 10P$$
$$0 = 111 - 10P$$
$$10P = 111$$
$$P = 11.1$$
$$Q^S = -39 + 5P$$
$$0 = -39 + 5P$$
$$5P = 39$$
$$P = 7.8$$

Thus, the demand choke price is $11.10 and the supply choke price is $7.80. We use these points to graph the demand and supply curves (D and S on the following graph). To graph the supply curve facing buyers (S_B), we simply shift the seller supply curve up by $1.20 at each quantity. For example, the choke price for the buyer supply curve is $7.80 + $1.20 = $9.00.

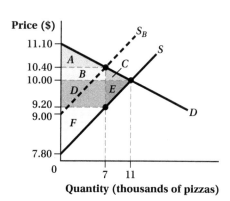

With no tax, the consumer surplus is the triangular area below the demand curve and above the equilibrium price (area $A + B + C$):

$$CS = 0.5 \times 11,000 \times (\$11.10 - \$10.00) = \$6,050$$

With the tax, the consumer surplus is the area above the price that buyers pay and below the demand curve (area A):

$$CS_{new} = 0.5 \times 7,000 \times (\$11.10 - \$10.40) = \$2,450$$

Thus, the tax decreases the consumer surplus by $\$6,050 - \$2,450 = \$3,600$.

With no tax, the producer surplus is the triangular area below the equilibrium price and above the supply curve (area $D + E + F$):

$$PS = 0.5 \times 11,000 \times (\$10.00 - \$7.80) = \$12,100$$

With the tax, the producer surplus reduces to the area below the price that sellers receive and above the supply curve (area F):

$$PS_{new} = 0.5 \times 7,000 \times (\$9.20 - \$7.80) = \$4,900$$

Thus, the producer surplus decreases by $\$12,100 - \$4,900 = \$7,200$.

c. The consumer surplus represented by area C and the producer surplus represented by area E have disappeared because of the tax. Since no one receives these surpluses anymore, this is a deadweight loss. The triangular area $C + E$ can be calculated as

$$DWL = 0.5 \times (\$10.40 - \$9.20) \times (11,000 - 7,000) = \$2,400$$

The deadweight loss can also be calculated as the difference between the total surplus that consumers and producers get with no tax and the total surplus they and the government receive with the tax. With no tax, the total surplus is

$$TS = CS + PS = \$6,050 + \$12,100 = \$18,150$$

With the tax, the surplus received by consumers and producers is

$$CS_{new} + PS_{new} = \$2,450 + \$4,900 = \$7,350$$

and the surplus received by the government (government tax revenue) is

$$GS = \$1.20 \times 7,000 = \$8,400$$

So the deadweight loss is

$$DWL = \$18,150 - (\$7,350 + \$8,400) = \$2,400$$

3.5 Subsidies

Subsidy

A payment by the government to a buyer or seller of a good or service. A subsidy is given to producers shifts the supply curve down by the amount of the per-unit subsidy.

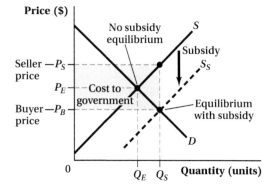

3.4 figure it out 1

Suppose that the demand and supply curves in a market for milk are given by the following equations:

$$Q^D = 95 - 12.5P$$
$$Q^S = -205 + 50P$$

Where Q^D is the quantity of milk demanded (in thousands of gallons), Q^S is the quantity supplied, and P is the price of milk (in dollars per gallon). The current equilibrium price is $4.80 per gallon, and the current equilibrium quantity is 35,000 gallons. Suppose the government wants to give milk producers a subsidy of $2 per gallon.

a. How will the subsidy change the price of milk that buyers pay? The price that sellers of milk receive? The quantity of milk sold?

b. How much will the subsidy cost the government?

Solution

a. The subsidy creates a dual-supply-curve situation. The supply curve for sellers is the same as the initial supply curve. But the supply curve facing buyers is shifted down by the amount of the subsidy ($2 per gallon). Since the government pays sellers $2 for each gallon of milk they sell, buyers pay $2 less per gallon than the full price that sellers receive. Thus, the price paid by buyers is

$$P_B = P_S - 2$$

Where P_S is the price received by sellers. To solve for the quantity and prices with the subsidy, we substitute this expression into our supply and demand equations:

$$Q^D = Q^S$$
$$95 - 12.5P_B = -205 + 50P_S$$
$$95 - 12.5 \times (P_S - 2) = -205 + 50P_S$$
$$95 - 12.5P_S + 25 = -205 + 50P_S$$
$$62.5P_S = 325$$
$$P_S = 5.2$$

Thus, the price that sellers receive is $5.20 per gallon. Then, the price that buyers pay is

$$P_B = \$5.20 - \$2.00 = \$3.20.$$

To solve for the equilibrium quantity of milk with the subsidy, we substitute the buyer price into the demand equation or the seller price into the supply equation:

$$Q^D = 95 - 12.5 \times 3.2 = 55$$
$$Q^S = -205 + 50 \times 5.2 = 55$$

That is, with the subsidy, the quantity of milk sold is 55,000 gallons. Thus, the subsidy reduces the price that buyers pay from $4.80 per gallon to $3.20 per gallon and raises the price that sellers receive from $4.80 per gallon to $5.20 per gallon. The subsidy increases the quantity of milk sold from 35,000 gallons to 55,000 gallons. The following diagram illustrates this solution.

b. The cost of the subsidy is the subsidy per gallon times the number of gallons sold: $2 \times 55,000 = \$110,000.$

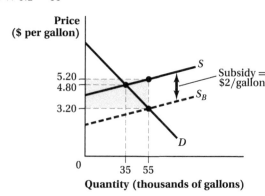

Practice Problems

Problem 1

Suppose the demand for strawberries in a local market is described by the following equation:

$$Q^D = 190 - 20P$$

Where Q^D is the quantity of strawberries demanded (in thousands of pounds) and P is the price of strawberries (in dollars per pound).

a. Suppose the current price of strawberries is $3.50 per pound. What is the consumer surplus?
b. Now suppose that unfavorable weather conditions decrease the supply of strawberries. As a result, the price rises to $6 per pound. What will happen to the consumer surplus? How much will it change?
∂ c. Use calculus to calculate the change in consumer surplus, and show that it is the same as in part (b).

Problem 2

Suppose the supply of tomatoes in a local market is described by the following equation:

$$Q^S = -40 + 40P$$

Where Q^S is the quantity of tomatoes supplied (in thousands of pounds) and P is the price of tomatoes (in dollars per pound).

a. Suppose the current price of tomatoes is $2.25 per pound. What is the producer surplus?
b. Now suppose that the demand for tomatoes increases, so the price rises to $3.25 per pound. What will happen to the producer surplus? How much will it change?
∂ c. Use calculus to calculate the change in producer surplus, and show that it is the same as in part (b).

Problem 3

Suppose the government is considering a tax on sellers of cigarettes, $1.10 per pack sold. With no tax, the demand and supply curves in the market for cigarettes are given by the following equations:

$$Q^D = 23 - 2P$$
$$Q^S = -10 + 20P$$

Where Q^D is the quantity of cigarettes demanded (in millions of packs), Q^S is the quantity supplied, and P is the price of cigarettes (in dollars per pack). With no tax, the equilibrium price of cigarettes is $1.50 per pack, and the equilibrium quantity is 20 million packs.

a. At the equilibrium price and quantity, what is the price elasticity of demand for cigarettes? The price elasticity of supply?
b. Given the elasticities you've calculated in (a), what would be the share of the tax borne by consumers? What would be the share borne by producers?
c. With the tax, what price would buyers pay? What price would sellers receive?

Problem 4

Suppose the demand and supply curves for corn are

$$Q^D = 600 - 60P$$
$$Q^S = -30 + 30P$$

Where Q^D is the quantity demanded per year (in millions of bushels), Q^S is the quantity supplied, and P is the price (in dollars).

a. What is the consumer surplus? Producer surplus?
b. Now suppose the government ends subsidies to ethanol producers, and these producers account for a large proportion of the demand for corn. As a result, the quantity of corn demanded decreases by $180 million bushels at each given price. How does this affect consumer surplus? Producer surplus?
c. What is the change in the total surplus in the market for corn resulting from the decrease in demand?

Problem 5

Suppose the demand and supply curves for electronic tablets are given by

$$Q^D = 54 - 0.1P$$
$$Q^S = -24 + 0.1P$$

where Q^D is the quantity demanded per year (in millions), Q^S is the quantity supplied, and P is the price (in dollars). Suppose that a technological innovation dramatically increases productivity in the production of tablets, so the quantity of tablets supplied increases by 12 million at each given price.

a. What is the consumer surplus before the technological change?

b. What is the consumer surplus after the change? How much do consumers gain or lose as a result of the technological innovation?

c. What is the producer surplus before the technological change?

d. What is the producer surplus after the change? How much do producers gain or lose as a result of the technological innovation?

e. What is the change in total surplus resulting from the innovation?

Problem 6

Suppose the government imposes a tax on buyers of luxury yachts, $5 million per yacht bought. With no tax, the demand and supply curves in the market for luxury yachts are given by the following equations:

$$Q^D = 5,200 - 80P$$
$$Q^S = -1,100 + 20P$$

where Q^D is the quantity of yachts demanded, Q^S is the quantity supplied, and P is the price of a typical yacht (in millions of dollars). These demand and supply curves are shown on the graph below.

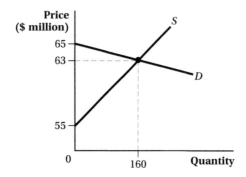

a. How does the tax affect the quantity of yachts sold? The price that buyers pay? The price that sellers receive?

b. What share of the tax is actually paid by buyers?

c. How does the tax affect consumer surplus? Producer surplus?

d. What is the deadweight loss resulting from the tax?

Problem 7

Suppose in the market for low-skilled labor, the supply curve is

$$L^S = -120 + 80W$$

Where L^S is the quantity of labor supplied (in millions of hours) and W is the wage, that is, the price of labor (in dollars per hour), and the demand curve is

$$L^D = 600 - 80W$$

where L^D is the quantity of labor demanded (in millions of hours). Suppose that currently, the minimum wage is $4 per hour.

a. What is the current wage of low-skilled workers? What is the quantity of low-skilled labor employed?
b. If the government raises the minimum wage to $6 per hour, what will be the quantity of labor employed? Will there be a shortage or surplus of labor? How large?
c. Are low-skilled workers better off or worse off as a result of the new minimum wage? By how much? Are employers better off or worse off? By how much?
d. What is the deadweight loss (if any) resulting from the new minimum wage?

Problem 8

Suppose that the demand and supply curves in a market for college education are given by the following equations:

$$Q^D = 45 - 1.5P$$
$$Q^S = -3 + 0.5P$$

where Q^D is the number of students who want to attend college (in millions), Q^S is the number of students that colleges are willing to enroll, and P is the average price of attending college (in thousands of dollars per year). Suppose that trying to encourage more people to get college degrees, the government gives each student a subsidy of $8,000 per year.
a. How will the subsidy change the price that a student pays for a year in college? The price that colleges receive per student? The number of students enrolled?
b. How much will the subsidy cost the government?
c. By how much are students better off as a result of the subsidy?

Problem 9

In the previous problem, how will your answers change if instead of giving the subsidy to students, the government pays colleges $8,000 per year for each student enrolled?

Problem 10

The following graph shows a market for pork. Suppose the government supports pork producers by imposing a price floor at $3 per pound and purchasing all unsold pork.

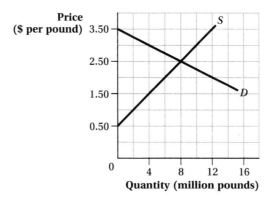

a. How much pork will the government purchase?
b. What is the cost of this program to consumers (in lost surplus)?
c. What is the cost to taxpayers of purchasing the unsold pork? Is there a loss of surplus associated with this purchase?
d. How much producer surplus do sellers of pork gain as a result of the program?
e. What is the cost to society of the pork support program?

Problem 11

Suppose a city government rules that no more than 4 million gallons of gasoline can be purchased per month in the city. The government enforces this quota by issuing permits that gas sellers must purchase in order to have the right to sell a certain quantity of gas in the city. The government sells these permits in a competitive auction. Before the quota is enforced, the market demand curve is

$$Q^D = 10 - 1.25P$$

and the market supply curve is

$$Q^S = -10 + 5P$$

where the quantity is measured in millions of gallons per month and the price is in dollars per gallon.

a. How will the quota influence the market price of gas? The quantity of gas sold?
b. How will the quota influence the consumer surplus? How will it change the producer surplus? (*Hint*: The easiest way to answer these questions is to draw the supply and demand curve, and show the effects of the quota on the graph.)
c. What will be the deadweight loss resulting from the quota (if any)?
∂ d. Use calculus to recalculate deadweight loss from the quota, and confirm that your answer is the same as in part (c).

∂ Problem 12

Suppose that the demand curve for a new spring dress is given by $P = 300 - 6Q^3$ and supply is $P = 30 + 4Q^3$, where price is in dollars and quantity is in thousands of dresses.

a. Find the equilibrium price and quantity.
b. Calculate the consumer and producer surplus at the equilibrium price.
c. Suppose that the local government sets a unit-tax of $10 on spring dresses. Calculate the new consumer and producer surplus.
d. Calculate the deadweight loss associated with the tax.

Consumer Behavior

4

4.1 The Consumer Preferences and the Concept of Utility

Utility

A measure of how satisfied a consumer is. You can think of utility as happiness or well-being. It is important to understand that utility is *not* a measure of how rich a consumer is, and it is *not* the dollar value of a consumption bundle. The units used to measure utility (utils) are arbitrary. Therefore, using the utility concept allows us to rank bundles of goods from best to worst, but we cannot say by how much one bundle is preferred to another.

Utility Function

A mathematical function that describes the relationship between the quantities of goods or services that a person consumes and the level of satisfaction (utility) that he gets from consuming this bundle. An example of a utility function is $U = Q_X^{0.5} Q_Y^{0.5}$, where U is the utility a person receives from consuming goods X and Y, Q_X is the quantity of good X that she consumes, and Q_Y is the quantity of good Y that she consumes.

Marginal Utility

The additional utility a consumer receives from an additional unit of a good or service. Marginal utility can be calculated for any given utility function.

Mathematically, the marginal utility of good X is the partial derivative of $U(Q_X, Q_Y)$ with respect to Q_X. This is because marginal utility is the additional utility that the consumer gains along with a marginal increase of quantity of good X, and therefore is the change in utility for a change in good X. For example, for the utility function $U = Q_X^{0.5} Q_Y^{0.5}$, the marginal utility of good X is $\frac{\partial U}{\partial Q_X} = 0.5 Q_X^{-0.5} \times Q_Y^{0.5} = 0.5 \times \left(\frac{Q_Y}{Q_X}\right)^{0.5}$, and the marginal utility of good Y is $\frac{\partial U}{\partial Q_Y} = 0.5 Q_X^{0.5} \times Q_Y^{-0.5} = 0.5 \left(\frac{Q_X}{Q_Y}\right)^{0.5}$.

Note that for this utility function, you can use these formulas to get the marginal utility of good X and of good Y, respectively for *any* levels of goods X and Y simply by subbing in for Q_X and Q_Y. For example, if $Q_X = 2$ and $Q_Y = 8$, then marginal utility of X is $0.5 \left(\frac{Q_X}{Q_Y}\right)^{0.5} = 0.5 \left(\frac{8}{2}\right)^{0.5} = 1$ and the marginal utility of Y is $0.5 \left(\frac{2}{8}\right)^{0.5} = 0.25$. Note that this means that you can use one set of formulas (marginal utilities derived from calculus) to calculate specific marginal utilities at many levels of goods X and Y. This may be *easier* than solving for marginal utility using algebraic methods over and over and over again to get these marginal utilities at different levels!

Monotonic Transformations

Utility functions tell us about ordinal rankings but not about cardinal rankings, and therefore the units of measurement ("utils") don't matter but the orderings generated by utility functions do. Monotonic transformations are changes to a utility function that preserve the ordering of preferences. We can tell whether different utility functions reflect the same preferences by solving for marginal rate of substitution using the methods discussed previously and then comparing these marginal rates of substitution. If they are the same, then the different utility functions represent the same preferences. If they are different, then the different utility functions represent different preferences.

4.2 Indifference Curves

Indifference Curves

An indifference curve shows consumption bundles that provide a consumer with the same utility. Each level of utility has a separate indifference curve. A higher indifference curve indicates a higher level of utility. A typical indifference curve is convex to the origin (i.e., bowed inward). The graph below shows typical indifference curves, U_1 and U_2. All combinations of good X and good Y that lie on U_1 are equally preferred, and so are all the bundles of X and Y that lie on U_2. But all the bundles on U_2 provide a higher level of utility than all the bundles on U_1 and therefore are preferred to all the bundles on U_1.

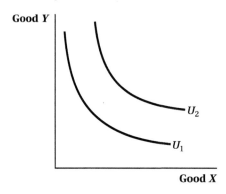

Marginal Rate of Substitution

The marginal rate of substitution of good X for good Y (MRS_{XY}) is the quantity of good Y that a consumer gives up to get a unit of good X while staying on the same indifference curve:

$$MRS_{XY} = -\frac{\Delta Y}{\Delta X}$$

With good X on the horizontal axis, the MRS_{XY} at a point equals the absolute value of the slope of the indifference curve at that point (see the following graph). Since an indifference curve is convex (i.e., becomes flatter when more of good X is consumed), the more of good X is consumed, the lower is the MRS_{XY}.

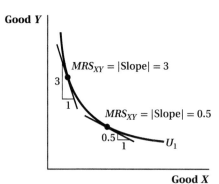

∂ Recall that MRS_{XY} is the absolute value of slope as opposed to slope itself. MRS_{XY} can be written using calculus as $-\dfrac{dY}{dX}$. Since this is a first derivative, we can test for convexity using calculus by calculating the derivative of MRS_{XY} with respect to good X and comparing this to zero (since this is effectively a second derivative test). Specifically, if $\dfrac{\partial MRS_{XY}}{\partial X} < 0$, then the indifference curve is convex. Similarly, if $\dfrac{\partial MRS_{XY}}{\partial X} > 0$, then the indifference curve is concave. Finally, if $\dfrac{\partial MRS_{XY}}{\partial X} = 0$, then the indifference curve is neither convex nor concave.

The marginal rate of substitution of good X for good Y also equals the ratio of the marginal utility of X (MU_X) to the marginal utility of Y (MU_Y):

$$MRS_{XY} = \frac{MU_X}{MU_Y}$$

∂ Since marginal utilities of X and Y, respectively, can be calculated as the partial derivatives of the utility function with respect to X and to Y, we can see that an easy way to calculate marginal rate of substitution of X for Y is to sub in for these partial derivatives:

$$MRS_{XY} = \frac{MU_X}{MU_Y} = \frac{\dfrac{\partial U}{\partial Q_X}}{\dfrac{\partial U}{\partial Q_Y}}$$

Note that the equation for marginal rate of substitution can also be derived using partial differentials (see the in-text appendix to Chapter 4).

For the example, $U = Q_X^{0.5} Q_Y^{0.5}$ as given in the preceding, marginal rate of substitution of X for Y is

$$MRS_{XY} = \frac{MU_X}{MU_Y} = \frac{0.5\left(\dfrac{Q_Y}{Q_X}\right)^{0.5}}{0.5\left(\dfrac{Q_X}{Q_Y}\right)^{0.5}} = \frac{Q_Y}{Q_X}$$

For the example that $Q_X = 2$ and $Q_Y = 8$, $MRS_{XY} = \dfrac{8}{2} = 4$. Again, it is evident that utilizing calculus is sometimes easier than relying on algebra!

The Shape of Indifference Curves

A consumer with steeper indifference curves is willing to give up more of good Y for a unit of good X than a consumer with flatter indifference curves. The curvature of the indifference curves characterizes the two goods' substitutability. Goods that are close substitutes have indifference curves that are close to straight lines, and indifference curves for perfect substitutes are straight lines. Goods that are complementary have very curved indifference curves, and indifference curves for perfect complements are L-shaped.

∂ The slope of an indifference curve indicates the rate at which a consumer is willing to trade away good Y for good X and therefore the marginal rate of substitution. Marginal rate of substitution is related to indifference curves, since it is just the absolute value of this slope. Since marginal rate of substitution can be written as the negative of a first derivative (as it is done in the previous section), we can therefore test for the shape of indifference curves (i.e., the extent of convexity or concavity), based on the marginal rate of substitution using calculus as we do in the previous section.

make the grade

The marginal rate of substitution and the slope of the indifference curve

Understanding the meaning of the marginal rate of substitution (MRS) is very important when you are solving problems on consumer choice. One thing about the MRS that is helpful to remember is that it equals the absolute value of the slope of the indifference curve along which the consumer substitutes. But this is only true if you substitute the good on the horizontal (X) axis for the good on the vertical (Y) axis. For example, suppose the following graph shows your indifference curve (U_1) for two goods, coffee (good X) and tea (good Y). At point A, you consume 3 cups of coffee and 7 cups of tea. Your indifference curve shows that if you give up 2 cups of tea and get 1 cup of coffee instead, moving to point B, you will be as well off as you are at point A. This means your marginal rate of substitution of coffee (good X) for tea (good Y) is

$$MRS_{XY} = -\frac{\Delta Y}{\Delta X} = -\frac{-2}{1} = 2$$

which is the absolute value of the slope of the indifference curve between point A and point B, as shown on the graph.

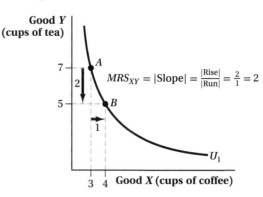

Note also that if you move from point B to point A, you substitute 2 cups of tea (good Y) for 1 cup of coffee (good X), so your marginal rate of substitution of tea for coffee is

$$MRS_{YX} = \frac{\Delta X}{\Delta Y} = -\frac{-1}{2} = 0.5$$

which is the absolute value of the inverse of the slope of the indifference curve.

4.2 figure it out 1

Ron enjoys pumpkin pasties and butterbeer. His utility function is $U = P^{0.5} + 0.8B^{0.5}$, where P is the number of pumpkin pasties he eats and B is the pints of butterbeer he drinks. Given this utility function, the marginal utility of pumpkin pasties is $MU_P = \dfrac{0.5}{P^{0.5}}$, and the marginal utility of butterbeer is $MU_B = \dfrac{0.4}{B^{0.5}}$.

a. At a dinner, Ron eats 10 pumpkin pasties and drinks 2 pints of butterbeers. What is his marginal rate of substitution of pumpkin pasties for butterbeer (MRS_{PB})?
b. Next day, Ron eats 9 pumpkin pasties and drinks 3 pints of butterbeer. Does he stay on the same indifference curve? Explain your answer in two different ways.
c. If Ron eats one more pumpkin pasty but drinks a half pint less of butterbeer, he stays on the same indifference curve. Are his indifference curves convex?
d. Given the utility function in this problem, show that the marginal utilities are as given, using calculus.
e. Show whether Ron's indifference curves are convex or concave, using calculus.

Solution:

a. The marginal rate of substitution of pumpkin pasties for butterbeer is defined as $MRS_{PB} = \dfrac{MU_P}{MU_B}$. Thus, Ron's MRS_{PB} is

$$MRS_{PB} = \frac{\dfrac{0.5}{P^{0.5}}}{\dfrac{0.4}{B^{0.5}}} = 1.25\left(\frac{B}{P}\right)^{0.5}$$

And when Ron consumes 10 pumpkin pasties and 2 butterbeers, his MRS_{PB} is

$$MRS_{PB} = 1.25 \times \left(\frac{2}{10}\right)^{0.5} = 0.56$$

b. Given Ron's utility function, when he consumes 10 pumpkin pasties and 2 butterbeers, his utility level is $U = 10^{0.5} + 0.8 \times 2^{0.5} = 4.29$. And when he consumes 9 pumpkin pasties and 3 butterbeers, his utility level is $U = 9^{0.5} + 0.8 \times 3^{0.5} = 4.38$. Since 9 pumpkin pasties and 3 butterbeers provide Ron with a higher level of utility than 10 pumpkin pasties and 2 butterbeers, he gets on a higher indifference curve when he consumes one more butterbeer instead of a pumpkin pasty. Another way to answer this question is to realize that Ron's $MRS_{PB} = 0.56$ suggests that if he gives up one pumpkin pasty and gets 0.56 pints of butterbeer instead, he will stay on the same indifference curve. But Ron actually gets the whole additional pint of butterbeer for one pumpkin pasty hat he gives up. Thus, he reaches a higher utility level, i.e., he gets on a higher indifference curve.

c. To see whether Ron's indifference curve is convex, we calculate his MRS_{PB} at $P = 11$ and $B = 1.5$ and compare it with his MRS_{PB} at $P = 10$ and $B = 2$. Using the formula in (a), at $P = 11$ and $B = 1.5$, $MRS_{PB} = 1.25 \times \left(\frac{1.5}{11}\right)^{0.5} = 0.46$. Thus, Ron's marginal rate of substitution of pumpkin pasties for butterbeer decreases as he consumes more pumpkin pasties, which means his indifference curve becomes less steep. That is, Ron's indifference curve is convex to the origin.

d. Marginal utilities can be calculated as partial derivatives of the utility function. Since $U = P^{0.5} + 0.8B^{0.5}$, the marginal utility of pumpkin pasties is $MU_P = \frac{\partial U}{\partial P} = 0.5P^{0.5-1} + 0 = 0.5P^{-0.5}$, and the marginal utility of butterbeer is $MU_B = \frac{\partial U}{\partial B} = 0 + 0.8(0.5)B^{0.5-1} = 0.4B^{-0.5}$. These are the same as the marginal utilities as given.

e. A way to check concavity versus convexity is to take the partial derivative of MRS_{PB} with respect to P and compare it to zero. This marginal rate of substitution is calculated in part (a). Specifically,

$$MRS_{PB} = \frac{MU_P}{MU_B} = \frac{0.5P^{-0.5}}{0.4B^{-0.5}} = 1.25B^{0.5}P^{-0.5}$$

The derivative of this with respect to P is $\frac{\partial MRS_{PB}}{\partial P} = 1.25(-0.5)B^{0.5}P^{-0.5-1} = -0.625B^{0.5}P^{-1.5}$. Since this is always less than zero (for positive amounts of B and P), Ron's indifference curves are convex.

∂ 4.2 figure it out 2

Maria is a kindergarten teacher. Suppose Maria's utility function is $U = 0.6C^{0.4}M^{0.6}$, where C is the number of crayon boxes and M is the number of marker boxes that she has for her class.
a. Given this utility function, what is Maria's marginal utility of crayons? Use calculus to solve.
b. What is Maria's marginal utility of markers? Use calculus to solve.
c. What is Maria's marginal rate of substitution of crayons for markers?
d. What is the shape of Maria's indifference curves?
e. Does the utility function $U = 0.4C^{0.6}M^{0.4}$ represent the same preferences as Maria's?

Solution:

a. Using partial derivatives, we can see that $MU_C = \frac{\partial U}{\partial C} = 0.6(0.4)C^{0.4-1}M^{0.6} = 0.24C^{-0.6}M^{0.6}$.

b. Using partial derivatives, we can see that $MU_M = \frac{\partial U}{\partial M} = 0.6(0.6)C^{0.4}M^{0.6-1} = 0.36C^{0.4}M^{-0.4}$.

c. Marginal rate of substitution of C for M therefore is $MRS_{CM} = \frac{MU_C}{MU_M} = \frac{0.24C^{-0.6}M^{0.6}}{0.36C^{0.4}M^{-0.4}} = \frac{2M}{3C} = 0.67MC^{-1}$.

d. Maria's indifference curves are convex. We can see this by using MRS_{CM} as calculated in part (c), taking the derivative with respect to C, and comparing it to zero as in our test to determine convexity or concavity. Here, $\frac{\partial MRS_{CM}}{\partial C} = 0.67(-1)MC^{-1-1} = -0.67MC^{-2}$, which is less than zero for positive amounts of markers and crayons, and therefore Maria's indifference curves are convex.

e. For this new utility function, $MU_C = \frac{\partial U}{\partial C} = 0.24C^{-0.4}M^{0.4}$ and $MU_M = \frac{\partial U}{\partial M} = 0.16C^{0.6}M^{-0.6}$. Marginal rate of substitution of C for M therefore is $MRS_{CM} = \frac{MU_C}{MU_M} = \frac{0.24C^{-0.4}M^{0.4}}{0.16C^{0.6}M^{-0.6}} = \frac{3M}{2C}$. Since this is not the same as part (c), the proposed utility function does not represent Maria's preferences.

4.3 The Consumer's Income and the Budget Constraint
Budget Constraint

A budget constraint is a line that shows all consumption bundles that a person can purchase when spending all his income. The equation for a budget constraint is

$$B = P_X Q_X + P_Y Q_Y$$

where B is the amount available to spend on good X and good Y, P_X and P_Y are the prices per unit of good X and good Y, and Q_X and Q_Y are the quantities of good X and good Y.

The following graph illustrates the basics of budget constraint.

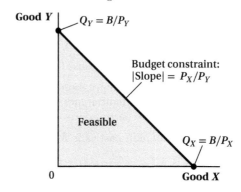

Factors that affect the budget constraint's position		
Factor	**If rises**	**If falls**
	Budget line:	
Price of *X*	Rotates clockwise around the vertical axis and becomes steeper	Rotates counterclockwise around the vertical axis and becomes flatter
Price of *Y*	Rotates counterclockwise around the horizontal axis and becomes flatter	Rotates clockwise around the horizontal axis and becomes steeper

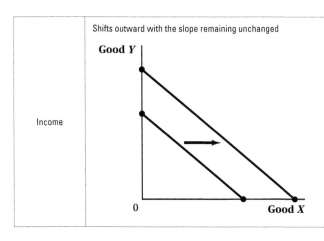

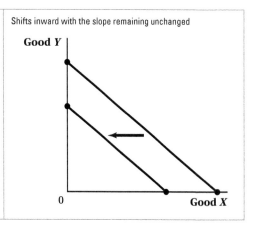

∂ Note that prices are the partial derivatives of the budget (B) with respect to relevant quantities $(Q_X$ and Q_Y, respectively), just as marginal utilities are the partial derivatives of the utility function (U) with respect to Q_X and Q_Y. Another way to think about the slope is to rewrite the budget constraint in point-slope form. Specifically,

$$Q_Y = \frac{B}{P_Y} - \left(\frac{P_X}{P_Y}\right)Q_X$$

Now, taking the derivative, $\dfrac{\partial Q_Y}{\partial Q_X} = -\left(\dfrac{P_X}{P_Y}\right)$. Note that this is the slope of the budget constraint. In absolute value form, we have the price ratio $\dfrac{P_X}{P_Y}$.

4.3 figure it out 1

Howard spends all his monthly allowance of $200 on coffee and donuts. The price of a cup of coffee is $2, and the price of a donut is $2. The following graph shows Howard's indifference curves.
a. What is Howard's optimal consumption bundle?
b. What is Howard's marginal rate of substitution of coffee for donuts at the point of his optimal choice?
c. Suppose the price of a donut falls to $1. How will Howard's optimal consumption bundle change?

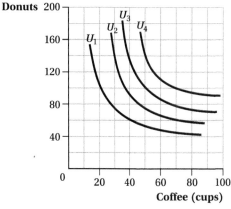

Solution:

a. To find Howard's optimal consumption bundle, we first draw his budget constraint. If Howard spends all his allowance on coffee, he will get $\dfrac{\$200}{\$2} = 100$ cups of coffee and no donuts. If he spends all his allowance on donuts, he will get $\dfrac{\$200}{\$2} = 100$ donuts and no coffee. Connecting these two points, we draw Howard's budget constraint $(BC_1$ on the following graph). Howard's optimal choice is the point of tangency between his budget line and the highest indifference curve he can reach, U_1. Thus, Howard's optimal consumption bundle is 40 cups of coffee and 60 donuts.

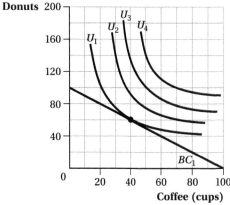

b. The marginal rate of substitution of coffee for donuts (MRS_{CD}) at a point equals the absolute value of the slope of the indifference curve at this point. And at the point of the consumer's optimal choice, the slope of the indifference curve equals the slope of the budget constraint, which is equal (by the absolute value) to the ratio of the price of the good on the horizontal axis (coffee) to the price of the good on the vertical axis (donuts). Thus, $MRS_{CD} = \dfrac{\$2}{\$2} = 1$.

c. With the new price of donuts, if Howard spends all his allowance on donuts, he will get $\dfrac{\$200}{\$1} = 200$ donuts and no coffee. If he spends all his allowance on coffee, he will still get $\dfrac{\$200}{\$2} = 100$ cups of coffee and no donuts. Connecting these two points, we get Howard's new budget constraint (BC_2 on the following graph). Howard's optimal choice is the point of tangency between this new budget line and the highest indifference curve he can reach, U_3. As we can see, Howard's optimal consumption bundle is now 50 cups of coffee and 100 donuts.

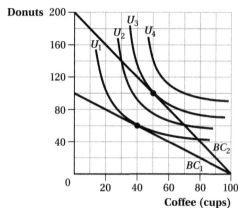

4.3 figure it out 2

Sally views Deer Park spring water and Zephyrhills spring water as perfect substitutes.
a. Draw Sally's indifference curves (with Deer Park water on the horizontal axis) when she consumes: (i) 24 bottles of Deer Park water and no Zephyrhills water; (ii) 20 bottles of Deer Park water and 20 bottles of Zephyrhills water; (iii) 32 bottles of Zephyrhills water and no Deer Park water.
b. Suppose Sally has $32 per month to spend on spring water. The price of Deer Park water is $1 per a half-liter bottle, and the price of Zephyrhills water is the same. Draw Sally's budget constraint on the same graph with the indifference curves. Can you tell how many bottles of Deer Park water and how many bottles of Zephyrhills water Sally will buy?
c. Now suppose the price of Deer Park water doubles, while the price of Zephyrhills water remains at $1. Draw Sally's new budget constraint. How many bottles of Deer Park water and how many bottles of Zephyrhills water will Sally buy now?
d. What is the utility function as a function of Deer Park (D) and Zephyrhills (Z) water implied by the information given in this problem?
e. Using calculus, derive the marginal utilities of the two types of water (MU_D and MU_Z) and the marginal rate of substitution between them (MRS_{DZ}).
f. Why does the Lagrangian approach break down in this circumstance?

Solution:

a. The fact that Deer Park water and Zephyrhills water are perfect substitutes to Sally means that no matter how much spring water she consumes, when she substitutes one bottle of Deer Park water for an equal-size bottle of Zephyrhills water, she stays on the same indifference curve. That is, her indifference curves are straight lines whose slope equals -1. Thus, to draw Sally's indifference curves, we simply draw straight lines with the slope equal to -1 through the points that represent Sally's consumption bundles (see the following graph).

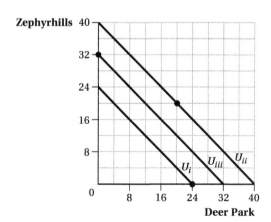

b. If Sally spends all $32 on Deer Park water, she'll buy $\dfrac{\$32}{\$1} = 32$ bottles of that water and no Zephyrhills water. If she spends all her budget on Zephyrhills water, she'll buy $\dfrac{\$32}{\$1} = 32$ bottles of that water and no Deer Park water. Connecting these two points on the graph, we get Sally's budget constraint. As you can see, it coincides with the indifference curve U_{iii} on the graph. Since any combination of goods on Sally's budget constraint gives her the same level of utility, we cannot tell how many bottles of Deer Park water and how many bottles of Zephyrhills water she will actually buy. We can only tell that she will buy 32 bottles of spring water.

c. With the new price, if Sally spends all her money on Deer Park water, she'll buy $\frac{\$32}{\$2} = 16$ bottles of that water and no Zephyrhills water. And if she spends all her budget on Zephyrhills water, she'll still buy $\frac{\$32}{\$1} = 32$ bottles of that water and no Deer Park water. Connecting these two points on the graph, we get Sally's budget constraint (BC_2 on the following graph). That is, Sally's budget constraint rotates clockwise around the vertical axis as a result of the higher price of Deer Park water. As the graph shows, Sally reaches her highest level of utility if she spends all her money on Zephyrhills water (this is called a corner solution). All the other feasible bundles (e.g., 8 bottles of Deer Park water and 16 bottles of Zephyrhills water) lie on lower indifference curves.

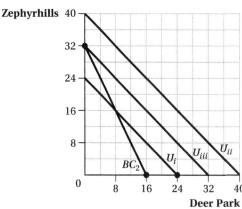

d. The utility function consistent with the graph for part a is $U(D,Z) = D + Z$.

e. Using partial derivatives, we can see that $MU_D = \frac{\partial U}{\partial D} = 1 + 0 = 1$ and $MU_Z = \frac{\partial U}{\partial Z} = 0 + 1 = 1$. Marginal rate of substitution of D for Z therefore is $MRS_{DZ} = \frac{MU_D}{MU_Z} = \frac{1}{1} = 1$.

f. The Lagrangian approach is based on solving for an interior optimum. Here, the solution is a corner solution as indicated in part (c). At this solution, therefore, the marginal rate of substitution actually does not equal the price ratio. (Challenge: Write out the Lagrangian and its first-order conditions to see this more formally. There is no way to solve the system of equations that is generated because this leads to a mathematical contradiction quickly!)

4.3 figure it out 3

Suppose Irene has $25 per month to spend on her mobile phone plan, which charges 5 cents per minute for phone calls and 10 cents to send a text message. Irene's indifference curves ($U_1 - U_4$) are shown on the following graph.

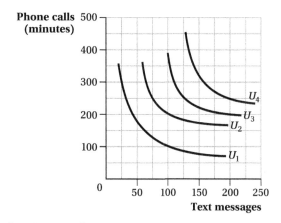

a. How many phone calls does Irene make per month? How many text messages does she send?
b. Suppose that the cell phone company faces difficulties when trying to accommodate the growing number of customers. The company changes Irene's plan and now charges 5 cents per minute only for the first 100 minutes. After that, the rate becomes 10 cents per minute. Draw Irene's budget constraint with the new phone plan.
c. With the new phone plan, how many phone calls does Irene make per month? How many text messages does she send? How does the new plan affect the utility that Irene gets?

Solution:

a. To find Irene's optimal consumption bundle, we draw her budget constraint. If Irene spends all her phone budget on text messages, she will send $\frac{\$25}{\$0.10} = 250$ messages. If she spends all her budget on phone minutes, she will get $\frac{\$25}{\$0.05} = 500$ minutes. We draw Irene's budget constraint (BC_1 on the following graph) by connecting these two points. Irene's optimal choice is the point of tangency between her budget line and the highest indifference curve she can reach, U_3. Thus, Irene's optimal consumption bundle is 125 text messages and 250 phone calls.

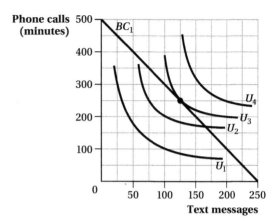

b. For the first 100 minutes of phone calls, Irene's budget constraint is the same as before. But her budget line has a kink at 100 minutes. It becomes flatter because phone minutes become more expensive. To find where this budget constraint intercepts the vertical axis, we need to figure out how many minutes Irene can buy if she buys only phone call time. We can find it from the following equation: $(\$0.05 \times 100) + (\$0.10 \times M) = \$25$, where M is the additional minutes after 100 minutes that Irene can buy. Solving the equation for M, we get $\$5 + 0.10M = \$25$, from which $M = 200$. Thus, the budget constraint intercepts the vertical axis at $100 + 200 = 300$ minutes. Now we can draw Irene's budget constraint (BC_2) as shown on the following graph.

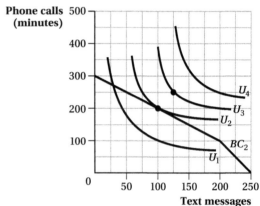

c. Irene's optimal choice is the point of tangency between her new budget constraint and the highest indifference curve she can reach, which is now U_2. Thus, Irene's optimal consumption bundle is 100 text messages and 200 phone calls. As we can see, Irene is now on a lower indifference curve, which means the utility level that she can reach with the new plan is lower than that with the old plan.

4.4 Combining Utility, Income, and Prices: What Will the Consumer Consume?

The consumer's optimal choice

A rational consumer chooses the bundle of good X and good Y that is at the point of tangency between his budget constraint (BC) and the highest indifference curve he can reach (U_1). At this point, the consumer's utility is maximized because

$$MRS_{XY} = \frac{P_X}{P_Y}$$

Note that this is the same thing as setting the absolute value of the slope of the indifference curve equal to the absolute value of the slope of the budget constraint. This is also the same as:

$$\frac{MU_X}{MU_Y} = \frac{P_X}{P_Y}$$

where the four partial derivatives (of the utility function and budget constraint with respect to X and Y, respectively) can be subbed in.

The following graph illustrates a consumer's optimal choice.

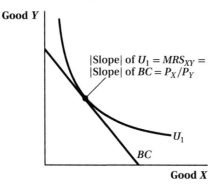

For the continuing example where $U = Q_X^{0.5}Q_Y^{0.5}$, assume that we know now that the prices of X and Y, respectively, are 10 and 5. (Recall that the consumer takes these prices as given, since they are determined by the market (the intersection of supply and demand) and not by the consumer.) The marginal rate of substitution of X for Y, or ratio of marginal utilities of X to Y, is shown in the preceding to equal $\dfrac{Q_Y}{Q_X}$. This, therefore, can be substituted on the left side of the equation and the given prices can be substituted on the right. Specifically,

$$\frac{Q_Y}{Q_X} = \frac{10}{5}$$
$$Q_Y = 2Q_X$$

Note that this by itself is not enough to solve the consumer's optimization problem, since this is one equation with two unknowns (Q_X and Q_Y). The good news, however, is that it is relatively straight-forward to find the optimal quantities. To do so, we just need to include the information contained in the budget constraint. Suppose that the amount of income that the consumer has at his or her disposal is equal to 100 and prices are as given in the preceding. Then, the consumer's budget constraint is simply:

$$100 = 10Q_X + 5Q_Y$$

Now, we have two equations with two unknowns and therefore can solve the system of equations. Plugging the first equation into the second:

$$100 = 10Q_X + 5(2Q_X)$$
$$100 = 20Q_X$$
$$Q_X = 5$$

Using the first equation, we see that:

$$Q_Y = 2Q_X$$
$$Q_Y = 2(5) = 10$$

Thus, $(Q_X, Q_Y) = (5,10)$ represents the coordinates of the tangency in the consumer's optimal choice figure, as shown.

The consumer's optimal choice also can be derived using the Lagrange multiplier that is introduced in the appendix to Chapter 4 in the textbook. The consumer's constrained optimization problem can be written as:

$$\max_{Q_X, Q_Y} U(Q_X, Q_U) \text{ subject to } (s.\ t.)\ B = P_X Q_X + P_Y Q_Y$$

Recall that the Lagrangian is basically a math tool to solve a constrained optimization problem. When you are solving an unconstrained optimization problem in a standard calculus class, recall that you take the derivative of the objective equation and set it equal to zero (first order condition). Then, you solve for your variable and you have found your maximum or minimum (depending on which way the curvature goes). The Lagrangian approach is similar. Particularly, we are interested in isolating an optimum. The only difference is that we have an additional constraint out there. The idea of the Lagrangian approach is to reduce the whole optimization to one equation that incorporates both the objective and the constraint. We then do the same thing as we would for a standard unconstrained optimization problem, we take the derivative (here partial derivatives) and set each of these equal to zero. Therefore, instead of one first-order condition, we have several, but then this is just a system of equations that we can solve using standard algebraic techniques. The Lagrangian can be written:

$$\mathcal{L}(Q_X, Q_Y, \lambda) = f(Q_X, Q_Y) + \lambda[g(Q_X, Q_Y)]$$

where $f(.,.)$ is the objective function (what you want to maximize here), $g(.,.)$ is the modification of the constraint (constraint written in the $= 0$ format), and λ is the Lagrange multiplier. You can think of the Lagrange multiplier as representing a math trick. We are using it to turn on and turn off the constraint and therefore analyzing our optimum such that the constraint is satisfied. For our preceding example, the Lagrangian therefore is:

$$\mathcal{L}(Q_X, Q_Y, \lambda) = Q_X^{0.5}Q_Y^{0.5} + \lambda[100 - 10Q_X - 5Q_Y]$$

The first-order conditions (partial derivatives of this equation with respect to quantity of X, quantity of Y, and the Lagrange multiplier λ, respectively, are:

$$\frac{\partial \mathcal{L}}{\partial Q_X} = 0.5Q_X^{-0.5}Q_Y^{0.5} - \lambda(10) = 0$$

$$\frac{\partial \mathcal{L}}{\partial Q_Y} = 0.5Q_X^{0.5}Q_Y^{-0.5} - \lambda(5) = 0$$

$$\frac{\partial \mathcal{L}}{\partial \lambda} = 100 - 10Q_X - 5Q_Y = 0$$

These equations represent the three equations with three unknowns (Q_X, Q_Y, and λ) that we want to solve to find our solution. Solving the first two for λ and setting them equal to each other, we find:

$$\lambda = \frac{0.5Q_X^{-0.5}Q_Y^{0.5}}{10} = \frac{0.5Q_X^{0.5}Q_Y^{-0.5}}{5}$$

Dividing both sides by 0.5 and multiplying by 5, we find that:

$$\frac{Q_X^{-0.5}Q_Y^{0.5}}{2} = Q_X^{0.5}Q_Y^{-0.5}$$

Using the fact that a variable to a negative exponent is equal to one divided by that variable to a positive exponent:

$$\frac{Q_Y^{0.5}}{2Q_X^{0.5}} = \frac{Q_X^{0.5}}{Q_Y^{0.5}}$$

Cross-multiplying, we see that:

$$Q_Y^{0.5}Q_Y^{0.5} = 2Q_X^{0.5}Q_X^{0.5}$$

Adding the exponents, we conclude that:

$$Q_Y = 2Q_X$$

The last of the three conditions tells us the budget constraint relationship:

$$100 = 10Q_X + 5Q_Y$$

Notice that we now have two equations with two unknowns instead of three equations with three unknowns. Our method is the same as if we were solving a simple supply and demand system with two equations and two unknowns. We just need to sub one relationship into the other and solve. Here,

$$100 = 10Q_X + 5(2Q_X)$$

$$100 = 20Q_X$$

$$Q_X = 5$$

$$Q_Y = 2(5) = 10$$

Note that this is the same answer as what we get from the previous shortcut approach, where we solve for marginal rate of substitution and set it equal to the price ratio and combine this with the budget constraint relationship. This is no surprise, however, since that first approach came out of our graphical interpretation of what the optimum should look like.

∂ Corner solutions

Corner solutions are defined by the characteristic that $MRS_{XY} \neq \dfrac{P_X}{P_Y}$ at the optimum. A common example of this is when it is optimal for consumers to consume all good X and no good Y, or all good Y and no good X. In these cases, the Lagrangian method breaks down (i.e., there will not be a solution to the first-order conditions). A way to figure out which corner a consumer will choose is to calculate his or her utility at each corner of the relevant budget constraint and then select the highest utility.

4.4 figure it out 1

Sebastian has \$420 per month to spend on concert tickets and restaurant meals. His marginal utility of a concert is $MU_C = \dfrac{4}{C}$, where C is the number of concerts he attends per month. And his marginal utility of a restaurant meal is $MU_M = \dfrac{2}{M}$, where M is the number of restaurant meals he has per month. The price of a concert ticket is \$40, and the price of a restaurant meal is \$20. As a rational consumer, how many concerts will Sebastian attend and how many restaurant meals will he have?

Solution:

Sebastian will maximize his utility at the point where the marginal rate of substitution of concerts for restaurant meals equals the ratio of the price of a concert ticket to the price of a restaurant meal, that is:

$$MRS_{CM} = \frac{MU_C}{MU_M} = \frac{P_C}{P_M}$$

Given that $MU_C = \dfrac{4}{C}$, $MU_M = \dfrac{2}{M}$, $P_C = \$40$, and $P_M = \$20$, we can write:

$$\frac{4}{C} \div \frac{2}{M} = \frac{40}{20}$$

$$\frac{4M}{2C} = \frac{40}{20}$$

$$\frac{2M}{C} = 2$$

$$\frac{M}{C} = 1$$

That is, Sebastian maximizes his utility when the number of concerts he attends and the number of restaurant meals he has are equal. But what are these numbers? To figure this out, we use Sebastian's budget constraint, which can be written as:

$$\$40 \times C + \$20 \times M = \$420$$

Since $M = C$, we can substitute C for M in the preceding equation, which gives us

$$\$40 \times C + \$20 \times C = \$420$$

$$\$60 \times C = \$420$$

$$C = 7$$

And since $M = C$, we know that $M = 7$ as well. Thus, Sebastian maximizes his utility by attending 7 concerts and having 7 restaurant meals per month.

∂ 4.4 figure it out 2

Suppose that the price of a box of crayons is \$1 and the price of a box of markers is \$2. If Maria's utility function is $U = 0.6C^{0.4}M^{0.6}$, where C is the number of crayon boxes and M is the number of marker boxes and her budget is \$20, how many boxes of crayons and how many boxes of markers should she choose? Use the Lagrangian approach to solve.

Solution:

The Lagrangian is:

$$\mathcal{L}(C,M,\lambda) = 0.6C^{0.4}M^{0.6} + \lambda[20 - C - 2M]$$

The first-order conditions (partial derivatives of this equation with respect to C, M, and the Lagrange multiplier λ, respectively) are:

$$\frac{\partial \mathcal{L}}{\partial C} = 0.24C^{-0.6}M^{0.6} - \lambda = 0$$

$$\frac{\partial \mathcal{L}}{\partial M} = 0.36C^{0.4}M^{-0.4} - \lambda(2) = 0$$

$$\frac{\partial \mathcal{L}}{\partial \lambda} = 20 - C - 2M = 0$$

Solving the first two equations for λ and setting them equal to each other, we find:

$$\lambda = 0.24C^{-0.6}M^{0.6} = 0.18C^{0.4}M^{-0.4}$$

Rearranging, we see that:

$$4M = 3C$$

$$M = \frac{3C}{4}$$

The third equation tells us the budget constraint relationship:

$$20 = C + 2\left(\frac{3C}{4}\right)$$

$$20 = 2.5C$$

$$C = 8$$

$$M = \frac{3(8)}{4} = 6$$

∂ 4.4 figure it out 3

Suppose again that the price of a box of crayons is \$1 and the price of a box of markers is \$2, as in figure it out 2, but now assume that Maria's utility function is $U = 0.4C + 0.6M$, where C is the number of crayon boxes and M is the number of marker boxes and her budget is still \$20.

a. Set up a Lagrangian and derive the first-order conditions for the maximization problem.

b. Is there a solution to the first-order conditions? If so, solve for the optimal quantities of boxes of crayons and markers. If not, what is the solution to the maximization problem?

Solution:

a. The Lagrangian is:

$$\mathcal{L}(C,M,\lambda) = 0.4C + 0.6M + \lambda(20 - C - 2M)$$

FOC:

$$\frac{\partial \mathcal{L}}{\partial C} = 0.4 - \lambda = 0$$

$$\frac{\partial \mathcal{L}}{\partial M} = 0.6 - 2\lambda = 0$$

$$\frac{\partial \mathcal{L}}{\partial \lambda} = 20 - C - 2M = 0$$

b. The first-order conditions require that $\lambda = 0.4$ and $\lambda = 0.3$. Therefore, the system of equations has no solution. Utility must be maximized at a consumption bundle where Maria buys all crayons or all markers (or if the slopes of her indifference curves and budget constraint are exactly the same, she could buy any affordable combination). In other words, there is a corner solution. Note that

$$\frac{MU_C}{P_C} = \frac{0.4}{1} > \frac{MU_M}{P_M} = \frac{0.6}{2}$$

So the additional utility per dollar is higher for crayons; therefore, Maria will want to buy only crayons. Given Maria's budget constraint, she can afford 20 boxes of crayons.

Practice Problems

Problem 1

Boris likes sausage and bread. His utility function is $U = 0.4S^{0.5}B^{0.5}$, where S is the pounds of sausage and B is the loaves of bread he eats. This utility function suggests that Boris's marginal utility of sausage is $MU_S = \dfrac{0.2B^{0.5}}{S^{0.5}}$, and his marginal utility of bread is $MU_B = \dfrac{0.2S^{0.5}}{B^{0.5}}$.

a. One week, Boris eats 9 pounds of sausage and 4 loaves of bread. What is his marginal rate of substitution of sausage for bread (MRS_{SB})?

b. Next week, Boris eats 6 pounds of sausage and 6 loaves of bread. Does he stay on the same indifference curve? Explain your answer.

c. Are Boris's indifference curves convex? Explain your answer.

d. Given the utility function in this problem, show that the marginal utilities are as given, using calculus.

e. Show whether Boris's indifference curves are convex or concave, using calculus.

f. Does the utility function $U = 0.1S + 0.1B$ represent the same preferences as Boris's?

Problem 2

Suppose Beatrice is indifferent between consuming bundle A, which consists of 2 burgers and 6 orders of fries, and bundle B, which consists of 6 burgers and 2 orders of fries.

a. Assume that Beatrice has typical indifference curves. If she is offered bundle C, which consists of 4 burgers and 4 orders of fries, will she prefer it to bundle A? Draw Beatrice's indifference curves to illustrate your answer.

b. Now suppose that Beatrice views burgers and fries as perfect substitutes. Will your answer in (a) change? Draw indifference curves to illustrate your answer.

c. Now suppose that Beatrice views burgers and fries as perfect complements. Will your answer in (a) change? Draw indifference curves to illustrate your answer.

Problem 3

Cornelius enjoys treacle tarts and cauldron cakes. His utility function is $U = 4T + 2C$, where T is the number of treacle tarts and C is the number of cauldron cakes.

a. One day, Cornelius eats 5 treacle tarts and 4 cauldron cakes. What is his marginal utility of consuming one more tart? What is his marginal rate of substitution of treacle tarts for cauldron cakes (MRS_{TC})?

b. Does Cornelius view treacle tarts and cauldron cakes as perfect complements? Perfect substitutes? Neither perfect complements nor perfect substitutes? Explain.

c. Next day, Cornelius eats 7 treacle tarts and no cauldron cakes. Does he stay on the same indifference curve? Explain your answer in two different ways.

d. Are Cornelius's indifference curves convex? Explain your answer.

e. Using calculus, derive the marginal utilities of treacle tarts and cauldron cakes (MU_T and MU_C) and the marginal rate of substitution between them (MRS_{TC}).

f. Is the Lagrangian approach an appropriate way to solve for an optimum, given this utility function? Why? (Hint: What will Cornelius's final optimum look like? Note that without prices, you cannot solve precisely but you still can describe the characteristics of equilibrium for him.)

Problem 4

Titus has \$100 per month to spend on cupcakes (C) and music downloads (M). The price of a cupcake is \$2, and the price of a music download is \$1.

a. Write an equation for Titus's budget constraint. Graph his budget constraint (with cupcakes on the horizontal axis). What is the slope of the budget line?

b. Given that Titus spends all his money, how many music downloads does he buy if he decides to eat 40 cupcakes per month?

c. Suppose that the price of a music download falls to \$0.50, while the price of a cupcake remains unchanged. Draw Titus's new budget constraint. What is the slope of the new budget line? With the new budget constraint, how many music downloads does Titus buy if he eats 40 cupcakes per month?

Problem 5

Benedict spends all his monthly allowance of $144 on audiobooks and pizza. The price of pizza is $4 per slice, and the price of an audiobook is $16. The following graph shows Benedict's indifference curves.

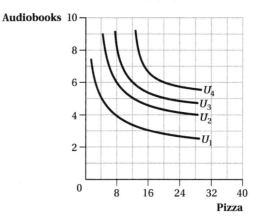

a. What is Benedict's optimal consumption bundle?
b. What is Benedict's marginal rate of substitution of pizza for audiobooks at the point of his optimal choice?
c. Suppose the price of pizza rises to $6 per slice. How will Benedict's optimal consumption bundle change?

Problem 6

Vassilios has $72 to spend on t-shirts and socks. His budget constraint (BC_1) and indifference curves $(U_1 - U_4)$ are shown on the following graph.

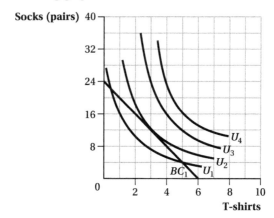

a. What are the prices of the two goods?
b. As a rational consumer, how many t-shirts and how many pairs of socks does Vassilios buy?
c. Suppose Vassilios's budget increases to $108. How many t-shirts and how many pairs of socks does he buy now?

Problem 7

Danny has a monthly budget of $72 to spend on music video downloads and phone calls. The price of a video download is $3, and Danny's phone plan charges 12 cents per minute.
a. Which of the following combinations of video downloads and phone calls can Danny afford?
  i.   20 downloads and 120 phone minutes
  ii. 12 downloads and 300 phone minutes
  iii. 6 downloads and 600 phone minutes
  iv. 15 downloads and 200 phone minutes

b. Draw Danny's budget constraint (with video downloads on the horizontal axis). If Danny downloads 6 videos, how many phone minutes can he afford?

c. Now suppose that Danny's phone company offers a new plan, which charges 12 cents per minute for the first 300 minutes per month and 6 cents per minute after that. Draw Danny's budget constraint with this new plan.

d. With the new plan, if Danny downloads 9 videos, can he afford 400 phone minutes? If Danny downloads 6 videos, how many phone minutes can he afford?

Problem 8

Christa spends all her monthly allowance of $128 on music CDs and iTunes music downloads. The price of a music CD is $16, and the price of iTunes downloads is $8 per album. The following graph shows Christa's indifference curves.

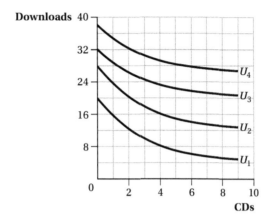

a. Does Christa view music CDs and albums downloads as perfect substitutes? Explain your answer.

b. As a rational consumer, how many CDs will Christa buy and how many albums will she download?

c. Suppose now that the price of iTunes downloads falls to $4 per album. How many CDs and how many iTunes albums will Christa buy?

Problem 9

Ben enjoys hotdogs. But a hotdog without a bun is useless to him, and so is a bun without a hotdog. To be able to pick the kinds of hotdogs and buns he likes most, Ben buys hotdogs and buns separately. He has $36 per week to spend on hotdogs and buns. The price of a hotdog is $2, and the price of a bun is $1.

a. Draw Ben's indifference curve on which he consumes 4 hotdogs and 12 buns.

b. As a rational consumer, how many hotdogs and how many buns will Ben buy per week?

c. Suppose Ben's budget for hotdogs and buns decreases to $24 per week. How many hotdogs and how many buns will he buy?

d. Will the Lagrangian approach work to solve for an interior optimum in this circumstance? Why or why not?

Problem 10

Suppose that Papa John's Pizza offers a special promotion: buy one medium pizza and get the second free. The price of a medium pizza is $8. Suppose that your daily income is $40 and your indifference curves are shown on the following graph. Assume that the price of all other goods is $1 per unit.

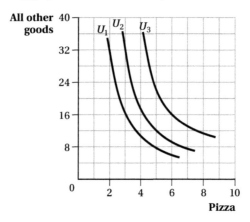

a. Draw your budget constraint before the special promotion. How many pizzas will you buy?
b. Draw your budget constraint with the special promotion. How many pizzas will you buy? Will Papa John's special promotion increase the quantity of pizza you buy?

∂ Problem 11

Delia is a toddler who only likes to consume milk and bananas. Suppose Delia's utility function is $U = 4MB$, where M is total ounce of milk and B is the number of banana pieces.
a. Given this utility function, what is Delia's marginal utility of milk? Use calculus to solve.
b. What is Delia's marginal utility of bananas? Use calculus to solve.
c. What is Delia's marginal rate of substitution of milk for bananas?
d. Show whether Delia's indifference curves are convex or concave, using calculus.
e. Does the utility function $U = 4M^{0.5}B^{0.5}$ represent the same preferences as Delia's?

∂ Problem 12

Suppose that the price of a box of chocolates is $10 and the price of a bottle of wine $15 and that Doug only has $60 to surprise his wife for Valentine's Day. If Doug's wife's utility function is $U = C^2W^2$, where C is the number of chocolate boxes and W is the number of wine bottles, how many boxes of chocolate and bottles of wine should Doug purchase to maximize his wife's happiness? Use the Lagrangian approach to solve.

∂ Problem 13

As in problem 12, suppose that the price of a box of chocolates is $10 and the price of a bottle of wine $15 and that Doug only has $60 to surprise his wife for Valentine's Day. If Doug's wife's utility function is $U = 2C + 2W$, where C is the number of chocolate boxes and W is the number of wine bottles, how many boxes of chocolate and bottles of wine should Doug purchase to maximize his wife's happiness? (Hint: Is the Lagrangian approach appropriate in this case?)

Individual and Market Demand

5

5.1 How Income Changes Affect an Individual's Consumption Choices

Income effect

The change in a consumer's consumption choices that results from a change in the purchasing power of the consumer's income.

Normal good

A good for which consumption rises when income rises.

∂ We can check if a good is a normal good using a partial derivative. Specifically, if the partial derivative of the demand function with respect to income $\frac{\partial Q}{\partial I} > 0$, then the good in question would be considered a normal good as opposed to an inferior good.

Inferior good

A good for which consumption decreases when income rises.

∂ We can check if a good is an inferior good using a partial derivative. Specifically, if the partial derivative of the demand function with respect to income $\frac{\partial Q}{\partial I} < 0$, then the good in question would be considered an inferior good as opposed to a normal good.

Income elasticity

The percentage change in the quantity consumed of a good in response to a 1% change in income. Formally, the income elasticity is

$$E_I^D = \frac{\%\Delta Q}{\%\Delta I} = \frac{\frac{\Delta Q}{Q}}{\frac{\Delta I}{I}} = \frac{\Delta Q}{\Delta I}\frac{I}{Q}$$

where Q is the quantity of the good consumed (ΔQ is the change in quantity), and I is income (ΔI is the change in income).

The sign of the income elasticity is the same as the sign of the income effect. For normal goods, $\frac{\Delta Q}{\Delta I} > 0$, and the income elasticity is positive. For inferior goods, $\frac{\Delta Q}{\Delta I} < 0$, and the income elasticity is negative.

∂ The income elasticity formula can be rewritten using calculus as $E_I^D = \frac{\partial Q}{\partial I} \times \frac{I}{Q}$, where $\frac{\partial Q}{\partial I}$ is the partial derivative of the demand function with respect to income. In this equation, I and Q are, respectively, the values of income and quantity demanded at the point along the demand curve at which you want to measure this elasticity.

Necessity good

A normal good for which income elasticity is between 0 and 1.

Luxury good

A good with an income elasticity greater than 1.

Income expansion path

A curve that connects a consumer's optimal bundles at each income level.

Engel curve

A curve that shows the relationship between the quantity of a good consumed and a consumer's income.

5.1 figure it out 1

Jim receives a weekly allowance of $54 from his parents. He spends all this money on hamburgers and coffee. The price of a hamburger is $1.50, and the price of a cup of coffee is $2.25. The following graph shows Jim's indifference curves ($U_1 - U_4$).

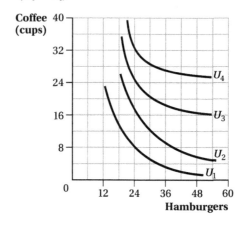

a. How many hamburgers and how many cups of coffee does Jim buy per week?
b. Now suppose that Jim's parents increase his weekly allowance by $18. Jim's preferences and the prices of the goods remain unchanged. What combination of hamburgers and coffee does Jim consume?
c. Suppose further that Jim's parents increase his weekly allowance again, by $18 more. Neither Jim's preferences nor the prices of the goods change. What combination of hamburgers and coffee does Jim consume now?
d. Draw Jim's income expansion path and Engel curves for hamburgers and coffee.
e. Are hamburgers a normal or an inferior good? What about coffee? Explain your answers.

Solution

a. To find Jim's optimal consumption bundle, we draw his budget constraint. If Jim spends all his allowance on hamburgers, he will get $\frac{\$54}{\$1.5} = 36$ hamburgers and no coffee. If he spends all his allowance on coffee, he will get $\frac{\$54}{\$2.25} = 24$ cups of coffee and no hamburgers. Connecting these two points, we draw Jim's budget constraint (BC_1 on the following graph). Jim's optimal choice is the point of tangency between his budget line and the highest indifference curve he can reach, U_1. Thus, he consumes 24 hamburgers and 8 cups of coffee.

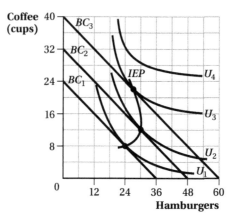

b. With Jim's allowances increased to $54 + $18 = $72, he can get $\frac{\$72}{\$1.5} = 48$ hamburgers and no coffee or $\frac{\$72}{\$2.25} = 32$ cups of coffee and no hamburgers. Connecting these two points, we draw Jim's new budget constraint (BC_2). Jim's optimal choice now is the point of tangency between the budget line BC_2 and the highest indifference curve Jim can reach, U_2. Thus, Jim consumes 30 hamburgers and 12 cups of coffee.

c. Now Jim's budget is $72 + $18 = $90, so he can get $\frac{\$90}{\$1.5} = 60$ hamburgers and no coffee or $\frac{\$90}{\$2.25} = 40$ cups of coffee and no hamburgers. Connecting these two points, we draw Jim's budget constraint (BC_3). Jim's optimal choice now is the point of tangency between the budget line BC_3 and the highest indifference curve he can reach, i.e., 27 hamburgers and 22 cups of coffee.

d. Jim's income expansion path is the curve that connects his optimal bundles at each income level (curve IEP on the preceding graph). Jim's Engel curves for hamburgers and coffee are shown on the following graphs. They reflect the relationship between the quantity of each good consumed and Jim's income.

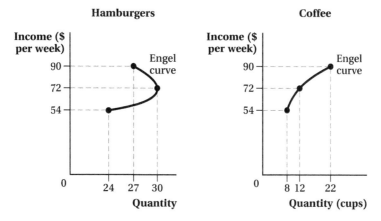

e. As Jim's income increases from $54 to $72, his consumption of hamburgers increases. Thus, in this income range, hamburgers are a normal good. But, as Jim's income increases more, from $72 to $90, his consumption of hamburgers decreases. Thus, at these income levels, hamburgers are an inferior good. Jim's consumption of coffee increases as his income increases, from $54 to $72 to $90. Thus, coffee is a normal good over the whole income range in question.

5.2 How Price Changes Affect Consumption Choices

5.2 figure it out 1

Misty earns $300 per week. She spends all her income on sandwiches and singing lessons. The price of a sandwich is $5, and the price of a singing lesson is $30. The following graph shows Misty's indifference curves.

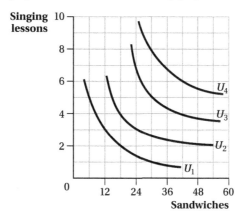

a. What is the slope of Misty's budget constraint?

b. What combination of sandwiches and singing lessons does Misty consume?

c. Suppose the price of a singing lesson rises to $60. How many sandwiches and how many singing lessons does Misty consume now?

d. On a separate diagram, draw Misty's demand curve for singing lessons, based on your answers in (b) and (c).

Solution

a. The slope of a budget constraint equals the negative of the ratio of the price of the good on the horizontal axis (sandwiches) to the price of the good on the vertical axis (singing lessons). Thus, the slope of Misty's budget line is $-\left(\dfrac{\$5}{\$30}\right) = -0.167$.

b. To find Misty's optimal consumption bundle, we draw her budget constraint. If Misty spends all her income on sandwiches, she will get $\dfrac{\$300}{\$5} = 60$ sandwiches and no singing lessons. If she spends all her income on singing lessons, she will get $\dfrac{\$300}{\$30} = 10$ lessons and no sandwiches. Connecting these two points, we get Misty's budget constraint (BC_1 on the following graph). Misty's optimal choice is the point of tangency between her budget line and the highest indifference curve she can reach, U_3. Thus, Misty gets 30 sandwiches and 5 singing lessons.

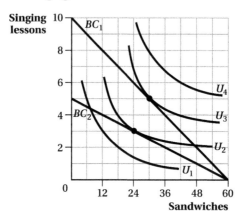

c. When the price of a singing lesson rises to \$60, even if Misty spends all her income on singing lessons, she can only get $\dfrac{\$300}{\$60} = 5$ lessons. The horizontal intercept of Misty's budget constraint does not change, since neither her income nor the price of sandwiches changes. Thus, Misty's budget line rotates counterclockwise around the horizontal axis, and her new budget constraint is BC_2. Misty's optimal choice is now the point of tangency between the budget line BC_2 and the highest indifference curve she can reach, U_2. Thus, Misty gets 24 sandwiches and 3 singing lessons.

d. Misty's demand curve for singing lessons shows the relationship between the price of singing lessons and Misty's quantity of singing lessons demanded. We can use the information from our indifference curve diagram to plot two points on this demand curve:

Price	Quantity of singing lessons demanded
\$30	30
\$60	24

Misty's demand curve for singing lessons (D) is shown on the following graph.

∂ 5.2 figure it out 2

Suppose that the demand curve for a product can be expressed as: $Q = 1,000 - 5P + 10P - I_0$, where P is the price of the good in question, P_0 is the price of a related good, and I is income. Remember that the demand function is a function describing the demand for the good in question, not the other good.

a. Use calculus to argue whether the related good is a complement or a substitute.

b. Use calculus to argue whether the good in question is a normal good or an inferior good.

c. If the price of the good is 10, the price of the related good is 5 and income is 500. Then, what is the income elasticity of demand? Use calculus to express this elasticity, and interpret its magnitude in words.

Solution

a. Since $\frac{\partial Q}{\partial P_0} = 0 - 0 + 10 - 0 = 10 > 0$, and therefore quantity is increasing with the price of the related good, we know that the related good is a substitute.

b. Since $\frac{\partial Q}{\partial I} = 0 - 0 + 0 - 1 = -1 < 0$, and therefore quantity is decreasing as income increases, we know that the good is an inferior good.

c. We need three things for the income elasticity formula—income, quantity, and the partial derivative of the demand function with respect to quantity. Income is given. To get quantity, we can substitute the values that we know into the demand function: $Q = 1,000 - 5(10) + 10(5) - 500 = 500$. The partial derivative of quantity with respect to income was calculated in part (b): $\frac{\partial Q}{\partial I} = -1$. The income elasticity of demand at the current allocation therefore is: $E_I^D = \frac{\partial Q}{\partial I} \times \frac{I}{Q} = -1\left(\frac{500}{500}\right) = -1$. This elasticity means that a 1% increase in income translates into a 1% decrease in quantity demanded. This is therefore exactly the case of a unit elasticity, since the elasticity is neither less than 1 in absolute value (inelastic), nor greater than 1 in absolute value (elastic).

5.3 Decomposing Consumer Responses to Price Changes into Income and Substitution Effects

Substitution effect

The change in a consumer's consumption choices that results from a change in the relative prices of two goods.

Total effect

The total change (substitution effect + income effect) in a consumer's optimal consumption bundle as a result of a price change.

Giffen good

A good for which price and quantity demanded are positively related. A Giffen good must be an inferior good.

∂ In calculus terms, a Giffen good has the properties that the partial derivative of the demand function with respect to income $\frac{\partial Q}{\partial I} < 0$, and the partial derivative of the demand function with respect to price $\frac{\partial Q}{\partial P} > 0$. Note that this second condition corresponds to an upward-sloping demand function, which is rare.

∂ Marshallian demand

Demand curves that show the relationship between price and quantity demanded, assuming that the consumer's income stays constant. Marshallian, or "uncompensated", demand curves include both income and substitution effects. The Marshallian demand curve can be solved for from the Lagrangian utility maximization problem—as used to solve for the consumer's optimum in Chapter 4—by treating income and the price of Y (and of any other goods) as fixed.

Hicksian demand

Demand curves that show the relationship between price and quantity demanded, assuming that the consumer's utility stays constant. Hicksian or "compensated" demand curves only include substitution effects. The Hicksian demand curve can be solved for from the Lagrangian expenditure minimization problem—as used to solve for the consumer's optimum in Chapter 4—by treating utility and the price of Y (and of any other goods) as fixed.

Slutsky equation

Decomposition of substitution and income effects. The Slutsky equation can be written:

$$\frac{\partial X(P_X, P_Y, I)}{\partial P_X} = \frac{\partial H(P_X; P_Y, \overline{U})}{\partial P_X} - X\frac{\partial X(P_X, P_Y, I)}{\partial I}$$

The first term (the partial derivative of the Hicksian demand curve with respect to price) represents the substitution effect. The second term (a function of the partial derivative of the Marshallian demand curve with respect to price) is the income effect.

make the grade

Separating the substitution and income effects of a price change

The following steps will help you correctly identify the substitution and income effects:
- Start at the point where the consumer initially maximizes her utility (point A on the graph below), i.e., where her indifference curve (U_1) is tangent to her budget constraint (BC_1).

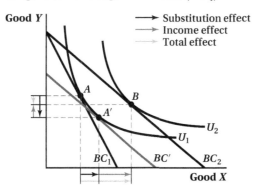

- Draw the new budget constraint reflecting the price change. As shown on the graph, a decrease in the price of good X rotates the budget constraint counterclockwise around the vertical axis. Find the new optimal bundle of goods (point B),

i.e., the point where this new budget constraint (BC_2) is tangent to a new indifference curve (U_2).
- Draw a new line (BC') that is parallel to the new budget constraint (BC_2) and tangent to the original indifference curve (point A'). The movement along the original indifference curve from point A (the original, pre-price change bundle) to this new tangency point (A') is the substitution effect. This movement shows how quantities change when relative prices change, holding the purchasing power of income constant.
- The income effect of the price change is the movement from point A' to point B. Here, relative prices are held constant (the budget lines are parallel), but the purchasing power of income changes.
- The total effect of a price change (for either good) on quantity consumed depends on the relative size of the substitution and income effects. If the price of one good falls, the quantities of both goods consumed may rise, or consumption of one good may rise and consumption of the other good may decline. However, the quantities consumed of the two goods cannot both decline, since this would mean the consumer would not be on her budget constraint.

∂ Separating the substitution and income effects of a price change, using calculus

It takes several steps to use calculus to decompose the income and substitution effects. The method can be thought of in terms of solving for the initial optimum (A, as in the preceding figure), the new optimum (B, as in the preceding figure), and the bundle that minimizes expenditure at the new prices subject to the original utility level (A', as in the preceding figure). The steps are as follows:

- Solve the original constrained optimization problem $\max_{X,Y} U(X,Y)$ $s.t.$ $I = P_X X + P_Y Y$, using the Lagrangian approach. The Lagrangian corresponding to this is:

$$\max_{X,Y,\lambda} \mathcal{L}(X,Y,\lambda) = U(X,Y) + \lambda(I - P_X X - P_Y Y).$$

The first-order conditions are:

$$\frac{\partial \mathcal{L}}{\partial X} = \frac{\partial U(X,Y)}{\partial X} - \lambda P_X = 0$$

$$\frac{\partial \mathcal{L}}{\partial Y} = \frac{\partial U(X,Y)}{\partial Y} - \lambda P_Y = 0$$

$$\frac{\partial \mathcal{L}}{\partial \lambda} = I - P_X X - P_Y Y = 0$$

This is a system of three equations with three unknowns (X, Y, and λ).

The solution (X,Y) is the allocation at point A in the preceding figure.

- Now suppose that the price of good X, P_X, changes to P_X' and therefore the new budget constraint is $I = P_X' X + P_Y Y$. The new allocation, point B in the preceding figure is the solution to: $\max_{X,Y} U(X,Y) s.t. I = P_X' X + P_Y Y$. The Lagrangian corresponding to this is: $\max_{X,Y,\lambda} \mathcal{L}(X,Y,\lambda) = U(X,Y) + \lambda(I - P_X' X - P_Y Y)$ and the first-order conditions are:

$$\frac{\partial \mathcal{L}}{\partial X} = \frac{\partial U(X,Y)}{\partial X} - \lambda P_X' = 0$$

$$\frac{\partial \mathcal{L}}{\partial Y} = \frac{\partial U(X,Y)}{\partial Y} - \lambda P_Y = 0$$

$$\frac{\partial \mathcal{L}}{\partial \lambda} = I - P_X' X - P_Y Y = 0$$

This is a system of three equations with three unknowns (X, Y, and λ).

The solution (X,Y) is the allocation at point B in the preceding figure, and the difference between A and B is the total effect of the price change.

- To decompose this total effect into income and substitution effects, we need the allocation A' in the preceding figure. To get A', we can solve the expenditure minimization problem: $\min_{X,Y} P_X' X + P_Y Y$ $s.t.$ $\overline{U}_A = U(X,Y)$, where $\overline{U}_A$ is the level of utility at the initial allocation A. The Lagrangian corresponding to this is: $\mathcal{L}(X,Y,\lambda) = P_X' X + P_Y Y + \lambda\big(\overline{U}_A - U(X,Y)\big)$ and the first-order conditions are:

$$\frac{\partial \mathcal{L}}{\partial X} = P_X' - \lambda\frac{\partial U(X,Y)}{\partial X} = 0$$

$$\frac{\partial \mathcal{L}}{\partial Y} = P_Y - \lambda\frac{\partial U(X,Y)}{\partial Y} = 0$$

$$\frac{\partial \mathcal{L}}{\partial \lambda} = \overline{U}_A - U(X,Y) = 0$$

This is now a system of three equations with three unknowns that can be solved for X, Y, and λ. X and Y give the allocation at A'. The substitution effect of the price change is the difference between A and A'. The income effect of the price change is the difference between A' and B.

The key distinctions between substitution and income effects

Keeping in mind the following key distinctions between the two effects will help you identify them.

Substitution effects	Income effects
Involve comparisons of bundles that lie on the same indifference curve.	Involve comparisons of bundles that lie on two different indifference curves.
The direction of the effect on quantity consumed for a given change in the relative price of the good is unambiguous.	The direction of the effect on quantity consumed for a given change in the relative price of the good is ambiguous and depends on whether the good is normal or inferior.
If the good's relative price falls, the substitution effect causes the consumer to want more of it.	If the good is normal, then a fall in either its price or the price of the other good will cause the consumer to want more of it. (A drop in any price, even of another good, increases the effective income of the consumer.) If the good is inferior, then a price drop will cause the consumer to want less of it.
If the good's relative price rises, the substitution effect causes the consumer to want less of it.	If the good is normal, then a rise in either its price or the price of the other good will cause the consumer to want less of it. If the good is inferior, then a rise in either price will cause the consumer to want more of it.

5.3 figure it out 1

Petunia spends all her weekly income, $48, on potatoes and tomatoes. The price of potatoes is $4 per pound, and the price of tomatoes is also $4 per pound. Petunia's indifference curves ($U_1 - U_3$) and her budget constraint (BC_1) are shown on the following graph. Suppose the price of potatoes falls to $2 per pound, while Petunia's income and the price of tomatoes remain unchanged.

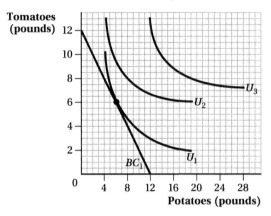

a. How does the fall in the price of potatoes affect the combination of goods that Petunia consumes?
b. What is the change in Petunia's consumption of potatoes due to the substitution effect? Due to the income effect? How does Petunia's consumption of tomatoes change due to the substitution effect? Due to the income effect?
c. Are potatoes a normal good or an inferior good? What about tomatoes? Explain your answers.

Solution

a. See the following graph. Initially, Petunia's optimal choice is the point of tangency between her budget constraint, BC_1, and the highest indifference curve she can reach, U_1 (point A). Thus, Petunia consumes 6 pounds of potatoes and 6 pounds of tomatoes. When the price of potatoes falls to $2 per pound, the horizontal (X) intercept of Petunia's budget line (i.e., the quantity of potatoes that she can get if she consumes only potatoes) is $\dfrac{\$48}{\$2} = 24$ pounds. The vertical intercept of Petunia's budget constraint does not change, since neither her income nor the price of tomatoes changes. Thus, Petunia's budget line rotates counterclockwise around the vertical axis, so her new budget constraint is BC_2. Petunia's optimal choice is now the point of tangency between the budget line BC_2 and the highest indifference curve she can reach, U_2 (point B). Thus, after the fall in the price of potatoes, Petunia's optimal consumption bundle is 8 pounds of potatoes and 8 pounds of tomatoes. That is, Petunia's consumption of potatoes increases by 2 pounds, and her consumption of tomatoes also increases by 2 pounds.

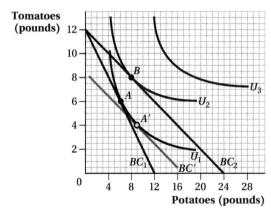

b. To separate the income effect and the substitution effect of the price change, we draw a new line (BC') that is parallel to the new budget constraint (BC_2) and tangent to the original indifference curve (U_1). The movement along U_1 from point A (the original, pre-price change bundle) to this new tangency point (A') is the substitution effect. This movement shows how quantities change when relative prices change, holding the purchasing power of income constant. Due to the substitution effect, Petunia's consumption of potatoes increases from 6 pounds to 9 pounds and her consumption of tomatoes decreases from 6 pounds to 4 pounds. The income effect of the price change is shown by the movement from point A' to point B. Here, relative prices are held constant (the budget lines BC' and BC_2 are parallel), but the purchasing power of income changes. Due to the income effect, Petunia's consumption of potatoes decreases from 9 pounds to 8 pounds and her consumption of tomatoes increases from 4 pounds to 8 pounds.

c. Potatoes are an inferior good because Petunia purchases fewer potatoes (8 pounds instead of 9 pounds) when the purchasing power of her income increases due to the price fall. Tomatoes, however, are a normal good because the increase in Petunia's purchasing power leads to an increase in her tomato consumption (from 4 pounds to 8 pounds).

5.3 figure it out 2

Elwood spends all his weekly income, $96, on bread and gasoline. The price of bread is $4 per loaf, and the price of gasoline is $2 per gallon. Elwood's indifference curves $(U_1 - U_3)$ and his budget constraint (BC_1) are shown on the following graph. Suppose the price of gasoline rises to $4 per gallon, while Elwood's income and the price of bread remain unchanged.

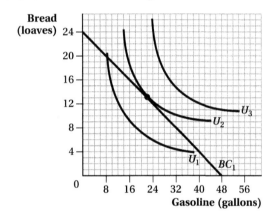

a. How does the higher price of gasoline affect the combination of goods that Elwood consumes?
b. What is the change in Elwood's consumption of gasoline because of the substitution effect? Because of the income effect? How does Elwood's consumption of bread change because of the substitution effect? Because of the income effect?
c. Is gasoline a normal good or an inferior good? What about bread? Explain your answers.

Solution

a. See the following graph. Initially, Elwood's optimal choice is the point of tangency between his budget constraint, BC_1, and the highest indifference curve he can reach, U_2 (point A). Thus, Elwood consumes 22 gallons of gas and 13 loaves of bread. When the price of gasoline rises to $4, the horizontal intercept of Elwood's budget line (i.e., the quantity of gasoline that he can get if he consumes only gasoline) is $\frac{\$96}{\$4} = 24$ gallons. The vertical intercept of Elwood's budget constraint does not change, since neither his income nor the price of bread changes. Thus, Elwood's budget line rotates clockwise around the vertical axis, so his new budget constraint is BC_2. Elwood's optimal choice is now the point of tangency between the budget line BC_2 and the highest indifference curve he can reach, U_1 (point B). Thus, after the rise in the price of gasoline, Elwood's optimal consumption bundle is 12 gallons of gasoline and 12 loaves of bread. That is, Elwood's consumption of gasoline decreases by 10 gallons, and his consumption of bread decreases by 1 loaf.

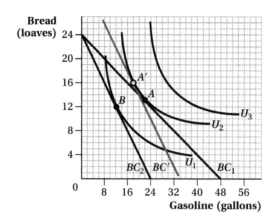

b. To separate the income effect and the substitution effect of the price change, we draw a new line (BC') that is parallel to the new budget constraint (BC_2) and tangent to the original indifference curve (U_2). The movement along U_2 from point A (the original, pre-price change bundle) to this new tangency point (A') is the substitution effect. This movement shows how quantities change when relative prices change, holding the purchasing power of income constant. Due to the substitution effect, Elwood's consumption of gasoline decreases from 22 gallons to 18 gallons and his consumption of bread increases from 13 loaves to 16 loaves. The income effect of the price change is shown by the movement from point A' to point B. Here, relative prices are held constant (the budget lines are parallel), but the purchasing power of income changes. Due to the income effect, Elwood's consumption of gasoline decreases from 18 gallons to 12 gallons and his consumption of bread decreases from 16 loaves to 12 loaves.

c. Gasoline is a normal good because Elwood purchases less gasoline (12 gallons instead of 18) when the purchasing power of his income falls due to the price increase. Bread is also a normal good because the fall in purchasing power leads to a decrease in Elwood's bread consumption (from 16 loaves to 12 loaves).

∂ 5.3 figure it out 3

Suppose that Kaden is only interested in hockey sticks (H) and superhero figures (S). Kaden has a utility function that can be expressed as $U(H,S) = H^{0.5}S^{0.5}$. His income is $300 and the prices of hockey sticks and superhero figures are $30 and $10, respectively.

a. What is Kaden's optimal consumption bundle of hockey sticks and superhero figures and his utility at these two prices?

b. If the price of hockey sticks increases to $40 and the price of superhero figures stays constant at $10, what does Kaden consume at the optimum at these new prices? Fractional answers are okay.

c. What are the magnitudes of the total, substitution, and income effects for hockey sticks and superhero figures?

d. Are hockey sticks a normal or an inferior good for Kaden?

Solution

a. We need to solve Kaden's original constrained optimization problem, $\max_{H,S} H^{0.5}S^{0.5}$ $s.t.$ $300 = 30H + 10S$, using the Lagrangian approach. The Lagrangian corresponding to this is:

$$\max_{H,S,\lambda} \mathcal{L}(H,S,\lambda) = H^{0.5}S^{0.5} + \lambda(300 - 30H - 10S)$$

The first-order conditions are:

$$\frac{\partial \mathcal{L}}{\partial H} = 0.5H^{0.5-1}S^{0.5} + 0 - \lambda(30) - 0 = 0.5H^{-0.5}S^{0.5} - \lambda(30) = 0$$

$$\frac{\partial \mathcal{L}}{\partial S} = 0.5H^{0.5}S^{0.5-1} + 0 - 0 - \lambda(10) = 0.5H^{0.5}S^{-0.5} - \lambda(10) = 0$$

$$\frac{\partial \mathcal{L}}{\partial \lambda} = 0 + 300 - 30H - 10S = 300 - 30H - 10S = 0$$

This is a system of three equations with three unknowns (H, S, and λ). The solution (H,S) is the allocation that we are interested in. Combining the first two equations, we see that:

$$\lambda = \frac{0.5H^{-0.5}S^{0.5}}{30} = \frac{0.5H^{0.5}S^{-0.5}}{10}$$

Simplifying by cancelling out 0.5 in the numerator and 10 in the denominator:

$$\frac{H^{-0.5}S^{0.5}}{3} = H^{0.5}S^{-0.5}$$

Using the rule that a variable to a negative exponent equals 1 divided by that variable to a positive exponent:

$$\frac{S^{0.5}}{3H^{0.5}} = \frac{H^{0.5}}{S^{0.5}}$$

Cross-multiplying, we see that:

$$S^{0.5}S^{0.5} = 3H^{0.5}H^{0.5}$$

Adding the exponents on each side, we can conclude that $S = 3H$.
Combining this with the third of the first-order conditions:

$$300 = 30H + 10(3H)$$
$$300 = 60H$$
$$H = 5$$
$$S = 3(5) = 15$$

Kaden should buy 5 hockey sticks and 15 superheroes at these prices.
We also want to find Kaden's level of utility at this original allocation: $U(5,15) = 5^{0.5}15^{0.5} \approx 8.66$.

b. We need to solve Kaden's new constrained optimization problem: $\max_{H,S} H^{0.5}S^{0.5}$ s.t. $300 = 40H + 10S$, using the Lagrangian approach. Notice that the only thing that has changed relative to part (a) is the price of hockey sticks. The Lagrangian corresponding to this, then, is:

$$\max_{H,S,\lambda} \mathcal{L}(H,S,\lambda) = H^{0.5}S^{0.5} + \lambda(300 - 40H - 10S)$$

The first-order conditions are:

$$\frac{\partial \mathcal{L}}{\partial H} = 0.5H^{-0.5}S^{0.5} - \lambda(40) = 0$$

$$\frac{\partial \mathcal{L}}{\partial S} = 0.5H^{0.5}S^{-0.5} - \lambda(10) = 0$$

$$\frac{\partial \mathcal{L}}{\partial \lambda} = 300 - 40H - 10S = 0$$

This is a system of three equations with three unknowns (H, S, and λ). The solution (H,S) is the allocation that we are interested in. Combining the first two equations, we see that:

$$\lambda = \frac{0.5H^{-0.5}S^{0.5}}{40} = \frac{0.5H^{0.5}S^{-0.5}}{10}$$

Rearranging, we can see that $S = 4H$.
Combining this with the third of the first-order conditions:

$$300 = 40H + 10(4H)$$
$$300 = 80H$$
$$H = 3.75$$
$$S = 4(3.75) = 15$$

Kaden should buy 3.75 hockey sticks and 15 superheroes at these prices. The total effect of the price change on Kaden's optimal bundle therefore is a decrease of 1.25 hockey sticks, and no change to the number of superhero figures. The increase in the price of hockey sticks had no effect on the optimal quantity of superhero figures in this case, since the income and the substitution effects are exactly offsetting. This is expected for the Cobb-Douglas utility function case.

c. To decompose this total effect into income and substitution effects, we can solve the expenditure minimization problem: $\min_{H,S} 40H + 10S$ s.t. $8.66 = H^{0.5}S^{0.5}$. The Lagrangian corresponding to this is: $\mathcal{L}(H,S,\lambda) = 40H + 10S + \lambda(8.66 - H^{0.5}S^{0.5})$, and the first-order conditions are:

$$\frac{\partial \mathcal{L}}{\partial H} = 40 - \lambda(0.5)H^{-0.5}S^{0.5} = 0$$

$$\frac{\partial \mathcal{L}}{\partial S} = 10 - \lambda(0.5)H^{0.5}S^{-0.5} = 0$$

$$\frac{\partial \mathcal{L}}{\partial \lambda} = 8.66 - H^{0.5}S^{0.5} = 0$$

This is now a system of three equations with three unknowns that can be solved for H, S, and λ. H and S give the allocation that we allow us to separate the substitution and income effects.

$$\lambda = \frac{40}{0.5H^{-0.5}S^{0.5}} = \frac{10}{0.5H^{0.5}S^{-0.5}}$$

Therefore, $4H = S$.

Combining this with the third of the first-order conditions:

$$8.66 = H^{0.5}(4H)^{0.5}$$
$$8.66 = 2H$$
$$H = 4.33$$
$$S = 4(4.33) = 17.32$$

The substitution effect for hockey sticks therefore is the difference between 5 (the optimal number of hockey sticks in part (a) before the price change) and 4.33. This corresponds to a decrease of 0.67 hockey sticks. The income effect for hockey sticks is the difference between 4.33 and 3.75 (the optimal number of hockey sticks in part (b) after the price change). This is a decrease of 0.58 hockey sticks. The total effect on the optimal number of hockey sticks therefore is a decrease of 1.25 sticks, as in part (b). For superheroes, we find that the substitution effect is a positive 2.32 superheroes (the difference between the original 15 and the 17.32 that we find here). The income effect, however, is an offsetting decrease of 2.32 superheroes (the difference between the 17.32 here and the new 15), and hence the total effect on the optimal number of superhero figures is zero. This is what we expect for this Cobb-Douglas utility function case.

d. Hockey sticks are a normal good for Kaden. As the price here increases (and therefore as Kaden experiences a drop in purchasing power), Kaden decreases his consumption of hockey sticks (the income effect). Another way to answer is to note that the income and substitution effects for hockey sticks (the good experiencing a price change) are moving in the same direction (here, both are decreasing).

∂ 5.3 figure it out 4

Reconsider Kaden in 5.3 figure it out 3. Continue to assume that Kaden has a utility function that can be expressed as $U(H, S) = H^{0.5}S^{0.5}$, where H and S are, respectively, hockey sticks and superhero figures.
a. Derive Kaden's Marshallian demand curve for hockey sticks using calculus, and show that the law of demand is satisfied.
b. Derive Kaden's Hicksian demand curve for hockey sticks, using calculus.

Solution:

a. Kaden's constrained optimization problem is: $\max_{H,S} H^{0.5}S^{0.5} \ s.t. \overline{I} = p_H H + \overline{p_s}S$, using the Lagrangian approach. The Lagrangian corresponding to this is:

$$\max_{H,S,\lambda} \mathcal{L}(H,S,\lambda) = H^{0.5}S^{0.5} + \lambda(\overline{I} - p_H H - \overline{p_S}S)$$

The first-order conditions are:

$$\frac{\partial \mathcal{L}}{\partial H} = 0.5H^{-0.5}S^{0.5} - \lambda(p_H) = 0$$

$$\frac{\partial \mathcal{L}}{\partial S} = 0.5H^{0.5}S^{-0.5} - \lambda(\overline{p_S}) = 0$$

$$\frac{\partial \mathcal{L}}{\partial \lambda} = \overline{I} - p_H H - \overline{p_s}S = 0$$

Combining the first two equations, we see that:

$$\lambda = \frac{0.5H^{-0.5}S^{0.5}}{p_H} = \frac{0.5H^{0.5}S^{-0.5}}{\overline{p_S}}$$

Therefore, $\overline{p_S}S = p_H H$

Combining this with the third of the first-order conditions:

$$\overline{I} = p_H H + \overline{p_s}S$$
$$\overline{I} = p_H H + p_H H$$

Kaden's Marshallian demand curve for hockey sticks is: $H = \dfrac{\overline{I}}{2p_H}$. Since $\dfrac{\partial H}{\partial p_H} = -\dfrac{\overline{I}}{2p_H^2} < 0$, the Law of Demand, which states that demand is decreasing as price holds.

b. Kaden's constrained optimization problem is: $\min_{H,S} p_H H + \overline{p_S} S$ $s.t.$ $\overline{U} = H^{0.5}S^{0.5}$, using the Lagrangian approach. The Lagrangian corresponding to this is:

$$\max_{H,S,\lambda} \mathcal{L}(H,S,\lambda) = p_H H + \overline{p_S} S + \lambda(\overline{U} - H^{0.5}S^{0.5})$$

The first-order conditions are:

$$\frac{\partial \mathcal{L}}{\partial H} = p_H - \lambda(0.5H^{-0.5}S^{0.5}) = 0$$

$$\frac{\partial \mathcal{L}}{\partial S} = \overline{p_S} - \lambda(0.5H^{0.5}S^{-0.5}) = 0$$

$$\frac{\partial \mathcal{L}}{\partial \lambda} = \overline{U} - H^{0.5}S^{0.5} = 0$$

Combining the first two equations, we see that:

$$\lambda = \frac{p_H}{0.5H^{-0.5}S^{0.5}} = \frac{\overline{p_S}}{0.5H^{0.5}S^{-0.5}}$$

Therefore, $\overline{p_S}S = p_H H$ or $S = \frac{p_H H}{\overline{p_S}}$.

Combining this with the third of the first-order conditions,

$$U = H^{0.5}S^{0.5}$$

$$\overline{U} = H^{0.5}\left(\frac{p_H H}{\overline{p_S}}\right)^{0.5} = H\left(\frac{p_H}{\overline{p_S}}\right)^{0.5}$$

Kaden's Hicksian demand curve for hockey sticks, then, is:

$$H = \overline{U}\left(\frac{\overline{p_S}}{p_H}\right)^{0.5}$$

5.4 The Impact of Changes in Another Good's Price: Substitutes and Complements

Substitute

A good that can be used in place of another good. The demand for a good increases when the price of a substitute rises and decreases when the price of a substitute falls.

∂ In calculus terms, a good is considered a substitute good if the partial derivative of the demand function with respect to the price of another good $\frac{\partial Q}{\partial P_0} > 0$, where P_0 is the price of the other good. Note that this is the relationship between the price in one market (the substitute market) and the quantity in another market (the market for Q).

Complement

A good that is purchased and used in combination with another good. The demand for a good decreases when the price of a complement rises and increases when the price of a complement falls.

∂ In calculus terms, a good is considered a complement good if the partial derivative of the demand function with respect to the price of another good $\frac{\partial Q}{\partial P_0} < 0$, where P_0 is the price of the other good. Note that this is the relationship between the price in one market (the complement market) and the quantity in another market (the market for Q).

5.5 Combining Individual Demand Curves to Obtain the Market Demand Curve

Add demand curves horizontally, not vertically

When moving from individual demand curves to market demand, you should add quantities on individual demand curves, not prices. This is called adding individual demands horizontally. The following graph illustrates how it's done. When you add horizontally, you are summing up all the individual quantities demanded, holding price fixed. This is exactly what you want to do because market demand is the total quantity demanded at any given price.

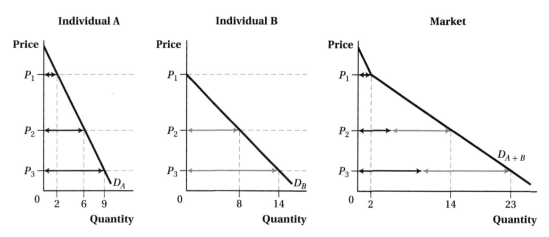

Similarly, if you are combining individual demand curves algebraically, make sure you've written out the individual demand curves as quantities demanded as a function of price (not as inverse demand curves). When you add those equations, you'll just be adding the quantities, which is again what you want to do.

5.5 figure it out 1

Suppose Tom and Jerry are the only consumers in the market for cheese in a small village. Tom's demand curve is $Q_T = 12 - 2P$, where Q_T is Tom's quantity of cheese demanded (in pounds) and P is the price of cheese (in dollars per pound). Jerry's demand curve is $Q_J = 16 - 4P$, where Q_J is Jerry's quantity of cheese demanded.

a. Find the equation for the market demand curve.
b. Graph the market demand curve.
c. What is the market quantity demanded when the price of cheese is $5 per pound? When the price of cheese is $2 per pound?

Solution

a. The market demand curve is derived by adding horizontally the individual buyers' demand curves. And summing horizontally means to add up quantities demanded at each price. Thus, we can get the market demand (Q_M) by adding Q_T and Q_J:

$$Q_M = Q_T + Q_J$$
$$Q_M = (12 - 2P) + (16 - 4P)$$
$$Q_M = 28 - 6P$$

We should note, however, that Tom is not willing to buy any cheese if the price is greater than or equal to $6 per pound because that is his demand choke price:

$$Q_T = 12 - 2P$$
$$0 = 12 - 2P$$
$$2P = 12$$
$$P = 6$$

But Jerry's demand choke price is only $4:

$$Q_J = 16 - 4P$$
$$0 = 16 - 4P$$
$$4P = 16$$
$$P = 4$$

Thus, as long as the price is below $4 per pound, the market demand is the horizontal sum of the two buyers' demand curves. But when the price is between $4 and $6, Jerry's quantity demanded is zero, so the market demand curve is the same as Tom's demand curve.

b. The following graph shows the market demand curve for cheese. The first point on the curve is Tom's demand choke price, $6. The second point is where $P = \$4$, so Jerry's quantity demanded is zero; therefore, the market quantity demanded equals Tom's quantity demanded: $Q_T = 12 - 2 \times 4 =$

4 pounds. The third point can be any point where the price is below $4, so we can use the preceding Q_M equation to find the quantity demanded by both buyers together. For example, when $P = \$1$, $Q_M = 28 - 6 \times 1 = 22$ pounds. Notice that the market demand curve is kinked as a result of the buyers' different choke prices.

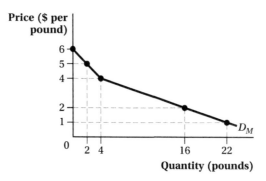

c. When the price of cheese is $5 per pound, Jerry's quantity demanded is zero, so the market demand curve is Tom's demand curve. And from Tom's demand curve, when $P = \$5$, $Q_T = 12 - 2 \times 5 = 2$ pounds. When the price of cheese is $2 per pound, the market demand curve is $Q_M = 28 - 6P$, so $Q_M = 28 - 6 \times 2 = 16$ pounds.

Practice Problems
Problem 1

Suppose an empirical study shows that when per capita income in the United States decreases by 3%, with all other influences on the demand for cigarettes held constant, the quantity of cigarettes demanded decreases by 0.15%.Given this information:

a. What is the income elasticity of demand for cigarettes in the United States?
b. Are cigarettes a normal good? An inferior good? A luxury good? A necessity good? A Giffen good? Explain and justify your answers.
c. Suppose per capita income in the United States is expected to rise by 5%. Other things being equal, what percentage change in the demand for cigarettes do you predict?
d. Suppose another empirical study estimates the income elasticity of demand for cigarettes at 0.08. Given the expected increase in income, which of the two studies would predict a greater effect on the demand for cigarettes? Explain your answer.

Problem 2

Suppose you spend $70 per month on orange juice and potato chips. You read a report suggesting that orange juice products may contain a fungicide. As a result, your preferences for orange juice change unfavorably. Assuming that the total amount you spend on orange juice and potato chips does not change, and the prices of the two goods remain the same, which of the following will happen? Explain why or why not.

a. Your budget constraint will become steeper (with orange juice on the horizontal axis).
b. Your indifference curves will become flatter (with orange juice on the horizontal axis).
c. Your demand curve for orange juice will shift rightward.
d. Your budget constraint will shift leftward.

Problem 3

Suppose there are 5,000 identical consumers in the market for gasoline in a small town. The demand curve for each consumer is given by:

$$Q = 20 - 5P$$

Where Q is the individual quantity demanded (gallons per day) and P is the price of gasoline ($ per gallon).

a. Find the equation for the market demand curve.
b. Graph the market demand curve.
c. What is the market quantity demanded when the price of gasoline is $2.50? When the price of gasoline is $4.50?

Problem 4

Steven receives a weekly allowance of $72 from his parents. He spends all this money on sandwiches and movie tickets. The price of a sandwich is $4, and the price of a movie ticket is $8. The following graph shows Steven's indifference curves.

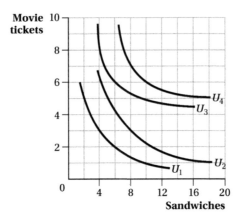

a. How many sandwiches and how many movie tickets does Steven buy per week?
b. Suppose that Steven's parents cut his weekly allowance to $56. Steven's preferences and the prices of the goods remain unchanged. What combination of sandwiches and movie tickets does Steven consume now?
c. Based on your preceding analysis, draw Steven's Engel curves for sandwiches and movie tickets.
d. Are sandwiches a normal or an inferior good? What about movie tickets? Explain and justify your answers.

Problem 5

Molly works part time, earning $80 per week. She spends all her income on coffee and donuts. The price of coffee is $2 per cup, and the price of a donut is $2. The following graph shows Molly's indifference curves.

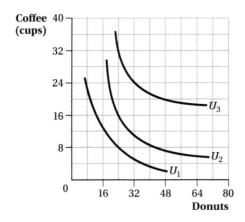

a. What is the slope of Molly's budget constraint?
b. What combination of coffee and donuts does Molly consume?
c. Suppose the price of a donut falls to $1. How much coffee and how many donuts does Molly consume now?
d. On a separate diagram, draw Molly's demand curve for donuts based on your answers in (b) and (c).

Problem 6

Jake's spends all his income on fried chicken and Coke. Jake's indifference curves (U_1 and U_2) and potential budget constraints (BC_1, BC_2, and BC_3) are shown on the following diagram.

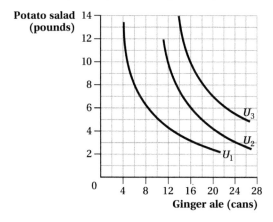

a. If the price of chicken is $4 per pound and the price of Coke is $1 per can, what combination of the two goods does Jake consume?

b. Given the prices in (a) and Jake's potential budget constraints on the preceding graph, what is the income Jake spends on fried chicken and Coke?

c. Now suppose that the price of chicken falls to $2 per pound. How does this change the combination of the two goods that Jake consumes?

d. When the price of chicken falls, what is the change in Jake's consumption of chicken due to the substitution effect? Due to the income effect? How does Jake's consumption of Coke change due to the substitution effect? Due to the income effect?

e. Is chicken a normal good or an inferior good? What about Coke? Explain your answers.

Problem 7

Nadya's budget for ginger ale and potato salad is $28. Her indifference curves are shown on the following graph. Initially, the price of ginger ale is $1 per can, and the price of potato salad is $2 per pound. But then the price of ginger ale rises to $2 per can, while the price of potato salad remains the same.

a. How does the higher price of ginger ale affect Nadya's consumption of ginger ale? Potato salad?

b. When the price of ginger ale rises, what is the change in Nadya's consumption of ginger ale due to the substitution effect? Due to the income effect? How does Nadya's consumption of potato salad change due to the substitution effect? Due to the income effect?

c. When the price of ginger ale rises, which effect on Nadya's consumption of potato salad is larger, the substitution effect or the income effect? Explain your answer.

d. "The substitution effect of a higher price of ginger ale on Nadya's consumption of potato salad is positive, while the income effect is negative." True or false? Explain.

e. Is ginger ale a normal good or an inferior good? What about potato salad? Explain your answers.

Problem 8

Andrew enjoys watching movies, both in theaters and on his new large-screen high-definition LED TV. He devotes $160 per month to spend on movie tickets and Blu-ray disc rentals. The following graph shows his indifference curves (U_1, U_2, and U_3) and his budget constraint BC_1 when the price of a movie ticket is $8, and the price of a Blu-ray rental is $4. Suppose the price of a Blu-ray rental falls to $2, while the price of a movie ticket and the amount Andrew spends on the two goods remain unchanged.

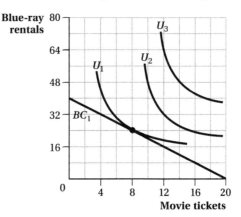

a. Draw Andrew's budget constraint after the price of a Blu-ray rental falls. How many movie tickets will Andrew buy? How many Blu-ray disks will he rent?
b. Are movie tickets and Blu-ray rentals substitutes or complements? Explain your answer.
c. How will the lower price of Blu-ray rentals affect Andrew's demand curve for movie tickets? How will it affect his demand curve for Blu-ray rentals? Explain your answers.
d. Is the substitution effect of the lower price of Blu-ray rentals on the number of movies Andrew watches in theaters negative or positive? Explain your answer.
e. Are movie tickets a normal good or an inferior good? What about Blu-ray rentals? Explain your answers.

Problem 9

Suppose Art and Bob are the only consumers in the market for ice cream in a small northern village in January. Art's demand curve is $Q_A = 7 - 2P$, where Q_A is Art's quantity of ice cream cones demanded and P is the price per cone. Bob's demand curve is $Q_B = 5 - P$, where Q_B is Bob's quantity of ice cream cones demanded.
a. Find the equation for the market demand curve.
b. Graph the market demand curve.
c. What is the market quantity demanded when the price of ice cream is $4 per cone? When the price of ice cream is $2 per cone?

Problem 10

Suppose the price of gasoline is initially $2 per gallon, but then the government imposes a new $2 tax on gas, which raises the buyer price of gas to $4 per gallon. The government compensates consumers for the higher price of gas by sending each of them a check for $400. Suppose Peter, a typical consumer, has $800 to spend on gasoline and other goods. The following graph shows Peter's indifference curves ($U_1 - U_4$), with gasoline on the horizontal axis and other goods as a composite good, whose price is $1, on the vertical axis.

Other goods (dollars) vs Gasoline (gallons), with indifference curves U_1, U_2, U_3, U_4.

a. How will Peter's consumption of gasoline change as a result of the new government policy?
b. Does the new policy make Peter better off or worse off? Explain your answer.
c. Will the new policy benefit the government (in terms of revenue)? Explain.

Problem 11

Suppose that the demand curve for a product can be expressed as: $Q = 6{,}000 - 20P - 50P_0 + 0.5I$ where P is the price of the good, P_0 is the price of a related good, and I is income.
a. Use calculus to argue whether the related good is a complement or a substitute.
b. Use calculus to argue whether the good itself is a normal good or an inferior good.
c. If the price of the good is 100, the price of the related good is 20 and income is 2,000, what is the income elasticity of demand? Use calculus to express this elasticity, and interpret its magnitude in words. Also indicate whether this elasticity is elastic or inelastic.

Problem 12

Suppose that Ed likes to hike (H) and watch football (F). Ed has a utility function $U(H,F) = 2H^{0.2} F^{0.6}$. Ed's income to spend on leisure activities is $2,400 and the prices of a hiking trip and watching a football game (inclusive of travel and supplies for hiking and going to football games) are $300 and $150, respectively.
a. What is Ed's optimal consumption bundle and utility at the original prices?
b. If the price of watching football decreases to $75 due to a promo and the price of hiking stays constant at $300. What does Ed consume at the optimum at these new prices?
c. What are the magnitudes of the total, substitution, and income effects?

Problem 13

Reconsider Ed in Problem 12. Continue to assume that Ed has a utility function that can be expressed as $U(H,F) = 2H^{0.2}F^{0.6}$, where H and F are hiking and football, respectively.
a. Use calculus to derive Ed's Marshallian demand curve for hiking, and show that the law of demand is satisfied.
b. Use calculus to derive Ed's Hicksian demand curve for hiking.

Producer Behavior

6

6.1 The Basics of Production
Production

The process by which a person, company, government, or non-profit agency creates a good or service that others are willing to pay for.

Final good

A good that is bought by a consumer.

Intermediate good

A good that is used to produce another good.

Production function

A mathematical relationship that describes how much output can be made from different combinations of inputs.

A production function is a formula that describes the output (Q) as a function of inputs, capital (K) and labor (L):

$$Q = f(K,L)$$

where f is a mathematical function that describes how capital and labor are combined to produce the output, for example,

$$Q = 14K^{0.5}L^{0.5}$$

6.2 Production in the Short Run
Short run

A period of time during which a firm cannot change the amount of capital, so it chooses how much labor to hire to minimize its cost of making the output quantity.

Marginal product

The additional output that a firm can produce by using an additional unit of an input (holding use of the other inputs constant).

In the short run, the marginal product that is most relevant is the marginal product of labor (since capital is fixed). The marginal product of labor (MP_L) is the change in quantity (ΔQ) resulting from a one-unit change in labor inputs (ΔL):

$$MP_L = \frac{\Delta Q}{\Delta L}$$

∂ Mathematically, the marginal product of labor (MP_L) is the partial derivative of $Q = f(K,L)$ with respect to L. This is because marginal product is the additional quantity that the producer can achieve along with a marginal increase of L input, and therefore is the change in quantity for a change in labor (L).

For example, for the production function $Q = K^{0.5}L^{0.5}$, the marginal product of labor is $\frac{\partial Q}{\partial L} = 0.5K^{0.5}L^{0.5-1} = 0.5\left(\frac{K}{L}\right)^{0.5}$, and the marginal product of capital is $\frac{\partial Q}{\partial K} = 0.5K^{0.5-1}L^{0.5} = 0.5\left(\frac{L}{K}\right)^{0.5}$. Note that for this production function, you can use these formulas to get the marginal product of labor and of capital, respectively, for any levels of L and K inputs simply by subbing in for L and K. For example, if $L = 5$ and $K = 5$, then marginal product of L is $0.5\left(\dfrac{5}{5}\right)^{0.5} = 0.5$ and the marginal product of K is similarly $0.5\left(\dfrac{5}{5}\right)^{0.5} = 0.5$. Note that this means that you can use one set of formulas (marginal products derived from calculus) to calculate specific marginal products at many input levels. This may be *easier* than solving for marginal product using algebraic methods repeatedly to get these marginal products at different levels.

Diminishing marginal product

A feature of a typical production function; as a firm hires additional units of a given input, the marginal product of that input falls.

A typical short-run production function

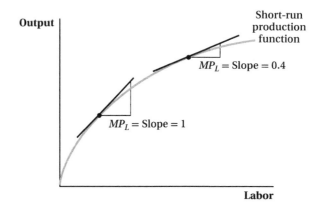

Since marginal products of labor and of capital are first partial derivatives of the product function of labor and capital, respectively, diminishing marginal product of labor and capital can be expressed as second-order conditions involving second-partial derivatives. Specifically, in terms of calculus, diminishing marginal product of labor is the statement that $\dfrac{\partial^2 Q}{\partial L^2} < 0$ and diminishing marginal product of capital is the statement that $\dfrac{\partial^2 Q}{\partial K^2} < 0$.

Average product

The quantity of output produced per unit of input.
For example, the average product of labor (AP_L) is the quantity produced Q divided by the amount of labor L used to produce it:

$$AP_L = \frac{Q}{L}$$

6.2 figure it out 1

Suppose the production function for a coffee shop is

$$Q = 25K^{0.6}L^{0.4}$$

where Q is the number of cups of coffee produced per day, K is the number of espresso machines, which is fixed at 2 in the short run, and L is the number of workers employed.
a. What is the equation for the firm's short-run production function?
b. Calculate the total output produced per day for $L = 2$, 3, and 4.
c. Calculate the marginal product of labor (MP_L) of the 3rd and the 4th workers. Is the marginal product diminishing?
d. Calculate the average product of labor for $L = 2$, 3, and 4.
e. Use calculus to determine a function for the marginal product of labor.

Solution:

a. To write the short-run production function, we plug the fixed value of capital, $K = 2$, into the production function equation in question, so we get:

$$Q = 25 \times 2^{0.6} \times L^{0.4}$$
$$Q = 37.89L^{0.4}$$

b. To calculate total output for each given number of workers, we plug the different values of L into the preceding equation:

$$L = 2 \quad Q = 37.89 \times 2^{0.4} = 50.00$$
$$L = 3 \quad Q = 37.89 \times 3^{0.4} = 58.80$$
$$L = 4 \quad Q = 37.89 \times 4^{0.4} = 65.97$$

c. The marginal product of labor is the additional output generated by an additional unit of labor, holding capital constant. We can use our results from (b) to calculate the marginal product of the 3rd and 4th workers. With 2 workers, $Q = 50.00$, while with 3 workers, $Q = 58.80$. Thus, the marginal product of the 3rd worker is

$$MP_L = 58.80 - 50.00 = 8.80$$

With 4 workers, $Q = 65.98$. Thus, the marginal product of the 4th worker is

$$MP_L = 65.97 - 58.80 = 7.17$$

Thus, the marginal product of labor is diminishing: as more labor added to the fixed amount of capital, output increases at a decreasing rate.

d. The average product of labor is calculated by dividing total output (Q) by the quantity of labor input (L):

$$L = 2 \quad Q = \frac{50.00}{2} = 25.00$$

$$L = 3 \quad Q = \frac{58.80}{3} = 19.60$$

$$L = 4 \quad Q = \frac{65.97}{4} = 16.49$$

e. Marginal product of labor is the partial derivative of the production function with respect to labor:

$$MP_L = \frac{\partial Q}{\partial L} = 25(0.4)K^{0.6}L^{0.4-1} = 10K^{0.6}L^{-0.6}.$$

6.4 The Firm's Cost Minimization Problem

Isoquant

A curve representing all the combinations of inputs that allow a firm to make a particular quantity of output.

Marginal rate of technical substitution of labor for capital ($MRTS_{LK}$)

The rate at which the firm can trade labor (L) for capital (K), holding output (Q) constant.

$$MRTS_{LK} = -\frac{\Delta K}{\Delta L} = \frac{MP_L}{MP_K}$$

Recall from the in-text appendix to Chapter 6 that $MRTS_{LK}$ is the absolute value of slope of the isoquant as opposed to slope itself. Using calculus, $MRTS_{LK}$ can be written as $-\dfrac{dK}{dL}$. Since this is a first derivative, we can use calculus to test for convexity by calculating the derivative of $MRTS_{LK}$ with respect to labor L and comparing this to zero. Note that this is effectively a second-derivative test since we are taking a derivative of $MRTS_{LK}$, which itself is a derivative. Specifically, if $\dfrac{\partial MRTS_{LK}}{\partial L} < 0$, then we know that the isoquant is convex. Similarly, if $\dfrac{\partial MRTS_{LK}}{\partial L} > 0$, then the isoquant is concave. Finally, if $\dfrac{\partial MRTS_{LK}}{\partial L} = 0$, then the isoquant is neither convex nor concave.

Since marginal products of L and K, respectively, can be calculated as the partial derivatives of the production function to L and to K, we can see that an easy way to calculate marginal rate of technical substitution of L for K is to substitute in for these partial derivatives.

$$MRTS_{LK} = \frac{MP_L}{MP_K} = \frac{\dfrac{\partial Q}{\partial L}}{\dfrac{\partial Q}{\partial K}}$$

Note that the equation for marginal rate of technical substitution can also be derived using partial differentials. (See the in-text appendix to Chapter 6.)

For the example, $Q = K^{0.5}L^{0.5}$, as given in the preceding, marginal rate of technical substitution of L for K is

$$MRTS_{LK} = \frac{MP_L}{MP_K} = \frac{0.5\left(\dfrac{K}{L}\right)^{0.5}}{0.5\left(\dfrac{L}{K}\right)^{0.5}} = \frac{K}{L}$$

For the example, $L = 5$ and $K = 5$, $MRTS_{XY} = \dfrac{5}{5} = 1$.

Isocost line

A curve that shows all of the input combinations yielding the same cost. Mathematically, the isocost line, corresponding to a total expenditure level of C, is given by

$$C = RK + WL$$

where R is the price (the rental rate) per unit of capital, W is the price (the wage) per unit of labor, and K and L are the number of units of capital and labor that the firm hires. The vertical intercept of the isocost line is $\dfrac{C}{R}$, and the slope is the (negative of the) inputs' price ratio, $-\dfrac{W}{R}$.

 Note that input prices (R and W) are the partial derivatives of the cost (C) with respect to relevant quantities (K and L, respectively) just as marginal products are the partial derivatives of the production function (Q) with respect to L and K. Another way to think about the slope is to rewrite the isocost line in point-slope form. Specifically,

$$K = \frac{C}{R} - \left(\frac{W}{R}\right)L$$

Now, taking the derivative $\dfrac{\partial K}{\partial L} = -\left(\dfrac{W}{R}\right)$. Note that this is the slope of the isocost line. In absolute value form, we have the input price ratio $\left(\dfrac{W}{R}\right)$.

Cost minimization

On the following graph, the point of tangency between the isocost line C_2 and the isoquant Q_1 is the firm's cost-minimizing capital and labor combination (L_1, K_1) to produce Q_1.

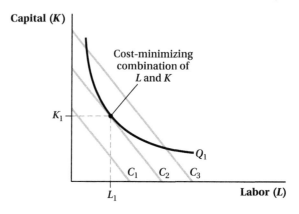

The tangency implies that at the combination of inputs minimizing the cost of producing a given quantity of output (Q_1), the ratio of input prices equals the $MRTS$:

$$|Slope| = MRTS_{LK} = \frac{W}{R} = \frac{MP_L}{MP_K}$$

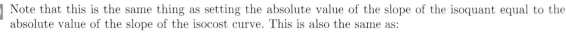 Note that this is the same thing as setting the absolute value of the slope of the isoquant equal to the absolute value of the slope of the isocost curve. This is also the same as:

$$\frac{MP_L}{MP_K} = \frac{W}{R}$$

where the four partial derivatives (of the production function and isocost curve for L and K, respectively) can be subbed in. Specifically, recall that $MP_L = \frac{\partial Q}{\partial L}$, $MP_K = \frac{\partial Q}{\partial K}$, $W = \frac{\partial C}{\partial L}$, and $R = \frac{\partial C}{\partial K}$.

An important economic interpretation that follows from this is that the cost is minimized when

$$\frac{MP_K}{R} = \frac{MP_L}{W}$$

For the continuing example where $Q = K^{0.5}L^{0.5}$, assume that we know now that the wage and rental rates are, respectively, 4 and 16. (Recall that the producer takes these input prices as given, since they are determined by the market (the intersection of supply and demand in labor and capital markets, respectively, not determined by the producer). The marginal rate of technical substitution of L for K, or the ratio of marginal products of L to K, is shown in the preceding to equal $\frac{K}{L}$. Therefore, this can be substituted for the left-hand side of the equation, while the given prices can be substituted on the right-hand side of the equation. Specifically,

$$\frac{K}{L} = \frac{4}{16}$$
$$K = \frac{L}{4}$$

Note that this by itself is not enough to solve the producer's optimization problem, since this is one equation with two unknowns (L and K). The good news, however, is that it is relatively straightforward to find the optimal quantities. To do so, we just need to include the information contained in the isoquant curve. Suppose that the producer wants to deliver 100 units of its product to the market. Then, the producer's production constraint is simply:

$$100 = K^{0.5}L^{0.5}$$

Now, we have two equations with two unknowns and therefore can solve the system of equations.

Plugging the first equation into the second:

$$100 = \left(\frac{L}{4}\right)^{0.5}L^{0.5}$$
$$100 = \frac{L}{2}$$
$$L = 200$$

Using the first equation, we see that:

$$K = \frac{L}{4}$$
$$K = \frac{200}{4} = 50$$

Thus, $(L, K) = (200, 50)$ represent the coordinates of the tangency in the preceding producer's optimal choice graph.

The producer's optimal choice also can be derived using the Lagrangian Method in the producer framework that is introduced in the appendix to Chapter 6 in the textbook. The consumer's constrained optimization problem can be written as:

$$\min_{L,K} RK + WL \text{ subject to } (s.t.) \ \overline{Q} = Q(K, L)$$

where $\overline{Q}$ is a fixed quantity level. Recall that the Lagrangian is basically a math tool to solve a constrained optimization problem. The idea of the Lagrangian approach is to reduce the whole optimization to one equation that incorporates both the objective and the constraint. Then, we do the same thing as we would for a standard unconstrained optimization problem; we take the derivative (here, partial derivatives) and set each of these equal to zero. Rather than one first-order condition, therefore, we may have several, but then this is just a system of equations that we can solve using standard algebraic techniques. The Lagrangian can be written:

$$\mathcal{L}(K,L,\lambda) = f(K,L) + \lambda[g(K,L)]$$

where $f(.,.)$ is the objective function (what you want to minimize here), $g(.,.)$ is the modification of the constraint (constraint written in the $= 0$ format), and λ is the Lagrange multiplier. We are using the Lagrange multiplier to turn on and turn off the constraint and therefore analyzing our optimum such that the constraint is satisfied. Thus, for our preceding example, the Lagrangian is:

$$\mathcal{L}(K,L,\lambda) = 16K + 4L + \lambda[100 - K^{0.5}L^{0.5}]$$

The first-order conditions (partial derivatives of this equation with respect to K, L, and the Lagrange multiplier λ, respectively) are:

$$\frac{\partial \mathcal{L}}{\partial K} = 16 - \lambda(0.5K^{-0.5}L^{0.5}) = 0$$

$$\frac{\partial \mathcal{L}}{\partial L} = 4 - \lambda(0.5K^{0.5}L^{-0.5}) = 0$$

$$\frac{\partial \mathcal{L}}{\partial \lambda} = 100 - K^{0.5}L^{0.5} = 0$$

These equations represent the three equations with three unknowns (K, L, and λ) that we want to solve to find our solution. Solving the first two for λ and setting them equal to each other, we find:

$$\lambda = \frac{16}{0.5K^{-0.5}L^{0.5}} = \frac{4}{0.5K^{0.5}L^{-0.5}}$$

Dividing both sides by 0.5 and multiplying by 5, we find that:

$$8K^{0.5}L^{-0.5} = 2K^{-0.5}L^{0.5}$$
$$4K^{0.5}K^{0.5} = L^{0.5}L^{0.5}$$
$$4K = L$$

The last of the three conditions tells us the production function constraint relationship:

$$100 = K^{0.5}L^{0.5}$$

Notice that we now have two equations with two unknowns rather than three equations with three unknowns. Our method is the same as if we were solving a simple supply and demand system with two equations and two unknowns. We just need to sub one relationship into the other and solve. Here,

$$100 = K^{0.5}(4K)^{0.5}$$
$$100 = 2K$$
$$K = 50$$
$$L = 4(50) = 200$$

Note that this is the same answer as what we get from the preceding shortcut approach, where we solve for marginal rate of technical substitution and set it equal to the input price ratio and combine this with the production function relationship.

6.4 figure it out 1

Suppose that the wage rate is $12 per hour and the rental rate of capital is $48 per hour.
a. Write an equation for the isocost line for a firm whose total expenditure level (C) is $960.
b. Draw a graph (with labor on the horizontal axis and capital on the vertical axis) that shows the isocost line for $C = \$960$. Indicate the horizontal and vertical intercepts along with the slope.
c. Suppose the price of labor falls to $8 per hour. Draw the new isocost line for $C = \$960$ on the same graph. What happens to the new intercepts of the isocost line? To the slope of the isocost line?

Solution

a. The equation for the isocost line can be written as

$$C = RK + WL$$
$$960 = 48K + 12L$$

b. An easy way to plot an isocost line is to find its horizontal and vertical intercepts. The horizontal intercept is the amount of labor the firm could hire if it only hired labor, i.e, when $K = 0$. Given our isocost equation, we can write: $960 = 12L$, from which $L = \frac{960}{12} = 80$ units. Similarly, the vertical intercept is the amount of capital the firm could hire if it used only capital, i.e., when $L = 0$. Then, $960 = 48K$, from which $K = \frac{960}{48} = 20$ units. We draw the isocost line (C_1) by connecting these two points (see the following graph). The slope of the isocost line is the rise over the run: $-\frac{20}{80} = -0.25$. The slope can also be calculated as the (negative of the) inputs' price ratio: $-\frac{W}{R} = -\frac{\$12}{\$48} = -0.25$.

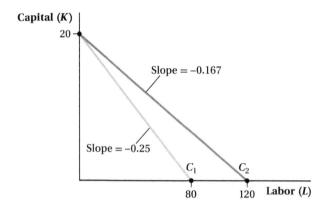

c. If the wage falls to $8, the vertical intercept is unaffected, because if the firm uses only capital, a change in the price of labor will have no impact on it. But the horizontal intercept increases to $\frac{\$960}{\$8} = 120$, so the isocost line becomes flatter (C_2). The slope is now $-\frac{20}{120} = -0.167$ or $-\frac{\$8}{\$48} = -0.167$.

6.4 figure it out 2

A firm employs 20 workers at $20 per hour and uses 10 units of capital at $40 per hour. With this combination of inputs used, the marginal product of labor is 5 units of output and the marginal product of capital is 20 units of output.
a. Draw the firm's isocost line.
b. What is the firm's current marginal rate of substitution of labor for capital?
c. Is the firm producing its current level of output at the minimum cost, or is there a way to produce it at a lower cost? Explain and graphically illustrate your answer.

Solution

a. To graph an isocost line, we first calculate the firm's current total cost:

$$C = RK + WL$$
$$C = \$40 \times 10 + \$20 \times 20 = \$800$$

Now we can find the horizontal and vertical intercepts of the isocost line. The horizontal intercept is the amount of labor the firm could hire if it only hired labor: $\frac{\$800}{\$20} = 40$. The vertical intercept is the amount of capital the firm could use if it used only capital: $\frac{\$800}{\$40} = 20$. We draw the isocost line (C_1) by connecting these two points (see the following graph).

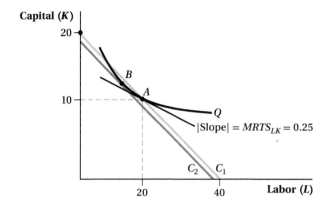

b. The firm's marginal rate of substitution is

$$MRTS_{LK} = \frac{MP_L}{MP_K} = \frac{5}{20} = 0.25$$

c. A firm minimizes its cost if the absolute value of the slope of its isocost line is equal to the marginal rate of substitution, which is the absolute value of the slope of the isoquant at the point that indicates the chosen combination of inputs. For the firm in question, the absolute value of the slope of the isocost line (the rise over the run) is $\frac{20}{40} = 0.5$. But, as we found in (b), the $MRTS_{LK}$ is $0.25 < 0.5$. Therefore, the firm is not minimizing its costs. The preceding graph shows how the firm can reduce its costs while keeping its output at the same level. The firm's current input choice is at point A. At this point, the isoquant is flatter than the isocost line, so it intersects the isocost line rather than being tangent to it. As the graph shows, the firm can reduce its costs, that is, shift its isocost line leftward (from C_1 to C_2) if it moves along the isoquant from point A to point B, increasing its capital input while decreasing its labor input.

6.5 Returns to Scale

Returns to scale

A change in the amount of output in response to a proportional increase or decrease in all of the inputs.

Constant returns to scale

A production function for which changing all inputs by the same proportion changes the quantity of output by the same proportion.

Increasing returns to scale

A production function for which changing all inputs by the same proportion changes output more than proportionately.

Decreasing returns to scale

A production function for which changing all inputs by the same proportion changes output less than proportionately.

Fixed cost

An input cost that does not vary with the amount of output.

Learning by doing

The process by which a firm becomes more efficient at production as it produces more output.

make the grade

How to determine a production function's returns to scale

A common question on an intermediate microeconomics test is whether a given production function exhibits constant, increasing, or decreasing returns to scale. If the production function is a Cobb–Douglas function, which is one of the most common types of production functions used by economists, you can answer this question easily. The Cobb–Douglas production function has the following form:

$$Q = A \times L^{\alpha} \times K^{\beta}$$

where A is a constant. To see whether there are constant, increasing, or decreasing returns to scale, all you need to do is add up the exponents on the inputs ($\alpha + \beta$). If they add up to 1, then the production function exhibits constant returns to scale. If they sum to more than 1, it indicates increasing returns to scale, and if they add up to less than 1, it shows decreasing returns to scale. For example, suppose you are given the production function

$$Q = 0.8L^{0.3} \times K^{0.6}$$

so $\alpha + \beta = 0.3 + 0.6 = 0.9$. Since $0.9 < 1$, this production function exhibits decreasing returns to scale.

But what if the production is not Cobb–Douglas? For example,

$$Q = 5L + 12K + 0.5LK$$

Then, an easy way to determine returns to scale is as follows. First, calculate the quantity when both capital and labor equal 1. Next, multiply the inputs by 2 and calculate the quantity. If the total quantity doubles, the production function exhibits constant returns to scale. If it less than doubles, then it exhibits decreasing returns to scale. And if the quantity more than doubles, there are increasing returns to scale. For the preceding production function, when $L = 1$ and $K = 1$, $Q = 5 + 12 + 0.5 = 17.5$. And when $L = 2$ and $K = 2$, $Q = 10 + 24 + 2 = 36$. Since $\frac{36}{17.5} = 2.06 > 2$, the production function exhibits increasing returns to scale.

6.5 figure it out 1

For each of the following production functions, determine if they exhibit constant, decreasing, or increasing returns to scale.

a. $Q = K^{0.7}L^{0.4}$
b. $Q = 0.7K + 0.4L$
c. $Q = \min(0.7K, 0.4L)$

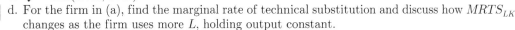

d. For the firm in (a), find the marginal rate of technical substitution and discuss how $MRTS_{LK}$ changes as the firm uses more L, holding output constant.
e. Suppose that the wage rate is $10 per hour and the rental rate of capital is $5 per hour. If the firm in (a) wants to produce 1,000 units of output, what is the cost-minimizing bundle of capital and labor?
f. Derive the firm's expansion path in (a).
g. Derive the firm's demand for labor in (a).
h Confirm that the demand for labor for the firm in (a) satisfies the Law of Demand.

Solution

a. This is a Cobb–Douglas production function. Thus, to see whether there are constant, increasing, or decreasing returns to scale, we add up the exponents on the inputs: $0.7 + 0.4 = 1.1$. Since $1.1 > 1$, this production function exhibits increasing returns to scale.
b. For this production function, the easiest way to see whether there are constant, increasing, or decreasing returns to scale is to calculate Q for $K = 1$ and $L = 1$ and then for $K = 2$ and $L = 2$. When $K = 1$ and $L = 1$, $Q = 0.7 \times 1 + 0.4 \times 1 = 1.1$. And when $K = 2$ and $L = 2$, $Q = 0.7 \times 2 + 0.4 \times 2 = 2.2$. Since output exactly doubles when inputs double, the production function exhibits constant returns to scale.
c. We repeat the exercise in (b). When $K = 1$ and $L = 1$, $Q = \min(0.7 \times 1, 0.4 \times 1) = 0.4$. And when $K = 2$ and $L = 2$, $Q = \min(0.7 \times 2, 0.4 \times 2) = 0.8$. Since output exactly doubles when input doubles, the production function exhibits constant returns to scale.

d. Use the marginal products to solve for the $MRTS$:

$$MRTS_{LK} = \frac{MP_L}{MP_K} = \frac{0.4K^{0.7}L^{-0.6}}{0.7K^{-0.3}L^{0.4}} = \frac{4K}{7L} = \frac{4}{7}KL^{-1}$$

We can take the partial of the $MRTS$ with respect to L to see how the $MRTS$ changes as L increases

$$\frac{\partial MRTS_{LK}}{\partial L} = -\frac{4}{7}KL^{-2} < 0$$

Thus, the $MRTS$ declines as the firm uses more labor. We know this because K and L must always be non-negative because you cannot have negative capital or labor. If both of these are always positive, then the second derivative will always be less than 0. Therefore, the $MRTS$ declines as indicated above.

e. First, we set up the firm's cost minimization problem as

$$\min_{K,L} 5K + 10L \; s.t. \; 1{,}000 = K^{0.7}L^{0.4}$$

Recall that we can use the Lagrangian approach to solve minimization problems where there is a constraint to consider. Specifically, the problem above is equivalent to:

$$\min_{K,L,\lambda} \mathcal{L}(K,L,\lambda) = 5K + 10L + \lambda(1{,}000 - K^{0.7}L^{0.4})$$

Finding the first-order conditions for the Lagrangian, we see that:

$$\frac{\partial \mathcal{L}}{\partial K} = 5 - \lambda(0.7K^{-0.3}L^{0.4}) = 0$$

$$\frac{\partial \mathcal{L}}{\partial L} = 10 - \lambda(0.4K^{0.7}L^{-0.6}) = 0$$

$$\frac{\partial \mathcal{L}}{\partial \lambda} = 1{,}000 - K^{0.7}L^{0.4} = 0$$

Since we now have three equations with three unknowns (K, L, λ), we can solve this system of equations to come up with the solution to the cost minimization problem. Specifically, we can use the first 2 conditions to solve for λ as a first step.

$$\lambda = \frac{5}{0.7K^{-0.3}L^{0.4}} = \frac{10}{0.4K^{0.7}L^{-0.6}}$$

Next, we can rearrange what we have found to solve for K as a function of L:

$$5(0.4K^{0.7}L^{-0.6}) = 10(0.7K^{-0.3}L^{0.4})$$
$$2(K^{0.7}K^{0.3}) = 7(L^{0.6}L^{0.4})$$
$$2K = 7L$$
$$K = 3.5L$$

Now plug K into the third first-order condition and solve for the optimal number of labor and machine-hours, L^* and K^*:

$$1{,}000 = K^{0.7}L^{0.4}$$
$$1{,}000 = (3.5L)^{0.7}L^{0.4}$$
$$(3.5)^{0.7}L^{0.7}L^{0.4} = 1{,}000$$
$$L^{1.1} \approx 416.06$$
$$L^* \approx 240.46 \text{ labor-hours}$$
$$K^* \approx 3.5(240.46) \approx 841.61 \text{ machine-hours}$$

f. The firm's expansion path tells us the relationship between the optimal amounts of labor and capital input. Within the Lagrangian procedure in (e), we found that $K = 3.5L$. This is the firm's expansion path.

g. We set up the firm's cost minimization problem as before but this time with a generic wage rate, W. In other words, we are solving as a function of W instead of as a function of a particular wage rate expressed as a number:

$$\min_{K,L} 5K + WL \; s.t. \; 1{,}000 = K^{0.7}L^{0.4}$$

Or, as a Lagrangian:

$$\min_{K,L,\lambda} \mathcal{L}(K,L,\lambda) = 5K + WL + \lambda(1{,}000 - K^{0.7}L^{0.4})$$

Finding the first-order conditions for the Lagrangian, we see that:

$$\frac{\partial \mathcal{L}}{\partial K} = 5 - \lambda(0.7K^{-0.3}L^{0.4}) = 0$$

$$\frac{\partial \mathcal{L}}{\partial L} = W - \lambda(0.4K^{0.7}L^{-0.6}) = 0$$

$$\frac{\partial \mathcal{L}}{\partial \lambda} = 1{,}000 - K^{0.7}L^{0.4} = 0$$

Since we now have three equations with three unknowns (K, L, λ), we can solve this system of equations to come up with the solution to the cost minimization problem. Specifically, we can use the first 2 conditions to solve for λ as a first step.

$$\lambda = \frac{5}{0.7K^{-0.3}L^{0.4}} = \frac{W}{0.4K^{0.7}L^{-0.6}}$$

$$5(0.4K^{0.7}L^{-0.6}) = W(0.7K^{-0.3}L^{0.4})$$

$$2(K^{0.7}K^{0.3}) = 0.7W(L^{0.6}L^{0.4})$$

$$2K = 0.7WL$$

$$K = 0.35WL$$

Substitute into the quantity constraint:

$$1{,}000 = (0.35WL)^{0.7}L^{0.4}$$

$$1{,}000 = 0.35^{0.7}W^{0.7}L^{1.1}$$

$$L^{1.1} \approx 2{,}085.22W^{-0.7}$$

$$L \approx 1{,}040.90W^{-0.64}$$

We have therefore arrived at the firm's demand curve for labor as have expressed this in terms of quantity of labor as a function of the price of labor (which, of course, is the wage rate).

h. Take the derivative of labor demand with respect to the wage rate

$$\frac{\partial L(W)}{\partial W} = 1{,}040.90(-0.64)W^{-1.64} \approx -666.18W^{-1.64}$$

which is negative since wages are positive in economics for the problem to make sense. This is what we expect from the Law of Demand since the Law of Demand tells us that as price increases, quantity demanded decreases. Here, if the price of labor (the wage rate) increases, the firm demands less labor.

6.6 Technological Change

Total factor productivity growth (or technological change)

An improvement in technology that changes the firm's production function such that more output is obtained from the same amount of inputs.

6.6 figure it out 1

A manufacturing firm's production function is

$$Q = 8K^{0.6}L^{0.4}$$

where Q is the quantity of output (units per hour), K is the amount of capital used (machine-hours), and L is the amount of labor hired (worker-hours). For this production function, the marginal product of labor is $MP_L = \frac{3.2K^{0.6}}{L^{0.6}}$, and the marginal product of capital is $MP_K = \frac{4.8L^{0.4}}{K^{0.4}}$. The firm rents capital at a rate of $R = \$30$ per hour and hires labor at $W = \$15$ per hour. The firm plans to produce 120 units of output per hour.

a. How much labor and how much capital should the firm use to minimize its cost of producing 120 units of output?

b. Suppose that a technological improvement increases the firm's total factor productivity, so the production function is now

$$Q = 12K^{0.6}L^{0.4}$$

for which the marginal product of labor is $MP_L = \dfrac{4.8K^{0.6}}{L^{0.6}}$, and the marginal product of capital is $MP_K = \dfrac{7.2L^{0.4}}{K^{0.4}}$. How much labor and how much capital should the firm use now to minimize the cost of producing 120 units of output per hour?

c. How does the technological improvement change the firm's costs of producing 120 units of output?

d. Use calculus to show that the marginal products of labor and of capital in (b) are as given.

Solution

a. A firm's costs are minimized when

$$\frac{MP_L}{MP_K} = \frac{W}{R}$$

For the firm in question, we can write:

$$\frac{\dfrac{3.2K^{0.6}}{L^{0.6}}}{\dfrac{4.8L^{0.4}}{K^{0.4}}} = \frac{15}{30}$$

$$\frac{3.2K^{0.6}K^{0.4}}{4.8L^{0.6}L^{0.4}} = 0.5$$

$$\frac{3.2K}{4.8L} = 0.5$$

$$3.2K = 2.4L$$

$$K = 0.75L$$

Now we substitute this expression for K into the production function and solve it for L, given that $Q = 120$:

$$Q = 8K^{0.6}L^{0.4}$$
$$120 = 8 \times (0.75L)^{0.6}L^{0.4}$$
$$120 = 8 \times 0.75^{0.6}L^{0.6}L^{0.4}$$
$$6.732L = 120$$
$$L = 17.83$$

Then, we calculate K as

$$K = 0.75 \times 17.83 = 13.37$$

Thus, to produce 120 units of output with minimum cost, the firm should use 17.8 worker-hours and 13.4 machine-hours.

b. With the increased total factor productivity, the cost-minimizing condition is

$$\frac{\dfrac{4.8K^{0.6}}{L^{0.6}}}{\dfrac{7.2L^{0.4}}{K^{0.4}}} = \frac{15}{30}$$

$$\frac{4.8K^{0.6}K^{0.4}}{7.2L^{0.6}L^{0.4}} = 0.5$$

$$\frac{4.8K}{7.2L} = 0.5$$

$$4.8K = 3.6L$$

$$K = 0.75L$$

Substituting this expression into the production function and solving it for L and K, given that $Q = 120$, we get:

$$Q = 12K^{0.6}L^{0.4}$$
$$120 = 12 \times (0.75L)^{0.6}L^{0.4}$$
$$10 = 0.75^{0.6}L^{0.6}L^{0.4}$$
$$0.8415L = 10$$
$$L = 11.88$$
$$K = 0.75 \times 11.88 = 8.91$$

Thus, with the improved technology, to produce 120 units of output with minimum cost, the firm should use 11.9 worker-hours and 8.9 machine-hours. Notice that the new technology allows the firm to produce the same quantity of output while using less capital and less labor.

c. Before the technological change, the cost of the firm's cost-minimizing combination of inputs is

$$\$15 \times 17.8 + \$30 \times 13.4 = \$669$$

And with the new technology, it is

$$\$15 \times 11.9 + \$30 \times 8.9 = \$445.50$$

Thus, the new technology allows the firm to reduce the cost of producing 120 units of output by $223.50.

∂ d. Marginal product of labor is the partial derivative of the production function with respect to labor: $MP_L = \dfrac{\partial Q}{\partial L} = 12(0.4)K^{0.6}L^{0.4-1} = 4.8K^{0.5}L^{-0.6}$. Marginal product of capital is the partial derivative of the production function with respect to capital: $MP_K = \dfrac{\partial Q}{\partial K} = 12(0.6)K^{0.6-1}L^{0.4}$ $= 7.2K^{-0.4}L^{0.4}$.

6.7 The Firm's Expansion Path and Total Cost Curve

Expansion path

A curve that illustrates how the optimal mix of inputs varies with total output.

∂ The firm's expansion path can be derived from the Lagrangian approach as the combination of the first two of the Lagrangian first-order conditions in which K is expressed as a function of L or vice versa.

Total cost curve

A curve that shows a firm's cost of producing particular quantities.

∂ Demand curve for capital

The demand curve for capital gives the relationship of how changes in the rental rate of capital affect the cost-minimizing combination of capital. The demand curve for capital can be solved for via the Lagrangian approach by holding output and the wage rate constant and solving for the optimal K as a function of these parameters.

∂ Demand curve for labor

The demand curve for labor gives the relationship of how changes in the wage rate affect the cost-minimizing combination of labor. The demand curve for labor can be solved for via the Lagrangian approach by holding output and the rental rate of capital constant and solving for the optimal L as a function of these parameters.

∂ **6.7 figure it out 1**

A firm has the production function $Q = 30K^{0.1}L^{0.9}$, where Q measures output, K represents machine-hours, and L measures labor-hours. Suppose that the wage rate is \$27 and the firm wants to produce 90,000 units of output.

a. Use calculus to derive the demand for capital.

b. Use calculus to confirm that the demand for capital satisfies the Law of Demand.

c. What is the optimal level of capital if the rental rate on capital is \$10?

Solution

a. We know that the firm will minimize costs when

$$MRTS_{LK} = \frac{MP_L}{MP_K} = \frac{W}{R}$$

(Alternately, we could use a Lagrangian.)

For this problem, the marginal rate of technical substitution is

$$MRTS_{LK} = \frac{MP_L}{MP_K} = \frac{30(0.9)K^{0.1}L^{-0.1}}{30(0.1)K^{-0.9}L^{0.9}} = \frac{9K}{L}$$

Applying the cost minimization condition gives us

$$MRTS_{LK} = \frac{9K}{L} = \frac{W}{R} = \frac{27}{R}$$

Now solve for L as a function of K:

$$\frac{9K}{L} = \frac{27}{R}$$
$$9KR = 27L$$
$$L = \frac{KR}{3}$$

We can then substitute into the output constraint, and solve for K as a function of R:

$$90,000 = 30K^{0.1}L^{0.9}$$
$$3,000 = K^{0.1}\left(\frac{KR}{3}\right)^{0.9}$$
$$3,000 = \left(\frac{1}{3}\right)^{0.9}R^{0.9}K^{0.1}K^{0.9}$$
$$3,000 \approx 0.372R^{0.9}K$$
$$K \approx 8,064.516R^{-0.9}$$

So the demand for capital is

$$K(R) \approx 8,064.516R^{-0.9}$$

b. Take the derivative of capital demand with respect to the rental rate

$$\frac{\partial K(R)}{\partial R} = 8,064.516(-0.9)R^{-1.9} = -7,258.064R^{-1.9}$$

which is negative, as we expect from the Law of Demand since here if the price of capital (the rental rate) increases, the firm demands less capital.

c. Substitute \$10 for R in the capital demand.

$$K \approx 8,064.516R^{-0.9} \approx 8,064.516(10)^{-0.9} \approx 1,015.262 \text{ machine-hours}$$

Practice Problems

Problem 1

Suppose the production function for a pizzeria is

$$Q = 36K^{0.5}L^{0.5}$$

where Q is the number of pizzas produced per day, K is the number of ovens, which is fixed at 4 in the short run, and L is the number of workers employed.

a. What is the equation for the firm's short-run production function?
b. If the pizzeria employs 4 workers, how much output can it produce?
c. What is the marginal product of the 5th worker?
d. When the pizzeria hires the 5th worker, does it experience diminishing marginal returns? Explain your answer.
e. Use calculus to determine functions for the marginal products of labor and of capital.

Problem 2

Fill in the blanks in the following table.

Labor Input	Output	Marginal Product	Average Product
1	100		
2	142		
3		32	
4			50
5		25	

Problem 3

A firm can hire workers for $8 per hour and rent capital (machines) for $16 per hour. The firm's total cost (C) is $1,600.
a. Write the equation for the firm's isocost line. Draw the graph of the isocost line, with labor-hours on the horizontal axis and machine-hours on the vertical axis.
b. Suppose the price of labor rises to $10 per hour. Draw the new isocost line for $C = \$1,600$. What happens to the isocost line?

Problem 4

A firm is employing 500 worker-hours at $16 per hour and 100 machine-hours at $40 per machine-hour. With the current combination of inputs used, the marginal rate of technical substitution of labor for capital ($MRTS_{LK}$) is 0.5.
a. Suppose the marginal product of labor is currently 12 units of output. What is the marginal product of capital?
b. Is the firm minimizing its costs? Explain your answer.
c. What can the firm do to improve its situation? Explain.

Problem 5

For each of the following production functions, determine if they exhibit constant, decreasing, or increasing returns to scale.
a. $Q = K^{0.8}L^{0.2}$
b. $Q = 0.4K^{0.5} + 0.6L^{0.5}$
c. $Q = \min(0.8K^{0.5}, 0.5L^{0.5})$
d. For the firm in (a), find the marginal rate of technical substitution and discuss how $MRTS_{LK}$ changes as the firm uses more L, holding output constant.
e. Suppose that the wage rate is $10 per hour and the rental rate of capital is $10 per hour. If the firm in (a) wants to produce 500 units of output, what is the cost-minimizing bundle of capital and labor?
f. Derive the expansion path of the firm in (a).
g. Derive the demand for capital of the firm in (a).
h. Confirm that the demand for capital for the firm in (a) satisfies the Law of Demand.

Problem 6

A manufacturing firm's production function is

$$Q = 10K^{0.5}L^{0.5}$$

where Q is the quantity of output (units), K is the amount of capital used (machine-hours), and L is the amount of labor hired (worker-hours). For this production function, the marginal product of labor is $MP_L = \dfrac{5K^{0.5}}{L^{0.5}}$, and the marginal product of capital is $MP_K = \dfrac{5L^{0.5}}{K^{0.5}}$. The firm rents capital at a rate of $R = \$4$ per hour and hires labor at $W = \$16$ per hour. The firm plans to produce 720 units of output.

a. How much labor and how much capital should the firm use to minimize its cost of production?
b. Suppose that a technological improvement increases the firm's total factor productivity, so the production function is now

$$Q = 12K^{0.5}L^{0.5}$$

for which the marginal product of labor is $MP_L = \dfrac{6K^{0.5}}{L^{0.5}}$, and the marginal product of capital is $MP_K = \dfrac{6L^{0.5}}{K^{0.5}}$. How much labor and how much capital should the firm use now to minimize the cost of producing 720 units of output?
c. How does the technological improvement change the firm's costs of producing 720 units of output?
d. Use calculus to show that the marginal products of labor and of capital of the new technology are as given.

Problem 7

A firm's isoquants are shown on the following graph. The firm hires labor at $18 per worker-hour and rents capital at $9 per machine-hour, using a cost-minimizing combination of inputs that costs $6,480.

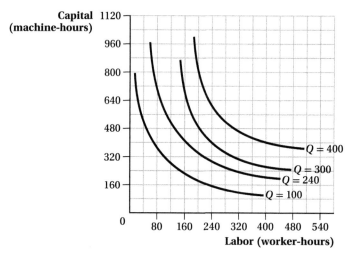

a. How much labor and how much capital does the firm use?
b. What is the firm's marginal rate of substitution of labor for capital?
c. How much output does the firm produce?
d. Now suppose the cost of capital falls to $6 per machine-hour, while the cost of labor remains the same. If the firm wants to keep its total cost at the same level ($6,480), how much output will the firm be able to produce? How will the combination of inputs used by the firm change?
e. How does the lower cost of capital affect the firm's cost per unit of output?

Problem 8

Suppose that the production function for new iPhones is

$$Q = 0.2K^{0.25}L^{0.75}$$

For this production function, the marginal product of labor is $MP_L = \dfrac{0.15K^{0.25}}{L^{0.25}}$, and the marginal product of capital is $MP_K = \dfrac{0.05L^{0.75}}{K^{0.75}}$. Assume that Apple can hire labor for $24 per hour, and the rental rate of

capital is \$6 per machine-hour. Suppose Apple is currently producing 96.7 iPhones per hour at the lowest possible cost.
a. What is the firm's marginal rate of technical substitution of labor for capital?
b. What is the lowest-cost combination of labor and capital that allows Apple to produce 96.7 iPhones?
c. Given the current level of production, what is the minimum cost of producing an iPhone?
d. Suppose Apple has \$19,200 to spend per hour on producing iPhones. What is the maximum number of iPhones it can produce?
e. Use calculus to show that the marginal products of labor and of capital are as given.

Problem 9

A company is advertising its new product on local TV and on the Internet. An economic consultant estimates that consumers are influenced by the company's commercials, according to the following function:

$$S = 40T^{0.4}N^{0.2}$$

where S is the quantity of the firm's product sold (units), T is the number of TV ads, and N is the number of Internet ads. For this production function, the marginal product of a TV ad is $MP_T = \dfrac{16N^{0.2}}{T^{0.6}}$, and the marginal product of an Internet ad is $MP_N = \dfrac{8T^{0.4}}{N^{0.8}}$.
A local television ad costs \$500, and an Internet ad costs \$100.
a. If the company wants to sell 500 units of the product, what combination of TV ads and Internet ads should it use? How much will it cost the company?
b. If the company wants to increase its sales to about 600 units, should it rely more on additional TV ads or additional Internet ads? Explain your answer.

Problem 10

Suppose that a firm's production function is

$$Q = 4K^{0.5}L^{0.5}$$

The firm currently hires 1,600 hours of labor and rents 2,500 machine-hours of capital.
a. How many units of output does the firm produce?
b. Suppose that the firm decides to lay off workers and use only 1,000 hours of labor. How much additional capital must the firm rent to keep the level of production in (a)?
c. Suppose now that advances in technology change the firm's production function. It is now

$$Q = 4K^{0.75}L^{0.25}$$

How will this change your answer in (b)?

Problem 11

A firm has the production function $Q = 6K^{0.4}L^{0.6}$, where Q measures output, K represents machine-hours, and L measures labor-hours.
a. If the rental rate of capital is $R = \$35$, the wage rate is $W = \$15$, and the firm wants to produce 80,000 units of output, what is the cost-minimizing bundle of capital and labor? Use calculus to solve.
b. Derive the firm's expansion path.

Problem 12

A firm has the production function $Q = 0.5K^{0.7}L^{0.3}$, where Q measures output, K represents machine-hours, and L measures labor-hours. Suppose that the rental rate of capital is \$40 and the firm wants to produce 60,000 units of output.
a. Use calculus to derive the demand for labor.
b. Confirm, using calculus, that the demand for labor satisfies the Law of Demand.
c. What is the optimal level of labor if the wage rate is \$25?

Costs

7.1 Costs That Matter for Decision Making: Opportunity Costs

Accounting cost

The direct cost of operating a business, including costs for raw materials.

Accounting profit

A firm's total revenue minus its accounting cost.

Opportunity cost

The value of what a producer gives up by using an input.

Economic cost

The sum of a producer's accounting and opportunity costs. Production decisions should be made based on economic cost, not accounting cost.

Economic profit

A firm's total revenue minus its economic cost. When making decisions, a firm should consider its economic profit, not accounting profit.

make the grade

The cost of capital

To be able to correctly answer exam questions and solve problems involving costs, it is important to understand and correctly interpret the costs of inputs. With the labor input, it is pretty straightforward: the price of labor (W) is how much the firm pays per unit of labor (usually worker-hour). There is much confusion, however, when it comes to measuring the cost of capital. It is easier in the case when the firm rents its capital from someone else. Then, the price of capital (R) is simply the amount paid per unit of capital (e.g., machine-hour). But what if the firm uses its own capital?

For example, suppose you invest $10,000 of your own funds to buy computers and other equipment for your web design business. Is the cost of your capital $10,000? It is a common mistake to think so. A firm's costs are the ongoing (hourly, monthly, annual, etc.) costs for the owner (which are compared with the ongoing revenue to calculate the firm's profit), not an amount invested once. But perhaps the cost of your capital is the amount of its depreciation calculated according to the accounting rules. Wrong again. Accounting rules are used for making financial statements and for the tax purposes, not to determine economic costs.

Recall that to determine the economic cost of something we should consider opportunity costs. Thus, to see what the actual cost of your capital is, you should ask yourself what the best alternative use of it would be. Suppose the highest annual rate of return that you could have received on your $10,000 if you had invested it in a different way is 4%. Assuming that at the end of the year you can still sell your computers and other equipment for $10,000, your cost of capital is $10,000 × 0.04 = $400 per year. More realistically, the market price of your capital is likely to fall, since computers may become obsolete rather quickly. Suppose at the end of the year, the highest price you can get for your capital is $8,000, that is, $2,000 less than it cost you at the beginning of the year. This lost value of capital, called economic depreciation, is part of your opportunity cost because you would not lose it if you invested your money in the best alternative way. (Note that the concept of economic depreciation is different from that of accounting depreciation, which is calculated according to standard accounting rules, rather than based on opportunity cost.) Thus, the economic cost of your capital is $2,000 (economic depreciation) + $400 (investment income forgone) = $2,400 per year. We can also calculate your cost of capital (R) at a monthly rate ($200), daily rate ($6.57), or even hourly rate ($0.27).

7.1 figure it out 1

Molly owns a candy store. Last year, her business had the following statement of revenues and costs:

Revenues	$360,000
Supplies	$200,000
Utilities	$10,000
Wages of employees	$85,000

As the sole owner of the business, Molly receives all its profit and does not formally pay herself a salary. Molly owns the building where her store is located and can always close the store and rent the space to someone else for $36,000 per year. Molly currently has a job offer from another store to work as the store manager for $50,000 per year. Assume that Molly can work only one job at a time.
a. What is Molly's accounting cost? Accounting profit?
b. What is Molly's economic cost? Economic profit?
c. Should Molly continue to operate her store or should she accept the job offer?

Solution:

a. Accounting cost is the direct cost of operating a business. It includes supplies, utilities, and employees' wages. Thus, Molly's accounting cost is $200,000 + $10,000 + $85,000 = $295,000. Molly's accounting profit is the difference between her total revenues and her accounting cost: $360,000 − $295,000 = $65,000.
b. Economic cost includes both accounting cost and the opportunity costs of owner supplied resources. Molly's opportunity costs are the rent she could earn if she rented the store space to someone else ($36,000) and the cost of her time given up to run her own store rather than working for the other store, where she can earn $50,000 per year. Thus, Molly's opportunity cost is $36,000 + $50,000 = $86,000, so her economic cost is $295,000 + $86,000 = $381,000. Molly's economic profit is the difference between her total revenue and her economic cost: $360,000 − $381,000 = −$21,000. That is, Molly's economic profit is negative. In other words, she incurs an economic loss of $21,000.
c. That Molly's economic profit is negative shows that she would be better off if she closed the store, rented the space to someone else, and took the job at the other store.

7.2 Costs That Do Not Matter for Decision Making: Sunk Costs

Sunk cost

A cost that, once paid, the firm cannot recover. Sunk costs, once they are paid, should *not* affect current and future production decisions. If a firm allows sunk costs to affect its decisions, it commits the **sunk cost fallacy.**

Specific capital

Capital that cannot be used outside of its original application. Whether capital is specific is an important determinant of sunk costs.

Operating revenue

The money a firm earns from selling its output.

Operating cost

The cost a firm incurs in producing its output.

7.3 Costs and Cost Curves

Cost curve

The mathematical relationship between a firm's production costs and its output.

Fixed cost (FC)

The cost of the firm's fixed inputs, independent of the quantity of the firm's output.

Variable cost (VC)

The cost of inputs that vary with the quantity of the firm's output.

Total cost (TC)

The sum of a firm's fixed and variable costs:

$$TC = FC + VC$$

7.4 Average and Marginal Costs

Average fixed cost (AFC)

A firm's fixed cost per unit of output (Q):

$$AFC = \frac{FC}{Q}$$

Average variable cost (AVC)

A firm's variable cost per unit of output (Q):

$$AVC = \frac{VC}{Q}$$

Average total cost

A firm's total cost per unit of output (Q):

$$ATC = \frac{TC}{Q}$$

$$ATC = AFC + AVC$$

Marginal cost

The additional cost of producing an additional unit of output:

$$MC = \frac{\Delta TC}{\Delta Q}$$

Since $TC = FC + VC$, and fixed cost is constant (i.e. $\Delta FC = 0$), all additional costs are variable costs. Therefore, marginal cost can also be calculated as

$$MC = \frac{\Delta VC}{\Delta Q}$$

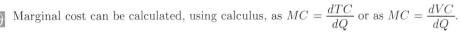 Marginal cost can be calculated, using calculus, as $MC = \frac{dTC}{dQ}$ or as $MC = \frac{dVC}{dQ}$.

The relationship between average and marginal costs

When the marginal cost curve is below the average cost curve, the average cost curve is downward-sloping. When the marginal cost curve is above the average cost curve, the average cost curve slopes upward. The marginal cost curve intersects the average total and average variable cost curves at their minimums. (Note that this relationship holds for both total costs and variable costs. In fact, it holds for any average and marginal values.)

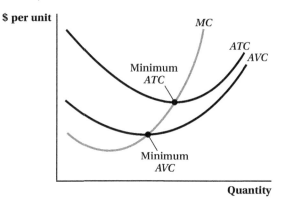

∂   The quantity that minimizes ATC is that which solves the equation $\dfrac{dATC}{dQ} = 0$ and satisfies $\dfrac{d^2ATC}{dQ^2} > 0$ (to assure that we are dealing with a minimum and not a maximum). Recall that this is a second derivative test and therefore $\dfrac{d^2ATC}{dQ^2} > 0$ indicates that ATC is convex (and therefore we are dealing with a minimum) just as $\dfrac{d^2ATC}{dQ^2} < 0$ would mean that ATC is concave (and in that case we would be dealing with a maximum. These are the first- and second-order conditions for an unconstrained minimization problem of average total cost (i.e., $\min_Q ATC$).

7.4 figure it out 1

Carlo's Pizza is a small pizzeria. Suppose Carlo's uses only two inputs to produce pizza: labor and capital. The cost of labor is \$300 per worker-week, and the cost of capital is \$400 per week. The pizzeria's short-run production function (with the capital input fixed) is described in the following table.

Labor (workers per week)	Output (pizzas per week)
1	74
2	152
3	228
4	296
5	350
6	384

a. If Carlo's produces 228 pizzas per week, what is the firm's average fixed cost?
b. If Carlo's produces 296 pizzas per week, what is the firm's average variable cost?
c. If Carlo's produces 350 pizzas per week, what is the firm's average total cost?
d. Suppose Carlo is currently employing 3 workers. If he hires one more worker, what will be the marginal cost per additional pizza produced?

Solution

a. Carlo's fixed cost is the cost of capital (\$400), as it does not vary with output. Thus, the average fixed cost is $AFC = \dfrac{FC}{Q} = \dfrac{\$400}{228} = \$1.75$.

b. Carlo's variable cost is the cost of labor, since it varies with output. To produce 296 pizzas, Carlo needs to employ 4 workers, so his variable cost is $VC = \$300 \times 4 = \$1,200$. And his average variable cost is $AVC = \dfrac{VC}{Q} = \dfrac{\$1,200}{296} = \$4.05$.

c. To produce 350 pizzas, Carlo needs 5 workers, so his variable cost is $VC = \$300 \times 5 = \$1,500$. Carlo's fixed cost remains the same ($400) at all levels of output. Thus, the total cost of producing 350 pizzas is $TC = FC + VC = \$400 + \$1,500 = \$1,900$. Then, the average total cost is $ATC = \dfrac{TC}{Q} = \dfrac{\$1,900}{350} = \$5.43$.

d. If Carlo's hires the 4th worker, its output will increase by $\Delta Q = 296 - 228 = 68$ pizzas. And the cost of an additional worker is $\Delta VC = \Delta TC = \$300$. ($\Delta VC = \Delta TC$ because the fixed cost does not change, i.e. $\Delta FC = 0$.) Thus, the marginal cost per additional pizza is $\dfrac{\Delta VC}{\Delta Q} = \dfrac{\$300}{68} = \$4.41$.

7.4 figure it out 2

Suppose a firm's total cost curve is

$$TC = 36Q^2 + 6Q + 60$$

where Q is the quantity produced (in thousands of units). The firm's marginal cost curve (which can be derived from its total cost curve) is

$$MC = 72Q + 6$$

a. Find the firm's fixed cost, variable cost, average total cost, and average variable cost.
b. Find the output level that minimizes average total cost.
c. Find the output level at which average variable cost is minimized.
d. Use calculus to show that the firm's marginal cost is as given.
e. Use calculus to minimize average total cost and confirm that your answer is the same as in (b).
f. Use calculus to minimize average variable cost and confirm that your answer is the same as in (c).

Solution

a. We know that when a firm's output is zero, there is no variable cost, which means the firm's total cost is all fixed cost. Thus, we can find the fixed cost by calculating total cost at zero units of output:

$$FC = 36 \times 0^2 + 6 \times 0 + 60$$
$$FC = 60$$

Variable cost can be found by subtracting fixed cost from total cost:

$$VC = (36Q^2 + 6Q + 60) - 60$$
$$VC = 36Q^2 + 6Q$$

Average total cost is total cost per unit of output:

$$ATC = \frac{TC}{Q}$$
$$ATC = \frac{36Q^2 + 6Q + 60}{Q}$$
$$ATC = 6 + 36Q + \frac{60}{Q}$$

Average variable cost is variable cost per unit of output:

$$AVC = \frac{VC}{Q}$$
$$AVC = \frac{36Q^2 + 6Q}{Q}$$
$$AVC = 36Q + 6$$

b. Minimum average total cost occurs when $ATC = MC$:

$$6 + 36Q + \frac{60}{Q} = 72Q + 6$$

Solving this equation for Q, we get:

$$36Q = \frac{60}{Q}$$

$$3Q^2 = 5$$

$$Q = \left(\frac{5}{3}\right)^{0.5}$$

$$Q = 1.291$$

That is, the average total cost is minimized when 1,291 units of output are produced.

c. Minimum average variable cost occurs when $AVC = MC$:

$$36Q + 6 = 72Q + 6$$

Solving this equation for Q, we get:

$$36Q = 0$$

$$Q = 0$$

That is, the average variable cost is minimized when no output is produced.

d. Using calculus, $MC = \dfrac{dTC}{dQ} = 36(2)Q^{2-1} + 6 + 0 = 72Q + 6$. This is as given.

e. Average total cost is shown in (a): $ATC = 36Q + 6 + \dfrac{60}{Q} = 36Q + 6 + 60Q^{-1}$. We can minimize this directly by calculating the first-order condition. Taking the derivative of ATC with respect to Q, we see that $\dfrac{dATC}{dQ} = 36 + 0 + 60(-1)Q^{-1-1} = 36 - 60Q^{-2}$. Setting this equal to zero, $36 - 60Q^{-2} = 0$ or $Q \approx 1.291$. To confirm that this is a minimum (and not a maximum), we can check the second-order condition: $\dfrac{d^2ATC}{dQ^2} = 0 - 60(-2)Q^{-2-1} = 120Q^{-3} > 0$. Since this is positive, we know that we have a minimum. This is the same answer as found in (b).

f. Average variable cost is shown in (a): $AVC = 36Q + 6$. We can minimize this directly by calculating the first-order condition. Taking the derivative of AVC with respect to Q, we see that $\dfrac{dAVC}{dQ} = 36 > 0$, indicates that AVC is increasing in Q. Since this derivative is positive and does not depend on Q, the function is minimized at $Q = 0$. This is the same answer as found in (c).

7.4 figure it out 3

Suppose a firm that produces TV sets has the following production function:

$$Q = 0.5K^{0.5}L^{0.5}$$

where Q is the number of TV sets produced per day, K is the amount of capital used (machine-hours), and L is the amount of labor employed (worker-hours). Given this production function, the marginal product of labor is $MP_L = \dfrac{0.25K^{0.5}}{L^{0.5}}$, and the marginal product of capital is $MP_K = \dfrac{0.25L^{0.5}}{K^{0.5}}$. The firm rents capital at a rate of $R = \$48$ per machine-hour and hires labor at a wage rate of $W = \$24$ per hour.

a. In the short run, the firm's capital input is fixed at 49 machine-hours per day. What is the firm's total cost of producing 24 TVs? The average total cost of producing 24 TVs?

b. What should the firm do in the long run to minimize the cost of producing 24 TV sets? How much will the firm be able to save?

c. Use calculus to show that the marginal products are as given.

Solution

a. When capital is fixed at $K = 49$, the firm's production function is

$$Q = 0.5 \times 49^{0.5}L^{0.5}$$

$$Q = 3.5L^{0.5}$$

Solving this equation for L, given that $Q = 24$, we have

$$24 = 3.5L^{0.5}$$

$$L^{0.5} = 6.857$$

$$L = 47$$

That is, given that $K = 49$, the firm has to employ 47 hours of labor to produce 24 TVs. With this combination of inputs, the total cost is

$$TC = \$24 \times 47 + \$48 \times 49$$

$$TC = \$3,480$$

and the average total cost is

$$ATC = \frac{\$3,480}{24}$$

$$ATC = \$145$$

b. As we learned in Chapter 6, in the long run, a firm minimizes costs when

$$\frac{MP_L}{MP_K} = \frac{W}{R}$$

So, the firm in question will minimize its cost when

$$\frac{\dfrac{0.25K^{0.5}}{L^{0.5}}}{\dfrac{0.25L^{0.5}}{K^{0.5}}} = \frac{24}{48}$$

$$\frac{0.25K^{0.5}K^{0.5}}{0.25L^{0.5}L^{0.5}} = 0.5$$

$$\frac{K}{L} = 0.5$$

$$K = 0.5L$$

We substitute this expression for K into the production function and solve for L and K, given that $Q = 24$:

$$Q = 0.5K^{0.5}L^{0.5}$$

$$24 = 0.5 \times (0.5L)^{0.5}L^{0.5}$$

$$24 = 0.5 \times 0.5^{0.5}L^{0.5}L^{0.5}$$

$$48 = 0.5^{0.5}L$$

$$0.707L = 48$$

$$L = 68$$

$$K = 0.5 \times 68 = 34$$

Thus, in the long run, to minimize its cost, the firm should increase labor from 47 to 68 worker-hours and reduce capital from 49 to 34 machine-hours. Then, the firm's total cost will fall to

$$TC = \$24 \times 68 + \$48 \times 34$$

$$TC = \$3,264$$

and the average total cost will fall to

$$ATC = \frac{\$3,264}{24}$$

$$ATC = \$136$$

That is, the firm will be able to save $\$3,480 - \$3,264 = \$216$ per day, or $\$145 - \$136 = \$9$ per TV set.

c. The marginal product of labor is the partial derivative of the production function with respect to labor, and the marginal product of capital is the partial derivative of the production function with respect to capital. Here, $MP_L = \dfrac{\partial Q}{\partial L} = 0.5(0.5)K^{0.5}L^{0.5-1} = 0.25K^{0.5}L^{-0.5}$ and $MP_K = \dfrac{\partial Q}{\partial K} = 0.5(0.5)K^{0.5-1}L^{0.5} = 0.25K^{-0.5}L^{0.5}$. These are equivalent to the marginal products as given.

∂ **7.4 figure it out 4**

Suppose a firm's total cost curve is $TC = 0.25Q^2 + 5Q + 2,000$.
a. Find the firm's marginal cost, average total cost, and average variable cost.
b. Use calculus to find the output level that minimizes average total cost.
c. Show that $ATC = MC$ at this output level.
d. Show that this is the minimum ATC by examining the second derivative.

Solution

a. Marginal cost is

$$MC = \frac{dTC}{dQ} = \frac{d(0.25Q^2 + 5Q + 2,000)}{dQ} = 0.25(2)Q^{2-1} + 5 + 0 = 0.5Q + 5$$

Average total cost is

$$ATC = \frac{TC}{Q} = \frac{0.25Q^2 + 5Q + 2,000}{Q} = 0.25Q + 5 + \frac{2,000}{Q} = 0.25Q + 5 + 2,000Q^{-1}$$

To find average variable cost, we need to recognize that fixed cost is 2,000 and $VC = 0.25Q^2 + 5Q$. Then average variable cost is

$$AVC = \frac{VC}{Q} = \frac{0.25Q^2 + 5Q}{Q} = 0.25Q + 5$$

b. To find the minimum of ATC, set its first derivative equal to zero and solve for Q:

$$\frac{dATC}{dQ} = \frac{d(0.25Q + 5 + 2,000Q^{-1})}{dQ} = .25 + 0 + 2,000^{-1}Q^{-1-1} = 0$$

$$0.25 = \frac{2,000}{Q^2}$$

$$Q^2 = 8,000$$

$$Q = \sqrt{8,000} \approx 89.443$$

Alternatively, we could find the quantity where $MC = ATC$:

$$MC = 0.5Q + 5 = 0.25Q + 5 + \frac{2,000}{Q} = ATC$$

$$0.25Q = \frac{2,000}{Q}$$

$$Q^2 = 8,000$$

$$Q = \sqrt{8,000} \approx 89.443$$

c. At this quantity, average total cost is

$$ATC \approx 0.25(89.443) + 5 + \frac{2,000}{(89.443)} \approx 49.722$$

and marginal cost is

$$MC \approx 0.5(89.443) + 5 \approx 49.722$$

d. Take the second derivative of average total cost:

$$\frac{d^2ATC}{dQ^2} = \frac{d(0.25 - 2,000Q^{-2})}{dQ} = 0 - 2,000(-2)Q^{-2-1} = \frac{4,000}{Q^3} > 0$$

for any $Q > 0$, so this is the minimum of ATC.

7.5 Short-Run and Long-Run Cost Curves
Short-run total cost curve

The mathematical representation of a firm's total cost of producing different quantities of output at a fixed level of capital.

7.6 Economies in the Production Process

Economies of scale

Total cost rises at a slower rate than output rises, so the average total cost falls as output increases.

Diseconomies of scale

Total cost rises at a faster rate than output rises, so the average total cost rises as output increases.

Constant economies of scale

Total cost rises at the same rate as output rises, so the average total cost remains constant as output increases.

Economies of scope

The simultaneous production of multiple products at a lower cost than if a firm made each product separately.

Diseconomies of scope

The simultaneous production of multiple products at a higher cost than if a firm made each product separately.

7.6 figure it out 1

Suppose that the long-run total cost function for a firm is

$$LTC = 24{,}000Q - 200Q^2 + Q^3$$

And the firm's long-run marginal cost function (which can be derived from its total cost function) is

$$LMC = 24{,}000 - 400Q + 3Q^2$$

a. At what levels of output will the firm face economies of scale? Diseconomies of scale? (*Hint*: These cost functions yield a typical U-shaped long-run average cost curve.)

b. Use calculus to minimize long-run average total cost.

Solution

a. We know that when $LMC < LATC$, long run average total cost is falling, so the firm experiences economies of scale. When $LMC > LATC$, the long-run average total cost is rising, so the firm faces diseconomies of scale. Thus, if we can find the quantity at which the minimum $LATC$ occurs, we can see where economies of scale end and diseconomies begin.

We also know that minimum average cost occurs at the level of output where $LMC = LATC$. To solve this equation, we first need to find the $LATC$ curve:

$$LATC = \frac{LTC}{Q}$$

$$LATC = \frac{24{,}000Q - 200Q^2 + Q^3}{Q}$$

$$LATC = 24{,}000 - 200Q + Q^2$$

Now, we set $LATC = LMC$ to find the quantity that minimizes $LATC$:

$$LATC = LMC$$

$$24{,}000 - 200Q + Q^2 = 24{,}000 - 400Q + 3Q^2$$

$$2Q^2 = 200Q$$

$$2Q = 200$$

$$Q = 100$$

Thus, long-run average total cost is minimized and economies of scale are constant when the firm produces 100 units of output (see the following graph). This means at $Q < 100$, the firm faces economies of scale. And at $Q > 100$, it faces diseconomies of scale. (You can prove this to yourself by substituting different quantities into the long-run average total cost equation and seeing if $LATC$ rises or falls as Q increases.)

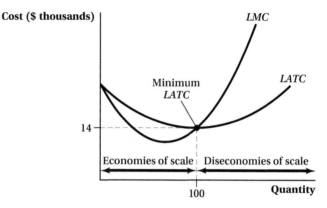

b. Long-run average total cost is shown in (a): $LATC = 24{,}000 - 200Q + Q^2$. We can minimize this directly by calculating the first-order condition. Taking the derivative of $LATC$ with respect to Q, we see that $\dfrac{dLATC}{dQ} = 0 - 200 + 2Q^{2-1} = 2Q - 200$. Setting this equal to zero, $2Q - 200 = 0$ or $Q = 100$. This is the same cutoff point as found in (a).

Practice Problems

Problem 1

Alan works for a law firm where he earns $150,000 per year. He is thinking about starting his own law practice. He has determined that his yearly costs would be $50,000 for rent on the office building, $300,000 for wages and salaries of employees, and $20,000 for supplies and utilities. To start the business, Alan would have to withdraw $250,000 from his savings account, which is currently earning interest at an annual rate of 2%. Running his own law practice would require Alan to quit his current job.

a. If Allan starts his law firm, what will be his annual accounting cost?

b. If Allan starts his law firm, what will be his annual economic cost?

c. Suppose that Alan's expected annual revenue from his law practice is $550,000. Should he start the business? Explain your answer.

Problem 2

Suppose Panasonic decided to develop a new digital camcorder. The project costs 10 billion yen to complete. The company's managers expected that the new camcorder would bring 12 billion yen in sales. Panasonic has already invested 7 billion yen in the project when the managers suddenly find out that the introduction of a similar product by Sony is expected to reduce Panasonic's revenue from its new camcorder to only 5 billion yen. Would you advise Panasonic to finish the project and launch the new camcorder, or would you suggest to discontinue it? Explain your answer.

Problem 3

Fill in the blanks in the following table.

Quantity (units)	Total Cost ($)	Variable Cost ($)	Average Total Cost ($)	Marginal Cost ($)
0	30		—	—
1	70			
2		60		
3			34	
4				18

Problem 4

Mauricio's barber shop hires labor and uses capital (building and equipment) to give haircuts. The cost of labor is $90 per worker-day. And the cost of capital, which is fixed in the short run, is $100 per day. The shop's short-run production function is described in the following table.

Labor (workers)	Output (haircuts)
1	20
2	35
3	48
4	60
5	72
6	84

a. If Mauricio's hires 5 workers, what is the shop's average fixed cost?
b. If Mauricio's produces 60 haircuts per day, what is the firm's average variable cost?
c. If Mauricio's produces 48 haircuts per day, what is the firm's average total cost?
d. Suppose Mauricio is currently employing 5 workers. If he hires one more worker, what will be the marginal cost per additional haircut produced?

Problem 5

Suppose a firm's total cost curve is

$$TC = 1{,}000 + 10Q + 4Q^2$$

where Q is the quantity of output (units). The firm's marginal cost curve (which can be derived from its total cost curve) is

$$MC = 10 + 8Q$$

a. Find the firm's fixed cost, variable cost, average total cost, and average variable cost.
b. Find the output level that minimizes average total cost.
c. Find the output level at which average variable cost is minimized.
d. Using calculus, show that the firm's marginal cost is as given.
e. Use calculus to minimize average total cost and confirm that your answer is the same as in (b).
f. Use calculus to minimize average variable cost and confirm that your answer is the same as in (c).

Problem 6

Giuseppe's Pizza is a family-owned pizzeria. It uses 4 pizza ovens and hires labor to make and sell pizza. Giuseppe's cost of capital is $128 per oven per day and its cost of labor is $64 per worker-day. The pizzeria's production function is

$$Q = 20K^{0.5}L^{0.5}$$

where Q is the number of pizzas produced per day, K is the number of ovens used, and L is the number of workers employed.

a. Find Giuseppe's short-run production function (i.e., when the number of ovens is fixed at 4).
b. If Giuseppe's employs 6 workers, what is the pizzeria's average fixed cost?
c. If Giuseppe's produces 80 pizzas per day, what is the firm's short-run average total cost? Average variable cost?
d. What is Giuseppe's short-run marginal cost of producing the 81st pizza (assuming that fractional worker-days, that is, part-time workers, are possible).
∂ e. Use calculus to solve for Giuseppe's marginal products of labor and capital.

Problem 7

A sweater factory has a choice of using a smaller plant, with 5 knitting machines, and a larger plant, with 10 knitting machines. If the firm uses the smaller plant, its total cost curve is

$$TC_1 = 200 + 30Q - 0.4Q^2 + 0.004Q^3$$

where Q is the quantity of sweaters produced per day. For the larger plant, the total cost curve is

$$TC_2 = 400 + 35Q - 0.6Q^2 + 0.004Q^3$$

The factory is currently using the smaller plant, producing 60 sweaters per day.

a. What is the firm's short-run average total cost?
b. What is the firm's long-run average total cost? Explain your answer.
c. If the factory plans to continue to produce 60 sweaters per day in the long run, should it expand its plant? Explain.
∂ d. Determine, using calculus, the firm's marginal cost if the firm uses the smaller plant.
e. For which values of Q is marginal cost increasing for this firm if it uses the smaller plant?
f. Determine, using calculus, the firm's marginal cost if the firm uses the larger plant.
g. For which values of Q is marginal cost increasing for this firm if it uses the larger plant?

Problem 8

Suppose that a producer of laptop computers has the following production function:

$$Q = 0.3K^{0.5}L^{0.5}$$

where Q is the number of laptops produced per day, K is the amount of capital used (machine-hours), and L is the amount of labor employed (worker-hours). Given this production function, the marginal product of labor is $MP_L = \dfrac{0.15K^{0.5}}{L^{0.5}}$, and the marginal product of capital is $MP_K = \dfrac{0.15L^{0.5}}{K^{0.5}}$. The firm rents capital at a rate of $R = \$120$ per machine-hour and hires labor at a wage rate of $W = \$30$ per hour.

a. In the short run, the firm's capital input is fixed at 100 machine-hours per day. What is the firm's total cost of producing 21 laptops? The average total cost?
b. What should the firm do in the long run to minimize the cost of producing 21 laptops? How much will the firm be able to save?
∂ c. Use calculus to show that the marginal products are as given.

Problem 9

Suppose that the long-run total cost curve for a firm is

$$LTC = 14{,}000Q - 80Q^2 + Q^3$$

where Q is the quantity of output (units). The firm's long-run marginal cost curve (which can be derived from its total cost curve) is

$$LMC = 14{,}000 - 160Q + 3Q^2$$

a. What quantity of output should the firm produce to minimize its long-run average total cost ($LATC$)?
b. If the firm is producing at the minimum possible $LATC$, how much does it cost the firm to produce an average unit of output?
c. At what levels of output will the firm face economies of scale? Diseconomies of scale? (*Hint*: The firm's cost functions yield a typical U-shaped long-run average cost curve.)
d. Show, using calculus, that the firm's long-run marginal cost is as given.
e. For which values of Q is long-run marginal cost increasing for this firm?

Problem 10

A small manufacturing firm has the following production function:

$$Q = 8K^{0.5}L^{0.5}$$

where Q is the quantity of output (units per day), K is the amount of capital used (machines), and L is the number of workers employed. The firm is currently using 9 machines and cannot change its capital input in the short run. The cost of capital (R) is $1,000 per machine-day, and the cost of labor (W) is $200 per worker-day.
a. What is the firm's short-run production function? Write the equation for the firm's short-run total cost curve (with total cost as a function of output).
b. If the firm produces 96 units of output per day, what is its average variable cost? Average total cost?
c. What is the marginal cost of producing the 97th unit?
d. Use calculus to solve for the firm's marginal products of labor and capital.

Problem 11

A firm has a production function of $Q = 0.5K^{0.5}L^{0.5}$, the rental rate of capital is $10, and the wage rate is $25. In the short-run, $\overline{K}$ is fixed at 100 units.
a. What is the short-run production function?
b. What is the short-run demand for labor?
c. What are the firm's short-run total cost and short-run marginal cost? Use calculus to solve.

Problem 12

Suppose a firm's total cost curve is $TC = 0.4Q^3 - 2Q^2 + 6Q + 8$. Find the quantity that minimizes average variable costs for the firm using calculus. Demonstrate that average variable cost is equal to marginal cost at this quantity.

Supply in a Competitive Market 8

8.1 Market Structures and Perfect Competition in the Short Run

Market structure

The competitive environment in which firms operate.

The Four Basic Market Structures

	Perfect competition	Monopolistic competition	Oligopoly	Monopoly
Number of firms	Many	Many	Few	One
Type of products sold	Identical	Differentiated	Identical or differentiated	Unique
Barriers to entry	None	None	Some	High

Perfect competition

A market with many firms producing identical products and no barriers to entry.

The demand curve facing a perfectly competitive firm

The demand curve facing a firm in a perfectly competitive market is perfectly elastic (horizontal) at the market equilibrium price.

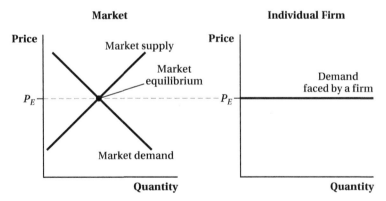

8.2 Profit Maximization in a Perfectly Competitive Market

Profit

The difference between a firm's revenue and its total cost:

$$\pi = TR - TC$$

Marginal cost

The additional cost of producing an additional unit of output:

$$MC = \frac{\Delta TC}{\Delta Q}$$

∂ Recall from the Chapter 7 Online Appendix that marginal cost can be calculated, using calculus, as $MC = \frac{dTC}{dQ}$.

Marginal revenue

The additional revenue from selling one additional unit of output:

$$MR = \frac{\Delta TR}{\Delta Q}$$

∂ Marginal revenue can be calculated, using calculus, as $MR = \frac{dTR}{dQ}$.

Marginal revenue of a perfectly competitive firm

In a perfectly competitive market, a firm's marginal revenue equals the market price:

$$MR = P$$

Profit maximization for a perfectly competitive firm

A perfectly competitive firm maximizes its profit at the quantity of output where

$$MR = P = MC$$

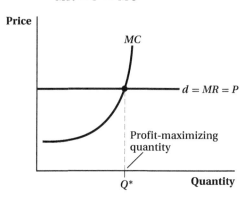

∂ The firm's maximization problem is $\max_{Q} \pi = TR - TC$ and therefore the first-order condition is $\frac{dTR}{dQ} - \frac{dTC}{dQ} = 0$ or $MR - MC = 0$ or $MR = MC$. For a perfectly competitive firm, this simplifies to $P = MC$.

Deciding whether to operate at a loss or shut down in the short run

	Shut down	Operate
Revenue	None	Some (*TR*)
Cost	Fixed (*FC*)	Fixed (*FC*) + Variable (*VC*)
Loss	–*FC*	*TR* – (*FC* + *VC*)

Using per unit cost curves to analyze firms' decisions

There are many questions about situations in perfectly competitive markets, and firms' decisions can be easily answered by looking at three cost curves: marginal cost (MC), average total cost (ATC), and average variable cost (AVC). Each of these cost curves explains part of the situation at hand. The following table summarizes the questions that you can answer by looking at each curve.

Curve	Question	Answer
MC	What is the profit-maximizing level of output?	It is the level of output at which $MC = MR$. And since for a perfectly competitive firm $MR = P$, it is the level of output at which $MC = P$.
ATC	Is the firm earning economic profit?	If at the profit-maximizing level of output $P > ATC$, then the firm is making a positive economic profit. If $ATC = P$, then the firms is making zero economic profit. And if $ATC > P$, the firm is incurring an economic loss. Profit is measured as the rectangle with a base equal to output and a height equal to the difference between P and ATC at that quantity of output: If a perfectly competitive firm is earning a positive profit, the story ends there. You don't need to consider the firm's average variable cost curve.
AVC	If the firm is incurring an economic loss, should it continue to operate or should it shut down?	If at the profit-maximizing level of output $P > AVC$, the firm should continue to operate; if $AVC > P$, the firm should shut down.

Knowing which curve is used to answer which question makes it easier to analyze complicated diagrams and answer questions for homework, quizzes, and exams. Remember that each curve has its own role and focus on that curve to simplify your analysis. The following graph shows an example. The firm's profit-maximizing level of output (Q^*) is where $MC = MR$, and since for a perfectly competitive firm $MR = P$, the profit-maximizing output corresponds to the point where $MC = P$. Since at this level of output $ATC > P$, the firm is incurring an economic loss. But it will continue to operate in the short run because at its profit-maximizing level of output $P > AVC$.

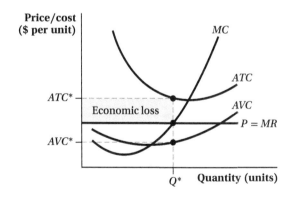

make the grade

Can a firm have two profit-maximizing levels of output?

Consider the following graph. As you can see, the firm's marginal cost equals price at both Q_1 and Q^*. Does this mean there are two profit-maximizing levels of output? To answer this question, notice that when the output is Q_1, the marginal cost is *decreasing* while the price is constant. That is, if the firm produces another unit of output, this unit will cost less than the firm gains from selling it ($MC < P_M$). Therefore, the firm's profit will increase if it produces more than Q_1. This means Q_1 is not the firm's profit-maximizing level of output. The firm will continue to increase its output as far as $MC < P_M$, that is, until the output is Q^* and $MC = P_M$ again. But the situation is very different here, since the marginal cost is now *increasing* with output. That is, the marginal cost of the next unit produced will be greater than the firm's revenue from this unit (P_M), so the firm's profit will fall if it increases output beyond Q^*. This means Q^* is the firm's profit-maximizing level of output. Thus, even though the MC curve intersects the price line twice, the firm's profit-maximizing output is only where the marginal cost curve intersects the price line from below, which happens at the larger level of Q.

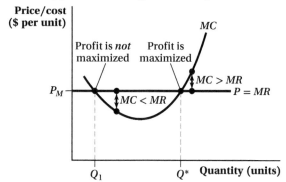

make the grade

Solving quadratic equations

The equation for a firm's marginal cost curve often has a quadratic form, since a typical MC curve is U-shaped. This means to find the profit-maximizing level of output, we need to be able to solve quadratic equations. Although this may sound intimidating, it's not that difficult. For example, consider the following marginal cost curve:

$$MC = 7.6 - 3.6Q + 0.6Q^2$$

where MC is the marginal cost (in dollars) and Q is the quantity of output (in units). Suppose the market price is $P = \$4.60$. To find the profit-maximizing quantity, we set the marginal cost equal to the marginal revenue, which for a perfectly competitive firm equals the market price, and solve this equation for Q:

$$MC = P$$
$$7.6 - 3.6Q + 0.6Q^2 = 4.6$$

To use the quadratic formula, we need to write the preceding equation in the standard form, which is

$$ax^2 + bx + c = 0$$

So we write:

$$0.6Q^2 - 3.6Q + 3 = 0$$

where $x = Q$, $a = 0.6$, $b = 3.6$, and $c = 3$. Now, all we need to do is to use the following quadratic formula to solve the equation:

$$x = \frac{-b \pm \sqrt{b^2 - 4ac}}{2a}$$

Given that a firm's profit-maximizing output is only where the marginal cost curve intersects the price line from below (see the previous Make the Grade advice), out of the two possible solutions only the one with the larger Q is relevant. Therefore, we solve our profit-maximizing condition as follows:

$$Q = \frac{3.6 + \sqrt{(-3.6)^2 - 4 \times 0.6 \times 3}}{2 \times 0.6}$$

$$Q = \frac{3.6 + \sqrt{5.76}}{1.2}$$

$$Q = \frac{3.6 + 2.4}{1.2}$$

$$Q = 5$$

Thus, the firm in question maximizes its profit when it produces 5 units of output.

8.2 figure it out 1

Suppose that consumers see all tomatoes as identical and that there are many tomato producers in the market. The current market equilibrium price of tomatoes is $2.30 per pound. Pedro's small hydroponic tomato farm has the following short-run total cost curve:

$$TC = 10 + 3.8Q - 0.9Q^2 + 0.1Q^3$$

where TC is the total cost in thousands of dollars and Q is the quantity of tomatoes produced in thousands of pounds per month. Pedro's marginal cost curve (which can be derived from the TC curve) is

$$MC = 3.8 - 1.8Q + 0.3Q^2$$

a. What quantity of tomatoes should Pedro produce in the short run to maximize his profit?
b. If the farm maximizes profit, how much profit will it earn per month?
∂ c. Use calculus to show that marginal cost is as given.
d. Express profit as a function of Q, use calculus to maximize this function, and show that the solution is the same as your answer to (a).

Solution

a. Given that consumers see all tomatoes as identical and that there are many tomato producers in the market, Pedro's farm can be considered perfectly competitive. And firms in perfect competition maximize profit by producing the quantity for which $P = MC$. To find this quantity for Pedro's farm, we set its MC equal to the market price and solve this equation for Q:

$$3.8 - 1.8Q + 0.3Q^2 = 2.3$$
$$0.3Q^2 - 1.8Q + 1.5 = 0$$
$$Q = \frac{1.8 + \sqrt{1.8^2 - 4 \times 0.3 \times 1.5}}{2 \times 0.3}$$
$$Q = 5$$

Thus, Pedro's profit-maximizing quantity of tomatoes is 5,000 pounds per month. This, however, is only the case if the farm's total revenue covers at least its variable cost; otherwise the farm is better off if it shuts down and produces no output. When Pedro produces 5,000 pounds of tomatoes per month, the farm's total revenue is $TR = P \times Q = \$2.30 \times 5,000 = \$11,500$. And its total cost (in thousands of dollars) calculated from the total cost curve is

$$TC = 10 + 3.8 \times 5 - 0.9 \times 5^2 + 0.1 \times 5^3$$
$$TC = 19$$

As we know, total cost is the sum of fixed cost and variable cost: $TC = FC + VC$, so $VC = TC - FC$. Further, fixed cost is the part of total cost that does not vary with output (changes in Q have no effect on FC). Therefore, if $TC = 10 + 3.8Q - 0.9Q^2 + 0.1Q^3$, then the FC must be 10, which means $VC = 19 - 10 = 9$. Since the farm's total revenue ($11,500) exceeds its variable cost ($9,000), Pedro maximizes his profit if he continues to operate producing 5,000 pounds of tomatoes per month.

b. Pedro's profit is

$$\pi = TR - TC$$
$$\pi = \$11,500 - \$19,000$$
$$\pi = -\$7,500$$

Thus, at its profit-maximizing level of output, the farm incurs a loss of $7,500 per month. (Note that we can still say that 5,000 pounds of tomatoes per month is Pedro's profit-maximizing level of output, since at that level his profit is the least negative. But we can also call it the "loss-minimizing level of output," since this is where Pedro's loss is at its minimum).

∂ c. Marginal cost is the derivative of the total cost function with respect to quantity: $MC = \dfrac{dTC}{dQ} = 0 + 3.8 - 0.9(2)Q^{2-1} + 0.1(3)Q^{3-1} = 3.8 - 1.8Q + 0.3Q^2$. This is the same equation for marginal cost as given in the problem.

d. The farm's profit function is $\pi = 2.3Q - (10 + 3.8Q - 0.9Q^2 + 0.1Q^3) = -0.1Q^3 + 0.9Q^2 - 1.5Q - 10$. Maximizing this function with respect to Q, we see that the first derivative of this function (which we then set equal to zero to solve) is: $-0.1(3)Q^{3-1} + 0.9(2)Q - 1.5 - 0 = -0.3Q^2 + 1.8Q - 1.5 = 0$ or

$0.3Q^2 - 1.8Q + 1.5 = 0$ as in (a). The quadratic formula in that part showed that $Q = 5$. To confirm that this is a maximum and not a minimum, we use the second derivative test (i.e., take the derivative of $-0.3Q^2 + 1.8Q - 1.5$). The second derivative then is $-0.3(2)Q^{2-1} + 1.8 - 0 = -0.6Q + 1.8$. This is negative for $Q > 3$. Since $Q = 5$, we therefore know that we are in this concave range and therefore have a maximum.

8.2 figure it out 2

Suppose picture frames are produced in a perfectly competitive market. Each identical firm has a short-run total cost curve of

$$TC = 40 + 14Q - 2Q^2 + 0.15Q^3$$

where Q is the quantity of picture frames produced (in thousands per month). The firm's marginal cost curve that corresponds to this total cost curve is

$$MC = 14 - 4Q + 0.45Q^2$$

a. What is the price below which a firm in the market will not produce any output in the short run (the shut-down price)?

b. Use calculus to show that marginal cost is as given.

c. Use calculus to minimize average variable cost to derive the shut-down price and confirm that your answer is the same as in (a).

Solution

a. A firm will not produce any output in the short run at a price below its minimum average variable cost (AVC). To find the minimum AVC, we need to know the firm's AVC curve. Recall that AVC is the variable cost per unit of output: $AVC = \dfrac{VC}{Q}$. We can find the VC curve from the TC curve, given that $VC = TC - FC$ and that fixed cost is the part of total cost that does not vary with output. That is, if $TC = 40 + 14Q - 2Q^2 + 0.15Q^3$, then FC must be 40 (recall that $FC = TC$ when $Q = 0$), which means

$$VC = 14Q - 2Q^2 + 0.15Q^3$$

and

$$AVC = \frac{(14Q - 2Q^2 + 0.15Q^3)}{Q}$$
$$AVC = 14 - 2Q + 0.15Q^2$$

To find the minimum AVC, recall from Chapter 7 that AVC is minimized when $AVC = MC$. So, we equate AVC and MC to find the output at which AVC is at its minimum:

$$AVC = MC$$
$$14 - 2Q + 0.15Q^2 = 14 - 4Q + 0.45Q^2$$
$$0.3Q^2 = 2Q$$
$$0.3Q = 2$$
$$Q = 6.667$$

That is, AVC is at its minimum at an output of 6,667 picture frames per month. To find the level of AVC at this output, we plug $Q = 6.667$ into the formula for AVC:

$$AVC = 14 - 2 \times 6.667 + 0.15 \times 6.667^2$$
$$AVC = 7.33$$

So, the minimum price at which the firm should operate is $7.33 per frame. If the price falls below this level, the firm should shut down in the short run and only pay its fixed cost.

b. Marginal cost is the derivative of the total cost function with respect to quantity: $MC = \dfrac{dTC}{dQ} = 0 + 14 - 2(2)Q^{2-1} + 0.15(3)Q^{3-1} = 14 - 4Q + 0.45Q^2$. This is the same equation for marginal cost as given in the problem.

c. Average variable cost is shown in (a): $AVC = 14 - 2Q + 0.15Q^2$. We can minimize this directly by calculating the first-order condition. Taking the derivative of AVC with respect to Q, we see that $\dfrac{dAVC}{dQ} = 0 - 2 + 0.15(2)Q^{2-1} = 0.3Q - 2$. Setting this equal to zero, $0.3Q - 2 = 0$, or $Q = 6.667$.

To confirm that this is a minimum (and not a maximum), we can check the second-order condition: $\dfrac{d^2AVC}{dQ^2} = 0.3 > 0$. Since this is positive, we know that we have a minimum. This is the same quantity as found in (a); therefore, the shut-down price is also the same. The firm should shut down if price is less than AVC at a quantity of 6.667: if $P < 14 - 2(6.667) + 0.15(6.667)^2 = \$7.33$. This is the same as what is found in (a).

8.3 Perfect Competition in the Short Run

8.3 figure it out 1

Suppose that the market for toothbrushes is perfectly competitive and has 100 producers. Out of these producers, 60 are "low-cost" producers whose individual average variable cost and marginal cost curves are

$$AVC = 1 + 0.4Q$$
$$MC = 1 + 0.8Q$$

and 40 firms are "high-cost" producers whose individual average variable cost and marginal cost curves are

$$AVC = 1 + 0.5Q$$
$$MC = 1 + Q$$

where Q is the quantity of toothbrushes produced (in thousands per day).
a. Derive the short-run supply curves for a low-cost producer and for a high-cost producer.
b. Derive the market short-run supply curve.
c. If the market demand curve for toothbrushes is given by $Q^D = 230 - 57.5P$, what are the market equilibrium price and quantity of toothbrushes?
d. At the market price, how many toothbrushes does each low-cost firm produce? Each high-cost firm?
e. When the market is in equilibrium, what is the industry producer surplus?
f. Use calculus to re-calculate producer surplus and show that the solution is the same as in (e). (Hint: Remember how producer surplus is calculated in the Appendix to Chapter 3.)
g. Write the short-run industry supply curve as a function of the number of high-cost firms (N_{hc}) and the number of low-cost firms (N_{lc}).
h. Suppose that the number of high-cost firms in the toothbrush industry decreases to 30. What is the number of low-cost firms under this new scenario which would support the original equilibrium found in (c)?

Solution

a. A perfectly competitive firm's supply curve is the portion of its marginal cost curve that is at or above its average variable cost curve. For both the low-cost and the high-cost firms in question, the marginal cost is above the average variable cost at any positive level of output. To see this, we calculate the difference between MC and AVC by subtracting the AVC curve from the MC curve. For the low-cost firms:

$$MC - AVC = (1 + 0.8Q) - (1 + 0.4Q) = 0.4Q$$

Thus, for all $Q > 0$, the MC curve is above the AVC curve. Similarly, for the high-cost firms:

$$MC - AVC = (1 + Q) - (1 + 0.5Q) = 0.5Q$$

Thus, the firms' individual supply curves are simply their marginal cost curves. The curves for a low-cost firm (S_L) and for a high-cost firm (S_H) are shown on the following graph.

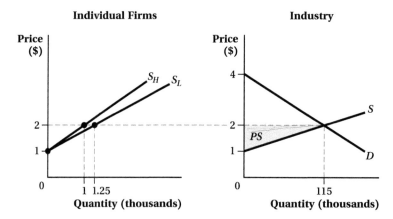

b. To derive the industry short-run supply curve, we sum each of the firm's short-run supply curves horizontally. That is, we add each firm's quantity supplied at each price. To be able to do this algebraically, we need to express the quantity supplied as a function of price. And since a perfectly competitive firm chooses to produce where $P = MC$, for a low-cost firm we can write

$$P = 1 + 0.8Q_{lc}$$

Solving this equation for Q, we get

$$0.8Q_{lc} = P - 1$$
$$Q_{lc} = -1.25 + 1.25P$$

For a high-cost firm:

$$P = 1 + Q_{hc}$$

and

$$Q_{hc} = P - 1$$

Now, since there are 60 low-cost firms with identical supply curves, we can sum them simply by multiplying the firm's individual supply curve by 60:

$$Q_{LC} = 60 \times (-1.25 + 1.25P)$$
$$Q_{LC} = -75 + 75P$$

Similarly, we can get the supply curve for the 40 high-cost firms:

$$Q_{HC} = 40 \times (-1 + P)$$
$$Q_{HC} = -40 + 40P$$

The short-run industry supply curve is the horizontal sum of the quantities supplied by low-cost producers and the quantities supplied by high-cost producers:

$$Q^S = Q_{LC} + Q_{HC}$$
$$Q^S = (-75 + 75P) + (-40 + 40P)$$
$$Q^S = -115 + 115P$$

This industry supply curve (S) is shown on the preceding graph.

c. Market equilibrium occurs where quantity demanded is equal to quantity supplied:

$$Q^D = Q^S$$
$$230 - 57.5P = -115 + 115P$$
$$172.5P = 345$$
$$P = 2$$

The equilibrium quantity can be found by substituting $P = 2$ into either the market supply or market demand equation:

$$Q^S = -115 + 115P$$
$$Q^S = -115 + 115 \times 2$$
$$Q^S = 115$$
$$Q^D = 230 - 57.5P$$
$$Q^D = 230 - 57.5 \times 2$$
$$Q^D = 115$$

Thus, the equilibrium price of a toothbrush is $2, and the equilibrium quantity is 115,000 toothbrushes per day (see the preceding graph).

d. At a price of $2 per toothbrush, each low-cost producer will produce $Q_{lc} = -1.25 + 1.25P = -1.25 + 1.25 \times 2 = 1.25$ thousand toothbrushes. And each high-cost producer will produce $Q_{hc} = -1 + P = -1 + 2 = 1$ thousand toothbrushes.

e. The easiest way to calculate industry producer surplus is to use the graph of the industry supply curve (see the preceding graph). Producer surplus is the triangular area below the market price ($2) and above the industry supply curve. The base of this triangle is 115,000 and its height is $2 - $1 = $1. Thus, the producer surplus is

$$PS = 0.5 \times \text{base} \times \text{height}$$
$$PS = 0.5 \times 115,000 \times \$1 = \$57,500$$

f. Supply is $Q^S = -115 + 115P$, so inverse supply is $P = 1 + \dfrac{Q^S}{115}$

Producer surplus is the area under the equilibrium price and above the supply curve. Recall from the Chapter 3 online appendix that we can use integration from calculus to figure out the magnitude of this area by integrating over the relevant quantity. Particularly,

$$PS = \int_0^{115} \left(2 - \left(1 + \frac{Q}{115} \right) \right) dQ$$
$$= \int_0^{115} 1\, dQ - \int_0^{115} \frac{Q}{115} dQ$$
$$= [Q]_0^{115} - \left[\frac{Q^2}{230} \right]_0^{115}$$
$$= [115 - 0] - \left[\frac{(115)^2}{230} - \frac{(0)^2}{230} \right]$$
$$= (115 - 0) - (57.5 - 0) = 57.5$$

Since quantity is in thousands, this is the same $57,500 producer surplus found in (e).

g. The short-run industry supply curve can be written generically as: $Q^S = N_{hc}(P - 1) + N_{lc}(1.25P - 1.25)$ where N_{hc} is the number of high-cost firms and N_{lc} is the number of low-cost firms. Note that you do not need calculus to write this, though this material is related to the online appendix to this chapter.

h. If $N_{hc} = 30$, we know that $Q^S = 30(P - 1) + N_{lc}(1.25P - 1.25) = 30P - 30 + N_{lc}(1.25P - 1.25)$. The equilibrium condition now is:

$$Q^D = Q^S$$
$$230 - 57.5P = 30P - 30 + N_{lc}(1.25P - 1.25)$$

The original equilibrium price was $2 as found in (c). At this price,

$$230 - 57.5(2) = 30(2) - 30 + N_{lc}(1.25(2) - 1.25)$$
$$115 = 30 + 1.25\, N_{lc}$$
$$N_{lc} = 68$$

Therefore, when the number of high-cost firms decreases to 30, the number of low-cost firms must be 68 for price and quantity to be as given.

8.4 Perfectly Competitive Industries in the Long Run

Free entry

The ability of a firm to enter an industry without encountering legal or technical barriers.

Free exit

The ability of a firm to exit an industry without encountering legal or technical barriers.

Long-run competitive equilibrium

The point at which the market price is equal to the minimum average total cost and firms would gain no profits by entering the industry.

Constant-cost industry

An industry whose firms' long-run average total costs do not change with total industry output.

Increasing-cost industry

An industry whose firms' long-run average total costs increase with increases in industry output.

Decreasing-cost industry

An industry whose firms' long-run average total costs decrease with increases in industry output.

8.4 figure it out 1

Suppose that the market for corn is currently in long-run competitive equilibrium at a price of $4 per bushel. Suppose further that ethanol subsidies lead to an increase in demand for corn (which is the major input into ethanol production). Assume that corn production is a constant-cost industry and that a firm's short-run marginal cost curve is the same as its long-run marginal cost curve.

a. In the short run, what will happen to the price of corn? Explain and illustrate your answer with graphs showing the market and a representative firm.

b. In the short run, how will firms respond to the change in price described in (a)? What will happen to each producer's profit in the short run? Use your graph to explain and illustrate your answer.

c. Given the situation described in (b), what can we expect to happen to the number of corn producers in the long run? Why?

d. What will happen to the price of corn in the long run?

Solution

a. As shown on the following graph, an increase in demand for corn, that is, a rightward shift of the demand curve (from D_1 to D_2) leads to a rise in the price of corn (from $4 to P_2).

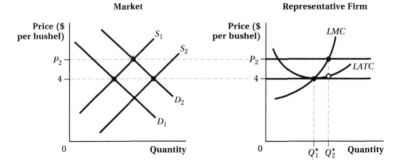

b. As shown on the graph, when the price of corn rises to P_2, each firm moves up and to the right along its marginal cost curve (LMC) to choose the profit-maximizing output (i.e., where $MC = P_2$, so each firm increases its output from Q_1^* to Q_2^*. Before the increase in demand, the industry was in long-run competitive equilibrium, which means when the price was $4 per bushel, each firm was earning zero economic profit. But when the price of corm rises to P_2, it is above the firm's average total cost ($LATC$) at the profit-maximizing level of output (Q_2^*). Thus, the increase in demand has led to positive economic profits for the firms.

c. Because firms in the industry are earning positive economic profits, new firms will want to take advantage of this opportunity. And since there are no barriers to entry (the market is perfectly competitive), we can expect the number of firms in the industry to increase.

d. As the number of producers in the industry increases, the market supply curve shifts rightward (from S_1 to S_2), causing the price of corn to fall. Firms will continue to enter the industry, the supply curve will continue to shift, and price will continue to fall until it is once again at the minimum $LATC$ of $4, which means there are no economic profits to be made by entering the industry, so firms no longer have an incentive to enter. At this point, the market is in long-run competitive equilibrium again.

8.4 figure it out 2

Suppose the olive oil industry is perfectly competitive. Every producer has the following long-run total cost curve:

$$LTC = 1,288Q - 9Q^2 + 0.025Q^3$$

where Q is the quantity of olive oil produced (in tons). The corresponding marginal cost curve is

$$LMC = 1,288 - 18Q + 0.075Q^2$$

The market demand curve for olive oil is

$$Q^D = 329 - 0.5P$$

where Q^D is the quantity demanded (in thousands of tons) and P is the price of olive oil (in dollars per ton).

a. Derive an individual producer's long-run average total cost curve.
b. What is the long-run equilibrium price of olive oil?
c. How much olive oil does each firm produce in the long run?
d. When the market is in long-run equilibrium, how much olive oil is sold?
e. When the market is in long-run equilibrium, how many firms are there in the industry?
f. Use calculus to show that long-run marginal cost is as given.

Solution

a. A firm's long-run average total cost curve is:

$$LATC = \frac{LTC}{Q}$$

$$LATC = \frac{(1,288Q - 9Q^2 + 0.025Q^3)}{Q}$$

$$LATC = 1,288 - 9Q + 0.025Q^2$$

b. The long-run equilibrium price is the price at which firms in the industry earn zero economic profits. This happens when $P = LMC = LATC$, that is, when the $LATC$ is at its minimum. To find this point, we set $LATC$ equal to LMC and solve this equation for Q:

$$LATC = LMC$$

$$1,288 - 9Q + 0.025Q^2 = 1,288 - 18Q + 0.075Q^2$$

$$0.05Q^2 = 9Q$$

$$0.05Q = 9$$

$$Q = 180$$

To find the $LATC$ at this output, we plug $Q = 180$ into the formula for $LATC$:

$$LATC = 1,288 - 9 \times 180 + 0.025 \times 180^2$$

$$LATC = 478$$

Thus, the long-run equilibrium price of olive oil is $478 per ton.

c. As we found in (b), when the market is in long-run equilibrium (i.e., $P = LMC = LATC = \$478$), $Q = 180$, that is, each firm produces 180 tons of olive oil.

d. Given the market demand curve, the quantity of olive oil demanded at the equilibrium price ($478 per ton) is $Q^D = 329 - 0.5 \times 478 = 90$ thousand tons. Since the market is in equilibrium, this is also the quantity of olive oil supplied and the quantity sold.

e. As we've found in (d), the quantity of olive oil produced by the industry is 90,000 tons. And as we've found in (b), each firm produces 180 tons. This means the number of firms in the industry is $\frac{90,000}{180} = 500$.

f. Long-run marginal cost is the derivative of the long-run total cost function with respect to quantity:

$$LMC = \frac{dLTC}{dQ} = 1{,}288 - 9(2)Q^{2-1} + 0.025(3)Q^{3-1} = 1{,}288 - 18Q + 0.075Q^2.$$ This is the same equation for long-run marginal cost as given in the problem.

∂ 8.4 figure it out 3

Suppose that the perfectly competitive market for horseradish is made up of identical firms with long-run total cost functions given by $TC(Q) = Q^3 - 3Q^2 + 81.25Q$, where Q is pounds of horseradish. Assume that these cost functions are independent of the number of firms in the market and that firms may enter or exit the market freely. Market demand is $Q^D = 1{,}001 - 6.5P$ and P is cents per pound.

a. Using calculus, find the long-run equilibrium price, the quantity produced by each firm, and the number of firms in the industry.

b. Suppose that market demand decreases to $Q_2^D = 900.5 - 6.5P$. Solve for the new long-run competitive equilibrium.

Solution

a. We know that the long-run competitive equilibrium price equals the minimum of average total cost. First, find average total cost:

$$ATC = \frac{TC}{Q} = \frac{Q^3 - 3Q^2 + 81.25Q}{Q} = Q^2 - 3Q + 81.25$$

Now find the quantity produced by each firm at the minimum average cost by solving the first-order condition:

$$\frac{dATC}{dQ} = \frac{d(Q^2 - 3Q + 81.25)}{dQ} = 2Q - 3 = 0$$

$$2Q = 3$$

$$Q = 1.5$$

Then plug this quantity into the average total cost equation to get the equilibrium price:

$$P = ATC = (1.5)^2 - 3(1.5) + 81.25 = 79$$

This corresponds to $0.79 per pound.

At this price, the quantity demanded in the market is

$$Q^D = 1{,}001 - 6.5P = 1{,}000 - 6.5(79) = 487.5 \text{ pounds}$$

So the number of firms is

$$N = \frac{market\ output}{firm\ output} = \frac{487.5}{1.5} = 325 \text{ firms}$$

b. Because the total cost curves for the firms do not change with the number of firms, the minimum average total cost, equilibrium price, and the output per firm will not change when demand changes. However, total market quantity and the number of firms will decrease when demand decreases. At a price of $0.79, the new market quantity demanded is

$$Q_2^D = 900.5 - 6.5P = 900.5 - 6.5(79) = 387$$

From (a), we know that each firm produces 1.5 units, so the number of firms is equal to

$$N_2 = \frac{market\ output}{firm\ output} = \frac{387}{1.5} = 258 \text{ firms}$$

8.5 Producer Surplus, Economic Rents, and Economic Profits

Economic rent

Returns to specialized inputs above what firms paid for them.

Practice Problems

Problem 1

Suppose that consumers see all paper towels as identical and that there are many paper towel producers in the market. The current market price of paper towels is $3 per 6-pack. Bonta, one of the paper towel producers in the market, has the following short-run average total cost curve:

$$ATC = 1 + \frac{10}{Q} + 0.05Q$$

where Q is the quantity of paper towels produced (in thousands of 6-packs per year). Bonta's marginal cost curve is

$$MC = 1 + 0.1Q$$

a. How many 6-packs of paper towels should Bonta produce to maximize its profit?
b. If Bonta maximizes profit, how much profit will it earn per year?

Problem 2

Suppose that red bell pepper is sold in a perfectly competitive market. The current market price is $2.50 per pound. Assume that all firms in the market are identical and have the short-run cost curves shown on the following graph.

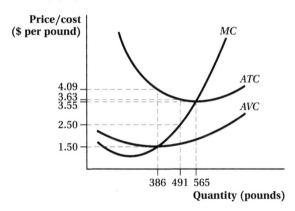

a. How much red bell pepper should a typical firm produce to maximize its profit?
b. If a firm maximizes its profit, how much profit does it earn?
c. What is the price below which a typical firm will not produce any output in the short run (the shut-down price)?
d. What is a typical firm's fixed cost? Are the firms able to cover their fixed costs? Explain your answer.

Problem 3

Suppose that romaine lettuce is sold for $3.50 per pound in a perfectly competitive market that is currently in short-run equilibrium. Each firm in the market has the following short-run total cost curve:

$$TC = 1.5 + 3.125Q - 0.75Q^2 + 0.125Q^3$$

where TC is the total cost in thousands of dollars per month and Q is the quantity of romaine lettuce sold in thousands of pounds per month. The corresponding marginal cost curve is

$$MC = 3.125 - 1.5Q + 0.375Q^2$$

a. How much romaine lettuce does each firm produce?
b. How much profit does each firm earn?
c. Use calculus to show that marginal cost is as given.
d. Express profit as a function of Q, use calculus to maximize this function, and show that the solution is the same as your answer to (a).

Problem 4

Suppose that the market for potatoes is perfectly competitive and has 110 firms. Out of these firms, 50 are "high-cost" producers, each with a short-run supply curve given by

$$Q_{hc} = 8P$$

and the remaining 60 firms are "low-cost" producers, with a short-run supply curve given by

$$Q_{lc} = 10P$$

Quantities are measured in thousands of pounds and prices are dollars per pound.
a. Derive the short-run industry supply curve for potatoes.
b. If the market demand curve for potatoes is given by $Q^D = 6{,}000 - 2{,}000P$, what are the market equilibrium price and quantity of potatoes?
c. At the price you found in (b), how many potatoes does each high-cost firm produce? Each low-cost firm?
d. At the price you found in (b), what is the industry producer surplus?
e. Use calculus to re-calculate producer surplus and show that the solution is the same as in (e). (Hint: Remember how producer surplus is calculated in the Appendix to Chapter 3.)
g. Write the short-run industry supply curve as a function of the number of high-cost firms (N_{hc}) and the number of low-cost firms (N_{lc}).
h. Suppose that the number of high-cost firms in the toothbrush industry increases to 60. What is the number of low-cost firms under this new scenario which would support the original equilibrium found in (b)?

Problem 5

The following graph shows the current equilibrium in a perfectly competitive market for wheat, and a representative firm's long-run marginal cost and long-run average total cost curves. Assume that wheat production is a constant-cost industry.

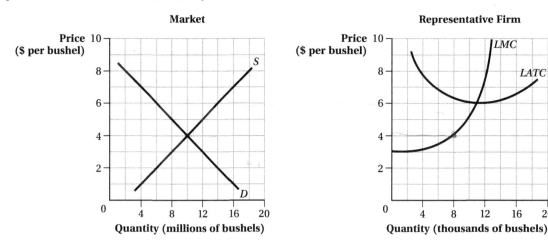

a. What quantity of wheat does a representative firm produce? Explain.
b. Are the firms in the industry earning economic profits or incurring losses? Explain.
c. In the long run, will firms enter or exit the market? Explain.
d. Show on the graph how the market will adjust in the long run. What will happen to the market price? The quantity of wheat sold?
e. In the long run, what will happen to the quantity of wheat sold by a representative firm?

Problem 6

Suppose milk is sold in a perfectly competitive market. All milk producers are identical and have the following short-run total cost curve:

$$TC = 19.2 + 2Q - 0.5Q^2 + 0.05Q^3$$

where TC is the total cost in thousands of dollars and Q is the quantity of milk produced in thousands of gallons. The firm's marginal cost curve that corresponds to this total cost curve is

$$MC = 2 - Q + 0.15Q^2$$

a. If the market price of milk is $3.60 per gallon, how much milk will each firm produce? How much economic profit will it earn?

b. Suppose the demand for milk decreases, so the market price of milk falls to $2.35 per gallon. How much milk will each firm produce? How much economic profit will it earn?

c. Now suppose that consumers hear rumors that milk sold in this market is contaminated with pesticides. As a result, the market demand for milk decreases further, so the price of milk falls to $0.75 per gallon. How much milk will each firm produce now? How much economic profit will it earn?

d. Use calculus to show that marginal cost is as given.

Problem 7

Suppose there are 1,000 firms in the market for soybeans, which is perfectly competitive. The following graph shows the firms' individual short-run supply curves. There are 300 high-cost firms in the industry whose individual supply curve is S_1, 500 medium-cost firms whose individual supply curve is S_2, and 200 low-cost firms with the individual supply curve S_3. Use the right-hand panel to graph the short-run industry supply curve.

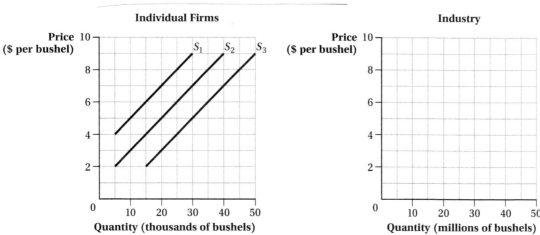

Problem 8

Suppose that bottled water is sold for $1.66 per bottle in a perfectly competitive market that is currently in short-run equilibrium. Each firm in the market has the following short-run total cost curve:

$$TC = 4.16 + 0.7Q - 0.3Q^2 + 0.07Q^3$$

where TC is the total cost in millions of dollars and Q is the quantity of bottled water sold in millions of bottles per year. The corresponding marginal cost curve is

$$MC = 0.7 - 0.6Q + 0.21Q^2$$

a. What quantity of bottled water does an individual firm produce?

b. How much profit does each firm earn?

c. What is a firm's producer surplus?

d. Use calculus to show that marginal cost is as given.

Problem 9

Suppose the market for sugar is perfectly competitive. Each producer has the following long-run total cost curve:

$$LTC = 1{,}300Q - 74Q^2 + 2Q^3$$

where LTC is the total cost in thousands of dollars and Q is the quantity sugar produced in thousands of tons. The corresponding marginal cost curve is

$$LMC = 1{,}300 - 148Q + 6Q^2$$

The market demand curve for sugar is

$$Q^D = 6{,}162 - 4P$$

where Q^D is the quantity demanded in thousands of tons and P is the price of sugar in dollars per ton.
a. Derive an individual producer's long-run average total cost curve.
b. What is the long-run equilibrium price of sugar?
c. How much sugar does each firm produce in the long run?
d. In long-run equilibrium, how much sugar is sold in the market?
e. When the market is in long-run equilibrium, how many firms are in the industry?
∂ f. Use calculus to show that long-run marginal cost is as given.

Problem 10

Suppose that the market for bread is perfectly competitive, and bread production is a constant-cost industry. Each firm must hire a manager. There is a potentially unlimited supply of managers with average skills, but there are only 10 managers that have extraordinary talent. All managers are paid \$72,000 per year. A firm with an average manager has the following long-run total cost and long-run marginal cost curves:

$$LTC_A = 72 + 0.02Q^2$$
$$LMC_A = 0.04Q$$

A firm with an extraordinary manager has the following LTC and LMC curves:

$$LTC_E = 72 + 0.01Q^2$$
$$LMC_E = 0.02Q$$

Total cost is measured in thousands of dollars, and output (Q) is measured in thousands of loaves of bread per year. The market demand for bread is given by

$$Q^D = 6{,}000 - 1{,}000P$$

where Q^D is the quantity of bread demanded (in thousands of loaves) and P is the price of bread (dollars per loaf).
a. Derive the long-run supply curve for a firm with an average manager and for a firm with an extraordinary manager.
b. Derive the supply curve for all firms with extraordinary managers. What would the equilibrium market price of bread be if only firms with extraordinary managers were in the industry? Would the market be in long-run equilibrium? Explain.
c. What is the long-run equilibrium price of bread?
d. When the market is in long-run equilibrium, how many firms with average managers are in the industry?
e. When the market is in long-run equilibrium, how much economic profit does a firm with an average manager earn? How much economic profit does a firm with an extraordinary manager earn? How much economic rent will an extraordinary manager generate for his firm?

Problem 11

Suppose that the market for luxury hotel rooms across the world is perfectly competitive. Hotels are identical and have long-run cost functions given by $TC(Q) = 25Q^3 - 10Q^2 + 500Q$ where Q is in thousands of rooms. Market demand is $Q^D = 5{,}000 - 2P$ and price is in U.S. dollars.

a. Derive the marginal and average cost curves for hotels in this industry. (Hint: Use calculus to find marginal cost.)

b. Using calculus, find the quantity at which average total cost is minimized for each hotel.

c. Find the long-run equilibrium price in this industry.

d. Use market demand to find the equilibrium total industry output.

e. Find the equilibrium number of hotels.

Market Power and Monopoly

9

9.1 Sources of Market Power

Market Power

A firm's ability to influence the market price of its product. For a given market demand curve, the firm's decision about how much to supply completely determines the market price. That is, a firm with market power is a price setter, not a price taker. However, since a firm with market power faces a downward-sloping demand curve, it cannot sell whatever quantity it produces at a fixed market price (as a perfectly competitive firm can). To sell more, a firm with market power has to lower its price. The extreme version of market power is a monopoly, but a firm does not need to be a monopoly to have market power.

Monopoly

A market served by only one firm.

Monopolist

The sole supplier and price setter of a good on the market.

Decision making is similar for all firms with market power

Once a firm has some market power (i.e. ,faces a downward sloping demand curve), and once the demand curve facing the firm is determined, the firm's decision-making process is the same whether it is a monopoly, an oligopolistic firm, or a monopolistically competitive firm.

Barriers to entry

Factors that prevent entry into markets with large producer surpluses.

Natural monopoly

A market in which it is efficient for a single firm to produce the entire industry output. This is because the firm's long-run average total cost curve exhibits economies of scale at any output level that the market can bear.

Network good

A good whose value to each consumer increases with the number of other consumers of the product.

Product differentiation

Imperfect substitutability across varieties of a product.

9.2 Market Power and Marginal Revenue

Oligopoly

Market structure in which a few competitors operate.

Monopolistic competition

Market structure with a large number of firms selling differentiated products.

Marginal revenue

The additional revenue a firm earns from selling one more unit. For a firm with market power who charges the same price to all customers the marginal revenue is less than the good's price.

On the following graph, when the firm increases production from 1 to 2 units, the price of the good falls from \$13 to \$10. The firm's initial total revenue is $TR_1 = P_1 \times Q_1 = \$13 \times 1 = \$13$ (area $A + B$), and its total revenue at the new production point is $TR_2 = P_2 \times Q_2 = \$10 \times 2 = \$20$ (area $B + C$). Thus, the firm's marginal revenue is

$$MR = TR_2 - TR_1 = \$20 - \$13$$
$$MR = \$7$$

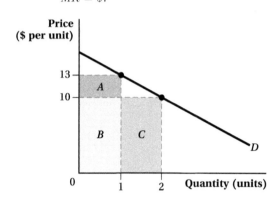

The firm gains area C (\$10 × 1 = \$10) because it increases output, but loses area A (\$3 × 1 = \$3) because it has to reduce price in order to sell an additional unit of output. Thus, the marginal revenue is

$$MR = \text{Area } C - \text{Area } A = \$10 - \$3 = \$7$$

Marginal revenue can be calculated using calculus as the first derivative of the revenue function (written as a function of Q) with respect to Q, meaning that $MR = \dfrac{dR}{dQ}$. Since Q is the only variable in the revenue function, we can use a standard derivative instead of a partial derivative here.

Marginal revenue for a linear demand curve

For any linear inverse demand curve of the form

$$P = a - bQ$$

Where P is the price, Q is the quantity demanded, and a and b are constants, the marginal revenue curve is

$$MR = a - 2bQ$$

For example, for the demand curve (D) on the following graph, $a = 16$ (the vertical intercept), and $b = \dfrac{3}{10} = 0.3$ (the negative of the slope), so the inverse demand curve is

$$P = 16 - 0.3Q$$

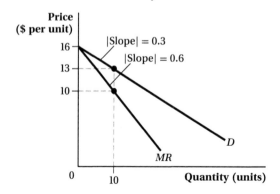

And the marginal revenue curve (MR) is

$$MR = 16 - 2 \times 0.3Q$$
$$MR = 16 - 0.6Q$$

That is, the MR curve has the same vertical intercept as the demand curve, but is twice as steep as the demand curve.

∂ We can show this rule using calculus. For a linear demand curve, $P = a - bQ$:

$$R = PQ = (a - bQ)Q = aQ - bQ^2.$$

Marginal revenue is the derivative of this function with respect to Q:

$$MR = \frac{dR}{dQ} = a - 2bQ.$$

This shows the short-cut rule as given for the linear demand case.

9.2 figure it out 1

Suppose a firm faces the following demand curve

$$Q = 1,500 - 100P$$

Where Q is the quantity demanded (units) and P is the price per unit (dollars).
a. What is the firm's marginal revenue curve?
b. What is the firm's marginal revenue when $Q = 600$? When $Q = 750$?
c. If the firm increases its output from 400 units to 600 units, how much additional revenue will it get? How much revenue will it receive from selling more output? How much revenue will it lose because it has to lower the price to sell more units?
∂ d. Determine what is the firm's marginal revenue curve using calculus and confirm that it is the same as in part (a).

Solution

a. To find the firm's marginal revenue curve, we first solve the demand equation for P to find the inverse demand curve:

$$Q = 1,500 - 100P$$
$$100P = 1,500 - Q$$
$$P = 15 - 0.01Q$$

This linear inverse demand curve can be written as

$$P = a - bQ$$

Where $a = 50$ and $b = 0.01$. So the marginal revenue curve that corresponds to this inverse demand curve is

$$MR = a - 2bQ$$
$$MR = 15 - 0.02Q$$

b. Given the marginal revenue curve found in (a):

When $Q = 600$, $MR = 15 - 0.02 \times 600 = 3$ (dollars per unit)

When $Q = 750$, $MR = 15 - 0.02 \times 750 = 0$ (dollars per unit)

Note that as the quantity sold increases, the marginal revenue falls, and when the level of output reaches 750 units, the firm can no longer increase its revenue by selling more units.
c. From the inverse demand curve, we can find that the price the firm must charge to sell 400 units of its product is $P = 15 - 0.01 \times 400 = 11$ (dollars per unit). So, when the firm sells 400 units, its total revenue is $11 \times 400 = \$4,400$. The price that the firm charges to sell 600 units is $P = 15 - 0.01 \times 600 = 9$ (dollars per unit), so the total revenue is $9 \times 600 = \$5,400$. Thus, the firm's additional revenue from increasing output from 400 units to 600 units is $5,400 - \$4,400 = \$1,000$. The firm receives $9 \times (600 - 400) = \$1,800$ more from selling 200 additional units at $9 (area C on the following graph). This is the "quantity effect" on the firm's revenue. But it loses ($11 - \$9) \times 400 = \$800$ (area A) because it sells the previous 400 units at $9 per unit instead of $11 per unit. This is the "price effect" on the firm's revenue. So, the firm's additional revenue ($1,800 - \$800 = \$1,000$) is the net of the quantity effect and the price effect.

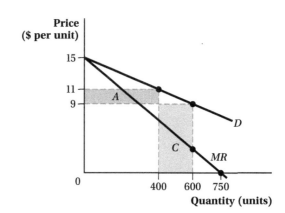

d. Using the inverse demand function found in part (a), the firm's revenue function is $R = P \times Q = (15 - 0.01Q)Q = 15Q - 0.01Q^2$. Marginal revenue is the derivative: $\frac{dR}{dQ} = 15 - 0.01(2)Q^{2-1} = 15 - 0.02Q$. This is the same as in part (a). The calculus method illustrates why we always multiply the slope of inverse demand by 2 in order to calculate marginal revenue for the case of a linear demand curve. Since in the case of linear demand, substituting in for P and multiplying by Q always leads to a quadratic term in Q, taking the derivative using the power rule from calculus means that the 2 drops down in front and 1 is subtracted from the exponent. Thus, the rule for multiplying the slope of inverse demand by 2 comes out of the math for the linear demand case.

9.3 Profit maximization for a firm with market power

How to Maximize Profit

To maximize its profit, a firm should choose its quantity where its marginal revenue equals its marginal cost:

$$MR = MC$$

This condition comes from the firm's profit maximization problem.

$$\max_{Q} \pi = TR - TC$$

Taking the first order-condition gives $\dfrac{d\pi(Q)}{dQ} = \dfrac{d(TR)}{dQ} - \dfrac{d(TC)}{dQ}$

$$= MR - MC = 0$$

As a result, $MR = MC$.

Markup

The percentage of the firm's price that is greater than its marginal cost:

$$markup = \frac{P - MC}{P}$$

For a profit-maximizing firm

$$\frac{P - MC}{P} = -\frac{1}{E^D}$$

Where E^D is the price elasticity of demand for the firm's product. The less elastic the demand that the firm faces, the greater is the markup.

Recall from Chapter 2 that elasticities can be calculated using calculus or algebraic methods for linear demand and supply cases. The calculus methods can be further used for nonlinear cases. In either case, these formulas can be substituted into the markup equations here.

Lerner index

A measure of a firm's markup, or its level of market power. The Lerner index shows how much market power a firm has. The less elastic the demand faced by the firm, the higher the index (i.e., the greater the markup), so the greater is the firm's market power. The Lerner index can range from 0 (perfect competition) to 1 (perfectly inelastic demand).

make the grade

Profit maximization with market power

Many exam problems on market power and monopoly involve profit maximization. When solving these problems, one important thing to remember is that the profit maximizing condition under market power is the same as that under perfect competition: $MR = MC$. However, for firms with market power the marginal revenue does *not* equal price. Therefore, to find a firm's profit-maximizing level of output, you need to derive its marginal revenue curve. When solving problems on profit maximization with market power, follow these three steps:

Step 1. Derive the marginal revenue curve from the demand curve.

For a linear demand curve, this will be another straight line with the same vertical intercept that is twice as steep (MR on the following graph). Algebraically, if the inverse demand curve is

$$P = a - bQ$$

then the marginal revenue curve is

$$MR = a - 2bQ$$

For example, the inverse demand curve on the graph below is

$$P = 16 - 0.5Q$$

In this case, $a = 16$ and $b = 0.5$, so the marginal revenue curve is

$$MR = 16 - (2 \times 0.5)Q$$
$$MR = 16 - Q$$

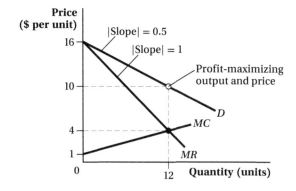

Step 2. Find the output quantity at which marginal revenue equals marginal cost.

To find the profit-maximizing level of output, we equate the firm's marginal cost and marginal revenue functions and solve this equation for Q. For example, on the preceding graph, the firm's marginal cost curve is

$$MC = 1 + 0.25Q$$

So, we equate this MC curve with the MR curve we've found above and solve this equation for Q:

$$MR = MC$$
$$16 - Q = 1 + 0.25Q$$
$$1.25Q = 15$$
$$Q = 12$$

Thus, the optimal level of output is 12 units. Graphically, this is the quantity at which the MC and MR curves intersect.

Step 3. Determine the price at which the quantity demanded equals the profit-maximizing quantity level.

To solve for the profit-maximizing price, we plug the profit-maximizing quantity into the inverse demand curve:

$$P = 16 - 0.5Q$$
$$P = 16 - 0.5 \times 12$$
$$P = 10$$

Thus, the profit-maximizing price is $10 per unit. To find this price graphically, we follow $Q = 12$ up to the demand curve and then read the price off the vertical axis (see the graph on the left). That is, we've found that if the firm produces the profit-maximizing output level of 12 units, the market price will be $10. Equivalently, if the firm charges a price of $10, it will sell 12 units.

∂ Of course, instead of Steps 1 and 2, you could set up the firm's profit maximization problem and solve the first-order condition to determine optimal output quantity before jumping to Step 3 to determine the profit-maximizing price. The setup is shown at the beginning of section 9.3 in this study guide.

9.3 figure it out 1

Suppose Dell faces the following demand curve for its notebook computers:

$$Q = 20 - 0.02P$$

Dell's marginal cost curve is

$$MC = 100 + 80Q$$

Where Q is in millions and P and MC are in dollars.

a. What is Dell's profit-maximizing level of output?

b. What price should Dell charge to maximize its profit?

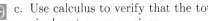 c. Use calculus to verify that the total cost function $TC = 100Q + 40Q^2$ is consistent with Dell's marginal cost curve as given.

d. Assuming that Dell's total cost function is $TC = 100Q + 40Q^2$, use calculus to re-answer parts (a) and (b).

e. Use calculus to confirm that Dell is maximizing and not minimizing profit.

Solution

a. Following the three-steps outlined in the preceding Make the Grade section, we first need to derive the firm's marginal revenue curve from the demand curve it faces. The easiest way to do it is to use the inverse demand curve. We find Dell's inverse demand curve by solving the demand curve equation for P:

$$Q = 20 - 0.02P$$
$$0.02P = 20 - Q$$
$$P = 1,000 - 50Q$$

In this inverse demand curve, $a = 1,000$ and $b = 50$. The marginal revenue curve that corresponds to this inverse demand curve is

$$MR = a - 2bQ$$
$$MR = 1,000 - 100Q$$

To find Dell's profit-maximizing level of output, we set $MR = MC$ and solve this equation for Q:

$$MR = MC$$
$$1,000 - 100Q = 100 + 80Q$$
$$180Q = 900$$
$$Q = 5$$

Thus, Dell's profit-maximizing level of output is 5 million notebook computers.

b. To find Dell's profit-maximizing price, we plug the profit-maximizing quantity found in (a) into the inverse demand curve:

$$P = 1,000 - 50Q$$
$$P = 1,000 - 50 \times 5$$
$$P = 750$$

Thus, to maximize its profit, Dell should charge \$750 per computer. The following diagram illustrates this solution.

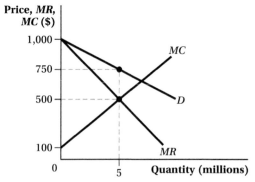

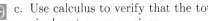 c. We find the marginal cost function by taking the first derivative of the total cost function. For the given total cost function, $\frac{dTC}{dQ} = 100 + 40(2)Q^{2-1} = 100 + 80Q$. This is the same as the marginal cost curve as given.

d. Dell's profit maximization problem is:

$$\max_{Q} \pi = TR(Q) - TC(Q) = PQ - TC(Q) = (1,000 - 50Q)Q - (100Q + 40Q^2) = 900Q - 90Q^2$$

Taking the first-order condition gives
$$\frac{d\pi(Q)}{dQ} = \frac{d(900Q - 90Q^2)}{dQ} = 900 - 180Q = 0$$
$$Q = 5$$

At this quantity, price is: $P = 1,000 - 50(5) = 750$ as it is in parts (a) and (b).

e. We need to check the second order condition for Dell. Here, $\frac{d^2\pi}{dQ^2} = -180$. Since this is less than zero, we have verified that Dell is indeed maximizing profits.

9.4 How a Firm with Market Power Reacts to Market Changes

9.4 figure it out 1

Suppose Frito-Lay faces the following demand curve for its tortilla chips:

$$Q = 200 - 50P$$

The firm's marginal cost curve is

$$MC = 2 + 0.01Q$$

Where Q is in millions of bags and P and MC are in dollars. Suppose further that a lower price of corn decreases the marginal cost of producing tortilla chips by \$1 at all output levels, so Frito-Lay's marginal cost curve becomes

$$MC = 1 + 0.01Q$$

The demand for Frito-Lay's tortilla chips remains unchanged.
a. How does the lower marginal cost affect Frito-Lay's profit-maximizing level of output? Profit-maximizing price?
b. How does the change in marginal cost affect Frito-Lay's markup?

Solution

a. To find Frito Lay's profit-maximizing level of output, we first need to derive the firm's marginal revenue curve from the inverse demand curve. We find the inverse demand curve by solving the demand curve equation for P:

$$Q = 200 - 50P$$
$$50P = 200 - Q$$
$$P = 4 - 0.02Q$$

In this inverse demand curve $a = 4$ and $b = 0.02$, so the corresponding marginal revenue curve is

$$MR = a - 2bQ$$
$$MR = 4 - 0.04Q$$

To find Frito-Lay's profit-maximizing level of output, we set $MR = MC$ and solve this equation for Q:

$$MR = MC$$
$$4 - 0.04Q = 2 + 0.01Q$$
$$0.05Q = 2$$
$$Q = 40$$

To find Frito-Lay's profit-maximizing price, we plug the profit-maximizing quantity ($Q = 40$) into the inverse demand curve:

$$P = 4 - 0.02Q$$
$$P = 4 - 0.02 \times 40$$
$$P = 3.2$$

Thus, before the decrease in costs, Frito-Lay's profit-maximizing level of output is 40 million bags, and its profit-maximizing price is $3.20 per bag. The following diagram illustrates this solution (point A).

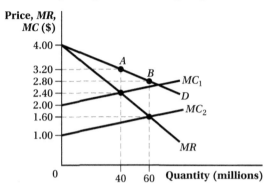

To find Frito-Lay's profit-maximizing level of output after the decrease in cost, we equate the MR curve with the new MC curve (MC_2 on the graph) and solve this equation for Q:

$$MR = MC$$
$$4 - 0.04Q = 1 + 0.01Q$$
$$0.05Q = 3$$
$$Q = 60$$

To find Frito-Lay's new profit-maximizing price, we plug the new profit-maximizing quantity ($Q = 60$) into the inverse demand curve:

$$P = 4 - 0.02 \times 60$$
$$P = 2.8$$

Thus, after the decrease in cost, Frito-Lay's profit-maximizing level of output is 60 million bags, and its profit-maximizing price is $2.80 per bag (point B). That is, the decrease in MC has increased the firm's profit maximizing quantity from 40 million to 60 million bags and lowered its profit-maximizing price from $3.20 to $2.80 per bag. Note that despite the fact that Frito-Lay's marginal cost falls by $0.80 (from $2.40 to $1.60, as shown on the graph), the firm lowers its price by only $0.40. That is, to maximize its profit, Frito-Lay's does not want to pass along to consumers the whole cost it saves.

b. Before the cost decrease, Frito-Lay's profit maximizing price is $3.20 per bag, and the marginal cost at the profit-maximizing level of output is $MC = 2 + 0.01 \times 40 = 2.40$ (dollars), so the markup is

$$\frac{P - MC}{P} = \frac{\$3.20 - \$2.40}{\$3.20} = 0.25$$

After the cost drop, the firm's profit maximizing price is $2.80, and the marginal cost at the profit-maximizing level of output is $MC = 1 + 0.01 \times 60 = 1.60$ (dollars), so the markup is

$$\frac{P - MC}{P} = \frac{\$2.80 - \$1.60}{\$2.80} = 0.429$$

Thus, Frito-Lay's markup increases from 25% to 42.9%.

9.4 figure it out 2

Suppose Panasonic faces the following demand curve for its digital camcorders:

$$Q = 40 - 0.05P$$

Panasonic's marginal cost curve is

$$MC = 200 + 20Q$$

Where Q is in thousands and P and MC are in dollars. Suppose further that Sony, a competitor of Panasonic, introduces a new camcorder. As a result, the demand curve faced by Panasonic changes to

$$Q = 56 - 0.1P$$

Panasonic's marginal cost curve remains unchanged.

a. How does the introduction of the competing product change Panasonic's profit-maximizing level of output? Profit-maximizing price?
b. How does the introduction of the new Sony camcorder change the price elasticity of demand for the Panasonic camcorders?
c. How does the change in demand faced by Panasonic affect its market power?

Solution

a. To find Panasonic's profit-maximizing level of output, we first derive the firm's marginal revenue curve from the inverse demand curve. We find the inverse demand curve faced by Panasonic before the competing product is introduced by solving the initial demand curve for P:

$$Q = 40 - 0.05P$$
$$0.05P = 40 - Q$$
$$P = 800 - 20Q$$

In this inverse demand curve $a = 800$ and $b = 20$, so the corresponding marginal revenue curve is

$$MR = a - 2bQ$$
$$MR = 800 - 40Q$$

The following graph shows the demand curve faced by Panasonic before the competing product is introduced (D_1) and the corresponding marginal revenue curve (MR_1). To find Panasonic's profit-maximizing level of output, we set $MR = MC$ and solve this equation for Q:

$$MR = MC$$
$$800 - 40Q = 200 + 20Q$$
$$60Q = 600$$
$$Q = 10$$

To find Panasonic's profit-maximizing price, we plug the profit-maximizing quantity ($Q = 10$) into the inverse demand curve:

$$P = 800 - 20Q$$
$$P = 800 - 20 \times 10$$
$$P = 600$$

Thus, before the new Sony camcorder is introduced, Panasonic's profit-maximizing level of output is 10,000 camcorders, and its profit-maximizing price is \$600 per camcorder. The following diagram illustrates this solution (point A).

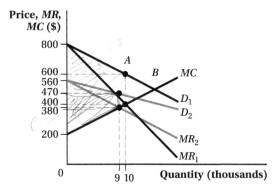

Now we find the inverse demand curve faced by Panasonic after the competing product is introduced by solving the new demand curve for P:

$$Q = 56 - 0.1P$$
$$0.1P = 56 - Q$$
$$P = 560 - 10Q$$

As you can see on the preceding graph, the new demand curve (D_2) is flatter; that is, the availability of the competing product makes Panasonic's potential customers more price-sensitive. In the new inverse demand curve, $a = 560$ and $b = 10$, so the corresponding marginal revenue curve is

$$MR = a - 2bQ$$
$$MR = 560 - 20Q$$

To find Panasonic's new profit-maximizing level of output, we set $MR = MC$ and solve this equation for Q:

$$MR = MC$$
$$560 - 20Q = 200 + 20Q$$
$$40Q = 360$$
$$Q = 9$$

To find Panasonic's profit-maximizing price, we plug the profit-maximizing quantity $(Q = 9)$ into the inverse demand curve:

$$P = 560 - 10Q$$
$$P = 560 - 10 \times 9$$
$$P = 470$$

That is, after the new Sony camcorder is introduced, Panasonic's profit-maximizing level of output is 9,000 camcorders, and its profit-maximizing price is $470 per camcorder (point B on the preceding diagram). Thus, as a result of the introduction of the competing product, Panasonic's profit-maximizing quantity of camcorders decreases from 10,000 to 9,000 and its profit-maximizing price of a camcorder falls from $600 to $470.

b. The easiest way to find the price elasticity of demand for the Panasonic camcorders is to use the Lerner index equation:

$$\frac{P - MC}{P} = -\frac{1}{E^D}$$

Before the competing product is introduced, Panasonic's profit-maximizing price is $600, and the marginal cost at the profit-maximizing level of output is $MC = 200 + 20 \times 10 = 400$ (dollars), so the markup is

$$\frac{P - MC}{P} = \frac{\$600 - \$400}{\$600} = 0.3333$$

Thus, we can write:

$$0.3333 = -\frac{1}{E^D}$$

Solving this equation for E^D, we get

$$-0.3333E^D = 1$$
$$E^D = -3.00$$

After the competing product is introduced, Panasonic's, profit-maximizing price is $470, and the marginal cost at the profit-maximizing level of output is $MC = 200 + 20 \times 9 = 380$ (dollars), so the markup is

$$\frac{P - MC}{P} = \frac{\$470 - \$380}{\$470} = 0.1915$$

So, we can write:

$$0.1915 = -\frac{1}{E^D}$$

Solving this equation for E^D, we get

$$-0.1915E^D = 1$$
$$E^D = -5.22$$

Thus, the price elasticity of demand for Panasonic's camcorders (the absolute value of the elasticity number) increases from 3.00 to 5.22, after a new substitute for the product becomes available.

c. A firm's market power can be measured by the Lerner index. The higher the index, the greater is the firm's ability to price above its marginal cost. As calculated in (b), before the competing product is introduced, the Lerner index for Panasonic is 0.3333, and after it is introduced, the Lerner index falls to 0.1915. This means the change in the price elasticity of demand for the Panasonic camcorders resulting from the introduction of the competing product leads to a decrease in Panasonic's market power.

∂ 9.4 figure it out 3

Suppose that Apple faces the following inverse demand curve for its largest-scale product designed to revolutionize the world:

$$P = 9{,}000 + 60Q - Q^2$$

Apple's total cost curve is:

$$TC = 7{,}500Q$$

Where Q is in thousands and P and TC are in dollars.
a. Use calculus to determine Apple's marginal revenue curve.
b. Use calculus to determine Apple's marginal cost curve.
c. What is Apple's profit-maximizing level of output?
d. What price should Apple charge to maximize its profit?

Solution

a. Revenue is:

$$R = P \times Q = (9{,}000 + 60Q - Q^2)Q = 9{,}000Q + 60Q^2 - Q^3$$
$$MR = \frac{dR}{dQ} = 9{,}000 + 120Q - 3Q^2$$

b. Marginal cost is the derivative of the total cost curve with respect to quantity: $MC = \frac{dTC}{dQ}$ = 7,500.

c. To maximize profit, Apple should set $MR = MC$:

$$9{,}000 + 120Q - 3Q^2 = 7{,}500$$
$$1{,}500 + 120Q - 3Q^2 = 0$$
$$(-3Q + 150)(Q + 10) = 0$$
$$Q = 50, -10$$

Since quantities must be positive, we know that:

$$Q = 50 \text{ or } 50 \text{ thousand units.}$$

d. Price comes from the inverse demand curve: $P = 9{,}000 + 60(50) - (50)^2 = \$9{,}500$.

9.5 The Winners and Losers from Market Power
Consumer surplus

The difference between the amount consumers would be willing to pay for a good or service and the amount they actually have to pay. Consumer surplus is the area under the demand curve and above the price.

Producer surplus

The difference between the price at which producers are willing to sell their good or service and the price they actually receive. Producer surplus is the area below the price and above the marginal cost curve. (Recall that in a perfectly competitive market, producer surplus is the area below the price and above the supply curve. But since the supply curve in a perfectly competitive market is actually part of the marginal cost curve, producer surplus also can be viewed as the area below the price and above the marginal cost curve just as it is under perfect competition.

Deadweight loss (DWL)

The reduction in total surplus that occurs as a result of a market inefficiency.

 Recall from Chapter 3 that consumer and producer surplus and deadweight loss can be calculated using integration methods from calculus, or using geometry for linear demand and supply cases. The calculus methods, however, can be further used for nonlinear cases.

9.5 figure it out 1

Suppose Hewlett-Packard (HP) faces the following demand curve for its inkjet printers:

$$Q = 40 - 0.2P$$

HP's marginal cost curve is

$$MC = 35 + Q$$

Where Q is in millions and P and MC are in dollars. Assume that HP maximizes its profit.
a. What is the consumer surplus in the market for HP inkjet printers?
b. What is HP's producer surplus?
c. What is the deadweight loss resulting from HP's market power?
d. Use calculus to confirm your answer to part (a).
e. Use calculus to confirm your answer to part (b).
f. Use calculus to confirm your answer to part (c).

Solution

a. To calculate the consumer surplus, we need to know HP's profit-maximizing level of output and price. To find HP's profit-maximizing quantity and price, we derive the firm's marginal revenue curve from the inverse demand curve, which we find by solving the demand curve equation for P:

$$Q = 40 - 0.2P$$
$$0.2P = 40 - Q$$
$$P = 200 - 5Q$$

In this inverse demand curve, $a = 200$ and $b = 5$, so the corresponding marginal revenue curve is

$$MR = a - 2bQ$$
$$MR = 200 - 10Q$$

To find HP's profit-maximizing level of output, we set $MR = MC$ and solve this equation for Q:

$$MR = MC$$
$$200 - 10Q = 35 + Q$$
$$11Q = 165$$
$$Q = 15$$

To find HP's profit-maximizing price, we plug the profit-maximizing quantity ($Q = 15$) into the inverse demand curve:

$$P = 200 - 5Q$$
$$P = 200 - 5 \times 15$$
$$P = 125$$

Thus, HP's profit-maximizing level of output is 15 million printers, and its profit-maximizing price is $125 per printer. The following diagram illustrates this solution. As always, drawing such a diagram, based on your algebraic calculations, is a good problem-solving strategy and the easiest way to find and calculate consumer and producer surpluses and deadweight losses.

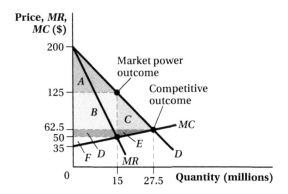

The consumer surplus is the area below the demand curve and above the price. As follows from the inverse demand curve, at $Q = 0$, $P = \$200$. Thus, the consumer surplus is the triangular area A on the graph, which can be calculated as

$$CS = 0.5 \times 15 \text{ million} \times (\$200 - \$125) = \$562.5 \text{ million}$$

b. The producer surplus is the area below the price and above the marginal cost curve up to the quantity sold. That is, HP's producer surplus is (area $B + D + F$). Given that at the profit-maximizing quantity $MC = 35 + 15 = 50$ (dollars), we can calculate the rectangular area $B + D$ as follows:

$$(\text{Area } B + D) = (\$125 - \$50) \times 15 \text{ million} = \$1,125 \text{ million}$$

And given that at $Q = 0$, $MC = \$35$, we can calculate the triangular area F as

$$\text{Area } F = 0.5 \times (\$50 - \$35) \times 15 \text{ million} = \$112.5 \text{ million}$$

So the producer surplus is

$$PS = \$1,125 \text{ million} + \$112.5 \text{ million} = \$1,237.5 \text{ million}$$

c. To find the deadweight loss from HP's market power, we need to compare the consumer and producer surpluses found in the preceding part with the consumer and producer surpluses that would be the case under perfect competition. If HP behaved like a competitive firm, it would price its printers at marginal cost. To see how many printers HP would sell at the competitive price, we equate the inverse demand curve to the MC curve and solve this equation for Q:

$$P = MC$$
$$200 - 5Q = 35 + Q$$
$$6Q = 165$$
$$Q = 27.5$$

Then, we plug this quantity into the inverse demand curve to find the competitive price:

$$P = 200 - 5Q$$
$$P = 200 - 5 \times 27.5$$
$$P = 62.5$$

The consumer surplus under perfect competition would be the triangular area below the demand curve and above this price (area $A + B + C$), which can be calculated as

$$CS_C = 0.5 \times 27.5 \text{ million} \times (\$200 - \$62.50) = \$1,890.625 \text{ million}$$

And the producer surplus would be the triangular area above the marginal cost curve and below the competitive price (area $D + E + F$), which can be calculated as

$$PS_C = 0.5 \times 27.5 \text{ million} \times (\$62.50 - \$35) = \$378.125 \text{ million}$$

So, under perfect competition the total surplus would be

$$CS_C + PS_C = \$1,890.625 \text{ million} + \$378.125 \text{ million} = \$2,268.75 \text{ million}$$

While in the situation when HP has market power, it is

$$CS + PS = \$562.5 \text{ million} + \$1{,}237.5 \text{ million} = \$1{,}800 \text{ million}$$

The difference, $\$2{,}268.75$ million – $\$1{,}800$ million = $\$468.75$ million, is the deadweight loss from HP's market power. By charging a higher price and reducing output, HP converts part of the consumer surplus (area B) into its producer surplus. But part of the consumer surplus (area C) and part of the competitive producer surplus (area E) are lost. This deadweight loss (triangular area $C + E$) can also be calculated directly as

$$DWL = 0.5 \times (\$125 - \$50) \times (27.5 \text{ million} - 15 \text{ million}) = \$468.75 \text{ million}$$

d. Consumer surplus can be calculated using integration as in the online appendix to Chapter 3. Here,

$$CS = \int_0^{15} \big((200 - 5Q) - 125)\big)\, dQ = \int_0^{15} (75 - 5Q)dQ = \int_0^{15} 75dQ - \int_0^{15} 5QdQ$$

$$= [75Q]_0^{15} - \left[\frac{5Q^2}{2}\right]_0^{15}$$

$$= [75(15) - 75(0)] - \left[\frac{5(15)^2}{2} - \frac{5(0)^2}{2}\right]$$

$$= (1{,}125 - 0) - (562.5 - 0) = 562.5. \text{ This corresponds exactly to consumer}$$
surplus in part a (to scale $\$562.5$ million).

e. Producer surplus can be calculated using integration as in the online appendix to Chapter 3.

$$PS = \int_0^{15} \big(125 - (35 + Q)\big)\, dQ = \int_0^{15} (90 - Q)dQ = \int_0^{15} 90dQ - \int_0^{15} QdQ$$

$$= [90Q]_0^{15} - \left[\frac{Q^2}{2}\right]_0^{15}$$

$$= [90(15) - 90(0)] - \left[\frac{(15)^2}{2} - \frac{(0)^2}{2}\right]$$

$$= (1{,}350 - 0) - (112.5 - 0) = 1{,}237.5. \text{ This corresponds exactly to}$$
producer surplus in part b (to scale $\$1{,}237.5$ million).

f. Deadweight loss can be calculated using integration as in the online appendix to Chapter 3. Here,

$$DWL = \int_{15}^{27.5} \big((200 - 5Q) - (35 + Q)\big)\, dQ = \int_{15}^{27.5} (165 - 6Q)dQ \int_{15}^{27.5} 165dQ - \int_{15}^{27.5} 6QdQ$$

$$= [165Q]_{15}^{27.5} - [3Q^2]_{15}^{27.5}$$

$$= [165(27.5) - 165(15)] - [3(27.5)^2 - 3(15)^2]$$

$$= (4{,}537.5 - 2{,}475) - (2{,}268.75 - 675) = 2{,}062.5 - 1{,}593.75 = 468.75. \text{ This corresponds}$$
in part (c), exactly to deadweight loss (to scale $\$468.75$ million).

9.6 Governments and Market Power: Regulation, Antitrust, and Innovation

Antitrust law

Laws designed to promote competitive markets by restricting firms from behaviors that limit competition.

Rent-seeking

A firm's attempts to gain government-granted monopoly power and, therefore, additional producer surplus. If spending on rent-seeking doesn't lead to more of the good being produced or to higher-quality output, it is deadweight loss.

Practice Problems

Problem 1

Figaro's is a small barbershop. It charges the same price per haircut to all its customers and faces the demand curve shown on the following diagram. Figaro's marginal cost of a haircut is constant at $6.

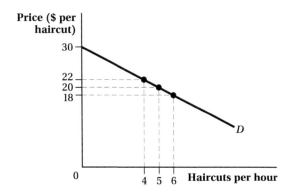

a. What is the barbershop's marginal revenue from the fifth haircut?
b. If Figaro's lowers its price from $22 per haircut to $20 per haircut, how much revenue will it lose because of the lower price? How much revenue will it gain because it sells more haircuts?
c. Suppose the barbershop is currently charging $20 per haircut but is considering lowering the price to $18. Should Figaro's lower its price? Explain your answer.
d. Use calculus to solve for Figaro's marginal revenue curve.

Problem 2

Suppose a firm faces the following demand curve

$$Q = 100 - P$$

Where Q is the quantity demanded (units) and P is the price per unit (dollars). The firm's marginal cost is constant at $25 per unit.
a. What is the firm's marginal revenue at the point where it produces 20 units?
b. Suppose the firm is currently charging $60 per unit. What is the firm's marginal revenue?
c. Should the firm raise its price, lower its price, or leave it at $60 per unit? Explain your answer.

Problem 3

Suppose Sony faces the following demand curve for its Blu-ray players:

$$Q = 30 - 0.2P$$

Sony's marginal cost curve is

$$MC = 40 + Q$$

where Q is in millions and P and MC are in dollars.
a. What is Sony's profit-maximizing level of output?
b. What price should Sony charge to maximize its profit?
c. Use calculus to verify that the total cost function $TC = 40Q + \dfrac{Q^2}{2}$ is consistent with Sony's marginal cost curve, as given.
d. Assuming that Sony's total cost function is $TC = 40Q + \dfrac{Q^2}{2}$, use calculus to re-answer parts (a) and (b).
e. Use calculus to confirm that Sony is maximizing and not minimizing profit.

Problem 4

Suppose the following diagram shows the demand curve (D) for Canon digital cameras. The diagram also shows Canon's marginal cost (MC) and average total cost (ATC).

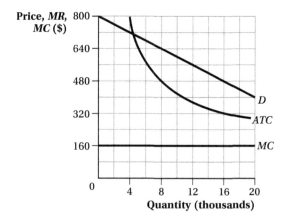

a. Draw Canon's marginal revenue curve.
b. What is Canon's profit-maximizing level of output?
c. What price should Canon charge to maximize its profit?
d. How much profit can Canon make?

Problem 5

Suppose Nature's Path faces the following demand curve for its organic oatmeal:

$$Q = 12 - 2P$$

The firm's marginal cost curve is

$$MC = 1.6 + 0.1Q$$

where Q is in millions of boxes and P and MC are in dollars. Suppose further that a higher price of oats increases the marginal cost of producing oatmeal by $1.10 at every level of output. The demand for Nature's Path oatmeal remains unchanged.
a. How does the change in marginal cost affect Nature's Path's profit-maximizing level of output? Profit-maximizing price?
b. How does the increased marginal cost affect the firm's markup?

Problem 6

Suppose Epson faces the following demand curve for its scanners:

$$Q = 24 - 0.2P$$

where Q is in millions and P is in dollars. Epson's marginal cost is constant at $50 per scanner. Assume that Epson maximizes its profit.
a. What is the consumer surplus in the market for Epson scanners?
b. What is Epson's producer surplus?
c. What is the deadweight loss resulting from Epson's market power?

Problem 7

Suppose Philips initially faces the following demand curve for its new model of LCD TV set:

$$Q = 100 - 0.1P$$

Then, due to favorable consumer reports, the demand curve faced by Philips changes to

$$Q = 60 - 0.05P$$

Philips's marginal cost curve (which has not changed) is

$$MC = 400 + 10Q$$

The quantity of TV sets (Q) is in millions and P and MC are in dollars.
a. How has the change in demand affected Philips's profit-maximizing level of output? Profit-maximizing price?
b. How has the change in consumer preferences affected the price elasticity of demand for the Philips's new TV sets? How has it affected Philips's market power?

Problem 8

Suppose that econometricians at Sargento have estimated the price elasticity of demand for Swiss cheese produced by the company at –4.

a. If Sargento's marginal cost of producing cheese is constant at $3 per pound, what price should the firm charge to maximize its profit?

b. Suppose that Sargento's managers want to know the price elasticity of demand faced by their competitor, Kraft, and you are hired to estimate it. The managers believe that Kraft's marginal cost of producing Swiss is the same as Sargento's. You collect data and find out that Kraft sells its Swiss cheese for an average price of $3.80 per pound. Assuming that Kraft is maximizing its profit, what is the price elasticity of demand for its Swiss cheese?

Problem 9

Suppose that Horizon faces the following demand curve for its organic milk:

$$Q = 170 - 20P$$

Horizon's marginal cost curve is

$$MC = 7 + 0.025Q$$

where Q is in millions of gallons and P and MC are in dollars per gallon. Assume that Horizon maximizes its profit.

a. What is the consumer surplus in the market for Horizon milk?

b. What is Horizon's producer surplus?

c. What is the deadweight loss resulting from Horizon's market power?

d. Use calculus to confirm your answer to part (a).

e. Use calculus to confirm your answer to part (b).

f. Use calculus to confirm your answer to part (c).

Problem 10

Suppose an electric company faces the following demand curve for electricity:

$$Q = 100 - 5P$$

The company's long-run average total cost curve is

$$LATC = \frac{140}{Q} + 4$$

where the quantity of electricity is in millions of kilowatt-hours (kWh), and the price and cost are in cents per kWh. The company's long-run marginal cost is constant at 4 cents.

a. What is the company's profit-maximizing level of output? What is its profit-maximizing price? If the company charges its profit-maximizing price, how much economic profit will it make?

b. If the company maximizes its profit, what is the consumer surplus? Producer surplus? What is the deadweight loss resulting from the company's market power?

c. Suppose the government imposes a price cap at 6 cents per kWh. How much electricity will the company produce? What price will it charge? How much economic profit will it make?

d. How does the price cap affect the consumer surplus? Producer surplus? Deadweight loss?

Problem 11

Reconsider the problem faced by Apple in Problem 6 in 9.4 figure it out 3. Again, suppose that Apple faces the following inverse demand curve for its largest-scale i product that is designed to revolutionize the world:

$$P = 9,000 + 60Q - Q^2$$

Apple's total cost curve is:

$$TC = 7,500Q$$

where Q is in thousands and P and TC are in dollars.

a. What is consumer surplus?

b. What is producer surplus?

Market Power and Pricing Strategies

10

10.1 The Basics of Pricing Strategy

Pricing strategy

A firm's method of pricing its product based on market characteristics.

Price discrimination

The practice of charging different prices to different customers for the same product.

Arbitrage

The practice of reselling a product at a price higher than its original selling price.

When can a firm pursue a pricing strategy?

<u>Requirement 1</u>: **The firm must have market power.**
Without market power, a firm can't choose its price at all, much less charge different prices to different consumers or use more advanced pricing strategies.
<u>Requirement 2</u>: **The firm must prevent resale and arbitrage.**
A firm must be able to prevent its customers from reselling its product among themselves. Otherwise, the customers able to buy the product at a low price would resell it to the customers who would otherwise have had to buy it from the firm at a higher price.

10.2 Direct Price Discrimination I: Perfect/First-Degree Price Discrimination

Price discrimination

Charging different prices to different customers. For price discrimination to be an option, a firm needs to have different types of customers with different price sensitivities of demand. The exact kind of price discrimination the firm should use depends on the kind of information the firm has:

- If a firm has complete information about each customer's demand curve before the customer buys the product, the firm can practice perfect (first-degree) price discrimination, that is, it can charge every customer a different price.
- If a firm can identify groups of customers with different price sensitivity before they buy the product, the firm can discriminate by customer group, that is, it can practice third-degree price discrimination.
- If a firm can identify its customers' differing demands only after they make a purchase, it can try indirect (second-degree) price discrimination, which involves offering different pricing packages (quantity discounts, different versions of the product at different prices, bundling together different products, etc.) and then identifying the customer's type from the pricing package she chooses.

Pricing strategies when customers have the same demand curves

A set of strategies such as offering different unit prices to the same customer for different quantities purchased or charging lump-sum fees on top of per-unit prices.

Direct price discrimination

A pricing strategy in which firms charge different prices to different customers based on observable characteristics of the customers.

Perfect price discrimination (first-degree price discrimination)

A type of direct price discrimination in which a firm charges each customer a price exactly equal to his willingness to pay.

∂ The perfect (first-degree) price discrimination model can be solved using either algebra or calculus (see the online appendix for Chapter 10), and the calculus methods can be used in a wider variety of circumstances than can algebra by itself (e.g., nonlinear demands).

make the grade

Is it really price discrimination?

You should be careful to always check whether you are dealing with price discrimination—the pricing strategy to charge different prices for the same product—or with price differences. It's often surprisingly hard to tell them apart. Prices can differ across different customer groups if a firm with market power price discriminates, but prices can also differ across the groups if the marginal cost of supplying the groups differs, even in a perfectly competitive market. For example, a professional-grade Canon digital SLR camera is much more expensive than a similar consumer-grade model, which is basically the same camera except that it lacks some advanced features used by professional photographers. Does this price difference reflect price discrimination? Not necessarily. Suppose the price difference exists because professional photographers find the advanced features of the camera more valuable and are willing to pay more for them. Thus, by disabling these advanced capabilities in the consumer-grade model, Canon is trying to segment the market. In this case, we deal with price discrimination. But maybe the cost of the model with advanced features is much higher than the cost of the consumer-grade model. In addition, there might be economies of scale, as more people buy consumer-grade cameras than high-end professional cameras. You can't tell just by looking at the prices. You also need to know the firm's marginal cost.

10.2 figure it out 1

Suppose an auto dealership faces the following demand curve for its cars:

$$Q = 160 - 4P$$

The dealership's marginal cost curve is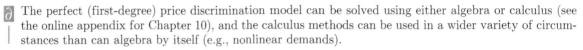

$$MC = 7 + 0.05Q$$

where Q is the number of cars sold and P and MC are measured in thousands of dollars.
a. If the dealership cannot price-discriminate, what is its profit-maximizing level of output and price?
b. If the dealership cannot price-discriminate, what are the consumer and producer surpluses in the market, assuming the firm maximizes its profit? What is the deadweight loss resulting from the dealership's market power?
c. If the dealership has the ability to practice perfect price discrimination, how many cars will it sell?
d. If the dealership practices perfect price discrimination, what are the consumer and producer surpluses in the market? What is the deadweight loss?

∂ e–h. Use calculus to redo (a)–(d) and confirm that your answers are the same.

Solution

a. To find the dealership's profit-maximizing level of output and price, we need to know its marginal revenue curve, which can be derived from the inverse demand curve. We find the inverse demand curve by solving the demand equation for P:

$$Q = 160 - 4P$$
$$4P = 160 - Q$$
$$P = 40 - 0.25Q$$

In this inverse demand curve, $a = 40$ and $b = 0.25$, so the corresponding marginal revenue curve is

$$MR = a - 2bQ$$
$$MR = 40 - 0.5Q$$

To find the dealership's profit-maximizing level of output, we set $MR = MC$ and solve this equation for Q:

$$MR = MC$$
$$40 - 0.5Q = 7 + 0.05Q$$
$$0.55Q = 33$$
$$Q = 60$$

To find the firm's profit-maximizing price, we plug the profit-maximizing quantity ($Q = 60$) into the inverse demand curve:

$$P = 40 - 0.25Q$$
$$P = 40 - 0.25 \times 60$$
$$P = 25$$

Thus, the dealership's profit-maximizing level of output is 60 cars, and its profit-maximizing price is $25,000 per car. The following graph illustrates this solution.

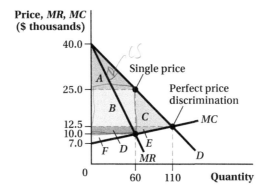

b. The consumer surplus is the area below the demand curve and above the price. As follows from the inverse demand curve, at $Q = 0$, $P = \$40,000$. Thus, the consumer surplus is the triangular area A on the graph, which can be calculated as

$$CS = 0.5 \times 60 \times (\$40,000 - \$25,000) = \$450,000$$

The producer surplus is the area below the price and above the marginal cost curve up to the quantity sold. That is, the dealership's producer surplus is area $(B + D + F)$. Given that at the profit-maximizing quantity $MC = 7 + 0.05 \times 60 = 10$ (thousand dollars), we can calculate the rectangular area $B + D$ as follows:

$$(\text{Area } B + D) = (\$25,000 - \$10,000) \times 60 = \$900,000$$

And given that at $Q = 0$, $MC = \$7$, we can calculate the triangular area F as

$$\text{Area } F = 0.5 \times (\$10,000 - \$7,000) \times 60 = \$90,000$$

So the producer surplus is

$$PS = \$900,000 + \$90,000 = \$990,000$$

To find the deadweight loss from the dealership's market power, we compare the consumer and producer surpluses found in the preceding with the consumer and producer surpluses that would exist under perfect competition. If the dealership behaved like a competitive firm, it would price its cars at marginal cost. To see how many cars would be sold at the competitive price, we equate the inverse demand curve to the MC curve and solve this equation for Q:

$$P = MC$$
$$40 - 0.25Q = 7 + 0.05Q$$
$$0.3Q = 33$$
$$Q = 110$$

Now we plug this quantity into the inverse demand curve to find the competitive price:

$$P = 40 - 0.25Q$$
$$P = 40 - 0.25 \times 110$$
$$P = 12.5$$

That is, the competitive price is \$12,500. The consumer surplus under perfect competition would be the triangular area below the demand curve and above this price (area $A + B + C$), which can be calculated as

$$CS_C = 0.5 \times 110 \times (\$40,000 - \$12,500) = \$1,512,500$$

And the producer surplus would be the triangle above the marginal cost curve and below the competitive price (area $D + E + F$), which can be calculated as

$$PS_C = 0.5 \times 110 \times (\$12,500 - \$7,000) = \$302,500$$

So, under perfect competition, the total surplus would be

$$CS_C + PS_C = \$1,512,500 + \$302,500 = \$1,815,000$$

While, under market power, it is

$$CS + PS = \$450,000 + \$990,000 = \$1,440,000$$

The difference, \$1,815,000 − \$1,440,000 = \$375,000 is the deadweight loss from the dealership's market power. This deadweight loss (triangular area $C + E$) can also be calculated directly as

$$DWL = 0.5 \times (\$25,000 - \$10,000) \times (110 - 60) = \$375,000$$

c. If the dealership practices perfect price discrimination, it charges each customer a price equal to her willingness to pay. Thus, the dealership will sell cars to all the customers whose willingness to pay is at least equal to the firm's marginal cost. This means the dealership will sell 110 cars (as calculated in [b]).

d. If the firm practices perfect price discrimination, the consumer surplus is zero because every consumer is charged a price equal to his willingness to pay. The producer surplus will be the whole triangular area below the demand curve and above the marginal cost curve (area $A + B + C + D + E + F$), since for every car sold the price paid by the customer equals his willingness to pay, which is the corresponding point on the demand curve. Thus, the firm captures the whole amount of available surplus, which equals the total surplus under perfect competition calculated in (b), \$1,815,000. This producer surplus can be calculated directly as the triangular area $(A + B + C + D + E + F)$:

$$PS = 0.5 \times (\$40,000 - \$7,000) \times 110 = \$1,815,000$$

Since as a result of perfect price discrimination the dealership sells the competitive quantity of cars, there is no deadweight loss.

e. The firm's inverse demand function is given as $P = 40 - 0.25Q$. This implies total revenue is given by $TR(Q) = P(Q) \times Q = 40Q - 0.25Q^2$. Marginal revenue is

$$MR = \frac{dTR(Q)}{dq} = 40 - 0.5Q$$

Without complete total cost information, we can still use calculus indirectly, by using marginal revenue as calculated using calculus in the preceding. Profit maximization requires the firm to select output such that $MR = MC$. This is

$$MR = 40 - 0.5Q = 7 + 0.05Q = MC$$
$$33 = 0.55Q$$
$$Q = 60$$

Thus, we conclude that $Q = 60$ is the profit-maximizing level of output. The optimal price is $P = 40 - 0.25(60) = 25$, as found in (a).

f. Consumer surplus is

$$CS = \int_0^{60}\big((40 - 0.25Q) - 25\big)dQ$$

$$= \int_0^{60}(15 - 0.25Q)dQ = \int_0^{60}15dQ - \int_0^{60}0.25QdQ$$

$$= [15Q]_0^{60} - \left[\frac{0.25Q^2}{2}\right]_0^{60} = [15Q]_0^{60} - [0.125Q^2]_0^{60}$$

$$= [15(60) - 15(0)] - [0.125(60)^2 - 0.125(0)^2]$$

$$= (900 - 0) - (450 - 0) = 450$$

Since price is in thousands, this corresponds to $450,000, as found in (b).
Producer surplus is

$$PS = \int_0^{60}\big(25 - (7 + 0.05Q)\big)dQ$$

$$= \int_0^{60}(18 - 0.05Q)dQ = \int_0^{60}18dQ - \int_0^{60}0.05QdQ$$

$$= [18Q]_0^{60} - \left[\frac{0.05Q^2}{2}\right]_0^{60} = [8Q]_0^{60} - [0.025Q^2]_0^{60}$$

$$= [18(60) - 18(0)] - [0.025(60)^2 - [0.025(0)^2]$$

$$= (1{,}080 - 0) - (90 - 0) = 990$$

This corresponds to $990,000, as found in (b).
Deadweight loss is

$$\text{DWL} = \int_{60}^{110}\big((40 - 0.25Q) - (7 + 0.05Q)\big)dQ = \int_{60}^{110}(33 - 0.3Q)dQ = \int_{60}^{110}33dQ - \int_{60}^{110}0.3QdQ$$

$$= [33Q]_{60}^{110} - \left[\frac{0.3Q^2}{2}\right]_{60}^{110} = [33Q]_{60}^{110} - [0.15Q^2]_{60}^{110}$$

$$= [33(110) - 33(60)] - [0.15(110)^2 - 0.15(60)^2]$$

$$= (3{,}630 - 1{,}980) - (1{,}815 - 540) = 375$$

Deadweight loss therefore is $375,000, as found in (b).

g. Using calculus methods in this context does not change the reasoning for the dealership choosing to sell 110 cars is unchanged using calculus methods.

h. As the perfect price-discriminating monopolist maximizes its producer surplus (which is equal to the total surplus):

$$PS = \int_0^{110}\big((40 - 0.25Q) - (7 + 0.05Q)\big)dQ = \int_0^{110}(33 - 0.3Q)dQ = \int_0^{110}33dQ - \int_0^{110}0.3QdQ$$

$$= [33Q]_0^{110} - \left[\frac{0.3Q^2}{2}\right]_0^{110} = [33Q]_0^{110} - [0.15Q^2]_0^{110}$$

$$= [33(110) - 33(0)] - [0.15(110)^2 - 0.15(0)^2]$$

$$= (3{,}630 - 0) - (1{,}815 - 0) = 1{,}815$$

This corresponds to $1,815,000, as found in (d).
Consumer surplus is then:

$$CS = \int_0^{110}\big((40 - 0.25Q) - (40 - 0.25Q)\big)dQ = \int_0^{110}0dQ = 0$$

And, deadweight loss is similarly zero, also as found in (d).

$$\text{DWL} = \int_{110}^{110}\big((40 - 0.25Q) - (7 + 0.05Q)\big)dQ = \int_{110}^{110}(33 - 0.3Q)dQ = 0$$

Note that this integral equals zero because the integration is over a zero quantity change.

∂ 10.2 figure it out 2

A firm with market power faces the demand function $q = 800 - 5P$. The firm's total cost function is $TC(q) = 3q + 0.5q^2 + 100$.

a. If the firm behaves as a single-price monopoly, identify the firm's optimal price and output level using calculus.

b. Use calculus to demonstrate that the single-price monopolist's profit-maximizing choice of price and output also maximize producer surplus.

c. Use calculus to identify the output level that would maximize total surplus.

d. Uses calculus to identify the output level that a perfect-price discriminating monopolist would produce.

Solution

a. Rearranging the firm's demand function to identify the inverse demand function, we have:

$$P = 40 - 0.2q$$

The firm's profit function is:

$$\pi = 40q - 0.2q^2 - 3q - 0.5q^2 - 100$$
$$= 37q - 0.7q^2 - 100$$

The firm's first-order condition for profit maximization is:

$$0 = \frac{d\pi}{dq} = 37 - 1.4q$$

Solving for q, we identify the firm's profit-maximizing choice of output as $q = 26.43$. The highest price the single-price monopolist can charge to sell 26.43 units is

$$P = 40 - 0.2(26.43)$$
$$= 34.71$$

b. Producer surplus is defined as $PS = TR(q_m) - \int_0^{q_m} MC(q)dq$, where q_m is the single-price monopolist's output level, $TR(q_m)$ is total revenue function $\left(TR(q_m) = 40q_m - 0.2q_m^2\right)$, and $MC(q_m)$ is the monopolist's marginal cost function. Given the total cost curve supplied in the problem, $MC(q_m) = \frac{dTC}{dq} = 3 + q_m$. As $TC(q_m) = \int_0^{q_m} MC(q)dq = 3q_m + 0.5q_m^2, + FC$ producer surplus is: $PS = 40q_m - 0.2q_m^2 - 3q_m - 0.5q_m^2$. Simplifying, we have: $PS = 37q_m - 0.7q_m^2$. (Recall that the difference between profit and producer surplus is that profit includes fixed costs.) The first-order condition to maximize producer surplus is: $0 = \frac{dPS}{dq_m} = 37 - 1.4q_m$. Since this first-order condition corresponds precisely with the single-price monopolist's first-order condition for profit maximization, the choice of output that maximizes profits corresponds exactly with the choice of output that maximizes producer surplus. In this case, solving the first-order condition for producer surplus maximization, we see that $q_m = 26.43$.

c. Total surplus is $TS = \int_0^{q_*} \left(MB(q) - MC(q)\right)dq$, where $MB(q)$ is the inverse demand function, and q_* is the number of units transacted in the market. For our application, $TS = \int_0^{q_*}(40 - 0.2q - 3 - q)dq = 37q_* - 0.6q_*^2$. The first-order condition for total surplus maximization is $0 = \frac{dTS}{dq_*} = 37 - 1.2q_*$. Solving for q_*, we have $q_* = 30.83$.

d. The perfect price-discriminating monopolist earns profits according to: $\pi = \int_0^{q_{ppdm}}(40 - 0.2q)dq - 3q_{ppdm} - 0.5q_{ppdm}^2 - 100$. Performing the integration on the first part, we have $\pi = 40q_{ppdm} - 0.1q_{ppdm}^2 - 3q_{ppdm} - 0.5q_{ppdm}^2 - 100$. Simplifying, the perfect price-discriminating monopolist's profit is: $\pi = 37q_{ppdm} - 0.6q_{ppdm}^2 - 100$. The first-order condition for profit maximization is $0 = \frac{d\pi}{dq_{ppdm}} = 37 - 1.2q_{ppdm}$. Solving for q_{ppdm}, we identify the perfect price-discriminating monopolist will bring 30.83 units to the market, which is the same as in (c).

10.3 Direct Price Discrimination II: Segmenting/Third-Degree Price Discrimination

Segmenting (third-degree price discrimination)

A type of direct price discrimination in which a firm charges different prices to different groups of customers based on the identifiable attributes of those groups.

10.3 figure it out 1

Suppose that a local movie theater has two groups of customers, ordinary moviegoers and students. The ordinary customers' demand curve is

$$Q_O = 23 - 2P$$

and the students' demand curve is

$$Q_S = 9 - P$$

where Q is the number of movie tickets in thousands and P is the price of a ticket in dollars. Assume that the theater's marginal cost is constant at \$1 per ticket.

a. If the movie theater charges the same price to all customers, what is its profit-maximizing price? How many tickets are sold at this price? What is the theater's producer surplus?

b. Now suppose the theater's manager is considering selling tickets to students at a discount. The theater can prevent resale by requiring students with discounted tickets to show their IDs at the admission. To maximize its profit, what price should the theater charge to students? What price should it charge to other customers? How will the theater's segmentation strategy change its producer surplus?

Solution

a. First, we need to find the market demand curve faced by the theater. Recall from Chapter 5 that the market demand curve can be calculated as the horizontal sum of the students' demand curve and the other customers' demand curve:

$$Q = Q_S + Q_O$$
$$Q = (9 - P) + (23 - 2P)$$
$$Q = 32 - 3P$$

To derive the market demand curve correctly, we also need to find the demand choke prices for each group of customers. We do this by setting $Q = 0$ and solving each group's demand curve for P. For students,

$$Q_S = 9 - P$$
$$0 = 9 - P$$
$$P = 9$$

And for other customers,

$$Q_O = 23 - 2P$$
$$0 = 23 - 2P$$
$$P = 11.5$$

This means in the price range between \$11.50 and \$9 students' quantity of movie tickets demanded is zero, so the market demand curve is the same as that of the ordinary customers. And at \$9 and below, it is the market demand curve calculated in the preceding. That is, the market demand curve is kinked, as shown on the following graph.

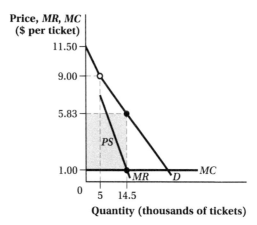

To find the movie theater's profit-maximizing price, we need to know its marginal revenue curve, which can be derived from the inverse demand curve. For the part of the market demand curve below the kink, the inverse demand curve can be found as follows:

$$Q = 32 - 3P$$
$$3P = 32 - Q$$
$$P = \frac{32}{3} - \frac{Q}{3}$$

In this inverse demand curve, $a = \dfrac{32}{3}$ and $b = \dfrac{1}{3}$, so the corresponding marginal revenue curve is

$$MR = a - 2bQ$$
$$MR = \frac{32}{3} - \frac{2Q}{3}$$

To find the profit-maximizing number of tickets sold, we set $MR = MC$ and solve this equation for Q:

$$\frac{32}{3} - \frac{2Q}{3} = 1$$
$$32 - 2Q = 3$$
$$2Q = 29$$
$$Q = 14.5$$

From the inverse demand curve, we can calculate the price at which the theater can sell this quantity of tickets:

$$P = \frac{32}{3} - \frac{Q}{3}$$
$$P = \frac{32}{3} - \frac{14.5}{3}$$
$$P = \frac{(32 - 14.5)}{3}$$
$$P = 5.83$$

This price is on the part of the demand curve below the kink, so the demand and marginal revenue curves that we used to find the profit-maximizing quantity are the ones that are relevant. Thus, when the movie theater charges the same price to all customers, its profit- maximizing price is \$5.83, and it sells 14,500 tickets at this price. The preceding diagram illustrates this solution.

The theater's producer surplus is the area below the price and above the marginal cost curve, which can be calculated as follows:

$$PS = 14{,}500 \times (\$5.83 - \$1) \approx \$70{,}000$$

b. If the theater can separate the two groups of customers and prevent resale, it will face two separate demand curves. Therefore, we derive the marginal revenue curves for each segment and solve for the profit-maximizing price separately for each group. First, we find each group's inverse demand curve:

Students:	Other customers:
$Q_S = 9 - P_S$	$Q_O = 23 - 2P_O$
$P_S = 9 - Q_S$	$2P_O = 23 - Q_O$
	$P_O = 11.5 - 0.5Q_O$

Next, we know that the marginal revenue curve is the inverse demand curve, with the coefficient on quantity twice as large. Thus, the marginal revenue curves for the two segments are

Students:	Other customers:
$MR_S = 9 - 2Q_S$	$MR_O = 11.5 - Q_O$

The theater wants to sell the quantities at which its marginal cost (\$1) equals its marginal revenue. Setting the marginal revenue equation for each group equal to the marginal cost tells us the optimal number of tickets sold to each group:

Students:	Other customers:
$MR_S = MC$	$MR_O = MC$
$9 - 2Q_S = 1$	$11.5 - Q_S = 1$
$2Q_S = 8$	$Q_S = 10.5$
$Q_S = 4$	

To find the ticket prices at which the theater can sell these quantities, we plug each quantity into the corresponding inverse demand curve:

Students:	Other customers:
$P_S = 9 - Q_S$	$P_O = 11.5 - 0.5Q_O$
$P_S = 9 - 4$	$P_O = 11.5 - 0.5 \times 10.5$
$P_S = 5$	$P_O = 6.25$

Thus, the theater should charge students $5 per ticket, and it should charge other customers $6.25 per ticket. The following graph illustrates this solution.

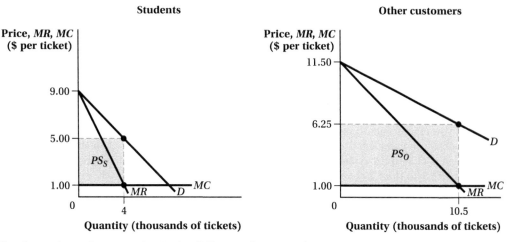

The theater's producer surplus is the difference between the price and the marginal cost for each segment times the number of tickets sold to that segment:

Students: **Other customers:**

$PS_S = (\$5 - \$1) \times 4{,}000$ $PS_O = (\$6.25 - \$1) \times 10{,}500$

$PS_S = \$16{,}000$ $PS_O = \$55{,}125$

So, the combined producer surplus from the two segments is

$$PS = \$16{,}000 + \$55{,}125 = \$71{,}125$$

Thus, the theater's price discrimination by segmenting increases its producer surplus from $70,000 to $71,125.

10.4 Indirect/Second-Degree Price Discrimination

Indirect price discrimination (second-degree price discrimination)

A pricing strategy in which customers pick among a variety of pricing options offered by the firm.

Quantity discount

The practice of charging a lower per-unit price to customers who buy larger quantities.

Incentive compatibility

The requirement under an indirect price discrimination strategy that the price offered to each consumer group is chosen by that group.

Versioning

A pricing strategy in which the firm offers different product options designed to attract different types of consumers.

10.4 figure it out 1

Suppose you've developed a new software program that is very effective in helping students learn economics, and you want to offer it to economics instructors. Your market research shows that you have (roughly) two types of potential customers. The first type (Type A) instructors work at small colleges and are evaluated mainly based on effectiveness of their teaching. Therefore, their demand for your software is relatively inelastic with respect to the price charged. You estimate that a Type A instructor's demand curve for your software is

$$Q_A = 220 - 100P$$

The second type (Type B) instructors work at big research universities and care less about teaching. Therefore, they are less willing to pay a higher price for your innovative teaching software. That is, their demand is relatively elastic with respect to price. In addition, since these instructors have to teach large classes, they are willing to pay much less per user (student) than Type A instructors are. You estimate that a Type B instructor's demand curve is

$$Q_B = 960 - 800P$$

The price is in dollars per user, and the quantity is the number of users (students). Assume that you can prevent sharing and resale of your software (including making students pay for their individual licenses). Your marginal cost is constant at $0.60 per user.

a. If you can tell which type of customer is buying your product before a purchase is made, what prices will you charge each type?

b. Suppose you cannot tell which type of customer each instructor is when she purchases your software, so you decide to use quantity discounting. Specifically, you intend to charge $1.40 per user for a package with less than 240 users and $0.90 per user for a package with 240 or more users. Is this pricing plan incentive-compatible? Explain your answer.

Solution

a. If you can separate the two groups of customers and prevent resale, you will face two separate demand curves. Therefore, to find your profit-maximizing solution, you need to know the marginal revenue curves for each segment, so you can solve for the profit-maximizing price separately for each group. First, you find each group's inverse demand curve:

Type A:	Type B:
$Q_A = 220 - 100P_A$	$Q_B = 960 - 800P_B$
$100P_A = 220 - Q_A$	$800P_B = 960 - Q_B$
$P_A = 2.2 - 0.01Q_A$	$P_B = 1.2 - 0.00125Q_B$

We know that the marginal revenue curve is the inverse demand curve with the coefficient on quantity twice as large (see the text, Chapter 9, pp. 330–331). Thus, the marginal revenue curves for the two segments are:

Type A:	Type B:
$MR_A = 2.2 - 2 \times 0.01Q_A$	$MR_B = 1.2 - 2 \times 0.00125Q_B$
$MR_A = 2.2 - 0.02Q_A$	$MR_B = 1.2 - 0.0025Q_B$

You want to sell the quantities (number of user licenses) for which your marginal cost ($0.60) equals your marginal revenue received from each type of customer:

Type A:	Type B:
$MR_A = MC$	$MR_B = MC$
$2.2 - 0.02Q_A = 0.6$	$1.2 - 0.0025Q_B = 0.6$
$0.02Q_A = 1.6$	$0.0025Q_B = 0.6$
$Q_A = 80$	$Q_B = 240$

Now, by plugging these quantities into the inverse demand curve, we can find the prices at which you can sell these quantities:

Type A:	Type B:
$P_A = 2.2 - 0.01Q_A$	$P_B = 1.2 - 0.00125Q_B$
$P_A = 2.2 - 0.01 \times 80$	$P_B = 1.2 - 0.00125 \times 240$
$P_A = 1.4$	$P_B = 0.9$

Thus, you should charge Type A instructors $1.40 per user and Type B instructors $0.90 per user. The diagram below illustrates this solution.

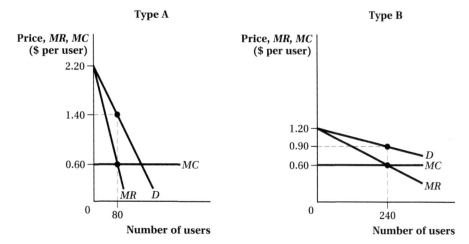

b. To see whether your pricing strategy is incentive compatible for a Type A instructor, we need to compare the consumer surpluses she receives under each plan. If a Type A instructor chooses to pay the regular price ($1.40 per user), her quantity demanded will be

$$Q_A = 220 - 100P_A$$
$$Q_A = 220 - 100 \times 1.40$$
$$Q_A = 80$$

so her consumer surplus will be the area below her demand curve and above the price up to this quantity (area A on the following graph):

$$CS = 0.5 \times (\$2.20 - \$1.40) \times 80 = \$32$$

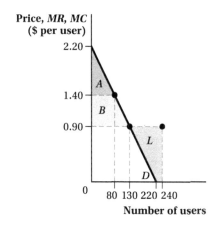

If a Type A instructor chooses the quantity discount plan, she will purchase a package with 240 users for $0.90 per user. In this case, her quantity demanded is

$$Q_A = 220 - 100 \times 0.90$$
$$Q_A = 130$$

This means her demand curve will be above the price only up to this quantity, that is, she will receive consumer surplus only from the first 130 user licenses purchased. This consumer surplus is the area below the demand curve and above the price ($0.90), that is, it is (area $A + B$), which is

$$(\text{Area } A + B) = 0.5 \times (\$2.20 - \$0.90) \times 130 = \$84.50$$

But to get the quantity discount, she has to buy 110 more user licenses. And for these licenses, the price she pays is above her demand curve, which means she values them less than she has to pay for them. Notice that the demand curve intersects the horizontal axis at $Q = 220$ (since at $P = 0$, $Q_A = 220 - 100 \times 0 = 220$), which means a Type A instructor's willingness to pay for the last 20 licenses is zero. The result is a loss in consumer surplus equal to the area below the price and above the demand curve (which runs along the horizontal axis once the demand curve hits the axis) between $Q = 130$ and $Q = 240$ (area L). This area is a trapezoid, so we can calculate it using the trapezoid area formula:

$$\text{Area of trapezoid} = 0.5 \times (a + b) \times h$$

where a is the trapezoid's longer parallel side, b is its shorter parallel side, and h is its height (i.e., the distance between the two parallel sides). For area L, the longer base is $240 - 130 = 110$, the shorter base is $240 - 220 = 20$, and the height is $\$0.90$. Thus:

$$\text{Area } L = 0.5 \times (110 + 20) \times \$0.90 = \$58.50$$

Thus, with the quantity discount, a Type A instructor's consumer surplus is

$$CS = \text{Area } (A + B) - \text{Area } C$$
$$CS = \$84.5 - \$58.5 = \$26$$

Since this is less than the consumer surplus a Type A instructor receives if she chooses the $\$1.40$ per-user option ($\$32$), she will take the offer designed for her. That is, your pricing plan is incentive-compatible for Type A instructors. We can also see this if we compare a Type A instructor's consumer surplus gain from the quantity discount option (area B) with her consumer surplus loss (area L). Area B is a trapezoid, where the longer base is 130, the shorter base is 80, and the height is $\$1.40 - \$0.90 = \$0.50$. Thus:

$$\text{Area } B = 0.5 \times (130 + 80) \times \$0.50 = \$52.50$$

Since this gain in consumer surplus is less than the consumer surplus loss calculated in the preceding ($\$58.50$), Type A instructors will not opt for the quantity discount offer.

A Type B instructor will surely prefer the quantity discount because, according to his inverse demand curve, his quantity demanded at prices above $\$1.20$ per user is zero (as the graph in (a) illustrates). And, as we could see in (a), at $\$0.90$, his quantity demanded is exactly 240 user licenses. This means he can take the quantity discount offer without sacrificing any consumer surplus, that is, without buying licenses that he values less than he has to pay for them. Therefore, a Type B instructor will also take the offer designed for him. Thus, your pricing plan is incentive-compatible for both types of customer.

10.5 Bundling

Bundling

A pricing strategy in which the firm sells two or more products together at a single price.

Mixed bundling

A type of bundling in which the firm simultaneously offers consumers the choice of buying two or more products separately or as a bundle.

Pure bundling

A type of bundling in which the firm offers the products only as a bundle.

10.5 figure it out 1

A cable company provides TV channels to its customers. Suppose, for the sake of simplicity, that there are only two cable networks available: CNN and HGTV. The marginal cost of supplying CNN is $\$10$ per month and is $\$6$ per month for HGTV. Suppose there are only three customers in the market, Bill, Erin, and Lindsey, and they value the networks (i.e., are willing to pay per month) as shown in the following table. The cable company is deciding what packages to offer and what prices to charge.

	Willingness to pay ($ per month)	
	CNN	**HGTV**
Bill	15	12
Erin	26	4
Lindsey	9	20

a. If the cable company offers access to the two networks separately, what price should it charge for each? What will be the company's producer surplus?

b. If the company offers the two networks as a bundle, what price should it charge? How much producer surplus will the company earn in this case?

c. If the company offers its customers a choice to either purchase access to the networks separately or as a bundle, how should it price each option? Will the company be able to earn a greater producer surplus as a result of this mixed bundling? Explain your answer.

Solution

a. To sell access to CNN to all three customers, the company would have to charge a price no higher than $9, which is the amount above which the costumer with the lowest willingness to pay (Lindsey) will not pay. This price, however, is below the marginal cost ($10), so the company will not be able to sell access to CNN to all three customers without a loss of producer surplus. Thus, it will charge $15 per month and sell CNN just to Bill and Erin. The company will not be able to sell HGTV to all three customers for the same reason: the customer with the lowest willingness to pay (Erin) values it at only $4, while the company's marginal cost is $6. Thus, the company will charge $12 per month and sell HGTV to just Bill and Lindsey. With these prices, the firm's producer surplus from selling access to CNN (the difference between the price charged and the marginal cost, times the number of customers who will buy it) will be

$$PS_C = (\$15 - \$10) \times 2$$
$$PS_C = \$10$$

and its surplus from selling access to HGTV will be

$$PS_H = (\$12 - \$6) \times 2$$
$$PS_H = \$12$$

so its total monthly producer surplus will be

$$PS = \$10 + \$12$$
$$PS = \$22$$

b. To determine the price that the company should charge, we calculate each customer's willingness to pay for the bundle by summing the customers' willingness to pay for each product as shown in the following table:

	Willingness to pay ($ per month)		
	CNN	**HGTV**	**Bundle**
Bill	15	12	27
Erin	26	4	30
Lindsey	9	20	29

The maximum price the company can charge for its bundle and still sell it to all three customers is the price that the customer who values the bundle the least (Bill) is willing to pay. That is, the company will charge $27 per month. The marginal cost of the bundle is $10 + $6 = $16. Thus, the company's producer surplus will be

$$PS = (\$27 - \$16) \times 3$$
$$PS = \$33$$

c. Recall that Erin values HGTV below the marginal cost, and Lindsey values CNN below the marginal cost. Since the cable company does not want to supply channels to customers who value them at less than the cost of providing them, it will try to split these customers off from the bundle. That is, the company would like to end up selling the bundle to Bill, only CNN to Erin, and only HGTV to Lindsey. Because Bill values the bundle at $27 per month, this is the maximum price the company can charge to sell it to him. But if this is the price of the bundle, the company can't charge Erin her full $26 valuation for CNN. If it tried, Erin would choose the bundle instead because it would give her $3 more of consumer surplus ($30 − $27) than if she purchased only CNN for $26, in which case her consumer surplus would be zero. A price of $26 for CNN is therefore not incentive compatible. To set an incentive-compatible price for CNN, the cable company has to leave Erin with at least $3 of consumer surplus. Thus, the incentive-compatible price for the purchase of CNN alone is $26 – $3 = $23 per month. And since Bill values CNN at less than $23, he will buy the bundle rather than take the CNN-only option. So incentive compatibility holds in the other direction as well.

We can do the same type of calculations with HGTV and Lindsey. The cable company can't charge $20 for HGTV alone, because Lindsey would opt for the bundle to get $29 – $27 = $2 of consumer surplus rather than receive zero consumer surplus from buying HGTV alone at $20. The company has to leave Lindsey with at least $2 of surplus if she opts to buy just HGTV. The highest price that will achieve this is $20 – $2 = $18. Again, offering this option won't move Bill away from the bundle, because he values HGTV at less than $18. So with the three different prices, the company will sell a bundle to Bill for $27 and earn a producer surplus of

$$PS_B = \$27 - \$16 = \$11$$

It will sell CNN alone to Erin for $23 to earn a surplus of

$$PS_C = \$23 - \$10 = \$13$$

and HGTV to Lindsey for $18, with a producer surplus of

$$PS_H = \$18 - \$6 = \$12$$

Thus, the total producer surplus from using mixed bundling is

$$PS = \$11 + \$13 + \$12 = \$36$$

This is more than the $22 per month the cable company would make by offering the channels separately and more than the $33 per month it will make using pure bundling. Producer surplus has increased because mixed bundling has allowed the company to avoid delivering a product to a customer who values it at less than it costs to produce.

10.6 Advanced Pricing Strategies

Block pricing

The practice of reducing the price of a good when the customer buys more of it.

∂ Block pricing can be solved using either algebra or calculus (see the online appendix for Chapter 10), and the calculus methods can be used in a wider variety of circumstances than can algebra alone (e.g., nonlinear demands).

Two-part tariff

A pricing strategy in which the payment has two components, a per-unit price and a fixed fee.

---

make the grade

Which price strategy to use?

With so many different pricing strategies and conditions that allow firms to implement them, it is easy to get lost when answering exam questions about pricing strategies. The following is a summary of the conditions under which a certain price strategy can be implemented to help firms make their pricing decisions. And it should help you do better on the test:

When to use perfect (first-degree) price discrimination
1. The firm has market power and can prevent resale.
2. The firm's customers have different demand curves.
3. The firm has complete information about every customer and can identify each one's demand before purchase.

When to use segmenting (third-degree) price discrimination

1. The firm has market power and can prevent resale.
2. The firm's customers have different demand curves.
3. The firm can directly identify specific groups of customers with different price sensitivities (but not the demand of every individual customer) before purchase.

When to use indirect (second-degree) price discrimination

1. The firm has market power and can prevent resale.
2. The firm's customers have different demand curves.
3. The firm cannot directly identify which customers have which type of demand before purchase.

When to use bundling

1. The firm has market power and can prevent resale.
2. The firm sells a second product and consumers' demand for that product is negatively correlated with their demand for the first product.

When to use block pricing and two-part tariffs

1. The firm has market power and can prevent resale.
2. The firm's customers may have either identical or different demand curves.

The following diagram (Figure 10.1 in the text) provides an overview of pricing strategies with references to the sections in the text where they are covered.

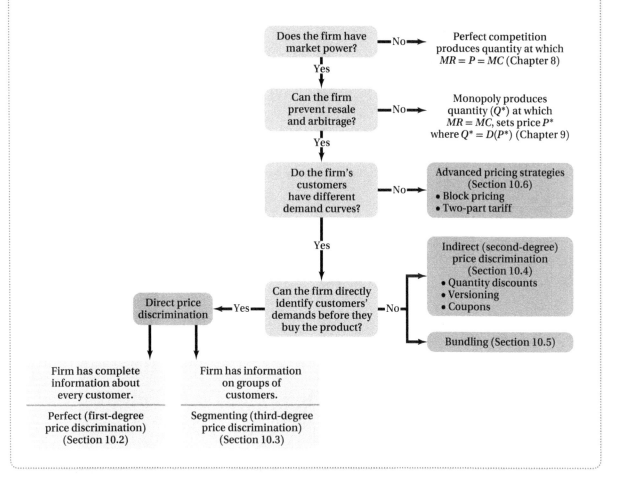

10.6 figure it out 1

Suppose all customers of a mobile phone company have the following demand curve for the phone calls:

$$Q = 400 - 20P$$

where Q is in minutes per month and P is in cents per minute. The company's marginal cost of providing the service is constant at 4 cents per minute. Assume that the company can prevent resale.

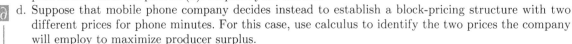

a. If the company charges a single price per minute regardless of how many minutes are used, what will be its profit-maximizing price? Producer surplus (per customer)?

b. Suppose that instead of a single price, the company is considering offering its customers the following plan: 12 cents per minute for the first 160 minutes, 9 cents per minute for the next 60 minutes, and 6 cents per minute after that. If the company hired you as an economic consultant, would you advise the company to use this plan instead of a single price? Explain your answer.

c. The company is also considering a plan with a fixed monthly fee and a per-minute price. What monthly fee and what per-minute price should it charge? Would you advise the company to use this plan rather than the plan in (b)? Explain your answer.

d. Suppose that mobile phone company decides instead to establish a block-pricing structure with two different prices for phone minutes. For this case, use calculus to identify the two prices the company will employ to maximize producer surplus.

e. If the phone company establishes a block-pricing structure with two different prices for minutes of service and maximizes producer surplus, use calculus to identify consumer surplus, producer surplus, and total surplus.

Solution

a. To find the single profit-maximizing price, we need to know the firm's marginal revenue curve, which can be derived from the inverse demand curve. And to find the inverse demand curve, we solve the demand equation for P:

$$Q = 400 - 20P$$
$$20P = 400 - Q$$
$$P = 20 - 0.05Q$$

The marginal revenue curve is the inverse demand curve with the coefficient on quantity twice as large. Thus, the firm's marginal revenue curve is:

$$MR = 20 - 0.1Q$$

Now we can find the profit-maximizing quantity by setting $MR = MC$ and solving for Q:

$$20 - 0.1Q = 4$$
$$0.1Q = 16$$
$$Q = 160$$

By plugging this quantity into the inverse demand curve, we can find the profit-maximizing price:

$$P = 20 - 0.05Q$$
$$P = 20 - (0.05 \times 160)$$
$$P = 12$$

Thus, the single profit-maximizing price is 12 cents per minute. This solution is shown on the following graph.

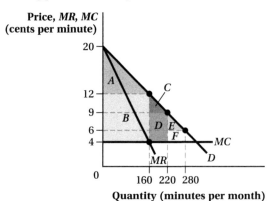

The company's producer surplus is the area above the marginal cost curve and below the demand curve up to the quantity sold (area B on the preceding graph), which is

$$PS = (\$0.12 - \$0.04) \times 160 = \$12.80$$

b. When a customer buys the first 160 minutes at 12 cents per minute, the consumer surplus is area A on the preceding graph. And when the company offers the next 60 minutes (i.e., minutes 161 – 220) at 9 cents per minute, the customer will take advantage of this offer because the incremental purchase at the lower price yields an additional consumer surplus equal to the area of triangle C. The company is also better off, because it adds an additional amount of producer surplus equal to the area of rectangle D:

$$\text{Area } D = (\$0.09 - \$0.04) \times 60 = \$3.00$$

And when the company offers all the following minutes at 6 cents per minute, the customer will buy 60 minutes more, because, according to the demand curve, the quantity demanded at 6 cents per minute is

$$Q = 400 - 20 \times 0.06$$
$$Q = 280$$

Again, the customer will take the deal because of an additional consumer surplus from minutes 221 – 280 (area E). And the company earns an additional producer surplus equal to the area of rectangle F:

$$\text{Area } F = (\$0.06 - \$0.04) \times 60 = \$1.20$$

Thus, with this pricing plan, the company's total producer surplus is area $(B + D + F)$:

$$PS = \$12.80 + \$3.00 + \$1.20 = \$17.00$$

Since this block pricing allows the company to earn a greater producer surplus ($17 compared with $12.80 when charging a single profit-maximizing price), it is a better strategy than a single price.

c. The company should charge the per-minute price that is equal to its marginal cost, 4 cents per minute. This will allow it to sell all the minutes for which customers are willing to pay a price above the marginal cost, increasing the number of minutes sold to

$$Q = 400 - 20 \times 0.04$$
$$Q = 320$$

If that was the only price that consumers pay for the service, the company's producer surplus would be zero, and the consumer surplus would be the entire area below the demand curve and above the marginal cost (area $A + B + C$ on the following graph). Since this consumer surplus represents the willingness of the consumers to pay above the per-minute price, the firm can charge a consumer a fixed monthly fee equal to (area $A + B + C$), in addition to that price, and the consumer will still buy 320 minutes. So the company should charge a fixed fee of

$$(\text{Area } A + B + C) = 0.5 \times (\$0.20 - \$0.04) \times 320 = \$25.60 \text{ per month}$$

in addition to the price of $0.04 per minute. That is, by using this two-part tariff, the firm will capture the entire surplus in the market for itself. Since this producer surplus ($25.60) is greater than the company's producer surplus with the block pricing ($17.00), you should advise the company to use the two-part tariff.

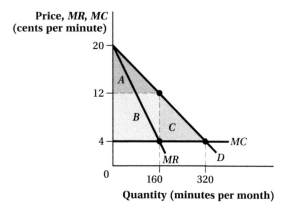

d. For a block-pricing structure with two different prices, we will first decompose total revenue from each price tier. Total revenue from the high-price tier is

$$TR_1 = TR(P_1) = P_1 \times Q(P_1) = P_1(400 - 20P_1) = 400P_1 - 20P_1^2$$

Excess demand for output at the lower-price tier is

$$Q_2 = 400 - 20P_2 - Q_1(P_1)$$
$$Q_2 = 400 - 20P_2 - (400 - 20P_1)$$
$$Q_2 = 20P_1 - 20P_2$$

Total revenue from this lower-price tier is

$$TR_2 = P_2 \times Q(P_2) = P_2(20P_1 - 20P_2) = 20P_1P_2 - 20P_2^2$$

The phone company's combined total revenue function is

$$TR = 400P_1 - 20P_1^2 + 20P_1P_2 - 20P_2^2$$

The phone company's total production cost for output associated with tier-one pricing is

$$TC_1 = \int_0^{400-20P_1} 4dQ = [4Q]_0^{400-20P_1}$$
$$= 4(400 - 20P_1) - 4(0) = 1{,}600 - 80P_1$$

The phone company's total production cost for output associated with tier-two pricing is

$$TC_2 = \int_{400-20P_1}^{400-20P_1+20P_1-20P_2} 4dQ = \int_{400-20P_1}^{400-20P_2} = [4Q]_{400-20P_1}^{400-20P_2}$$
$$= 4(400 - 20P_2) - 4(400 - 20P_1)$$
$$= 1{,}600 - 80P_2 - 1{,}600 + 80P_1$$
$$= 80P_1 - 80P_2$$

The company's total production cost for producing output across both pricing blocks is

$$TC = 1{,}600 - 80P_1 + 80P_1 - 80P_2$$
$$= 1{,}600 - 80P_2$$

The block-pricing monopoly producer surplus is

$$PS = TR - TC = 400P_1 - 20P_1^2 + 20P_1P_2 - 20P_2^2 - 1{,}600 + 80P_2$$

The company's objective is to choose P_1 and P_2, which maximizes PS. The relevant system of first-order conditions is

$$0 = \frac{\partial PS}{\partial P_1} = 400 - 40P_1 + 20P_2$$

$$0 = \frac{\partial PS}{\partial P_2} = 20P_1 - 40P_2 + 80$$

Using the first of these first-order conditions, we may solve for P_1. This produces

$$P_1 = 10 + 0.5P_2$$

Inserting the right-hand side of this statement for P_1 into the second of the first-order conditions and solving for P_2, we have

$$0 = 20(10 + 0.5P_2) - 40P_2 + 80$$
$$0 = 200 + 10P_2 - 40P_2 + 80$$
$$30P_2 = 280$$
$$P_2 \approx 9.33$$

Thus,

$$P_1 = 10 + 0.5(9.33) \approx 14.67$$

The corresponding block-one output is $Q_1 = 400 - 20P_1 = 400 - 20(14.67) = 106.6$. The block-two output is $Q_2 = 400 - 20P_2 - Q_1(P_1) = 400 - 20(9.33) - 106.6 = 106.8$.

e. Producer surplus is

$$PS = 400P_1 - 20P_1^2 + 20P_1P_2 - 20P_2^2 - 1{,}600 + 80P_2$$
$$= 400(14.67) - 20(14.67)^2 + 20(14.67)(9.33) - 20(9.33)^2 - 1{,}600 + 80(9.33)$$
$$\approx 1{,}706.67$$

The inverse demand curve is $P = 20 - 0.05Q$. Consumer surplus then is

$$CS = \int_0^{106.6}(20 - 0.05Q - 14.67)dQ + \int_{106.6}^{106.6+106.8}(20 - 0.05Q - 9.33)dQ$$

$$= \int_0^{106.6}(5.33 - 0.05Q)dQ + \int_{106.6}^{213.4}(10.67 - 0.05Q)dQ$$

$$= [5.33Q]_0^{106.6} - \left[\frac{0.05Q^2}{2}\right]_0^{106.6} + [10.67Q]_{106.6}^{213.4} - \left[\frac{0.05Q^2}{2}\right]_{106.6}^{213.4}$$

$$= [5.33Q]_0^{106.6} - [0.025Q^2]_0^{106.6} + [10.67Q]_{106.6}^{213.4} - [0.025Q^2]_{106.6}^{213.4}$$

$$= [5.33(106.6) - 5.33(0)] - [0.025(106.6)^2 - 0.025(0)^2] + [10.67(213.4) - 10.67(106.6)]$$

$$- [0.025(213.4)^2 - 0.025(106.6)^2]$$

$$= (568.18 - 0) - (284.09 - 0) + (2{,}276.98 - 1{,}137.42) - (1{,}138.49 - 284.09)$$

$$= 569.25$$

Total surplus in the market with block pricing (with two pricing tiers) is $1,706.67 + 569.25 = $2,275.92.

Practice Problems

Problem 1

The following graph shows the demand curve for airplane tickets (D) faced by an airline and the company's single-price marginal revenue curve (MR). The company's marginal cost is constant at $80 per ticket.

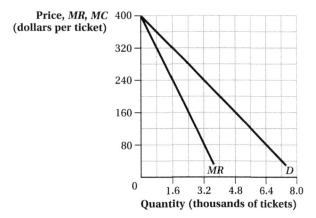

a. If the airline cannot price-discriminate, how much should it charge per ticket to maximize its profit?
b. If the airline sells all tickets at the same price, maximizing its profit, what is its customers' consumer surplus? What is the company's producer surplus? What is the deadweight loss resulting from the airline's market power?
c. If the airline has the ability to practice perfect price discrimination, how many tickets will it sell? What will be the consumer and producer surpluses? What will be the deadweight loss?

Problem 2

Suppose you manage two ice cream parlors: one in a city where there are several competing ice cream shops and another in a small town, where there is less competition among shops. In the city, your customer's price elasticity of demand is −4, while in the small town it is −2. In both locations, the marginal cost of your ice cream is constant at $1.50 per scoop.
a. How much should you charge per scoop in each location?
b. Why are your profit-maximizing prices different in the two locations?

Problem 3

Suppose PC Tools develops a new version of its Antivirus software and offers it both as a full version and as an upgrade from previous versions. The company estimates that the demand curve for the full version is

$$Q_F = 400 - 10P$$

and the demand curve for the upgrade is

$$Q_U = 320 - 20P$$

The marginal cost of the full version of the software is the same as that of the upgrade, constant at $4 per copy (since it's the same software, only the user licenses are different).

What price should PC Tools charge for the full version? For the upgrade? Explain your answers.

Problem 4

Suppose your friend owns a barbershop and asks you whether a discount to students will help him increase profit. You estimate that the price elasticity of demand for haircuts faced by the barbershop is −3 for students and −2 for all other customers. The barbershop's marginal cost of a haircut is the same, whatever type of customer it serves. Should the barbershop give a discount to students? If so, how big (in percentage terms) should the discount be?

Problem 5

Suppose that a concert hall faces the following demand curve for its evening shows:

$$Q_E = 40 - 0.8P$$

And the demand curve for its afternoon shows is

$$Q_A = 24 - 0.8P$$

where Q is the number of tickets in thousands and P is the price of a ticket in dollars. Assume that the concert hall's marginal cost is constant at $10 per ticket.

a. Suppose the concert hall charges the same price for all shows. What is its profit-maximizing price? How many tickets is sold at this price? What is the concert hall's producer surplus?

b. Now suppose the concert hall decides to charge more for evening shows than for afternoon shows. To maximize its profit, what price should the concert hall charge for evening shows? For afternoon shows? How will the concert hall's producer surplus change as a result of this pricing strategy?

Problem 6

Adobe offers two versions of its photo editing software: (1) Photoshop, which is the full-featured version designed for professional photographers and graphic designers, and (2) Photoshop Elements, a consumer-grade version of the program, which has only basic features and editing tools. Suppose that Adobe prices Photoshop at $200 per copy and Photoshop Elements at $80 per copy. Adobe's marginal cost is constant at $10, the same for both products. Suppose further half of Adobe's customers are amateur photographers and the other half are professionals. Each group's willingness to pay for each version of the software is shown in the following table.

	Willingness to pay ($)	
	Photoshop	**Photoshop Elements**
Amateurs	$220	$120
Professionals	$300	$140

a. Is the Adobe's pricing scheme incentive compatible? Explain your answer.

b. Suppose that Adobe sells 1 million copies of its software (one per customer). What is the company's producer surplus?

c. Suppose that Adobe raises the price of the full version of Photoshop to $250. Will this increase the company's producer surplus? Explain.

d. Now suppose that Adobe does not change the prices but upgrades Elements, so the professionals are willing to pay $50 more for it, while to the amateurs the upgrade does not matter. Will Adobe's producer surplus increase as a result of this? Explain.

Problem 7

Suppose Netflix's representative customer's demand curve in the market for DVD rentals is

$$Q = 20 - 10P$$

where Q is the number of DVDs rented per month and P is in dollars per DVD. The company's marginal cost of providing the service is constant at $0.40 per DVD. Assume that Netflix can prevent resale and sharing.

a. If Netflix charges a single price per DVD regardless of how many DVDs a customer rents, what will be its profit-maximizing price? Producer surplus?

b. Suppose that instead of a single price, the company is offering the following plans: (1) $9.60 for 8 DVDs per month and (2) $14.40 for 16 DVDs per month. Will this pricing strategy allow Netflix to increase its producer surplus? Explain your answer.

c. Suppose that Netflix decides instead to establish block pricing, with two different prices for rentals. Use calculus to identify the two prices the company will use to maximize producer surplus.

d. Suppose that Netflix establishes block pricing, with two different prices for rentals and maximizes producer surplus. Use calculus to identify consumer surplus, producer surplus, and total surplus.

Problem 8

Suppose a restaurant owner is considering giving a discount to senior citizens and hires you to help him determine how big the discount should be. You estimate that senior citizens' price elasticity of demand for the restaurant's meals is −4, while other customers' price elasticity of demand is −2. The restaurant's marginal cost of serving seniors is 50% higher than that of serving other customers. Should the restaurant give a discount to senior citizens? If so, how big (in percentage terms) should the discount be?

Problem 9

Suppose a golf club wants to create a pricing scheme with a fixed annual membership fee and a charge per round of golf. Each of the club members is estimated to have the following demand curve:

$$Q = 55 - 0.5P$$

where Q is the number of rounds of golf per year and P is the price in dollars per round. The club can provide rounds of golf at a constant marginal cost of $60 per round.

a. What monthly fee and what per-round price should the golf club charge? Explain your answer.

b. Suppose that the golf course decides instead to establish block pricing, with two different prices for rounds of golf. For this case, use calculus to identify the two prices the company will use to maximize producer surplus.

c. Suppose that the golf course establishes block pricing, with two different prices for golf rounds and maximizes producer surplus. Use calculus to identify consumer surplus, producer surplus, and total surplus.

Problem 10

Suppose Amazon faces two different types of consumer in the market for its music downloads. The first type (Type A) are music fans who download a lot of music and shop across different online download services in search of lower prices. Each of these customers is estimated to have the following demand curve for music downloads offered by Amazon:

$$Q_A = 200 - 200P$$

The second type (Type B) are customers who buy books from Amazon but are less interested in downloading music and searching for alternative music download services. Each of these customers is estimated to have the following demand curve:

$$Q_B = 90 - 50P$$

The price is in dollars per download, and the quantity is the number of downloads per month. Amazon's marginal cost is constant at $0.40 per download. The company cannot tell which demand curve represents which customer before purchase. Assume that Amazon has a fixed number of customers, with equal numbers of customers in each group. Also assume that Amazon can prevent sharing and resale of the downloaded music files.

a. If Amazon charges a single price, what price will maximize its profit? What will be Amazon's producer surplus (per customer)?

b. Now suppose that Amazon charges $1.10 per download if a customer buys less than 100 downloads per month and $0.70 per download if she buys 100 or more downloads per month. Is this pricing plan incentive compatible? Explain your answer.

c. Should Amazon charge a single price or should it use the price scheme in (b)? Explain your answer.

∂ Problem 11

Suppose that demand for olives by local Italian restaurants is given by $Q = 540 - 0.4P$, where P is cents per pound and olives are purchased from a local grocer.

a. Suppose that the local grocer charges only one price for olives irrespective of the number of pounds purchased. Use calculus to identify the price per pound that would maximize revenue for the grocer.

b. Suppose that the grocer adopts two-tier block pricing, Use calculus to identify the two-tier pricing that maximizes revenue for the grocer.

Imperfect Competition

11

11.1 What Does Equilibrium Mean in an Oligopoly?

Imperfect competition

Market structures with characteristics between those of perfect competition and monopoly.

Oligopoly

Competition between a small number of firms.

Monopolistic competition

A type of imperfect competition with a large number of firms in which each firm has some market power but makes zero economic profit in the long run.

Nash equilibrium

An equilibrium in which each firm is doing the best it can conditional on the actions taken by its competitors.

Prisoner's dilemma

A situation in which the Nash equilibrium outcome is worse for all involved than another (unstable) outcome.

11.2 Oligopoly with Identical Goods: Collusion and Cartels

Cartel or collusion

Oligopoly behavior in which firms coordinate and collectively act as a monopoly to gain monopoly profits.

11.2 figure it out 1

Problem 1

Suppose that Speedway and Gas Mart are the only two gas stations in a small, isolated town. The inverse market demand curve for gas is

$$P = 6.5 - 0.5Q$$

where Q is in thousands of gallons and P is in dollars per gallon. Assume that gasoline can be supplied by either station at a constant marginal cost of $2.50 per gallon, there are no fixed costs, and there are no taxes.

a. If the two gas stations collude and agree to evenly split the market, how much gas will each gas station supply and what will be the price of gas? How much profit will each gas station earn?

b. Does Speedway have an incentive to cheat on this agreement by selling an additional thousand gallons of gas? Explain your answer.

c. If Speedway decides to cheat and sell an additional thousand gallons of gas, how will Gas Mart's profit be affected? Explain.

d. Suppose the agreement allows the gas stations to exceed the sales quotas defined in (a) but by no more than 1,000 gallons. How much profit will each station earn? Do the gas stations have an incentive to cheat on this agreement by selling another thousand gallons of gas (i.e. exceeding the quotas defined in [a] by 2,000 gallons)? Explain.

e. Use calculus to redo (a) by solving for marginal revenue directly from the revenue function that is relevant to the collusion, and confirm that your answers are the same.

Solution

a. If the gas stations collude, they will act as a monopoly and choose to supply the quantity of gas that maximizes their combined profits by equating the cartel's marginal revenue to the marginal cost. We know that the marginal revenue curve is the inverse demand curve, with the coefficient on quantity twice as large, so the marginal revenue curve is

$$MR = 6.5 - Q$$

Now we can set $MR = MC$ to solve for the profit-maximizing output:

$$6.5 - Q = 2.5$$
$$Q = 4$$

Thus, the cartel will supply 4,000 gallons of gas, so each gas station will supply $\frac{4,000}{2} = 2,000$ gallons. To find the price that the gas stations will charge, we substitute the quantity supplied by the two gas stations ($Q = 4$) into the inverse demand curve:

$$P = 6.5 - 0.5 \times 4 = 4.5$$

Thus, if the two gas stations follow the agreement, they will charge \$4.50 per gallon, with each making a profit of \$4.50 − \$2.50 = \$2.00 per gallon and a total profit of \$2.00 × 2,000 = \$4,000.

b. If Speedway sells an additional thousand gallons of gas, the market quantity will increase to 5,000 gallons, so the price of gas will be

$$P = 6.5 - 0.5 \times 5 = 4 \text{ (dollars per gallon)}$$

Since the gas stations' marginal cost is constant and there is no fixed cost, $ATC = MC = \$2.50$. So Speedway's profit will be $\pi = (P - ATC) \times Q = (\$4.00 - \$2.50) \times 3,000 = \$4,500$. Since selling an additional thousand gallons of gas increases Speedway's profit from \$4,000 to \$4,500, it does have an incentive to cheat on the agreement.

c. With the market price of \$4.00 per gallon and Gas Mart's 2,000 gallon supply, Gas Mart's profit will be (\$4.00 − \$2.50) × 2,000 gallons = \$3,000. Thus, if Speedway cheats on the cartel agreement and sells an additional thousand gallons of gas, Gas Mart's profit will fall from \$4,000 to \$3,000.

d. As follows from (b), each gas station has an incentive to increase its sales of gas from 2,000 to 3,000 gallons, so each station will sell 3,000 gallons and together they will sell 6,000 gallons. As a result, the price of gas will be

$$P = 6.5 - 0.5 \times 6 = 3.5 \text{ (dollars per gallon)}$$

and each gas station's profit will be (\$3.50 − \$2.50) × 3,000 = \$3,000. (Note, however, that if the agreement allows the gas stations to exceed the sales quotas defined in (a), then neither each station's profit nor the cartel's total profit will be maximized.)

  Now, if one of the gas stations cheats and sells another thousand gallons of gas, the market quantity will increase to 7,000 gallons, so the price of gas will be

$$P = 6.5 - 0.5 \times 7 = 3 \text{ (dollars per gallon)}$$

The cheater's profit will be (\$3.00 − \$2.50) × 4,000 = \$2,000. That is, selling an additional thousand gallons of gas would decrease the cheater's profit from \$3,000 to \$2,000. Therefore, the gas stations do not have an incentive to cheat on this agreement.

e. The collusion's total revenue function is $R(Q) = P(Q) \times Q = (6.5 - 0.5Q) = 6.5Q - 0.5Q^2$. Marginal revenue is $\frac{dR}{dQ} = 6.5 - Q$. Notice that this is the same marginal revenue as noted in (a) and that the rest of the calculations are the same, so $Q = 4$ and $P = \$4.50$ per gallon. Alternately, we could set up the profit function by noting that marginal cost is constant, and there are no fixed costs and therefore $TC = 2.5Q$. With this information, the profit function is $\pi = R(Q) - TC = 6.5Q - 0.5Q^2 - 2.5Q = 4Q - 0.5Q^2$. Maximize this with respect to quantity by taking the derivative with respect to Q and setting it equal to zero to form the collusion's first-order condition. Here, $\frac{d\pi}{dQ} = 4 - Q = 0$, so $Q = 4$ as noted above.

11.3 Oligopoly with Identical Goods: Bertrand Competition

Bertrand competition

Oligopoly model in which each firm chooses the price of its product.

11.4 Oligopoly with Identical Goods: Cournot Competition

Cournot competition

Oligopoly model in which each firm chooses its production quantity.

Residual demand curve

In Cournot competition, the demand remaining for a firm's output given competitor firms' production quantities.

Residual marginal revenue curve

A marginal revenue curve corresponding to a residual demand curve.

Reaction curve

A function that relates a firm's best response to its competitor's possible actions.

11.4 figure it out 1

Suppose there are only two countries in the world that produce natural gas, the United States and Canada. The world's inverse demand curve for natural gas is

$$P = 10 - 0.1Q$$

Where P is the price of natural gas in dollars per 1,000 cubic feet, and Q is the quantity of natural gas in trillions of cubic feet per year. Suppose that the marginal cost of producing natural gas is $2 per 1,000 cubic feet in the United States and $3 per 1,000 cubic feet in Canada. Assume that there is no fixed cost. Assume further that there is only one firm that produces natural gas in each country. Use the Cournot model to analyze the firms' production decisions.

a. Derive and graph each country's reaction curve.
b. If the market is in Cournot equilibrium, how much natural gas does each country produce?
c. In Cournot equilibrium, what is the world price of natural gas?
d. How much profit does each firm earn?
e. Use calculus to solve for the United States and Canada's reaction functions and show that these are the same as in (a).

Solution

a. Let q_{US} be the quantity of natural gas produced in the United States and q_C, the quantity of natural gas produced in Canada. Then, $Q = q_{US} + q_C$. Substituting this expression into the market inverse demand curve, we get:

$$P = 10 - 0.1(q_{US} + q_C)$$
$$P = 10 - 0.1q_{US} - 0.1q_C$$

Because the slope of the marginal revenue curve is twice the slope of the inverse residual demand curve faced by each country, the U.S. firm's marginal revenue curve is

$$MR_{US} = 10 - 0.2q_{US} - 0.1q_C$$

And the Canadian firm's marginal revenue curve is

$$MR_C = 10 - 0.1q_{US} - 0.2q_C$$

Each firm will maximize its profit by setting $MR = MC$, so for the U.S. firm we can write:

$$MR_{US} = MC_{US}$$
$$10 - 0.2q_{US} - 0.1q_C = 2$$

Solving this equation for q_{US}, we get the U.S. firm's reaction curve:

$$0.2q_{US} = 8 - 0.1q_C$$
$$q_{US} = 40 - 0.5q_C$$

And for the Canadian firm:

$$MR_C = MC_C$$
$$10 - 0.1q_{US} - 0.2q_C = 3$$
$$0.2q_C = 7 - 0.1q_{US}$$
$$q_C = 35 - 0.5q_{US}$$

These reaction curves are shown on the following graph.

**Reaction curves: quantities of natural gas
in trillions of cubic feet per year**

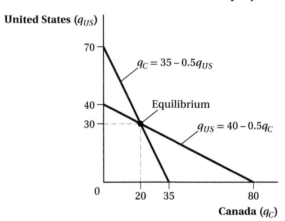

Reaction curve $q_{US} = 40 - 0.5q_C$ shows the U.S. firm's best response to any production choice of the Canadian firm. And reaction curve $q_C = 35 - 0.5q_{US}$ shows the Canadian firm's best response to any production choice of the U.S. firm. These reaction curves reflect the firms' strategic interaction, with each firm's actions affecting the optimal actions of the competitor, which in turn affect its own optimal action, and so on. This is why the equilibrium occurs where the reaction curves intersect, i.e. at the point where both firms are producing their optimal quantity given the other firm's actions.

b. The Cournot equilibrium is where both competitors are simultaneously producing optimally given the other's actions, that is, where the two firms' reaction curves intersect. To solve for this equilibrium, we substitute the Canadian firm's reaction curve into the reaction curve for the U.S. firm and solve the equation for q_{US}:

$$q_{US} = 40 - 0.5q_C$$
$$q_{US} = 40 - 0.5(35 - 0.5q_{US})$$
$$q_{US} = 40 - 17.5 + 0.25q_{US}$$
$$0.75q_{US} = 22.5$$
$$q_{US} = 30$$

Then,

$$q_C = 35 - 0.5 \times 30 = 20$$

Thus, in equilibrium, the United States produces 30 trillion cubic feet of natural gas and Canada produces 20 trillion cubic feet.

c. To find the world market price, we substitute the quantities of natural gas produced in both countries into the inverse market demand curve:

$$P = 10 - 0.1(q_{US} + q_C)$$
$$P = 10 - 0.1(30 + 20)$$
$$P = 5$$

That is, the world price of natural gas is $5 per 1,000 cubic feet.

d. The U.S. firm produces 30 trillion cubic feet and earns $\$5 - \$2 = \$3$ per 1,000 cubic feet, so its total profit is $\dfrac{\$3}{1,000} \times 30$ trillion $= \$90$ billion. The Canadian firm produces 20 trillion cubic feet and earns $\$5 - \$3 = \$2$ per 1,000 cubic feet, so its total profit is $\dfrac{\$2}{1,000} \times 20$ trillion $= \$40$ billion. Note that the firm with the lower marginal cost produces more output and earns a greater profit.

e. The United States' profit function can be written:

$$\pi_{US} = \big(10 - 0.1(q_{US} + q_C)\big)q_{US} - 2q_{US}$$
$$= 10q_{US} - 0.1q_{US}^2 - 0.1q_{US}q_C - 2q_{US}$$
$$= 8q_{US} - 0.1q_{US}^2 - 0.1q_{US}q_C$$

The United States' objective is to maximize π_{US} by choosing q_{US}. Its first-order condition is

$$0 = \frac{\partial \pi_{US}}{\partial q_{US}} = 8 - 0.2q_{US} - 0.1q_C$$

The United States' reaction function then is derived as:

$$0.2q_{US} = 8 - 0.1q_C$$
$$q_{US} = 40 - 0.5q_C$$

Canada's profit function can be written:

$$\pi_C = \big(10 - 0.1(q_{US} + q_C)\big)q_C - 3q_C$$
$$= 10q_C - 0.1q_C^2 - 0.1q_{US}q_C - 3q_C$$
$$= 7q_C - 0.1q_C^2 - 0.1q_{US}q_C$$

Canada's objective is to maximize π_C by choosing q_C. Its first-order condition is

$$0 = \frac{\partial \pi_C}{\partial q_C} = 7 - 0.2q_C - 0.1q_{US}$$

Canada's reaction function then is derived as:

$$0.2q_C = 7 - 0.1q_{US}$$
$$q_C = 35 - 0.5q_{US}$$

Since these reaction curves are the same as in part (a) of the problem, all subsequent analysis is the same and the solution is the same using calculus as using algebraic methods, as in (a–d).

11.5 Oligopoly with Identical Goods: Stackelberg Competition

First-mover advantage

In Stackelberg competition, the advantage gained by the initial firm in setting its production quantity.

Stackelberg competition

Oligopoly model in which firms make production decisions sequentially.

11.5 figure it out 1

Consider again the case in 11.4 figure it out 1, where there are only two countries in the world that produce natural gas, the United States and Canada, and the world's inverse demand curve for natural gas is

$$P = 10 - 0.1Q$$

Where P is the price of natural gas in dollars per 1,000 cubic feet and Q is the quantity of natural gas in trillions of cubic feet per year. Recall that the marginal cost of producing natural gas is $\$2$ per 1,000 cubic feet in the United States and $\$3$ per 1,000 cubic feet in Canada. Assume again that there is no fixed cost and there is only one firm that produces natural gas in each country. Use the Stackelberg oligopoly model to analyze the firms' production decisions.

a. Suppose that the U.S. firm is the first mover. How much does each firm produce? What is the world price of natural gas? How much profit does each firm earn?

b. Now suppose that the Canadian firm is the first mover. How much does each firm produce? What is the world price of natural gas? How much profit does each firm earn?

Solution

a. Given that the U.S. firm is going to move first and it knows from previous experience that the Canadian firm's output is a function of the U.S. firm's output, we can find the demand curve faced by the U.S. firm by substituting the Canadian firm's reaction curve into the market inverse demand curve. As we've found in 11.4 figure it out 1, the Canadian firm's reaction curve is

$$q_C = 35 - 0.5q_{US}$$

and the market demand curve can be expressed as

$$P = 10 - 0.1(q_{US} + q_C)$$
$$P = 10 - 0.1q_{US} - 0.1q_C$$

So we can write:

$$P = 10 - 0.1q_{US} - 0.1(35 - 0.5q_{US})$$
$$P = 10 - 0.1q_{US} - 3.5 + 0.05q_{US}$$
$$P = 6.5 - 0.05q_{US}$$

Because the slope of the U.S. firm's marginal revenue curve is twice the slope of the inverse demand curve it faces, the U.S. firm's marginal revenue curve is

$$MR_{US} = 6.5 - 0.1q_{US}$$

The U.S. firm maximizes its profit by setting $MR_{US} = MC_{US}$, so we can write:

$$6.5 - 0.1q_{US} = 2$$

Solving this equation for q_{US}, we get:

$$0.1q_{US} = 4.5$$
$$q_{US} = 45$$

Now we can find the Canadian firm's output by plugging $q_{US} = 45$ into its reaction curve:

$$q_C = 35 - 0.5 \times 45 = 12.5$$

Thus, the U.S. firm produces 45 trillion cubic feet of natural gas and the Canadian firm produces 12.5 trillion cubic feet.

We can find the market price by substituting these quantities into the world's inverse demand curve:

$$P = 10 - 0.1(q_{US} + q_C)$$
$$P = 10 - 0.1(45 + 12.5)$$
$$P = 4.25$$

That is, the world price of natural gas is $4.25 per 1,000 cubic feet.

Since the U.S. firm produces 45 trillion cubic feet and earns $4.25 - $2 = $2.25 per 1,000 cubic feet, its profit is $\frac{\$2.25}{1,000} \times 45$ trillion = $101.25 billion. The Canadian firm produces 12.5 trillion cubic feet and earns $4.25 - $3 = $1.25 per 1,000 cubic feet, so its profit is $\frac{\$1.25}{1,000} \times 12.5$ trillion = $15.625 billion. Note that the advantage of being the first-mover allows the U.S. firm to increase its profit from $90 billion (see 11.4 figure it out 1) to $101.25 billion, while the Canadian firm's profit falls from $40 billion to $15.625 billion.

b. Now the Canadian firm is moving first and knows from previous experience that the U.S. firm's output is a function of the Canadian firm's output. Therefore, we can find the demand curve faced by the Canadian firm by substituting the U.S. firm's reaction curve into the market inverse demand curve. As we've found in 11.4 figure it out 1, the U.S. firm's reaction curve is

$$q_{US} = 40 - 0.5q_C$$

so we can write:

$$P = 10 - 0.1(40 - 0.5q_C) - 0.1q_C$$
$$P = 10 - 4 + 0.05q_C - 0.1q_C$$
$$P = 6 - 0.05q_C$$

Because the slope of the Canadian firm's marginal revenue curve is twice the slope of the inverse demand curve it faces, the Canadian firm's marginal revenue curve is

$$MR_C = 6 - 0.1q_C$$

The Canadian firm maximizes its profit by setting $MR_C = MC_C$, so we can write:

$$6 - 0.1q_C = 3$$

Solving this equation for q_C, we get:

$$0.1q_C = 3$$
$$q_C = 30$$

Now we can find the U.S. firm's output by plugging $q_C = 30$ into its reaction curve:

$$q_{US} = 40 - 0.5 \times 30 = 25$$

Thus, the Canadian firm produces 30 trillion cubic feet of natural gas and the U.S. firm produces 25 trillion cubic feet.

We can find the market price by substituting these quantities into the world's inverse demand curve:

$$P = 10 - 0.1(q_{US} + q_C)$$
$$P = 10 - 0.1(25 + 30)$$
$$P = 4.5$$

That is, the world price of natural gas is $4.5 per 1,000 cubic feet.

Since the Canadian firm produces 30 trillion cubic feet and earns $4.5 - $3 = $1.5 per 1,000 cubic feet, its profit is $\frac{\$1.5}{1,000} \times 30$ trillion = $45 billion. The U.S. firm produces 25 trillion cubic feet and earns $4.5 - $2 = $2.5 per 1,000 cubic feet, so its profit is $\frac{\$2.5}{1,000} \times 25$ trillion = $62.5 billion. Note that the advantage of being the first-mover allows the Canadian firm to increase its profit from $40 billion (see 11.4 figure it out 1) to $45 billion, while the U.S. firm's profit falls from $90 billion to $62.5 billion.

11.6 Oligopoly with Differentiated Goods: Bertrand Competition

Differentiated product market

Market with multiple varieties of a common product.

11.6 figure it out 1

Suppose there are only two producers of desktop PCs of a certain class, Dell and Hewlett Packard (HP). Since consumers view their products as similar but not identical, the firms face different demand curves. The demand curve faced by Dell is

$$q_D = 130 - 0.125p_D + 0.05p_H$$

and the demand curve faced by HP is

$$q_H = 120 - 0.12p_H + 0.06p_D$$

where q_D and q_H are the quantities of Dell and HP computers, respectively, in thousands, and p_D and p_H are the prices that Dell and HP charge, respectively, in dollars. Assume, for simplicity, that the marginal cost is zero for both firms. Use the Bertrand model to analyze the firms' decisions.
a. Derive and graph each firm's reaction curve.
b. What is each firm's profit-maximizing price?

c. What is each firm's profit-maximizing output?

@ d. Use calculus to solve for Dell and Hewlett Packard's price reaction functions, and show that these are the same as in (a).

Solution

a. To derive the reaction curves we need to know each firm's marginal revenue curve expressed as a function of price. We can find these marginal revenue curves from the demand curves using the same rule as we used to find the marginal revenue curve as a function of quantity from an inverse demand curve. That is, if the demand curve is

$$Q = a - bP$$

then the marginal revenue curve is

$$MR = a - 2bP$$

In the demand curve faced by Dell, $a = 130 + 0.05p_H$ and $b = 0.125$. Thus, Dell's marginal revenue curve as a function of price can be written as

$$MR_D = (130 + 0.05p_H) - 2 \times 0.125p_D$$

or, rearranging the terms,

$$MR_D = 130 - 0.25p_D + 0.05p_H$$

Now we can derive Dell's reaction curve by setting $MR_D = MC_D = 0$ and solving this equation for p_D:

$$130 - 0.25p_D + 0.05p_H = 0$$
$$0.25p_D = 130 + 0.05p_H$$
$$p_D = 520 + 0.2p_H$$

Similarly, given the demand curve faced by HP, its marginal revenue curve as a function of price is

$$MR_H = 120 - 0.24p_H + 0.06p_D$$

And we can derive HP's reaction curve by setting $MR_H = MC_H = 0$ and solving this equation for p_H:

$$120 - 0.24p_H + 0.06p_D = 0$$
$$0.24p_H = 120 + 0.06p_D$$
$$p_H = 500 + 0.25p_D$$

These reaction curves are shown on the following graph.

Reaction curves: prices in dollars

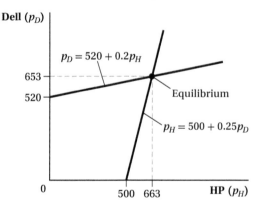

b. We can solve for Dell's equilibrium price by substituting HP's reaction curve into Dell's reaction curve:

$$p_D = 520 + 0.2p_H$$
$$p_D = 520 + 0.2(500 + 0.25p_D)$$
$$p_D = 520 + 100 + 0.05p_D$$
$$0.95p_D = 620$$
$$p_D = 652.63$$

And to find HP's equilibrium price we substitute $p_D = 652.63$ into HP's reaction curve:

$$p_H = 500 + 0.25 \times 652.63 = 663.16$$

Thus, Dell's optimal price is \$652.63 and HP's optimal price is \$663.16. (Note that the results would be the same if we first solved for HP's equilibrium price by substituting Dell's reaction curve into HP's reaction curve and then substituted that price into Dell's reaction curve to find Dell's optimal price.)

c. We can find each firm's profit-maximizing output by plugging the prices found in the preceding into the demand curves faced by each firm. For Dell:

$$q_D = 130 - 0.125p_D + 0.05p_H$$
$$q_D = 130 - 0.125 \times 652.63 + 0.05 \times 663.16$$
$$q_D = 81.58$$

And for HP:

$$q_H = 120 - 0.12p_H + 0.06p_D$$
$$q_H = 120 - 0.12 \times 663.16 + 0.06 \times 652.63$$
$$q_H = 79.58$$

Thus, Dell's optimal output is 81,580 computers, and HP's optimal output is 79,580 computers.

d. Dell's profit function can be written (which is equivalent to its revenue function, since marginal cost is assumed to be zero):

$$\pi_D = (130 - 0.125p_D + 0.05p_H)p_D$$
$$= 130p_D - 0.125p_D^2 + 0.05p_D p_H$$

Dell's objective is to maximize π_D by choosing p_D. The firm's first-order condition is

$$0 = \frac{\partial \pi_D}{\partial p_D} = 130 - 0.25p_D + 0.05p_H$$

Dell's reaction function then is derived as:

$$0.25p_D = 130 + 0.05p_H$$
$$p_D = 520 + 0.2p_H$$

Hewlett-Packard's profit function can be written (which also is equivalent to its revenue function, since marginal cost is assumed to be zero):

$$\pi_H = (120 - 0.12p_H + 0.06p_D)p_H$$
$$= 120p_H - 0.12p_H^2 + 0.06p_D p_H$$

Hewlett-Packard's objective is to maximize π_H by choosing p_H. The firm's first-order condition is

$$0 = \frac{\partial \pi_H}{\partial p_H} = 120 - 0.24p_H + 0.06p_D$$

Hewlett-Packard's reaction function then is derived as:

$$0.24p_H = 120 + 0.06p_D$$
$$p_H = 500 + 0.25p_D$$

Since these reaction curves are the same as in part (a) of the problem, all subsequent analyses are the same and the final solution is using calculus as using algebraic methods as in the text.

∂ 11.6 figure it out 2

The inverse demand for bubble bath is given by $P = 15 - 0.02Q$, where P is the price per bottle in dollars and Q is the total number of bottles brought to market in hundreds. There are two bubble bath manufacturers operating in the local market. Firm 1's cost function is given by $C_1 = 0.005q_1^2$, where q_1 is the number of bottles of bubble bath brought to market by firm 1. Firm 2's cost function is given by $C_2 = 0.005q_2^2$, where q_2 is the number of bottles of bubble bath brought to market by firm 2. The two firms are Cournot competitors that compete by setting output so that $Q = q_1 + q_2$.

a. Write firm 1's profit function and identify firm 1's reaction function to firm 2's output, using calculus.
b. Write firm 2's profit function and identify firm 2's reaction function to firm 1's output, using calculus.
c. Identify the equilibrium output level of each firm and the equilibrium price for bubble bath.

Solution

a. Firm 1's profit function is its total revenue minus costs. Total revenue for firm 1 is $P(q_1, q_2) \times q_1 = \left(15 - 0.02(q_1 + q_2)q_1\right)$. Profit then is $\pi_1 = \left(15 - 0.02(q_1 + q_2)\right)q_1 - 0.005q_1^2$. Firm 1's profit-maximizing condition is: $0 = \dfrac{d\pi_1}{dq_1} = 15 - 0.04q_1 - 0.02q_2 - 0.01q_1$, or $0 = 15 - 0.05q_1 - 0.02q_2$. Solving for q_1, we have: $q_1 = 300 - 0.4q_2$. This is firm 1's profit-maximizing response to firm 2's choice of output.

b. Similarly, firm 2's profit function is $\pi_2 = \left(15 - 0.02(q_1 + q_2)\right)q_2 - 0.005q_2^2$. Firm 2's profit-maximizing condition is: $0 = \dfrac{d\pi_2}{dq_2} = 15 - 0.04q_2 - 0.02q_1 - 0.01q_2$. Solving for q_2, we have: $q_2 = 300 - 0.4q_1$. This is firm 2's profit-maximizing response to firm 1's choice of output.

c. By substituting firm 2's reaction function into firm 1's reaction function, we have: $q_1 = 300 - 0.4(300 - 0.4q_1)$. Simplifying this we identify: $q_1 = 180 + 0.16q_1$. Thus, solving for q_1, we see that $q_1 \approx 214.29$. By symmetry, $q_2 \approx 214.29$. Therefore, each manufacturer brings approximately 21,429 bottles of bubble bath to the market. The market price per bottle is then $P = 15 - 0.02(214.29 + 214.29) \approx \$6.43$.

11.7 Monopolistic Competition

Monopolistic competition

A market structure characterized by many firms selling a differentiated product with no barriers to entry.

make the grade

Which model to use when analyzing imperfect competition?

With so many different imperfect competition models it is easy to get confused trying to figure out which model to use in which situation. The following summary of models used to analyze firms' decisions under imperfect competition—with references to the sections in the text where they are covered—provides a concise guide to each model's assumptions and situations in which this model is most appropriate to apply.

Collusion and cartels (Section 11.2)

Assumptions
- Firms sell identical products.
- Firms agree to coordinate their quantity and pricing decisions, and no firm deviates from the agreement, even if breaking it is in the firm's best self-interest.

Decisions and outcomes
Firms coordinate their production decisions and act collectively as a monopoly. The resulting market quantity and price are equal to those of a monopoly, and industry profit is maximized. While collusive behavior allows firms to capture monopoly profits, collusion and cartels are rarely stable because each firm has the incentive to increase its own profit by producing more (pricing lower).

Bertrand competition with identical goods (Section 11.3)

Assumptions
- Firms sell identical products.
- Firms compete by choosing the price at which they sell their products.
- Firms set their prices simultaneously.

Decisions and outcomes
Firms compete on price. Each firm simultaneously sets the price of its good, and consumers then choose to purchase all of the quantity demanded from whichever firm has the lowest price, even if the price is only one penny lower. This model shows that only two firms need to be in a market to achieve the perfectly competitive market outcome where price equals marginal cost. This is because firms in these situations have a strong incentive to try to undercut the prices of their rivals. Market output is equal to the competitive level of output and firm economic profits are zero.

Cournot competition (Section 11.4)

Assumptions
- Firms sell identical products.
- Firms compete by choosing a quantity to produce.

- All goods sell for the same price, which is determined by the sum of the quantities produced by all the firms in the market.
- Firms choose quantities simultaneously.

Decisions and outcomes

In contrast to firms in Bertrand competition, firms in Cournot competition simultaneously choose the quantity of a good to produce, and not the price at which the good sells. The Cournot equilibrium price is generally above the price in Bertrand competition, but below the monopoly price. The Cournot output is less than the Bertrand level of output, but greater than the output generated by a cartel. Firms in a Cournot oligopoly earn greater profits than those in the Bertrand model, but less than the monopoly profit.

∂ The Cournot model can be solved using either algebra or calculus (see the online appendix for Chapter 11), and the calculus methods can be used in a wider variety of circumstances than can algebra alone (e.g., nonlinear demands and/or total costs).

Stackelberg competition (Section 11.5)

Assumptions

- Firms sell identical products.
- Firms compete by choosing a quantity to produce.
- All goods sell for the same price, which is determined by the sum of the quantities produced by all the firms in the market.
- Firms do not choose quantities simultaneously. One firm chooses its quantity first. The next firm observes this and then chooses its quantity.

Decisions and outcomes

Firms make production decisions sequentially. Because the first firm in an industry can make production decisions independently of other firms and may be able to capture larger profits, a first-mover advantage exists for these firms.

Bertrand competition with differentiated goods (Section 11.6)

Assumptions

- Firms sell differentiated products.
- Each firm chooses the price at which it sells its product.
- Firms set prices simultaneously.

Decisions and outcomes

Consumers in these markets are willing to substitute across goods, but do not consider them identical, or perfect substitutes. As a result, small differences in prices do not lead to all demand being satisfied by the producer with the lowest price (as in the Bertrand oligopoly with identical products).

∂ The differentiated Bertrand model can be solved using either algebra or calculus (see the online appendix for Chapter 11), and the calculus methods can be used in a wider variety of circumstances than can algebra alone (e.g., nonlinear demands and/or total costs).

Monopolistic competition (Section 11.7)

Assumptions

- Firms sell differentiated products that consumers do not view as perfect substitutes.
- Other firms' choices affect a firm's residual demand curve, but the firm ignores any strategic interactions between its own quantity or price choice and its competitors'.
- There is free entry into the market.

Decisions and outcomes

Firms have some characteristics of both monopolies and perfectly competitive firms. Because there are no barriers to entry, economic profit is driven to zero through the entry of firms.

11.7 figure it out 1

Jim Cat is a firm that produces mouse traps. The demand curve it faces in a monopolistically competitive market is

$$Q = 60 - 10P$$

where Q is the quantity of mouse traps produced in thousands per year and P is the price of a mouse trap in dollars. The firm's marginal cost of a mouse trap is constant at \$3. The market for mouse traps is in long-run equilibrium.

a. How many mouse traps is Jim Cat producing per year?
b. What price does the firm charge per mouse trap?
c. What is the firm's fixed cost?
∂ d. Redo parts (a) and (b) using calculus, and confirm that your answers are the same.

Solution

a. Given that the market for mouse traps is in equilibrium, we know that Jim Cat is maximizing its profit. This means the firm's marginal revenue equals its marginal cost. Thus, to find how many mousetraps Jim Cat is producing, we should set $MR = MC$ and solve this equation for Q. To find the firm's MR curve, we first derive its inverse demand curve by solving the demand equation for P:

$$Q = 60 - 10P$$
$$10P = 60 - Q$$
$$P = 6 - 0.1Q$$

We know that the marginal revenue curve is the inverse demand curve with the coefficient on quantity twice as large, so the firm's marginal revenue curve is

$$MR = 6 - 0.2Q$$

Thus, we can write:

$$MR = MC$$
$$6 - 0.2Q = 3$$

And solving this equation for Q, we get:

$$0.2Q = 3$$
$$Q = 15$$

Thus, Jim Cat is producing 15,000 mouse traps per year.

b. We can find the price that the firm charges by substituting the quantity of mouse traps produced into the inverse demand curve:

$$P = 6 - 0.1 \times 15 = 4.5$$

Thus, Jim Cat charges $4.50 per mouse trap.

c. When a monopolistically competitive market is in long-run equilibrium, the firms in the market are making zero economic profits. This means Jim Cat's total revenue equals its total cost. Thus, we know that the firm's total cost is

$$TC = TR = P \times Q = \$4.50 \times 15,000 = \$67,500$$

Now, recall that $TC = FC + VC$, from which $FC = TC - VC$. Since Jim Cat's marginal cost is constant, it equals average variable cost: $MC = AVC = \$3$. And since $AVC = \dfrac{VC}{Q}$, we can find the firms variable cost as $VC = AVC \times Q = \$3 \times 15,000 = \$45,000$. So Jim Cat's fixed cost is

$$FC = \$67,500 - \$45,000 = \$22,500$$

d. Jim Cat's total revenue function is $R(Q) = P(Q) \times Q = (6 - 0.1Q)Q = 6Q - 0.1Q^2$. Marginal revenue is $\dfrac{dR}{dQ} = 6 - 0.2Q$. Notice that this is the same marginal revenue as noted in (a). Marginal cost is $\dfrac{dTC}{dQ} = 3$, so we know that total cost is $TC = 3Q + FC$. Since the calculations based on marginal revenue and marginal cost are the same, $Q = 15$ (15,000 traps) and $P = \$4.50$, as in parts (a) and (b). Alternately, we could set up the profit function using fixed cost as found in part (c): $\pi = R(Q) - TC = 6Q - 0.1Q^2 - 3Q - 22,500 = 3Q - 0.1Q^2 - 22,500$. We can then maximize this with respect to quantity by taking the derivative with respect to Q and setting it equal to zero to form Jim Cat's first-order condition. Here, $\dfrac{d\pi}{dQ} = 3 - 0.2Q = 0$, so $Q = 15$ (15,000 traps), as noted in the preceding, and price follows.

Practice Problems

Problem 1

Suppose that there are four gas stations in a small, isolated town. The inverse market demand curve for their gasoline is

$$P = 6 - 0.5Q$$

Where Q is in thousands of gallons and P is in dollars per gallon. Each station can supply any quantity of gasoline at a constant marginal cost of \$2 per gallon, with no fixed cost and no taxes. All gas stations sell the same regular gas, and the differences in location, service, and so forth don't matter to consumers.

a. If the gas stations compete in a free market, how much gas will each station supply? What will be the price of gas? How much profit will each gas station earn?

b. If the four gas stations collude and agree to evenly split the market, how much gas will each gas station supply and what will be the price of gas? How much profit will each gas station earn?

c. Is the agreement in (b) likely to be stable? To explain and justify your answer, suppose one of the gas stations cheats and sells a thousand gallons of gas more than its quota set by the agreement. What will happen to the cheater's profit? What will happen to the other gas stations' profits?

d. Redo (b), using calculus by solving for marginal revenue directly from the revenue function that is relevant to the collusion, and confirm that your answers are the same.

Problem 2

Suppose there are only two electricity suppliers in a city, Blue Line and Red Power. The city's inverse demand curve for electricity is

$$P = 8 - 0.05Q$$

where P is the price of electricity in cents per kilowatt-hour (kWh) and Q is the quantity of electricity in millions of kilowatt-hours. Blue Line's marginal cost of producing electricity is 4 cents per kWh, and Red Power's marginal cost is 5 cents per kWh. Assume, for simplicity, that there is no fixed cost. Both companies face capacity constraints, so there are limits on how much demand they can satisfy.

a. Derive and graph each company's reaction curve.

b. If the market is in equilibrium, how much electricity does each company produce?

c. In equilibrium, what is the market price of electricity?

d. How much profit does each company earn?

e. Use calculus to solve for the company's reaction functions, and show that these are the same as in (a).

Problem 3

Consider again the case in Problem 2, where Blue Line and Red Power are the only two electricity suppliers in a city and the inverse demand curve for electricity is

$$P = 8 - 0.05Q$$

Where P is the price of electricity in cents per kilowatt-hour (kWh) and Q is the quantity of electricity in millions of kilowatt-hours. Recall that Blue Line's marginal cost of producing electricity is 4 cents per kWh, and Red Power's marginal cost is 5 cents per kWh. Assume again that there is no fixed cost and both companies face capacity constraints, so there are limits on how much demand they can satisfy.

a. Suppose that Blue Line is the first mover. How much electricity does each firm produce? What is the market price of electricity? How much profit does each firm earn?

b. Now suppose that Red Power is the first mover. How much electricity does each firm produce? What is the market price of electricity? How much profit does each firm earn?

Problem 4

Suppose there are only two producers of electronic keyboards of a certain class, Roland and Yamaha. Since consumers view their products as similar but not identical, the firms face different demand curves. The demand curve faced by Roland is

$$q_R = 200 - 0.4p_R + 0.2p_Y$$

and the demand curve faced by Yamaha is

$$q_Y = 240 - 0.5p_Y + 0.1p_R$$

where q_R and q_Y are the quantities of Roland and Yamaha keyboards, respectively, in thousands, and p_R and p_Y are the prices of Roland and Yamaha keyboards, respectively, in dollars. Assume, for simplicity, that the marginal cost of producing keyboards is zero for both firms. Use the Bertrand model to analyze the firms' decisions.

a. Derive and graph each firm's reaction curve.
b. What is each firm's profit-maximizing price?
c. What is each firm's profit-maximizing output?
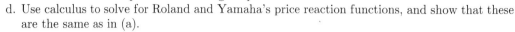 d. Use calculus to solve for Roland and Yamaha's price reaction functions, and show that these are the same as in (a).

Problem 5

Strelkin is a firm that produces cases for smartphones. The demand curve it faces in a monopolistically competitive market is

$$Q = 200 - 10P$$

where Q is the quantity of cases produced in thousands per year and P is the price of a case in dollars. The firm's marginal cost of producing a case is constant at $10. The market for smartphone cases is in long-run equilibrium.

a. How many cases is Strelkin producing per year?
b. What price does the firm charge per case?
c. What is the firm's average total cost of producing a smartphone case?
∂ d. Use calculus to redo (a) and (b), and confirm that your answers are the same.

Problem 6

Suppose there are only two oil producers in the world, Iran and Saudi Arabia. The world's inverse market demand curve for oil is

$$P = 200 - 4Q$$

where Q is in millions of barrels of oil per day and P is in dollars per barrel. Suppose that Saudi Arabia produces oil at a constant marginal cost of $4 per barrel and has a production capacity of 30 million barrels per day. Iran's marginal cost is constant at $12 per barrel, and its production capacity is 16 million barrels per day. For the sake of simplicity, ignore the fixed costs.

a. Suppose the two countries form a cartel and agree to evenly split the market, each producing 12 barrels of oil per day. If both countries follow the agreement, what will be the market price of oil? How much profit will each country earn?
b. Is the cartel in (a) likely to be stable? To justify your answer, suppose Iran cheats and sells one million barrels per day more than its quota set by the agreement. What will happen to Iran's profit? What will happen to Saudi Arabia's profit?
c. Suppose Saudi Arabia argues that since it can produce oil at a lower cost, the cartel's interests are better served if Saudi Arabia alone satisfies all the world's demand for oil. If Saudi Arabia produces all the oil for the cartel and Iran produces no oil, what will happen to the cartel's profit as compared with its profit in (a)?
d. Suppose Saudi Arabia offers Iran $1.15 billion per day in exchange for Iran's agreement not to produce any oil. Will Iran accept this offer? Justify your answer.
e. If Iran accepts Saudi Arabia's offer in (d), will it have an incentive to cheat on this agreement? To answer this question, suppose that Iran signs the agreement but then cheats and produces 1 million barrels of oil per day. If Saudi Arabia still follows the agreement, what will happen to Iran's profit? To Saudi Arabia's profit?

Problem 7

Suppose the cartel in Problem 6 dissolves because cheating has overwhelmed the countries' efforts to maintain an agreement. So now, Iran and Saudi Arabia choose the quantities of oil they supply to the world market separately. Use the information in Problem 6 to analyze each country's production decisions.

a. Derive and graph each country's reaction curve.
b. If the market is in equilibrium, how much oil does each country produce?
c. In equilibrium, what is the world price of oil?

d. How much profit does each country earn?

e. How do the total oil production, the market price of oil, and the total industry profit in this scenario compare with the most profitable cartel outcome in Problem 6?

Problem 8

Let's continue our analysis of the world oil oligopoly in Problems 6 and 7. Suppose again that Iran and Saudi Arabia cannot hold to a cartel agreement, so they make their oil production decisions individually. But now, instead of choosing its production level based on what it believes its competitor might do, each country tries to choose its output level first and force its competitor to react on that move.

a. Suppose that Saudi Arabia moves first. How much oil will each country produce? What will be the market price of oil? How much profit will each country earn? How do these outcomes compare with those in Problem 7?

b. Now suppose that Iran is the first mover. How much oil will each country produce? What will be the market price of oil? How much profit will each country earn? (*Hint:* Recall from Problem 6 that Iran's oil production capacity is limited to 16 million barrels per day.)

Problem 9

Suppose Nature's Path faces the following demand curve in a monopolistically competitive market for organic cereals:

$$Q = 12.5 - 2.5P$$

where Q is the quantity demanded in millions of boxes per year and P is the price in dollars per box. The firm's marginal cost is constant at $2 per box, and its fixed cost is $5 million per year.

a. How many boxes of cereal is Nature's Path producing per year? What price does the firm charge per box?

b. What is Nature's Path's economic profit? Is the market in long-run equilibrium? Explain your answer.

c. Now suppose more firms enter the market for organic cereals, so the demand curve that Nature's Path faces is now

$$Q = 20 - 5P$$

How does the entry of new firms affect the quantity of cereal that Nature's Path produces? How does it affect the price that the firm charges per box and the firm's economic profit? Is the market now in long-run equilibrium? Explain your answer.

Problem 10

Suppose there are only two producers of touch-screen laptop computers, Asus and Toshiba. Since consumers view their products as being similar but not identical, the firms face different demand curves. The demand curve faced by Asus is

$$q_A = 100 - 0.1p_A + 0.05p_T$$

and the demand curve faced by Toshiba is

$$q_T = 90 - 0.08p_T + 0.04p_A$$

where q_A and q_T are the quantities of Asus and Toshiba laptops, respectively, in thousands, and p_A and p_T are the prices of Asus and Toshiba laptops, respectively, in dollars. Suppose that Asus's marginal cost is constant at $100 per laptop, and Toshiba's marginal cost is constant at $80 per laptop. Assume that there is no fixed cost. Use the Bertrand model to analyze the firms' decisions.

a. Derive and graph each firm's reaction curve. (*Hint:* When setting $MR = MC$, express marginal cost as the change in total cost resulting from a $1 change in price: $\frac{\Delta TC}{\Delta P}$.)

b. What is each firm's profit-maximizing price?

c. What is each firm's profit-maximizing output?

Problem 11

Paradise Plaza offers small modern apartments in a local area. Turtle Terrace offers much larger but traditional style apartments in the same area. The two apartment complexes compete in a Bertrand market structure with differentiated products. The demand curve for Paradise Plaza's apartments is given by: $q_P = 900 - p_P + 0.5p_T$, where p_P is the rental price at Paradise Plaza and p_T is the rental price at Turtle Terrace in dollars per month. The demand curve for Turtle Terrace's apartments is given by: $q_T = 1,000 - 0.5p_T + p_P$. Paradise Plaza's cost of providing an apartment is $C_P = 15q_P$ while Turtle Terrace's cost of providing the special is $C_T = 20q_T$.

a. Identify Paradise Plaza's profit function and its reaction function to Turtle Terrace's apartment rental price, using calculus.

b. Identify Turtle Terrace's profit function and its reaction function to Paradise Plaza's apartment rental price, using calculus.

c. Identify the equilibrium prices charged for apartment rentals at Paradise Plaza and at Turtle Terrace.

Game Theory

12.1 What is a Game?

Game theory

The study of strategic interactions among two or more economic actors.

Strategic decision

An action made based on the anticipation of others' actions.

Simultaneous game

A game in which participants choose their actions simultaneously without knowing their opponents' strategies.

Repeated games

A series of simultaneous games among the same set of economic actors.

Sequential game

Economic game in which players take consecutive turns.

Player

A participant in an economic game, who must decide on actions based on the actions of others.

Strategy

The plan of action that a player takes in an economic game.

Payoff

The outcome a player receives from playing the game.

Optimal strategy

The action that has the highest expected payoff.

Dominant strategy

A winning strategy for a player, regardless of her opponents' strategies.

Dominated strategy

A losing strategy for a player, regardless of his opponents' strategies.

Payoff matrix

A table that lists the players, strategies, and payoffs of an economic game.

12.2 Nash Equilibrium in One-Period Games

Nash equilibrium

An equilibrium in which each firm is doing the best it can, conditional on the actions taken by its competitors.

Prisoner's dilemma

A situation in which the Nash equilibrium outcome is worse for all involved than another (unstable) outcome.

Normal form

The common organization of an economic game into its players, strategies, and the payoffs in a payoff matrix.

Pure strategy

A strategy in which the player chooses a particular action with certainty.

Mixed strategy

A strategy in which the player randomizes her actions.

Maximin strategy

A strategy in which the player minimizes his exposure to loss.

---

make the grade

The check method of solving games

Solving games can be challenging. The method, explained in the following, will help you simplify games and find a Nash equilibrium (or whether it exists) easily. Suppose you are trying to solve a game with two players, Company X and Company Y. Each company can take one of two actions: produce Product A or Produce Product B. The following payoff matrix shows each company's profits (in millions of dollars) that result from every possible combination of strategies. (The payoff matrix is shown in pure black and white to show how you can read it and solve the game if it appears that way on your assignment or exam.)

	Company Y	
	Product A	Product B
Company X Product A	150 , 115	120 , 60
Company X Product B	90 , 85	60 , 110

First, remember that you should always look at each player's decision-making process separately. Start by considering the "row" player's choices (Company X in our case). The row player's payoffs are always shown to the left of the comma in payoff matrices. We ask:

1. *What is the best action for Company X to take if Company Y chooses Product A?* As you can see from the payoff matrix, if Company Y chooses Product A, Company X is better off choosing Product A too (since 150 > 90). Let's place a check mark next to Company X's payoff for that action (150), as shown in the following payoff matrix.

	Company Y	
	Product A	Product B
Company X Product A	✓150 , 115✓	✓120 , 60
Company X Product B	90 , 85	60 , 110✓ ✗

2. *What is the best action for Company X to take if Company Y chooses Product B?* As you can see, if Company Y chooses Product B, then Company X is again better off choosing Product A (120 > 60). Therefore, we place a check mark next to Company X's payoff for that action (120).

Now we repeat the exercise from Company Y's ("column" player's) perspective. The column player's payoffs are always shown to the right of the comma in payoff matrices. We ask:

1. *What is the best action for Company Y to take if Company X chooses Product A?* You can see from the payoff matrix that if Company X chooses Product A, Company Y is better off choosing Product A too (since 115 > 60). So, we place a check mark next to Company Y's payoff for that action (115).

2. *What is the best action for Company Y to take if Company X chooses Product B?* If Company X chooses Product B, then Company Y is better off choosing Product B too (110 > 85). Therefore, we place a check mark next to Company Y's payoff for that action (110).

Note that there is only one box in the payoff matrix in which two check marks appear: both companies selecting Product A. This is the *Nash equilibrium* of the game.

You can also use this method to look for dominant and dominated strategies for each player. Recall that a dominant strategy is a strategy that is best for a player no matter what action the other player takes. Consider Company X's decision explained in the preceding. As our check marks show, its answer to both questions is the same: Company X always chooses Product A no matter what action Company Y takes. That strategy is Company X's *dominant strategy*. We can then cross out Company X's alternative (dominated) strategy

(Product B), allowing us to reduce the game to fewer options. Dominated strategies are indicated by rows or columns without any check marks next to a player's payoffs. As we can see, the Product B row has no check marks next to Company X's payoffs. Now we repeat the process for Company Y. Since Company Y's decision changes, depending on Company X's decision, Company Y has no dominant strategy. And since both columns have check marks next to Company Y's payoffs, we cannot cross out any column to indicate a dominated strategy for Company Y.

When solving games, you should also remember that when the players follow their dominant strategies, a Nash equilibrium will necessarily occur, but a Nash equilibrium does not always result from each player's dominant strategies. In our example, Company X does not care what Company Y does. No matter what action Company Y takes, Company X is always better off choosing Product A. This means Company X has a dominant strategy. Company Y's best option, however, is influenced by Company X's choice. But we know that Company X will always choose Product A because this is its dominant strategy. And given that, we also know that Company Y will choose Product A too. Therefore, a Nash equilibrium occurs when both companies choose Product A.

∂ Solving for mixed strategy equilibria

The check method provides a way to solve for pure strategy equilibria in which each player plays a particular strategy with probability one. In other words, pure strategy equilibria are equilibria in which players play a particular strategy *for sure*. In some cases, however, there may be no pure strategy equilibrium, but there will be a mixed strategy equilibrium in which one or both players choose to randomize over available strategies. In other cases, there may be both pure strategy and mixed strategy equilibria. Pure strategy equilibria can be identified using the check box method which is detailed in your textbook and reviewed in the preceding. Mixed strategy equilibria can be identified using the method described in the online appendix and reviewed in the following. In mixed strategy equilibria, players play particular strategies with probabilities less than one and therefore randomize.

To figure out the mixed strategy equilibria, we can consider conditions (describing mutual best responses) for which each player is indifferent between the strategies available to her. Let's consider a game similar to the one in the preceding check method example. Note, however, we have listed probabilities next to each of the strategies for Companies X and Y, respectively, and that the payoff to Company X for the case that it chooses Product B is changed.

		Company Y	
		q Product A	$1-q$ Product B
p Product A		150 , 115	120 , 60
Company X			
$1-p$ Product B		160 , 85	60 , 110

From each company's perspective, its value depends on what the other company does. If Company X chooses Product A, for example, it receives 150, if Company Y also chooses Product A (this happens with probability q) and receives 120 if Company Y chooses Product B (this happens with probability

$1 - q$). Recall that probabilities always range from 0 to 1 and that the summation of probabilities over all possible states of the world equals 1. Therefore, in the context of this example, $q + (1 - q) = 1$, so we know that we have accounted for all possible outcomes. Company X's expected value from playing a particular strategy is a weighted sum of possible payoffs with the probabilities as weights, and this is similar for Company Y. For Company X, the expected payoff of Product A is:

$$q(150) + (1 - q)(120) = 30q + 120$$

Similarly, the expected payoff of Product B is:

$$q(160) + (1 - q)(60) = 100q + 60$$

These expected payoffs must be equal to keep Company Y indifferent between the available products. Otherwise, one or both of the companies would have an incentive to deviate (in other words, there would be a profitable deviation to choose a different strategy), and this would mean that we would not be dealing with an equilibrium.

Therefore, $30q + 120 = 100q + 60$, or $q = \dfrac{6}{7}$.

We can similarly set these equations up from Company Y's perspective. For that company, the expected value from Product A is:

$$p(115) + (1 - p)(85) = 30p + 85$$

From Product B, it is:

$$p(60) + (1 - p)(110) = 110 - 50p$$

Setting these equal, $30p + 85 = 110 - 50p$, or $80p = 25$, or $p = \dfrac{5}{16}$. The equilibrium therefore has Company X choosing Product A, with probability $\dfrac{5}{16}$ and Product B, with probability $\dfrac{11}{16}$, and has Company Y choosing Product A, with probability $\dfrac{6}{7}$ and Product B, with probability $\dfrac{1}{7}$. Note that we used the equilibrium condition from Company Y to solve for p (the probability that Company X chooses Product A), and we used the equilibrium condition from Company X to solve for q (the probability that Company Y chooses Product A).

12.1 figure it out 1

Suppose Canon and Nikon are considering developing new models of their digital SLR cameras. Each company can introduce a completely new model, upgrade its existing model, or do nothing, leaving its existing model as it is. The following payoff matrix shows each company's profits (in millions of dollars) resulting from each strategy (with Canon's payoffs listed before the comma and Nikon's, after it).

		Nikon		
		New model	**Upgrade**	**Leave as is**
	New model	180 , 170	220 , 190	300 , 150
Canon	**Upgrade**	140 , 200	200 , 170	260 , 160
	Leave as is	100 , 180	120 , 210	160 , 190

a. Is there a dominant strategy for Canon? For Nikon? Explain.
b. Are there any dominated strategies for Canon? For Nikon? Explain.
c. Is there a Nash equilibrium in this game? Explain.

Solution

a. A dominant strategy is a strategy that is best for a player no matter what strategy its opponent follows. To see whether Canon has a dominant strategy, we consider its choices, given each of the possible actions by Nikon. As we can see from the payoff matrix, if Nikon chooses to develop a new model of its camera, Canon's best option is also to develop a new model, since its payoff in this case (180) is greater than its payoffs from upgrading the camera (140) or leaving it as it is (100). So, we place a check mark next to Canon's payoff for that action (180) (see the following playoff matrix). Next, if Nikon chooses to upgrade its camera, Canon's best option is again to develop a new model, since $220 > 200$ and $220 > 120$. We place another check mark next to the Canon's payoff of 220. Finally, if Nikon chooses to leave its camera as it is, Canon's best option is still to develop a new model, since $300 > 260$ and $300 > 160$. We place a check mark next to that highest payoff. Our three check marks next to the Canon's payoffs in the same row indicate that, whatever Nikon's choice is, Canon's best option is always to develop a new model of its camera. Therefore, this is Canon's dominant strategy.

		Nikon		
		New model	**Upgrade**	**Leave as is**
	New model	✓180 , 170	✓220 , 190✓	✓300 , 150
Canon	**Upgrade**	140 , 200✓	200 , 170	260 , 160 ✗
	Leave as is	100 , 180	120 , 210✓	160 , 190 ✗
			✗	

To see whether Nikon has a dominant strategy, we consider its choices given each of the possible actions by Canon. As we can see from the payoff matrix, if Canon chooses to develop a new model, Nikon's best option is to upgrade, since its payoff in this case (190) is greater than its payoffs from developing a new model (170) or leaving its camera as it is (150). Next, if Canon chooses to upgrade its camera, Nikon's best option is to develop a new model, since $200 > 170$ and $200 > 160$. Finally, if Canon chooses to leave its camera as it is, Nikon's best option is to upgrade its camera, since $210 > 180$ and $210 > 190$. As you can see, the three check marks next to Nikon's payoffs are not in the same column. This means Nikon's best option depends on what Canon does. That is, Nikon does not have a dominant strategy.

b. A dominated strategy is a losing strategy for a player, regardless of what its opponent does. Canon's dominated strategies are indicated by the rows of the payoff matrix with no check marks next to Canon's payoffs. That is, no check marks in the "Upgrade" and "Leave as is" rows mean that under no circumstances is it best for Canon to choose these options. These are Canon's dominated strategies, and we can cross out these rows.

Nikon's dominated strategies are indicated by the columns of the payoff matrix with no check marks next to Nikon's payoffs. The only such column is "Leave as is," which means that under no circumstances is this the best choice for Nikon. This is Nikon's dominated strategy, and we can cross out this column.

c. There is a box in the payoff matrix in which two check marks appear. It is where Canon chooses to develop a new model and Nikon chooses to upgrade its existing camera. This is the Nash equilibrium of the game. This is because, as we could see in (a), Canon chooses the "New Model" option no matter what Nikon does, and given that Canon's choice, Nikon's best option is to upgrade.

∂ 12.2 figure it out 2

Suppose that two players (A and B) play a game where player A has the opportunity to move a game piece up or down, while player B can choose left or right. Payoffs for this game are given in the following table.

		B	
		Left	**Right**
	Up	1 , 5	15 , 3
A	**Down**	5 , 2	10 , 6

a. What are the pure strategy Nash equilibria, if any?
b. What is the mixed strategy Nash equilibrium, if any?

Solution

a. By the check method:

		B	
		Left	**Right**
	Up	1 , 5✓	✓15 , 3
A	**Down**	✓5 , 2	10 , 6✓

There are no pure strategy Nash equilibria, since there are no boxes with two checks (using the check method).

b.

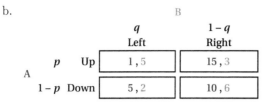

The equilibrium conditions and their solutions are:

$$q + 15(1 - q) = 5q + 10(1 - q)$$
$$4q = 5(1 - q)$$
$$4q = 5 - 5q$$
$$q = \frac{5}{9}$$

and $5p + 2(1 - p) = 3p + 6(1 - p)$

$$2p = 4(1 - p)$$
$$2p = 4 - 4p$$
$$p = \frac{2}{3}$$

Since neither player knows exactly what the other will do, both find it optimal to mix their strategies (randomize) over their possible actions until the point that each is exactly indifferent between the pure strategies available to him or her. The optimal degree of randomization then depends on the possible payoffs at stake. There is a mixed strategy Nash equilibrium in which player A plays up, with probability $\frac{2}{3}$, and down, with probability $\frac{1}{3}$, and B plays left, with probability $\frac{5}{9}$, and right, with probability $\frac{4}{9}$.

12.3 Repeated Games

Backward induction

The process of solving a multistep game by first solving the last step and then working backward.

Grim trigger strategy (or grim reaper strategy)

A strategy in which cooperative play ends permanently when one player cheats.

Tit-for-tat

A strategy in which the player mimics her opponent's prior-period action in each round; for example, the player cheats when her opponent cheated in the preceding round, and cooperates when her opponent cooperated in the previous round.

12.3 figure it out 1

Suppose there are two wine makers in the market, Celebrity and Rosso. The following payoff matrix shows each firm's profits (in millions of dollars) resulting from each of the two alternative strategies: make mostly high-end wines and make mostly cheap wines (with Celebrity's payoffs listed before the comma and Rosso's, after it).

		Rosso	
		High end	Cheap
Celebrity	High end	−20 , 25	10 , 100
	Cheap	30 , 120	20 , 60

a. If both wine producers act rationally to maximize their profits, what will be the outcome of the game? Explain.
b. Now suppose that Rosso suspects that Celebrity might be committed to producing high-end wines because of motives other than profit. Which option is Rosso likely to choose? Explain your answer.

c. Suppose that the demand for Celebrity's wine plummets when both companies produce cheap wines, since consumers of Celebrity's cheap wine decide that Rosso's wine is better and substitute toward it. (Further suppose that Rosso's costs are such that its total profit does not change in response to changes in preferences in the market.) Payoffs can now then be expressed as:

		Rosso	
		High end	**Cheap**
Celebrity	**High end**	−20 , 25	10 , 100
	Cheap	30 , 120	−20 , 60

What are the pure strategy Nash equilibria, if any?

d. For the payoffs in (c), what is the mixed strategy Nash equilibrium?

Solution

a. We can use the check method to solve this game (see the following payoff matrix). First, we consider Celebrity's choices, given each possible Rosso's action. As we can see from the payoff matrix, if Rosso chooses to produce high-end wines, Celebrity's best option is to produce cheap wines, since its profit in this case is $30 million, while it incurs a loss of $20 million from producing high-end wines. If Rosso chooses to produce cheap wines, Celebrity's best option is, again, to produce cheap wines, since $20 million > $10 million.

		Rosso	
		High end	**Cheap**
Celebrity	**High end**	−20 , 25	10 , 100✓
	Cheap	✓30 , 120✓	✓20 , 60

Now consider Rosso's choices, given each Celebrity's action. If Celebrity chooses to produce high-end wines, Rosso's best option is to produce cheap wines, since its profit in this case is $100 million rather than $25 million earned from producing high-end wines. If Celebrity chooses to produce cheap wines, Rosso's best option is, to produce high-end wines, since $120 million > $60 million.

As we can see, there is a box in the payoff matrix in which two check marks appear. It is where Celebrity chooses to produce cheap wines and Rosso chooses to produce high-end wines. This is the Nash equilibrium of the game. This is because producing cheap wines is a dominant strategy for Celebrity: it chooses this option whatever Rosso does. And given that is Celebrity's choice, Rosso's best option is to produce high-end wines.

b. It makes sense for Rosso to go with a maximin strategy, which is to produce cheap wines. The worst Rosso could do in this case is make $60 million. If Rosso decides to made high-end wines instead, its profit could fall as low as $25 million, if Celebrity also decides to produce high-end wines.

c. By the check method:

		Rosso	
		High end	**Cheap**
Celebrity	**High end**	−20 , 25	✓10 , 100✓
	Cheap	✓30 , 120✓	−20 , 60

There are two pure strategy Nash equilibria. In one, Celebrity produces cheap wine and Rosso produces high-end wine, and in the other, the companies reverse these choices.

d.

		Rosso	
		q **High end**	$1-q$ **Cheap**
Celebrity	p **High end**	−20 , 25	10 , 100
	$1-p$ **Cheap**	30 , 120	−20 , 60

To check for a mixed strategy Nash equilibrium, we can assign probability p that Celebrity produces high-end wine and probability q that Rosso also produces wine that is high end. Accordingly, the probabilities Celebrity and Rosso produce cheap wine are $(1 - p)$, and $(1 - q)$, respectively. For Celebrity, the expected value of high-end wine must equal the expected value of cheap wine. For Rosso, the expected value of high-end wine also must equal the expected value of cheap wine. Celebrity's expected value depends on the probabilities that Rosso produces either high or low-end wine, and Rosso's expected value depends on the probabilities that Celebrity chooses one type of wine or the other. The equilibrium conditions and their solutions are as follows.

For Celebrity:

$$-20q + 10(1 - q) = 30q + (-20)(1 - q)$$
$$50q = 30(1 - q)$$
$$50q = 30 - 30q$$
$$q = \frac{3}{8}$$

For Rosso:

$$25p + 120(1 - p) = 100p + 60(1 - p)$$
$$75p = 60(1 - p)$$
$$75p = 60 - 60p$$
$$p = \frac{4}{9}$$

Since neither producer knows exactly what the other will produce, both find it optimal to mix their strategies (randomize) oversupplying high- or low-end wine to the market until the point that each producer is exactly indifferent between the available pure strategy options. The optimal degree of randomization then depends on the possible payoffs at stake. There is a mixed strategy Nash equilibrium in which Celebrity produces high-end wine, with probability $\frac{4}{9}$ (because p was the probability assigned to high end for Celebrity) and cheap wine, with the remaining $\frac{5}{9}$ probability, and Rosso produces high end, with probability $\frac{3}{8}$ (because q was Rosso's probability of high end) and cheap wine, with the remaining $\frac{5}{8}$ probability.

12.3 figure it out 2

Suppose Samsung and LG are considering offering extended warranty for their refrigerators. This warranty is expensive to offer, but each firm can lose a substantial market share and profit if it does not offer it while its competitor does. The following payoff matrix shows each company's profits (in millions of dollars) that result from each of the two alternative strategies: offer the warranty and not to offer the warranty (with Samsung's payoffs listed before the comma and LG's, after it).

		LG	
		Offer warranty	Don't offer warranty
Samsung	Offer warranty	30 , 30	60 , 20
	Don't offer warranty	20 , 60	40 , 40

a. If the game is played once, what is the likely outcome?

b. Suppose the game is repeated three times. How will your answer in (a) change? Explain.

c. Now suppose the two companies have agreed not to offer the warranty. The game is repeated infinitely, and each company uses a grim trigger strategy to encourage compliance with the agreement. At what level of the discounting of the future factor d will LG choose to follow the agreement? Explain.

Solution

a. We can use the check method to solve for the Nash equilibrium in a one-period game (see the following diagram). First, we consider Samsung's choices, given each possible LG's action. As we can see from the payoff matrix, if LG chooses to offer the warranty, Samsung's best option is also to offer the warranty, since Samsung's payoff in this case ($30 million) is greater than its payoffs when it does not offer the warranty ($20 million). If LG chooses not to offer the warranty, Samsung's best option is, again, to offer it, since $60 million > $40 million.

LG

	Offer warranty	Don't offer warranty
Samsung Offer warranty	✓30 , 30✓	✓60 , 20
Samsung Don't offer warranty	20 , 60✓	40 , 40

Now consider LG's choices given Samsung's actions. If Samsung chooses to offer the warranty, LG's best option is to offer it too, since LG's payoff in this case ($30 million) is greater than its payoffs with no warranty offered ($20 million). If Samsung chooses not to offer the warranty, LG's best option is to offer it, since $60 million > $40 million.

The upper-left box in the payoff matrix is where check marks appear for both companies. Thus, the outcome of the game is when both firms offer the warranty. This is not the best cooperative outcome for the game, but it is the only stable equilibrium.

b. If the game is played for three periods, there would be no change in the players' behavior. In the third period, both companies would offer warranties because that is the Nash equilibrium. Knowing this and using backward induction, players will opt to offer warranties in both the second and the first periods as well.

c. LG's payoff from cheating and offering the warranty is the $60 million from the first period—when Samsung does not offer the warranty and LG cheats—and $30 million for each period after that, since Samsung will also start offering the warranty. Thus, in an infinitely repeated game, LG's total expected payoff when cheating is

$$60 + d \times 30 + d^2 \times 30 + d^3 \times 30 + \ldots$$

LG's payoff from following the agreement (when neither of the companies offers the warranty) is $40 million in each period. So, in an infinitely repeated game, LG's total expected payoff when following the agreement is

$$40 + d \times 40 + d^2 \times 40 + d^3 \times 40 + \ldots$$

LG will be indifferent between these two options when the preceding payoff streams are equal:

$$60 + d \times 30 + d^2 \times 30 + d^3 \times 30 + \ldots = 40 + d \times 40 + d^2 \times 40 + d^3 \times 40 + \ldots$$

Solving this equation for d, we get:

$$60 + 30 \times (d + d^2 + d^3 + \ldots) = 40 + 40 \times (d + d^2 + d^3 + \ldots)$$
$$10 \times (d + d^2 + d^3 + \ldots) = 20$$
$$d + d^2 + d^3 + \ldots = 2$$

Since $d + d^2 + d^3 + \ldots = \dfrac{d}{1-d}$ for any d between zero and one ($0 \le d < 1$), we can write:

$$\frac{d}{1-d} = 2$$
$$d = 2(1-d)$$
$$d = 2 - 2d$$
$$3d = 2$$
$$d = 0.667$$

Thus, LG is indifferent between keeping the agreement and cheating on if its discounting of the future factor is 0.667. This means LG will follow the agreement if it views each dollar earned in the next period to be worth more than 66.7 cents in the present.

12.4 Sequential Games

Sequential games

Games where one player moves first and other players observe this action before making their decisions.

Extensive form or decision tree

Representation of a sequential game that shows both the choice and timing of players' actions.

make the grade

Backward induction and trimming decision trees in sequential games

Solving sequential games requires us to work backward, using a technique called *backward induction*. That is, we start with the player who moves last. This may seem strange, given that the player who moves first often has a first-mover advantage. Remember, however, that we assume all players know the strategies available to every player in the game and the payoffs from every possible outcome. Suppose, for example, that there are two players, Player 1 and Player 2, and Player 1 moves first. Before Player 1 chooses her strategy, she must consider what Player 2 is likely to do because Player 1's payoff is determined both by her choice and that of her opponent. When we are solving the game, we want to think like the players. Therefore, to determine the best strategy for Player 1 to use, we must first examine what Player 2 is likely to do, given every possible choice that Player 1 might make. While it seems like we are acting as if Player 2 is moving first, in reality we are just putting ourselves in Player 1's shoes as she considers her best strategy, and that begins with predicting Player 2's moves.

Another useful technique that you can apply to solve sequential games is called "trimming the branches." It is very similar to removing dominated strategies in a normal-form game. This method allows you to narrow the solution options by eliminating branches that represent any actions that a player would never take. Consider the following decision tree for choosing a movie release date by two producers, Studio 1 and Studio 2 (with the payoffs in millions of dollars):

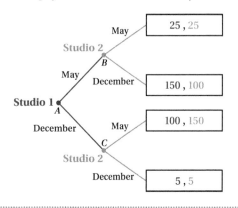

We can use backward induction to solve this game. Studio 1—which is moving first—is considering what Studio 2 will do in response to its choice. Look at node B, where Studio 1 chooses to release its movie in May. What will Studio 2 do? It will choose to release its movie in December because in that case its payoff is greater ($100 > 25$). We place a check mark next to the December payoff, but we can also eliminate May as an option at node B, since Studio 2 will not choose it. That is, we can cut that branch as shown in the following decision tree. Now, consider what Studio 2 will do if Studio 1 chooses to release its movie in December (node C). In this case, Studio 2 will choose to release its movie in May (since $150 > 5$), so we can put a check mark next to that payoff and cut the December branch at node C.

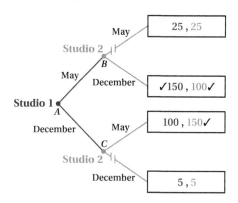

The final step is to choose Studio 1's best strategy. Given Studio 2's expected moves, Studio 1 is only left with two options (those not trimmed from the tree): choose "May" and earn a payoff of $150 million or choose "December" and earn a payoff of $100 million. Since $150 > 100$, Studio 1 will choose "May" and we can place a check mark by this payoff.

Backward induction and trimming the tree greatly simplify even the most complex sequential games. The trick is to place yourself in the first mover's shoes by considering the actions that will be chosen by the second (third, fourth, etc.) mover.

12.4 figure it out 1

Suppose AT&T and Verizon are considering a new television advertising campaign for their mobile phone services. Television ads are expensive, so when neither of the companies advertise, each earns a profit of $100 million, while if both companies advertise, each earns only $60 million. However, if one company advertises while the other does not, the company that advertises earns a profit of $140 million, while its competitor earns only $30 million.

a. Construct a normal-form payoff matrix for this game.
b. Find all Nash equilibria (if any).
c. If this game is played sequentially and AT&T makes its decision before Verizon does, what will the likely outcome be?
d. Is there a first-mover advantage in this game? Explain.

Solution

a. The following shows the normal-form payoff matrix (the payoffs are in millions of dollars, with AT&T's profits before the comma and Verizon's, after it).

		Verizon	
		Advertise	Don't advertise
AT&T	Advertise	60 , 60	140 , 30
	Don't advertise	30 , 140	100 , 100

b. We can use the check method to find out if there is a Nash equilibrium. First, we consider AT&T's choices given each possible Verizon's action. If Verizon advertises, AT&T's best option is to also advertise, since $60 million > $30 million. If Verizon does not advertise, AT&T's best option is, again, to advertise ($140 million > $100 million). That is, advertising is a dominant strategy for AT&T. It is AT&T's best strategy whatever Verizon does. We could analyze Verizon's options the same way, but since Verizon's payoffs are simply the mirror images of those of AT&T, we can conclude immediately that advertising is also a dominant strategy for Verizon. Because advertising is a dominant strategy for both companies, the outcome of this game is that both firms advertise and earn $60 million each. This is the (only) Nash equilibrium in the game because neither company has an incentive to change its strategy, given the strategy of the other.

		Verizon	
		Advertise	Don't advertise
AT&T	Advertise	✓60 , 60✓	✓140 , 30
	Don't advertise	30 , 140✓	100 , 100

c. The extensive form of this game, with AT&T moving first, is shown in the following. We can use backward induction to solve the game. When making its choice as the first mover, AT&T will consider how Verizon responds. Suppose AT&T chooses to advertise. This takes us to node B, where Verizon makes its choice. Which option will Verizon choose? It will choose to advertise, because in that case its payoff is greater ($60 million > $30 million). Next, let's see what Verizon will do if AT&T chooses not to advertise, so we are at node C. In this case, Verizon will, again, choose to advertise (since $140 million > $100 million). The final step is to choose AT&T's best strategy. Given Verizon's expected moves, AT&T faces two options: (1) choose to advertise and earn $60 million, or (2) choose not to advertise and earn $30 million. Since $60 million > $30 million, AT&T will choose to advertise. Thus, the likely outcome of the game is, again, both firms advertise and earn $60 million each.

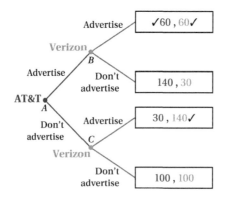

d. Since the outcome of the game in (b) is the same as the outcome in (c), that is, both companies advertise and earn $60 million each, there is no first-mover advantage in this game. This is because each company has a dominant strategy, that is, the best strategy to follow whatever the opponent does. Since each company will always choose its dominant strategy, it is irrelevant if one of them makes its decision before the other.

12.4 figure it out 2

Suppose Apple has developed a new model of its iPhone that has innovative interface. If the new iPhone is released, Apple's competitor in the market for smartphones, Samsung, will be able to imitate the new interface and offer a similar smartphone at a lower price. Assume that the patent laws permit this kind of imitation. The extensive form of this game is shown in the following (payoffs are profits in millions of dollars).

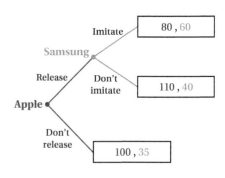

a. Will Apple release its new iPhone for sale? Explain why or why not.
b. Would your answer in (a) change if Samsung promised not to imitate Apple's new design? Explain.
c. Would your answer in (a) change if Samsung signed a legal agreement with Apple promising to pay $21 million if it imitates Apple's new design? Explain.

Solution

a. See the following figure. Using backward induction, Apple can see that if it releases its new iPhone, Samsung will choose to imitate it, since in that case Samsung's profit will be greater ($60 million rather than $40 million). Given this reality, if Apple releases its new iPhone, it will earn $80 million, and if it does not release it, it will be able to earn $100 million. Thus, to a great disappointment of its fans, Apple will not release its new iPhone.
b. The outcome of the game won't change. Samsung's promise would not be credible. Since Samsung has a strong incentive to imitate Apple's interface ($20 million of additional profit), Apple would not believe Samsung's promise and would not release its new iPhone.
c. See the following figure. The promised payment reduces Samsung's payoff when it imitates Apple's interface from $60 million to $39 million. As a result, Samsung's preferred option now is not to imitate. Realizing this, Apple chooses to release its new iPhone, because it now earns more ($110 million) when it does than when it doesn't ($100 million). Note that Samsung never actually pays anything to Apple, since it does not use the "imitate" option. But the promised payment allows Samsung to earn $5 million more ($40 million instead of $35 million).

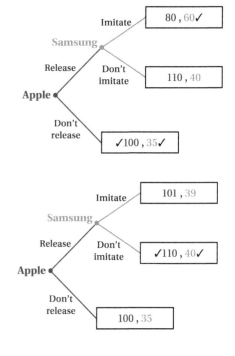

12.5 Strategic Moves, Credibility, and Commitment
Strategic move
An action taken early in a game that favorably influences the ultimate outcome of the game.

Side payment
A type of bribe that influences the outcome of a strategic game.

Noncredible threat
A threat made in a game that is not rational for the player to follow through on, and as such is an empty threat.

Credible commitment
A choice or a restriction of choices that guarantees a player will take a particular future action if certain conditions occur.

Practice Problems
Problem 1
Suppose two competing satellite TV services, Dish Network and DirecTV, are considering a new television advertising campaign. When neither of the companies advertises, Dish Network's profit is $24 million, and DirecTV's profit is $22 million. If both companies advertise, Dish Network's profit decreases to $11 million, and DirecTV's profit falls to $12 million. This is because running TV ads is expensive, and although advertising can convince people to subscribe to a company's service instead of to a competitor's it cannot increase the overall number of customers by much. If, however, Dish Network advertises while DirecTV does not, Dish Network's profit is $27 million and DirecTV's profit is only $8 million. If DirecTV advertises while Dish Network does not, DirecTV earns $25 million and Dish Network earns only $7 million. Assume this is a simultaneous one-period game.
a. Construct a normal-form payoff matrix for this game.
b. Is there a dominant strategy for Dish Network? For DirecTV? Explain.
c. Are there any dominated strategies for Dish Network? For DirecTV? Explain.
d. Is there a Nash equilibrium in this game? Is this a prisoner's dilemma? Explain.
e. What is the likely outcome of this game? Explain.

Problem 2
Suppose there are two competing breweries in the market, Noble Hops and Malty Twist. The following payoff matrix shows each firm's profits (in millions of dollars) resulting from each of the two alternative strategies: (1) produce mostly cheap low-end beer and (2) produce mostly high-quality beer.

		Malty	
		Cheap	High quality
Noble	Cheap	18 , 25	30 , 10
	High quality	40 , 20	12 , –5

a. If both breweries act rationally to maximize their profits, what will be the outcome of the game? Explain.
b. Now suppose that Noble Hops suspects that Malty Twist might choose to produce high-quality beer to establish its reputation, even if this hurts Malty Twist's profits in the short run. Which option is Noble Hops likely to choose? Explain your answer.

∂ c. Suppose that Malty Twist's hires a new brewmaster who can help the company gain market share but only if Malty Twist competes with Noble Hops in the high-quality beer market (i.e., only if they both produce high-quality beer). Profits, given their respective strategies, are now, as in the following.

		Malty	
		Cheap	High quality
Noble	Cheap	18 , 25	30 , 10
	High quality	40 , 20	12 , 30

What are the pure strategy Nash equilibria, if any?

d. What is the mixed strategy Nash equilibrium, if any?

Problem 3

Suppose the U.S. government is reassessing the benefits of the country's membership in the NAFTA and considering imposing a tariff on imports of tomatoes from Mexico. If the tariff is imposed, there is a possibility that Mexico will retaliate by imposing a tariff on corn imports from the United States. Suppose that the United States' surplus resulting from free trade with Mexico in the markets for tomatoes and corn is $10 billion, and Mexico's surplus resulting from free trade with the United States is $8 billion. If the United States imposes the tariff and Mexico does not retaliate, the United States will increase its surplus to $12 billion (since the terms-of-trade gain for the United States will exceed the deadweight loss from restricting trade), and Mexico's surplus will fall to $4 billion. But if Mexico retaliates, the United States' surplus will fall to $7 billion, while Mexico's surplus will be $6 billion.

a. Construct the extensive form (decision tree) for the game.

b. Is there a Nash equilibrium in this game? If the U.S. government's goal is to maximize the nation's surplus, will it impose the tariff? Explain.

Problem 4

Suppose two competing popular restaurants in a city, Art's Place and Bob's Place, are considering expending their facilities to be able to serve more customers. The following payoff matrix shows the restaurants' profits (in thousands of dollars), depending on whether each of them expands or holds the line.

		Bob's	
		Expand	Don't expand
Art's	Expand	30 , 38	47 , 28
	Don't expand	25 , 49	35 , 41

a. If this is a simultaneous one-period game, what decision each restaurant is likely to make?

b. If the game is repeated twice, how will the outcome change compared to your answer in (a)? Explain.

c. Suppose that Art and Bob have agreed not to expand their facilities and use a grim trigger strategy to encourage each other's compliance with the agreement. Assume that the game is repeated infinitely. At what level of the discounting of the future factor (d) will Art choose to follow the agreement? What about Bob? Explain.

Problem 5

Suppose there are only two oil producers in the world, Iran and Saudi Arabia. The two countries form a cartel and agree to evenly split the market, each producing 12 million barrels of oil per day. If both countries follow the agreement, Iran's profit is $1,104 million per day and Saudi Arabia's profit is $1,200 million per day. If Iran cheats and sells one million barrels per day more than its quota set by the agreement while Saudi Arabia follows the agreement, Iran's profit increases to $1,144 million and Saudi Arabia's profit falls to $1,152 million. If Saudi Arabia cheats by producing an additional million barrels of oil while Iran follows the agreement, Saudi Arabia's profit increases to $1,248 million and Iran's profit falls to $1,056 million. If both countries cheat, Iran's profit is $1,092 million and Saudi Arabia's profit is $1,196 million. Assume that the preceding strategies are the only possible options for the two countries, the countries make simultaneous moves, and the game is played once.

a. Construct a payoff matrix for this game.
b. Is there a dominant strategy for Iran? For Saudi Arabia? Explain.
c. Are there any dominated strategies for Iran? For Saudi Arabia? Explain.
d. Is there a Nash equilibrium in this game? Explain.

Problem 6

Consider again the scenario in Problem 5. Suppose now that the game is played repeatedly, and each country uses a grim trigger strategy to encourage the other country's compliance with the agreement. Suppose that Iran views $1 earned in the next period to be worth $0.85 in the present period, and Saudi Arabia views it to be worth $0.93.
a. If the game is repeated four times, how will its outcome change compared with that in Problem 5? Explain.
b. If the game is repeated infinitely, how will its outcome change compared with that in Problem 5? Explain.

Problem 7

Suppose Sony and Panasonic are considering developing new models of their digital camcorders. Each company can introduce a completely new model, upgrade its existing model, or do nothing, leaving its existing model as it is. The following payoff matrix shows each company's profits (in millions of dollars) resulting from each strategy.

		Panasonic		
		New model	**Upgrade**	**Leave as is**
	New model	120 , 110	125 , 100	140 , 80
Sony	**Upgrade**	110 , 115	130 , 140	125 , 85
	Leave as is	95 , 130	100 , 120	90 , 95

a. Is there a dominant strategy for Sony? For Panasonic? Explain.
b. Are there any dominated strategies for Sony? For Panasonic? Explain.
c. Is there a Nash equilibrium in this game? Explain.

Problem 8

Consider again the scenario in Problem 7. But now suppose that Sony makes its decision before Panasonic does.
a. Construct the extensive form (decision tree) for the game.
b. Is there a Nash equilibrium in this game? Is the outcome of the game different from that in Problem 7? Explain.

Problem 9

Suppose GM and Toyota are the only two firms in the world capable of making fully electric cars with characteristics and costs comparable to those of conventional vehicles. Neither firm has started to produce the new car yet. Assume that each firm can make only a yes/no decision: either to produce these breakthrough electric cars or not. The following payoff matrix shows the companies' profits from producing the new electric cars (in billions of dollars), depending on their decisions.

		Toyota	
		Produce	**Don't produce**
	Produce	–2 , –1	12 , 0
GM	**Don't produce**	0 , 15	0 , 0

a. If GM and Toyota make their decisions simultaneously, is there a Nash equilibrium in this game? Will GM produce the new car? Will Toyota? Explain.
b. Now suppose Toyota is ready to launch the new car before GM is. How will this change your answer in (a)? Is there a first-mover advantage in this game? Explain.
c. Suppose again that Toyota is ready to move first, but the U.S. government offers a subsidy of $3 billion to GM if the company launches its new electric car. How will this change your answer in (b)? Explain.

Problem 10

Suppose Intel introduces a new high-performance computer processor (CPU) and is currently the only producer of this kind of CPU on the market. Another CPU producer, AMD, is deciding whether to enter the market with a similar CPU. If AMD doesn't enter, Intel will earn $800 million from its new processor. If AMD does enter, its profit will depend on how Intel reacts. If Intel fights AMD's entry by starting a price war, AMD will lose $100 million and Intel will earn $300 million. If Intel does not fight, AMD will earn $200 million and Intel will earn $400 million.

a. Construct the extensive form of the game (with profits from the new CPU in millions of dollars as the companies' payoffs).
b. Will AMD decide to enter the market? Will Intel start a price war? Explain your answers.
c. Suppose that Intel promises to start a price war before AMD has made its decision. Will this change your answers in (b)? Explain.
d. Now suppose that, trying to deter AMD's entry, Intel builds all the capacity it would need if AMD were to enter and there was a price war (since with lower prices, quantity sold would increase). Intel's investment in extra capacity lowers its profit to $580 million when it's the only seller in the market (because the extra capacity sits idle) and to $290 billion if AMD enters and Intel decides not to fight. The extra capacity does not affect Intel's profit in the event of a price war, because the company will be fully utilizing the capacity it has already built. AMD's expected payoffs are also unaffected by Intel's extra capacity. In this scenario, will AMD enter the market? Will there be a price war? Is building the extra capacity a good strategy for Intel? Explain.

Problem 11

Suppose that John and Mike are owners of neighboring coffee shops. They can choose to specialize in either espresso or regular coffee. Their profits given their respective strategies are as follows.

		Mike	
		Espresso	**Coffee**
	Espresso	100 , 100	120 , 110
John			
	Coffee	110 , 120	90 , 90

a. What are the pure strategy Nash equilibria, if any?
b. What is the mixed strategy Nash equilibrium, if any?

Investment, Time, and Insurance | 13

13.1 Present Discounted Value Analysis

Investment

The purchase of capital in the present with the intent of reaping future benefits.

Interest

A periodic payment tied to an amount of assets borrowed or lent.

Principal

The amount of assets on which interest payments are made.

Interest rate

Interest expressed as a fraction of the principal. Interest rates are quoted on a per-period basis (yearly, monthly, etc.), so the payment of interest is a "flow payment," paid out per unit of time. For example, if a savings account has $1,000 in it (the principal) at a 2% annual interest rate, it pays $1,000 \times 0.02 = $20 of interest at the end of the year. In general, the amount of interest paid (I) is

$$I = A \times r$$

where A is the principal and r is the interest rate (expressed as a fraction).

Compounding or compound interest

A calculation of interest based on the sum of the original principal and the interest paid over past periods. The value of the investment after t periods (V_t) is calculated as follows:

$$V_t = A \times (1 + r)^t$$

where A is the principal and r is the interest rate (expressed as a fraction). For example, if a savings account has $1,000 in it, and the annual interest rate is 2%, the value of the account after five years will be $1,000 \times (1 + 0.02)^5 = $1,104.08.

The "rule of 72"

A rule-of-thumb for approximating how long it will take for a balance growing at any constant interest rate to double. To use it, divide 72 by the per-period interest rate. The result will be the approximate number of periods until the balance doubles. For example, an account compounding at 8% per year should double every $\frac{72}{8} = 9$ years.

Present discounted value (PDV)

The value of a future payment in terms of equivalent present-period dollars. The present discounted value (PDV) of a payment in period t (V_t) is calculated as follows:

$$PDV = \frac{V_t}{(1 + r)^t}$$

where r is the interest rate (expressed as a fraction). For example, if a payment of $1,000 occurs five years from now, and the annual interest rate is 4%, the PDV of the payment is

$$PDV = \frac{\$1,000}{(1 + 0.04)^5} = \$821.93$$

Special cases of PDVs

- A set of regular payments M made for T periods:

$$PDV = \frac{M}{r} \times \left[1 - \frac{1}{(1+r)^T} \right]$$

- A *perpetuity*—a set of regular payments M occurring forever (i.e., when T goes to infinity):

$$PDV = \frac{M}{r}$$

Bond

Financial instrument that indicates the issuer is indebted to the purchaser.

Face value (par value)

The principal that the bond issuer pays interest on.

Coupon rate

The rate of the regular periodic amount paid out to bondholders. The coupon rate is the rate of interest applied to the principal.

Coupon payments

Set of scheduled interest payments that recur over a bond's entire life.

Maturity

The length of a bond's life. A bond's maturity is the time between when the bond is issued and when the borrower pays the face value to the bondholder.

Yield to maturity (or just yield)

The interest rate that makes a bond's present discounted value equal to its current market price.

At par (or at face value)

Description of a bond whose price equals its face value, or whose yield equals its coupon rate.

Below par

Description of a bond with a price less than its face value, or whose yield to maturity is greater than its coupon rate.

Above par

Description of a bond with a price above its face value, or whose yield to maturity is less than its coupon rate.

13.1 figure it out 1

Suppose you've just purchased a newly issued corporate bond with a face value of $2,000, an annual coupon rate of 5% (with one coupon payment per year), and a maturity of three years. The real interest rate is 4%.

a. What is the present discounted value of your bond?

b. Suppose your friend has purchased a bond with the same attributes, except that its maturity is five years. What is the present discounted value of your friend's bond?

c. Suppose again that the bond matures in three years, but the interest rate is 4% in the first year, 5% in the second year, and 6% in the third year. How will this affect your bond's PDV?

Solution

a. First, we find the amount of each coupon payment by multiplying the bond's face value by the coupon rate: $2,000 × 0.05 = $100. The other component of a bond's payoffs to its bearer is its face-value redemption at maturity. Thus, you expect to receive $2,000 three years from now. Putting this all together, the PDV of your bond is

$$PDV = \frac{\$100}{1 + 0.04} + \frac{\$100}{(1 + 0.04)^2} + \frac{\$100}{(1 + 0.04)^3} + \frac{\$2,000}{(1 + 0.04)^3} = \$2,055.50$$

b. Since the bond's maturity is five years, your friend will receive five coupon payments, $100 each year, plus the face value of her bond five years from now. Therefore, the PDV of her bond is

$$PDV = \frac{\$100}{1 + 0.04} + \frac{\$100}{(1 + 0.04)^2} + \frac{\$100}{(1 + 0.04)^3} + \frac{\$100}{(1 + 0.04)^4} + \frac{\$100}{(1 + 0.04)^5} + \frac{\$2,000}{(1 + 0.04)^5} = \$2,089.04$$

c. Substituting the interest rates for each year into the PDV formula in (a), we calculate the PDV of your bond as follows:

$$PDV = \frac{\$100}{1 + 0.04} + \frac{\$100}{(1 + 0.05)^2} + \frac{\$100}{(1 + 0.06)^3} + \frac{\$2,000}{(1 + 0.06)^3} = \$1,950.06$$

13.2 Evaluating Investment Choices

Net present value (NPV) analysis

The use of the present discounted value to evaluate the expected long-term return on an investment. This allows us to properly account for the costs and benefits that occur in different periods of time. If the PDV of an investment project's benefits outweighs the PDV of its costs, the project's NPV (the sum of these PDVs) will be positive and the investment is a worthwhile undertaking. If the PDVs of the costs are greater than the benefits, the project's NPV will be negative and the investment is not worthwhile. The generic formula for computing the NPV of any investment decision is

$$NPV = (B_0 - C_0) + \frac{B_1 - C_1}{1 + r} + \frac{B_2 - C_2}{(1 + r)^2} + \ldots + \frac{B_T - C_T}{(1 + r)^T}$$

where r is the interest rate (expressed as a fraction), 0, 1, 2, …T are the periods spanned by the investment project (with 0 being the current period and T, the last period), B_0, B_1, … B_T are the investment's benefits in the respective periods, and C_0, C_1, … C_T are the costs, so $B_T - C_T$ is the net benefit in any particular period, t.

Payback period

The length of time required for an investment's initial costs to be recouped in future benefits without discounting future flows. Payback periods are easy to compute, but their disadvantage is that they don't take into account that future costs and benefits must be discounted, to properly compare them with the initial costs.

13.2 figure it out 1

Margo, a freelance artist, is selling her prints online. She is considering buying her own printer to save the cost of using local printing services. A printer that would meet Margo's quality standards costs at least $1,200. Margo expects to use it for three years and won't be able to resell it. Paper and ink will cost her $100 per year. Using her own printer instead of the printing services will save Margo $600 per year. Assume, for simplicity, that Margo's costs and benefits of using the printer come in one payment at the end of the year and the inflation rate is zero.

a. If Margo could invest her money at an annual interest rate of 4%, what is the net present value of Margo's investment in the printer? Should she buy the printer? Explain.

b. Now suppose that Margo has a credit card debt with an annual interest rate of 16%, and her best alternative to buying the printer is to repay this debt. In this situation, what is the net present value of Margo's investment in the printer? Should she buy the printer? Explain.

Solution

a. Margo's costs are \$1,200 now ($C_0 = \$1,200$) and \$100 in each of the next three years ($C_1 = C_2 = C_3 = \$100$). And her benefits are $B_1 = B_2 = B_3 = \$600$. Thus, the net present value of her investment is

$$NPV = (B_0 - C_0) + \frac{B_1 - C_1}{1 + r} + \frac{B_2 - C_2}{(1 + r)^2} + \frac{B_3 - C_3}{(1 + r)^3}$$

$$NPV = (\$0 - \$1,200) + \frac{\$600 - \$100}{1 + 0.04} + \frac{\$600 - \$100}{(1 + 0.04)^2} + \frac{\$600 - \$100}{(1 + 0.04)^3}$$

$$NPV = \$187.55$$

Thus, the NPV of Margo's investment is positive, which means the PDV of the investment's benefits outweighs the PDV of its costs. Therefore, purchasing the printer is worthwhile.

b. Since Margo's best alternative to investing in the printer is to use this money to repay her credit card debt, the interest rate on that debt is her opportunity cost of investing. That is, the relevant interest rate to use in the NPV formula is 16%. Given this, the net present value of Margo's investment is

$$NPV = (\$0 - \$1,200) + \frac{\$600 - \$100}{1 + 0.16} + \frac{\$600 - \$100}{(1 + 0.16)^2} + \frac{\$600 - \$100}{(1 + 0.16)^3}$$

$$NPV = -\$77.06$$

Thus, the NPV of Margo's investment is now negative, which means the PDV of the investment's costs outweighs the PDV of its benefits. Therefore, Margo should repay her credit card debt and not purchase the printer.

13.3 The Correct Interest Rate to Use, and Capital Markets

Nominal interest rate

Rate of return expressed in raw currency values.

Real interest rate (or inflation-adjusted interest rate)

Rate of return expressed in terms of purchasing power. As long as inflation rates aren't very high, the basic rule is that the real interest rate, r, is approximately the nominal interest rate, i, minus the inflation rate, π:

$$r \approx i - \pi$$

make the grade

Which interest rate to use?

As explained in the text, you should use the real, rather than nominal, interest rate when calculating PDVs and evaluating individuals' and firms' investment decisions. Nominal interest rates are rates of return expressed only in currency values without regard for how much purchasing power those values hold. Real interest rates express rates of return in terms of purchasing power, the amount of goods and services that the payment can purchase. If inflation has reduced a future payment's purchasing power because a dollar buys less in the future than it does in the present, real interest rates take that into account. So, you should use real interest rates to calculate present values in constant dollars. And, as long as inflation rates aren't very high, the real interest rate is approximately the nominal interest rate minus the inflation rate. But, what is the ap-

propriate nominal interest rate to use when calculating the real interest rate?

To answer this question, recall that the interest rate captures the opportunity cost of investing. It is an opportunity cost because when you use a certain amount of money to purchase capital, you give up other ways to use it. This means that the interest rate used to compute PDVs and NPVs should be the best alternative rate of return that is forgone if the investment is made. For example, if a firm is considering whether to invest in building a new plant, it is in essence deciding between building the plant and putting the money in the financial market, where it would earn interest at the market rate. Thus, you should use that interest rate when calculating the NPV for this investment. Similarly, if members of a household are deciding whether to invest in building an addition to their home, the best alternative use of the money they consider investing could be holding it in a mutual fund. In this case, the appropriate interest rate to use in PDV and NPV calculations is the rate paid by the mutual fund. And if you are considering buying a new computer for your business, and you have a credit card debt, your best alternative use of the money could be repaying that debt to avoid paying a 20% interest on it. If so, your relevant interest rate to use when calculating your investment's NPV is 20%.

13.3 figure it out 1

Suppose that the demand for capital curve is

$$Q^D = 40 - 400r$$

and the supply of capital curve is

$$Q^S = 400r$$

Where r is the real interest rate (expressed as a fraction) and Q is the quantity of capital (in billions of dollars).

a. What is the market interest rate? What is the equilibrium quantity of capital invested?

b. Suppose that business confidence falls, so firms are willing to invest $8 billion less at each given interest rate. How will this influence the market interest rate? The equilibrium quantity of capital invested? Draw a diagram to explain your answer.

Solution

a. An equilibrium interest rate is the rate at which the quantity of capital demanded equals the quantity of capital supplied. Thus, we set $Q^D = Q^S$ and solve this equation for r:

$$Q^D = Q^S$$
$$40 - 400r = 400r$$
$$800r = 40$$
$$r = 0.05$$

Now we can find the quantity of capital invested by substituting the interest rate into either the demand or the supply equation:

$$Q^D = 40 - 400 \times 0.05 = 20$$
$$Q^S = 400 \times 0.05 = 20$$

Thus, the market interest rate is 5%, and $20 billion is invested at this rate.

b. The fact that firms are willing to invest $8 billion less at each given interest rate means that the demand for capital curve shifts leftward by $8 billion (see the following diagram). To derive the new demand curve algebraically, we subtract 8 from the original demand curve:

$$Q_2^D = 40 - 400r - 8$$
$$Q_2^D = 32 - 400r$$

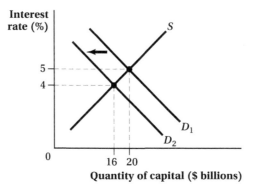

To find the new market equilibrium, we set $Q_2^D = Q^S$ and solve this equation for r:

$$Q_2^D = Q^S$$
$$32 - 400r = 400r$$
$$800r = 32$$
$$r = 0.04$$

Now we can find the quantity of capital invested by substituting the interest rate into either the demand or the supply equation:

$$Q^D = 32 - 400 \times 0.04 = 16$$
$$Q^S = 400 \times 0.04 = 16$$

Thus, the market interest rate falls from 5% to 4%, and the quantity of capital invested decreases from $20 billion to $16 billion.

13.4 Evaluating Risky Investments

Expected value

The probability-weighted average payout. For an uncertain outcome with N possible payments,

$$\text{Expected value} = (p_1 \times M_1) + (p_2 \times M_2) + \ldots (p_N \times M_N)$$

where p_1, p_2, $\ldots$ are, respectively, the probabilities of Payments 1, 2, and so on, and M_1, M_2, $\ldots$ are the payments themselves.

Option value of waiting

The value created if an investor can postpone his investment decision until the uncertainty about an investment's returns is wholly or partially resolved.

13.4 figure it out 1

Consider again the scenario in 13.2 figure it out Problem 1. But now suppose that although Margo can estimate her cost of paper and ink fairly accurately, she is not that certain about how much she can save by using her own printer instead of local printing services. Calculating this depends on the demand for her prints, which cannot be predicted with certainty. Based on her experience and some market research, Margo estimates that there is a 60% chance that her saving from using the printer will be $500 per year, a 30% chance that it will be $700 per year, and a 10% chance that there will be no saving at all. Assume that Margo could invest her money at an annual interest rate of 4%.
a. Calculate the expected value of Margo's annual benefit from using her own printer.
b. What is the net present value of Margo's investment in the printer? Should she buy the printer? Explain.

Solution

a. The expected value of Margo's annual benefit is the probability-weighted average saving from using the printer:

$$\text{Expected value} = (p_1 \times M_1) + (p_2 \times M_2) + (p_3 \times M_3)$$
$$= (0.6 \times \$500) + (0.3 \times \$700) + (0.1 \times \$0)$$
$$= \$510$$

b. To calculate the net present value of Margo's investment, we substitute the expected value of her benefit calculated in (a) into the NPV formula:

$$NPV = (B_0 - C_0) + \frac{B_1 - C_1}{1 + r} + \frac{B_2 - C_2}{(1 + r)^2} + \frac{B_3 - C_3}{(1 + r)^3}$$
$$NPV = (\$0 - \$1{,}200) + \frac{\$510 - \$100}{1 + 0.04} + \frac{\$510 - \$100}{(1 + 0.04)^2} + \frac{\$510 - \$100}{(1 + 0.04)^3}$$
$$NPV = -\$62.21$$

Since the NPV of the investment is negative, i.e., the PDV of the investment's costs outweighs the PDV of its expected benefits, purchasing the printer is not worthwhile.

13.5 Uncertainty, Risk, and Insurance

Risk-averse

Suffering an expected utility loss from uncertainty, or equivalently, being willing to pay to have that risk reduced. A risk-averse person prefers having a guaranteed amount to having a risky but equivalent-in-expected-value amount. That is, uncertainty reduces the utility of a risk-averse person.

Certainty equivalent

The guaranteed income level at which an individual would receive the same expected utility level as from an uncertain income.

Risk premium

The compensation an individual would require to bear risk without suffering a loss in expected utility.

Insurance

A payment one economic actor pays another to reduce the risk facing the payer.

Complete insurance (full insurance)

An insurance policy that leaves the insured individual equally well off regardless of the outcome.

Diversification

A strategy to reduce risk by combining uncertain outcomes. An important part of making diversification work is that risks being added together must be at least partially unrelated.

Actuarially fair

Description of an insurance policy with expected net payments equal to zero.

Risk-free interest rate

Rate of return on an investment that an asset paying a guaranteed return would pay.

13.5 figure it out 1

Mario owns a Ferrari worth $256,000, and this is his only wealth. Mario is a rather reckless driver, so there is a 25% chance that he will get into an accident, after which his car will be worth only $16,000. Mario's utility of wealth function is

$$U = 10W^{0.5}$$

where W is Mario's wealth in thousands of dollars.
a. What is Mario's expected wealth?
b. What is Mario's expected utility?
c. What is Mario's risk premium?
d. Suppose an insurance company offers Mario a policy that pays him $153,000 if there is an accident, in exchange for a $60,000 premium paid to the insurer in the case of no accident. Should Mario accept this offer?

Solution

a. The probability that Mario's wealth will be reduced to $16,000 is 0.25, and the probability that it will remain at $256,000 is $1 - 0.25 = 0.75$. Therefore, Mario's expected wealth is

$$0.75 \times \$256,000 + 0.25 \times \$16,000 = \$196,000$$

b. If Mario does not have an accident, his utility is

$$U = 10 \times 256^{0.5} = 160$$

And if he gets into an accident, his utility is

$$U = 10 \times 16^{0.5} = 40$$

Since the probability of an accident is 0.25, and the probability of no accident is 0.75, Mario's expected utility is

$$0.75 \times 160 + 0.25 \times 40 = 130$$

c. Mario's risk premium is the extra amount of expected wealth he must receive to make him as well off when his wealth is uncertain as when it is guaranteed. To calculate Mario's risk premium, we first need to determine the guaranteed wealth that would offer him the same utility level (130) as his uncertain wealth. To find this certainty equivalent, we substitute $U = 130$ into Mario's utility function and solve this equation for W:

$$130 = 10W^{0.5}$$
$$W^{0.5} = 13$$
$$W = 169$$

Thus, Mario derives the same utility from a guaranteed $169,000 wealth as he does from his $196,000 wealth expected with uncertainty. This means Mario is willing to give up $196,000 − $169,000 = $27,000 to eliminate his wealth uncertainty. This is Mario's risk premium. The following diagram illustrates this solution.

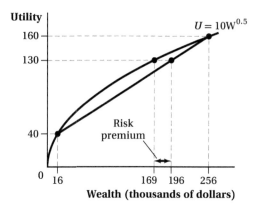

d. With the insurance, if no accident occurs, Mario's wealth is $256,000 − $60,000 = $196,000, so his utility is $10 \times 196^{0.5} = 140$. And in the case of an accident, Mario's wealth is $16,000 + $153,000 = $169,000, so his utility is $10 \times 169^{0.5} = 130$. Therefore, his expected utility is

$$0.75 \times 140 + 0.25 \times 130 = 137.5$$

Since Mario's expected utility is greater with the insurance (137.5) than without insurance (130), he should accept the insurer's offer. Note that with this insurance policy, Mario's expected wealth (0.75 × $196,000 + 0.25 × $169,000 = $189,250) is less than his expected wealth with no insurance ($196,000). But since the insurance reduces his risk, he derives more utility from the lower expected wealth and therefore is happy to give up $196,000 − $189,250= $6,750 (which goes to the insurance company) in exchange for more certainty.

Practice Problems
Problem 1

Robert is thinking about buying a convenience store. He is confident the store can earn a profit of $80,000 per year for the foreseeable future. The current owner of the store is asking $1.1 million for it. The annual interest rate at which Robert can lend his money on the financial market is 7%. The expected rate of inflation is 2% per year.

a. Assuming that the store will earn an annual profit of $80,000 forever, what is the present discounted value of the store?

b. If Robert pays $1.1 million for the store, what will be the net present value of his investment? Should he buy the store for $1.1 million? Explain.

c. How would your answer in (b) change if Robert could earn an annual interest rate of 10% (rather than 7%) in the financial market? Explain.

Problem 2

Alicia has purchased a bond that matures in four years. The face value of the bond is $1,000, and its annual coupon rate is 4% (with one coupon payment per year). The real interest rate is expected to stay constant at 2%.

a. What is the present discounted value of the bond?

b. Suppose after one year, Alicia's friend offers her $1,100 for her bond. Should Alicia sell the bond? Explain.

Problem 3

Suppose that the demand for capital curve is

$$Q^D = 80 - 800r$$

and the supply of capital curve is

$$Q^S = 800r$$

where r is the real interest rate (expressed as a fraction) and Q is the quantity of capital (in billions of dollars).

a. What is the market interest rate? What is the equilibrium quantity of capital invested?

b. Suppose that consumer confidence falls, so households spend less on consumption and are willing to save $16 billion more at each given interest rate. How will this influence the market interest rate? The equilibrium quantity of capital invested? Draw a diagram to explain your answer.

Problem 4

Suppose you won $1 million in a lottery and you are offered the following options to receive your prize: (1) $200,000 now and then $200,000 each year for the next four years, (2) a single payment of $900,000 now, and (3) $50,000 every year forever.

a. If the expected real interest rate is 5%, which option will you choose? Explain.

b. How will your answer in (a) change if the expected real interest rate is 6%? Explain.

Problem 5

George and Emma own a Web design business as partners. They are considering the purchase of a new computer, which will enable the partnership to earn $450 more per year. The price of the computer is $1,600. The partners plan to hold on to this computer for three years and then will be able to resell it for $500. Assume, for simplicity, that the partnership's additional profit comes in one payment at the end of each year.

a. If the market interest rate is 10% and the expected rate of inflation is 2%, what is the net present value of the investment?

b. Suppose George believes that purchasing the computer would be a worthwhile investment. "We will get $1,350 back in three years," he argues, "and then we'll get $500 more when we sell it, so our total benefits from the computer will be $1,850, while it will cost us only $1,600." Do you agree with George? Explain.

c. How will your answer in (a) change if the market interest rate is 7% and the expected rate of inflation is 3%? Explain.

Problem 6

Bob, a restaurant owner, is considering expanding his kitchen. The project would cost him $85,000. Bob is confident that expanding will allow the restaurant to earn an additional profit of $20,000 per year for the next five years, but he is not sure what will happen after that. Assume, for simplicity, that Bob invests the whole amount at the beginning of the first year, and his additional profit comes in one payment at the end of each year. Assume also that the inflation rate is zero.

a. Suppose Bob plans to invest his own funds, and the best alternative use of this money would be to lend it on the financial market at an interest rate of 4%. What is the net present value of Bob's investment project? (To make a conservative estimate of the NPV, assume that there will be no additional profit after five years.) Should Bob expand his kitchen? Explain.

b. Now suppose that Bob has to borrow funds to invest in his expansion project. He can get an $85,000 bank loan, which he'd repay with a down payment of $30,000 and two annual installments of $30,000. Should Bob expand his kitchen? Explain.

Problem 7

Consider again the scenario in Problem 6. But now suppose that a market research consultant tells Bob that there is a 70% chance that the additional profit from his investment project in the next five years will be $20,000 per year, a 20% chance that it will be $30,000 per year, and a 10% chance that it will be only $5,000 per year.

a. Calculate the expected value of Bob's additional annual profit.

b. If Bob invests his own funds, what is the net present value of his investment project? (To make a conservative estimate of the NPV, assume that there will be no additional profit after five years.) Should Bob expand his kitchen?

Problem 8

Agatha, a homeowner, faces a risk that her house will suffer a fire, causing a $160,000 loss with a probability of 0.03. Agatha's utility function is $U = 10W^{0.5}$, where W is her wealth (as measured by the value of her house in thousands of dollars). Suppose that the market value of the house is $196,000.

a. What is Agatha's expected wealth?

b. What is Agatha's expected utility?

c. What is Agatha's risk premium?

d. Suppose an insurance company offers Agatha a policy that pays her $154,000 if there is a fire in exchange for a $6,000 premium paid to the insurer if no fire occurs. Should Agatha buy this insurance policy?

Problem 9

An airline is considering replacing its planes. It has two options: buy replacement planes at $40 million each or renovate and update the old planes at a cost of $5 million each and delay having to purchase new planes for another five years. Since the old planes are less fuel-efficient, an old plane costs $1.2 million more to operate than a new one does. Assume that operating costs are paid once at the end of each year, the inflation rate is zero, and the price of a new plane five years from now is still $40 million.

a. Suppose that the market interest rate the airline faces is 5%. Which of the two options should the airline choose? Explain.

b. How will your answer change if the market interest rate is 7%? Explain.

Problem 10

Monica is considering the purchase of an old convenience store building, which she plans to convert to an upscale wine store. The building can be purchased for $250,000, and the new wine store will generate an annual profit of $40,000 for its lifetime (you can assume forever), starting one year after its opening. However, there is a 25% chance that the city council will rezone the district to forbid establishments selling alcohol. A hearing is scheduled one year from now. If the district is rezoned, Monica's profit will be zero. Assume, for simplicity, that Monica has no other options for her business and won't be able to resell the building. Also assume that the store's profit comes in one payment at the end of each year of operation, the market interest rate is 5%, and the inflation rate is zero.

a. What is the net present value of opening the store today?

b. What is the net present value of the project if Monica decides to wait until the zoning decision has been made?

c. Based on your answers in (a) and (b), should Monica open the store today, or should she wait until the zoning commission makes its decision? What is Monica's option value of waiting (if any)? Explain.

General Equilibrium

14

14.1 General Equilibrium Effects in Action

General equilibrium analysis

The study of market behavior that accounts for cross-market influences and is concerned with conditions present when all markets are simultaneously in equilibrium.

Partial equilibrium analysis

Determination of the equilibrium in a particular market that assumes there are no cross-market spillovers.

14.1 figure it out 1

Assume that wheat and rye are the only two goods in the world. Suppose that the demand for wheat is given by

$$Q_w^d = 16 - P_w + 0.4P_r$$

and the demand for rye is

$$Q_r^d = 10 - P_r + 0.4P_w$$

The supply of wheat is given by

$$Q_w^s = 2 + 0.8P_w$$

and the supply of rye is

$$Q_r^s = 2 + P_r$$

The quantities are in millions of bushels, and the prices are in dollars per bushel.

a. Solve for the general equilibrium prices and quantities of wheat and rye.

b. Suppose that the demand for rye increases by 4 million bushels at any given set of wheat and rye prices. How will this affect the general equilibrium prices and quantities of wheat and rye?

Solution

a. We first solve for the price of wheat as a function of the price of rye by setting quantity demanded and quantity supplied equal in the wheat market:

$$Q_w^d = Q_w^s$$
$$16 - P_w + 0.4P_r = 2 + 0.8P_w$$
$$1.8P_w = 14 + 0.4P_r$$
$$P_w = \frac{14 + 0.4P_r}{1.8}$$

By multiplying both the numerator and the denominator on the right-hand side by 5, we get an expression for P_w that is more convenient to use:

$$P_w = \frac{70 + 2P_r}{9}$$

Similarly, we solve for the equilibrium in the rye market, expressing the price of rye as a function of the price of wheat:

$$Q_r^d = Q_r^s$$
$$10 - P_r + 0.4P_w = 2 + P_r$$
$$2P_r = 8 + 0.4P_w$$
$$P_r = 4 + 0.2P_w$$

219

Now, to find the general equilibrium price of wheat, we insert the preceding equation into the equation for the price of wheat and solve it for P_w:

$$P_w = \frac{70 + 2(4 + 0.2P_w)}{9}$$

$$9P_w = 70 + 8 + 0.4P_w$$

$$8.6P_w = 78$$

$$P_w = 9.07$$

To find the price of rye in general equilibrium, we insert the wheat price $P_w = 9.07$ into the equation for the price of rye:

$$P_r = 4 + 0.2 \times 9.07 = 5.81$$

We can calculate the general equilibrium quantities of wheat and rye by inserting the equilibrium prices we have found into the supply or demand curve equations for wheat and rye. For wheat:

$$Q_w^d = 16 - 9.07 + (0.4 \times 5.81) = 9.3$$
$$Q_w^s = 2 + (0.8 \times 9.07) = 9.3$$

And for rye:

$$Q_r^d = 10 - 5.81 + (0.4 \times 9.07) = 7.8$$
$$Q_r^s = 2 + 5.81 = 7.8$$

Thus, the general equilibrium price of wheat is \$9.07 per bushel, and the quantity of wheat produced is 9.3 million bushels. The general equilibrium price of rye is \$5.81 per bushel, and the quantity of rye is 7.8 million bushels.

b. When the demand for rye increases, both markets are affected. We follow the same steps as in (a) to solve for the new equilibrium prices and quantities. Since the demand for wheat is not directly affected, the equation for the price of wheat as a function of the price of rye remains the same:

$$P_w = \frac{70 + 2P_r}{9}$$

But the equation for the equilibrium price of rye changes. Since the demand for rye increases by 4 million bushels at any given P_r and P_w, we derive the new equation by adding 4 to the right-hand side of the original equation. So the demand equation for rye is now

$$Q_r^{d*} = (10 - P_r + 0.4P_w) + 4$$
$$= 14 - P_r + 0.4P_w$$

Now we solve for the price of rye as a function of the price of wheat as follows:

$$Q_r^{d*} = Q_r^s$$
$$14 - P_r + 0.4P_w = 2 + P_r$$
$$2P_r = 12 + 0.4P_w$$
$$P_r = 6 + 0.2P_w$$

To find the new general equilibrium price of wheat, we insert the preceding equation into the equation for the price of wheat and solve it for P_w:

$$P_w = \frac{70 + 2(6 + 0.2P_w)}{9}$$

$$9P_w = 70 + 12 + 0.4P_w$$

$$8.6P_w = 82$$

$$P_w = 9.53$$

And to find the price of rye in the new general equilibrium, we insert $P_w = 9.53$ into the new equation for the price of rye:

$$P_r = 6 + 0.2 \times 9.53 = 7.91$$

Now we can calculate the new general equilibrium quantities of wheat and rye by inserting the equilibrium prices we have found into the supply or demand equations for wheat and rye. For wheat:

$$Q_w^d = 16 - 9.53 + 0.4 \times 7.91 = 9.6$$
$$Q_w^s = 2 + 0.8 \times 9.53 = 9.6$$

And for rye:

$$Q_r^{d*} = 14 - 7.91 + 0.4 \times 9.53 = 9.9$$
$$Q_r^s = 2 + 7.91 = 9.9$$

Thus, as a result of the increased demand for rye, the general equilibrium price of wheat rises from $9.07 per bushel to $9.53 per bushel, and the quantity of wheat produced increases from 9.3 million bushels to 9.6 million bushels. The general equilibrium price of rye rises from $5.81 per bushel to $7.91 per bushel, and the quantity of rye increases from 7.8 million bushels to 9.9 million bushels. Since the demand for wheat is affected by the price of rye, the increased demand for rye affects not only the equilibrium price and quantity in the rye market but also both of these in the wheat market.

14.2 General Equilibrium: Equity and Efficiency

Social welfare function

Mathematical function that combines individuals' utility levels into a single measure of society's total utility level.

Utilitarian social welfare function

Mathematical function that computes society's welfare as the sum of every individual's welfare:

$$W = u_1 + u_2 + \ldots + u_N$$

Where W is the value of the social welfare function and the subscripts denote individuals (with a total of N people in the economy).

Rawlsian social welfare function

Mathematical function that computes society's welfare as the welfare of the worst-off individual:

$$W = \min[u_1 + u_2 + \ldots + u_N]$$

where W is the value of the social welfare function and the subscripts denote individuals (with a total of N people in the economy).

Egalitarian

Belief that the ideal society is one in which each individual is equally well off.

Pareto efficiency

An economic allocation of goods in which the goods cannot be reallocated without making at least one individual worse off.

14.2 figure it out 1

Imagine a hypothetical country with a population of 300 million. Suppose that 1% of this population are the "rich", whose income is $625,000 per person, 70% are the "middle class", whose income is $49,000 per person, and 29% are the "poor", whose income is $9,000 per person. Assume that the individual incomes within each group are equal. Suppose that the individual utility function is

$$u = w^{0.5}$$

where u is the level of utility and w is the individual's income in thousands of dollars.
a. Using the utilitarian social welfare function, what is the country's level of social welfare?
b. Using the Rawlsian social welfare function, what is the country's level of social welfare?
c. Now suppose that to reduce income inequality in the country, the government introduces a more progressive tax system. As a result, $675 billion is redistributed from the rich to the poor. How will this affect the level of social welfare in the country evaluated using the utilitarian social welfare function? Rawlsian social welfare function?

Solution

a. The utilitarian social welfare function computes society's welfare as the sum of every individual's welfare:

$$W = u_1 + u_2 + \ldots + u_N$$

where W is the value of the social welfare and the subscripts denote individuals (with a total of N people in the economy). Given the individual utility function, we can calculate the levels of utility for an individual in each group. For a rich individual it is $625^{0.5} = 25$, for a middle class person it is $49^{0.5} = 7$, and for a poor person it is $9^{0.5} = 3$. Since the individual incomes within each group are equal, we can calculate the total utility received by each group by multiplying the individual level of utility by the number of individuals in the group. There are 0.01×300 million $= 3$ million rich individuals, so this group's total utility level is 25×3 million $= 75$ million. There are $0.70 \times 300 = 210$ million individuals in the middle class group, so this group's total utility level is 7×210 million $= 1{,}470$ million. And there are $0.29 \times 300 = 87$ million poor individuals, so this group's total utility level is 3×87 million $= 261$ million. Now we can calculate the country's level of social welfare by summing up the total utility levels of the three groups:

$$W = 75 \text{ million} + 1{,}470 \text{ million} + 261 \text{ million} = 1{,}806 \text{ million}$$

b. The Rawlsian social welfare function computes society's welfare as the welfare of the worst-off individual:

$$W = \min[u_1, u_2, \ldots, u_N]$$

As calculated in (a), the lowest individual level of utility, that is, the one received by a poor person, is 3. Therefore, according to the Rawlsian social welfare function, the country's level of social welfare is 3.

c. With the old tax system, the total income of the rich is

$$\$625{,}000 \times 3 \text{ million} = \$1{,}875 \text{ billion}$$

and the total income of the poor is

$$\$9{,}000 \times 87 \text{ million} = \$783{,}000 \text{ billion}$$

With the new tax system, the rich receive

$$\$1{,}875 \text{ billion} - \$675 \text{ billion} = \$1{,}200 \text{ billion}$$

which is

$$\frac{\$1{,}200 \text{ billion}}{3 \text{ million}} = \$400{,}000 \text{ per person}$$

And the poor receive

$$\$783 \text{ billion} + \$675 \text{ billion} = \$1{,}458 \text{ billion}$$

which is

$$\frac{\$1{,}458 \text{ billion}}{87 \text{ million}} = \$16{,}759 \text{ per person.}$$

Given the individual utility function, the level of utility received by a rich individual is now $400^{0.5} = 20$, and the level of utility received by a poor individual is $16.759^{0.5} = 4.09$. Using the utilitarian social welfare function, we can calculate the total utility received by the rich group as

$$20 \times 3 \text{ million} = 60 \text{ million}$$

and the total utility received by the poor group as

$$4.09 \times 87 \text{ million} = 356 \text{ million}$$

Since the income of the middle class is not affected, the level of utility received by this group remains unchanged. Thus, the country's level of social welfare is now:

$$W = 60 \text{ million} + 1{,}470 \text{ million} + 356 \text{ million} = 1{,}886 \text{ million}$$

Comparing this level of social welfare with that achieved under the old tax system (as calculated in (a)), we can see that according to the utilitarian social welfare function, income redistribution through a more progressive tax system has increased the country's social welfare by $1{,}886$ million $- 1{,}806$ million $= 80$ million (units of utility), or 4.4%. This is because, due to diminishing marginal utility, a dollar taken from a rich person lowers her utility level by less than a dollar given to a poor person increases his level of utility.

To use the Rawlsian social welfare function, note that, as calculated in the preceding, the lowest individual level of utility (the one received by a poor person) is 4.09 with the new tax system and 3 with the old system. That is, according to the Rawlsian social welfare function, the country's level of social welfare has increased from 3 to 4.09 (units), or by 36.3%.

14.3 Efficiency in Markets: Exchange Efficiency

Edgeworth box

Graph of an economy with two economic actors and two goods that is used to analyze market efficiency.

Marginal rate of substitution

Recall from Chapter 4 that the marginal rate of substitution of good X for good Y (MRS_{XY}) is the quantity of good Y that a consumer gives up to get a unit of good X while staying on the same indifference curve:

$$MRS_{XY} = -\frac{\Delta Y}{\Delta X}$$

With good X on the horizontal axis, the MRS_{XY} at a point equals the absolute value of the slope of the indifference curve at that point (see the following graph).

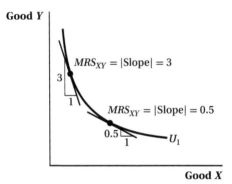

The marginal rate of substitution of good X for good Y also equals the ratio of the marginal utility of good X (MU_X) to the marginal utility of good Y (MU_Y):

$$MRS_{XY} = \frac{MU_X}{MU_Y}$$

Consumption contract curve

Curve that shows all possible Pareto-efficient allocations of goods across consumers.

Marginal rate of technical substitution of labor for capital ($MRTS_{LK}$)

Recall from Chapter 6 that $MRTS_{LK}$ is the rate at which the firm can trade labor (L) for capital (K), holding output (Q) constant.

$$MRTS_{LK} = -\frac{\Delta K}{\Delta L} = \frac{MP_L}{MP_K}$$

where MP_L is the marginal product of labor and MP_K is the marginal product of capital.

14.3 figure it out 1

The following Edgeworth box shows the quantities of coffee and cupcakes available to two consumers, Daniel and Adele. Daniel's preferences are represented by an indifference curve U_D, and Adele's preferences are represented by an indifference curve U_A.

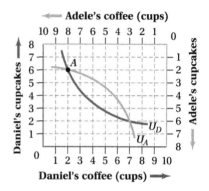

a. Suppose that Daniel and Adele are initially at point A. How many cups of coffee does each have? How many cupcakes?
b. Suppose that Daniel gives Adele 4 cupcakes in exchange for 5 cups of coffee. Does this exchange result in a Pareto improvement? Explain your answer.
c. Now (starting from point A) suppose that Adele gives Daniel 2 cups of coffee in exchange for 2 cupcakes. Does this exchange result in a Pareto improvement? Explain your answer.

Solution

a. At point A, Daniel has 2 cups of coffee and 6 cupcakes. And Adele has 8 cups of coffee and 2 cupcakes.
b. If Daniel gives Adele 4 cupcakes in exchange for 5 cups of coffee, he will end up with $2 + 5 = 7$ cups of coffee and $6 - 4 = 2$ cupcakes. And Adele will end up with $8 - 5 = 3$ cups of coffee and $2 + 4 = 6$ cupcakes. This allocation is represented by point B on the following graph. A Pareto improvement would occur if one of the individuals was made better off without making the other worse off. Because point B is on the same indifference curves as point A, neither Daniel nor Adele is better off. Therefore, this is not a Pareto improvement.

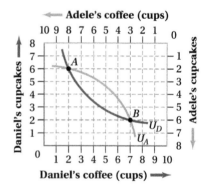

c. If Adele gives Daniel 2 cups of coffee in exchange for 2 cupcakes, Daniel will end up with $2 + 2 = 4$ cups of coffee and $6 - 2 = 4$ cupcakes. And Adele will end up with $8 - 2 = 6$ cups of coffee and $2 + 2 = 4$ cupcakes. This allocation is represented by point C on the following graph. A Pareto improvement occurs if at least one of the individuals is made better off without making the other worse off. As the graph shows, a higher indifference curve can be drawn through point C for both Daniel (U_{D2}) and Adele (U_{A2}). This means both individuals are better off as a result of the exchange. Therefore, it is a Pareto improvement.

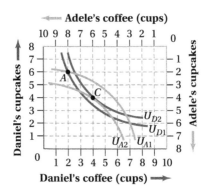

14.4 Efficiency in Markets: Input Efficiency

Production contract curve

Curve that shows all Pareto-efficient allocations of inputs across producers.

Production possibilities frontier (PPF)

Curve that connects all possible efficient output combinations of two goods.

14.4 figure it out 1

Suppose that there are 10 units of labor and 8 units of capital available in an economy where there are only two industries, agriculture and manufacturing. The marginal rate of technical substitution of labor for capital ($MRTS_{LK}$) is 0.5 in agriculture and 2 in manufacturing.

a. Is the economy input efficient? Explain your answer.

b. Suggest a reallocation of labor and capital that will lead to a Pareto improvement if such an improvement is possible, or explain why a Pareto improvement is not possible. Draw an Edgeworth box to illustrate your answer.

Solution

a. Production efficiency is achieved when the marginal rates of technical substitution is equal across industries. Since the $MRTS_{LK}$ in agriculture (0.5) is not equal to that in manufacturing (2), the economy is not productively efficient. The following graph illustrates this situation. The economy is currently at point A, where the isoquant for manufacturing (Q_M) is steeper than the isoquant for agriculture (Q_A), reflecting the fact that the $MRTS_{LK}$ in manufacturing is greater than that in agriculture.

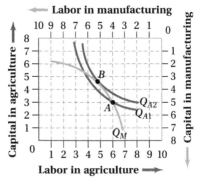

b. The fact that the $MRTS_{LK}$ in manufacturing is greater than that in agriculture means that the marginal product of labor relative to the marginal product of capital $\left(\dfrac{MP_L}{MP_K}\right)$ is greater in manufacturing than in agriculture. Therefore, labor should be reallocated from agriculture to manufacturing, and capital should be reallocated in the opposite direction.

As an example, suppose that the economy moves from point A to point B (on the preceding graph). Since the amount of labor employed in agriculture decreases and the amount of capital in agriculture increases, the marginal product of labor (MP_L) increases and the marginal product of capital (MP_K) decreases, so the $MRTS_{LK} = \dfrac{MP_L}{MP_K}$ rises. In manufacturing, the amount of labor increases and the amount of capital decreases. As a result, the marginal product of labor (MP_L) decreases and the marginal product of capital (MP_K) increases, so the $MRTS_{LK}$ falls.

This results in a Pareto improvement. As you can see on the graph, at point B, agriculture is producing more output than at point A (as indicated by a higher isoquant Q_{A1}), while manufacturing is producing the same level of output (Q_M). That is, agriculture's output increases without decreasing manufacturing's output, which is a Pareto improvement. (In this particular example, the slopes of the isoquants Q_{A2} and Q_M at point B are equal (since the isoquants are tangent to each other); that is, the $MRTS_{LK}$ in agriculture equals that in manufacturing. This means the allocation of inputs at point B is Pareto-efficient.)

14.5 Efficiency in Markets: Output Efficiency
Marginal rate of transformation (MRT)

The tradeoff between the production of any goods on the market. The MRT shows how much of one good must be given up to obtain one more unit of another.

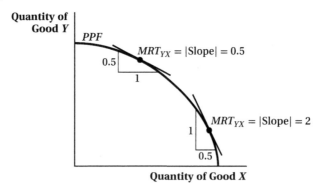

$$MRT_{YX} = \frac{MP_L^Y}{MP_L^X} = \frac{MP_K^Y}{MP_K^X}$$

where MP_L^Y is the marginal product of labor in the production of good Y, MP_L^X is the marginal product of labor in the production of good X, and MP_K^X, MP_K^Y are the marginal products of capital in the production of good X and good Y, respectively.

make the grade

Three conditions of an efficient general equilibrium

You may find the concept of an efficient general equilibrium rather complicated and hard to understand. Also, the links among different kinds of efficiency may seem difficult to untangle. The following overview of the three efficiency requirements should help you grasp the essentials of each of these conditions and see the relationships among them more clearly.

1. **Exchange efficiency.** A Pareto-efficient allocation of a set of goods across consumers: no consumer can be made better off without making someone else worse off.

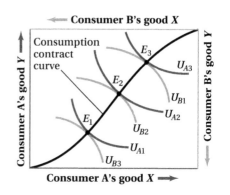

A Pareto-efficient allocation of good X and good Y occurs at a point of tangency between consumer A's and consumer B's indifference curves, where consumer A's marginal rate of substitution of good X for good $Y(MRS_{XY})$ equals that of consumer B. On the preceding diagram, points E_1, E_2, and E_3 are efficient. The consumption contract curve shows all possible Pareto-efficient allocations of good X and good Y between consumer A and consumer B. An efficient market will also result in the good's price ratio $\left(\dfrac{P_X}{P_Y}\right)$ equaling consumers' marginal rate of substitution. That is, exchange efficiency is achieved when

$$MRS_{XY}^A = MRS_{XY}^B = \frac{P_X}{P_Y}$$

2. **Input efficiency.** A Pareto-efficient allocation of inputs across producers: inputs must be allocated to producing the goods in the economy in such a way that making a higher quantity of one good means a smaller quantity must be made of at least one other good.

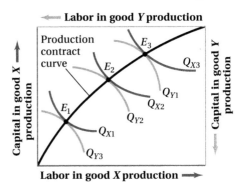

A Pareto-efficient allocation of labor and capital inputs occurs at a tangency between good X and good Y isoquants, where the marginal rate of technical substitution of labor for capital $(MRTS_{LK})$ in good X production equals that in good Y production. On the preceding diagram, points E_1, E_2, and E_3 are efficient. The production contract curve shows all possible Pareto-efficient allocations of labor and capital between good X production and good Y pro-

duction. Also, since the $MRTS_{LK}$ is the ratio of the inputs' marginal products, input efficiency requires those ratios to be equal in the two industries. That is, input efficiency is achieved when

$$MRTS_{LK}^X = MRTS_{LK}^Y = \frac{MP_L^X}{MP_K^X} = \frac{MP_L^Y}{MP_K^Y}$$

3. **Output efficiency.** A mix of outputs that simultaneously supports exchange and input efficiency; the mix and amount of goods that the economy produces cannot be changed without making some consumer or producer worse off. The first two conditions take the set of goods produced in the economy as a predetermined starting point and then evaluate efficiency in how they are allocated among consumers (exchange efficiency) and producers (input efficiency). Output efficiency deals with which goods are produced and in what quantities.

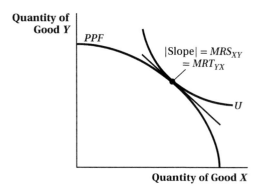

Output efficiency occurs at the point of tangency between the consumers' indifference curves (U) and the production possibilities frontier (PPF), where the marginal rate of substitution (MRS_{XY}) equals the marginal rate of transformation (MRT_{YX}). The marginal rate of substitution between goods equals the goods' price ratio, and production is efficient when the marginal cost of producing a good equals its price. Therefore, for complete efficiency to hold, the marginal rate of substitution must equal not only the ratio of the goods' prices but also the ratio of the goods' marginal costs of production. That is, output efficiency is achieved when

$$MRT_{XY} = MRS_{XY} = \frac{P_X}{P_Y} = \frac{MC_X}{MC_Y}$$

14.5 figure it out 1

Consider an economy that produces only two goods, oranges and t-shirts. At the current production levels, the marginal cost of producing a pound of oranges is $2 and the marginal cost of producing a t-shirt is $4. Suppose that at the current levels of production, consumers are willing to give up two t-shirts for one pound of oranges. Assume that the economy is both input-efficient and exchange-efficient, and both markets are perfectly competitive.

a. What is the marginal rate of transformation from t-shirts to oranges? What is the marginal rate of substitution of oranges for t-shirts?

b. Is the economy output-efficient? Draw a *PPF* graph to illustrate and explain your answer.

c. What is likely to happen to the output mix that is currently being produced? Will it change? If so, how? Use your *PPF* graph to explain your answer.

Solution

a. The marginal rate of transformation from t-shirts to oranges (MRT_{TO}) shows how many t-shirts firms are willing to give up to produce one more pound of oranges. Given that the marginal cost of producing a pound of oranges is \$2 and the marginal cost of producing a t-shirt is \$4, the firms' opportunity cost of producing a pound of oranges is $\frac{\$2}{\$4} = 0.5$ t-shirts. That is, for every pound of oranges produced, the company is giving up the chance to make 0.5 of a t-shirt. This means $MRT_{TO} = \frac{MC_O}{MC_T} = \frac{\$2}{\$4} = 0.5$.

The marginal rate of substitution of oranges for t-shirts (MRS_{OT}) is the quantity of t-shirts that consumers are willing to give up to get a pound of oranges. Since consumers are willing to give up two t-shirts for one pound of oranges, $MRS_{OT} = 2$.

b. Output efficiency is achieved when the marginal rates of transformation equals the marginal rate of substitution. Since the $MRT_{TO}(0.5)$ is not equal to the $MRS_{OT}(2)$, the economy is not output-efficient. The following graph illustrates this situation. The economy is currently at point A. Since we've assumed the economy is input-efficient, the combination of the two goods produced is on the PPF. However, since $MRS_{OT} > MRT_{TO}$, the consumers' indifference curve (U_1) at this point is steeper than the PPF.

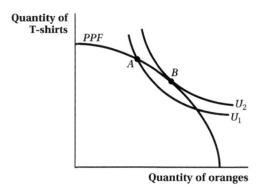

c. The fact that $MRS_{OT} > MRT_{TO}$ means that consumers are willing to pay a higher price for oranges in terms of t-shirts (two t-shirts per pound of oranges) than the firms' opportunity cost of oranges in terms of t-shirts (0.5 t-shirts per pound of oranges). Therefore, it is profitable for firms to increase the production of oranges and decrease the production of t-shirts. And as they do, the economy moves to the right and down along the PPF, so the PPF becomes steeper at the point of production, which means MRT_{TO} rises. At the same time, as more oranges and fewer t-shirts are produced, the marginal utility of oranges (MU_O) decreases while the marginal utility of t-shirts (MU_T) increases, so $MRS_{OT} = \frac{MU_O}{MU_T}$ falls. The production of oranges will continue to increase and the production of t-shirts will continue to fall until MRS_{OT} and MRT_{TO} are equalized (point B on the graph) and firms maximize their profits. Note that at point B, the PPF is tangent to a higher indifference curve (U_2), which means consumers are better off as a result of the output adjustment. And since the slopes of the PPF and the indifference curve (U_2) are equal, that is, $MRS_{OT} = MRT_{TO}$, the economy is now output-efficient.

14.6 Markets, Efficiency, and the Welfare Theorems

Summary of main concepts and relationships
First Welfare Theorem

Theorem stating that perfectly competitive markets in general equilibrium distribute resources in a Pareto-efficient way. The First Welfare Theorem relies on the following assumptions: (1) firms and consumers take as given all the prices of goods and inputs, i.e., there is no market power; (2) all participants in an economic transaction know the relevant information; (3) there are no externalities, i.e., costs or benefits that affect a third party not directly involved in an economic transaction; (4) there are no public goods, i.e., goods that benefit an individual consumer even as others consume it.

Second Welfare Theorem

Theorem stating that any given Pareto-efficient allocation in a perfectly competitive market is a general equilibrium outcome for some initial allocation. That is, under the assumptions made for the First Welfare Theorem, any Pareto-efficient equilibrium can be achieved by choosing the right initial allocation of goods. For example, if we want an efficient outcome that is also equitable, we can get to that outcome by initially allocating goods among consumers along the contract curve close to a point we feel is equitable.

Lump-sum transfer

Transfer to or from an individual for which the size is unaffected by the individual's choices. Lump-sum transfers are (almost) never used in real life because it is difficult to legislate taxes or subsidies that bear absolutely no relation to people's actions.

Practice Problems

Problem 1

Corn chips and salsa are complements. Suppose that the demand for corn chips is given by

$$Q_c^d = 10 - P_c - 0.5P_s$$

and the demand for salsa is

$$Q_s^d = 10 - P_s - 0.5P_c$$

The supply of corn chips is given by

$$Q_c^s = 1 + P_c$$

and the supply of salsa is

$$Q_s^s = 1 + P_s$$

The quantities are in millions of pounds, and the prices are in dollars per pound.
a. Are the markets for corn chips and salsa linked on the supply side or on the demand side? Explain.
b. Solve for the general equilibrium prices and quantities of corn chips and salsa.
c. Suppose that the demand for corn chips decreases, so consumers are willing to buy 3 million pounds less at any given set of prices for corn chips and salsa. How will this affect the general equilibrium prices and quantities of the two goods?

Problem 2

Corn production and soybean production use common inputs. Suppose that the demand for corn is given by

$$Q_c^d = 10 - P_c$$

and the demand for soybeans is

$$Q_s^d = 10 - P_s$$

The supply of corn is given by

$$Q_c^s = 1 + P_c - 0.5P_s$$

and the supply of soybeans is

$$Q_s^s = 1 + P_s - 0.5P_c$$

The quantities are in millions of bushels, and the prices are in dollars per bushel.

a. Are the markets for corn and soybeans linked on the supply side or on the demand side? Explain.
b. Solve for the general equilibrium prices and quantities of corn and soybeans.
c. Suppose that the demand for corn increases, so consumers are willing to buy 3 million bushels more at any given price of corn. How will this affect the general equilibrium prices and quantities of the two goods?

Problem 3

Archibald, Benedict, and Carole are members of a small commune. Archibald's wealth is $225,000, Benedict's is $25,000, and Carole's is $1.6 million. The individual utility of wealth function is

$$u = w^{0.5}$$

where u is the level of utility and w is the individual's wealth in thousands of dollars. Suppose the social welfare function is a Rawlsian function:

$$W = \min[u_A,\ u_B,\ u_C]$$

where W is the value of the social welfare and the subscripts denote the three individuals.
a. What is the commune's level of social welfare?
b. Recommend a transfer that will increase the commune's social welfare if any such transfer is possible.
c. What is the highest level of welfare that the commune can achieve by redistributing wealth among the three individuals? How must wealth be redistributed to achieve this level?

Problem 4

Consider the scenario in Problem 3, but now suppose that the social welfare function is a utilitarian function:

$$W = u_A + u_B + u_C$$

a. What is the commune's level of social welfare?
b. Recommend a transfer that will increase the commune's social welfare if any such transfer is possible.
c. What is the highest level of welfare that the commune can achieve by redistributing wealth among the three individuals? How must wealth be redistributed to achieve this level?

Problem 5

The following Edgeworth box shows the quantities of cauldron cakes and chocolate frogs available to two consumers, Harry and Ron. Harry's preferences are represented by an indifference curve U_H, and Ron's preferences are represented by an indifference curve U_R.

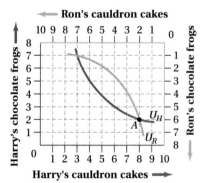

a. Suppose that Harry and Ron are initially at point A. How many cauldron cakes does each have? How many chocolate frogs? With this allocation, which of the two has a higher preference for cauldron cakes relative to chocolate frogs? Explain.
b. Suppose that Ron gives Harry one chocolate frog in exchange for two cauldron cakes. Does this exchange result in a Pareto improvement? Explain your answer.

c. Now (starting at point A) suppose that Ron offers Harry three chocolate frogs in exchange for three cauldron cakes. Will Harry accept the offer? Why? If the exchange takes place, will it result in a Pareto improvement? Explain.

Problem 6

The following Edgeworth box shows how two castaways, Robin and Quinn, are allocating labor (measured in hours) and capital (measured in units) to fishing and picking berries. The current input allocation is at point A.

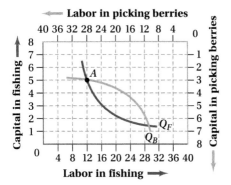

a. How many units of labor and capital are used in the production of each good?
b. Suggest a reallocation of labor and capital between fishing and picking berries that will enable Robin and Quinn to produce more of both goods. Use the preceding diagram to illustrate and explain your answer.

Problem 7

Suppose that there are 20 movie tickets and 8 concert tickets available to two consumers, Billy and Jean. Currently, Billy has 6 movie tickets and 5 concert tickets, and his marginal rate of substitution of movies for concerts (MRS_{MC}) is 1. Jean's MRS_{MC} is 0.1.
a. How many movie tickets and how many concert tickets does Jean have? Is the current allocation of goods Pareto-efficient? Draw an Edgeworth box to illustrate and explain your answer.
b. Suggest a reallocation of movie tickets and concert tickets that will lead to a Pareto improvement if such reallocation is possible, or explain why a Pareto improvement is not possible. Use your Edgeworth box to illustrate and explain your answer.

Problem 8

A small economy uses labor and capital to produce cotton and wheat. The following Edgeworth box shows how the two inputs can be allocated to produce certain quantities of the two goods. Isoquants Q_C indicate the quantities of cotton (in millions of pounds), and isoquants Q_W indicate the quantities of wheat (in millions of bushels). If the economy devotes all labor and capital to cotton production, 160 million pounds of cotton can be produced. If all labor and capital are devoted to wheat production, the economy can produce 300 million bushels of wheat.

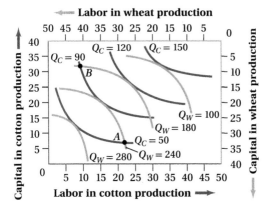

a. Draw the economy's production contract curve.
b. Draw the economy's production possibilities frontier (with cotton on the horizontal axis).
c. Plot points A and B on your PPF graph. Are these points input-efficient? Explain.

Problem 9

Consider an economy that produces only two goods, corn and textiles. At the current production levels, the marginal cost of producing a bushel of corn is $6 and the marginal cost of producing a square yard of textiles is $4. And consumers' marginal rate of substitution of corn for textiles (MRS_{CT}) is 1. Assume that the economy is both input-efficient and exchange-efficient, and both markets are perfectly competitive.
a. What is the marginal rate of transformation from textiles to corn?
b. Is the economy output-efficient? Draw a PPF graph to illustrate and explain your answer.
c. What is likely to happen to the output mix that is currently being produced? Will the combination of the goods produced change? If so, how? Use your PPF graph to explain your answer.

Problem 10

Corn and soybeans are substitutes in consumption. And common inputs are used to produce corn and soybeans. Suppose that the demand for corn is given by

$$Q_c^d = 10 - P_c + 0.5P_s$$

where P_C is the price of corn and P_S is the price of soybeans. And the demand for soybeans is

$$Q_s^d = 10 - P_s + 0.5P_c$$

The supply of corn is given by

$$Q_c^s = 1 + P_c - 0.25P_s$$

and the supply of soybeans is

$$Q_s^s = 1 + P_s - 0.25P_c$$

The quantities are in millions of bushels, and the prices are in dollars per bushel.
a. Are the markets for corn and soybeans linked on the supply side or on the demand side? Explain.
b. Solve for the general equilibrium prices and quantities of corn and soybeans.
c. Suppose that the demand for corn increases, so consumers are willing to buy 3 million bushels more at any given price of corn and of soybeans. How will this affect the general equilibrium prices and quantities of the two goods?

Asymmetric Information

15.1 The Lemons Problem and Adverse Selection

Complete information

Situation in which all participants in an economic transaction know the relevant information.

Asymmetric information

A situation in which there is an imbalance of information across participants in an economic transaction.

Lemons problem

An asymmetric information problem that occurs when a seller knows more about the quality of the good he is selling than does the buyer.

Adverse selection

A situation in which market characteristics lead to more low-quality goods and fewer high-quality goods being put on the market.

15.1 figure it out 1

Suppose that consumers value a high-quality used car at a price of $8,000 and a low-quality used car at $2,000. The supply of high-quality used cars is given by

$$Q_H = -800 + 0.2P_H$$

And the supply of low-quality used cars is

$$Q_L = -200 + 0.2P_L$$

Where Q_H and Q_L are the quantities of high-quality and low-quality cars, respectively, and P_H and P_L are the prices of high-quality and low-quality cars in dollars. Suppose that potential buyers cannot tell the difference between high-quality and low-quality cars when purchasing a used car.

a. Suppose buyers believe there is 50% probability that a used car on the market will be low quality. What is the price that they are willing to pay for a used car?

b. If buyers offer the price determined in (a), how many high-quality used cars will be made available in the market? How many low-quality cars will be available? Are buyers correct in their assumption that 50% of the used cars available for sale are of low quality? Explain.

c. What do you expect to happen over time, as information about the true odds of buying a low-quality used car becomes available to buyers? Explain.

Solution

a. If buyers expect that 50% of the used cars available are of low quality (which means they expect the other 50% to be of high quality), then the expected value of a used car is

$$(0.5 \times \$2,000) + (0.5 \times \$8,000) = \$5,000$$

Therefore, the price that buyers are willing to pay for a used car is $5,000.

b. If buyers offer $5,000 for a used car, the quantity of high-quality cars supplied is

$$Q_H = -800 + 0.2 \times 5,000 = 200$$

and the quantity of low-quality cars supplied is

$$Q_L = -200 + (0.2 \times 5,000) = 800$$

That is, the buyers' assumption that the percentage of low-quality used cars available for sale is 50% is incorrect. The probability that a used car on the market will be of low quality is actually $\dfrac{800}{(800 + 200)}$ = 0.8, or 80%.

c. If buyers expect that 80% of the used cars available are of low quality (which means they expect only 20% to be of high quality), then the expected value of a used car is

$$0.8 \times \$2,000 + 0.2 \times \$8,000 = \$3,200$$

That is, the price that buyers are willing to pay falls to $3,200. This is below the lowest price that owners of high-quality cars are willing to accept (i.e., below the supply choke price). To see that, set $Q_H = 0$ and solve this equation for P_H:

$$Q_H = 0$$
$$-800 + 0.2P_H = 0$$
$$0.2P_H = 800$$
$$P_H = 4,000$$

Thus, the lowest price that owners of high-quality cars are willing to accept is $4,000, while buyers are willing to pay only $3,200. This means only low-quality used cars will be on the market.

15.2 Moral Hazard

Moral hazard

A situation that arises when one party in an economic transaction cannot observe the other party's behavior.

make the grade

Adverse selection vs. moral hazard

Although both adverse selection and moral hazard are problems that exist because of asymmetric information, it is important to understand the difference between these two problems. For example, suppose you are asked the following question on a test:

Consider this statement: "In the market for health insurance, asymmetric information is all about adverse selection, while in the auto insurance market it's all about moral hazard." True or false? Explain.

The answer to this question is that the statement is false. Both problems are usually present in each of the markets. When we talk about adverse selection in insurance, we mean the unobservable riskiness of individuals seeking insurance coverage. Risky drivers are more likely to seek full auto insurance coverage, and unhealthy individuals are more likely to seek health insurance. Therefore, adverse selection is a concern to insurers *before* a policy is written. Moral hazard, in contrast, has to do with situations when individuals make less effort to reduce their risks once they are covered by insurance. For example, they may drive more recklessly or eat unhealthier food. Moral hazard is therefore a concern to insurers *after* a policy has been purchased.

15.2 figure it out 1

Calbert is deciding whether to quit smoking. He currently spends $800 per year on cigarettes, and since smoking adversely influences his health, his medical expenses are as high as $5,000 per year. If Calbert quit smoking, he would be able to reduce his medical expenses to $2,500 per year. However, he enjoys smoking and believes that the monetary equivalent of the utility he derives from it is $2,000 per year.

a. Suppose Calbert does not have health insurance. Should he quit smoking? Explain.

b. Now suppose that Calbert has purchased a health insurance policy that for an annual premium of $2,000 pays 60% of his medical expenses after a deductible of $500 per year. Will this insurance coverage change Calbert's decision regarding smoking? Explain.

c. After the insurance company has sold the insurance policy to Calbert, what kind of information asymmetry problem does it face? Explain. Suggest how the insurer can avoid this problem in this particular situation.

Solution

a. Calbert's cost of quitting smoking is the monetary equivalent of the utility he gives up, or $2,000. His benefits are the $2,500 saved on medical expenses, plus $800 saved on cigarettes, so his total benefit is $2,500 + $800 = $3,300. Since Calbert's benefit from quitting exceeds his cost, he should quit smoking.

b. If Calbert smokes, he pays the first $500 of his $5,000 medical expenses plus 40% of the rest, or $4,500; that is, he pays $500 + (0.4 × $4,500) = $2,300 per year. And if he does not smoke, he pays $500 + (0.4 × $2,000) = $1,300 per year. Thus, Calbert saves $1,000 on medical expenses if he quits smoking. Given that he also saves $800 on cigarettes, his total saving resulting from quitting is $1,000 + $800 = $1,800. Since this is less than the monetary equivalent of the utility he gives up if he quits ($2,000), Calbert will continue to smoke. (Note that since Calbert pays the same insurance premium regardless of whether he smokes, the amount of insurance premium does not influence his decision and therefore is irrelevant here.)

c. After purchasing the insurance policy, Calbert has changed his behavior and now makes less effort to reduce his medical expenses. This means the insurance company faces a moral hazard problem. If Calbert smokes, the insurance company pays ($5,000 − $500) × 0.6 = $2,700 a year to cover his medical expenses. Since this is less than the insurance premium it receives from Calbert ($2,000), the company incurs a loss. If, however, Calbert quit smoking (i.e., made the same effort to reduce his medical expenses as he would without insurance), then the insurance company would pay only ($2,500 − $500) × 0.6 = $1,200 to cover his medical expenses, which is less than the insurance premium it receives from Calbert.

To avoid this moral hazard situation, the insurance company could specify Calbert's not smoking as a condition of coverage, but it would be hard to verify whether Calbert complies. A better approach would be to come up with an insurance policy that does not change Calbert's decision to quit smoking. For example, suppose the insurance policy pays only 50% of Calbert's medical expenses after a deductible of $500. Then, if Calbert smokes, he pays $500 + 0.5 × $4,500 = $2,750 per year in medical expenses. And if he does not smoke, he pays $500 + 0.5 × $2,000 = $1,500 per year. Thus, Calbert now saves $1,250 on medical expenses if he quits smoking. Given that he also saves $800 on cigarettes, his total saving resulting from not smoking is $1,250 + $800 = $2,050. Since this is more than the monetary equivalent of the utility Calbert gives up if he quits ($2,000), Calbert is better off by not smoking. So, he quits, and the insurance company pays ($2,500 − $500) × 0.5 = $1,000 to cover his medical expenses, which is less than the insurance premium it receives from Calbert ($2,000).

15.2 figure it out 2

Bill's medical expenses function is given by

$$X = 3,000 - (200H - 5H^2)$$

where X is his medical expenses in dollars per year, and H is the number of hours per week that he devotes to exercise. From this expenses function, we can conclude that if Bill does not exercise, his medical expenses are $3,000, and exercise saves him

$$B = 200H - 5H^2$$

in medical expenses. (For example, exercising for 5 hours per week will save Bill $875 per year ($200 × 5 − 5 × 5^2 = 875$), so his expenses will be $2,125 per year, rather than $3,000 per year with no exercise.) These saved expenses can be viewed as Bill's benefits from exercising.

Given this benefit function, we can find Bill's marginal benefit curve. It can be proven (using calculus) that if the benefit function has the form

$$B = aH - bH^2$$

then, the marginal benefit curve is given by

$$MB = a - 2bH$$

Given Bill's benefit function, this means his marginal benefit curve is

$$MB = 200 - (2 \times 5H)$$
$$MB = 200 - 10H$$

Suppose Bill's marginal cost of exercising (i.e., the opportunity cost of his time spent on an additional hour of exercise) is given by

$$MC = 10H$$

a. If Bill does not have health insurance, what is his optimal number of hours to exercise?
b. Now suppose that Bill buys a health insurance plan that pays 80% of his medical expenses. How will this change his optimal number of hours to exercise? Explain.

Solution

a. Bill's optimal number of hours to exercise is where his marginal benefit of saving on medical expenses equals the marginal cost of his time. Therefore, to find this number, we set $MB = MC$ and solve this equation for H:

$$200 - 10H = 10H$$
$$-20H = -200$$
$$20H = 200$$
$$H = 10$$

Thus, Bill's optimal length of time to exercise is 10 hours per week.

b. Since the insurance plan pays 80% of Bill's medical expenses, Bill pays only 20% out of pocket. Therefore, with insurance, his expenses function is

$$X_I = 0.2X$$
$$X_I = 0.2 \times [3,000 - (200H - 5H^2)]$$
$$X_I = 600 - (40H - H^2)$$

which means his benefit from exercise is now given by

$$B_I = 40H - H^2$$

In this function, $a = 40$ and $b = 1$, so the corresponding marginal benefit curve is

$$MB_I = 40 - 2H$$

Now we can set $MB_I = MC$ and solve this equation for H:

$$40 - 2H = 10H$$
$$12H = 40$$
$$H = 3\frac{1}{3}$$

Thus, the insurance coverage reduces Bill's optimal time to devote to exercise from 10 hours per week to 3 hours and 20 minutes per week.

15.3 Asymmetric Information in Principal–Agent Relationships

Summary of main concepts and relationships
Principal–agent relationships

Economic transactions that feature information asymmetry between a principal and his hired agent, whose actions the principal cannot fully observe.

15.3 figure it out 1

Shareholders of a small corporation are trying to determine how to structure the compensation of the new CEO. Two options are under consideration. The first option is to offer the CEO a flat salary of $250,000 per year. The second option is to offer her a profit-sharing plan with a base salary of $80,000 plus 10% of the firm's profit. If the CEO puts high effort into the job, the firm's annual profit will be $2 million, with 80% probability and $1 million, with 20% probability. If the CEO exerts low effort, the probability of the firm's profit will be reversed, that is, there will be 80% probability of $1 million profit and 20% probability of $2 million. The CEO's opportunity cost of putting high effort into the job is $140,000, while her opportunity cost of exerting low effort is $85,000.

a. Draw the game tree for the interaction between the shareholders and the CEO, assuming that the shareholders move first.

b. What is the equilibrium outcome for this game? What kind of contract should the shareholders offer? What level of effort will the CEO choose?

Solution

a. First, let's calculate the expected payoffs for each option. If the CEO works hard, the corporation's expected profit is (0.8 × $2 million) + (0.2 × $1 million) = $1.8 million. If she works with low efforts, the expected profit is (0.2 × $2 million) + (0.8 × $1 million) = $1.2 million.

With the flat salary option, if the CEO puts high effort into the job, the shareholders' expected payoff (the company's expected profit minus the compensation paid to the CEO) will be $1,800,000 – $250,000 = $1,550,000, while the CEO's payoff (the difference between her compensation and her opportunity cost of exerting high effort) will be $250,000 – $140,000 = $110,000. If, however, the CEO puts low effort into her job, the shareholder's expected payoff will be $1,200,000 – $250,000 = $950,000, while the CEO's payoff will be $250,000 – $85,000 = $165,000 (the difference between her compensation and her opportunity cost of exerting low effort).

With the profit-sharing plan, the CEO's compensation will be $80,000 plus 10% of the expected profit. So, if the CEO works with high effort, she will earn $80,000 + 0.1 × $1,800,000 = $260,000. In this case, the shareholder's expected payoff (the company's expected profit minus the compensation paid to the CEO) will be $1,800,000 – $260,000 = $1,540,000, while the CEO's expected payoff (the difference between her compensation and her opportunity cost) will be $260,000 – $140,000 = $120,000. If the CEO works with low effort, her expected compensation will be $80,000 + 0.1 × $1,200,000 = $200,000. Then, the shareholder's payoff will be $1,200,000 – $200,000 = $1,000,000, while the CEO's payoff will be $200,000 – $85,000 = $115,000 (the difference between her compensation and her opportunity cost of low effort). The following game tree shows each player's payoffs (in thousands of dollars) associated with each of the two options.

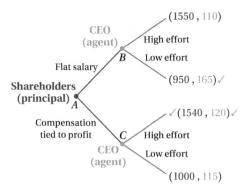

b. As with any sequential game, we can find the equilibrium, using backward induction. Suppose the shareholders choose the flat salary option. This takes the game to node B, where the CEO decides whether to work hard or put only modest effort into the job. Since the CEO's payoff from choosing low effort is greater (165 > 110), she will choose to work with low effort. Now suppose shareholders choose to offer the profit-sharing plan. This takes us to node C, where the CEO makes her decision. Here, since the CEO's expected payoff is greater when she works hard (120 > 115), she will prefer this choice. Now that we've solved for the last stage of the game, we can figure out the shareholders' choice in the first stage. If the shareholders choose the flat salary option, the CEO will not work hard and the shareholders' expected payoff will be $950,000. If the shareholders choose to link the CEO's pay to the company's profit, the CEO will work hard and the shareholders' expected payoff will be $1,540,000. Since $1,540,000 > $950,000, the shareholders' preferred option is the compensation structure linked to the company's profit. Thus, the equilibrium of this principal–agent game is where the shareholders offer the CEO the profit-sharing compensation plan and the CEO chooses to work hard.

15.3 figure it out 2

Suppose that there are two types of workers on the job market: high-productivity workers (let's call them "achievers") and low-productivity workers (let's call them "slackers"). Firms are willing to pay $350,000 over the course of a worker's lifetime (in present value terms) to an achiever and $200,000 to a slacker (since these are the values a worker of each type produces for a firm). But employers cannot tell on sight whether a job applicant is an achiever of a slacker, so they try to separate high-productivity workers from low-productivity workers by offering $350,000 to job applicants with a college degree and $200,000 to those without a college degree. For an achiever, it takes four years to obtain a college degree, and each year costs $30,000 (including the psychological monetary cost equivalent of studying). For a slacker, it takes five years, and each year costs $40,000. Assume, for the sake of simplicity, that college education adds nothing to either worker's productivity.

a. What is the net benefit of completing college for an achiever? For a slacker?
b. Will employers be able to separate high-productivity workers from low-productivity workers? Explain.

Solution

a. For an achiever, the cost of completing college is

$$C_A = \$30,000 \times 4 = \$120,000$$

and for a slacker, it is

$$C_S = \$40,000 \times 5 = \$200,000$$

Since the wage premium offered by employers to workers with a college degree is $350,000 – $200,000 = $150,000, the net benefit of completing college for an achiever is

$$NB_A = \$150,000 - \$120,000 = \$30,000$$

and for a slacker, it is

$$NB_S = \$150,000 - \$200,000 = -\$50,000$$

b. As the net benefits calculated in (a) suggest, high-productivity workers are $30,000 better off if they finish college, so they will. And low-productivity workers are worse off (since their net benefit of completing college is negative), so they won't go to college. This means all job applicants with a college degree will be high-productivity workers, and all those without higher education will be slackers. Thus, paying a wage premium to college graduates will enable employers to separate high-productivity workers from low-productivity workers.

15.4 Signaling to Solve Asymmetric Information Problems

Signaling

A solution to the problem of asymmetric information in which the knowledgeable party alerts the other party to an unobservable characteristic of the good.

Signal

A costly action taken by an economic actor to indicate something that would otherwise be difficult to observe.

make the grade

Understanding signaling

Recall that signaling is a solution to the problem of asymmetric information in which the knowledgeable party alerts the other party to an unobservable characteristic of the good. It is important to understand how signaling can help solve the problem of asymmetric information. In order for a signal to work, it must be cheaper for higher-quality producers to send it than it is for lower-quality producers.

For example, suppose a computer repair firm is considering two strategies to signal that its services are of high quality (and they in fact are): (1) change the firm's name from WYZ Tweaks to WYZ Quality Tweaks and (2) offer a three-month warranty for its services. Which of these two strategies do you think is more effective as a signal of high quality? The change of the firm's name is just "cheap talk." Any firm can insert the word "quality" into its name, and the cost of doing so will not differ between firms providing high-quality services and those providing low-quality services. Offering the warranty is a much more effective signal. Since WYZ Tweak provides high-quality services, offering a warranty is less expensive for it than for firms that provide low-quality services. Thus, consumers will believe that a firm offering a warranty provides higher-quality services than firms that do not.

Practice Problems
Problem 1

Suppose that half of the contractors in the market for home remodeling offer high-quality services and the other half is incompetent. Homeowners value a typical high-quality remodeling at $25,000, but remodeling done by an incompetent contractor has no value to them. However, homeowners don't know what quality of workmanship to expect from a contractor when purchasing the service. High-quality contractors value their work at $20,000 per typical remodeling, and incompetent contractors value their service at $10,000.
a. What is the most that a homeowner is willing to pay for a typical remodeling?
b. What will be the market outcome in this situation? Will homeowners hire high-quality contractors? Incompetent contractors? Explain.

Problem 2

Suppose that consumers value a high-quality used car at $9,000, and a low-quality used car at $4,000. The supply of high-quality used cars is given by

$$Q_H = -1,250 + 0.25P_H$$

and the supply of low-quality used cars is

$$Q_L = -1,250 + 0.5P_L$$

where Q_H and Q_L are the quantities of high-quality and low-quality cars, respectively, and P_H and P_L are the prices of high-quality and low-quality cars in dollars. Potential buyers cannot tell the difference between high-quality and low-quality cars when purchasing a used car.
a. Suppose that buyers believe there is a 60% chance that a used car on the market is of low quality and a 40% chance that it is of high quality. What is the price that buyers are willing to pay for a used car?
b. If buyers offer the price determined in (a), how many high-quality used cars will be made available for sale? How many low-quality cars will be available? Are buyers correct in their assumption that 60% of the used cars available for sale are of low quality? Explain.
c. What will happen over time, as information about the true odds of buying a low-quality used car become available to buyers? Explain.

Problem 3

Caroline likes junk food, but she has recently realized that eating junk food increases her risk of various health problems. Her friend, a student of public health, estimates that if Caroline continues to eat junk food, her medical expenses will be $4,000 per year, but if she switches to healthy food, she can reduce her medical expenses to $2,000 per year. Assume that healthy food costs Caroline the same as junk food, but the monetary equivalent of the utility derived from food enjoyment that Caroline gives up if she switches to healthy food is $700 per year.

a. Suppose Caroline does not have health insurance. Should she stop eating junk food? Explain.
b. Now suppose that Caroline has purchased a health insurance policy that for an annual premium of $1,800 pays 80% of her medical expenses. Will this insurance coverage change Caroline's decision with regard to junk food? Explain.
c. After the insurance company has sold its insurance policy to Caroline, what kind of information asymmetry problem does it face? Explain. Will the insurance company avoid this problem if it pays only 60% of Caroline's medical expenses? Explain.

Problem 4

Simona's medical expenses function is given by

$$X = 4{,}000 - (100H - 5H^2)$$

where X is her medical expenses in dollars per year, and H is the number of hours per week that she devotes to exercise. Note that according to this medical expenses function, Simona's benefit from exercise can be expressed as

$$B = 100H - 5H^2$$

Suppose Simona's marginal cost of exercising (i.e., her opportunity cost of time spent on an additional hour of working out) is

$$MC = 1 + H$$

a. If Simona does not have health insurance, what is her optimal number of hours to exercise? (*Hint*: Derive Simona's marginal benefit curve as explained in 15.2 figure it out, Problem 2.)
b. Now suppose that Simona gets a health insurance plan that pays 90% of her medical expenses. How will this change her optimal number of hours to exercise? Explain.

Problem 5

Consider an online market for desktop computers. Suppose both buyers and sellers are price takers, that is, no one has market power. Assume, for simplicity, that there are only two types of computers on the market, high-quality and low-quality. Assume also that every potential buyer is willing to pay $800 for a high-quality computer and $300 for a low-quality one. The supply of high-quality computers is given by

$$Q_H = -55 + 0.1P_H$$

and the supply of low-quality computers is

$$Q_L = -50 + 0.25P_L$$

where Q_H and Q_L are in thousands and P_H and P_L are in dollars.

a. Suppose all buyers and sellers have full information about the quality of computers being offered. How many high-quality computers and how many low-quality computers will be sold?
b. Now suppose that potential buyers believe that there is a 50% chance that a computer on the market is of low quality, but they can't tell whether a computer is high-quality or low-quality when purchasing it. In this situation, what is the immediate market outcome? What price are buyers willing to pay for a computer? How many high-quality computers and how many low-quality computers will be sold?
c. If the market outcome is as determined in (b), what is the deadweight loss resulting from asymmetric information? (*Hint*: Draw the supply and demand curves for high-quality computers in the market where full information is available and in the market with asymmetric information; then, on a separate diagram, do the same for low-quality computers.)

Problem 6

Suppose there are two types of potential buyers in the market for individual health insurance: Type A and Type B. There are 40 million of Type A individuals and 60 million of Type B individuals. Type A are young and healthy individuals whose expected medical expenses are $1,000 per year. Type B are older individuals who are more likely to have health problems and whose expected medical expenses are $5,000 per year. All insurance policies offered in the market have the same terms: they cover 80% of all medical expenses with no deductible. Both Type A and Type B individuals are risk averse, and the risk premium they agree to pay if offered this insurance plan is equal to 10% of their expected medical expenses with no insurance. Assume that the insurance companies have no market power, and their average total cost of providing insurance (operating costs, etc.) is constant at $200 per customer.

a. Suppose that insurance companies can distinguish between Type A and Type B individuals by screening their potential customers, but screening costs them extra $150 per insured customer. Will the companies be able to insure Type A individuals? Type B individuals? Explain.

b. Suppose that insurance companies know, without screening, that 40% of their potential customers are Type A and 60% are Type B, but they are not allowed to discriminate based on the type of the insured. Will the insurance companies be able to sell their policies to Type A individuals? To Type B individuals? Explain.

c. Now, given the situation in (b), suppose that the government mandates that every individual must buy health insurance. How will the mandate affect insurance coverage and gains from trade in the market for health insurance?

Problem 7

A hotel owner is trying to determine how to structure his manager's compensation. One option he considers is a flat salary of $70,000 per year. The second option is a base salary of $30,000 plus 15% of the hotel's profit. If the manager puts a lot of effort into her job, the hotel's annual profit will be $500,000 with 75% probability and $100,000 with 25% probability. If the manager exerts only modest effort, the hotel's profit will be $500,000 with 25% probability and $100,000 with 75% probability. The manager's opportunity cost of putting a lot of effort into her job is $50,000, while her opportunity cost of exerting only modest effort is $25,000.

a. Draw the game tree for the interaction between the hotel owner and the manager. Assume that the hotel owner moves first.

b. What is the equilibrium outcome for this game? What kind of contract should the hotel owner offer? What level of effort will the manager choose? Explain.

Problem 8

Suppose there are two types of individuals on the job market: one half of the job seekers are "hard workers" and the other half are "slackers." A hard worker's reservation wage (in present value terms) is $450,000 over the course of the worker's lifetime (i.e., she won't work for less), and a slacker's reservation wage is $300,000. Firms are willing to pay $450,000 to a hard worker (since this is the value a hard worker produces for a firm), and $300,000 to a slacker (since this is the value a slacker produces). Employers, however, cannot tell on sight whether a job applicant is a hard worker or a slacker. They try to separate hard workers from slackers by offering a wage premium to job applicants with a college degree. Assume that the job market is competitive, that is, neither firms nor workers have market power.

Suppose that a hard worker can obtain a college degree in four years, and each year costs him $25,000 (including the psychic monetary cost equivalent of studying). For a slacker, it takes six years to complete college, and each year costs $35,000. Assume, for simplicity, that college education by itself adds nothing to a worker's productivity.

Will firms be able to separate hard workers from slackers by offering a wage premium to job applicants with a college degree? Explain your answer.

Problem 9

Consider the scenario in Problem 8 again, but now suppose that colleges practice grade inflation. This does not affect "hard workers," but "slackers" can now obtain a college degree in five years, and each year costs them $28,000. How will this affect the job market outcome? Will firms still be able to separate hard workers from slackers by offering a wage premium to job applicants with a college degree? Does grade inflation benefit students? Explain your answers.

Problem 10

Mr. Fairfield suspects that his wife is cheating on him and files for divorce. If he can prove his wife's adultery, he will receive a $2 million settlement. If he cannot, his settlement will be $1 million. His lawyer presents him with the following payment options: (1) a $100,000 flat fee, (2) 10% of the settlement. The lawyer promises to hire a private detective at his (the lawyer's) own expense, $30,000, to prove Mrs. Fairfield's infidelity, but the client cannot verify whether the lawyer actually does this. If hired, the detective will prove Mrs. Fairfield's adultery for sure, while without a private detective there is only a 10% chance that her adultery will be proved.

a. Draw the game tree for the interaction between Mr. Fairfield and his lawyer. Who is the principal and who is the agent?

b. Which option should Mr. Fairfield choose? What is the equilibrium outcome for this game? Explain.

Externalities and Public Goods

16

16.1 Externalities

Externality

A cost or benefit that affects a third party not directly involved in an economic transaction.

Negative externality

A cost imposed on a third party not directly involved in an economic transaction.

Positive externality

A benefit conferred on a third party not directly involved in an economic transaction.

External marginal cost

The cost imposed on a third party when an additional unit of a good is produced or consumed.

External marginal benefit

The benefit conferred on a third party when an additional unit of a good is produced or consumed.

Social cost

The cost of an economic transaction to society, equal to the private cost plus the external cost.

Social benefit

The benefit of an economic transaction to society, equal to the private benefit plus the external benefit.

16.1 figure it out 1

Suppose newsprint is sold in a free perfectly competitive market. The industry short-run supply curve is

$$Q^S = -40 + 0.1P$$

and the market demand for newsprint is given by

$$Q^D = 60 - 0.1P$$

where the quantity is measured in millions of tons and the price is in dollars per ton. Suppose that the external marginal cost of the pollution generated by the industry is estimated to be $50 for each ton of newsprint produced.
a. What is the market equilibrium price and quantity of newsprint?
b. What is the socially optimal level of output and price of newsprint?
c. What is the deadweight loss in the market for newsprint (if any)?

Solution

a. In a free perfectly competitive market, firms don't take into account external costs when making their production decisions. They choose their optimal level of output at the point where price—which equals marginal revenue and is represented by the demand curve—is equal to the industry's private marginal cost, which is represented by the (inverse) supply curve. Thus, we can find the market equilibrium price by setting $Q^S = Q^D$ and solving this equation for P:

$$Q^S = Q^D$$
$$-40 + 0.1P = 60 - 0.1P$$
$$0.2P = 100$$
$$P = 500$$

Now we can find the equilibrium quantity by substituting $P = 500$ into either the demand or the supply equation:

$$Q^D = 60 - 0.1 \times 500 = 10$$
$$Q^S = -40 + 0.1 \times 500 = 10$$

Thus, the market equilibrium price is \$500 per ton and the equilibrium quantity is 10 million tons.

b. The socially optimal level of output is where consumers' marginal benefit equals social marginal cost. The marginal benefit received by consumers is reflected by the price they are willing to pay, so the inverse demand curve—which shows the prices that consumers are willing to pay at each given level of output—is also the marginal benefit curve. (The concept of inverse demand curve is explained in detail in Chapter 2.) To derive this curve, we solve the demand equation for P:

$$Q^D = 60 - 0.1P$$
$$0.1P = 60 - Q$$
$$P^D = 600 - 10Q$$
$$MB = 600 - 10Q$$

Social marginal cost (SMC) equals the sum of the industry's private marginal cost (MC_I) and the external marginal cost (EMC). The industry's marginal cost is represented by its inverse supply curve, which can be derived by solving the supply equation for P:

$$Q^S = -40 + 0.1P$$
$$0.1P = 40 + Q$$
$$P^S = 400 + 10Q$$
$$MC = 400 + 10Q$$

Since $SMC = MC_I + EMC$, and $EMC = \$50$ (as given in the question), we can calculate the SMC of producing newsprint as follows:

$$SMC = (400 + 10Q) + 50$$
$$SMC = 450 + 10Q$$

Now we can solve for the socially optimal level of newsprint output by setting $MB = SMC$:

$$600 - 10Q = 450 + 10Q$$
$$20Q = 150$$
$$Q = 7.5$$

Substituting $Q = 7.5$ into either SMC or MB equation, we find the socially optimal price of newsprint:

$$SMC = 450 + 10 \times 7.5 = 525$$
$$MB = 600 - 10 \times 7.5 = 525$$

Thus, the socially optimal output of newsprint is 7.5 million tons, and the socially optimal price is \$525 per ton. The diagram on the right illustrates this solution.

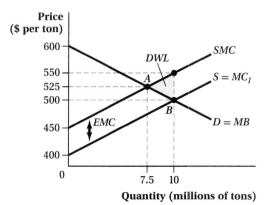

c. The deadweight loss arises because firms in the industry choose their level of output without taking into account external costs (which they don't pay), so they produce more newsprint than the efficient level of output. At the socially optimal level of output (point A on the preceding graph), every buyer of newsprint values it at least as much as it costs society to produce it, including the external costs. The industry produces at point B, however, and the portion of the demand curve between points A and B represents buyers who value the newsprint less than it costs society to produce. If the price reflected the true cost of the product, buyers would not purchase this newsprint. Therefore, the deadweight loss arising from the externality is the triangular area below the social marginal cost curve (SMC) and above the demand (marginal benefit) curve ($D = MB$), between the socially optimal level of output (7.5 million tons) and the market equilibrium output (10 million tons). This triangle is the sum of the losses from each ton of newsprint for which society's costs are greater than its benefits. Since at $Q = 10$, $SMC = 450 + 10 \times 10 = 550$, the base of the DWL triangle is $\$550 - \$500 = \$50$. And its height is 10 million $-$ 7.5 million $= 2.5$ million. Thus, we calculate the deadweight loss as follows:

$$DWL = 0.5 \times \$50 \times 2.5 \text{ million} = 62.5 \text{ million}$$

16.2 Fixing Externalities

Efficient level of pollution

The level of emissions necessary to produce the efficient quantity of the good tied to the externality.

Marginal abatement cost (MAC)

The cost of reducing emissions by one unit.

Pigouvian tax

A tax imposed on an activity that creates a negative externality.

Pigouvian subsidy

A subsidy paid for an activity that creates a positive externality.

Quota

A regulation mandating that the production or consumption of a certain quantity of a good or externality be limited (negative externality) or required (positive externality).

Tradable permit

A government-issued permit that allows a firm to emit a certain amount of pollution during production and that can be traded to other firms.

16.2 figure it out 1

Consider again the scenario in 16.1 figure it out 1. Suppose that the government imposes a \$50 tax on each ton of newsprint sold.
a. With the tax, what is the market equilibrium price and quantity of newsprint?
b. What is the deadweight loss in the market for newsprint (if any)?

Solution

a. See the following graph. The tax increases the private marginal cost of producing newsprint, that is, it shifts the industry's private marginal cost curve (MC_I) up by the amount of the per ton tax ($T = \$50$). That is, the industry's inverse supply curve with the tax is

$$P^{ST} = MC_I + T$$
$$P^{ST} = (400 + 10Q) + 50$$
$$P^{ST} = 450 + 10Q$$

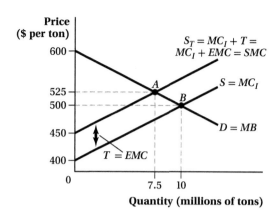

We can solve for the market equilibrium quantity by equating this inverse supply curve (which shows the prices at which producers are willing to supply each given quantity of newsprint), and the inverse demand curve derived in 16.1 figure it out 1 (which shows the prices at which consumers are willing to buy each given quantity):

$$P^{ST} = P^D$$
$$450 + 10Q = 600 - 10Q$$
$$20Q = 150$$
$$Q = 7.5$$

Now we can find the equilibrium price by substituting $Q = 7.5$ into either the demand or the supply equation:

$$P^D = 600 - (10 \times 7.5) = 525$$
$$P^{ST} = 450 + (10 \times 7.5) = 525$$

Thus, the market equilibrium price is $525 per ton and the equilibrium quantity is 7.5 million tons (point A on the preceding graph).

b. Because the per ton tax equals the external marginal cost of producing newsprint ($T = EMC$), with the tax, the industry's marginal cost curve (inverse supply curve) (S_T) is the same as the social marginal cost curve (SMC):

$$S_T = MC_I + T = MC_I + EMC = SMC$$

Therefore, with the tax, when the market is in equilibrium, the social marginal cost of producing newsprint equals the marginal benefit. This means the efficient level of output is achieved, so there is no deadweight loss.

16.2 figure it out 2

Suppose there are only two coal-burning power plants in the electricity industry, Alpha and Beta. In the absence of regulation, Alpha emits 60 tons of pollutants, and Beta emits 70 tons. Government regulators estimate that the optimal level of pollution for the industry is 80 tons and would like to lower the total pollution by the two plants to this level. Alpha's total abatement cost curve is

$$TAC_A = 2e_A + 0.5e_A^2$$

which means its marginal abatement cost is given by

$$MAC_A = 2 + e_A$$

Where e_A is the number of tons of pollution cut by Alpha. The costs are in thousands of dollars. Beta's total abatement cost curve is

$$TAC_B = 4e_B + 1.5e_B^2$$

so its marginal abatement cost is

$$MAC_B = 4 + 3e_B$$

Where e_B is the number of tons of pollution cut by Beta.

a. Suppose that the regulators implement a quantity regulation, dividing the optimal level of pollution equally between the firms, that is, allowing each firm to produce no more than 40 tons of pollution. How much will this regulation cost each firm? What will be the total cost of reducing the pollution to its optimal level?

b. Now suppose that the regulators issue 80 tradable pollution permits and divide them equally between the two firms. Each permit allows the firm that owns it to emit 1 ton of pollutant. How many tons of pollution will each plant emit? What will be the price of a permit? What will be the total cost of reducing the pollution to its optimal level? How does it compare with the total cost of the quantity regulation in (a)?

Solution

a. Alpha will have to cut $60 - 40 = 20$ tons of pollution, so the regulation will cost it

$$TAC_A = 2 \times 20 + 0.5 \times 20^2 = 240 \text{ (thousand dollars)}$$

Beta will have to cut $70 - 40 = 30$ tons of pollution, so its cost will be

$$TAC_B = 4 \times 30 + 1.5 \times 30^2 = 1{,}470 \text{ (thousand dollars)}$$

Thus, the total cost of reducing the pollution to its optimal level will be

$$\$240{,}000 + \$1{,}470{,}000 = \$1{,}710{,}000$$

b. The firms will trade the permits until their marginal abatement costs are equalized, that is,

$$MAC_A = MAC_B$$

$$2 + e_A = 4 + 3e_B$$

We also know that, since the number of permits is 80, the industry must reduce the pollution by $(60 + 70) - 80 = 50$ tons. That is

$$e_A + e_B = 50$$

from which

$$e_B = 50 - e_A$$

We can substitute this expression into the marginal abatement cost equality condition and solve it for e_A:

$$2 + e_A = 4 + 3(50 - e_A)$$
$$2 + e_A = 4 + 150 - 3e_A$$
$$4e_A = 152$$
$$e_A = 38$$

Now we can find e_B by substituting e_A into the preceding equation:

$$e_B = 50 - 38 = 12$$

That is, Alpha will emit $60 - 38 = 22$ tons of pollution, and Beta will emit $70 - 12 = 58$ tons.

When the market for tradable permits is in equilibrium, the price of a permit is equal to each firm's marginal cost of abatement:

$$P_{per} = MAC_A = MAC_B$$
$$P_{per} = 2 + e_A = 2 + 38 = 40$$
$$P_{per} = 4 + 3e_B = 4 + (3 \times 12) = 40$$

So, the price of a permit will be $40,000.

Since Alpha has to cut 38 tons of pollution, its total cost of abatement is

$$TAC_A = (2 \times 38) + (0.5 \times 38^2) = 798 \text{ thousand dollars}$$

And since Beta must cut 12 tons of pollution, its total cost of abatement is

$$TAC_B = (4 \times 12) + (1.5 \times 12^2) = 264 \text{ thousand dollars}$$

Thus, the total cost of reducing the pollution to its optimal level is $798,000 + $264,000 = $1,062,000. This is $648,000 less than the $1,710,000 total abatement cost of the quantity regulation in (a). Note that both firms are better off with the tradable permits than with the quantity regulation. Alpha's total abatement cost is higher with the permits ($798,000) than with the quantity regulation ($240,000). But it makes money by selling its permits to Beta. That is, Alpha sells 40 − 22 = 18 permits at $40,000 per permit, receiving a revenue of $40,000 × 22 = $880,000, which is more than its total cost of abatement. Beta pays $880,000 for the permits, but its total cost of abatement plus the amount paid for the permits ($264,000 + $880,000 = $1,144,000) is still less than its total abatement cost under the pollution quota ($1,470,000).

16.3 Further Topics in Externalities and Their Remedies

Tragedy of the commons

The phenomenon that a common resource is used more intensively than it would be if it were privately owned.

Common resource

An economic good that all individuals can access freely and whose value to the individual consumer decreases as others use it.

Nonexcludability

A defining property of a common resource, that consumers cannot be prevented from consuming the good.

Coase theorem

Theorem that states that costless negotiation among market participants will lead to the efficient market outcome regardless of who holds legal property rights.

make the grade

Understanding externalities

There are three important things about externalities that you should be sure to remember and understand:

First, an externality is a cost or a benefit that affects someone who is not directly involved in the economic transaction in question. For example, a paper mill is a seller in the market for paper. But if it dumps waste that resulted from paper production into a river, it affects people and businesses using the river (for recreation, fishing, etc.) and may have nothing to do with buying or selling paper. (Therefore, we call such a person or business "a third party.")

Second, a negative externality imposes a cost on a third party (an external cost) that is not taken into account by the market participants. Therefore, it results in overproduction, that is, a market equilibrium quantity that is above the efficient level. For example, fossil-fuel-fired power plants create air pollution when they generate electricity. They decide how much electricity to produce by equating their marginal revenue to their private marginal cost, without taking into account external costs that the pollution imposes on other people. Therefore, the industry overproduces electricity. A positive externality, in contrast, provides a benefit to a third party (an external benefit) that is not taken into account by the market. Therefore, it results in underproduction, that is, a market equilibrium where the quantity is below the efficient level. For example, when people decide whether to go to college, they compare their own benefits of getting a college degree with their own costs. But they don't take into account the fact that when more people acquire a college degree, the pay and job prospects of other people rise. Therefore, a free market for higher education leads people to purchase less of it than would be socially optimal. Thus, left to its own devices, a free market with negative externalities produces more than the optimal welfare-maximizing quantity of the good. And a free market with positive externalities produces less than the optimal quantity.

Third, governments can impose Pigouvian taxes or subsidies on markets with externalities to bring the private costs and benefits in line with the true costs and benefits to society. However, this is not the only way to correct for the market failures due to externalities. As the Coase theorem states, if negotiation among market participants costs low enough, it may lead to the efficient market outcome with no government intervention.

16.3 figure it out 1

A paper mill dumps waste into a lake used by a catfish farmer. The farmer's marginal cost of the pollution is given by

$$EMC = 0.5Q$$

Where Q is the quantity of paper (tons per week) produced by the mill. The marginal cost of producing paper is

$$MC = 5 + 0.5Q$$

And the society's marginal benefit from consuming paper (the inverse demand curve for paper) is given by

$$MB = 65 - Q$$

Assume that the markets are perfectly competitive, with no regulation, and that the paper mill and the farmer can bargain costlessly.

a. If the farmer owns the lake, how much paper will be produced? How will this outcome be reached? Will any money change hands between the mill and the farmer? Is this outcome socially optimal?

b. Now suppose the paper mill owns the lake and rents it to the farmer. A pollution-free lake rents for $1,000 a week. How much paper will be produced? For how much will the farmer rent the lake from the mill? Is this outcome socially optimal?

Solution

a. If the farmer owns the lake, he charges the paper mill his cost of the pollution. Thus, it becomes part of the mill's private marginal cost. That is, the private marginal cost of producing paper is

$$MC_P = MC + EMC$$
$$MC_P = 5 + 0.5Q + 0.5Q$$
$$MC_P = 5 + Q$$

In a perfectly competitive market, this is also the paper mill's inverse supply curve. Therefore, we can solve for the equilibrium quantity of paper by equating this inverse supply curve with the inverse demand/marginal benefit curve:

$$MC_P = MB$$
$$5 + Q = 65 - Q$$
$$2Q = 60$$
$$Q = 30$$

Thus, 30 tons of paper per week will be produced. The farmer then will charge the paper mill $(0.5 \times 30) = 15$ dollars per ton of paper produced or $(15 \times 30) = \$450$ per week for polluting his lake.

Since the transacting parties take the external costs of producing paper (i.e., the cost of the pollution to the farmer) into account, in equilibrium, the social marginal cost of producing paper equals the marginal benefit. Therefore, the market outcome is socially optimal.

b. Since the pollution reduces the market value of the lake, the rent that the farmer is willing to pay is lower than he would pay for a pollution-free lake by the amount of $EMC = 0.5Q$ per ton. This is the paper mill's opportunity cost of polluting the lake, which is essentially an increase in the mill's private marginal cost. That is, the mill's private marginal cost is, again,

$$MC_P = MC + EMC$$
$$MC_P = 5 + Q$$

Therefore, the equilibrium quantity of paper will be the same as in (a), 30 tons per week. But the cost of pollution is now borne by the paper mill, since it receives a lower rent than it would if the lake were pollution free. The rent is reduced by $(0.5 \times 30) = 15$ dollars per ton of paper produced or by $(\$15 \times 30) = \$450$ per week, so rather than receiving $1,000, the mill receives only $1,000 - \$450 = \$550$ per week.

Again, since the transacting parties take the external costs of producing paper into account, the market equilibrium occurs where the social marginal cost of producing paper equals the marginal benefit. Therefore, the market outcome is socially optimal.

16.4 Public Goods

Public good

Public goods are goods (such as national defense, a fireworks display, or clean air) that are accessible to anyone who wants to consume them and that remain just as valuable to the consumer even as other people consume them.

Nonrival

Defining property of a public good that describes how one individual's consumption of the good does not diminish another consumer's enjoyment of the same good.

Private good

A good that is rival (one person's consumption affects the ability of another to consume it) and excludable (individuals can be prevented from consuming it).

Club good

A good that is nonrival and excludable.

Total marginal benefit

The vertical sum of the marginal benefit curves of all of a public good's consumers.

Free-rider problem

A source of inefficiency resulting from individuals consuming a public good or service without paying for it.

make the grade

Goods categorized by rivalry and excludability

The following table will help you categorize goods based on rivalry and excludability.

	Excludable: Individuals can be kept from consuming	**Nonexcludable:** Individuals cannot be kept from consuming
Rival: One individual's consumption affects another's consumption	**Private good:** pizza, gasoline, pencil, candy bar	**Common resource:** shared property, fisheries, interstate highways
Nonrival: One individual's consumption has no effect on another's consumption	**Club good:** Satellite TV services, private park, movie	**Public good:** fireworks display, mosquito abatement, national defense, clean air

16.4 figure it out 1

Suppose there are five stores in a mall. Each store's demand for guard services, which reflects the store's marginal benefit from a reduction in thefts, is given by

$$Q^D = 100 - 5P$$

The competitive supply of guard services is given by

$$Q^S = -50 + 5P$$

The quantity of guard services is measured in guard-hours per week, and the price is in dollars per guard-hour. Guards patrolling the mall provide the service without rivalry; that is, all the stores are protected simultaneously and one store's protection does not diminish another store's security. The stores are considering forming an association to share the costs of the guard services.

a. Suppose the stores form an association, with each member paying an equal share for the guard services. How many guard-hours will they hire? Will they get the optimal level of the service? Explain.

b. If each store purchased its own guard services, how many guard-hours would it hire? Would the stores get the optimal level of protection? Explain.

Solution

a. The stores will hire the quantity of the service for which the stores' total marginal benefit equals the marginal cost of the services. Since the guard services are nonrival and the stores receive them simultaneously, the total marginal benefit curve is the vertical sum of the stores' individual marginal benefit curves. We can find each store's marginal benefit (which is its inverse demand curve) by solving the demand equation for P:

$$Q^D = 100 - 5P$$
$$5P = 100 - Q$$
$$P^D = MB = 20 - 0.2Q$$

Since the stores have the same MB curves, we can find the total marginal benefit curve simply by multiplying the individual MB curve by five:

$$MB_T = 5 \times MB = 5(20 - 0.2Q)$$
$$MB_T = 100 - Q$$

The guard service providers' marginal cost curve is their inverse supply curve, so we can find it by solving the supply equation for P:

$$Q^S = -50 + 5P$$
$$5P = 50 + Q$$
$$P^S = MC = 10 + 0.2Q$$

Now we can find the equilibrium quantity of the guard services by setting $MB_T = MC$ and solving this equation for Q:

$$MB_T = MC$$
$$100 - Q = 10 + 0.2Q$$
$$1.2Q = 90$$
$$Q = 75$$

Thus, the stores will hire 75 guard-hours per week (point A on the following diagram). The stores receive the optimal level of the service because their total marginal benefit equals the marginal cost of providing the service.

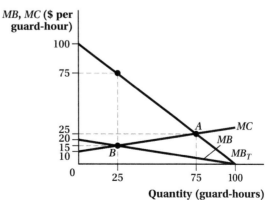

b. If each store purchased its own guard service, it would choose the level of service at which the store's individual marginal benefit equals the price (i.e., the marginal cost of the service). So we can find the equilibrium quantity of the guard services by setting $MB = MC$ and solving this equation for Q:

$$MB = MC$$
$$20 - 0.2Q = 10 + 0.2Q$$
$$0.4Q = 10$$
$$Q = 25$$

Thus, each store would hire 25 guard-hours per week (point B on the preceding diagram). The stores would receive the service below the optimal level. At this level, their total marginal benefit when the service is provided as a club good ($MB_T = 100 - Q = 75$ dollars) is greater than the marginal cost of providing the service ($15). Note also that the service is more costly to a store when its purchased as a private good at $15 per guard-hour than when it is received as a club good, when the association pays $P = MC = 10 + 0.2Q = 10 + 0.2 \times 75 = 25$ dollars per guard-hour, with each store paying only $\frac{\$25}{5} = \$5$ per guard-hour.

Practice Problems
Problem 1

A small community of 10 households is considering implementing a neighborhood watch program. The following table shows each homeowner's willingness to pay for the program.

Homeowner	Willingness to pay ($ per year)
Aaron	300
Betty	450
Cindy	200
Don	350
Elliot	400
Frank	425
George	340
Haley	270
Ivan	340
Jayson	285

The program would cost $3,300 per year.
a. Is it efficient for the community to implement this program? Explain your answer.
b. Will any of the households implement the watch program privately? Explain.
c. Suppose that the program is put to a vote at a homeowners meeting, with the suggestion that the cost would be split evenly among the ten households. Will the program pass by majority vote? Explain.

Problem 2

A large farm is located near a resort. The farm uses pesticides, and the chemical waste flows into the river, making the resort a less desirable vacation place, which reduces its profit by $20,000 per year. The farm can alter its production process, which would reduce the pollution to a level that does not affect the resort. This pollution abatement would cost the farm $18,000 per year. Assume that the farm and the resort can bargain costlessly.
a. Suppose that the resort has the property right to the pollution-free river. Will the farm alter its production process? Will the socially optimal outcome be reached? Explain your answer.
b. Now suppose that the farm has the property right to the river. Will the farm alter its production process? Will the socially optimal outcome be reached? Explain your answer.

Problem 3

Suppose that the market for higher education is perfectly competitive, and all college degrees are of equal value. The market supply curve is given by

$$Q^S = -25 + 0.5P$$

and the market demand curve is

$$Q^D = 45 - 0.5P$$

where the quantity is the number of college degrees awarded per year in millions, and the price is in thousands of dollars per degree. Suppose that the external marginal benefit from each person with a college degree is $20,000.
a. With no government intervention, how many college degrees are produced? What is the price of obtaining a college degree?
b. What is the socially optimal number of college degrees?
c. What is the deadweight loss in the unregulated market for higher education (if any)?

Problem 4

Consider again the scenario in Problem 3. Suppose that the government gives a subsidy of $20,000 to each student who completes college.
a. With the subsidy, how many college degrees are produced? What price does a student pay to obtain a college degree?
b. What is the deadweight loss in the market for college education (if any)? Explain.

Problem 5

Suppose gasoline is sold in an unregulated perfectly competitive market, where the market supply curve is

$$Q^S = -100 + 100P$$

and the market demand curve is

$$Q^D = 200 - 25P$$

where the quantity is in billions of gallons per year and the price is in dollars per gallon. Suppose that the external marginal cost of gasoline depends on the quantity of gasoline consumed as follows:

$$EMC = 0.01Q$$

a. What is the market equilibrium price and quantity of gasoline?
b. What is the socially optimal level of output and price of gasoline?
c. What is the deadweight loss in the market for gasoline (if any)?

Problem 6

Consider again the scenario in Problem 5. Suppose that the government imposes a $0.50 tax on each gallon of gasoline sold.
a. With the tax, what is the market equilibrium price and quantity of gasoline?
b. What is the deadweight loss in the market for gasoline (if any)?

Problem 7

Suppose there are two chemical plants in the industry, ABC and DEF. In the absence of regulation, ABC releases 30 tons of pollution into the air, and DEF emits 20 tons. Government regulators estimate the optimal level of pollution for the industry at 30 tons and would like to lower the total pollution by the two plants to this level. ABC's total abatement cost curve is

$$TAC_A = e_A + 1.5e_A^2$$

which means its marginal abatement cost is given by

$$MAC_A = 1 + 3e_A$$

Where e_A is the number of tons of pollution cut by ABC. The costs are in thousands of dollars. DEF's total abatement cost curve is

$$TAC_D = 2e_D + e_D^2$$

so its marginal abatement cost is

$$MAC_D = 2 + 2e_D$$

Where e_D is the number of tons of pollution cut by DEF.

a. Suppose that the government implements a quantity regulation, dividing the optimal level of pollution equally between the firms, that is, allowing each firm to produce no more than 15 tons of pollution. How much will the pollution reduction cost each firm? What will be the total cost of reducing the pollution to its optimal level?

b. Now suppose that the regulators issue 300 tradable pollution permits and divide them equally between the two firms. Each permit allows the firm that owns it to release 0.1 tons of pollution. How many tons of pollution will each plant emit? What will be the price of a permit? What will be the total cost of reducing the pollution to its optimal level? How does it compare with the total cost of pollution abatement in part (a)?

Problem 8

A pulp mill dumps waste into a lake used by a resort. The resort's marginal cost of the pollution (resulting from losing customers and lower prices for the accommodations) is given by

$$EMC = 0.4Q$$

Where Q is the quantity of pulp produced by the mill (tons per week). The marginal cost of producing pulp is

$$MC = 4 + 0.6Q$$

And the society's marginal benefit from pulp (the inverse demand curve for pulp) is given by

$$MB = 40 - Q$$

Assume that the markets are perfectly competitive, with no regulation, and that the pulp mill and the resort can bargain costlessly.

a. If the resort owns the lake, how much pulp will be produced? Will any money change hands between the mill and the resort? Is this outcome socially optimal? Explain.

b. Now suppose the pulp mill owns the lake and rents it to the resort. A pollution-free lake rents for $800 a week. How much pulp will be produced? For how much will the resort rent the lake from the mill? Is this outcome socially optimal? Explain.

Problem 9

Suppose four households in an isolated community are considering putting on a fireworks display. Each household's marginal benefit from fireworks can be expressed as

$$MB = 100 - 2Q$$

The marginal cost of putting on a fireworks show is given by

$$MC = 60 + 0.5Q$$

The marginal benefits and marginal costs of the fireworks are measured in dollars, and the length of the show (Q) is measured in minutes. Assume that no one else can see the fireworks.

a. Suppose the households have agreed to share the costs of the fireworks equally. What is the socially optimal length of the fireworks?

b. If each household put on its own fireworks, for how long would the show last?

Problem 10

Two dairy farmers, Albert and Brandon, share a common pasture. Each has a choice of grazing 1 or 2 cows on the pasture. If 2 cows graze on the pasture, each will give 2,500 gallons of milk per year. If 3 cows graze on the pasture, the grass will be thinner and each will give 1,900 gallons of milk. If 4 cows graze on the pasture, the grass will have a hard time to recover, so each cow will give only 1,000 gallons of milk. The market price of milk is $2 per gallon.

a. If each farmer tries to maximize his revenue from selling milk, how many cows will each keep on the pasture? Explain your answer. (*Hint*: Construct a payoff matrix for the game where Albert and Brandon are deciding whether to keep 1 cow or 2 cows in the pasture and find the Nash equilibrium.)

b. What is the optimal number of cows to keep on the common pasture? Explain.

Behavioral and Experimental Economics

17

Behavioral economics

Branch of economics that incorporates insights from human psychology into models of economic behavior.

17.1 When Human Beings Fail to Act the Way Economic Models Predict

Overconfidence

A belief that skill and judgment are better than they truly are, or that better outcomes are more likely to happen than their true probability.

Hyperbolic discounting

Tendency of people to place much greater importance on the immediate present than even the near future when making economic decisions.

Time-consistent

Consistencies in a consumer's economic preferences in a given economic transaction, whether the economic transaction is far off or imminent.

Endowment effect

The phenomenon where simply possessing a good makes it more valuable; that is, the possessor must be paid more to give up the good than he would have paid to buy it in the first place.

Loss aversion

A type of framing bias in which a consumer chooses a reference point around which losses hurt much more than gains feel good.

Anchoring

A type of framing bias in which a person's decision is influenced by specific pieces of information given.

Mental accounting

A type of framing bias in which people divide their current and future assets into separate, nontransferable portions, instead of basing purchasing decisions on their assets as a whole.

Sunk cost fallacy

The mistake of allowing sunk costs to affect decisions.

Altruism

Acts motivated primarily by a concern for the welfare of others.

17.3 Testing Economic Theories with Data: Experimental Economics

Econometrics

Field that develops and uses mathematical and statistical techniques to test economic theory.

Experimental economics

Branch of economics that relies on experiments to illuminate economic behavior.

Lab experiment

Test of an economic theory in a laboratory setting.

Natural experiment

A randomization or near-randomization that arises by happenstance.

Field experiment

Research method in which randomizations are carried out in real-world settings.

Practice Problems

Problem 1

Two online stores, BDigit and C&G, are selling the same model of a digital camera, with the same accessories included. Both sellers offer the camera for $699.99. However, while C&G simply states that price, BDigit announces that it is "50% off the $1,400 regular price." Suppose that more customers order the camera from BDigit than from C&G. What behavioral bias is likely to be responsible for this? Explain you answer.

Problem 2

Antonio pays $40 for a concert ticket. After 15 minutes of listening to the music, he realizes that he does not like it at all. He still decides to stay because he wants to get his money's worth. What behavioral bias has Antonio fallen victim to? Explain.

Problem 3

At the end of November, a company's manager is considering two plans to motivate his sales force during the holiday season. Plan A promises everyone a $1,000 holiday bonus but stipulates that the bonus will be withdrawn if a sales person does not increase her sales by at least 15% by the end of the month. Plan B announces that a $1,000 bonus will be given at the end of the month to those who increase their sales by 15% or more.
a. If the company's sales people are rational, will Plan B motivate them more effectively than Plan A? Explain.
b. If the sales people are influenced by the endowment effect, which of the two plans will motivate them more effectively? Explain your answer.

Problem 4

Yolanda has made a New Year's resolution to be more fit. She intends to work out three times a week in the upcoming year and is willing to pay $15 per week for the access to a local gym. She made the same resolution last year and worked out three times a week in January, but then her visits to the gym became less and less frequent, and at the end of the year she did not work out at all. But now Yolanda is confident that she will stick to her resolution for the entire year. The gym offers her two payment options: (1) $5 per visit and (2) $700 for an annual health club membership, which must be paid up front.
a. If Yolanda is a rational consumer, which option will she choose? Explain.
b. By offering the membership option, the gym is trying to take advantage of a behavioral bias that Yolanda and other customers are likely to be prone to. What behavioral bias is it? How does the gym benefit from it?

Problem 5

An aerospace company decided to develop a new aircraft. The estimated cost of the project was $20 billion. The company's managers expected that the new plane would bring $23 billion in sales over its lifetime (in present value terms). After the company has already invested $15 billion in the project, the managers find out that the development cost will be twice as high as it was originally projected.

a. If the managers are rational, will they stop the project or will they decide to continue it? Explain.

b. Suppose that the managers decide to continue the project because they believe the company has already invested too much to give it up. What behavioral bias are they falling victim to? Explain.

Problem 6

Alex wants to buy a big screen LED TV set. He's just found one he likes online, available for sale. The seller offers two payment options: (1) $2,500 up front and (2) three quarterly payments of $1,000, starting from the next quarter (i.e., three months from the date of purchase). In either case, the TV ships in 24 hours after the purchase. Suppose that Alex's best alternative use of money is to lend it on the financial market at a quarterly interest rate of 2.5%.

a. If Alex is a rational consumer, which option will he choose? Explain. (*Hint*: A rational consumer would compare the present value of the quarterly payments with the amount of the up-front payment.)

b. By offering the quarterly payment option, the seller of the TV is trying to take advantage of a behavioral bias that Alex could fall victim to. What behavioral bias is it, and how can the seller benefit from it?

Problem 7

Larry was willing to pay $60 for a football ticket, but was able to purchase it for $40. Now tickets to the game sell for $90. Suppose that Larry can sell his ticket at the going price, with no transaction costs.

a. If Larry is rational, will he sell his ticket or will he go to the game? Explain.

b. Suppose Larry decides to go to the game because he thinks he got a good deal when he purchased the ticket, so he wants to take advantage of it. What behavioral bias could Larry be falling victim to? Explain.

Problem 8

Suppose that you are selling video games online. Your customers discount future payments at a rate of 25% for the first month, 10% for the second month, and 5% per month after that. You are a rational seller, with a monthly discount rate of 0.5%. You offer your customers two options to pay for a video game they purchase: (1) $51 up-front and (2) three monthly payments of $20, starting a month from the day of purchase. In either case, you ship video games to the buyer in 24 hours after the purchase. Which option will your customers choose? Will you benefit from your customers' behavioral bias? Explain.

Problem 9

David is a homeowner in Savannah, Georgia. He recently got a new job in Ohio and has to move there, so he puts his house on sale. David values the house at $200,000, but lists it for $250,000, since that is the price he paid for it. Fernando is looking for a house in Savannah. He is willing to pay $230,000 for David's house and offers him that price, but David declines Fernando's offer because he does not want to sell his house for less than he paid for it.

a. What behavioral bias has influenced David's decision? Explain.

b. David's wife Laura says: "If we had accepted Fernando's offer, we would have lost $20,000." True or false? Explain.

Problem 10

"According to behavioral economics, people don't actually behave the way the conventional economic models predict they would. Therefore, everything that you've learned from your microeconomics course is rather useless." Give three reasons why this statement is incorrect.

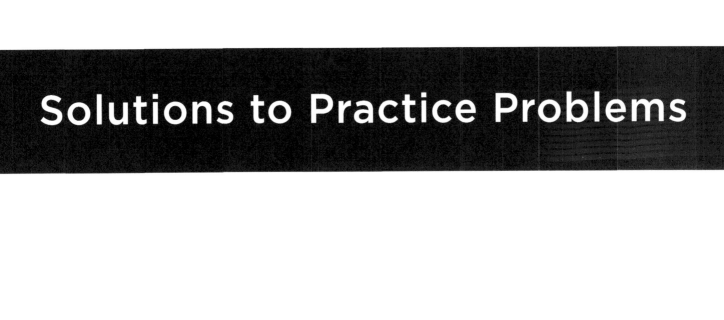

Solutions to Practice Problems

Adventures in Microeconomics (including the Math Review Appendix and Notes on How to Gain the Most from This Guide)

1

Solutions for Practice Problems

Problem 1

a. The slope-intercept equation for a line can be expressed as follows:

$$y = mx + b$$

where m is the slope and b is the vertical (y) intercept. For $m = 2$ and $b = 8$, the equation is

$$y = 2x + 8$$

b. See the following graph. To graph a line, we only need to know the coordinates of its two points. Because the equation is in the slope-intercept form, we already know the coordinates of one point, the vertical (y) intercept. Since $b = 8$, the intercept occurs at point $(0, 8)$. That is, when $x = 0$, $y = 2 \times 0 + 8 = 8$. To find another point on the line, we substitute any number for x, say, set $x = 10$, and calculate y from the equation:

$$y = 2 \times 10 + 8 = 28$$

That is, our second point on the line is $(10, 28)$. Now we can graph the line by connecting these two points.

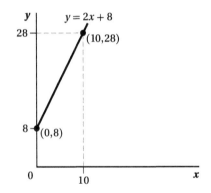

c. Since the slope of the line is positive, the relationship between x and y is positive, which means an increase in x results in an increase in y. This is also evident from the fact that the line is upward sloping.

d. The slope of the line (2) shows that when x increases by one unit, y increases by 2 units.

Problem 2

a. The slope-intercept equation for a line can be expressed as follows:

$$y = mx + b$$

where m is the slope and b is the vertical (y) intercept. With $m = -0.5$ and $b = 20$, the equation is

$$y = -0.5x + 20$$

b. Since the slope of the line is negative, the relationship between x and y is negative, which means an increase in x results in a decrease in y.

c. To find the x when $y = 0$, we substitute $y = 0$ into our equation and solve it for x:

$$y = -0.5x + 20$$

$$0 = -0.5x + 20$$

Subtracting 20 from the both sides of the equation and flipping the sides, we get

$$-0.5x = -20$$

Now we divide the both sides by −0.5, to get

$$x = 40$$

d. See the graph that follows. The easiest way to graph the line in this case is to connect its vertical and horizontal intercepts. Since $b = 20$, the vertical intercept occurs at point $(0, 20)$. That is, when $x = 0$, $y = -0.5 \times 0 + 20 = 20$. And the horizontal (x) intercept is the point we've found in (c). That is, when $y = 0$, $x = 40$, so the horizontal intercept occurs at point $(40, 0)$. We graph the line by connecting these two points.

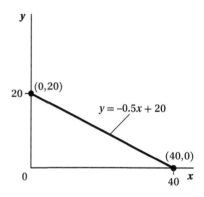

Problem 3

a. See the following graph. The slope of a line can be calculated as "rise over run," that is, the change in the variable measured on the vertical axis (y) divided by the change in the variable measured on the horizontal axis (x). We can pick any two points on the line and calculate the rise over the run between these points. For example, between point A and point B, the rise is $60 - 120 = -60$ (it is negative because y decreases when we move from point A to point B). And the run is $25 - 10 = 15$. Thus, the slope of the line is

$$\frac{Rise}{Run} = \frac{-60}{15} = -4$$

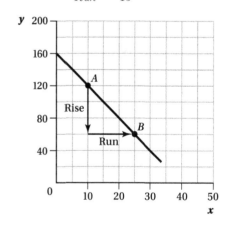

b. The slope-intercept equation for a line is expressed as follows:

$$y = mx + b$$

where m is the slope and b is the vertical (y) intercept. As calculated in (a), the slope of the line is $m = -4$. And as the graph shows, the vertical intercept is $b = 160$. Thus, the equation for the line is

$$y = -4x + 160$$

c. The slope of the line (-4) shows that when x increases by one unit, y decreases by 4 units. Therefore, when x increases by 5 units, y decreases by $4 \times 5 = 20$ units.

Problem 4

a. See the following graph. The slope of a curve at a point is equal to the slope of the line tangent to the curve at this point. And the slope of a line is measured as "rise over run," that is, the change in the variable measured on the vertical axis (y) divided by the change in the variable measured on the horizontal axis (x). To calculate the slope of the line tangent to curve U at point A, we take any two points on the line and calculate the rise over the run between these points. For example, between point C and point A, the rise is $240 - 320 = -80$ (it is negative because y decreases when we move from point C to point A). And the run is $80 - 40 = 40$. Thus, the slope of the line and therefore the slope of the curve at point A is

$$\frac{Rise}{Run} = \frac{-80}{40} = -2$$

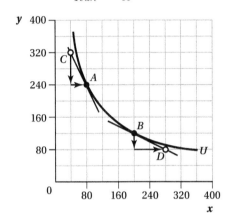

b. We can calculate the slope of the line tangent to curve U at point B as the rise over the run between points B and D as follows:

$$\frac{Rise}{Run} = \frac{80 - 120}{280 - 200} = \frac{-40}{80} - 0.5$$

Thus, the slope of the curve at point B is -0.5.

c. When $x = 200$, $y = 120$; that is, we are at point B. As calculated in (b), the slope of the curve at this point is -0.5, which means that if x increases by one unit, y decreases by 0.5 units.

Problem 5

To solve an equation for an unknown, we need to isolate the unknown on one side of the equation and put everything else on the other side of the equation. We can do this by performing the same operations on both sides of the equation. We can first add 20 to the both sides of the equation and flip the sides, so we get

$$64 = 4x - 20$$

$$64 + 20 = 4x - 20 + 20$$

$$84 = 4x$$

$$4x = 84$$

Now we divide both sides by 4 and get

$$x = 21$$

Problem 6

To solve the equation for P, we isolate P on the left-hand side of the equation and put everything else on the right-hand side. We first add 24 and $2P$ to both sides of the equation and flip the sides:

$$126 - 2P = -24 + 3P$$

$$126 + 24 - 2P + 2P = -24 + 24 + 3P + 2P$$

$$150 = 5P$$

$$5P = 150$$

Now we divide both sides by 5 to get the solution:

$$x = 30$$

Problem 7

Since $Q^D = Q^S$, we can write:

$$75 - 0.5P = -25 + 2P$$

and solve this equation for P. To do so, we isolate P on the left-hand side of the equation and put everything else on the right-hand side. We first add 25 and $0.5P$ to both sides of the equation and flip the sides:

$$75 + 25 - 0.5P + 0.5P = -25 + 25 + 2P + 0.5P$$

$$100 = 2.5P$$

$$2.5P = 100$$

Now we divide both sides by 2.5 and get:

$$P = 40$$

Next, we substitute $P = 40$ into either the Q^D equation or the Q^S equation to find Q^D and Q^S, which should be equal:

$$Q^D = 75 - 0.5 \times 40 = 55$$

$$Q^S = -25 + 2 \times 40 = 55$$

Thus, $Q^D = Q^S = 55$.

Problem 8

To answer this question, we write the following equation and solve it for K:

$$80 = 16K^{0.5}$$

Although this equation is not linear, we can use the same method as we use to solve linear equations. That is, we isolate K on the left-hand side of the equation and put everything else on the other side. To do so, we divide both sides of the equation by 16 and flip the sides:

$$\frac{80}{16} = \frac{16K^{0.5}}{16}$$

$$5 = K^{0.5}$$

$$K^{0.5} = 5$$

Now we raise both sides to the second power and get

$$(K^{0.5})^2 = 5^2$$

$$K = 25$$

Thus, the firm needs 25 units of capital to produce 80 units of output.

Problem 9

See the following graph. The shaded area on the graph is a triangle, so we can calculate it using the following formula:

$$\text{Area of triangle} = 0.5 \times b \times h$$

where b is the base of the triangle and h is its height. For the triangle in question, the base is $b = 16 - 8 = 8$, and the height is $h = 5 - 3 = 2$. Therefore, the area is

$$\text{Area} = 0.5 \times 8 \times 2 = 8$$

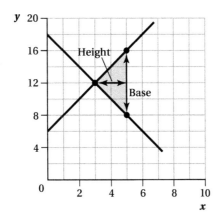

Problem 10

Area A is a triangle. And the area of a triangle can be calculated using the following formula:

$$\text{Area of triangle} = 0.5 \times b \times h$$

where b is the base of the triangle and h is its height. The base here is $b = 4 - 0 = 4$, and the height is $h = 8 - 6 = 2$. Thus,

$$\text{Area } A = 0.5 \times 4 \times 2 = 4$$

Area B is a rectangle, and the area of a rectangle can be calculated using the following formula:

$$\text{Area of rectangle} = b \times h$$

where b is the base of the rectangle and h is its height. The base of rectangle B is $b = 4 - 0 = 4$, and its height is $h = 6 - 3 = 3$. Thus,

$$\text{Area } B = 4 \times 3 = 12$$

Area C is a trapezoid. And the area of a trapezoid can be calculated, using the following formula:

$$\text{Area of trapezoid} = 0.5 \times (a + b) \times h$$

Where a is the trapezoid's longer parallel side, b is its shorter parallel side, and h is its height (i.e., the distance between the two parallel sides). For trapezoid C, $a = 4 - 0 = 4$, $b = 2 - 0 = 2$, and $h = 8 - 0 = 8$. Thus,

$$\text{Area } C = 0.5 \times (4 + 2) \times 8 = 24$$

🔊 Problem 11

Using the standard derivative rules:

a. $\dfrac{df(x)}{dx} = \dfrac{d(400x)}{dx} = 400$

b. $\dfrac{df(x)}{dx} = \dfrac{d(x^2 + 50x)}{dx} = (2)x^{2-1} + 50 = 2x + 50$

c. $\dfrac{df(x)}{dx} = \dfrac{d(x^3 - 2x^2 + 3x - 4)}{dx} = 3x^{3-1} - 2(2)x^{2-1} + 3 - 0 = 3x^2 - 4x + 3$

d. $\dfrac{df(x)}{dx} = \dfrac{d(2{,}000)}{dx} = 0$

∂ **Problem 12**

Building off of the answer in problem 11:

a. $\dfrac{d^2f(x)}{dx^2} = \dfrac{d(400)}{dx} = 0$

b. $\dfrac{d^2f(x)}{dx^2} = \dfrac{d(2x+50)}{dx} = 2 + 0 = 2$

c. $\dfrac{d^2f(x)}{dx^2} = \dfrac{d(3x^2 - 4x + 3)}{dx} = 3(2)x^{2-1} - 4 + 0 = 6x - 4$

d. $\dfrac{d^2f(x)}{dx^2} = \dfrac{d(0)}{dx} = 0$

∂ **Problem 13**

Functions are concave when the second derivative is less than zero, and are convex when the second derivative is greater than zero.

a. Since the second derivative is exactly zero, this function is neither concave nor convex for different values of x.

b. Since the second derivative is always greater than zero, the function is convex.

c. The second derivative is less than zero, and the function is concave when $6x - 4 < 0$, or $x < \dfrac{2}{3}$.

   Similarly, the second derivative is more than zero, and the function is convex when $x > \dfrac{2}{3}$.

d. Since the second derivative is exactly zero, this function is neither concave nor convex for different values of x.

∂ **Problem 14**

To calculate these derivatives, we treat y as if it is a constant:

a. $\dfrac{\partial f(x,y)}{\partial x} = 400 + 0 = 400$

b. $\dfrac{\partial f(x,y)}{\partial x} = 2x^{2-1}y + 50y = 2xy + 50y$

c. $\dfrac{\partial f(x,y)}{\partial x} = 3x^{3-1}y^3 - 2y^2 + 3 - 0 + 0 = 3x^2y^3 - 2y^2 + 3$

d. $\dfrac{\partial f(x,y)}{\partial x} = 0$

∂ **Problem 15**

Building off of the answer in problem 14:

a. $\dfrac{\partial^2 f(x,y)}{\partial x^2} = \dfrac{d(400)}{dx} = 0$

b. $\dfrac{\partial^2 f(x,y)}{\partial x^2} = \dfrac{d(2xy + 50y)}{dx} = 2y + 0 = 2y$

c. $\dfrac{\partial^2 f(x,y)}{\partial x^2} = \dfrac{d(3x^2y^3 - 2y^2 + 3)}{dx} = 3(2)x^{2-1}y^3 - 0 + 0 = 6xy^3$

d. $\dfrac{\partial^2 f(x,y)}{\partial x^2} = \dfrac{d(0)}{dx} = 0$

⌐ Problem 16

To calculate these derivatives, we treat x as if it is a constant:

a. $\dfrac{\partial f(x,y)}{\partial x} = 0 + 300 = 300$

b. $\dfrac{\partial f(x,y)}{\partial x} = x^2 + 50x$

c. $\dfrac{\partial f(x,y)}{\partial x} = 3x^3 y^{3-1} - 2(2)xy^{2-1} + 0 - 4 + 0 = 3x^3 y^2 - 4xy - 4$

d. $\dfrac{\partial f(x,y)}{\partial x} = 0$

⌐ Problem 17

Building off of the answer in problem 16:

a. $\dfrac{\partial^2 f(x,y)}{\partial y} = \dfrac{d(300)}{dy} = 0$

b. $\dfrac{\partial^2 f(x,y)}{\partial y^2} = \dfrac{d(x^2 + 50x)}{dy} = 0 + 0 = 0$

c. $\dfrac{\partial^2 f(x,y)}{\partial y^2} = \dfrac{d(3x^3 y^2 - 4xy - 4)}{dy} = 3(2)x^3 y^{2-1} - 4x - 0 = 6x^3 y - 4x$

D. $\dfrac{\partial^2 f(x,y)}{\partial y^2} = \dfrac{d(0)}{dy} = 0$

⌐ Problem 18

To totally differentiate the function, we can use calculations from problems 14 and 16—part (c) of each. Particularly, since $\dfrac{\partial f(x,y)}{\partial x} = 3x^2 y^3 - 2y^2 + 3$ and $\dfrac{\partial f(x,y)}{\partial y} = 3x^3 y^2 - 4xy - 4$ for this function:

$$df(x,y) = \frac{\partial f(x,y)}{\partial x} dx + \frac{\partial f(x,y)}{\partial y} dy$$

$$df(x,y) = (3x^2 y^3 - 2y^2 + 3)dx + (3x^3 y^2 - 4xy - 4)dy$$

2

Supply and Demand

Solutions for Practice Problems

Problem 1

a. Crude oil is an input used to produce gasoline. When the price of oil rises, gasoline production becomes more costly. Therefore, the supply of gasoline decreases, that is, the supply curve shifts leftward.

b. An alternative motor fuel is a substitute for gasoline. When the prices of alternative fuels fall, motorists will want to use more of those fuels, substituting them for gasoline. Thus, the demand curve for gasoline will shift leftward.

c. Higher wages at oil refineries mean a higher cost of the labor input in gasoline production. As the production of gasoline becomes more costly, the supply of gasoline decreases, which is reflected by a leftward shift of the supply curve.

d. As consumers become more conscious of the adverse effects of burning gasoline, they will want to consume less gasoline at every given price. Thus, the demand curve shifts leftward.

e. With a more fuel-efficient car, less gasoline is needed to drive the same distance. Thus, the demand for gasoline decreases, that is, the demand curve shifts leftward.

f. Cars and gasoline are complements. When the price of a car falls, consumers will buy more cars and therefore will need more gasoline. Thus, the demand for gasoline increases, that is, the demand curve shifts rightward.

Problem 2

a. When the price of conventional milk is $3 per gallon and the consumer income is $30 thousand per year, the demand equation is

$$Q^D = -20 - 10P + 20 \times 3 + 2 \times 30$$
$$Q^D = 100 - 10P$$

This demand curve (D_1) is shown on the following graph. When the price of organic milk is $6 per gallon, the quantity of organic milk demanded is $Q^D = 100 - 10 \times 6 = 40$ thousand gallons (point A on the graph).

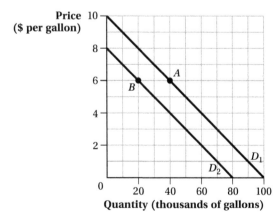

b. The positive coefficient of P_C in the demand equation shows that as the price of conventional milk rises, the demand for organic milk increases. This suggests that the two goods are substitutes. The positive coefficient of I shows that as consumer income increases, the demand for organic milk increases. This suggests that organic milk is a normal good.

c. When the price of conventional milk is $2.50 per gallon and the consumer income is $25 thousand per year, the demand equation is

$$Q^D = -20 - 10P + 20 \times 2.50 + 2 \times 25$$
$$Q^D = 80 - 10P$$

This demand curve (D_2) is shown on the preceding graph. The lower price of conventional milk shifts the demand curve for organic milk leftward by $20 \times (3 - 2.50) = 10$ thousand gallons at each given price. And the lower consumer income shifts the demand curve farther leftward by $2 \times (30 - 25) = 10$ thousand gallons at each given price. At a price of $6 per gallon, the quantity of organic milk demanded decreases from 40 thousand gallons to $80 - 10 \times 6 = 20$ thousand gallons, that is, by 20 thousand gallons (point B on the graph).

d. When $P = 5$, $Q^D = 100 - 10 \times 5 = 50$. The coefficient of P in the equation is the inverse of the slope of the demand curve. Thus, the price elasticity of demand is $-10 \times \left(\dfrac{5}{50}\right) = -1$. That is, the demand is unit elastic.

e. At these prices and income level, $Q = -20 - 10(6) + 20(3) + 2(30) = 40$. Using the derivative of a constant and power rules of derivatives, $\dfrac{\partial Q^D}{\partial I} = 0 - 0 + 0 + 2(1)I^{1-1} = 2I^0 = 2$. The income elasticity of demand, then, is $E^D = \dfrac{\partial Q^D}{\partial I}\dfrac{I}{Q^D} = 2\dfrac{30}{40} = 1.5$.

f. Using the derivative of a constant and power rules of derivatives, $\dfrac{\partial Q^D}{\partial P_C} = 0 - 0 + 20(1)P_C^{1-1} + 0 = 2P_C^0 = 20$. Using quantity as calculated in the previous section and the price of conventional milk as given, the cross-price elasticity of demand (where subscript O refers to organic and subscript C refers to conventional milk) then is: $E_{OC}^D = \dfrac{\partial Q_O^D}{\partial P_C}\dfrac{P_C}{Q_O^D} = 20\dfrac{3}{40} = 1.5$.

g. Conventional milk is a substitute good for organic milk, since the partial derivative of quantity demanded with respect to the price of conventional milk, $\dfrac{\partial Q^D}{\partial P_C} = 20 > 0$. Organic milk is a normal good, since the partial derivative of quantity demanded with respect to income, $\dfrac{\partial Q^D}{\partial I} = 2 > 0$. These are the same answers as in part (b).

Problem 3

a. The quantity demanded at the current market price is $Q^D = 900 - 100 \times 6 = 300$ million bushels. The quantity supplied is $Q^S = -600 + 200 \times 6 = 600$ million bushels. Although the sellers are willing to sell 600 million bushels, buyers are willing to buy only 300 million bushels. Thus, only 300 million bushels will be actually sold.

b. Since the quantity supplied exceeds the quantity demanded, the situation in the market can be characterized as a surplus (excess supply). The surplus is $Q^S - Q^D = 600 - 300 = 300$ million bushels.

c. To eliminate the surplus, sellers will have to lower the price. And as the price falls, the quantity of wheat demanded increases along with the quantity sold.

d. We can solve for the market equilibrium price as follows:

$$Q^D = Q^S$$
$$900 - 100P = -600 + 200P$$
$$300P = 1,500$$
$$P = 5$$

At this price,

$$Q^D = 900 - 100 \times 5 = 400$$
$$Q^S = -600 + 200 \times 5 = 400$$

Thus, the equilibrium price of wheat is $5, and the equilibrium quantity is 400 million bushels.

e. Since $\dfrac{\partial Q^D}{\partial P} = 0 - 100(1)P^{1-1} = -100P^0 = -100 < 0$, the Law of Demand holds.

f. Since $\dfrac{\partial Q^S}{\partial P} = 0 + 200(1)P^{1-1} = 200P^0 = 200 > 0$, the Law of Supply holds.

Problem 4

a. To solve for the equilibrium price, we equate the quantity demanded and quantity supplied:

$$Q^D = Q^S$$
$$2{,}100 - 140P = -420 + 140P$$
$$280P = 2{,}520$$
$$P = 9$$

To solve for the equilibrium quantity, we substitute the equilibrium price into either the demand equation or the supply equation:

$$Q^D = 2{,}100 - 140 \times 9 = 840$$
$$Q^S = -420 + 140 \times 9 = 840$$

Thus the price is \$9 per pizza, and the quantity sold is 840 pizzas.

b. When the school is not in session, the demand curve is

$$Q_2^D = 2{,}100 - 140P - 420$$
$$Q_2^D = 1{,}680 - 140P$$

To solve for the equilibrium price, we equate:

$$Q_2^D = Q^S$$
$$1{,}680 - 140P = -420 + 140P$$
$$280P = 2{,}100$$
$$P = 7.5$$

To solve for the equilibrium quantity, we substitute the equilibrium price into either the demand equation or the supply equation:

$$Q_2^D = 1{,}680 - 140 \times 7.5 = 630$$
$$Q^S = -420 + 140 \times 7.5 = 630$$

Thus, when the school is out of session, the equilibrium price is \$7.50 per pizza, and the equilibrium quantity is 630 pizzas. As we would expect, both the equilibrium price and the equilibrium quantity fall as a result of lower demand.

c. When the school is in session, $P = 9$, $Q^S = 840$, and the inverse of the slope of the supply curve is 140 (the coefficient of P in the supply equation). Thus, the price elasticity of supply is $140 \times \left(\dfrac{9}{840}\right)$ $= 1.5$.

 d. Using the derivative of a constant and power rules of derivatives, $\dfrac{\partial Q^S}{\partial P} = 0 + 140(1)P^{1-1} = 140P^0 = 140.$

The price elasticity of supply then is $E^S = \dfrac{\partial Q^S}{\partial P} \dfrac{P}{Q^S} = 140\dfrac{9}{840} = 1.5$. This is the same as in part (c).

e. Using the derivative of a constant and power rules of derivatives, $\dfrac{\partial Q^D}{\partial P} = 0 - 140(1)P^{1-1} = -140P^0 =$

-140. The price elasticity of demand then is $E^D = \dfrac{\partial Q^D}{\partial P} \dfrac{P}{Q^D} = -140\dfrac{9}{840} = -1.5$.

Problem 5

a. On the following diagram, the initial equilibrium is at the point of intersection of the demand curve, D_1, and the supply curve, S_1. The news about the health benefits of drinking orange juice is likely to make consumers want to drink more of it. As a result, the demand curve for orange juice shifts rightward (from D_1 to D_2). Less favorable weather conditions for growing oranges shift the supply curve for oranges leftward, increasing the price of oranges. Since oranges are used to produce orange juice, the production of orange juice becomes more costly. As a result, the supply of orange juice decreases, that is, the supply curve shifts leftward. The new equilibrium is at the point where the new demand curve (D_2) intersects the new supply curve (S_2).

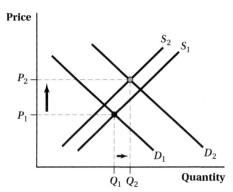

b. Both the rightward shift of the demand curve and the leftward shift of the supply curve lead to a higher equilibrium price. Thus, we can unambiguously predict that the equilibrium price of orange juice will rise. But since the rightward shift of the demand curve increases the equilibrium quantity, while a leftward shift in the supply curve causes the equilibrium quantity to decrease, we cannot unambiguously predict the direction in which the equilibrium quantity will change (unless we know the relative magnitudes of these effects). On the preceding diagram, the effect of the decreased supply (i.e., the impact of unfavorable weather) is greater than the effect of the increased demand (i.e., the impact of the favorable change in consumer preferences) and therefore the equilibrium quantity decreases. But if the changed consumer preferences had a greater impact on the market than the unfavorable weather conditions, the equilibrium quantity could increase, as shown on the following diagram.

Problem 6

a. The price elasticity of demand is calculated as

$$E = \frac{1}{slope} \times \frac{P}{Q}$$

The inverse of the slope $\left(\frac{1}{slope}\right)$ is the coefficient of P in the demand equation, so $\frac{1}{slope} = -250$. The quantity demanded at $P = 3$ is $Q = 3{,}000 - 250 \times 3 = 2{,}250$. Then the elasticity is $E = -250 \times \left(\frac{3}{2{,}250}\right) = -0.333$. Since $|{-0.333}| < 1$, the demand at this point is inelastic.

b. When the price is \$10, the quantity demanded is $Q = 3{,}000 - 250 \times 10 = 500$. Plugging into the elasticity formula, we get $-250 \times \left(\frac{10}{500}\right) = -5$. Since $|{-5}| > 1$, the demand at this point is elastic.

c. Along a linear demand curve, the demand is unit elastic at the price equal to $\frac{1}{2}$ of the demand choke price (i.e., the price at which the quantity demanded equals zero). The demand choke price is shown by the vertical intercept of the inverse demand curve. For the demand equation in question, the inverse demand curve can be found as follows:

$$Q = 3{,}000 - 250P$$
$$250P = 3{,}000 - Q$$
$$P = 12 - 0.004Q$$

The vertical intercept of the inverse demand curve is where $Q = 0$, that is, where

$$P = 12 - 0.004 \times 0$$
$$P = 12$$

Thus, the demand choke price is \$12, and the price at which the demand is unit elastic is $\dfrac{\$12}{2} = \$6$. We can verify this by calculating the price elasticity of the demand at this point. When the price is \$6, the quantity demanded is $Q = 3,000 - 250 \times 6 = 1,500$. Plugging into the elasticity formula, we get $-250 \times \left(\dfrac{6}{1,500}\right) = -1$.

d. Total expenditure is maximized when the price elasticity of demand is exactly unit elastic. This is true when:

$$E^D = \frac{\partial Q^D}{\partial P}\frac{P}{Q^D} = -1$$

Using the derivative of a constant and power rules of derivatives,

$$\frac{\partial Q^D}{\partial P} = 0 - 250(1)P^{1-1}$$
$$= -250P^0$$
$$= -250$$

So, $-250\dfrac{P}{Q^D} = -1$

Rearranging by cross-multiplying, we can see that this holds when $250P = Q^D$. Substituting into the demand equation:

$$Q^D = 3,000 - 250P$$
$$250P = 3,000 - 250P$$
$$500P = 3,000$$
$$P = 6$$
$$Q^D = 3,000 - 250(6) = 1,500$$

Notice that this is the point identified in part (c).

Problem 7

a. To find the inverse demand curve, we solve the demand equation for P:

$$Q^D = 70 - 20P^D$$
$$20P^D = 70 - Q^D$$
$$P^D = 3.5 - 0.05Q^D$$

And the inverse supply curve can be derived from the supply equation the same way:

$$Q_1^S = -80 + 80P_1^S$$
$$80P_1^S = 80 + Q_1^S$$
$$P_1^S = 1 + 0.0125Q_1^S$$

On the following graph, D is the demand curve and S is the supply curve.

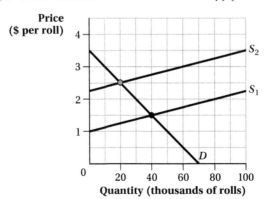

b. We can solve for the equilibrium price by equating Q^D and Q_1^S. But we can also solve for the equilibrium quantity using the inverse demand and inverse supply equations as follows:

$$P^D = P_1^S$$
$$3.5 - 0.05Q = 1 + 0.0125Q$$
$$0.0625Q = 2.5$$
$$Q = 40$$

The equilibrium price can be found using either the inverse demand or the inverse supply curve:

$$P^D = 3.5 - 0.05 \times 40 = 1.5$$
$$P_1^S = 1 + 0.0125 \times 40 = 1.5$$

c. The new inverse supply curve is

$$P_2^S = 1 + 0.0125Q + 1.25$$
$$P_2^S = 2.25 + 0.0125Q$$

It is labeled S_2 on the preceding graph. The upward shift of the inverse supply curve is also a leftward shift of the original supply curve, showing that the quantity supplied decreases at each given price. Thus, it is a decrease in supply. The upward shift of the inverse supply curve is most likely a result of increased costs of production. Since producers need to cover their higher costs, the minimum price that they are willing to accept to supply a certain quantity of paper towels increases.

d. With the new supply curve, we solve for the equilibrium quantity as follows:

$$P^D = P_2^S$$
$$3.5 - 0.05Q = 2.25 + 0.0125Q$$
$$0.0625Q = 1.25$$
$$Q = 20$$

The equilibrium price can be found using either the inverse demand or the new inverse supply curve:

$$P^D = 3.5 - 0.05 \times 20 = 2.5$$
$$P_2^S = 2.25 + 0.0125 \times 20 = 2.5$$

e. Substituting $P_c = 0.5$ into the expanded supply curve, we can see that $Q^S = -77 + 80P - 6(0.5) = -80 + 80P$, which is the supply curve as given.

f. Since $\dfrac{\partial Q^S}{\partial P_C} = -6 < 0$, we know that the quantity supplied of paper towels decreases as the price of paper increases, which is the expected relationship given that paper is an input to the production of paper towels.

g. Now, $Q^S = -77 + 80P - 6(0.4) = -79.4 + 80P$. Note that the decrease in the price of paper increases quantity supplied at each price and results in a parallel shift of the supply curve to the right.

h. Setting quantity demanded equal to the new quantity supplied from part (g):

$$70 - 20P = -79.4 + 80P$$
$$100P = 9.4$$
$$P = 0.094$$

To get quantity, we can substitute P into the demand or the supply equation (or both to check): $Q^D = 70 - 20(0.094) = 68.12$. Note that as the price of the input decreased, price fell and quantity increased as in the graph on the right. (The graph is not to scale.)

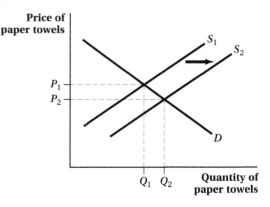

Problem 8

The first step is to see what happens to the quantity of HP computers demanded when the price of Dell computers falls by 10%. We can use the cross-price elasticity to find this. The cross-price elasticity of demand for HP computers with respect to the price of Dell computers is

$$E_{HD} = \frac{\%\Delta Q_H}{\%\Delta P_D}$$

We know that $\%\Delta P_D = -10\%$, and $E_{HD} = 0.8$. Thus, we can write:

$$\frac{\%\Delta Q_H}{-10} = 0.8$$

from which $\%\Delta Q_H = 0.8 \times (-10) = -8\%$. Thus, when the price of Dell computers falls by 10%, the quantity of HP computers demanded decreases by 8%. Now let's see how this decrease in the quantity of HP computers demanded can be offset with a change in the price of HP computers. Clearly, the price of HP computers must fall in order for the quantity of HP computers demanded to increase. Using the price elasticity of demand for HP computers we can determine how far the price needs to fall. The price elasticity of demand for HP computers is

$$E_H = \frac{\%\Delta Q_H}{\%\Delta P_H} = -1.6$$

To offset the decrease in the quantity of HP computers demanded caused by the fall in the price of Dell computers, $\%\Delta Q_H$ needs to be 8%. Thus, we can write:

$$E_H = \frac{8}{\%\Delta P_H} = -1.6$$

from which $\%\Delta P_H = \frac{8}{(-1.6)} = -5\%$. Thus, the price of HP computers would have to fall by 5% to exactly offset the effect of the fallen price of Dell computers on the quantity of HP computers demanded.

Problem 9

See the following graphs. In both cities growth in population (number of consumers) led to a rightward shift of the demand curve for housing (from D_1 to D_2). As a result, the equilibrium price of housing rose, and the equilibrium quantity of housing increased in both cities. However, in City A, the supply curve was flatter and therefore the shift of the demand curve caused a small rise in price and a large increase in quantity. In City B, the supply curve was steeper; therefore, the price increase was larger and the quantity increase was smaller.

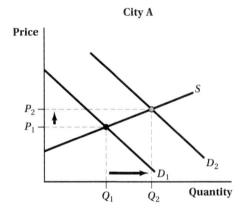

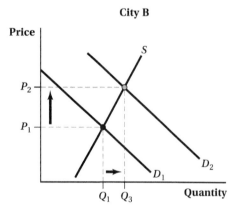

Problem 10

The first step is to see what would happen to the quantity of oil demanded when world income increases if we hold the price of oil constant. We can use the income elasticity to find this. The income elasticity of demand for oil (0.4) suggests that for each 1% increase in income, the quantity of oil demanded will increase by 0.4%. So, if income increases by 16%, holding the price constant, the quantity of oil demanded will increase by $0.4 \times 16 = 6.4\%$ (see the following diagram). This increase in the quantity demanded creates excess demand at the initial price, so the price must rise to eliminate this excess demand. The price elasticity of demand for oil (−0.11) tells us that for each 1% rise in price, the quantity of oil demanded will decrease by 0.11%. And the price elasticity of supply (0.21) tells us that for each 1% rise in price, the quantity of oil supplied will increase by 0.21%. That is, each 1% increase in price will decrease the excess demand by 0.11 + 0.21 = 0.32 percentage points. Thus, to eliminate the whole excess demand, the price must rise by $\dfrac{6.4}{0.32} = 20\%$.

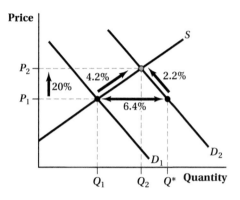

⟨∂⟩ Problem 11

When 20,000 bottles are sold, quantity is 20 as expressed in the given inverse supply curve. Price, then, is

$$P = -190 + 0.5(20)^2 = \$10$$

Using the supply equation, $\dfrac{\partial P}{\partial Q^S} = 0 + 0.5(2)Q^{2-1} = Q$.

At $Q = 20$, this value is then just 20.

The price elasticity of supply is: $E^S = \dfrac{1}{\dfrac{\partial P}{\partial Q^S}}\dfrac{P}{Q^S} = \dfrac{1}{20}\dfrac{10}{20} = 0.025$.

Therefore, supply for this particular shampoo is very inelastic.

3

Using Supply and Demand to Analyze Markets

Solutions for Practice Problems

Problem 1

a. The easiest way to find the consumer surplus is to graph the demand curve. Since it is a straight line, we only need to identify two points to graph it. The first point is where $P = 3.50$. At this point, $Q^D = 190 - 20 \times 3.50 = 120$. The second point that can be easily identified (and is useful for calculating consumer surplus) is the choke price for demand. To find this point, we set Q^D equal to zero and solve for P:

$$Q^D = 190 - 20P$$
$$0 = 190 - 20P$$
$$20P = 190$$
$$P = 8.5$$

Thus, the demand choke price is $8.50. Now we can graph the demand curve (see the following graph).

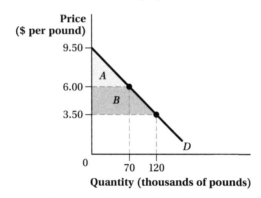

The consumer surplus is the triangular area below the demand curve and above the price (area $A + B$). We calculate it as

$$CS = 0.5 \times 120{,}000 \times (\$9.50 - \$3.50) = \$360{,}000$$

b. When the price rises to $6 per pound, $Q^D = 190 - 20 \times 6 = 70$. The consumer surplus now is the triangular area below the demand curve and above the new price (area A). We calculate it as

$$CS_{\text{new}} = 0.5 \times 70{,}000 \times (\$9.50 - \$6.00) = \$122{,}500$$

Thus, the consumer surplus decreases by $360,000 − $122,500 = $237,500

c. Since the consumer surplus formula using calculus requires substituting in the inverse demand curve, we first solve for it. We can rearrange the standard demand curve to get the inverse demand relationship.

$$Q^D = 190 - 20P$$
$$20P = 190 - Q^D$$
$$P = 9.5 - 0.05Q^D$$

The change in consumer surplus is the difference between the consumer surplus under the lower price and the consumer surplus under the higher price.

$$\Delta CS = \int_0^{120}(9.5 - 0.05Q - 3.5)dQ - \int_0^{70}(9.5 - 0.05Q - 6)dQ$$

Integrating below the demand curve up to the quantity corresponding to the lower price:

$$\int_0^{120}(9.5 - 0.05Q - 3.5)dQ = \int_0^{120} 6dQ - \int_0^{120}0.05QdQ = [6Q]_0^{120} - \left[\frac{0.05Q^2}{2}\right]_0^{120}$$

$$= [6(120) - 6(0)] - \left[\frac{0.05(120)^2}{2} - \frac{0.05(0)^2}{2}\right]$$

$$= (720 - 0) - (360 - 0) = 360$$

Integrating below the demand curve up to the quantity corresponding to the higher price:

$$\int_0^{70}(9.5 - 0.05Q - 6)dQ = \int_0^{70} 3.5dQ - \int_0^{70} 0.05QdQ = [3.5Q]_0^{70} - \left[\frac{0.50Q^2}{2}\right]_0^{70}$$

$$= [3.5(70) - 3.5(0)] - \left[\frac{0.05(70)^2}{2} - \frac{0.05(0)^2}{2}\right]$$

$$= (245 - 0) - (122.5 - 0) = 122.5$$

Therefore, the change in consumer surplus is the difference: $360,000 − 122,500 = $237,500 as found in part (b) of the problem.

Problem 2

a. To find the producer surplus, we graph the supply curve. Since it is a straight line, we only need to identify two points to graph it. The first point is where $P = 2.25. At this point, $Q^S = -40 + 40 \times 2.25 = 50$. The second point that can be easily identified (and is useful for calculating producer surplus) is the choke price for supply. To find this point, we set Q^S equal to zero and solve for P:

$$Q^S = -40 + 40P$$
$$0 = -40 + 40P$$
$$40P = 40$$
$$P = 1$$

Thus, the supply choke price is $1.00. Now we can graph the supply curve (see the following graph).

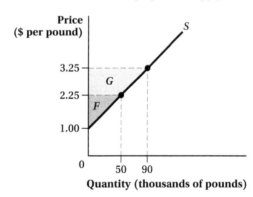

The producer surplus is the triangular area above the supply curve and below the price (area F). We calculate it as

$$PS = 0.5 \times 50,000 \times (\$2.25 - \$1.00) = \$31,250$$

b. When the price rises to $3.25 per pound, $Q^S = -40 + 40 \times 3.25 = 90$. The producer surplus now is the triangular area above the supply curve and below the new price (area $F + G$). We calculate it as

$$PS_{\text{new}} = 0.5 \times 90,000 \times (\$3.25 - \$1.00) = \$101,250$$

Thus, the producer surplus increases by $101,250 − $31,250 = $70,000.

c. Since the producer surplus formula using calculus requires substituting in the inverse supply curve, we first solve for it. We can rearrange the standard supply curve to get the inverse supply relationship.

$$Q^S = 40P - 40$$
$$40P = 40 + Q^S$$
$$P = 1 + 0.025Q^D$$

The change in producer surplus is the difference between the producer surplus under the higher price and the producer surplus under the lower price:

$$\Delta PS = \int_0^{90}(3.25 - (1 + 0.025Q))dQ - \int_0^{50}(2.25 - (1 + 0.025Q))dQ$$

Integrating above the supply curve up to the quantity corresponding to the higher price:

$$\int_0^{90}(3.25 - (1 + 0.025Q))dQ = \int_0^{90} 2.25dQ - \int_0^{90}0.025QdQ = [2.25Q]_0^{90} - \left[\frac{0.025Q^2}{2}\right]_0^{90}$$

$$= [2.25(90) - 2.25(0)] - \left[\frac{0.025(90)^2}{2} - \frac{0.02(0)^2}{2}\right]$$

$$= (202.5 - 0) - (101.25 - 0) = 101.25$$

Integrating above the supply curve up to the quantity corresponding to the lower price:

$$\int_0^{50}(2.25 - (1 + 0.025Q))dQ = \int_0^{50} 1.25dQ - \int_0^{50}0.025QdQ = [1.25Q]_0^{50} - \left[\frac{0.025Q^2}{2}\right]_0^{50}$$

$$= [1.25(50) - 1.25(0)] - \left[\frac{0.025(50)^2}{2} - \frac{0.025(0)^2}{2}\right]$$

$$= (62.5 - 0) - (31.25 - 0) = 31.25$$

Therefore, the change in producer surplus is the difference: $101,250 - 31,250 = \$70,000$ as found in part (b) of the problem.

Problem 3

a. The formula for the price elasticity of demand is

$$E^D = \frac{\Delta Q^D}{\Delta P} \times \frac{P}{Q}$$

The coefficient of price in the demand equation (–2) shows that for each $1 increase in price, quantity demanded decreases by 2 million. Therefore, $\frac{\Delta Q^D}{\Delta P} = -2$. Substituting into the elasticity formula, we get

$$E^D = -2 \times \frac{1.50}{20} = -0.15$$

The formula for the price elasticity of supply is

$$E^S = \frac{\Delta Q^S}{\Delta P} \times \frac{P}{Q}$$

The coefficient of price in the supply equation (20) shows that for each $1 increase in price, quantity supplied increases by 20 million. Therefore, $\frac{\Delta Q^S}{\Delta P} = 20$. Thus, the price elasticity of supply is

$$E^S = 20 \times \frac{1.50}{20} = 1.5$$

b. The proportion of the tax borne by buyers would be

$$\frac{E^S}{E^S + |E^D|} = \frac{1.5}{1.5 + 0.15} = 0.909 \text{ or } 90.9\%$$

The proportion of the tax borne by sellers would be

$$\frac{E^D}{E^S + |E^D|} = \frac{0.15}{1.5 + 0.15} = 0.091 \text{ or } 9.1\%$$

c. Buyers would bear 90.9% of the tax, so the buyer price would increase by $1.10 \times 0.909 = \$1.00$. Thus, buyers would pay $1.50 + $1.00 = $2.50 per pack. Sellers would receive the price paid by buyers minus the tax: $2.50 - $1.10 = $1.40.

Problem 4

a. To find the consumer and producer surpluses, we graph the demand and supply curves. Since both curves are straight lines, we only need to identify two points for each curve. The first point, common for the two curves and necessary to find consumer and producer surpluses, is the market equilibrium.

We solve for the equilibrium price by equating the demand and supply curves:

$$Q^D = Q^S$$
$$600 - 60P = -30 + 30P$$
$$90P = 630$$
$$P = 7$$

To find the equilibrium quantity, we substitute the equilibrium price into either the demand equation or the supply equation:

$$Q^D = 600 - 60 \times 7 = 180$$
$$Q^S = -30 + 30 \times 7 = 180$$

Thus, the equilibrium price is $7 per bushel, and the equilibrium quantity is 180 million bushels. The second point on each curve that is useful for the calculations of consumer and producer surpluses is the choke price for demand and supply. To find these points, we set Q^D and Q^S equal to zero and solve for P:

$$Q^D = 600 - 60P$$
$$0 = 600 - 60P$$
$$60P = 600$$
$$P = 10$$
$$Q^S = -30 + 30P$$
$$0 = -30 + 30P$$
$$30P = 30$$
$$P = 1$$

Thus, the demand choke price is $10 per bushel and the supply choke price is $1 per bushel. Now we can use these points to graph the demand and supply curves (D_1 and S on the following graph).

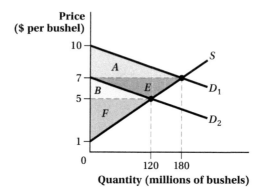

The consumer surplus is the triangular area below the demand curve and above the equilibrium price (area A). It can be calculated as

$$CS = 0.5 \times 180 \text{ million} \times (\$10 - \$7) = \$270 \text{ million}$$

The producer surplus is the triangular area above the supply curve and below the equilibrium price ($B + E + F$). It can be calculated as

$$PS = 0.5 \times 180 \text{ million} \times (\$7 - \$1) = \$540 \text{ million}$$

b. To find the consumer and producer surpluses after the change in demand, we need to find and graph the new demand curve. Since the quantity demanded decreases by 180 million bushels at each price, we subtract 180 from the demand equation:

$$Q_2^D = 600 - 60P - 180$$
$$Q_2^S = 420 - 60P$$

To solve for the new equilibrium price, we equate Q_2^D and Q^S:

$$420 - 60P = -30 + 30P$$
$$90P = 450$$
$$P = 5$$

To solve for the new equilibrium quantity, we substitute the new equilibrium price into either the new demand equation or the supply equation:

$$Q_2^D = 420 - 60 \times 5 = 120$$
$$Q^S = -30 + 30 \times 5 = 120$$

Thus, the new equilibrium price is \$5 per bushel, and the new equilibrium quantity is 120 million bushels. To find the new demand choke price, we set Q_2^D equal to zero and solve for P:

$$Q_2^D = 420 - 60P$$
$$0 = 420 - 60P$$
$$60P = 420$$
$$P = 7$$

Now we can draw the new demand curve (D_2 on the preceding graph). After the decrease in demand, the consumer surplus is the triangular area below the new demand curve and above the new equilibrium price (area B):

$$CS_{\text{new}} = 0.5 \times 120 \text{ million} \times (\$7 - \$5) = \$120 \text{ million}$$

As we can see, consumer surplus decreases by \$270 million − \$120 million = \$150 million.

After the decrease in demand, the producer surplus is the triangular area above the supply curve and below the new equilibrium price (area F):

$$PS_{\text{new}} = 0.5 \times 120 \text{ million} \times (\$5 - \$1) = \$240 \text{ million}$$

Thus, producer surplus decreases by \$540 million − \$240 million = \$300 million.

c. The loss in total surplus resulting from the decreased demand is the sum of the losses in consumer surplus and producer surplus: \$150 million + \$300 million = \$450 million.

Problem 5

a. To find the consumer surplus, we graph the demand and supply curves. Since both curves are straight lines, we only need to identify two points for each curve. The first point, common for the two curves and necessary to find consumer and producer surpluses, is the market equilibrium. We can solve for the equilibrium price by equating the demand and supply curves:

$$Q^D = Q^S$$
$$54 - 0.1P = -24 + 0.1P$$
$$0.2P = 78$$
$$P = 390$$

To solve for the equilibrium quantity, we substitute the equilibrium price into either the demand equation or the supply equation:

$$Q^D = 54 - 0.1 \times 390 = 15$$
$$Q^S = -24 + 0.1 \times 390 = 15$$

Thus, the equilibrium price is \$390, and the equilibrium quantity is 15 million tablets. The second point on each curve that is useful for the calculations of consumer and producer surpluses is the choke price for demand and supply. To find these points, we set Q^D and Q^S equal to zero and solve for P:

$$Q^D = 54 - 0.1P$$
$$0 = 54 - 0.1P$$
$$0.1P = 54$$
$$P = 540$$
$$Q^S = -24 + 0.1P$$
$$0 = -24 + 0.1P$$
$$0.1P = 24$$
$$P = 240$$

Thus, the demand choke price is \$540 and the supply choke price is \$240. Now we can use these points to graph the demand and supply curves (D and S_1 on the following graph).

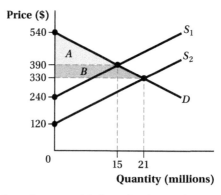

The consumer surplus is the triangular area A below the demand curve and above the initial equilibrium price. So the consumer surplus is:

$$CS = 0.5 \times 15 \text{ million} \times (\$540 - \$390) = \$1{,}125 \text{ million}$$

b. To find the consumer surplus after the change in supply, we need to find and graph the new supply curve. Since quantity supplied increases by 12 million at each price, we add 12 to the supply equation:

$$Q_2^S = -24 + 0.1P + 12$$
$$Q_2^S = -12 + 0.1P$$

To solve for the new equilibrium price, we equate Q^D and Q_2^S:

$$54 - 0.1P = -12 + 0.1P$$
$$0.2P = 66$$
$$P = 330$$

To find the new equilibrium quantity, we substitute the new equilibrium price into either the demand equation or the new supply equation:

$$Q^D = 54 - 0.1 \times 330 = 21$$
$$Q_2^S = -12 + 0.1 \times 330 = 21$$

Thus, the new equilibrium price is \$330, and the new equilibrium quantity is 21 million tablets. To find the new supply choke price, we set Q_2^S equal to zero and solve for P:

$$Q_2^S = -12 + 0.1P$$
$$0 = -12 + 0.1P$$
$$0.1P = 12$$
$$P = 120$$

Now we can draw the new supply curve (S_2 on the preceding graph). After the increase in supply, the consumer surplus is the triangular area below the demand curve and above the new equilibrium price (area $A + B$):

$$CS_{\text{new}} = 0.5 \times 21 \text{ million} \times (\$540 - \$330) = \$2{,}205 \text{ million}$$

As we can see, consumer surplus increases by \$2,205 − \$1,125 = 1,080 million (area B). That is, consumers gain \$1.08 billion as a result of the technological innovation.

c. The producer surplus is initially the triangular area above the supply curve S_1 and below the initial equilibrium price (area $E + C$) (see the following graph). It can be calculated as

$$PS = 0.5 \times 15 \text{ million} \times (\$390 - \$240) = \$1{,}125 \text{ million}$$

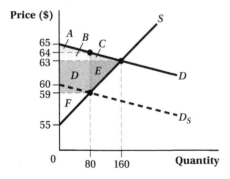

d. With the increased supply, the producer surplus is the triangular area above the new supply curve (S_2) and below the new equilibrium price (area $E + F$):

$$PS_{new} = 0.5 \times 21 \text{ million} \times (\$330 - \$120) = \$2,205 \text{ million}$$

Producer surplus increases by $2,205 - $1,125 = $1,080 million, that is, producers gain $1.08 billion. Producers lose area C, but gain area F.

e. The gain in total surplus resulting from the technological innovation is the sum of the gains in consumer surplus and producer surplus: $1.08 billion + $1.08 billion = $2.16 billion.

Problem 6

a. The tax creates a dual-demand-curve situation. The demand curve for buyers is the same as the demand curve with no tax. But the demand curve facing sellers (D_S on the following graph) is shifted down by the amount of the tax ($5 million), since the price that sellers receive at each given quantity demanded is the price paid by buyers minus the tax. Thus, the price received by sellers is

$$P_S = P_B - 5$$

where P_B is the price paid by buyers. To solve for the quantity and prices with the tax, we substitute this expression into our supply and demand equations:

$$5,200 - 80P_B = -1,100 + 20P_S$$
$$5,200 - 80P_B = -1,100 + 20 \times (P_B - 5)$$
$$5,200 - 80P_B = -1,100 + 20P_B - 100$$
$$100P_B = 6,400$$
$$P_B = 64$$
$$P_S = 64 - 5 = 59$$

To find the equilibrium quantity with the tax, we substitute the buyer price into the demand equation or the seller price into the supply equation:

$$Q^D = 5,200 - 80 \times 64 = 80$$
$$Q^S = -1,100 + 20 \times 59 = 80$$

Comparing this after-tax equilibrium with the no-tax equilibrium, we can see that the price buyers pay rises from $63 million to $64 million, and the price that sellers receive falls from $63 million to $59 million. The tax decreases the quantity of yachts bought from 160 to 80.

b. With no tax, buyers of yachts pay $63 million per yacht. With the tax, they pay $64 million. Thus, out of the $5 million per yacht tax, the burden that actually falls on buyers is $1 million. That is, the buyers' share of the tax is $\frac{\$1 \text{ million}}{\$5 \text{ million}} = 0.2$, or 20%.

c. With no tax, the consumer surplus is the triangular area below the demand curve and above the equilibrium price (area $A + B + C$):

$$CS = 0.5 \times 160 \times (\$65 \text{ million} - \$63 \text{ million}) = \$160 \text{ million}$$

With the tax, the consumer surplus is the area above the price that buyers pay and below the demand curve (area A):

$$CS_{\text{new}} = 0.5 \times 80 \times (\$65 \text{ million} - \$64 \text{ million}) = \$40$$

Thus, the tax decreases consumer surplus by $160 million – $40 million = $120 million.

With no tax, the producer surplus is the triangular area below the equilibrium price and above the supply curve (area $D + E + F$):

$$PS = 0.5 \times 160 \times (\$63 \text{ million} - \$55 \text{ million}) = \$640 \text{ million}$$

With the tax, the producer surplus reduces to the area below the price that sellers receive and above the supply curve (area F):

$$PS_{\text{new}} = 0.5 \times 80 \times (\$59 \text{ million} - \$55 \text{ million}) = \$160 \text{ million}$$

Thus, the producer surplus decreases by $640 million – $160 million = $480 million.

d. The consumer surplus represented by area C and the producer surplus represented by area E have disappeared because of the tax. Since no one receives these surpluses anymore, this is a deadweight loss. The triangular area $C + E$ can be calculated as

$$\text{DWL} = 0.5 \times (\$64 \text{ million} - \$59 \text{ million}) \times (160 - 80) = \$200$$

The deadweight loss can also be calculated as the difference between the total surplus, which consumers and producers get with no tax and the total surplus they and the government receive with the tax. With no tax, the total surplus is

$$TS = CS + PS = \$160 \text{ million} + \$640 \text{ million} = \$800 \text{ million}$$

With the tax, the surplus received by consumers and producers is

$$CS_{\text{new}} + PS_{\text{new}} = \$40 \text{ million} + \$160 \text{ million} = \$200 \text{ million}$$

and the surplus received by the government (government tax revenue) is

$$GS = \$5 \text{ million} \times 80 = \$400 \text{ million}.$$

So the deadweight loss is

$$\text{DWL} = \$800 \text{ million} - (\$200 \text{ million} + \$400 \text{ million}) = \$200 \text{ million}$$

Problem 7

a. The minimum wage is a price floor. To find whether it is binding, we solve for the market equilibrium wage by equating the quantity of labor supplied and the quantity of labor demanded:

$$L^S = L^D$$
$$-120 + 80W = 600 - 80W$$
$$160W = 720$$
$$W = 4.5$$

Thus, the equilibrium wage is $4.50 per hour. Since the minimum wage ($4.00) is below the equilibrium wage, the price floor is nonbinding; that is, it has no effect on the market wage or the quantity of labor employed. To solve for the equilibrium quantity of labor, we substitute the equilibrium wage into either the supply equation or the demand equation:

$$L^S = -120 + 80 \times 4.5 = 240$$
$$L^D = 600 - 80 \times 4.5 = 240$$

Thus, the current wage is $4.50 per hour, and the quantity of labor employed is 240 million hours.

b. If the government raises the minimum wage to $6 per hour, the minimum wage will be above the equilibrium wage, so the price floor will become binding, and the actual wage will be the minimum wage. At $6 per hour, the quantity of labor supplied will be

$$L^S = -120 + 80 \times 6 = 360$$

while the quantity of labor demanded will be

$$L^D = 600 - 80 \times 6 = 120$$

so there will be a surplus of labor of $360 - 120 = 240$ million hours. Although workers will want to work 360 million hours, employers will want to hire only 120 million hours, so only 120 million hours will be actually employed.

c. Workers are the sellers in the labor market. Therefore, to see whether workers are better off or worse off, we need to calculate and compare the producer surpluses before and after the new minimum wage is introduced. The easiest way to do it is to graph the demand and supply curves, using the equilibrium point and the choke prices for demand and supply. To find the choke prices, we set L^S and L^D equal to zero and solve for W:

$$L^S = -120 + 80W$$
$$0 = -120 + 80W$$
$$80W = 120$$
$$W = 1.50$$
$$L^D = 600 - 80W$$
$$0 = 600 - 80W$$
$$80W = 600$$
$$W = 7.50$$

Thus, the supply choke price is $1.50 per hour and the demand choke price is $7.50 per hour. We use these points to graph the demand and supply curves (D and S on the following graph).

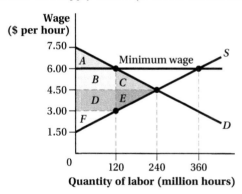

When the minimum wage is $4, the labor market is in equilibrium, so the producer surplus is the triangular area above the supply curve and below the equilibrium price (area $D + E + F$):

$$PS = 0.5 \times 240 \text{ million} \times (\$4.50 - \$1.50) = \$360 \text{ million}$$

With the new minimum wage, the producer surplus is the area below the minimum wage and above the supply curve, up to the quantity of labor employed (area $B + D + F$). An easy way to calculate the value of this surplus is to add the area of triangle F to the area of the rectangle $B + D$. To find these areas, we need to know the wage at which the quantity of labor supplied is 120. So we solve the following equation:

$$L^S = 120$$
$$-120 + 80W = 120$$
$$80W = 240$$
$$W = 3$$

Now we can calculate the area of triangle F:

$$F = 0.5 \times 120 \text{ million} \times (\$3.00 - \$1.50) = \$90 \text{ million}$$

and the area of rectangle $B + D$:

$$B + D = 120 \text{ million} \times (\$6.00 - \$3.00) = \$360 \text{ million}$$

So the producer surplus with the new minimum wage is

$$PS_{\text{new}} = \$90 \text{ million} + \$360 \text{ million} = \$450 \text{ million}$$

Thus, producer surplus increases from $360 million to $450 million; that is, workers are better off by $450 million − $360 million = $90 million.

Employers are the buyers in the labor market. Therefore, to see whether they are better off or worse off, we calculate and compare the consumer surpluses before and after the new minimum wage is introduced. When the minimum wage is $4, the labor market is in equilibrium, so the consumer surplus is the triangular area below the demand curve and above the equilibrium price (area $A + B + C$):

$$CS = 0.5 \times 240 \text{ million} \times (\$7.50 - \$4.50) = \$360 \text{ million}$$

With the new minimum wage, consumer surplus reduces to area A above the minimum wage and below the demand curve:

$$CS_{\text{new}} = 0.5 \times 120 \text{ million} \times (\$7.50 - \$6.00) = \$90 \text{ million}$$

Thus, consumer surplus decreases from $360 million to $90 million; that is, employers are worse off by $360 million − $90 million = $270 million.

d. As we can see from (c), employers are worse off by $270 million while workers are better off only by $90. That is, while the new minimum wage transfers part of the consumer surplus (area B) to producers, it results in the loss of consumer surplus represented by area C and the loss of producer surplus represented by area E. This deadweight loss (area $C + E$) can be calculated as

$$DWL = 0.5 \times (\$6.00 - \$3.00) \times (240 \text{ million} - 120 \text{ million}) = \$180 \text{ million}$$

The deadweight loss can also be calculated as the difference between the employers' loss and the workers' gain:

$$DWL = \$270 \text{ million} - \$90 \text{ million} = \$180 \text{ million}$$

Problem 8

a. With no subsidy, the equilibrium price is where $Q^D = Q^S$:

$$45 - 1.5P = -3 + 0.5P$$
$$2P = 48$$
$$P = 24$$

To find the equilibrium quantity, we substitute the equilibrium price into either the demand or the supply equation:

$$Q^D = 45 - 1.5 \times 24 = 9$$
$$Q^S = -3 + 0.5 \times 24 = 9$$

Thus, with no subsidy, the price of a year in college is $24,000 per year, and the number of students attending is 9 million.

With the subsidy, the students' demand curve is the same as with no subsidy. But the demand curve faced by colleges is shifted up by the amount of the subsidy ($8,000), since the price that colleges receive at each given quantity demanded is the price paid by students plus the subsidy. Thus, the price received by sellers is

$$P_S = P_B + 8$$

where P_B is the price paid by buyers. To solve for the quantity and prices with the subsidy, we substitute this expression into our supply and demand equations:

$$45 - 1.5P_B = -3 + 0.5P_S$$
$$45 - 1.5P_B = -3 + 0.5 \times (P_B + 8)$$
$$45 - 1.5P_B = -3 + 0.5P_B + 4$$
$$2P_B = 44$$
$$P_B = 22$$
$$P_S = 22 + 8 = 30$$

Thus, the price that students pay is $22,000 per year, and the price that colleges receive is $30,000 per year. To solve for the equilibrium quantity with the subsidy, we substitute the buyer price into the demand equation or the seller price into the supply equation:

$$Q^D = 45 - 1.5 \times 22 = 12$$
$$Q^S = -3 + 0.5 \times 30 = 12$$

That is, with the subsidy, the number of students enrolled is 12 million. Thus, the subsidy lowers the price that students pay from $24,000 per year to $22,000 per year, raises the price that colleges receive from $24,000 per year to $30,000 per year, and increases the number of students attending college from 9 million to 12 million.

b. The cost of the subsidy is the subsidy per student times the number of students enrolled: $8,000 × 12 million = $96 billion.

c. To see how students are better off as a result of the subsidy, we calculate and compare the consumer surpluses with and without the subsidy. The easiest way to do it is to graph the demand and supply curves, using the equilibrium point and the choke prices for demand and supply. To find the choke prices, we set Q^D and Q^S equal to zero and solve for P:

$$Q^D = 45 - 1.5P$$
$$0 = 45 - 1.5P$$
$$1.5P = 45$$
$$P = 30$$
$$Q^S = -3 + 0.5P$$
$$0 = -3 + 0.5P$$
$$0.5P = 3$$
$$P = 6$$

Thus, the demand choke price is $30,000 per year and the supply choke price is $6,000 per year. We use these points to graph the demand and supply curves (D and S on the following graph). With no subsidy, the consumer surplus is the area below the demand curve and above the price (area A):

$$CS = 0.5 \times 9 \text{ million} \times (\$30,000 - \$24,000) = \$27 \text{ billion}$$

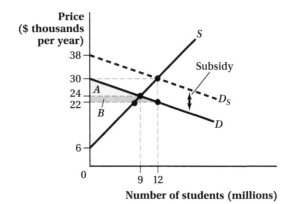

With the subsidy, the consumer surplus is the area below the demand curve and above the price students pay when given the subsidy (area $A + B$):

$$CS_{\text{new}} = 0.5 \times 12 \text{ million} \times (\$30,000 - \$22,000) = \$48 \text{ billion}$$

Thus, students gain $48 billion – $27 billion = $21 billion as a result of the subsidy.

Problem 9

Nothing will really change. With the subsidy, colleges' supply curve is the same as their supply curve with no subsidy. But the supply curve faced by students is shifted down by the amount of the subsidy ($8,000), since, at each given quantity, the price they pay is less than the price that the college receives by the amount of the subsidy. Thus, the price paid by buyers is

$$P_B = P_S - 8$$

where P_S is the price received by sellers. To solve for the quantity and prices with the subsidy, we substitute this expression into our supply and demand equations:

$$45 - 1.5P_B = -3 + 0.5P_S$$
$$45 - 1.5 \times (P_S - 8) = -3 + 0.5P_S$$
$$45 - 1.5P_S + 12 = -3 + 0.5P_S$$
$$2P_S = 60$$
$$P_S = 30$$
$$P_B = 30 - 8 = 22$$

Thus, the price that students pay is still $22,000 per year, and the price that colleges receive is still $30,000 per year. Since the buyer demand equation and the seller supply equation are the same as in the previous problem, the equilibrium number of students enrolled is also the same: 12 million (see the following graph).

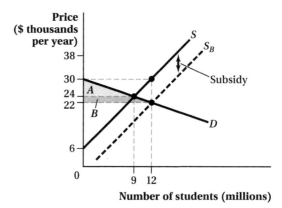

Thus, no matter whether the subsidy is given to students or to colleges, it lowers the price that students pay from $24,000 per year to $22,000 per year, raises the price that colleges receive from $24,000 per year to $30,000 per year, and increases the number of students attending college from 9 million to 12 million. The change in students' consumer surplus resulting from the subsidy is also the same: students gain $21 billion (area B on the preceding graph).

Problem 10

a. As shown on the graph at right, the price floor is above the market equilibrium, so it is binding. With the price floor in effect, the quantity of pork supplied rises to 10 million pounds, while the quantity demanded falls to 4 million pounds. Thus, the government will have to purchase 10 million − 4 million = 6 million pounds of pork.

b. With no price floor, when the market is in equilibrium, the price of pork is $2.50 per pound, and the quantity of pork sold is 8 million pounds. The consumer surplus is the area below the demand curve and above the equilibrium price (area $A + B$):

$$CS = 0.5 \times 8 \text{ million} \times (\$3.50 - \$2.50) = 4 \text{ million}$$

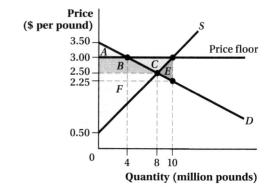

With the price floor, the consumer surplus is the area below the demand curve and above the price floor (area A):

$$CS_{\text{new}} = 0.5 \times 4 \text{ million} \times (\$3.50 - \$3.00) = 1 \text{ million}$$

Thus, consumers lose \$3 million as a result of the program.

c. The government purchases 6 million pounds of pork at \$3 per pound. Thus, taxpayers pay \$3.00 $\times$ 6 million = \$18 million. The value of this purchase, however, is only what consumers in a free market are willing to pay, which is the trapezoid area under the demand curve over the quantity purchased. This area can be calculated as

$$0.5 \times (\$3.00 + \$2.25) \times (10 \text{ million} - 4 \text{ million}) = \$15.75 \text{ million}$$

We can view this as a lost government surplus of \$18 million − \$15.75 million = \$2.25 million (area $C + E$). This deadweight loss can also be calculated directly:

$$(\text{Area } C + E) = 0.5 \times (10 \text{ million} - 4 \text{ million}) \times (\$3.00 - \$2.25) = \$2.25 \text{ million}$$

d. With no price floor, the producer surplus is the area above the supply curve and below the market price (area F):

$$PS = 0.5 \times 8 \text{ million} \times (\$2.50 - \$0.50) = 8 \text{ million}$$

With the price floor, the producer surplus is the area above the supply curve and below the price floor, up to the quantity sold to both consumers and the government (area $B + C + F$):

$$PS_{\text{new}} = 0.5 \times 10 \text{ million} \times (\$3.00 - \$0.50) = 12.5 \text{ million}$$

Thus, producers gain \$4.5 million as a result of the program.

e. Part of the loss in government surplus (area C) is a transfer to pork producers, but the rest of it (area E) is a deadweight loss, which can be calculated as

$$\text{DWL} = 0.5 \times (\$3.00 - \$2.25) \times (10 \text{ million} - 8 \text{ million}) = 0.75 \text{ million}$$

Another way to calculate this deadweight loss is

$$\text{DWL} = \text{Loss in consumer surplus} + \text{Loss in government surplus} - \text{Gain in producer surplus}$$
$$\text{DWL} = \$3 \text{ million} + \$2.25 \text{ million} - 4.5 \text{ million} = 0.75 \text{ million}$$

Problem 11

a. To find the equilibrium price of gas with no quota, we equate the quantities of gas demanded and supplied and solve this equation for P:

$$Q^D = Q^S$$
$$10 - 1.25P = -10 + 5P$$
$$6.25P = 20$$
$$P = 3.2$$

The equilibrium quantity of gas can be found by substituting the equilibrium price into either the demand or the supply equation:

$$Q^D = 10 - 1.25 \times 3.2 = 6$$
$$Q^S = -10 + 5 \times 3.2 = 6$$

The quota creates a regulatory bend in the supply curve so that it becomes vertical at the quantity of 4 million gallons (see the following graph). That is, no matter what the price of gas is, gas sellers cannot supply more than 4 million gallons. Now the demand curve intersects the supply curve at $Q = 4$, so we can find the equilibrium price of gas by substituting $Q = 4$ into the demand equation and solving it for P:

$$4 = 10 - 1.25P$$
$$1.25P = 6$$
$$P = 4.8$$

Thus, the quota raises the price of gas from \$3.20 to \$4.80 per gallon and reduces the quantity of gas sold from 6 million gallons to 4 million gallons.

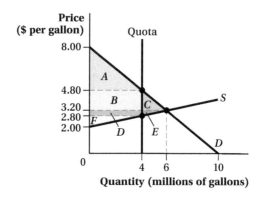

b. With no quota in effect, the consumer surplus is the triangular area below the demand curve and above the equilibrium market price $(A + B + C)$. To calculate this area, we need to know the demand choke price, that is, the price at which $Q^D = 0$. We can find the demand choke price from the demand curve:

$$Q^D = 10 - 1.25P = 0$$
$$1.25P = 10$$
$$P = 8$$

The consumer surplus therefore is

$$CS = 0.5 \times 6 \text{ million} \times (\$8 - \$3.20) = \$14.4 \text{ million}$$

With the quota in effect, the consumer surplus reduces to the area below the demand curve and above the price with the quota in effect ($4.80 per gallon). So the consumer surplus is area A, which can be calculated as follows:

$$CS = 0.5 \times 4 \text{ million} \times (\$8 - \$4.80) = \$6.4 \text{ million}$$

Thus, the quota reduces the consumer surplus from $14.4 million to $ 6.4 million.

Let's turn to producer surplus now. With no quota in effect, it is the triangular area above the supply curve and below the equilibrium price $(D + E + F)$. To calculate this area, we need to know the supply choke price, that is, the price at which $Q^S = 0$. We can find it from the supply curve:

$$Q^S = -10 + 5P = 0$$
$$5P = 10$$
$$P = 2$$

The producer surplus therefore is

$$PS = 0.5 \times 6 \text{ million} \times (\$3.20 - \$2) = \$3.6 \text{ million}$$

With the quota enforced, the producer surplus is the area above the supply curve and below the price when the quota is in effect ($4.80 per gallon), up to the quota quantity (4 million gallons). That is, the producer surplus is area $B + D + F$. To calculate this area, we need to know the price at which the quantity supplied is equal to the quota. We can determine it my setting $Q^S = 4$ and solving the supply equation for P:

$$Q^S = -10 + 5P = 4$$
$$5P = 14$$
$$P = 2.8$$

This means

$$(\text{Area } B + D) = 4 \text{ million} \times (\$4.80 - \$2.80) = \$8 \text{ million}$$

and

$$\text{Area } F = 0.5 \times 4 \text{ million} \times (\$2.80 - \$2.00) = \$1.6 \text{ million}$$

so the producer surplus is

$$PS = (\text{Area } B + D + F) = \$8 \text{ million} + \$1.6 \text{ million} = \$9.6 \text{ million}$$

Thus, the producer surplus increases from $3.6 million to $9.6 million.

Note, however, that to be able to sell gas in the city, sellers have to buy permits from the government. And once they've purchased all the permits, they are able to sell 4 million gallons of gas for $4.80 per gallon. As the supply curve shows, sellers are willing to sell this quantity for only $2.80 per gallon. This means sellers will pay up to $2 per gallon for the right to sell gas in the city. And since sellers compete with each other in the auction, the government will be able to get that exact price, so its revenue from selling the permits (government surplus) will be $2 × 4 million = $8 million (area $B + D$). Thus, $8 million out of the $9.6 million producer surplus is transferred to the government, so the sellers are left with only $1.6 million.

c. The consumer surplus represented by area C and the producer surplus represented by area E disappear because of the quota. Since no one receives these surpluses anymore, this is a deadweight loss. The triangular area $C + E$ can be calculated as

$$\text{DWL} = 0.5 \times (\$4.80 - \$2.80) \times (6 \text{ million} - 4 \text{ million}) = \$2 \text{ million}$$

d. To calculate deadweight loss, note from the figure that we are are interested in the area under the demand curve and above the supply curve between a quantity of 4 and 6 (in millions). We can therefore form the integral by taking the difference between the inverse demand and inverse supply equations. We can rearrange demand and supply to get inverse demand and supply, respectively.

$$Q^D = 10 - 1.25P$$
$$1.25P = 10 - Q^D$$
$$P = 8 - 0.8Q^D$$

and

$$Q^S = 5P - 10$$
$$5P = 10 + Q^S$$
$$P = 2 + 0.2Q^S$$

We then want to evaluate this integral between quantity levels of 4 and 6:

$$\text{DWL} = \int_4^6 \big((8 - 0.8Q) - (2 + 0.2Q)\big)dQ = \int_4^6 (6 - Q)dQ$$

$$= [6Q]_4^6 - \left[\frac{Q^2}{2}\right]_4^6$$

$$= [6(6) - 6(4)] - \left[\frac{(6)^2}{2} - \frac{(4)^2}{2}\right]$$

$$= (36 - 24) - (18 - 8) = 2$$

Deadweight loss therefore is $2 million in dollar terms as found in the preceding part (c) .

Problem 12

a. The equilibrium condition is: $300 - 6Q^3 = 30 + 4Q^3$.

$$10Q^3 = 270$$
$$Q^3 = 27$$
$$Q = 3$$
$$P = 300 - 6(3)^3 = 138$$

The price of the spring dress therefore is $138, and 3,000 of these are sold in equilibrium.

b. The consumer surplus calculation is:

$$CS = \int_0^3 \big((300 - 6Q^3) - 138\big)dQ = \int_0^3 (162 - 6Q^3)dQ = [162Q]_0^3 - \left[\frac{6Q^4}{4}\right]_0^3 = [162(3) - 162(0)] - \left[\frac{6(3)^4}{4} - \frac{6(0)^4}{4}\right]$$

$$= (486 - 0) - (121.5 - 0) = 364.5$$

$$PS = \int_0^3 \big(138 - (30 + 4Q^3)\big)dQ = \int_0^3 (108 - 4Q^3)dQ = [108Q]_0^3 - \left[\frac{4Q^4}{4}\right]_0^3 = [108Q]_0^3 - [Q^4]_0^3$$

$$= [108(3) - 108(0)] - [(3)^4 - (0)^4] = (324 - 0) - (81 - 0) = 243$$

The consumer and producer surpluses are $364,500 and $243,000, respectively.

c. With a tax of $10, the equilibrium conditions become:

$$P_b = 300 - 6Q^3$$
$$P_s = 30 + 4Q^3$$
$$P_b - P_s = 10$$

Solving this system of equations, we find that:

$$P_s + 10 = 300 - 6Q^3$$
$$P_s = 290 - 6Q^3$$
$$290 - 6Q^3 = 30 + 4Q^3$$
$$10Q^3 = 260$$
$$Q^3 = 26$$
$$Q \approx 2.96$$
$$P_b = 300 - 6(2.96)^3$$
$$P_b \approx 144.39$$
$$P_s = 144.39 - 10 = 134.39$$

$$CS = \int_0^{2.96}\big((300 - 6Q^3) - 144.39\big)dQ = \int_0^{2.96}(155.61 - 6Q^3)dQ = [155.61Q]_0^{2.96} - \left[\frac{6Q^4}{4}\right]_0^{2.96}$$

$$= [155.61(2.96) - 155.61(0)] - \left[\frac{6(2.96)^4}{4} - \frac{6(0)^4}{4}\right] = (460.61 - 0) - (115.15 - 0) = 345.46$$

$$PS = \int_0^{2.96}\big(134.39 - (30 + 4Q^3)\big)dQ = \int_0^{2.96}(104.39 - 4Q^3)dQ = [104.39Q]_0^{2.96} - \left[\frac{4Q^4}{4}\right]_0^{2.96}$$

$$= [104.39Q]_0^{2.96} - [Q^4]_0^{2.96} = [104.39(2.96) - 104.39(0)] - [(2.96)^4 - (0)^4]$$

$$= (308.99 - 0) - (76.77 - 0) = 232.22$$

The consumer and producer surpluses are $345,460 and $232,220, respectively.

d. The deadweight loss calculation is:

$$\text{DWL} = \int_{2.96}^3\big((300 - 6Q^3) - (30 + 4Q^3)\big)dQ = \int_{2.96}^3(270 - 10Q^3)dQ = [270Q]_{2.96}^3 - \left[\frac{10Q^4}{4}\right]_{2.96}^3$$

$$= [270(3) - 270(2.96)] - \left[\frac{10(3)^4}{4} - \frac{10(2.96)^4}{4}\right] = (810 - 799.2) - (202.5 - 191.91) = 0.21$$

Deadweight loss is $21,000.

Consumer Behavior

4

Solutions for Practice Problems

Problem 1

a. Boris's MRS_{SB} is

$$MRS_{SB} = \frac{MU_S}{MU_B} = \frac{\left(\dfrac{0.2B^{0.5}}{S^{0.5}}\right)}{\left(\dfrac{0.2S^{0.5}}{B^{0.5}}\right)} = \frac{0.2B^{0.5}B^{0.5}}{0.2S^{0.5}S^{0.5}} = \frac{B}{S} = \frac{4}{9} = 0.44$$

b. When Boris consumes 9 pounds of sausage and 4 loaves of bread, his utility is $0.4 \times 9^{0.5} \times 4^{0.5} = 2.4$. And when he consumes 6 pounds of sausage and 6 loaves of bread, his utility is $0.4 \times 6^{0.5} \times 6^{0.5} = 0.4 \times 36^{0.5} = 2.4$. Since the two bundles provide the same utility, they are on the same indifference curve.

c. Suppose sausage is on the horizontal axis (the results would be the same if bread was on the horizontal axis). As calculated in (a), when Boris eats 9 pounds of sausage and 4 loaves of bread, his MRS_{SB} is 0.44. And when he decreases his consumption of sausage from 9 pounds to 6 pounds and increases his consumption of bread from 4 loaves to 6 loaves, moving up along his indifference curve, his $MRS_{SB} = \dfrac{B}{S} = \dfrac{6}{6} = 1$. Thus, Boris's MRS_{SB} increases as he consumes less sausage, which means his indifference curve becomes steeper when less of the good that is on the horizontal axis is consumed, i.e., the indifference curve is convex to the origin.

d. Marginal utilities can be calculated as partial derivatives of the utility function. Since $U = 0.4S^{0.5}B^{0.5}$, the marginal utility of sausage is $MU_S = \dfrac{\partial U}{\partial S} = 0.4(0.5)S^{0.5-1}B^{0.5} = \dfrac{0.2B^{0.5}}{S^{0.5}}$, and the marginal utility of bread is $MU_B = \dfrac{\partial U}{\partial B} = 0.2(0.5)S^{0.5}B^{0.5-1} = \dfrac{0.2S^{0.5}}{B^{0.5}}$.

e. A way to check concavity versus convexity is to take the partial derivative of MRS_{SB} with respect to S and compare it to zero. This marginal rate of substitution is calculated in part (c). Specifically, $MRS_{SB} = \dfrac{B}{S}$. The derivative of this with respect to S is $\dfrac{\partial MRS_{SB}}{\partial S}$ is $-\dfrac{B}{S^2}$. Since this is always less than or equal to zero (for positive B and S), Boris's indifference cures are convex.

f. For this new utility function, $MU_S = \dfrac{\partial U}{\partial S} = 0.1$ and $MU_B = \dfrac{\partial U}{\partial B} = 0.1$. Marginal rate of substitution of S for B therefore is $MRS_{SB} = \dfrac{MU_S}{MU_B} = \dfrac{0.1}{0.1} = 1$. Since this is not the same as his original marginal rate of substitution as calculated in part (a) of $\dfrac{B}{S}$, the proposed utility function does not represent Boris's preferences.

Problem 2

a. Since Beatrice is indifferent between bundles A and B, these bundles are on the same indifference curve (U_1 on the following graph). As a typical indifference curve, U_1 is convex to the origin. As the graph shows, given that U_1 is convex, bundle C must lie above it, that is, on a higher indifference curve (U_2). Thus, Beatrice prefers bundle C to bundle A.

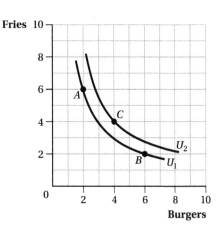

b. If Beatrice views the two goods as perfect substitutes, her indifference curves are straight lines. And, as the following graph shows, if the indifference curve on which bundles A and B lie (U_1) is a straight line, then bundle C is also on that indifference curve. Thus, Beatrice is indifferent between bundle C and bundle A.

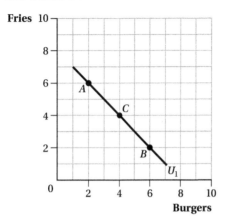

c. If Beatrice views the two goods as perfect complements, her indifference curves are L-shaped (see the following graph). Mathematically, they can be represented as $U = \min\{Q_B, Q_F\}$, where U is the level of utility that Beatrice gets, and Q_B and Q_F are the quantities of burgers and fries that she consumes. So, when Beatrice consumes bundle A, her utility is $U_1 = \min\{2, 6\} = 2$, which is the same as her utility when she consumes bundle B: $\min\{6, 2\} = 2 = U_1$. But if she consumes bundle C, her utility is $U_2 = \min\{4, 4\} = 4$. Thus, bundle C lies on a higher indifference curve than bundle A, and Beatrice prefers Bundle C to bundle A.

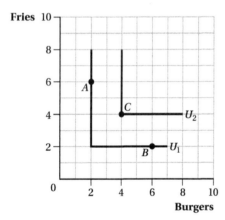

Problem 3

a. Cornelius has a linear utility function of the form $U = aT + bC$, where a and b are the marginal utilities of consuming one more treacle tart and one more cauldron cake, respectively. Thus, Cornelius's marginal utility of consuming one more treacle tart is 4, and his marginal utility of consuming one more cauldron cake is 2. The marginal rate of substitution of treacle tarts for cauldron cakes is defined as $MRS_{TC} = \dfrac{MU_T}{MU_C}$. Thus, Cornelius's $MRS_{TC} = \dfrac{4}{2} = 2$. Notice that Cornelius's marginal rate of substitution does not depend on the quantities of cauldron cakes and treacle tarts that he consumes.

b. Cornelius's linear utility function with a constant marginal rate of substitution of treacle tarts for cauldron cakes tells us that he views these two goods as perfect substitutes. That is, no matter how many treacle tarts Cornelius consumes, he is always as well-off eating one more treacle tart instead of two cauldron cakes.

c. Given Cornelius's utility function, when he consumes 5 treacle tarts and 4 cauldron cakes, his utility level is $4 \times 5 + 2 \times 4 = 28$. And when he consumes 7 treacle tarts and no cauldron cakes, his utility level is $4 \times 7 + 2 \times 0 = 28$. Since the two bundles provide Cornelius with the same level of utility, they are on the same indifference curve. Another way to answer this question is to realize that

Cornelius's $MRS_{TC} = 2$ suggests that if he substitutes one tart for 2 cauldron cakes, he will stay on the same indifference curve. And since the MRS_{TC} is constant, we also know that if Cornelius substitutes 2 tarts for 4 cakes (i.e., consumes 7 tarts instead of 5 and no cakes instead of 4), he will stay on the same indifference curve.

d. Cornelius's utility function is linear, with a constant marginal rate of substitution of treacle tarts for cauldron cakes. This means his indifference curves are straight lines and not convex curves.

e. Using partial derivatives, we can see that $MU_T = \dfrac{\partial U}{\partial T} = 4$ and $MU_C = \dfrac{\partial U}{\partial C} = 2$. Marginal rate of substitution of T for C therefore is $MRS_{TC} = \dfrac{MU_T}{MU_C} = \dfrac{4}{2} = 2$.

f. The Lagrangian approach is based on solving for an interior optimum. Here, Cornelius's utility function is one of perfect substitutes (because it's additive in the goods). Depending on the specific price ratio, his final solution, therefore, will either be a corner solution (where he chooses all T or all C) or will correspond to the full set of points on the budget constraint (infinite solutions). There is no way to solve the system of equations that is generated as the first-order conditions of the Lagrangian, because this leads to a mathematical contradiction quickly! Corneilius's solution, therefore, will likely be a corner solution, where $MRS_{TC} \neq \dfrac{P_T}{P_C}$. If $MRS_{TC} > \dfrac{P_T}{P_C}$, he will consume all T and no C. If $MRS_{TC} < \dfrac{P_T}{P_C}$, he will consume all C and no T. If by chance, $MRS_{TC} = \dfrac{P_T}{P_C}$, then there is no unique solution and he will consume any combination of T and C that is affordable because he will be indifferent among all of these allocations.

Problem 4

a. The equation of Titus's budget constraint is $\$100 = \$2C + \$1M$. To graph this budget constraint, we first find the horizontal and vertical intercepts. The horizontal intercept is where Titus spends all of his $\$100$ on cupcakes, buying $\dfrac{\$100}{\$2} = \$50$ cupcakes. The vertical intercept is where Titus spends all his money on music downloads, buying $\dfrac{\$100}{\$1} = \$100$ downloads. The budget constraint is a straight line that connects these points (BC_1 on the following graph). The slope of the budget constraint can be calculated as the rise over the run: $-\dfrac{-100}{50} = -2$. It can also be calculated as $-\left(\dfrac{P_C}{P_M}\right) = -\left(\dfrac{\$2}{\$1}\right) = -2$.

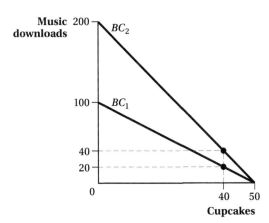

b. If Titus eats 40 cupcakes, he spends $\$2 \times 40 = \$80$ on them. This leaves him $\$100 - \$80 = \$20$ to spend on music downloads. At a price of $\$1$ per download, he buys $\dfrac{\$20}{\$1} = 20$ downloads.

c. The new budget constraint is BC_2 on the preceding graph. At a price of $\$0.50$, Titus can afford $\dfrac{\$100}{\$0.50} = 200$ downloads. Since the price of a cupcake remains unchanged, the horizontal intercept does not change. Titus still spends $\$80$ on cupcakes, which leaves him $\$20$ to spend on music downloads. But at a price of $\$0.50$ per download, he buys $\dfrac{\$20}{\$0.50} = 40$ downloads.

Problem 5

a. To find Benedict's optimal consumption bundle, we draw his budget constraint. If Benedict spends all his allowance on pizza, he will get $\frac{\$144}{\$4} = 36$ slices of pizza and no audiobooks. If he spends all his allowance on audiobooks, he will get $\frac{\$144}{\$16} = 9$ audiobooks and no pizza. Connecting these two points, we get Benedict's budget constraint (BC_1 on the following graph). Benedict's optimal choice is the point of tangency between his budget line and the highest indifference curve he can reach, U_3, at which he consumes 12 slices of pizza and 6 audiobooks.

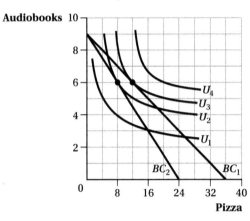

b. The marginal rate of substitution of pizza for audiobooks (MRS_{PA}) at a point equals the absolute value of the slope of the indifference curve at this point. And at the point of the consumer's optimal choice, the slope of the indifference curve equals the slope of the budget constraint, which is equal (by the absolute value) to the ratio of the price of the good on the horizontal axis (pizza) to the price of the good on the vertical axis (audiobooks). Thus, $MRS_{PA} = \frac{\$4}{\$16} = 0.25$.

c. With the new price of pizza, if Benedict spends all his allowance on pizza, he will get $\frac{\$144}{\$6} = 24$ slices of pizza. Thus, the horizontal intercept for the new budget line is 24. The vertical intercept remains the same, since the price of audiobooks does not change. The new budget constraint (BC_2) is shown on the preceding graph. Benedict's optimal choice is the point of tangency between the new budget line and the highest indifference curve he can reach, U_2, at which he consumes 8 slices of pizza and 6 audiobooks. That is, Benedict now consumes 4 slices of pizza less, but the quantity of audiobooks he buys remains at 6.

Problem 6

a. As Vassilios's budget constraint shows, when he spends all his money on t-shirts, he buys 6 t-shirts. Thus, the price of a t-shirt is $\frac{\$72}{6} = \$12$. Similarly, when Vassilios spends all his money on socks, he buys 24 pairs of socks. Thus, the price of socks is $\frac{\$72}{24} = \$3$ a pair.

b. Vassilios's optimal choice is the point of tangency between the budget line and the highest indifference curve he can reach, U_2, at which he buys 3 t-shirts and 12 pairs of socks (point A on the following graph).

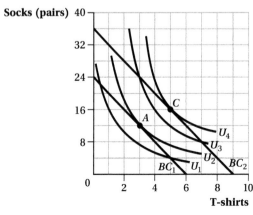

c. To find Vassilios's optimal consumption bundle, we draw his new budget constraint. If Vassilios spends all his money on t-shirts, he will buy $\dfrac{\$108}{\$12} = 9$ t-shirts and no socks. If he spends his entire budget on socks, he will get $\dfrac{\$108}{\$3} = 36$ pairs of socks and no t-shirts. Connecting these two points, we get Vassilios's new budget constraint (BC_2 on the preceding graph). Vassilios's optimal choice is the point of tangency between his new budget line and the highest indifference curve he can reach, U_4, at which he consumes 5 t-shirts and 16 pairs of socks (point C).

Problem 7

a. Twenty downloads and 120 phone minutes would cost Danny $\$3 \times 20 + \$0.12 \times 120 = \$74.40$, which exceeds his budget of $72, so this bundle is not feasible. Combination (ii) costs $\$3 \times 12 + \$0.12 \times 300 = \$72$, which is within Danny's budget, so it is feasible. Combination (iii) costs $\$3 \times 6 + \$0.12 \times 600 = \$90$, which exceeds Danny's budget and therefore is not feasible. Combination (iv) costs $\$3 \times 15 + \$0.12 \times 200 = \$69$, which is within the budget and therefore is feasible.

b. If Danny spends all his budget on video downloads, he will be able to buy $\dfrac{\$72}{\$3} = 24$ downloads and no phone minutes. If he spends all his money on phone calls, he will get $\dfrac{\$72}{\$0.12} = 600$ phone minutes and no video downloads. Danny's budget constraint is a straight line connecting these points (BC_1 on the following graph). If Danny downloads 6 videos, he spends $\$3 \times 6 = \$18$ on videos, which leaves him $\$72 - \$18 = \$54$ to spend on phone calls. And at a price of $0.12 per minute, he will be able to get $\dfrac{\$54}{\$0.12} = 450$ phone minutes (point A on the graph).

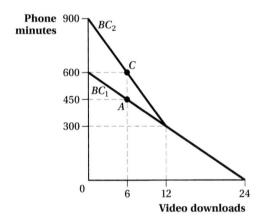

c. For the first 300 minutes of phone calls, Danny's budget constraint is the same as before. But his budget line becomes steeper at 300 minutes because phone calls become cheaper. To find where the new budget constraint intercepts the vertical axis, we need to figure out how many minutes Danny can buy if he buys only phone time. We can find this from the following equation: $(\$0.12 \times 300) + (\$0.06 \times M) = \$72$, where M is the additional minutes, after 300 minutes, that Danny can buy. Solving this equation, we get $M = 600$. Thus, Danny's budget constraint intercepts the vertical axis at $300 + 600 = 900$ minutes. Now, we can draw Danny's budget constraint as shown on the preceding graph (BC_2).

d. With the new plan, 9 video downloads and 400 phone minutes would cost Danny $\$3 \times 9 + (\$0.12 \times 300 + 0.06 \times 100) = \$69$, which is within his budget of $72. If Danny downloads 6 videos, he spends $\$3 \times 6 = \$18$ on videos. And for the first 300 minutes, he spends $\$0.12 \times 300 = \$36$, which leaves him $\$72 - \$18 - \$36 = \$18$ to spend on phone calls at $0.06, so he will be able to get $\dfrac{\$18}{\$0.06} = 300$ phone minutes more. Thus, the new plan allows Danny to afford 6 video downloads and 600 phone minutes. (point C on the graph).

Problem 8

a. If Christa considered music CDs and iTunes albums downloads perfect substitutes, her indifference curves would be straight lines. Since Christa's indifference curves are not straight lines, she does not view CDs and downloads as perfect substitutes.

b. To find Christa's optimal consumption bundle, we draw her budget constraint. If Christa spends all her allowance on CDs, she will get $\dfrac{\$128}{\$16} = 8$ CDs and no iTunes downloads. If she spends all her allowance on downloads, she will get $\dfrac{\$128}{\$8} = 16$ albums. Connecting these two points, we get Christa's budget constraint (BC_1 on the following graph). Christa's optimal choice is the point of tangency between her budget line and the highest indifference curve she can reach, U_1, at which she buys 3 CDs and downloads 10 albums.

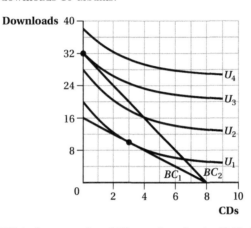

c. With the new price of iTunes downloads, if Christa spends all her allowance on downloads, she will get $\dfrac{\$128}{\$4} = 32$ albums. Thus, the vertical intercept for the new budget line is 32. The horizontal intercept remains the same, since the price of CDs does not change. The new budget constraint (BC_2) is shown on the preceding graph. As the graph shows, the highest indifference curve that Christa can reach, given her budget constraint, is U_3, and at the point where she reaches it, she buys only iTunes downloads (32 albums) and no CDs. This is called a corner solution.

Problem 9

a. Ben's indifference curve (U_1) is shown on the following graph. Ben views hotdogs and buns as perfect complements. When he has 4 hotdogs and 12 buns (point A), 8 extra buns add no utility to him, so the utility level he gets is the same as with 4 hotdogs and 4 buns (point B). The same would be true if Ben had 4 buns and more than 4 hotdogs: adding another hotdog while keeping the quantity of buns the same would not increase his utility. Therefore, his indifference curves are L-shaped. Mathematically, they can be represented as $U = \min\{Q_H, Q_B\}$, where U is the utility that Ben gets, and Q_H and Q_B are the quantities of hotdogs and buns that he consumes. For example, if Ben consumes 4 hotdogs and 12 buns, his utility, $U = \min\{4, 12\} = 4$, is the same as when he consumes 4 hotdogs and 4 buns ($U = \min\{4, 4\} = 4$) and also the same as when he consumes 12 hotdogs and 4 buns ($U = \min\{12, 4\} = 4$).

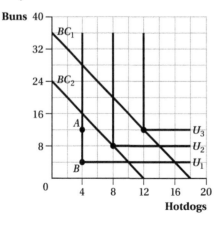

b. To find Ben's optimal consumption bundle, we draw his budget constraint. If Ben spends his entire budget on hotdogs, he will get $\dfrac{\$36}{\$2} = 18$ hotdogs and no buns. If he spends his entire budget on buns, he will get $\dfrac{\$36}{\$1} = 36$ buns and no hotdogs. Connecting these two points, we get Ben's budget constraint (BC_1 on the preceding graph). Ben's optimal choice is the point of tangency between his budget line and the highest indifference curve he can reach, U_3, at which he buys 12 hotdogs and 12 buns. How do we find this point? We know that Ben's optimal choice is always a bundle with equal quantities of hotdogs and buns. This is because adding another unit of one good while keeping the quantity of the other good constant does not increase utility but only causes additional spending. Thus, we can write the equation for Ben's optimal choice, given his budget constraint, as $36 = 2Q + Q$, where Q is the quantity of hotdogs (which is equal to the quantity of buns) that Ben buys. Solving this equation for Q, we get $Q = 12$.

c. Ben's budget constraint (BC_2) is shown on the preceding graph. As explained in (b), given that hotdogs and buns are perfect complements, we can write the equation for Ben's budget constraint as $24 = 2Q + Q$. Solving this equation for Q, we get $Q = 8$. Ben's optimal choice—the point of tangency between his budget line (BC_2) and the highest indifference curve he can reach (U_2)—is shown on the preceding graph.

d. Even though the Lagrangian approach is based on solving for an interior optimum and solutions are interior optima here, the Lagrangian approach will not work in this circumstance. Write out the Lagrangian to see this more formally:

$$\max_{H,B} \mathcal{L} = \min(H,\, B) + \lambda(36 - 2H - B) \text{ where } H \text{ represents hotdogs and } B \text{ denotes buns.}$$

Note that it is impossible to take the derivative of a minimum correspondence (the first term of the Lagrangian as written). Therefore, it is impossible to take the first-order conditions, which are key to the Lagrangian approach.

Problem 10

a. Your budget constraint (BC_1) is shown on the following graph. If you spend all your income on pizza, you will be able to buy $\dfrac{\$40}{\$8} = 5$ pizzas and no other goods. If you spend all your income on other goods, you will get $\dfrac{\$40}{\$1} = 40$ units of the other goods and no pizza. Your budget constraint is a straight line connecting these points. Your optimal choice is the point of tangency between your budget line and the highest indifference curve you can reach, U_1, at which you buy 3 pizzas and 16 units of other goods.

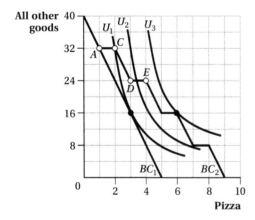

b. With the special promotion, you still buy 40 units of other goods if you buy no pizza. And when you buy 1 pizza, you pay $8, leaving $32 for purchasing 32 units of the other goods (point A). But since you can get the second pizza free, you'll still have $32 left to buy 32 units of the other goods after you get the second pizza (point C). Now, if you want the third pizza, you have to pay $8 more, leaving $24 to purchase 24 units of other goods (point D). But the fourth pizza is free, so you can buy 4 pizzas and still have $24 to purchase 24 units of the other goods (point E). Continuing the same way, you can draw the rest of your budget line (BC_2 on the preceding graph). Your optimal choice now is the point of tangency between the budget line BC_2 and the highest indifference curve you can reach, U_3, at which you buy 6 pizzas and 16 units of other goods. Thus, Papa John's promotion increases the quantity of pizza you buy from 3 to 6 pizzas.

∂ Problem 11

a. Using partial derivatives, we can see that $MU_M = \dfrac{\partial U}{\partial M} = 4B$.

b. Using partial derivatives, we can see that $MU_B = \dfrac{\partial U}{\partial B} = 4M$.

c. Marginal rate of substitution of M for B, therefore, is $MRS_{MB} = \dfrac{MU_M}{MU_B} = \dfrac{4B}{4M} = \dfrac{B}{M}$.

d. A way to check concavity versus convexity is to take the partial derivative of MRS_{MB} with respect to M and compare it to zero. This marginal rate of substitution is calculated in part (c). Specifically, $MRS_{MB} = \dfrac{B}{M}$. The derivative of this with respect to M is $\dfrac{\partial MRS_{MB}}{\partial M}$ is $-\dfrac{B}{M^2}$. Since this is always less than or equal to zero (for positive M and B), Delia's indifference cures are convex.

e. For this new utility function $MU_M = \dfrac{\partial U}{\partial M} = 2M^{-0.5}B^{0.5}$ and $MU_B = \dfrac{\partial U}{\partial B} = 2M^{0.5}B^{-0.5}$. Marginal rate of substitution of M for B therefore is $MRS_{MB} = \dfrac{MU_M}{MU_B} = \dfrac{2M^{-0.5}B^{0.5}}{2M^{0.5}B^{-0.5}} = \dfrac{B}{M}$. Since this is the same as Delia's original marginal rate of substitution as calculated in part (c), the proposed utility function does represent her preferences.

∂ Problem 12

The Lagrangian is:

$$\mathcal{L}(C,W,\lambda) = C^2W^2 + \lambda[60 - 10C - 15W]$$

The first-order conditions (partial derivatives of this equation with respect to C, W, and the Lagrange multiplier λ, respectively) are:

$$\frac{\partial \mathcal{L}}{\partial C} = 2CW^2 - \lambda(10) = 0$$

$$\frac{\partial \mathcal{L}}{\partial W} = 2C^2W - \lambda(15) = 0$$

$$\frac{\partial \mathcal{L}}{\partial \lambda} = 60 - 10C - 15W = 0$$

Solving the first two equations for λ and setting them equal to each other, we find:

$$\lambda = \frac{2CW^2}{10} = \frac{2C^2W}{15}$$

Rearranging, we see that:

$$3W = 2C$$

$$W = \frac{2C}{3}$$

The third of the first-order conditions tells us the budget constraint relationship:

$$60 = 10C + 15\left(\frac{2C}{3}\right)$$

$$60 = 20C$$

$$C = 3$$

$$W = \frac{2(3)}{3} = 2$$

∂ Problem 13

The Lagrangian approach is not appropriate, since this is the perfect substitutes case. Note that marginal utilities are first partial derivatives of the utility function and therefore

$$\frac{MU_C}{P_C} = \frac{2}{10} > \frac{MU_W}{P_W} = \frac{2}{15}$$

So the additional utility per dollar is higher for chocolates than for wine. Therefore, Doug should buy only chocolate. Given his budget constraint, he can afford 6 boxes.

Individual and Market Demand 5

Solutions for Practice Problems

Problem 1

a. The income elasticity of demand is

$$E_I^D = \frac{\%\Delta Q}{\%\Delta I}$$

where Q is the quantity of the good consumed (ΔQ is the change in quantity), and I is income (ΔI is the change in income). Thus, the income elasticity of demand for cigarettes is

$$E_I^D = \frac{-0.15}{-3} = 0.05$$

b. Since the income elasticity is positive, cigarettes are a normal good. Since the income elasticity is greater than 0 but less than 1, cigarettes are a "necessity" good. A Giffen good must be an inferior good. Since cigarettes are a normal rather than an inferior good, they can't be a Giffen good.

c. Using the income elasticity formula in (a), we can write:

$$0.05 = \frac{\%\Delta Q}{5}$$

from which

$$\%\Delta Q = 0.05 \times 5 = 0.25$$

Thus, we predict that, other things being equal, the quantity of cigarettes demanded will increase by 0.25% in response to a 5% increase in income.

d. The second study suggests a more income elastic demand for cigarettes, since $0.08 > 0.05$. That is, according to the second study for each 1% increase in income, the quantity of cigarettes demanded will increase by 0.08%, while according to the first study the quantity demanded will increase by only 0.05% in response to a 1% increase in income. Thus, the second study predicts a greater effect of a given increase in income on the demand for cigarettes.

Problem 2

a. No. Your budget constraint is affected by the amount you devote to the goods and by the prices of the goods. Since the total amount you spend on orange juice and potato chips remains unchanged and the prices of the two goods remain the same, your budget constraint is not affected.

b. Yes. When your preferences for orange juice change unfavorably, your indifference curves flatten because you are willing to give up fewer potato chips to get one more glass of orange juice. For example, suppose you consume 2 glasses of orange juice and 15 potato chips (point A on the following graph). Initially, your indifference curve is U, so you agree to give up 7 potato chips to get one more glass of orange juice, that is, to move to point B. Then, when your preferences for orange juice change unfavorably, you agree to give up only 4 potato chips to get one more glass of orange juice, that is, to move from point A to point B'. This means your indifference curve is now U_2, which is flatter than U_1.

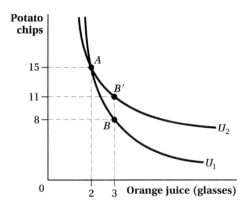

Another way to think about this is to recall that the absolute value of the slope of an indifference curve is the marginal rate of substitution (MRS). In our example, the marginal rate of substitution of orange juice for potato chips is

$$MRS_{OP} = \frac{MU_O}{MU_P}$$

Where MU_O is the marginal utility of orange juice and MU_P is the marginal utility of potato chips. The unfavorable change in your preferences lowers your marginal utility of orange juice at any quantity, reducing your MRS_{OP}, that is, flattening your indifference curves.

c. No. When your preferences for orange juice change unfavorably, at each given price you are willing to buy less orange juice. Thus, your demand curve for orange juice shifts leftward, not rightward.

d. No. Your budget constraint would shift leftward if the amount you devote to the two goods decreased or if the prices of the two goods both rose. Since the total amount you spend on orange juice and potato chips remains unchanged and the prices of the two goods remain the same, your budget constraint is unaffected.

Problem 3

a. The market demand curve is the horizontal sum of all the buyers' demand curves. Summing horizontally means to add up quantities demanded at each price. And adding up 5,000 identical demand curves is the same as multiplying an individual demand curve by 5,000. Thus, the market demand curve (Q_M) is:

$$Q_M = 5{,}000 \times (20 - 5P)$$

$$Q_M = 100{,}000 - 25{,}000P$$

b. To graph the market demand curve, we first find the market demand choke price:

$$Q_M = 100{,}000 - 25{,}000P$$

$$0 = 100{,}000 - 25{,}000P$$

$$25{,}000P = 100{,}000$$

$$P = 4$$

Since the demand curve is linear, we only need one more point to graph it. For example, when $P = 1$, $Q_M = 100{,}000 - 25{,}000 \times 1 = 75{,}000$. We graph the demand curve by connecting these two points (see the following graph).

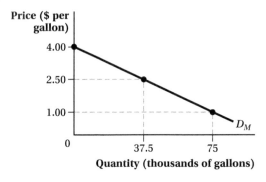

c. When the price of gasoline is $2.50, the market quantity demanded is $Q_M = 100{,}000 - 25{,}000 \times 2.50$ $= 37{,}500$. When the price is $4.50, it is above the demand choke price ($4), so the quantity demanded is zero.

Problem 4

a. To find Steven's optimal consumption bundle, we draw his budget constraint. If Steven spends all his allowance on sandwiches, he will get $\dfrac{\$72}{\$4} = 18$ sandwiches and no movie tickets. If he spends all his allowance on movie tickets, he will get $\dfrac{\$72}{\$8} = 9$ movie tickets and no sandwiches. Connecting these two points, we draw Steven's budget constraint (BC_1 on the following graph). Steven's optimal choice is the point of tangency between his budget line and the highest indifference curve he can reach, U_3. Thus, Steven's optimal consumption bundle is 6 sandwiches and 6 movie tickets.

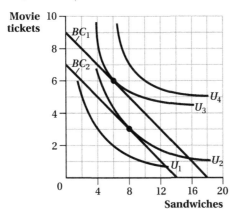

b. With Steven's allowances cut to $56, he can get $\dfrac{\$56}{\$4} = 14$ sandwiches and no movie tickets or $\dfrac{\$56}{\$8} = 7$ movie tickets and no sandwiches. Connecting these two points, we draw Steven's new budget constraint (BC_2). Steven's optimal choice now is the point of tangency between the budget line BC_2 and the highest indifference curve he can reach, U_1. Thus, Steven's optimal consumption bundle is now 8 sandwiches and 3 movie tickets.

c. Steven's Engel curves for sandwiches and movie tickets are shown on the following graphs. They reflect the relationship between the quantity of each good consumed and Steven's income.

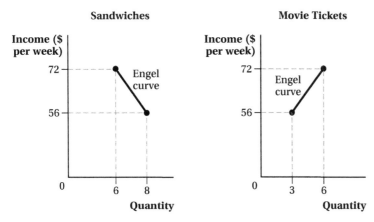

d. As Steven's income decreases from $72 to $56, his consumption of sandwiches increases from 6 to 8. Thus, sandwiches are an inferior good. Steven's demand for movies decreases from 6 to 3 as his income decreases. Thus, movies are a normal good.

Problem 5

a. The slope of a budget constraint equals the negative of the ratio of the price of the good on the horizontal axis (donuts) to the price of the good on the vertical axis (coffee). Thus, the slope of Molly's budget line is $-\left(\dfrac{\$2}{\$2}\right) = -1$.

b. To find Molly's optimal consumption bundle, we draw her budget constraint. If Molly spends all her income on donuts, she will get $\dfrac{\$80}{\$2} = 40$ donuts and no coffee. If she spends all her income on coffee she will get $\dfrac{\$80}{\$2} = 40$ cups of coffee and no donuts. Connecting these two points, we draw Molly's budget constraint (BC_1 on the following graph). Molly's optimal choice is the point of tangency between this budget line and the highest indifference curve she can reach, U_2. Thus, Molly consumes 24 donuts and 16 cups of coffee.

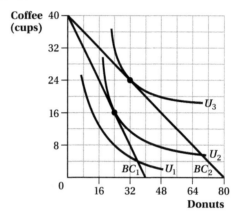

c. When the price of a donut falls to $1, if Molly spends all her income on donuts, she can get $\dfrac{\$80}{\$1} = 80$ donuts. The vertical intercept of Molly's budget constraint does not change, since neither her income nor the price of coffee changes. Thus, Molly's budget line rotates counterclockwise around the vertical axis, and her new budget constraint is BC_2. Molly's optimal choice is now the point of tangency between the budget line BC_2 and the highest indifference curve she can reach, U_3. Thus, Molly consumes 32 donuts and 24 cups of coffee.

d. Molly's demand curve for donuts shows the relationship between the price of donuts and her quantity of donuts demanded. We can use the information from our indifference curve diagram to plot two points on Molly's demand curve:

Price	Quantity of donuts demanded
$2	24
$1	32

Molly's demand curve for donuts (D) is shown on the following graph.

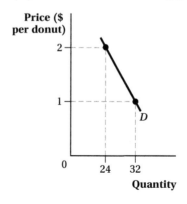

Problem 6

a. See the following graph. First, we need to find Jake's actual budget constraint. We know that the absolute value of slope of the budget line equals the ratio of the price of the good on the horizontal axis to the price of the good on the vertical axis. That is, the absolute value of the slope of Jake's budget constraint should be $\frac{\$4}{\$1} = 4$. The budget line BC_3 on the graph satisfies this condition (since its slope is $\frac{-256}{64} = -4$). Jake's optimal choice then is where this budget line is tangent to the highest possible indifference curve (U_2). Thus, Jake consumes 24 pounds of chicken and 160 cans of Coke.

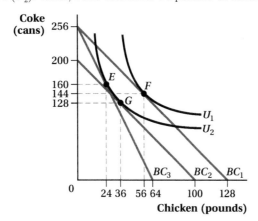

b. Given the budget constraint BC_3, if Jake spends all his income on chicken, he can buy 64 pounds of chicken at $4 per pound. From this we can conclude that Jake's income is $4 × 64= $256.

c. When the price of chicken falls to $2 per pound, Jake can buy $\frac{\$256}{\$2} = 128$ pounds of chicken and no Coke or $\frac{\$256}{\$1} = 256$ cans of Coke and no chicken. Thus, his budget constraint is now BC_1. Jake's optimal choice is where this budget line is tangent to the highest possible indifference curve (U_1). Thus, Jake now consumes 56 pounds of chicken and 144 cans of Coke.

d. To separate the income effect and the substitution effect of the price change, we use the line BC_2, which is parallel to the new budget constraint (BC_1) and tangent to the original indifference curve (U_2). The movement along U_2 from point E (the original, pre-price change bundle) to this tangency point (G) is the substitution effect. Due to the substitution effect, Jake's consumption of chicken increases from 24 pounds to 36 pounds and his consumption of Coke decreases from 160 cans to 128 cans. The income effect of the price change is shown by the movement from point G to point F. Due to the income effect, Jake's consumption of chicken increases from 36 pounds to 56 pounds and his consumption of Coke increases from 128 cans to 144 cans.

e. Chicken is a normal good because Jake purchases more chicken (56 pounds instead of 36 pounds) when the purchasing power of his income increases because of the price drop. Coke is also a normal good because the rise in purchasing power leads to an increase in Jake's Coke consumption (from 128 cans to 144 cans).

Problem 7

a. See the following graph. Initially, the horizontal intercept of Nadya's budget line (i.e., the quantity of ginger ale that she can get if she consumes only ginger ale) is $\frac{\$28}{\$1} = 28$ cans. And the vertical intercept of her budget line (i.e., the quantity of potato salad she can get if she consumes only potato salad) is $\frac{\$28}{\$2} = 14$ pounds. Connecting these points, we draw Nadya's initial budget constraint (BC_1). Nadya's optimal choice is the point of tangency between this budget line and the highest indifference curve she can reach, U_2 (point A). Thus, initially, Nadya consumes 17 cans of ginger ale and 5.5 pounds of potato salad. When the price of ginger ale rises to $2, the horizontal intercept of Nadya's budget line is $\frac{\$28}{\$2} = 14$ cans. The vertical intercept of her budget constraint does not change, since neither her income nor the price of potato salad changes. Thus, Nadya's budget line rotates clockwise around the vertical axis, so her new budget constraint is BC_2. Nadya's optimal choice is now the point of tangency between the budget line BC_2 and the highest indifference curve she can reach, U_1 (point B). Thus, after the rise in the price of ginger ale, Nadya's optimal consumption bundle is 7 cans of ginger ale and 7 pounds of potato salad. That is, Nadya's consumption of ginger ale decreases by 10 cans, and her consumption of potato salad increases by 1.5 pounds.

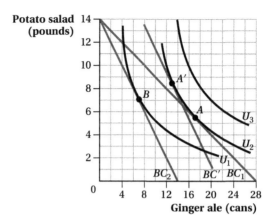

b. To separate the income effect and the substitution effect of the price change, we draw the line BC', which is parallel to the new budget constraint (BC_2) and tangent to the original indifference curve (U_2). The movement along U_2 from point A (the original, pre-price change bundle) to this tangency point (A') is the substitution effect. Due to the substitution effect, Nadya's consumption of ginger ale decreases from 17 cans to 13 cans, and her consumption of potato salad increases from 5.5 pounds to 8.5 pounds. The income effect of the price change is shown by the movement from point A' to point B. Due to the income effect, Nadya's consumption of ginger ale decreases from 13 cans to 7 cans and her consumption of potato salad decreases from 8.5 pounds to 7 pounds.

c. As follows from (b), the substitution effect increases Nadya's consumption of potato salad by 3 pounds. The income effect decreases her consumption of potato salad by 1.5 pounds. Since the positive substitution effect is larger than the negative income effect, Nadya's consumption of potato salad increases (by 1.5 pounds).

d. True. As ginger ale becomes more expensive relative to potato salad, Nadya substitutes potato salad for ginger ale, consuming 3 more pounds of potato salad. And as the price of ginger ale rises, the purchasing power of Nadya's income falls, so she consumes less potato salad (by 1.5 pounds, as explained in [b]).

e. Ginger ale is a normal good because Nadya purchases less ginger ale (7 cans instead of 13 cans) when the purchasing power of her income decreases due to the price rise. Potato salad is also a normal good because the fall in purchasing power leads to a decrease in Nadya's consumption of potato salad (from 8.5 pounds to 7 pounds).

Problem 8

a. See the following graph. When the price of Blu-ray rentals falls to \$2, the vertical intercept of Andrew's budget line is $\frac{\$160}{\$2} = 80$. The horizontal intercept of his budget constraint does not change, since neither his income nor the price of movie tickets changes. Thus, Andrew's budget line rotates clockwise around the horizontal axis, so his new budget constraint is BC_2. Andrew's optimal choice is now the point of tangency between the budget line BC_2 and the highest indifference curve he can reach, U_2 (point B). Thus, after the fall in the price of Blu-ray rentals, Andrew's optimal consumption bundle is 12 movie tickets and 32 Blu-ray rentals.

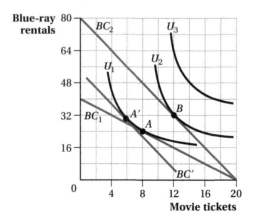

b. When the price of a Blu-ray rental falls, Andrew's optimal choice moves from point A to point B, where he buys more of both movie tickets and Blu-ray rentals. Since Andrew's demand for movie tickets increases as the price of Blu-ray rentals falls, these two goods are complements.

c. From (b), we know that the two goods are complements. And a fall in the price of a complement of a good increases the quantity of this good demanded at every price, shifting the demand curve rightward. Thus, when the price of Blu-ray rentals falls, Andrew's demand curve for movie tickets shifts rightward. The demand curve for Blu-ray rentals is not affected: Andrew simply moves down along his demand curve for Blu-ray rentals from the point when the price is $4 and the quantity demanded is 24 to the point where the price is $2 and the quantity demanded is 32.

d. To isolate the substitution effect of the price change, we use the line (BC') that is parallel to the new budget constraint (BC_2) and tangent to the original indifference curve (U_1). The movement along U_2 from point A (the original, pre-price change bundle) to this tangency point (A') is the substitution effect. Due to this effect, the number of movies Andrew watches in theaters decreases from 8 to 6. Thus, the substitution effect of the lower price of Blu-ray rentals on the number of movies Andrew watches in theaters is negative.

e. To see whether a good is normal or inferior, we look at the income effect of the price change. The income effect of the lower price of Blu-ray rentals is shown by the movement from point A' to point B, holding the price of Blu-ray rentals relative to movie tickets constant (the budget lines are parallel) but changing the purchasing power of income. Due to the income effect, the number of movies Andrew watches in theaters increases from 6 to 12, and the number of Blu-ray discs he rents increases from 30 to 32. Since Andrew's consumption of both goods increases as the purchasing power of his income increases due to the lower price of Blu-ray rentals, both movie tickets and Blu-ray rentals are normal goods.

Problem 9

a. The market demand curve is derived by adding horizontally the individual buyers' demand curves. And summing horizontally means to add up quantities demanded at each price. Thus, we can get the market demand (Q_M) by adding Q_A and Q_B:

$$Q_M = Q_A + Q_B$$
$$Q_M = (7 - 2P) + (5 - P)$$
$$Q_M = 12 - 3P$$

However, Art is not willing to buy any ice cream if the price is greater than or equal to $3.50 per cone because that is his demand choke price:

$$Q_A = 7 - 2P$$
$$0 = 7 - 2P$$
$$2P = 7$$
$$P = 3.50$$

And Bob's demand choke price is $5:

$$Q_B = 5 - P$$
$$0 = 5 - P$$
$$P = 5$$

Thus, as long as the price is below $3.50 per cone, the market demand is the horizontal sum of the two buyers' demand curves. But when the price is between $3.50 and $5, the market demand is the same as Bob's demand.

b. The following graph shows the market demand curve for ice cream. The first point on the curve is Bob's demand choke price, $5 per cone. The second point is where $P = \$3.50$ and Art's quantity demanded is zero, so the market quantity demanded equals Bob's quantity demanded: $Q_B = 5 - 3.50 = 1.5$ cones per month. The third point can be any point where the price is below $3.50 per cone, so we can use the preceding Q_M equation to find the quantity demanded by both buyers together. For example, when $P = \$1$, $Q_M = 12 - 3 \times 1 = 9$ cones. The market demand curve is kinked as a result of the buyers' different choke prices.

c. When the price of ice cream is $4 per pound, Art's quantity demanded is zero, so the market demand curve is Bob's demand curve. And from Bob's demand curve, when $P = \$4$, $Q_T = 5 - 4 = 1$ cone. When the price of ice cream is $2 per cone, the market demand curve is $Q_M = 12 - 3P$, so $Q_M = 12 - 3 \times 2 = 6$ cones.

Problem 10

a. See the following graph. When the price of gasoline is $2 per gallon, the horizontal intercept of Peter's budget line (i.e., the quantity of gas he can get if he spends all his budget on gas) is $\dfrac{\$800}{\$2} = 400$ gallons. And the vertical intercept of his budget line (i.e., the quantity of other goods he can get if he spends his entire budget on other goods) is $\dfrac{\$800}{\$1} = 800$ dollars. Connecting these points, we draw Peter's budget constraint (BC_1). Peter's optimal choice is the point of tangency between this budget line and the highest indifference curve he can reach, U_2. Thus, before the new government policy, Peter consumes 160 gallons of gasoline and 480 dollars of other goods. When the price of gasoline rises to $4 per gallon, the horizontal intercept of Peter's budget line is $\dfrac{\$800}{\$4} = 200$ gallons, with the vertical intercept unchanged. That is, the higher price of gas resulting from the tax rotates Peter's budget line clockwise around the vertical axis, so his budget constraint is BC'. But since the government's check adds $400 to Peter's budget, he can afford $\dfrac{\$400}{\$4} = 100$ gallons more of gas at each given quantity of other goods (or $\dfrac{\$400}{\$1} = 400$ dollars more of other goods at each given quantity of gas). That is, Peter's budget constraint shifts rightward by 100 gallons of gas at each quantity of other goods (or upward by 400 dollars of other goods at each quantity of gas). The resulting budget constraint is BC_2. Thus, with the new government policy, Peter's optimal choice is the point of tangency between the budget line BC_2 and the highest indifference curve he can reach, U_3, where Peter consumes 160 gallons of gas and 560 dollars of other goods. That is, Peter's consumption of gasoline does not change, but his consumption of other goods increases by 80 dollars.

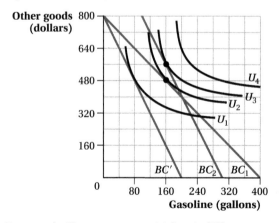

b. As shown on the preceding graph, Peter gets on a higher indifference curve as a result of the new government policy. That is, the new policy makes Peter better off.

c. The new tax increases the government revenue by $\$2 \times 160 = \$320$ per consumer. But the amount that the government pays to each consumer (400) exceeds this additional revenue. Thus, the new policy makes the government worse off.

∂ Problem 11

a. Since $\dfrac{\partial Q}{\partial P_0} = -50 < 0$, and therefore quantity is decreasing as the price of the related good increases, we know that the related good is a complement.

b. Since $\dfrac{\partial Q}{\partial I} = 0.5 > 0$, and therefore quantity is increasing with income, we know that the good is a normal good.

c. We need three things for the income elasticity formula—income, quantity, and the partial derivative of the demand function with respect to quantity. Income is given. To get quantity, we can substitute the values that we know into the demand function: $Q = 6{,}000 - 20(100) - 50(20) + 0.5(2{,}000) = 4{,}000$.

The partial derivative of quantity with respect to income was calculated in part (b): $\dfrac{\partial Q}{\partial I} = 0.5$. The

income elasticity of demand at the current allocation therefore is: $E_I^D = \dfrac{\partial Q}{\partial I} \times \dfrac{I}{Q} = 0.5\left(\dfrac{2{,}000}{4{,}000}\right) = 0.25$.

This elasticity means that a one percent increase in income translates into a 0.25 percent increase in quantity demanded. This is an inelastic response (as described in Chapter 2), since this is less than one in absolute value.

∂ Problem 12

a. We need to solve Ed's original constrained optimization problem: $\max_{H,F} 2H^{0.2}F^{0.6}$ s.t. $2{,}400 = 300H + 150F$, using the Lagrangian approach. The Lagrangian corresponding to this is:

$$\max_{H,F,\lambda} \mathcal{L}(H,F,\lambda) + 2H^{0.2}F^{0.6} + \lambda(2{,}400 - 300H - 150F)$$

The first-order conditions are:

$$\frac{\partial \mathcal{L}}{\partial H} = 2(0.2)H^{-0.8}S^{0.6} - \lambda(300) = 0$$

$$\frac{\partial \mathcal{L}}{\partial F} = 2(0.6)H^{0.2}F^{-0.4} - \lambda(150) = 0$$

$$\frac{\partial \mathcal{L}}{\partial \lambda} = 2{,}400 - 300H - 150F = 0$$

This is a system of three equations with three unknowns $(H, S,$ and $\lambda)$. The solution (H,S) is the allocation that we are interested in. Combining the first two equations, we see that:

$$\lambda = \frac{2(0.2)H^{-0.8}F^{0.6}}{300} = \frac{2(0.6)H^{0.2}F^{-0.4}}{150}$$

Therefore, $F = 6H$

Combining this with the third of the first-order conditions:

$$2{,}400 = 300H + 150(6H)$$
$$2{,}400 = 1{,}200H$$
$$H = 2$$
$$F = 6(2) = 12$$

At these prices, Ed should engage in 2 hiking trips and watch 12 football games.

We also want to find Ed's level of utility at this original allocation: $U(2,12) = 2(2)^{0.2}12^{0.6} \approx 10.20$.

b. We need to solve Ed's new constrained optimization problem: $\max_{H,F} 2H^{0.2}F^{0.6}$ s.t. $2{,}400 = 300H + 75F$, using the Lagrangian approach. The Lagrangian corresponding to this is:

$$\max_{H,F,\lambda} \mathcal{L}(H,F,\lambda) = 2H^{0.2}F^{0.6} + \lambda(2{,}400 - 300H - 75F)$$

The first-order conditions are:

$$\frac{\partial \mathcal{L}}{\partial H} = 2(0.2)H^{-0.8}F^{0.6} - \lambda(300) = 0$$

$$\frac{\partial \mathcal{L}}{\partial F} = 2(0.6)H^{0.2}F^{-0.4} - \lambda(75) = 0$$

$$\frac{\partial \mathcal{L}}{\partial \lambda} = 2{,}400 - 300H - 75F = 0$$

This is a system of three equations with three unknowns (H, F, and λ). The solution (H,F) is the allocation that we are interested in. Combining the first two equations, we see that:

$$\lambda = \frac{2(0.2)H^{-0.8}F^{0.6}}{300} = \frac{2(0.6)H^{0.2}F^{-0.4}}{75}$$

Therefore, $F = 12H$.

Combining this with the third of the first-order conditions:

$$2{,}400 = 300H + 75(12H)$$

$$2{,}400 = 1{,}200H$$

$$H = 2$$

$$F = 12(2) = 24$$

Ed should go on 2 hiking trips and watch 24 football games at these prices. The total effect of the price change therefore is an increase of 12 football games, and no changes in hiking trips.

c. To decompose this total effect into income and substitution effects, we can solve the expenditure minimization problem: $min_{H,F}300H + 75F$ s.t. $10.20 = 2H^{0.2}F^{0.6}$. The Lagrangian corresponding to this is: $\mathcal{L}(H,F,\lambda) = 300H + 75F + \lambda(10.20 - 2H^{0.2}F^{0.6})$, and the first-order conditions are:

$$\frac{\partial \mathcal{L}}{\partial H} = 300 - \lambda(2)(0.2)H^{-0.8}F^{0.6} = 0$$

$$\frac{\partial \mathcal{L}}{\partial F} = 75 - \lambda(2)(0.6)H^{0.2}F^{-0.4} = 0$$

$$\frac{\partial \mathcal{L}}{\partial \lambda} = 10.20 - 2H^{0.2}F^{0.6} = 0$$

This is now a system of three equations with three unknowns that can be solved for H, F, and λ. H and F give the allocation that allow us to separate the substitution and income effects.

$$\lambda = \frac{300}{2(0.2)H^{-0.8}F^{0.6}} = \frac{75}{2(0.6)H^{0.2}F^{-0.4}}$$

Therefore, $12H = F$.

Combining this with the third of the first-order conditions:

$$10.20 = 2H^{0.2}(12H)^{0.6}$$

$$5.10 = H^{0.8}(12)^{0.6}$$

$$H^{0.8} \approx 1.15$$

$$H \approx (1.15)^{1.25} \approx 1.19$$

$$F \approx 12(1.19) \approx 14.28$$

The substitution effect for football therefore is the difference between 12 and 14.28 (an increase of 2.28 football games), and the income effect for football is an increase of $24 - 14.28 = 9.72$ games. The total effect therefore is an increase of 12 games as in part (b). For hiking, we find that the substitution effect is $1.19 - 2 = -0.81$ trips, and the income effect is $2 - 1.19 = 0.81$, and hence the total effect is zero.

∂ Problem 13

a. Ed's constrained optimization problem is: $max_{H,F}H^{0.2}F^{0.6}$ s.t. $\overline{I} = p_H H + \overline{p_F}F$, using the Lagrangian approach. The Lagrangian corresponding to this is:

$$\max_{H,F,\lambda} \mathcal{L}(H,F,\lambda) = 2H^{0.2}F^{0.6} + \lambda(\overline{I} - p_H H - \overline{p_F}F)$$

The first-order conditions are:

$$\frac{\partial \mathcal{L}}{\partial H} = 2(0.2)H^{-0.8}F^{0.6} - \lambda(p_H) = 0$$

$$\frac{\partial \mathcal{L}}{\partial F} = 2(0.6)H^{0.2}F^{-0.4} - \lambda(\overline{p_F}) = 0$$

$$\frac{\partial \mathcal{L}}{\partial \lambda} = \overline{I} - p_H H - \overline{p_F}F = 0$$

Combining the first two equations, we see that:

$$\lambda = \frac{2(0.2)H^{-0.8}F^{0.6}}{p_H} = \frac{2(0.6)H^{0.2}F^{-0.4}}{\overline{p_F}}$$

Therefore, $\overline{p_F}F = 3p_H H$.

Combining this with the third of the first-order conditions:

$$\overline{I} = p_H H + \overline{p_F} F$$

$$\overline{I} = p_H H + 3 p_H H$$

Ed's Marshallian demand curve for hiking is: $H = \dfrac{\overline{I}}{4 p_H}$. Since $\dfrac{\partial H}{\partial p_H} = -\dfrac{\overline{I}}{4 p_H^2} < 0$, the Law of Demand that demand is decreasing in price holds.

b. Ed's constrained optimization problem is: $\min_{H,F} p_H H + \overline{p_F} F \ s.t. \ \overline{U} = 2 H^{0.2} F^{0.6}$, using the Lagrangian approach. The Lagrangian corresponding to this is:

$$\max_{H,F,\lambda} \mathcal{L}(H,F,\lambda) = p_H H + \overline{p_F} F + \lambda(\overline{U} - 2 H^{0.2} F^{0.6})$$

The first-order conditions are:

$$\frac{\partial \mathcal{L}}{\partial H} = p_H - \lambda\big(2(0.2) H^{-0.8} F^{0.6}\big) = 0$$

$$\frac{\partial \mathcal{L}}{\partial S} = \overline{p_F} - \lambda\big(2(0.6) H^{0.2} F^{-0.4}\big) = 0 \quad \frac{\partial \mathcal{L}}{\partial \lambda} = \overline{U} - H^{0.2} F^{0.6} = 0$$

Combining the first two equations, we see that:

$$\lambda = \frac{p_H}{2(0.2) H^{-0.8} F^{0.6}} = \frac{\overline{p_F}}{2(0.6) H^{0.2} F^{-0.4}}$$

Therefore, $\overline{p_F} F = 3 p_H H$ or $F = \dfrac{3 p_H H}{\overline{p_F}}$.

Combining this with the third of the first-order conditions,

$$\overline{U} = H^{0.2} F^{0.6}$$

$$\overline{U} = H^{0.2} \left(\frac{3 p_H H}{\overline{p_F}}\right)^{0.6} = H^{0.8} \left(\frac{3 p_H}{\overline{p_F}}\right)^{0.6}$$

Ed's Hicksian demand curve for hiking, then, is:

$$H^{0.8} = \overline{U} \left(\frac{\overline{p_F}}{3 p_H}\right)^{0.6}$$

$$H = \overline{U}^{1.25} \left(\frac{p_F}{3 p_H}\right)^{0.75}$$

6

Producer Behavior

Solutions for Practice Problems

Problem 1

a. To write the short-run production function, we plug the fixed value of capital, $K = 3$, into the production function, so we get:

$$Q = 36 \times 4^{0.5} \times L^{0.5}$$
$$Q = 72L^{0.5}$$

b. Using the short-run production function in (a), we can calculate that when $L = 4$,

$$Q = 72 \times 4^{0.5}$$
$$Q = 144$$

c. The marginal product of labor is the additional output generated by an additional unit of labor, holding capital constant. From (b) we know that with 4 workers, $Q = 144$. And given the production function in (a), with 5 workers

$$Q = 72 \times 5^{0.5}$$
$$Q = 161$$

Thus, the marginal product of the 5th worker is $161 - 144 = 17$ pizzas.

d. To see whether the pizzeria experiences diminishing marginal returns when it hires the 5th worker, we compare the marginal product of the 5th worker with that of the 4th worker. With 3 workers

$$Q = 72 \times 3^{0.5}$$
$$Q = 125$$

Thus, the marginal product of the 4th worker is $144 - 125 = 19$ pizzas. Since the marginal product of the 5th worker (17 pizzas) is smaller than that of the 4th worker (19 pizzas), the pizzeria is experiencing diminishing marginal returns.

e. Marginal product of labor is the partial derivative of the production function with respect to labor:

$$MP_L = \frac{\partial Q}{\partial L} = 36(0.5)K^{0.5}L^{0.5-1} = 18K^{0.5}L^{-0.5}.$$

Marginal product of capital is the partial derivative of the production function with respect to capital:

$$MP_K = \frac{\partial Q}{\partial K} = 36(0.5)K^{0.5-1}L^{0.5} = 18K^{-0.5}L^{0.5}.$$

Problem 2

See the following table.

Labor Input	Output	Marginal Product	Average Product
1	100	100	100
2	142	42	71
3	174	32	58
4	200	26	50
5	225	25	45

When no labor is employed, the output is zero, so the MP_L of the first worker is $100 - 0 = 100$. And when $L = 1$, the average product of labor is $\frac{100}{1} = 100$. When the second worker is hired, the additional output is $142 - 100 = 42$, so the $MP_L = 42$. And $AP_L = \frac{142}{2} = 71$. Since the marginal product of the 3rd worker is 32, we know that the additional output resulting from hiring this worker is 32, so the total output is $142 + 32 = 174$. Then, $AP_L = \frac{174}{3} = 58$. Further, given that when 4 workers are employed the average product is 50, we can calculate the output with 4 workers as $50 \times 4 = 200$, and then the marginal product of the 4th worker as $200 - 174 = 26$. Finally, given that the output with 4 workers is 200, and the marginal product of the 5th worker is 25, we calculate the output with 5 workers as $200 + 25 = 225$ and then the average product with 5 workers as $\frac{225}{5} = 45$.

Problem 3

a. The equation for the isocost line is

$$C = RK + WL$$
$$1{,}600 = 16K + 8L$$

An easy way to graph an isocost line is to compute its horizontal and vertical intercepts. The horizontal intercept is the amount of labor the firm could hire if it only hired labor, i.e., $K = 0$. Given our isocost equation, we can write: $1{,}600 = 8L$, from $L = \frac{1{,}600}{8} = 200$ units. The vertical intercept is the amount of capital the firm could use if it used only capital (i.e. $L = 0$), so we can write $1{,}600 = 16K$, from which $K = \frac{1{,}600}{16} = 100$ units. We draw the isocost line (C_1) by connecting these two points (see the following graph).

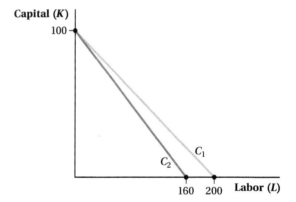

b. When the wage rises to \$10, the vertical intercept is unaffected, since if the firm used only capital, the higher price of labor would not affect its costs. But the horizontal intercept is now $\frac{\$1{,}600}{\$10} = 160$, so the isocost line rotates clockwise around the vertical axis and becomes steeper (C_2).

Problem 4

a. The marginal rate of technical substitution can be expressed as

$$MRTS_{LK} = \frac{MP_L}{MP_K}$$

So we can write:

$$0.5 = \frac{12}{MP_K}$$

And solving for MP_K, we get

$$0.5 MP_K = 12$$
$$MP_K = 24$$

b. A firm minimizes its costs when

$$MRTS_{LK} = \frac{W}{R}$$

For the firm in question, $MRTS_{LK} = 0.5$, while $\dfrac{W}{R} = \dfrac{\$16}{\$40} = 0.4$. Thus, the firm is not minimizing its costs.

c. The cost-minimizing condition can also be written as

$$\frac{MP_K}{R} = \frac{MP_L}{W}$$

For the firm in question, $\dfrac{MP_K}{R} = \dfrac{24}{40} = 0.6$, while $\dfrac{MP_L}{L} = \dfrac{12}{16} = 0.75$. That is,

$$\frac{MP_K}{R} < \frac{MP_L}{W}$$

which means, given the current combination of inputs, an additional dollar spent on labor would yield a greater marginal product (i.e., additional output) than the marginal product lost as a result of spending one dollar less on capital. Therefore, the firm would do better if it increases its use of labor and reduces its use of capital.

Problem 5

a. This is a Cobb-Douglas production function. Thus, to see whether there are constant, increasing, or decreasing returns to scale, we add up the exponents on the inputs: $0.8 + 0.2 = 1$. Since the exponents add up to 1, this production function exhibits constant returns to scale.

b. For this production function, the easiest way to see whether there are constant, increasing, or decreasing returns to scale is to calculate Q for $K = 1$ and $L = 1$ and then for $K = 2$ and $L = 2$. When $K = 1$ and $L = 1$, $Q = 0.4 \times 1^{0.5} + 0.6 \times 1^{0.5} = 1$. And when $K = 2$ and $L = 2$, $Q = 0.4 \times 2^{0.5} + 0.6 \times 2^{0.5} = 1.41$. Since output less than doubles when inputs double, the production function exhibits decreasing returns to scale.

c. We repeat the exercise in (b). When $K = 1$ and $L = 1$, $Q = \min(0.8 \times 1^{0.5}, 0.5 \times 1^{0.5}) = 0.5$. And when $K = 2$ and $L = 2$, $Q = \min(0.8 \times 2^{0.5}, 0.5 \times 2^{0.5}) = 0.71$. Since output less than doubles when inputs double, the production function exhibits decreasing returns to scale.

d. Use the marginal products to solve for the $MRTS$:

$$MRTS_{LK} = \frac{MP_L}{MP_K} = \frac{0.2K^{0.8}L^{-0.8}}{0.8K^{-0.2}L^{0.2}} = \frac{K}{4L} = 0.25KL^{-1}$$

We can take the partial of the $MRTS$ with respect to L to see how the $MRTS$ changes, as L increases

$$\frac{\partial MRTS_{LK}}{\partial L} = -0.25KL^{-2} < 0$$

Thus, the $MRTS$ declines as the firm uses more labor for the standard case where K and L are positive.

e. First, we set up the firm's cost minimization problem as

$$\min_{K,L} 10K + 10L \; s.t. \; 500 = K^{0.8}L^{0.2}$$

Or, as a Lagrangian:

$$\min_{K,L,\lambda} \mathcal{L}(K,L,\lambda) = 10K + 10L + \lambda(500 - K^{0.8}L^{0.2})$$

Finding the first-order conditions for the Lagrangian, we see that:

$$\frac{\partial \mathcal{L}}{\partial K} = 10 - \lambda(0.8K^{-0.2}L^{0.2}) = 0$$

$$\frac{\partial \mathcal{L}}{\partial L} = 10 - \lambda(0.2K^{0.8}L^{-0.8}) = 0$$

$$\frac{\partial \mathcal{L}}{\partial \lambda} = 500 - K^{0.8}L^{0.2} = 0$$

Since we now have three equations with three unknowns (K,L,λ), we can solve this system of equations to come up with the solution to the cost minimization problem. Specifically, we can use the first 2 conditions to solve for λ as a first step.

$$\lambda = \frac{10}{0.8K^{-0.2}L^{0.2}} = \frac{10}{0.2K^{0.8}L^{-0.8}}$$

$$10(0.2K^{0.8}L^{-0.8}) = 10(0.8K^{-0.2}L^{0.2})$$

$$2(K^{0.8}K^{0.2}) = 8(L^{0.8}L^{0.2})$$

$$2K = 8L$$

$$K = 4L$$

Now plug K into the third first-order condition and solve for the optimal number of labor- and machine-hours, L^* and K^*:

$$500 = K^{0.8}L^{0.2}$$

$$500 = (4L)^{0.8}L^{0.2}$$

$$(4)^{0.8}L^{0.8}L^{0.2} = 500$$

$$L^* \approx 164.94 \text{ labor-hours}$$

$$K^* \approx 4(164.94) \approx 659.76 \text{ machine-hours}$$

f. The firm's expansion path tells us the relationship between the optimal amounts of labor and capital input. Within the Lagrangian procedure in (e), we found that $K = 4L$. This is the firm's expansion path.

g. We set up the firm's cost minimization problem as before, but this time we set it with a generic rental rate of capital R:

$$\min_{K,L} RK + 10L \text{ s.t. } 500 = K^{0.8}L^{0.2}$$

Or, as a Lagrangian:

$$\min_{K,L,\lambda} \mathcal{L}(K,L,\lambda) = RK + 10L + \lambda(500 - K^{0.8}L^{0.2})$$

Finding the first-order conditions for the Lagrangian, we see that:

$$\frac{\partial \mathcal{L}}{\partial K} = R - \lambda(0.8K^{-0.2}L^{0.2}) = 0$$

$$\frac{\partial \mathcal{L}}{\partial L} = 10 - \lambda(0.2K^{0.8}L^{-0.8}) = 0$$

$$\frac{\partial \mathcal{L}}{\partial \lambda} = 500 - K^{0.8}L^{0.2} = 0$$

Since we now have three equations with three unknowns (K,L,λ), we can solve this system of equations to come up with the solution to the cost minimization problem. Specifically, we can use the first 2 conditions to solve for λ as a first step.

$$\lambda = \frac{R}{0.8K^{-0.2}L^{0.2}} = \frac{10}{0.2K^{0.8}L^{-0.8}}$$

$$R(0.2K^{0.8}L^{-0.8}) = 10(0.8K^{-0.2}L^{0.2})$$

$$0.2R(K^{0.8}K^{0.2}) = 8(L^{0.8}L^{0.2})$$

$$0.2RK = 8L$$

$$L = 0.025RK$$

Substitute into the quantity constraint:

$$500 = K^{0.8}L^{0.2}$$

$$500 = K^{0.8}(0.025RK)^{0.2}$$

$$0.025^{0.2}R^{0.2}K = 500$$

$$K \approx 1{,}045.64R^{-0.2}$$

h. Take the derivative of capital demand with respect to the rental rate

$$\frac{\partial K(R)}{\partial R} = 1{,}045.64(-0.2)R^{-1.2} = -209.13R^{-1.2}$$

which is negative, as we expect from the Law of Demand since the Law of Demand tells us that as price increases, quantity demanded decreases. Here, if the price of capital (the rental rate) increases, the firm demands less capital.

Problem 6

a. A firm's costs are minimized when

$$\frac{MP_L}{MP_K} = \frac{W}{R}$$

For the firm in question, we can write:

$$\frac{\dfrac{5K^{0.5}}{L^{0.5}}}{\dfrac{5L^{0.5}}{K^{0.5}}} = \frac{16}{4}$$

$$\frac{5K^{0.5}K^{0.5}}{5L^{0.5}L^{0.5}} = 4$$

$$\frac{K}{L} = 4$$

$$K = 4L$$

Now we substitute this expression for K into the production function and solve it for L, given that $Q = 720$:

$$Q = 10K^{0.5}L^{0.5}$$

$$720 = 10 \times (4L)^{0.5}L^{0.5}$$

$$720 = 10 \times 4^{0.5}L^{0.5}L^{0.5}$$

$$20L = 720$$

$$L = 36$$

Then, we calculate K as

$$K = 4 \times 36 = 144$$

Thus, to produce 720 units of output with minimum cost, the firm should use 36 hours of labor and 144 machine-hours.

b. With the increased total factor productivity, the cost-minimizing condition is

$$\frac{\dfrac{6K^{0.5}}{L^{0.5}}}{\dfrac{6L^{0.5}}{K^{0.5}}} = \frac{16}{4}$$

$$\frac{6K^{0.5}K^{0.5}}{6L^{0.5}L^{0.5}} = 4$$

$$\frac{K}{L} = 4$$

$$K = 4L$$

Substituting this expression into the production function and solving it for L and K, given that $Q = 720$, we get:

$$Q = 12K^{0.5}L^{0.5}$$

$$720 = 12 \times (4L)^{0.5}L^{0.5}$$

$$720 = 12 \times 4^{0.5}L^{0.5}L^{0.5}$$

$$24L = 720$$

$$L = 30$$

$$K = 4 \times 30 = 120$$

Thus, with the improved technology, to produce 720 units of output with minimum cost, the firm should use 30 hours of labor and 120 machine-hours. Notice that the new technology allows the firm to produce the same quantity of output using less capital and less labor.

c. Before the technological change, the cost of the firm's cost-minimizing combination of inputs is

$$\$16 \times 36 + \$4 \times 144 = \$1{,}152$$

And with the new technology, it is

$$\$16 \times 30 + \$4 \times 120 = \$960$$

Thus, the new technology allows the firm to reduce the cost of producing 720 units of output by $192.

d. Marginal product of labor is the partial derivative of the production function with respect to labor: $MP_L = \dfrac{\partial Q}{\partial L} = 12(0.5)K^{0.5}L^{0.5-1} = 6K^{0.5}L^{-0.5}$. Marginal product of capital is the partial derivative of the production function with respect to capital: $MP_K = \dfrac{\partial Q}{\partial L} = 12(0.5)K^{0.5-1}L^{0.5} = 6K^{-0.5}L^{0.5}$. These are equivalent to the given functions.

Problem 7

a. To find the firm's cost-minimizing combination of inputs, we draw the isocost line. The horizontal intercept of the isocost line is where the firm uses only labor, so its total cost is

$$C = WL$$
$$6{,}480 = 18L$$

from which

$$L = \frac{6{,}480}{18} = 360$$

The vertical intercept of the isocost line is where the firm uses only capital, so its total cost is

$$C = RK$$
$$6{,}480 = 9K$$

from which

$$K = \frac{6{,}480}{9} = 720$$

We draw the firm's isocost line (C_1 on the following graph) by connecting these two points. The firm choses the combination of inputs at the point where this isocost line is tangent to the highest achievable isoquant ($Q = 240$). At this point, the firm uses 160 worker-hours and 400 machine-hours.

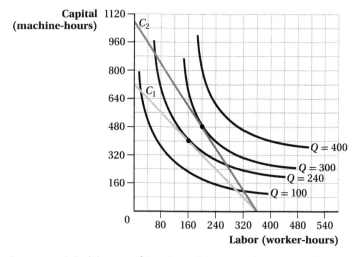

b. When the firm uses its cost-minimizing combination of inputs, the marginal rate of substitution (which is the absolute value of the slope of the isoquant at the point of tangency) equals the absolute value of the slope of the isocost line, which can be calculated as $\dfrac{720}{360} = 2$. (The absolute value of the slope of the isocost line is also equal to $\dfrac{W}{R} = \dfrac{\$18}{\$9} = 2$.) Thus, the firm's $MRTS_{LK} = 2$.

c. The isoquant, $Q = 240$, tangent to the firm's isocost line indicates that the firm produces 240 units of output.

d. When the cost of capital is $6 per machine-hour, the vertical intercept of the isocost line (that is, where $L = 0$ and the firm spends all $6,480 on capital) is $\dfrac{6{,}480}{6} = 1{,}080$. The horizontal intercept does not change, since the cost of labor remains the same. Thus, the new isocost line is C_2 on the preceding graph. As we can see, this isocost line is tangent to the isoquant along which the firm produces 300 units of output. We can also see that at the point of tangency, the firm uses 200 hours of labor and 480 machine-hours. Thus, because of the lower cost of capital, the firm is able to use 40 more hours of labor and 80 more machine-hours and produce 60 more units of output at the same total cost.

e. Initially, the per-unit cost is $\dfrac{\$6,480}{240} = \$27$. And after the fall in the cost of capital, it is $\dfrac{\$6,480}{300} = \$21.60$. Thus, the per-unit cost of output falls by $5.40.

Problem 8

a. We know that at the point where the firm is minimizing its cost of producing a given level of output, the marginal rate of technical substitution of labor for capital equals $\dfrac{W}{R}$. Thus, Apple's $MRTS_{LK}$ is $\dfrac{\$24}{\$6} = 4$.

b. Apple minimizes its cost if

$$\frac{MP_L}{MP_K} = \frac{W}{R}$$

Thus, we can write:

$$\frac{\dfrac{0.15K^{0.25}}{L^{0.25}}}{\dfrac{0.05L^{0.75}}{K^{0.75}}} = \frac{24}{6}$$

$$\frac{0.15K^{0.25}K^{0.75}}{0.05L^{0.25}L^{0.75}} = 4$$

$$3K = 4L$$

$$L = 0.75K$$

We substitute this expression for L into the production function and solve it for K, given that $Q = 96.7$:

$$Q = 0.2K^{0.25}L^{0.75}$$
$$96.7 = 0.2 \times K^{0.25}(0.75K)^{0.75}$$
$$96.7 = 0.2 \times 0.75^{0.75}K^{0.25}K^{0.75}$$
$$0.1612K = 96.7$$
$$K = 600$$

Then, we calculate L as

$$L = 0.75 \times 600 = 450$$

Thus, the lowest-cost combination of labor and capital that allows Apple to produce 96.7 iPhones is 450 worker-hours and 600 machine-hours.

c. Given the optimal input combination in (b), producing 96.7 iPhones costs $24 \times 450 + \$6 \times 600 = \$14,400$, so producing one iPhone costs $\dfrac{\$14,000}{96.7} = \$149$.

d. The cost-minimizing condition found in (b), $L = 0.75K$, holds for any level of cost, so we substitute this expression into the isocost equation and solve it for K and L given that $C = \$19,200$:

$$19,200 = 6K + 24(0.75K)$$
$$24K = 19,200$$
$$K = 800$$
$$L = 0.75 \times 800 = 600$$

Substituting K and L into the production function, we calculate the maximum number of iPhones that Apple can produce:

$$Q = 0.2 \times 800^{0.25} \times 600^{0.75} = 128.9 \text{ (iPhones per hour)}$$

e. Marginal product of labor is the partial derivative of the production function with respect to labor: $MP_L = \dfrac{\partial Q}{\partial L} = 0.2(0.75)K^{0.25}L^{0.75-1} = 0.15K^{0.25}L^{-0.25}$. Marginal product of capital is the partial derivative of the production function with respect to capital: $MP_K = \dfrac{\partial Q}{\partial K} = 0.2(0.25)K^{0.25-1}L^{0.75} = 0.05K^{-0.25}L^{-0.25}$. These are equivalent to the given functions.

Problem 9

a. We can find the company's cost-minimizing combination of TV ads and Internet ads by using the following condition:

$$\frac{MP_T}{MP_N} = \frac{P_T}{P_N}$$

where P_T is the price of a TV ad and P_N is the price of an Internet ad. Thus, we can write:

$$\frac{\dfrac{16N^{0.2}}{T^{0.6}}}{\dfrac{8T^{0.4}}{N^{0.8}}} = \frac{500}{100}$$

$$\frac{16N^{0.2}N^{0.8}}{8T^{0.6}T^{0.4}} = 5$$

$$2N = 5T$$

$$N = 2.5T$$

We substitute this expression for N into the production function and solve it for T and N, given that $S = 500$:

$$S = 40T^{0.4}N^{0.2}$$
$$500 = 40 \times T^{0.4}(2.5T)^{0.2}$$
$$500 = 40 \times 2.5^{0.2}T^{0.4}T^{0.2}$$
$$48.045 \times T^{0.6} = 500$$
$$T^{0.6} = 10.407$$
$$T = 10.407^{1/0.6}$$
$$T = 49.607 \approx 50$$
$$N = 2.5 \times 49.607 = 124.018 \approx 124$$

Thus, the company should run 50 TV ads and 124 Internet ads. Running these ads will cost the company $500 \times 50 + \$100 \times 124 = \$37,400$.

b. The cost-minimizing condition is the same:

$$\frac{MP_T}{MP_N} = \frac{P_T}{P_N}$$

from which

$$N = 2.5T$$

But now we substitute the expression for N into the production function and solve it for T and N, given that $S = 600$:

$$48.045 \times T^{0.6} = 600$$
$$T^{0.6} = 12.488$$
$$T = 12.488^{1/0.6}$$
$$T = 67.218 \approx 67$$
$$N = 2.5 \times 67.218 \approx 168$$

Thus, the new optimal combination is 67 TV ads and 168 Internet ads. Thus, the company should rely more on additional Internet adds than on additional TV ads, running 44 more Internet ads and only 17 more TV ads.

Problem 10

a. The quantity of output can be calculated directly from the firm's production function:

$$Q = 4 \times 2,500^{0.5} \times 1,600^{0.5}$$
$$Q = 8,000$$

b. To find the amount of capital that the firm must use to produce 8,000 units of output, given that it hires 1,000 hours of labor, we plug these numbers into the production function and solve the equation for K:

$$8,000 = 4K^{0.5} \times 1,000^{0.5}$$
$$2,000 = K^{05} \times 1,000^{0.5}$$
$$1,000K = 4,000,000$$
$$K = 4,000$$

Thus, the firm must increase its capital input by $4,000 - 2,500 = 1,500$ machine-hours.

c. To find the amount of capital that the firm must use to produce 8,000 units of output, given its new production function and that it hires 1,000 hours of labor, we plug these numbers into the new production function and solve the equation for K:

$$8,000 = 4K^{0.75} \times 1,000^{0.25}$$
$$K^{0.75} = \frac{2,000}{1,000^{0.25}}$$
$$K^{0.75} = 355.7$$
$$K = 355.7^{1/0.75}$$
$$K = 2,520$$

Thus, with the new technology, the firm must increase its capital input by only 20 machine-hours $(2,520 - 2,500)$.

∂ Problem 11

a. Using the Lagrangian (alternately we could use the cost minimization condition directly), we set up the firm's cost minimization problem as

$$\min_{K,L} 35K + 15L \ s.t. \ 80,000 - 6K^{0.4}L^{0.6} = 0$$

Or, as a Lagrangian:

$$\min_{K,L,\lambda} \mathcal{L}(K,L,\lambda) = 35K + 15L + \lambda(80,000 - 6K^{0.4}L^{0.6})$$

Finding the first-order conditions for the Lagrangian, we see that:

$$\frac{\partial \mathcal{L}}{\partial K} = 35 - \lambda\big(6(0.4)K^{0.4-1}L^{0.6}\big) = 35 - \lambda(2.4K^{-0.6}L^{0.6}) = 0$$

$$\frac{\partial \mathcal{L}}{\partial L} = 15 - \lambda\big(6(0.6)K^{0.4}L^{0.6-1}\big) = 15 - \lambda(3.6K^{0.4}L^{-0.4}) = 0$$

$$\frac{\partial \mathcal{L}}{\partial \lambda} = 80,000 - 6K^{0.4}L^{0.6} = 0$$

Since we now have three equations with three unknowns (K,L,λ), we can solve this system of equations to come up with the solution to the cost minimization problem. Specifically, we can use the first 2 conditions to solve for λ as a first step.

$$\lambda = \frac{35}{2.4K^{-0.6}L^{0.6}} = \frac{15}{3.6K^{0.4}L^{-0.4}}$$
$$35(3.6K^{0.4}L^{-0.4}) = 15(2.4K^{-0.6}L^{0.6})$$
$$126(K^{0.4}K^{0.6}) = 36(L^{0.4}L^{0.6})$$
$$126K = 36L$$
$$L = 3.5K$$

Now plug L into the third first-order condition and solve for the optimal number of labor- and machine-hours, L^* and K^*:

$$80,000 - 6K^{0.4}L^{0.6} = 0$$
$$6K^{0.4}(3.5K)^{0.6} = 80,000$$
$$6(3.5)^{0.6}K = 80,000$$
$$K^* \approx 6,287.79 \text{ machine-hours}$$
$$L^* \approx 3.5(6,287.79) \approx 22,007.27 \text{ labor-hours}$$

b. The firm's expansion path was derived along the way in (a). Particularly, we found that $L = 3.5K$ or alternately that $K = \dfrac{L}{3.5} = \dfrac{2L}{7}$.

Therefore, when minimizing costs, this firm will always choose a combination of inputs in which there is 3.5 times as much labor as capital, whatever its desired output is. This, of course, relies on having positive amounts of K and L.

∂ Problem 12

a. We know that the firm will minimize costs when

$$MRTS_{LK} = \frac{MP_L}{MP_K} = \frac{W}{R}$$

(Alternately, we could use a Lagrangian as we'll show below.)
For this problem, the marginal rate of technical substitution is

$$MRTS_{LK} = \frac{MP_L}{MP_K} = \frac{0.5(0.3)K^{0.7}L^{-0.7}}{0.5(0.7)K^{-0.3}L^{0.3}} = \frac{3K}{7L}$$

Applying the cost minimization condition gives us

$$MRTS_{LK} = \frac{3K}{7L} = \frac{W}{R} = \frac{W}{40}$$

Now solve for K as a function of L:

$$\frac{3K}{7L} = \frac{W}{40}$$
$$120K = 7LW$$
$$K = \frac{7LW}{120}$$

Substitute into the output constraint, and solve for L as a function of W:

$$60{,}000 = 0.5K^{0.7}L^{0.3}$$
$$120{,}000 = \left(\frac{7LW}{120}\right)^{0.7}L^{0.3}$$
$$120{,}000 = \left(\frac{7}{120}\right)^{0.7}W^{0.7}L^{0.7}L^{0.3}$$
$$120{,}000 \approx 0.137W^{0.7}L$$
$$L \approx 875{,}912.409W^{-0.7}$$

So the demand for labor is

$$L(W) \approx 875{,}912.409W^{-0.7}$$

If we instead want to set this up as a Lagrangian, we can write the firm's cost minimization problem with a generic wage rate, W.

$$\min_{K,L} 40K + WL \ s.t. \ 60{,}000 = 0.5K^{0.7}L^{0.3}, \text{ or}$$
$$\min_{K,L,\lambda} \mathcal{L}(K,L,\lambda) = 40K + WL + \lambda(60{,}000 - 0.5K^{0.7}L^{0.3})$$

Finding the first-order conditions for the Lagrangian, we see that:

$$\frac{\partial \mathcal{L}}{\partial K} = 40 - \lambda\big(0.5(0.7)K^{-0.3}L^{0.3}\big) = 0$$
$$\frac{\partial \mathcal{L}}{\partial L} = W - \lambda\big(0.5(0.3)K^{0.7}L^{-0.7}\big) = 0$$
$$\frac{\partial \mathcal{L}}{\partial \lambda} = 60{,}000 - 0.5K^{0.7}L^{0.3} = 0$$

Since we now have three equations with three unknowns (K,L,λ), we can solve this system of equations to come up with the solution to the cost minimization problem. Specifically, we can use the first 2 conditions to solve for λ as a first step.

$$\lambda = \frac{40}{0.35K^{-0.3}L^{0.3}} = \frac{W}{0.15K^{0.7}L^{-0.7}}$$

$$40(0.15K^{0.7}L^{-0.7}) = W(0.35K^{-0.3}L^{0.3})$$

$$6(K^{0.7}K^{0.3}) = 0.35W(L^{0.7}L^{0.3})$$

$$6K = 0.35WL$$

$$K = \frac{0.35WL}{6}$$

This is the same condition as $K = \frac{7LW}{120}$ (if you multiply by 20) and therefore the remaining math is the same as in the shorter approach at the beginning of this solution.

b. Take the derivative of labor demand with respect to the wage

$$\frac{\partial L(W)}{\partial W} = 875{,}912.409(-0.7)W^{-1.7} = -613{,}138.686W^{-1.7}$$

which is negative, as we expect from the Law of Demand since the Law of Demand tells us that as price increases, quantity demanded decreases. Here, if the price of labor (the wage rate) increases, the firm demands less labor.

c. Substitute \$25 for W in the labor demand.

$$L \approx 875{,}912.409W^{-0.7} \approx 875{,}912.409(25)^{-0.7} \approx 92{,}024.332 \text{ labor hours}$$

Costs

7

Solutions for Practice Problems

Problem 1

a. Accounting cost is the direct cost of operating a business, including supplies, utilities, and employees' wages. Thus, Alan's accounting cost is $50,000 + $300,000 + $20,000 = $370,000.

b. Economic cost includes both accounting cost and the opportunity costs of owner supplied resources. Alan's opportunity costs include the forgone salary at his current firm ($150,000) and the interest on his savings given up: $0.02 \times \$250,000 = \$5,000$. So, Alan's opportunity cost is $150,000 + $5,000 = $155,000, and his economic cost is $370,000 + $155,000 = $525,000.

c. Alan should start the business if he expects a positive economic profit, which is the difference between his revenue and his economic cost. Given Alan's expected revenue and his economic cost calculated in (b), Alan's economic profit is $550,000 – $525,000 = $25,000 > 0. Thus, Alan should quit his current job and start his own law firm.

Problem 2

Panasonic should finish the project. The 7 billion yen is a sunk cost that should not affect the company's decision. What matters is that the revenues from launching the new camcorder (5 billion yens) exceed the additional cost of completing the project (3 billion yen). Panasonic would lose the 7 billion yen of sunk costs, but that would also be true if the company discontinued the project. Abandoning the project would allow the company to avoid the incremental 3 billion yen cost, but it would then forgo the 5 billion yen in expected revenue. Looking forward and ignoring sunk costs, Panasonic faces a choice between an expected incremental gain of 2 billion yen (5 billion in revenues minus 3 billion in costs) from launching the new camcorder and an expected incremental loss (opportunity cost) of 2 billion yen (3 billion yen in saved costs minus 5 billion yen in lost revenues) from cancelling the project.

Problem 3

See the following table.

Quantity (units)	Total Cost ($)	Variable Cost ($)	Average Total Cost ($)	Marginal Cost ($)
0	30	0	—	—
1	70	40	70	40
2	90	60	45	20
3	102	72	34	12
4	120	90	30	18

When no output is produced, the variable cost is zero, so the whole total cost is fixed cost. Thus, we know that $FC = \$30$. Now we can calculate the variable cost for $Q = 1$: $VC = TC - FC = \$70 - \$30 = \$40$. The average total cost for $Q = 1$ is $ATC = \dfrac{TC}{Q} = \dfrac{\$70}{1} = \$70$, and the marginal cost of the first unit of output is $MC = \dfrac{\Delta TC}{\Delta Q} = \dfrac{\$70 - \$30}{1} = \$40$ or $MC = \dfrac{\Delta VC}{\Delta Q} = \dfrac{\$40 - \$0}{1} = \$40$.

For $Q = 2$, the total cost is $TC = FC + VC = \$30 + \$60 = \$90$. Then, $ATC = \dfrac{\$90}{2} = \$45$, and $MC = \dfrac{\$60 - \$40}{1} = \$20$.

For $Q = 3$, we can calculate total cost as follows: $TC = ATC \times Q = \$34 \times 3 = \$102$. Then, $VC = \$102 - \$30 = \$72$, and $MC = \dfrac{\$72 - \$60}{1} = \$12$.

For $Q = 4$, we calculate total cost by adding the marginal cost of the 4th unit to the total cost with $Q = 3$: $102 + 18 = 120$. Then, $VC = 120 - 30 = 90$, and $ATC = \dfrac{\$120}{4} = \$30$.

Problem 4

a. Mauricio's fixed cost is the cost of capital ($100). The shop's short-run production function shows that if it employs 5 workers, it will be able to produce 72 haircuts. Thus, the average fixed cost is $AFC = \dfrac{FC}{Q} = \dfrac{\$100}{72} = \$1.39$.

b. Mauricio's variable cost is the cost of labor, as it varies with output. To produce 60 haircuts, Mauricio needs 4 workers, so his variable cost is $VC = \$90 \times 4 = \$360$. Thus, the average variable cost is $AVC = \dfrac{VC}{Q} = \dfrac{\$360}{60} = \$6.00$.

c. To produce 48 haircuts, Mauricio needs 3 workers, so his variable cost is $VC = \$90 \times 3 = \$270$. Mauricio's fixed cost remains the same ($100) at all levels of output. Thus, the total cost of producing 48 haircuts is $TC = FC + VC = \$100 + \$270 = \$370$. Then, the average total cost is $ATC = \dfrac{TC}{Q} = \dfrac{\$370}{48} = \$7.71$.

d. If Mauricio's hires the 6th worker, its output will increase by $\Delta Q = 84 - 72 = 12$ haircuts. The cost of an additional worker is $\Delta TC = \Delta VC = \$90$. Thus, the marginal cost per additional haircut is $\dfrac{\Delta TC}{\Delta Q} = \dfrac{\$90}{12} = \$7.50$.

Problem 5

a. We know that when the firm's output is zero, there is no variable cost, that is, the firm's total cost is all fixed cost. Thus, we can find the fixed cost by calculating total cost at zero units of output:

$$TC = 1{,}000 + 10 \times 0 + 4 \times 0^2$$
$$TC = 1{,}000$$

Variable cost can be found by subtracting fixed cost from total cost:

$$VC = (1{,}000 + 10Q + 4Q^2) - 1{,}000$$
$$VC = 10Q + 4Q^2$$

Average total cost is total cost per unit of output:

$$ATC = \frac{TC}{Q}$$
$$ATC = \frac{1{,}000 + 10Q + 4Q^2}{Q}$$
$$ATC = \frac{1{,}000}{Q} + 10 + 4Q$$

Average variable cost is variable cost per unit of output:

$$AVC = \frac{VC}{Q}$$
$$AVC = \frac{10Q + 4Q^2}{Q}$$
$$AVC = 10 + 4Q$$

b. Minimum average total cost occurs when $ATC = MC$:

$$\frac{1{,}000}{Q} + 10 + 4Q = 10 + 8Q$$

Solving this equation for Q, we get:

$$4Q = \frac{1{,}000}{Q}$$
$$Q^2 = 250$$
$$Q = 250^{0.5}$$
$$Q = 15.8$$

That is, the average total cost is minimized when 15.8 units of output are produced.

c. Minimum average variable cost occurs when $AVC = MC$:

$$10 + 4Q = 10 + 8Q$$

Solving this equation for Q, we get:

$$4Q = 0$$
$$Q = 0$$

That is, the average variable cost is minimized when no output is produced.

d. Using calculus, $MC = \dfrac{dTC}{dQ} = 0 + 10 + 4(2)Q^{2-1} = 10 + 8Q$. This is as given.

e. Average total cost is shown in (a): $ATC = 1{,}000Q^{-1} + 10 + 4Q$. We can minimize this directly by calculating the first-order condition. Taking the derivative of ATC with respect to Q, we see that $\dfrac{dATC}{dQ} = 1{,}000(-1)Q^{-1-1} + 0 + 4 = -1{,}000Q^{-2} + 4$. Setting this equal to zero, $-1{,}000Q^{-2} + 4 = 0$ or $Q \approx 15.8$. To confirm that this is a minimum (and not a maximum), we can check the second-order condition: $\dfrac{d^2ATC}{dQ^2} = -1{,}000(-2)Q^{-2-1} = 2{,}000Q^{-3} > 0$. Since $Q > 0$, this is the minimum of ATC. This is the same answer as found in (b).

f. Average variable cost is shown in (a): $AVC = 10 + 4Q$. We can minimize this directly by calculating the first-order condition. Taking the derivative of AVC with respect to Q, we see that $\dfrac{dAVC}{dQ} = 4 > 0$, which indicates that AVC is increasing in Q. Since this derivative is positive and does not depend on Q, the function is minimized at $Q = 0$. This is the same answer as found in (c).

Problem 6

a. When K is fixed at 4, Giuseppe's production function is

$$Q = 20 \times 4^{0.5}L^{0.5}$$
$$Q = 40L^{0.5}$$

b. Plugging $L = 6$ into Giuseppe's short-run production function, we get

$$Q = 40 \times 6^{0.5} = 98$$

That is, with 6 workers, Giuseppe's produces 98 pizzas per day. Giuseppe's fixed cost, that is, the cost of the pizzeria's capital, is $\$128 \times 4 = \$512$ per day. Thus, the average fixed cost is

$$AFC = \frac{FC}{Q}$$
$$AFC = \frac{\$512}{98}$$
$$AFC = \$5.22$$

c. To calculate the cost of producing 80 pizzas, we need to find how much labor needs to be employed to produce this quantity of pizza. Substituting $Q = 80$ into Giuseppe's short-run production function and solving the equation for L, we get:

$$80 = 40L^{0.5}$$
$$L^{0.5} = 2$$
$$L = 4$$

That is, Giuseppe's needs 4 workers to produce 80 pizzas. So, the pizzeria's variable cost is $VC = \$64 \times 4 = \$256$, and its average variable cost is $AVC = \dfrac{VC}{Q} = \dfrac{\$256}{80} = \$3.20$. To find Giuseppe's total cost, we add its fixed cost to its variable cost: $TC = \$256 + \$512 = \$768$. Then, the pizzeria's average total cost is $ATC = \dfrac{TC}{Q} = \dfrac{\$768}{80} = \$9.60$.

d. The marginal cost of producing the 81st pizza can be calculated as the difference between the variable cost of producing 81 pizzas and the variable cost of producing 80 pizzas. To calculate the cost of producing 81 pizzas, we need to find how much labor is needed to produce this quantity of pizza. Substituting $Q = 81$ into Giuseppe's short-run production function and solving the equation for L, we get:

$$81 = 40L^{0.5}$$
$$L^{0.5} = 2.025$$
$$L = 4.1$$

So, the variable cost of producing 81 pizzas is $64 \times 4.1 = \$262.40$. As we've found in (c), the variable cost of producing 80 pizzas is $256. Thus, the marginal cost of the 81st pizza is $MC = \$262.40 - \$256.00 = \$6.40$.

 e. The marginal product of labor is the partial derivative of the production function with respect to labor, and the marginal product of capital is the partial derivative of the production function with respect to capital. Here, marginal products of labor and capital respectively are:

$$MP_L = \frac{\partial Q}{\partial L} = 20(0.5)K^{0.5}L^{0.5-1} = 10K^{0.5}L^{-0.5}$$

$$MP_K = \frac{\partial Q}{\partial K} = 20(0.5)K^{0.5-1}L^{0.5} = 10K^{-0.5}L^{0.5}$$

Problem 7

a. The firm's short-run average total cost $(SATC)$ is its ATC with the current plant. The firm's $SATC$ curve can be derived from its total cost curve for the current plant as follows:

$$SATC_1 = \frac{TC_1}{Q}$$

$$SATC_1 = \frac{200 + 30Q - 0.4Q^2 + 0.004Q^3}{Q}$$

$$SATC_1 = \frac{200}{Q} + 30 - 0.4Q + 0.004Q^2$$

Substituting $Q = 60$ into the $SATC_1$ equation, we have

$$SATC_1 = \frac{200}{60} + 30 - 0.4 \times 60 + 0.004 \times 60^2$$

$$SATC_1 = 23.73$$

Thus, the firm's short-run average total cost is $23.73 per sweater.

b. To find the firm's long-run average total cost, we need to compare its short-run average total costs for the two plants. The firm's SATC curve for the larger plant can be derived from its total cost curve for that plant:

$$SATC_2 = \frac{TC_2}{Q}$$

$$SATC_2 = \frac{400 + 35Q - 0.6Q^2 + 0.004Q^3}{Q}$$

$$SATC_2 = \frac{400}{Q} + 35 - 0.6Q + 0.004Q^2$$

Substituting $Q = 60$ into the $SATC_2$ equation, we have

$$SATC_2 = \frac{400}{60} + 35 - 0.6 \times 60 + 0.004 \times 60^2$$

$$SATC_2 = 20.07$$

Thus, the firm's short-run average total cost for the larger plant is $20.07 per sweater. A firm's long-run average total cost for a given level of output is the lowest ATC that can be achieved when the firm can adjust its capital input (plant size) as well as its labor input. Since out of the two possible choices, the ATC with the larger plant ($20.07) is lower than the ATC with the smaller plant ($23.73), the firm's long-run average total cost equals $SATC_2 = \$20.07$.

c. As follows from (b), if the factory switches from the smaller plant to the larger plant, it will be able to produce 60 sweaters at a lower average cost ($20.07 per sweater instead of $23.73 per sweater). Thus, the factory should expand its plant.

 d. Using calculus,

$$MC_1 = \frac{dTC_1}{dQ}$$

$$= 0 + 30 - 0.4(2)Q^{2-1} + 0.004(3)Q^{3-1}$$

$$= 30 - 0.8Q + 0.012Q^2$$

e. To find the quantities for which marginal cost is increasing, we need to find values for which the derivative of marginal cost with respect to Q is positive. Here, $\frac{dMC}{dQ} = 0 - 0.8 + 0.012(2)Q^{2-1} = -0.8 + 0.024Q$. This is increasing when $-0.8 + 0.024Q > 0$ or $Q > 0.03$.

f. Using calculus,

$$MC_2 = \frac{dTC_2}{dQ}$$
$$= 0 + 35 - 0.6(2)Q^{2-1} + 0.004(3)Q^{3-1}$$
$$= 35 - 1.2Q + 0.012Q^2$$

g. To find the quantities for which marginal cost is increasing, we need to find values for which the derivative of marginal cost with respect to Q is positive. Here, $\frac{dMC}{dQ} = 0 - 1.2 + 0.012(2)Q^{2-1} = -1.2 + 0.024Q$. This is increasing when $-1.2 + 0.024Q > 0$ or $Q > 0.02$.

Problem 8

a. When capital is fixed at $K = 100$, the firm's production function is

$$Q = 0.3 \times 100^{0.5}L^{0.5}$$
$$Q = 3L^{0.5}$$

Solving this equation for L, given that $Q = 21$, we have

$$21 = 3L^{0.5}$$
$$L^{0.5} = 7$$
$$L = 49$$

That is, with the capital input fixed at 100 machine-hours, the firm needs to employ 49 worker-hours to produce 21 laptops. With this combination of inputs, the total cost is

$$TC = \$30 \times 49 + \$120 \times 100$$
$$TC = \$13{,}470$$

and the average total cost is

$$ATC = \frac{\$13{,}470}{21}$$
$$ATC = \$641$$

b. In the long run, a firm minimizes costs when

$$\frac{MP_L}{MP_K} = \frac{W}{R}$$

For the firm in question:

$$\frac{\dfrac{0.15K^{0.5}}{L^{0.5}}}{\dfrac{0.15L^{0.5}}{K^{0.5}}} = \frac{30}{120}$$

$$\frac{0.15K^{0.5}K^{0.5}}{0.15L^{0.5}L^{0.5}} = 0.25$$

$$\frac{K}{L} = 0.25$$

$$K = 0.25L$$

We substitute this expression for K into the production function and solve it for L and K, given that $Q = 21$:

$$Q = 0.3K^{0.5}L^{0.5}$$
$$21 = 0.3 \times (0.25L)^{0.5}L^{0.5}$$
$$21 = 0.3 \times 0.25^{0.5}L^{0.5}L^{0.5}$$
$$70 = 0.25^{0.5}L$$
$$0.5L = 70$$
$$L = 140$$
$$K = 0.25 \times 140 = 35$$

Thus, in the long run, to minimize its cost, the firm should increase labor from 49 to 140 hours and reduce capital from 100 to 35 hours. Then, the firm's total cost will fall to

$$TC = \$30 \times 140 + \$120 \times 35$$
$$TC = \$8,400$$

and the average total cost will fall to

$$ATC = \frac{\$8,400}{21}$$
$$ATC = \$400$$

That is, the firm will be able to save $13,470 − $8,400 = $5,070 per day or $641 − $400 = $241 per laptop produced.

c. The marginal product of labor is the partial derivative of the production function with respect to labor, and the marginal product of capital is the partial derivative of the production function with respect to capital. Here, 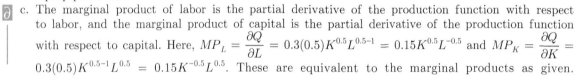 $MP_L = \dfrac{\partial Q}{\partial L} = 0.3(0.5)K^{0.5}L^{0.5-1} = 0.15K^{0.5}L^{-0.5}$ and $MP_K = \dfrac{\partial Q}{\partial K} = 0.3(0.5)K^{0.5-1}L^{0.5} = 0.15K^{-0.5}L^{0.5}$. These are equivalent to the marginal products as given.

Problem 9

a. The minimum average total cost occurs at the level of output where $LMC = LATC$. To solve this equation, we first need to find the $LATC$ curve:

$$LATC = \frac{LTC}{Q}$$
$$LATC = \frac{(14,000Q - 80Q^2 + Q^3)}{Q}$$
$$LATC = 14,000 - 80Q + Q^2$$

Now, we set $LATC = LMC$ to find the quantity that minimizes $LATC$:

$$LATC = LMC$$
$$14,000 - 80Q + Q^2 = 14,000 - 160Q + 3Q^2$$
$$2Q^2 = 80Q$$
$$2Q = 80$$
$$Q = 40$$

Thus, the firm's cost-minimizing level of output is 40 units.

b. To calculate the firm's minimum possible cost of producing an average unit of output, we plug the cost-minimizing quantity ($Q = 40$) into the $LATC$ equation:

$$LATC = 14,000 - 80 \times 40 + 40^2$$
$$LATC = 12,400$$

Thus, when the firm is producing at the minimum possible $LATC$, an average unit of output costs it $12,400.

c. We know that when $LMC < LATC$, long-run average total cost is falling, so the firm experiences economies of scale. And when $LMC > LATC$, the long-run average total cost is rising, so the firm faces diseconomies of scale. As we found in (a), the firm's long-run average total cost is minimized (and economies of scale are constant) when the firm produces 40 units of output. This means at $Q < 40$, the firm faces economies of scale. And at $Q > 40$, it faces diseconomies of scale.

 d. Using calculus, $LMC = \dfrac{dLTC}{dQ} = 14{,}000 - 80(2)Q^{2-1} + 3Q^{3-1} = 14{,}000 - 160Q + 3Q^2$. This is as given.

e. To find the quantities for which marginal cost is increasing, we need to find values for which the derivative of marginal cost with respect to Q is positive. Here, $\dfrac{dLMC}{dQ} = 0 - 160 + 3(2)Q^{2-1} = -160 + 6Q$. This is increasing when $-160 + 6Q > 0$ or $Q > 26.667$.

Problem 10

a. When $K = 9$, the firm's production function is

$$Q = 8 \times 9^{0.5}L^{0.5}$$
$$Q = 24L^{0.5}$$

To find the firm's short-run cost curve, we first solve its short-run production function for L, to see how much labor it needs to produce a given quantity of output:

$$Q = 24L^{0.5}$$
$$L^{0.5} = \frac{Q}{24}$$
$$L = \frac{Q^2}{576}$$

Now we can write the firm's total cost function as follows:

$$TC = WL + RK$$
$$TC = 200L + 1{,}000 \times 9$$
$$TC = 200\left(\frac{Q^2}{576}\right) + 9{,}000$$
$$TC = 0.347Q^2 + 9{,}000$$

b. In the total cost function we found in (a), the variable cost is the cost of labor:

$$VC = 0.347Q^2$$

so the average variable cost is

$$AVC = \frac{VC}{Q}$$
$$AVC = \frac{0.347Q^2}{Q}$$
$$AVC = 0.347Q$$
$$AVC = 0.347 \times 96 = 33.31$$

We can calculate the total cost by plugging $Q = 96$ into the total cost function in (a):

$$TC = 0.347Q^2 + 9{,}000$$
$$TC = 0.347 \times 96^2 + 9{,}000$$
$$TC = 12{,}198$$

Then, the average total cost is

$$ATC = \frac{TC}{Q}$$
$$ATC = \frac{12{,}198}{96} = 127.06$$

Thus, when the firm produces 96 units of output, its average variable cost is \$33.31, and its average total cost is \$127.06.

c. The marginal cost of producing the 97th unit is the difference between the variable cost of producing 97 units and the variable cost of producing 96 units. Given the VC function found in (b), we can write:

$$MC = (0.347 \times 97^2) - (0.347 \times 96^2)$$

$$MC = 0.347(97^2 - 96^2)$$

$$MC = 66.97$$

Thus, the marginal cost of producing the 97th unit is $66.97.

d. The marginal product of labor is the partial derivative of the production function with respect to labor, and the marginal product of capital is the partial derivative of the production function with respect to capital. Here, $MP_L = \dfrac{\partial Q}{\partial L} = 8(0.5)K^{0.5}L^{0.5-1} = 4K^{0.5}L^{-0.5}$ and $MP_K = \dfrac{\partial Q}{\partial K} = 0.8(0.5)K^{0.5-1}L^{0.5} = 4K^{-0.5}L^{0.5}$.

Problem 11

a. Substitute the fixed level of capital for $\overline{K}$ in the production function:

$$Q = 0.5\overline{K}^{0.5}L^{0.5} = 0.5(100)^{0.5}L^{0.5} = 5L^{0.5}$$

b. Solve for L:

$$L^{05} = \frac{Q}{5}$$

$$L = \frac{Q^2}{25}$$

c. Substitute K, the short-run labor demand, and the price of the inputs into the total cost equation:

$$TC_{SR} = R\overline{K} + WL = 10(100) + 25\left(\frac{Q^2}{25}\right) = 1{,}000 + Q^2$$

$$MC_{SR} = \frac{dTC_{SR}}{dQ} = 2Q$$

Therefore MC_{SR}, increases as output increases in the short run for this production function. This is as expected because short run capital is fixed.

Problem 12

Fixed cost is 8 and variable cost is $VC = 0.4Q^3 - 2Q^2 + 6Q$. Then, average variable cost is

$$AVC = \frac{VC}{Q} = \frac{0.4Q^3 - 2Q^2 + 6Q}{Q} = 0.4Q^2 - 2Q + 6$$

Minimize AVC by setting the first derivative equal to zero:

$$\frac{dAVC}{dQ} = \frac{d(0.4Q^2 - 2Q + 6)}{dQ} = 0.8Q - 2 + 0 = 0$$

$$0.8Q = 2$$

$$Q = 2.5$$

At $Q = 2.5$, average variable cost is

$$AVC = 0.4Q^2 - 2Q + 6 = 0.4(2.5)^2 - 2(2.5) + 6 = 3.5$$

Marginal cost is

$$MC = \frac{dVC}{dQ} = \frac{d(0.4Q^3 - 2Q^2 + 6Q)}{dQ} = 0.4(3)Q^{3-1} - 2(2)Q^{2-1} + 6 = 1.2Q^2 - 4Q + 6$$

At $Q = 2.5$, marginal cost is

$$MC = 1.2Q^2 - 4Q + 6 = 1.2(2.5)^2 - 4(2.5) + 6 = 3.5$$

Thus, the equivalence is shown.

Solutions for Practice Problems

Problem 1

a. Given that consumers see all paper towels as identical and that there are many paper towel producers in the market, Bonta can be considered a perfectly competitive firm. And firms in perfect competition maximize profit by producing the quantity for which $P = MC$. To find this quantity for Bonta, we set its MC equal to the market price and solve this equation for Q:

$$1 + 0.1Q = 3$$
$$0.1Q = 2$$
$$Q = 20$$

Thus, Bonta's profit-maximizing quantity of paper towels is 20,000 six-packs per year.

b. Bonta's profit can be calculated as

$$\pi = (P - ATC) \times Q$$

At the firm's profit-maximizing level of output ($Q = 20$), the firm's average total cost is $ATC = 1 + \dfrac{10}{20} + 0.05 \times 20 = 2.5$. Thus, Bonta's profit is

$$\pi = (\$3 - \$2.5) \times 20{,}000$$
$$\pi = \$10{,}000$$

Problem 2

a. Since the price is above the minimum average variable cost, a typical firm will produce, rather than shutting down. And when producing, firms in perfect competition maximize profit at the level of output where $P = MC$. As can be seen on the following graph, this happens when a typical firm produces 491 pounds of pepper.

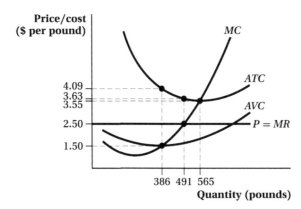

b. At the profit maximizing level of output (491 pounds), the profit is $\pi = (P - ATC) \times Q = (\$2.50 - \$3.63) \times 491 = -\$555$. Thus, a typical firm incurs a loss of $555.

c. A firm will not produce any output in the short run at a price below its minimum average variable cost (AVC). And the minimum AVC occurs where the AVC curve intersects the MC curve. As you can see on the graph, this is the point where the AVC is $1.50. Thus, a typical firm will shut down if the price of pepper falls below $1.50 per pound.

d. We can calculate a firm's fixed cost given that $FC = AFC \times Q$ and that $AFC = ATC - AVC$; that is, average fixed cost is measured by the distance between the ATC and AVC curves. Since fixed cost does not vary with output, we can calculate it at any output level. For example, using the information given on the graph, we can calculate FC at $Q = 386$ as follows: $FC = (\$4.09 - \$1.50) \times 386 = \$1{,}000$. At the profit-maximizing (i.e., loss-minimizing) level of output (491 pounds), the price is above the average variable cost, but below the average total cost. This means the firms cover all their variable costs, but only part of their fixed costs.

Problem 3

a. Since the market is in equilibrium, we know that each firm maximizes profit. And firms in perfect competition maximize profit by producing the quantity for which $P = MC$. To find this quantity, we set MC equal to the market price and solve this equation for Q:

$$3.125 - 1.5Q + 0.375Q^2 = 3.50$$
$$0.375Q^2 - 1.5Q - 0.375 = 0$$
$$Q = \frac{1.5 + \sqrt{1.5^2 + 4 \times 0.375 \times 0.375}}{2 \times 0.375}$$
$$Q = 4.236$$

Thus, each firm produces 4,236 pounds of romaine lettuce.

b. Each firm's total revenue is $TR = P \times Q = \$3.50 \times 4{,}236 = \$14{,}826$. And its total cost (in thousands of dollars) calculated from the total cost curve for the profit maximizing output level is

$$TC = 1.5 + 3.125 \times 4.236 - 0.75 \times 4.236^2 + 0.125 \times 4.236^3$$
$$TC = 10.781$$

Thus, each firm's profit is

$$\pi = TR - TC$$
$$\pi = \$14{,}826 - \$10{,}781$$
$$\pi = \$4{,}045$$

c. Marginal cost is the derivative of the total cost function with respect to quantity: $MC = \dfrac{dTC}{dQ} = 0 + 3.125 - 0.75(2)Q^{2-1} + 0.125(3)Q^{3-1} = 3.125 - 1.5Q + 0.375Q^2$. This is the same equation for marginal cost as given in the problem.

d. The firm's profit function is $\pi = 3.5Q - (1.5 + 3.125Q - 0.75Q^2 + 0.125Q^3) = -0.125Q^3 + 0.75Q^2 + 0.375Q - 1.5$. Maximizing this function with respect to Q, we see that the first-order condition is: $-0.125(3)Q^{3-1} + 0.75(2)Q + 0.375 - 0 = -0.375Q^2 + 1.5Q + 0.375 =$ or $0.375Q^2 - 1.5Q - 0.375 = 0$ as in (a). The quadratic formula in that part showed that $Q = 4.236$. Thus, each firm produces 4,236 pounds of romaine lettuce.

Problem 4

a. To derive the industry short-run supply curve, we sum each of the firm short-run supply curves horizontally. That is, we add each firm's quantity supplied at each price. Since there are 50 high-cost firms with identical supply curves, we can sum them simply by multiplying the firm's supply curve by 50:

$$Q_{HC} = 50Q_{hc} = 50 \times 8P$$
$$Q_{HC} = 400P$$

Similarly, we can get the supply curve for the 60 low-cost firms:

$$Q_{LC} = 60Q_{lc} = 60 \times 10P$$
$$Q_{LC} = 600P$$

The short-run industry supply curve is the horizontal sum of the quantities supplied by high-cost producers and the quantities supplied by low-cost producers:

$$Q^S = Q_{HC} + Q_{LC}$$
$$Q^S = 400P + 600P$$
$$Q^S = 1{,}000P$$

b. Market equilibrium occurs where quantity demanded is equal to quantity supplied:

$$Q^D = Q^S$$
$$6,000 - 2,000P = 1,000P$$
$$3,000P = 6,000$$
$$P = 2$$

The equilibrium quantity can be found by substituting $P = 2$ into either the market supply or market demand equation:

$$Q^S = 1,000P$$
$$Q^S = 1,000 \times 2$$
$$Q^S = 2,000$$
$$Q^D = 6,000 - 2,000P$$
$$Q^D = 6,000 - 2,000 \times 2$$
$$Q^D = 2,000$$

Thus, the equilibrium price of potatoes is $2 per pound, and the equilibrium quantity is 2 million pounds.

c. At a price of $2 per pound, each high-cost producer will produce $Q_{hc} = 8P = 8 \times 2 = 16$ thousand pounds of potatoes, and each low-cost producer will produce $Q_{lc} = 10P = 10 \times 2 = 20$ thousand pounds.

d. The easiest way to calculate industry producer surplus is to graph the industry supply curve (see the following graph). Producer surplus is the triangular area below the market price ($2) and above the industry supply curve. The base of this triangle is 2 million (the equilibrium quantity) and its height is $2 (the equilibrium price). Thus, the producer surplus is

$$PS = 0.5 \times 2 \text{ million} \times \$2 = \$2 \text{ million}$$

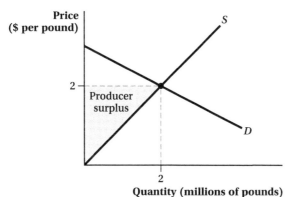

e. Supply is $Q^S = 1,000P$, so inverse supply is $P = \dfrac{Q^S}{1,000}$

Producer surplus is

$$PS = \int_0^{2,000} \left(2 - \left(\frac{Q}{1,000}\right)\right) dQ$$

$$= \int_0^{2,000} 2\,dQ - \int_0^{2,000} \frac{Q}{1,000} dQ$$

$$= [2Q]_0^{2,000} - \left[\frac{Q^2}{2,000}\right]_0^{2,000}$$

$$= [2(2,000) - 2(0)] - \left[\frac{(2,000)^2}{2,000} - \frac{(0)^2}{2,000}\right]$$

$$= (4,000 - 0) - (2,000 - 0) = 2,000$$

Since quantity is in thousands, this is the same $2,000,000 producer surplus found in (d).

g. The short-run industry supply curve can be written generically as: $Q^S = N_{hc}\left(\dfrac{P}{8}\right) + N_{lc}\left(\dfrac{P}{10}\right)$ where N_{hc} is the number of high-cost firms and N_{lc} is the number of low-cost firms and $\dfrac{P}{8}$ and $\dfrac{P}{10}$ are the respective inverse supply functions for these types.

h. If $N_{hc} = 60$, we know that $Q^S = 60\left(\dfrac{P}{8}\right) + N_{lc}\left(\dfrac{P}{10}\right) = 7.5P + N_{lc}\left(\dfrac{P}{10}\right)$. The equilibrium condition now is:

$$Q^D = Q^S$$

$$6{,}000 - 2{,}000P = 7.5P + N_{lc}\left(\dfrac{P}{10}\right)$$

The original equilibrium price was \$2, as found in (b). At this price,

$$6{,}000 - 2{,}000(2) = 7.5(2) + N_{lc}\left(\dfrac{(2)}{10}\right)$$

$$2{,}000 = 15 + \dfrac{N_{lc}}{5}$$

$$N_{lc} = 9{,}925$$

Problem 5

a. A profit-maximizing firm produces the quantity at which marginal cost equals price. The current market equilibrium price (the price at which the quantity of wheat demanded equals the quantity supplied) is \$4 per bushel. A representative firm takes this price as given and produces the quantity at which its marginal cost is $LMC = MR = P = \$4$. As shown on the following graph, this is the case when the firm produces 10,000 bushels of wheat (point A).

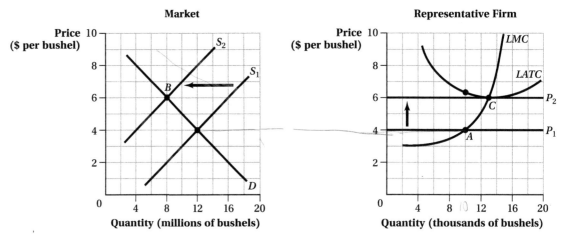

b. Since at their profit-maximizing level of output firms' average total cost (\$6.25) is higher than the market price (\$4), the firms are incurring economic losses (\$2.25 per each bushel of wheat sold).
c. Since firms incur economic losses, they will exit the market.
d. As firms exit the market, the market supply curve shifts leftward (from S_1 to S_2), and the equilibrium price rises until it equals $LATC$ and firms no longer incur economic losses. As shown on the graph, this happens when the market price is \$6 per bushel, and the quantity of wheat sold is 8 million bushels (point B).
e. As shown on the graph, after the market fully adjusts, a representative firm's marginal cost equals the new market price (\$6) when the firm produces 13,000 bushels of wheat (point C). Thus, the quantity of wheat sold by a representative firm increases from 10,000 bushels to 13,000 bushels.

Problem 6

a. A profit-maximizing firm produces the quantity at which marginal cost equals price. Thus, to find how much milk each firm will produce, we set $MC = \$3.60$ and solve this equation for Q:

$$MC = 3.6$$

$$2 - Q + 0.15Q^2 = 3.6$$

$$0.15Q^2 - Q - 1.6 = 0$$

$$Q = \dfrac{1 + \sqrt{1^2 + 4 \times 0.15 \times 1.6}}{2 \times 0.15}$$

$$Q = 8$$

That is, each firm produces 8,000 gallons of milk. The total cost at this quantity is

$$TC = 19.2 + 2 \times 8 - 0.5 \times 8^2 + 0.05 \times 8^3$$
$$TC = 28.8$$

so the average total cost is

$$ATC = \frac{TC}{Q}$$
$$ATC = \frac{28.8}{8}$$
$$ATC = 3.6$$

That is, the average total cost is $3.60 per gallon. Since the average total cost equals the market price ($3.60), the economic profit is zero, that is, the firms are breaking even.

b. We repeat the exercise in (a) with $MC = \$2.35$:

$$MC = 2.35$$
$$2 - Q + 0.15Q^2 = 2.35$$
$$0.15Q^2 - Q - 0.35 = 0$$
$$Q = \frac{1 + \sqrt{1^2 + 4 \times 0.15 \times 0.35}}{2 \times 0.15}$$
$$Q = 7$$

That is, each firm produces 7,000 gallons of milk. The total cost at this quantity is

$$19.2 + 2 \times 7 - 0.5 \times 7^2 + 0.05 \times 7^3$$
$$TC = 25.85$$

so the average total cost is

$$ATC = \frac{25.85}{7}$$
$$ATC = 3.69$$

Thus, the economic profit is

$$\pi = (P - ATC) \times Q$$
$$\pi = (2.35 - 3.69) \times 7$$
$$\pi = -9.38$$

This means each firm in the industry will incur an economic loss of $9,380, even if it produces its profit-maximizing (i.e., loss-minimizing) quantity of milk. So the question is, will the firms shut-down because of this loss or will they continue to produce? One way to answer this question, is to calculate a firm's average variable cost at $Q = 7$ and compare it with the market price. Recall that $TC = FC + VC$, so $VC = TC - FC$ and that fixed cost does not vary with output. Thus, if $TC = 19.2 + 2Q - 0.5Q^2 + 0.05Q^3$, then FC must be 19.2, which means

$$VC = 2Q - 0.5Q^2 + 0.05Q^3$$

Then:

$$AVC = \frac{2Q - 0.5Q^2 + 0.05Q^3}{Q}$$
$$AVC = 2 - 0.5Q + 0.05Q^2$$

And at $Q = 7$,

$$AVC = 2 - 0.5 \times 7 + 0.05 \times 7^2$$
$$AVC = 0.95$$

Since the price ($2.35) is higher than the AVC ($0.95), the firms in the industry can cover their variable costs, and even part of their fixed costs, so they continue to operate. If a firm shut-down its loss would be greater than $9,380: it would be equal to the whole amount of fixed cost, $19,200.

c. When the price falls to $0.75, we find the profit-maximizing level of output as follows:

$$MC = 0.75$$

$$2 - Q + 0.15Q^2 = 0.75$$

$$0.15Q^2 - Q + 1.25 = 0$$

$$Q = \frac{1 + \sqrt{1^2 + 4 \times 0.15 \times 1.25}}{2 \times 0.15}$$

$$Q = 5$$

At this level of output,

$$AVC = 2 - 0.5 \times 5 + 0.05 \times 5^2$$

$$AVC = 0.75$$

That is, $AVC = MC$, which means at this point, the AVC is at its minimum. In other words, this is the firms' shut-down point: when the price is $0.75 per gallon, the firms in the industry minimize their losses if they either produce 5,000 gallons of milk or shut down and produce no output. In either case a firm's economic loss equals the fixed cost. (You can verify that when $Q = 5$, $TC = 19.2 + 2 \times 5 - 0.5 \times 5^2 + 0.05 \times 5^3 = 22.95$, while $TR = P \times Q = 0.75 \times 5 = 3.75$, so the economic profit is $= 3.75 - 22.95 = -19.2$, that is, the economic loss is exactly equal to the amount of fixed cost.)

d. Marginal cost is the derivative of the total cost function with respect to quantity: $MC = \dfrac{dTC}{dQ} = $

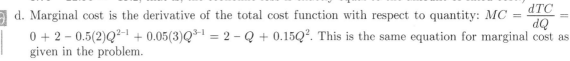

$0 + 2 - 0.5(2)Q^{2-1} + 0.05(3)Q^{3-1} = 2 - Q + 0.15Q^2$. This is the same equation for marginal cost as given in the problem.

Problem 7

See the following graph. The industry supply curve is the horizontal sum of the firms' supply curves. Only at prices $2 per bushel and higher does any firm produce. For prices between $2 and $4, the industry supply curve is the sum of low-cost and medium-cost firms' supply curves. At $P = \$2$, the 200 low-cost firms supply 15,000 bushels of soybeans each, and the 500 medium-cost firms supply 5,000 bushels each, so the industry supplies $200 \times 15,000 + 500 \times 5,000 = 5,500,000$ bushels. At a price of just below $4, the low-cost firms supply 25,000 bushels each, and the medium-cost firms supply 15,000 bushels each, so the industry supplies $200 \times 25,000 + 500 \times 15,000 = 12,500,000$ bushels. At $P = \$4$, the 300 high-cost firms start producing, so the industry supply curve shifts rightward by the quantity that they produce at $P = \$4$: $300 \times 5,000 = 1,500,000$. Thus, at $P = \$4$, the industry supplies $12,500,000 + 1,500,000 = 14,000,000$ bushels. And at $P = \$9$, the 200 low-cost firms supply 50,000 bushels each, the 500 medium-cost firms supply 40,000 bushels each, and the 300 high-cost firms supply 30,000 bushels each. Thus, the industry supplies $200 \times 50,000 + 500 \times 40,000 + 300 \times 30,000 = 39,000,000$ bushels. We draw the industry supply curve (S_{IND}) by connecting these four points.

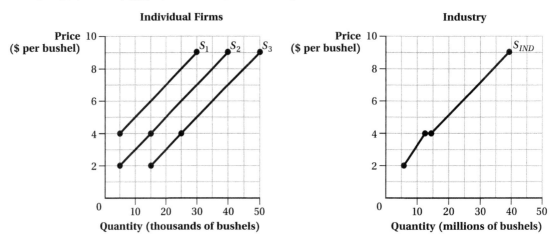

Problem 8

a. Since the market is in equilibrium, we know that each firm maximizes profit. And firms in perfect competition maximize profit by producing the quantity for which $P = MC$. To find this quantity, we set MC equal to the market price and solve this equation for Q:

$$0.7 - 0.6Q + 0.21Q^2 = 1.66$$

$$0.21Q^2 - 0.6Q - 0.96 = 0$$

$$Q = \frac{0.6 + \sqrt{(-0.6)^2 + 4 \times 0.21 \times 0.96}}{2 \times 0.21}$$

$$Q = 4$$

Thus, each firm produces 4 million bottles of water.

b. Each firm's total revenue is $TR = P \times Q = \$1.66 \times 4 = \$6.64$ million. And its total cost (in millions of dollars) calculated from the total cost curve for the profit-maximizing output level is

$$TC = 4.16 + 0.7 \times 4 - 0.3 \times 4^2 + 0.07 \times 4^3$$

$$TC = 6.64$$

Thus, $TC = TR$, which means firms earn zero economic profits.

c. Producer surplus can be calculated as a firm's total revenue minus its variable cost. Since $TC = FC + VC$, we can calculate VC as $TC - FC$. Fixed cost does not vary with output, so if $TC = 4.16 + 0.7Q - 0.3Q^2 + 0.07Q^3$, then 4.16 must be the fixed cost. Thus, a firm's variable cost is \$6.64 million – \$4.16 million = \$2.48 million. As we found in (b), a firm's total revenue is \$6.64 million. Thus, a firm's producer surplus is $PS = TR - VC = \$6.64$ million – \$2.48 million = \$4.16 million.

d. Marginal cost is the derivative of the total cost function with respect to quantity: $MC = \dfrac{dTC}{dQ} = 0 + 0.7 - 0.3(2)Q^{2-1} + 0.07(3)Q^{3-1} = 0.7 - 0.6Q + 0.21Q^2$. This is the same equation for marginal cost as given in the problem.

Problem 9

a. An individual producer's long-run average total cost curve is

$$LATC = \frac{LTC}{Q}$$

$$LATC = \frac{(1{,}300Q - 74Q^2 + 2Q^3)}{Q}$$

$$LATC = 1{,}300 - 74Q + 2Q^2$$

b. The long-run equilibrium price is the price at which firms in the industry earn zero economic profits. This happens when $P = LMC = LATC$, or when the $LATC$ is at its minimum. To find this point, we equate $LATC$ and LMC and solve this equation for Q:

$$LATC = LMC$$

$$1{,}300 - 74Q + 2Q^2 = 1{,}300 - 148Q + 6Q^2$$

$$4Q^2 = 74Q$$

$$4Q = 74$$

$$Q = 18.5$$

To find the $LATC$ at this output, we plug $Q = 18.5$ into the formula for $LATC$:

$$LATC = 1{,}300 - 74 \times 18.5 + 2 \times 18.5^2$$

$$LATC = 615.5$$

Thus, the long-run equilibrium price of sugar is \$615.50 per ton.

c. As we found in (b), when the market is in long-run equilibrium (i.e., $P = LMC = LATC = \$615.50$), $Q = 18.5$. Thus, each firm produces 18,500 tons of sugar.

d. Given the market demand curve, the quantity of sugar demanded at the equilibrium price is $Q^D = 6{,}162 - 4 \times 615.5 = 3{,}700$ thousand tons (3.7 million tons). Since the market is in equilibrium, this is also the quantity of sugar supplied and the quantity sold.

e. As we've found in (d), the quantity of sugar produced by the industry is 3,700 thousand tons. And as we've found in (b), each firm produces 18.5 thousand tons. Thus, the number of firms in the industry is $\dfrac{3{,}700}{18.5} = 200$.

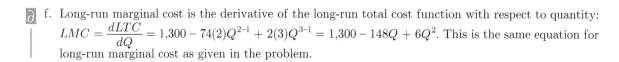

f. Long-run marginal cost is the derivative of the long-run total cost function with respect to quantity:
$LMC = \dfrac{dLTC}{dQ} = 1{,}300 - 74(2)Q^{2-1} + 2(3)Q^{3-1} = 1{,}300 - 148Q + 6Q^2$. This is the same equation for long-run marginal cost as given in the problem.

Problem 10

a. A perfectly competitive firm maximizes its profit when it chooses the level of output for which $LMC = P$, so the firm's supply curve is its LMC curve. But in the long run, a firm will produce only if the price is at or above its minimum long-run average total cost. So the relevant part of the LMC curve is the part that lies above the $LATC$ curve. To find the minimum $LATC$, we need to know the firm's $LATC$ curve. Given that $LATC = \dfrac{LTC}{Q}$, we can find the $LATC$ curve for a firm with an average manager as follows:

$$LATC_A = \frac{LTC_A}{Q}$$

$$LATC_A = \frac{72 + 0.02Q^2}{Q}$$

$$LATC_A = \frac{72}{Q} + 0.02Q$$

To find the minimum $LATC_A$, recall that ATC is minimized when $ATC = MC$. So, we equate $LATC_A$ and LMC_A and solve this equation for Q to find the output at which $LATC_A$ is at its minimum:

$$LATC_A = LMC_A$$

$$\frac{72}{Q} + 0.02Q = 0.04Q$$

$$0.02Q^2 = 72$$

$$Q^2 = 3{,}600$$

$$Q = 60$$

To find the level of $LAVC_A$ at this output, we plug $Q = 60$ into the formula for $LATC_A$:

$$LATC_A = \frac{72}{60} + 0.02 \times 60$$

$$LATC_A = 2.40$$

Thus, the long-run supply curve of a firm with an average manager is its long-run marginal cost curve above the $LMC_A = \$2.40$ (see the following graph). To write the equation for this supply curve with the quantity supplied as a function of price, we solve the profit-maximizing condition, $P = MC$, for Q:

$$P = LMC_A$$

$$P = 0.04Q_A$$

$$Q_A = 25P$$

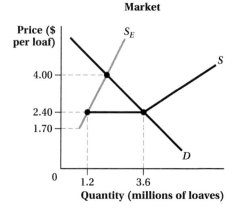

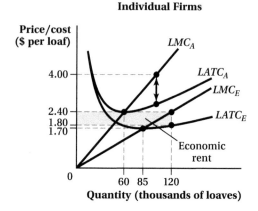

Similarly, we can find the $LATC$ curve for a firm with an exceptional manager as follows:

$$LATC_E = \frac{LTC_E}{Q}$$

$$LATC_E = \frac{72 + 0.01Q^2}{Q}$$

$$LATC_E = \frac{72}{Q} + 0.01Q$$

Then, we find the output at which $LATC_E$ is at its minimum:

$$LATC_E = LMC_E$$

$$\frac{72}{Q} + 0.01Q = 0.02Q$$

$$0.01Q^2 = 72$$

$$Q^2 = 7{,}200$$

$$Q = 84.853$$

And the $LAVC_E$ at this level of output is

$$LATC_E = \frac{72}{84.853} + 0.01 \times 84.853$$

$$LATC_E = 1.70$$

Thus, the long-run supply curve of a firm with an exceptional manager is its long-run marginal cost curve above the $LMS_E = \$1.70$ (see the preceding graph). To write the equation for this supply curve with the quantity supplied as a function of price, we solve the firm's profit-maximizing condition for Q:

$$P = LMC_E$$

$$P = 0.02Q_E$$

$$Q_E = 50P$$

b. To derive the supply curve for all firms with extraordinary managers, we sum the firms' individual supply curves horizontally. That is, we add each firm's quantity supplied at each price. Since there are 10 firms with identical supply curves, we can sum their supply curves simply by multiplying the individual firm's supply curve by 10:

$$Q_E = 10 \times 50P$$

$$Q_E = 500P$$

As we found in (a), in the long run, a firm with an extraordinary manager won't produce any output if the price is below \$1.70. Thus, the market supply curve for these firms is $Q_E = 500P$ if $P \geq \$1.70$ and $Q_E = 0$ if $P < \$1.70$ (S_E on the preceding graph). To see what the equilibrium price of bread would be if only the firms with extraordinary managers were in the market, we equate Q^E and Q^D and solve this equation for P:

$$Q^E = Q^D$$

$$500P = 6{,}000 - 1{,}000P$$

$$1{,}500P = 6{,}000$$

$$P = 4$$

Thus, with only extraordinary firms in the market, the equilibrium price of bread would be \$4 per loaf. This, however, is not a long-run equilibrium. Since the price (\$4) is above the lowest $LATC$ of the firms with average managers (\$2.40), those firms, attracted by potential economic profits, will enter the market. As a result, the market supply will increase, and the price of bread will fall.

c. As firms with average managers enter the market, the market supply increases, and the price falls until it reaches the minimum $LATC_A$ (\$2.40). At this price level, firms with average managers can no longer make economic profits, so they stop entering. And because all 10 firms with extraordinary managers are already in the market, there will be no more entry, so the market will be in long-run equilibrium. Thus, the long-run equilibrium price of bread is \$2.40 per loaf.

d. At the long-run equilibrium market price (\$2.40), the quantity of bread demanded is $Q^D = 6{,}000 - 1{,}000P = 6{,}000 - 1{,}000 \times \$2.40 = 3{,}600$ thousand (3.6 million) loaves. The firms with extraordinary managers supply $Q^E = 500P = 500 \times \$2.40 = 1{,}200$ thousand (1.2 million) loaves. And the rest of the demand, $3{,}600 - 1{,}200 = 2{,}400$ thousand (2.4 million) loaves is satisfied by firms with average managers. Given the individual supply curve of a firm with an average manager that we derived in (a), the quantity supplied by each firm at $P = \$2.40$ is $Q_A = 25P = 25 \times \$2.40 = 60$ thousand loaves. Thus, the number of firms that supply 2,400 thousand loaves must be $\dfrac{2,400}{60} = 40$.

e. When the market is in long-run equilibrium, a firm with an average manager earns zero economic profit, as its $LATC_A = P = \$2.40$. For a firm with an exceptional manager, the profit-maximizing level of output is where $LMC_E = P$. We find it by solving this condition for Q:

$$LMC_E = P$$
$$0.02Q = 2.40$$
$$Q = 120 \text{ thousand loaves}$$

At this level of output, $LATC_E = \dfrac{72}{120} + 0.01 \times 120 = \$1.80$. Thus, for each loaf of bread sold, a firm with an extraordinary manager makes $\$1.80$, and for the total output sold it makes $\$1.80 \times 120,000 = \$216,000$. This, however, is not economic profit but economic rent, that is, a return to a specialized input above what the firm paid for it. A firm with an extraordinary manager has lower cost because this manager can run the production process more efficiently than an average manager can for the same salary. And since there is a limited supply of exceptional managers, the manager's skills (human capital) earns economic rent for the firm. The difference between economic profit and economic rent is that when we calculate economic profit, we count inputs' opportunity costs, and economic rent is included in the opportunity cost of inputs that earn it. Thus, a firm with an extraordinary manager still earns zero economic profit, but the manager generates an economic rent of $\$216,000$ per year for the firm. (Note that an extraordinary manager in this scenario can request a huge salary raise from her firm, as other firms would be willing to pay her up to $\$216,000$ per year on top of the regular annual salary of $\$72,000$.)

∂ Problem 11

a. Marginal and average total cost are

$$MC = \frac{dTC}{dQ} = \frac{d(25Q^3 - 10Q^2 + 500Q)}{dQ} = 25(3)Q^{3-2} - 10(2)Q^{2-1} + 500 = 75Q^2 - 20Q + 500$$

$$ATC = \frac{TC}{Q} = \frac{25Q^3 - 10Q^2 + 500Q}{Q} = 25Q^2 - 10Q + 500$$

b. The minimum of average total cost occurs at the quantity where $MC = ATC$:

$$MC = ATC$$
$$75Q^2 - 20Q + 500 = 25Q^2 - 10Q + 500$$
$$50Q^2 = 10Q$$
$$Q = 0.2$$

This corresponds to 200 hotel rooms per hotel, since quantity is in thousands. Alternatively, we could find the quantity that minimizes ATC by taking its first-order condition with respect to Q:

$$\frac{dATC}{dQ} = \frac{d(25Q^2 - 10Q + 500)}{dQ} = 25(2)Q^{2-1} - 10 = 0$$
$$50Q = 10$$
$$Q = 0.2$$

c. Long-run equilibrium price must equal the minimum of average total cost. So find ATC at 0.2 units of output:

$$P = ATC = 25(0.2)^2 - 10(0.2) + 500 = \$499$$

d. Total industry output in equilibrium must satisfy the market demand at the equilibrium price. To find this output, we plug this price into the market demand curve:

$$Q^D = 5,000 - 2P = 5,000 - 2(499) = 4,002$$

This corresponds to 4,002,000 luxury rooms worldwide.

e. If each hotel offers 200 rooms (0.2 units), then the number of firms, N, is

$$N = \frac{market\ output}{firm\ output} = \frac{4,002}{0.2} = 20,010 \text{ hotels}$$

Market Power and Monopoly

9

Solutions for Practice Problems

Problem 1

a. If Figaro's sells 4 haircuts, its total revenue is $22 \times 4 = \$88$ (area $A + B$ on the following diagram). And if it sells 5 haircuts, the total revenue is $\$20 \times 5 = \$100$ (area $B + C$). Thus, the marginal revenue from the fifth haircut is $\$100 - \$88 = \$12$.

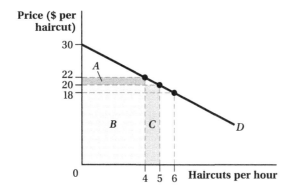

b. Since Figaro's charges the same price to all customers, it loses $(\$22 - \$20) \times 4 = \$8$ (area A) because it sells 4 haircuts at $20 per haircut instead of $22 per haircut. But the barbershop gains $\$20 \times 1 = \$20$ from selling an additional haircut (area C). Therefore, Figaro's marginal revenue from the fifth haircut is area $(B + C) - (A + B) = C - A = \$20 - \$8 = \$12$, which is the same as the MR calculated in (a).

c. If Figaro's lowers its price to $18 per haircut, it will sell 6 haircuts, so its total revenue will be $\$18 \times 6 = \$108$. And from (a) we know that Figaro's total revenue with 5 haircuts sold is $100. Thus, the marginal revenue from the sixth haircut is $\$108 - \$100 = \$8$. Since the marginal revenue ($8) is greater than the marginal cost ($6), Figaro's profit will increase if it lowers the price to $18. That is, the barbershop should lower its price.

d. We need Figaro's inverse demand curve in order to substitute into Figaro's revenue function to start this. Note from the figure that the vertical intercept is at 30. The slope is $\frac{\Delta P}{\Delta Q} = \frac{-2}{1} = -2$. Figaro's inverse demand curve, then, is $P = 30 - 2Q$. His revenue function, then, is $R = P \times Q = (30 - 2Q)Q$ $= 30Q - 2Q^2$. Marginal revenue is the derivative: $\frac{dR}{dQ} = 30 - 4Q$.

Problem 2

a. To find the firm's marginal revenue, we first solve the demand equation for P to find the inverse demand curve:

$$Q = 100 - P$$
$$P = 100 - Q$$

In this inverse demand curve, $a = 100$ and $b = 1$, so the corresponding marginal revenue curve is

$$MR = a - 2bQ$$
$$MR = 100 - 2Q$$

From this marginal revenue curve, we can calculate that when $Q = 20$, the marginal revenue is

$$MR = 100 - 2 \times 20 = 60 \text{ (dollars)}$$

b. Given the demand curve faced by the firm, when the price is $60, the quantity sold is

$$Q = 100 - 60 = 40 \text{ (units)}$$

Plugging this quantity into the firm's marginal revenue curve, we get

$$MR = 100 - 2 \times 40 = 20 \text{ (dollars)}$$

c. Since the firm's marginal revenue ($20) is less than its marginal cost ($25), the firm will increase its profit if it decreases output, increasing the marginal revenue to the level of the marginal cost. And to sell fewer units, the firm should raise its price.

Problem 3

a. Sony's maximizes its profit at the level of output where its marginal revenue equals its marginal cost. We can derive Sony's marginal revenue curve from the inverse demand curve, which we can find by solving the demand curve equation for P:

$$Q = 30 - 0.2P$$
$$0.2P = 30 - Q$$
$$P = 150 - 5Q$$

In this inverse demand curve, $a = 150$ and $b = 5$, so the marginal revenue curve that corresponds to this demand curve is

$$MR = a - 2bQ$$
$$MR = 150 - 10Q$$

To find Sony's profit-maximizing level of output, we set $MR = MC$ and solve this equation for Q:

$$MR = MC$$
$$150 - 10Q = 40 + Q$$
$$11Q = 110$$
$$Q = 10$$

Thus, Sony's profit-maximizing level of output is 10 million Blu-ray players.

b. To find Sony's profit-maximizing price, we plug the profit-maximizing quantity found in (a) into the inverse demand curve:

$$P = 150 - 5Q$$
$$P = 150 - 5 \times 10$$
$$P = 100$$

Thus, to maximize its profit, Sony should charge $100 per Blu-ray player.

c. Marginal cost is the derivative of total cost. For the given total cost function, $\frac{dTC}{dQ} = 40 + Q$. This is the same as the marginal cost curve as given.

d. Sony's profit-maximization problem is:

$$\max_{Q} \pi = TR(Q) - TC(Q) = PQ - TC(Q) = (150 - 5Q)Q - \left(40Q + \frac{Q^2}{2}\right) = 110Q - 5.5Q^2$$

Taking the first-order condition gives

$$\frac{d\pi(Q)}{dQ} = \frac{d(110Q - 5.5Q^2)}{dQ} =$$
$$110 - 11Q = 0$$
$$Q = 10$$

At this quantity, price is: $P = 150 - 5(10) = 100$ as in parts (a) and (b).

e. We need to check the second-order condition for Sony. Here, $\frac{d_{\pi}}{dQ^2} = -11$. Since this is less than zero, we have verified that Sony is indeed maximizing profits.

Problem 4

a. To derive Canon's marginal revenue curve, recall that for any linear demand curve faced by a firm, the marginal revenue curve can be found as follows:

$$MR = a - 2bQ$$

Where a is the vertical intercept and b is the (negative) slope of the (inverse) demand curve. As we can see on the graph, $a = 800$. And we can calculate the slope of the demand curve between its vertical intercept and any point on the curve. For example, if we take the point where $Q = 8$ and $P = 640$, then b can be calculated as follows:

$$b = \frac{(800 - 640)}{8} = 20$$

Thus, Canon's marginal revenue curve is

$$MR = 800 - 2 \times 20Q$$
$$MR = 800 - 40Q$$

To graph this curve, we only need to know two points. The first point is the vertical intercept at $P = \$800$. And the second point can be, for example, where $Q = 16$, so $MR = 800 - 40 \times 16 = 160$. We can draw Canon's marginal revenue curve (MR on the following graph) by connecting these two points.

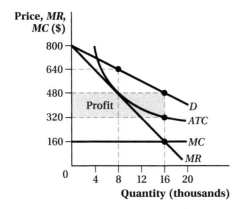

b. As we can see on the graph, the marginal revenue curve intersects the marginal cost curve (i.e., $MR = MC$) at the point where $Q = 16$. This means Canon's profit-maximizing level of output is 16,000 cameras.

c. As the demand curve faced by Canon shows, the quantity demanded is 16,000 when the price is \$480. Thus, to sell its profit-maximizing output, Canon should charge \$480 per camera.

d. As we can see on the graph, at the profit-maximizing level of output, Canon's average total cost is \$320. Thus, Canon's profit is

$$\pi = (P - ATC) \times Q$$
$$\pi = (\$480 - \$320) \times 16,000$$
$$\pi = \$2,560,000$$

Problem 5

a. To find the firm's profit-maximizing level of output, we need to know its marginal revenue curve, which can be derived from the inverse demand curve. We find the inverse demand curve by solving the demand equation for P:

$$Q = 12 - 2P$$
$$2P = 12 - Q$$
$$P = 6 - 0.5Q$$

In this inverse demand curve, $a = 6$ and $b = 0.5$, so the corresponding marginal revenue curve is

$$MR = a - 2bQ$$
$$MR = 6 - Q$$

To find Nature's Path's profit-maximizing level of output, we set $MR = MC$ and solve this equation for Q:

$$MR = MC$$
$$6 - Q = 1.6 + 0.1Q$$
$$1.1Q = 4.4$$
$$Q = 4$$

To find the firm's profit-maximizing price, we plug the profit-maximizing quantity ($Q = 4$) into the inverse demand curve:

$$P = 6 - 0.5Q$$
$$P = 6 - 0.5 \times 4$$
$$P = 4$$

Thus, before the increase in cost, Nature's Path's profit-maximizing level of output is 4 million boxes of oatmeal, and its profit-maximizing price is $4 per box.

Since the marginal cost has increased by $1.10 at every level of output, to derive Nature's Path's new marginal cost curve, we simply add $1.10 to the initial MC curve:

$$MC^* = MC + 1.1$$
$$MC^* = 1.6 + 0.1Q + 1.1$$
$$MC^* = 2.7 + 0.1Q$$

Now we can find the firm's profit-maximizing level of output after the increase in cost by equating the marginal revenue curve with the new marginal cost curve and solving this equation for Q:

$$MR = MC^*$$
$$6 - Q = 2.7 + 0.1Q$$
$$1.1Q = 3.3$$
$$Q = 3$$

To find Nature's Path's new profit-maximizing price, we plug the new profit-maximizing quantity ($Q = 3$) into the inverse demand curve:

$$P = 6 - 0.5 \times 3$$
$$P = 4.5$$

Thus, due to the higher marginal cost, Nature's Path's profit-maximizing level of output decreases from 4 million boxes of oatmeal to 3 million boxes, and its profit-maximizing price rises from $4 to $4.50 per box.

b. Initially, Nature's Path's profit maximizing price is $4 per box, and the marginal cost at the profit-maximizing level of output is $MC = 1.6 + 0.1 \times 4 = 2$ (dollars), so the markup is

$$\frac{P - MC}{P} = \frac{\$4 - \$2}{\$4} = 0.5$$

With the increased marginal cost, the firm's profit-maximizing price is $4.50, and the marginal cost at the profit maximizing level of output is $MC = 2.7 + 0.1 \times 3 = 3$ (dollars), so the markup is

$$\frac{P - MC}{P} = \frac{\$4.50 - \$3}{\$4.50} = 0.33$$

Thus, Nature's Path's markup decreases from 50% to 33%. That is, with the higher marginal cost, to maximize its profit, the firm has to reduce its markup rather than passing along the full increase in cost to consumers.

Problem 6

a. To calculate the consumer surplus, we first need to find Epson's profit-maximizing level of output and price. For that, we need to know the firm's marginal revenue curve, which can be derived from the inverse demand curve. We find the inverse demand curve by solving the demand curve faced by the firm for P:

$$Q = 24 - 0.2P$$
$$0.2P = 24 - Q$$
$$P = 120 - 5Q$$

In this inverse demand curve, $a = 120$ and $b = 5$, so the corresponding marginal revenue curve is

$$MR = a - 2bQ$$
$$MR = 120 - 10Q$$

To find Epson's profit-maximizing level of output, we set $MR = MC$ and solve this equation for Q:

$$MR = MC$$
$$120 - 10Q = 50$$
$$10Q = 70$$
$$Q = 7$$

To find Epson's profit-maximizing price, we plug the profit-maximizing quantity ($Q = 7$) into the inverse demand curve:

$$P = 120 - 5Q$$
$$P = 120 - 5 \times 7$$
$$P = 85$$

Thus, Epson's profit-maximizing level of output is 7 million scanners, and its profit-maximizing price is $85 per scanner. The following diagram illustrates this solution.

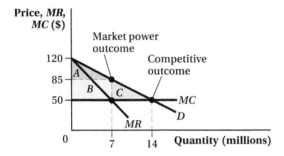

The consumer surplus is the area below the demand curve and above the price. As follows from the inverse demand curve, at $Q = 0$, $P = \$120$. Thus, the consumer surplus is the triangular area A on the graph, which can be calculated as

$$CS = 0.5 \times 7 \text{ million} \times (\$120 - \$85) = \$122.5 \text{ million}$$

b. The producer surplus is the area below the price and above the marginal cost curve up to the quantity sold. That is, Epson's producer surplus is area B, which can be calculated as:

$$PS = (\$85 - \$50) \times 7 \text{ million} = \$245 \text{ million}$$

c. To find the deadweight loss resulting from Epson's market power, we compare the consumer and producer surpluses found in the preceding parts with the consumer and producer surpluses that would be the case under perfect competition. If Epson behaved like a competitive firm, it would price its scanners at marginal cost, that is, at $50 per scanner. To see what quantity of scanners would be sold at this price, we first equate the inverse demand curve to the MC curve and solve this equation for Q:

$$P = MC$$
$$120 - 5Q = 50$$
$$5Q = 70$$
$$Q = 14$$

The consumer surplus under perfect competition would be the triangular area below the demand curve and above this price (area $A + B + C$), which can be calculated as

$$CS_C = 0.5 \times 14 \text{ million} \times (\$120 - \$50) = \$490 \text{ million}$$

And there would be no producer surplus, since all scanners would be sold at a price equal to the marginal cost. So, under perfect competition, the total surplus would be

$$TSc = CS_C = \$490 \text{ million}$$

While, under Epson's market power, it is

$$CS + PS = \$122.5 \text{ million} + \$245 \text{ million} = \$367.5 \text{ million}$$

The difference, \$490 million − \$367.5 million = \$122.5 million, is the deadweight loss resulting from Epson's market power. By charging a higher price and reducing output, Epson converts part of the consumer surplus (area B) into its producer surplus. But part of the consumer surplus (area C) is lost. This deadweight loss (triangular area C) can also be calculated directly as

$$DWL = 0.5 \times 7 \text{ million} \times (\$85 - \$50) = \$122.5 \text{ million}$$

Problem 7

a. To find Philips's initial profit-maximizing level of output, we need to know its marginal revenue curve, which can be derived from the inverse demand curve. To find the initial inverse demand curve, we solve the demand equation for P:

$$Q = 100 - 0.1P$$
$$0.1P = 100 - Q$$
$$P = 1,000 - 10Q$$

In this inverse demand curve, $a = 1,000$ and $b = 10$, so the corresponding marginal revenue curve is

$$MR = a - 2bQ$$
$$MR = 1,000 - 20Q$$

The following graph shows the initial demand curve faced by Philips (D_1) and the corresponding marginal revenue curve (MR_1). To find Philip's profit-maximizing level of output, we set $MR = MC$ and solve this equation for Q:

$$MR = MC$$
$$1,000 - 20Q = 400 + 10Q$$
$$30Q = 600$$
$$Q = 20$$

To find Philips's profit-maximizing price, we plug the profit-maximizing quantity ($Q = 20$) into the inverse demand curve:

$$P = 1,000 - 10Q$$
$$P = 1,000 - 10 \times 20$$
$$P = 800$$

Thus, initially, Philips's profit-maximizing level of output is 20 million TVs, and its profit-maximizing price is \$800 per TV set. The following diagram illustrates this solution (point A).

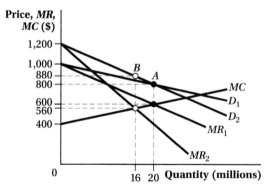

Now we need to find the inverse demand curve faced by Philips after the consumer preferences have changed, so we solve the new demand curve for P:

$$Q = 60 - 0.05P$$
$$0.05P = 60 - Q$$
$$P = 1,200 - 20Q$$

In this inverse demand curve, $a = 1{,}200$ and $b = 20$, so the corresponding marginal revenue curve is

$$MR = a - 2bQ$$
$$MR = 1{,}200 - 40Q$$

The new demand curve faced by Philips (D_2) and the corresponding marginal revenue curve (MR_2) are shown on the preceding graph. To find Philips's new profit-maximizing level of output, we set $MR = MC$ and solve this equation for Q:

$$MR = MC$$
$$1{,}200 - 40Q = 400 + 10Q$$
$$50Q = 800$$
$$Q = 16$$

To find Philips's new profit-maximizing price, we plug the profit-maximizing quantity $(Q = 16)$ into the new inverse demand curve:

$$P = 1{,}200 - 20Q$$
$$P = 1{,}200 - 20 \times 16$$
$$P = 880$$

Point B on the graph shows Philips's new profit-maximizing price-output choice. As we can see, the change in consumer preferences has decreased Philips's profit-maximizing level of output from 20 million to 16 million TV sets and has raised its profit-maximizing price from $800 to $880 per TV set.

b. The easiest way to find the price elasticity of demand for the Philips's new TV sets is to use the Lerner index equation:

$$\frac{P - MC}{P} = \frac{1}{E^D}$$

Before the change in consumer preferences, Philips's profit-maximizing price was $800, and the marginal cost at the profit-maximizing level of output was $MC = 400 + 10 \times 20 = 600$ (dollars), so the markup is

$$\frac{P - MC}{P} = \frac{\$800 - \$600}{\$800} = 0.25$$

Thus, we can write:

$$0.25 = \frac{1}{E^D}$$

Solving this equation for E^D, we get

$$-0.25E^D = 1$$
$$E^D = -4$$

After the change in consumer preferences, Philips's profit-maximizing price is $880, and the marginal cost at the profit-maximizing level of output is $MC = 400 + 10 \times 16 = 560$ (dollars), so the markup is

$$\frac{P - MC}{P} = \frac{\$880 - \$560}{\$880} = 0.364$$

So, we can write:

$$0.364 = -\frac{1}{E^D}$$

Solving this equation for E^D, we get

$$-0.364E^D = 1$$
$$E^D = -2.75$$

Thus, the price elasticity of demand for the Philips's new TVs (i.e., the absolute value of the elasticity number) has decreased from 4.00 to 2.75. Since consumer preferences for Philips's new TV sets have changed favorably, consumers are less willing to switch to a substitute as Philips raises its price.

c. A firm's market power can be measured by the Lerner index. The higher it is, the greater is the firm's ability to price above its marginal cost. As calculated in (b), the Lerner index for Philips is initially 0.25. And after the consumer preferences have changed, the Lerner index rises to 0.364. This means Philips's market power has increased.

Problem 8

a. We can find Sargento's profit-maximizing price, using the Lerner index equation:

$$\frac{P - MC}{P} = -\frac{1}{E^D}$$

Given that $MC = \$3$, and $E^D = -4$, we can write:

$$\frac{P - 3}{P} = -\frac{1}{-4}$$

$$\frac{P - 3}{P} = \frac{1}{4}$$

Solving this equation for P, we get

$$4P - 12 = P$$
$$3P = 12$$
$$P = 4$$

Thus, to maximize its profit, Sargento should charge $4 per pound.

b. Using the Lerner index equation, we can write:

$$\frac{3.80 - 3}{3.80} = -\frac{1}{E^D}$$

$$\frac{0.80}{3.80} = -\frac{1}{E^D}$$

Solving this equation for E^D, we get

$$0.8E^D = -3.80$$
$$E^D = -4.75$$

Thus, the price elasticity of demand for Kraft Swiss cheese is -4.75.

Problem 9

a. To calculate the consumer surplus, we need to find Horizon's profit-maximizing level of output and price. And to apply the profit-maximizing condition, $MR = MC$, we need to know the firm's marginal revenue curve, which can be derived from the inverse demand curve. We find the inverse demand curve by solving the demand equation for P:

$$Q = 170 - 20P$$
$$20P = 170 - Q$$
$$P = 8.5 - 0.05Q$$

In this inverse demand curve, $a = 8.5$ and $b = 0.05$, so the corresponding marginal revenue curve is

$$MR = a - 2bQ$$
$$MR = 8.5 - 0.1Q$$

To find Horizon's profit-maximizing level of output, we set $MR = MC$ and solve this equation for Q:

$$MR = MC$$
$$8.5 - 0.1Q = 7 + 0.025Q$$
$$0.125Q = 1.5$$
$$Q = 12$$

To find Horizon's profit-maximizing price, we plug the profit-maximizing quantity ($Q = 12$) into the inverse demand curve:

$$P = 8.5 - 0.05Q$$
$$P = 8.5 - 0.05 \times 12$$
$$P = 7.9$$

Thus, Horizon's profit-maximizing level of output is 12 million gallons of milk, and its profit-maximizing price is $7.90 per gallon. The following diagram illustrates this solution.

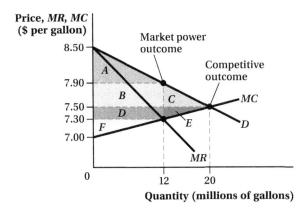

The consumer surplus is the area below the demand curve and above the price. As follows from the inverse demand curve, at $Q = 0$, $P = \$8.50$. Thus, the consumer surplus is the triangular area A on the graph, which can be calculated as

$$CS = 0.5 \times 12 \text{ million} \times (\$8.50 - \$7.90) = \$3.6 \text{ million}$$

b. The producer surplus is the area below the price and above the marginal cost curve up to the quantity sold. That is, Horizon's producer surplus is area $(B + D + F)$. Given that at the profit-maximizing quantity $MC = 7 - 0.025 \times 12 = 7.3$ (dollars), we can calculate the rectangular area $B + D$ as follows:

$$(\text{Area } B + D) = (\$7.90 - \$7.30) \times 12 \text{ million} = \$7.2 \text{ million}$$

And given that at $Q = 0$, $MC = \$7$, we can calculate the triangular area F as

$$\text{Area } F = 0.5 \times (\$7.3 - \$7) \times 12 \text{ million} = \$1.8 \text{ million}$$

So the producer surplus is

$$PS = \$7.2 \text{ million} + \$1.8 \text{ million} = \$9 \text{ million}$$

c. To find the deadweight loss from Horizon's market power, we compare the consumer and producer surpluses found in the preceding parts with the consumer and producer surpluses that would exist under perfect competition. If Horizon behaved like a competitive firm, it would price its milk at marginal cost. To see how much milk Horizon would sell at the competitive price, we equate the inverse demand curve to the MC curve and solve this equation for Q:

$$P = MC$$
$$8.5 - 0.05Q = 7 + 0.025Q$$
$$0.075Q = 1.5$$
$$Q = 20$$

Now we plug this quantity into the inverse demand curve to find the competitive price:

$$P = 8.5 - 0.05Q$$
$$P = 8.5 - 0.05 \times 20$$
$$P = 7.5$$

The consumer surplus under perfect competition would be the triangular area below the demand curve and above this price (area $A + B + C$), which can be calculated as

$$CS_C = 0.5 \times 20 \text{ million} \times (\$8.50 - \$7.50) = \$10 \text{ million}$$

And the producer surplus would be the triangle above the marginal cost curve and below the competitive price (area $D + E + F$), which can be calculated as

$$PS_C = 0.5 \times 20 \text{ million} \times (\$7.50 - \$7) = \$5 \text{ million}$$

So, under perfect competition the total surplus would be

$$CS_C + PS_C = \$10 \text{ million} + \$5 \text{ million} = \$15 \text{ million}$$

While, under market power, it is

$$CS + PS = \$3.6 \text{ million} + \$9 \text{ million} = \$12.6 \text{ million}$$

The difference, \$15 million – \$12.6 million = \$2.4 million, is the deadweight loss from Horizon's market power. By charging a higher price and reducing output, Horizon converts part of the consumer surplus (area B) into its producer surplus. But part of the consumer surplus (area C) and part of the producer surplus (area E) are lost. This deadweight loss (triangular area $C + E$) can also be calculated directly as

$$\text{DWL} = 0.5 \times (\$7.90 - \$7.30) \times (20 \text{ million} - 12 \text{ million}) = \$2.4 \text{ million}$$

d. Here,

$$CS = \int_0^{12}\big((8.5 - 0.05Q) - 7.9)\big)dQ = \int_0^{12}(0.6 - 0.05Q)dQ = \int_0^{12} 0.6dQ - \int_0^{12} 0.05QdQ$$

$$= [0.6Q]_0^{12} - \left[\frac{0.05Q^2}{2}\right]_0^{12}$$

$$= [0.6(12) - 0.6(0)] - \left[\frac{0.05(12)^2}{2} - \frac{0.05(0)^2}{2}\right]$$

$$= (7.2 - 0) - (3.6 - 0) = 3.6. \text{ This corresponds exactly to, in part (a), consumer}$$
surplus (to scale \$3.6 million).

e. $PS = \int_0^{12}\big(7.9 - (7 + 0.025Q)\big)dQ = \int_0^{15}(0.9 - 0.025Q)dQ = \int_0^{12} 0.9dQ - \int_0^{12} 0.025QdQ$

$$= [0.9Q]_0^{12} - \left[\frac{0.025Q^2}{2}\right]_0^{12}$$

$$= [0.9(12) - 0.9(0)] - \left[\frac{0.025(12)^2}{2} - \frac{0.025(0)^2}{2}\right]$$

$$= (10.8 - 0) - (1.8 - 0) = 9. \text{ This corresponds exactly to, in part (b), producer surplus}$$
(to scale \$9 million).

f. Here,

$$\text{DWL} = \int_{12}^{20}\big((8.5 - 0.05Q) - (7 + 0.025Q)\big)dQ = \int_{12}^{20}(1.5 - 0.075Q)dQ = \int_{12}^{20}1.5dQ - \int_{12}^{20}0.075QdQ$$

$$= [1.5Q]_{12}^{20} - \left[\frac{0.075Q^2}{2}\right]_{12}^{20}$$

$$= [1.5(20) - 1.5(12)] - \left[\frac{0.075(20)^2}{2} - \frac{0.075(12)^2}{2}\right]$$

$$= (30 - 18) - (15 - 5.4) = 12 - 9.6 = 2.4. \text{ This corresponds exactly to, in part (c),}$$
deadweight loss (to scale \$2.4 million).

Problem 10

a. To find the company's profit-maximizing level of output, we first derive its marginal revenue curve from the inverse demand curve. We find the inverse demand curve by solving the demand equation for P:

$$Q = 100 - 5P$$
$$5P = 100 - Q$$
$$P = 20 - 0.2Q$$

In this inverse demand curve, $a = 20$ and $b = 0.2$, so the corresponding marginal revenue curve is

$$MR = a - 2bQ$$
$$MR = 20 - 0.4Q$$

To find the company's profit-maximizing level of output, we set $MR = MC$ and solve this equation for Q:

$$MR = MC$$
$$20 - 0.4Q = 4$$
$$0.4Q = 16$$
$$Q = 40$$

To find the firm's profit-maximizing price, we plug the profit-maximizing quantity ($Q = 4$) into the inverse demand curve:

$$P = 20 - 0.2Q$$
$$P = 20 - 0.2 \times 40$$
$$P = 12$$

When the company produces its profit-maximizing output, its long-run average total cost is

$$LATC = \frac{140}{Q} + 4$$
$$LATC = \frac{140}{40} + 4$$
$$LATC = 7.5$$

so the company's economic profit is

$$\pi = (P - ATC) \times Q$$
$$\pi = (\$0.12 - \$0.075) \times 40 \text{ million}$$
$$\pi = \$1.8 \text{ million}$$

This solution is shown on the following graph. The company charges $0.12 per kWh and produces 40 million kilowatt-hours of electricity (point m), making an economic profit of $1.8 million (area B).

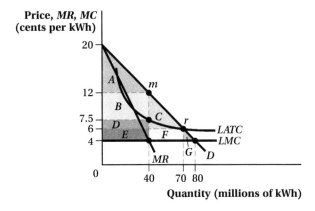

b. The consumer surplus is the area below the demand curve and above the price. As follows from the inverse demand curve, at $Q = 0$, $P = \$20$. Thus, the consumer surplus is the triangular area A on the graph, which can be calculated as

$$CS = 0.5 \times 40 \text{ million} \times (\$0.20 - \$0.12) = \$1.6 \text{ million}$$

The producer surplus is the area below the price and above the marginal cost curve up to the quantity sold. That is, the company's producer surplus is (area $B + D + E$), which can be calculated as:

$$PS = (\$0.12 - \$0.04) \times 40 \text{ million} = \$3.2 \text{ million}$$

To find the deadweight loss resulting from the company's market power, we compare the consumer and producer surpluses found in the preceding parts with the consumer and producer surpluses that would be the case under perfect competition. If the company behaved like a competitive firm, it would price electricity at the marginal cost, that is, at 4 cents per kWh. To see how much electricity would be sold at this price, we equate the inverse demand curve to the MC curve and solve this equation for Q:

$$P = MC$$
$$20 - 0.2Q = 4$$
$$0.2Q = 16$$
$$Q = 80$$

The consumer surplus under perfect competition would be the triangular area below the demand curve and above this competitive price, i.e., (area $A + B + C + D + E + F + G$), which can be calculated as

$$CS_C = 0.5 \times 80 \text{ million} \times (\$0.20 - \$0.04) = \$6.4 \text{ million}$$

And there would be no producer surplus, since all the electricity is sold at the price equal to the marginal cost. Thus, under perfect competition the total surplus would be

$$TS_C = CS_C = \$6.4 \text{ million}$$

while under market power it is

$$CS + PS = \$1.6 \text{ million} + \$3.2 \text{ million} = \$4.8 \text{ million}$$

The difference, $6.4 million – $4.8 million = $1.6 million, is the deadweight loss resulting from the company's market power. This deadweight loss, triangular area $(C + F + G)$, can also be calculated directly as

$$\text{DWL} = 0.5 \times (80 \text{ million} - 40 \text{ million}) \times (\$0.12 - \$0.04) = \$1.6 \text{ million}$$

c. Since the price cap is below the company's profit-maximizing price, it is binding, so the actual price of electricity will be 6 cents per kWh. And, given the demand curve faced by the company, if it charges this price, it will sell

$$Q = 100 - 5P$$
$$Q = 100 - 5 \times 6$$
$$Q = 70 \text{ million kWh}$$

At this level of output, the company's long-run average total cost is

$$LATC = \frac{140}{70} + 4$$
$$LATC = 6 \text{ cents per kWh}$$

which is the same as the price. Since $LATC = P$, the company's economic profit is zero. This solution is shown on the preceding graph (point r).

d. With the price cap, the consumer surplus is the area below the demand curve and above the price of 6 cents per kWh, that is, the (triangular area $A + B + C + D$) on the graph, which can be calculated as

$$CS = 0.5 \times 70 \text{ million} \times (\$0.20 - \$0.06) = \$4.9 \text{ million}$$

Thus, the price cap increases the consumer surplus from $1.6 million to $4.9 million.

The producer surplus is the area below the price and above the marginal cost curve up to the quantity sold. That is, the company's producer surplus is (area $E + F$), which can be calculated as:

$$PS = 70 \text{ million} \times (\$0.06 - \$0.04) = \$1.4 \text{ million}$$

Thus, the price cap reduces the company's producer surplus from $3.2 million to $1.4 million.

To find the deadweight loss, we compare the consumer and producer surpluses found in the preceding parts with the consumer and producer surpluses that would be the case under perfect competition. With the price cap, the total surplus is

$$CS + PS = \$4.9 \text{ million} + \$1.4 \text{ million} = \$6.3 \text{ million}$$

And as we've found in (c), under perfect competition the total surplus would be $6.4 million. The difference, $6.4 million – $6.3 million = $0.1 million, is the deadweight loss. This deadweight loss, (triangular area G), can also be calculated directly as

$$\text{DWL} = 0.5 \times (80 \text{ million} - 70 \text{ million}) \times (\$0.06 - \$0.04) = \$0.1 \text{ million}$$

Thus, the price cap reduces the deadweight loss from $1.6 million to $0.1 million.

Problem 11

a. In the Figure It Out exercise, we found that price was \$9,500 and quantity was 50 (50,000 units). Consumer surplus is

$$CS = \int_0^{50}\big((9{,}000 + 60Q - Q^2) - 9{,}500\big)dQ = \int_0^{50}(-500 + 60Q - Q^2)dQ = \int_0^{50} -500\,dQ + \int_0^{50} 60Q\,dQ - \int_0^{50} Q^2\,dQ$$

$$= [-500Q]_0^{50} + [30Q^2]_0^{50} - \left[\frac{Q^3}{3}\right]_0^{50}$$

$$= [-500(50) - (-500(0))] + [30(50)^2 - 30(0)^2] - \left[\frac{(50)^3}{3} - \frac{(0)^3}{3}\right]$$

$$= (-25{,}000 - 0) + (75{,}000) - (41{,}666.67 - 0) = 8{,}333.33.$$ This corresponds to approximately \$8.33 million.

b. Recall that we want to integrate between price and marginal cost. Marginal cost here is the derivative of total cost or 7,500. Producer surplus is

$$PS = \int_0^{50}(9{,}500 - 7{,}500)dQ = \int_0^{50}(2{,}000)dQ$$

$$= [2{,}000Q]_0^{50}$$

$$= [2{,}000(50) - 2{,}000(0)]$$

$$= (100{,}000 - 0) = 100{,}000.$$ This corresponds to \$100 million.

Market Power and Pricing Strategies

10

Solutions for Practice Problems

Problem 1

a. If the airline charges the same price for all tickets, its profit-maximizing number of tickets is where its marginal revenue equals marginal cost. As shown on the following graph, $MR = MC$ when the company sells 3,200 tickets. As the demand curve faced by the airline shows, the company will sell this profit-maximizing quantity of tickets if it charges $240 per ticket.

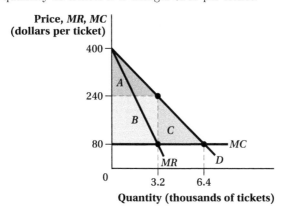

b. The consumer surplus is the area below the demand curve and above the price (area A on the graph), which can be calculated as

$$CS = 0.5 \times (\$400 - \$240) \times 3,200 = \$256,000$$

The company's producer surplus is the area below the price and above the marginal cost curve up to the quantity sold (area B), which is

$$PS = (\$240 - \$80) \times 3,200 = \$512,000$$

Thus, the total market surplus is

$$TS = CS + PS$$
$$TS = \$256,000 + \$512,000 = \$768,000$$

To find the deadweight loss from the airline's market power, we compare the consumer and producer surpluses found in the preceding with the consumer and producer surpluses that would exist under perfect competition. If the airline behaved like a competitive firm, it would price the tickets at marginal cost ($80 per ticket). As the demand curve on the graph shows, at this price 6,400 tickets would be sold, so the consumer surplus would be the (area $A + B + C$):

$$CS_C = 0.5 \times (\$400 - \$80) \times 6,400 = \$1,024,000$$

And there would be no producer surplus under perfect competition, since all tickets would be sold at marginal cost. So the total surplus in the market would be equal to the consumer surplus ($1,024,000). The difference between this surplus and the total surplus under the airline's market power, $1,024,000 − $768,000 = $256,000, is the deadweight loss from the company's market power. This deadweight loss (area C) can also be calculated directly as

$$DWL = 0.5 \times (\$240 - \$80) \times (6,400 - 3,200) = \$256,000$$

c. If the airline practices perfect price discrimination, it charges every customer a price equal to his willingness to pay. Thus, the airline will sell all tickets for which customers are willing to pay, at least the marginal cost, that is, 6,400 tickets. In this case, the consumer surplus will be zero because every consumer is charged a price equal to his willingness to pay. The producer surplus will be the whole triangular area below the demand curve and above the marginal cost curve (area $A + B + C$), since for every ticket sold, the price paid by the customer equals his willingness to pay. Thus, the airline captures the whole amount of available surplus, which equals the total surplus under perfect competition calculated in (b), $1,024,000. Since as a result of perfect price discrimination the company will sell the competitive quantity of tickets, there will be no deadweight loss.

Problem 2

a. We can use the Lerner index to find the profit-maximizing price of ice cream in each location:

$$\frac{P - MC}{P} = \frac{1}{-E^D}$$

For the city shop, we can write:

$$\frac{P - 1.50}{P} = \frac{1}{-(-4)}$$
$$4P - 6 = P$$
$$3P = 6$$
$$P = 2$$

And for the parlor in the small town,

$$\frac{P - 1.50}{P} = \frac{1}{-(-2)}$$
$$2P - 3 = P$$
$$P = 3$$

Thus, to maximize your profit, you should charge $2 per scoop in the city and $3 per scoop in the small town.

b. Because the demand you face in the small town is relatively less elastic than the demand you face in the city (i.e., the absolute value of the price elasticity of demand is lower), you are able to charge a higher price in the small town without losing as many customers as you would in the city.

Problem 3

To find the profit-maximizing prices, we derive the marginal revenue curves separately for the full version and for the upgrade version and solve for the profit-maximizing price for each segment of the market. First, we find each segment's inverse demand curve:

Full version:	Upgrade:
$Q_F = 400 - 10P_F$	$Q_U = 320 - 20P_U$
$10P_F = 400 - Q_F$	$20P_U = 320 - Q_U$
$P_F = 40 - 0.1Q_F$	$P_U = 16 - 0.05Q_U$

We know that the marginal revenue curve is the inverse demand curve, with the coefficient on quantity twice as large. Thus, the marginal revenue curves for the two segments are

Full version:	Upgrade:
$MR_F = 40 - 0.2Q_F$	$MR_U = 16 - 0.1Q_U$

PC Tools wants to sell the quantities at which its marginal cost ($4) equals its marginal revenue. Setting each marginal revenue above equal to marginal cost tells us the optimal quantity sold in each segment:

Full version:	Upgrade:
$MR_F = MC$	$MR_U = MC$
$40 - 0.2Q_F = 4$	$16 - 0.1Q = 4$
$0.2Q_F = 36$	$0.1Q = 12$
$Q_F = 180$	$Q_U = 120$

The last step is to find the prices at which the company can sell these quantities by plugging the quantities into the inverse demand curve:

Full version:	Upgrade:
$P_F = 40 - 0.1Q_F$	$P_U = 16 - 0.05Q_U$
$P_F = 40 - 0.1 \times 180$	$P_U = 16 - 0.05 \times 120$
$P_F = 22$	$P_U = 10$

Thus, PC Tools should charge $22 per copy for the full version and $10 per copy for the upgrade version. The following graph illustrates this solution.

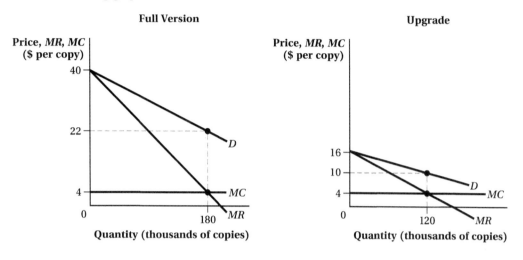

Problem 4

Students should be given a discount because their demand for haircuts is more elastic than that of other customers (i.e., students are more price sensitive), while the barbershop's marginal cost of a haircut is the same whatever type of customer it serves. To find out how big the discount should be, recall that—as shown in the text (Chapter 10, p. 409)—the Lerner index implies that for the barbershop to maximize its profit, the ratio of the prices in the two segments must be

$$\frac{P_S}{P_O} = \frac{\dfrac{E_S^D}{(1 + E_S^D)}}{\dfrac{E_O^D}{(1 + E_O^D)}}$$

where P_S is the price charged to students, P_O is the price charged to other customers, E_S^D is the price elasticity of students' demand, and E_O^D is the price elasticity of other customers' demand. Plugging the estimated elasticities into this formula, we get:

$$\frac{P_S}{P_O} = \frac{\dfrac{-3}{(1 - 3)}}{\dfrac{-2}{(1 - 2)}}$$

$$\frac{P_S}{P_O} = \frac{1.5}{2}$$

Thus, the student discount should be

$$\frac{P_O - P_S}{P_O} = \frac{2 - 1.5}{2} = 0.25$$

That is, students should get 25% off the regular price.

Problem 5

a. First, we need to find the market demand curve faced by the concert hall, which can be calculated as the horizontal sum of the demand curve for evening shows and the demand curve for afternoon shows:

$$Q = Q_E + Q_A$$
$$Q = (40 - 0.8P) + (24 - 0.8P)$$
$$Q = 64 - 1.6P$$

We should be aware, however, of the demand choke price for each segment (i.e., the price at which the quantity demanded is zero). For evening shows:

$$Q_E = 40 - 0.8P$$
$$0 = 40 - 0.8P$$
$$0.8P = 40$$
$$P = 50$$

And for the afternoon shows:

$$Q_A = 24 - 0.8P$$
$$0 = 24 - 0.8P$$
$$0.8P = 24$$
$$P = 30$$

That is, the demand choke price is $50 for evening shows and $30 for afternoon shows. Therefore, the market demand curve (D on the following graph) is kinked. In the price range between $50 and $30, it is the same as the demand curve for evening shows. And at $30 and below, it is the market demand curve calculated in the preceding.

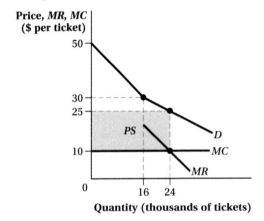

To find the concert hall's profit-maximizing price, we need to know its marginal revenue curve, which can be derived from the inverse demand curve. For the part of the market demand curve that is below the kink, we find the inverse demand curve as follows:

$$Q = 64 - 1.6P$$
$$1.6P = 64 - Q$$
$$P = 40 - 0.625Q$$

In this inverse demand curve, $a = 40$ and $b = 0.625$, so the corresponding marginal revenue curve is

$$MR = a - 2bQ$$
$$MR = 40 - 1.25Q$$

To find the profit-maximizing number of tickets sold, we set $MR = MC$ and solve this equation for Q:

$$40 - 1.25Q = 10$$
$$1.25Q = 30$$
$$Q = 24$$

From the inverse demand curve, we can calculate the price at which the theater can sell this quantity of tickets:

$$P = 40 - 0.625Q$$
$$P = 40 - 0.625 \times 24$$
$$P = 25$$

This price is on the part of the demand curve below the kink, so the demand and marginal revenue curves we have used to find the profit-maximizing quantity are the ones that are relevant. Thus, when the concert hall charges the same price to all customers, its profit-maximizing price is $25 per ticket, and it sells 24,000 tickets at this price. The preceding graph illustrates this solution.

The concert hall's producer surplus is the area below the price and above the marginal cost curve up to the quantity of tickets sold. This area can be calculated as follows:

$$PS = 24{,}000 \times (\$25 - \$10) = \$360{,}000$$

b. To find the profit-maximizing prices, we derive the marginal revenue curves separately for evening and afternoon shows and solve for the profit-maximizing price for each segment of the market. First, we find each segment's inverse demand curve:

Evening:	Afternoon:
$Q_E = 40 - 0.8P$	$Q_A = 24 - 0.8P$
$0.8P = 40 - Q_E$	$0.8P = 24 - Q_E$
$P_E = 50 - 1.25Q$	$P_A = 30 - 1.25Q$

We know that the marginal revenue curve is the inverse demand curve with the coefficient on quantity twice as large. Thus, the marginal revenue curves for the two segments are

Evening:	Afternoon:
$MR_E = 50 - 2.5Q$	$MR_A = 30 - 2.5Q$

The concert hall wants to sell the quantities at which its marginal cost ($10) equals its marginal revenue. Setting each marginal revenue curve in the preceding equal to marginal cost tells us the optimal number of tickets sold in each segment:

Evening:	Afternoon:
$MR_E = MC$	$MR_A = MC$
$50 - 2.5Q = 10$	$30 - 2.5Q = 10$
$2.5Q = 40$	$2.5Q = 20$
$Q_E = 16$	$Q_A = 8$

Now, we can find the ticket prices at which the concert hall can sell these quantities by plugging the quantities into the inverse demand curves:

Evening:	Afternoon:
$P_E = 50 - 1.25Q$	$P_A = 30 - 1.25Q$
$P_E = 50 - 2.5Q \times 16$	$P_A = 30 - 1.25 \times 8$
$P_E = 30$	$P_A = 20$

Thus, the concert hall should charge $30 per ticket for an evening show and $20 per ticket for an afternoon show. The following graph illustrates this solution.

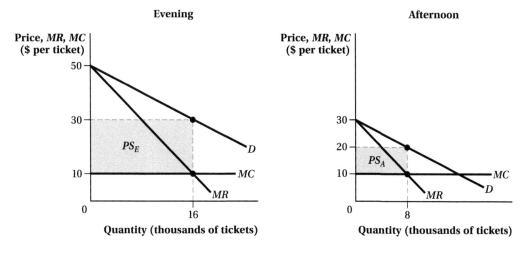

The concert hall's producer surplus is the difference between the price and the marginal cost for each segment times the number of tickets sold to that segment:

<table>
<tr><td align="center">**Evening:**</td><td align="center">**Afternoon:**</td></tr>
<tr><td align="center">$PS_E = (\$30 - \$10) \times 16{,}000$</td><td align="center">$PS_O = (\$20 - \$10) \times 8{,}000$</td></tr>
<tr><td align="center">$PS_E = \$320{,}000$</td><td align="center">$PS_O = \$80{,}000$</td></tr>
</table>

Therefore, the combined producer surplus from the two segments is

$$PS = \$320{,}000 + \$80{,}000 = \$400{,}000$$

Thus, the concert hall's price discrimination by segmenting increases its producer surplus from $360,000 to $400,000.

Problem 6

a. An amateur photographer gets $220 − $200 = $20 of consumer surplus from buying the full version and $120 − $80 = $40 of consumer surplus from buying Photoshop Elements, so he will choose Elements. A professional photographer gets $300 − $200 = $100 of consumer surplus from buying the full version and $140 − $80 = $60 of consumer surplus from buying Elements, so she will choose the full version. Thus, each group chooses the version designed to take advantage of the shape of its demand curve, which means these prices are incentive-compatible.

b. As shown in (a), Adobe's price scheme is incentive-compatible, so each group will choose the version of software that is intended for it. That is, the amateurs will buy 0.5 million copies of Elements, so Adobe will earn a producer surplus of ($80 − $10) × 0.5 million = $35 million. And the professionals will buy 0.5 million copies of the full Photoshop, so Adobe's producer surplus will be ($200 − $10) × 0.5 million = $95 million. Thus, Adobe's total producer surplus from selling the software will be $35 million + $95 million = $130 million.

c. If Adobe raises the price of the full version to $250, a professional will get only $300 − $250 = $50 of consumer surplus from buying it, which is less than the consumer surplus she gets from buying Elements ($60). Therefore, professionals will choose Elements and not the full version of Photoshop intended for them. That is, the new price of Photoshop is not incentive-compatible for professionals. As a result, all customers will buy Elements, and Adobe's producer surplus will fall from $130 to ($80 − $10) × 1 million = $70 million.

d. Since a professional is now willing to pay $190 for Elements, her consumer surplus from buying it is $190 − $80 = $110, which is more than her consumer surplus from buying the full version ($100). So professionals will choose Elements and not the full version of Photoshop intended for them. That is, the prices now are not incentive-compatible for professionals. Therefore, as in (c), all customers will buy Elements, and Adobe's producer surplus will fall from $130 to $70 million.

Problem 7

a. To find Netflix's profit-maximizing price, we need to know the firm's marginal revenue curve, which can be derived from the inverse demand curve. And to find the inverse demand curve, we solve the demand equation for P:

$$Q = 20 - 10P$$
$$10P = 20 - Q$$
$$P = 2 - 0.1Q$$

The marginal revenue curve is the inverse demand curve, with the coefficient on quantity twice as large. Thus, the firm's marginal revenue curve is:

$$MR = 2 - 0.2Q$$

Now we can find the profit-maximizing quantity by setting $MR = MC$ and solving for Q:

$$2 - 0.2Q = 0.4$$
$$0.2Q = 1.6$$
$$Q = 8$$

By plugging this quantity into the inverse demand curve, we can find the profit-maximizing price:

$$P = 2 - 0.1Q$$
$$P = 2 - 0.1 \times 8$$
$$P = 1.20$$

Thus, with single pricing, Netflix's profit-maximizing price is \$1.20 per D\
on the following graph.

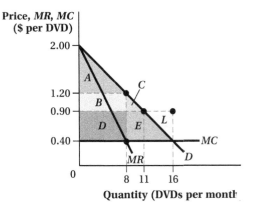

The company's producer surplus is the area above the marginal cost curve and below the den
curve up to the quantity sold (area $B + D$ on the preceding graph), which is

$$PS = (\$1.20 - \$0.40) \times 8 = \$6.40$$

b. With plan (1), consumers pay $\dfrac{\$9.60}{8} = \$1.20$ per DVD (i.e., the same price as in (a)). The consumer
surplus then is the area below the demand curve and above this price (area A on the preceding graph).
With plan (2), consumers pay $\dfrac{\$14.40}{16} = \$0.90$ per DVD. According to the demand curve, the quantity
of DVDs that consumers want to rent at this price is:

$$Q = 20 - 10P$$
$$Q = 20 - 10 \times 0.9$$
$$Q = 11$$

Thus, the consumer surplus increases by (area $B + C$), which is a trapezoid with a longer base of 11,
a shorter base of 8, and height of \$0.30, so

$$(\text{Area } B + C) = 0.5 \times (11 + 8) \times \$0.30 = \$2.85$$

But consumers also lose surplus because to be able to rent DVDs at the discount price, they have to
rent more DVDs than they want to at \$0.90 per DVD. This loss of consumer surplus is the area below
this price and above the demand curve up to the quantity of DVDs rented (area L), which is

$$\text{Area } L = 0.5 \times (\$0.90 - \$0.40) \times (16 - 11) = \$1.25$$

Since the gain in consumer surplus (\$2.85) exceeds the loss (\$1.25), consumers will choose option (2).
Then, Netflix's producer surplus will be the area below the price of \$0.90 per DVD and above the
marginal cost up to the quantity of DVDs rented (area $D + E + L$), which is

$$PS = (\$0.90 - \$0.40) \times 16 = \$8$$

Thus, a block pricing structure allows Netflix to increase its producer surplus from \$6.40 to \$8 per
customer per month.

c. For a block-pricing structure with two different prices, we will first decompose total revenue from
each price tier. Total revenue from the high-price (ordinary-customer) tier is

$$TR_1 = TR(P_1) = P_1 \times Q(P_1) = P_1(20 - 10P_1) = 20P_1 - 10P_1^2$$

Excess demand for output at the lower-price tier is

$$Q_2 = 20 - 10P_2 - Q_1(P_1)$$
$$Q_2 = 20 - 10P_2 - (20 - 10P_1)$$
$$Q_2 = 10P_1 - 10P_2$$

Total revenue from this lower-price tier is

$$TR_2 = P_2 \times Q(P_2) = P_2(10P_1 - 10P_2) = 10P_1P_2 - 10P_2^2$$

Netflix's combined total revenue function is

$$TR = 20P_1 - 10P_1^2 + 10P_1P_2 - 10P_2^2$$

total production cost for output associated with tier-one pricing is

$$TC_1 = \int_0^{20-10P_1} 0.4 dQ = [0.4Q]_0^{20-10P_1}$$

$$= 0.4(20 - 10P_1) - 0.4(0) = 8 - 4P_1$$

Netflix's total production cost for output associated with tier-two pricing is

$$TC_2 = \int_{20-10P_1}^{20-10P_1+10P_1-10P_2} 0.4 dQ = \int_{20-10P_1}^{20-10P_2} 0.4 dQ = [0.4Q]_{20-10P_1}^{20-10P_2}$$

$$= 0.4(20 - 10P_2) - 0.4(20 - 10P_1)$$

$$= 8 - 4P_2 - 4 + 4P_1$$

$$= 4P_1 - 4P_2$$

Netflix's total production cost for producing output across both pricing blocks is

$$TC = 8 - 4P_1 + 4P_1 - 4P_2$$

$$= 8 - 4P_2$$

The block pricing monopoly producer surplus is

$$PS = TR - TC = 20P_1 - 10P_1^2 + 10P_1P_2 - 10P_2^2 - 8 + 4P_2$$

Netflix's objective is to choose P_1 and P_2 that maximizes PS. The relevant system of first-order conditions is

$$0 = \frac{\partial PS}{\partial P_1} = 20 - 20P_1 + 10P_2$$

$$0 = \frac{\partial PS}{\partial P_2} = 10P_1 - 20P_2 + 4$$

Using the first of these first-order conditions, we may solve for P_1. This produces

$$P_1 = 1 + 0.5P_2$$

Inserting the right-hand side of this statement for P_1 into the second of the first-order conditions, and solving for P_2, we have

$$0 = 10(1 + 0.5P_2) - 20P_2 + 4$$

$$0 = 10 + 5P_2 - 20P_2 + 4$$

$$15P_2 = 14$$

$$P_2 \approx 0.93$$

Thus,

$$P_1 = 1 + 0.5(0.93) \approx 1.47$$

The corresponding block-one output is $Q_1 = 20 - 10P_1 = 20 - 10(1.47) = 5.3$. The block-two output is $Q_2 = 20 - 10P_2 - Q_1(P_1) = 20 - 10(0.93) - 5.3 = 5.4$.

d. Producer surplus is $PS = 20P_1 - 10P_1^2 + 10P_1P_2 - 10P_2^2 - 8 + 4P_2 = 20(1.47) - 10(1.47)^2 + 10(1.47)(0.93) - 10(0.93)^2 - 8 + 4(0.93) \approx 8.53$.

The inverse demand curve is $P = 2 - 0.1Q$. Consumer surplus then is

$$CS = \int_0^{5.3}(2 - 0.1Q - 1.47)dQ + \int_{5.3}^{5.3+5.4}(2 - 0.1Q - 0.93)dQ$$

$$= \int_0^{5.3}(0.53 - 0.1Q)dQ + \int_{5.3}^{10.7}(1.07 - 0.1Q)dQ$$

$$= [0.53Q]_0^{5.3} - \left[\frac{0.1Q^2}{2}\right]_0^{5.3} + [1.07Q]_{5.3}^{10.7} - \left[\frac{0.1Q^2}{2}\right]_{5.3}^{10.7}$$

$$= [0.53Q]_0^{5.3} - [0.05Q^2]_0^{5.3} + [1.07Q]_{5.3}^{10.7} - [0.05Q^2]_{5.3}^{10.7}$$

$$= [0.53(5.3) - 0.53(0)] - [0.05(5.3)^2 - 0.05(0)^2] + [1.07(10.7) - 1.07(5.3)]$$

$$- [0.05(10.7)^2 - 0.05(5.3)^2]$$

$$= (2.81 - 0) - (1.40 - 0) + (11.45 - 5.67) - (5.72 - 1.40)$$

$$= 2.87$$

Total surplus in the market with block pricing (with two-tier pricing) is $8.53 + 2.87 = \$11.40$.

Problem 8

As shown in the text (Chapter 10, p. 15), the Lerner index implies that for the firm to maximize its profit, the ratio of the prices in the two segments must be

$$\frac{P_S}{P_O} = \frac{[E_S^D/(1 + E_S^D)] \times MC_S}{[E_O^D/(1 + E_O^D)] \times MC_O}$$

where P_S is the price the restaurant charges to senior citizens, P_O is the price it charges to other customers, E_S^D is the price elasticity of seniors' demand, E_O^D is the price elasticity of other customers' demand, MC_S is the marginal cost of serving seniors, and MC_O is the marginal cost of serving other customers. You know that $MC_S = 1.5 \times MC_O$, so using your elasticity estimates, you can write:

$$\frac{P_S}{P_O} = \frac{[-4/(1 - 4)] \times 1.5 MC_O}{[-2/(1 - 2)] \times MC_O}$$

$$\frac{P_S}{P_O} = \frac{[-4/(1 - 4)] \times 1.5}{-2/(1 - 2)}$$

$$\frac{P_S}{P_O} = \frac{(4/3) \times 1.5}{2} = 1$$

This means $P_S = P_O$, i.e. no senior citizen discount should be offered (unless the restaurant owner wants to give it for reasons other than profit maximization).

Problem 9

a. The golf club should charge the per-round price that is equal to the marginal cost, $60 per round. This will allow the club to sell all the rounds for which customers are willing to pay a price that at least covers the marginal cost. To find this quantity, we substitute $P = \$60$ into the demand curve:

$$Q = 55 - 0.5 \times 60$$

$$Q = 25$$

If $60 per round was all customers pay for the service, the golf club's producer surplus would be zero, and the consumer surplus would be the entire area below the demand curve and above the marginal cost. To visualize and easily calculate this area, we graph the demand curve. We've already found one point on the curve, where $P = \$60$ and $Q = 25$. The second useful point is the demand choke price, which can be found by setting $Q = 0$ and solving the demand curve for P:

$$Q = 55 - 0.5P$$

$$55 - 0.5P = 0$$

$$0.5P = 55$$

$$P = 110$$

Now we can draw the demand curve (D on the following graph) by connecting these two points. As the graph shows, with a single price of $60 per round, the consumer surplus is area A. Since this consumer surplus represents the amount a golfer is willing to pay above the per-round price, the golf club can charge him a fixed annual fee equal to area A in addition to that price, and the golfer will still be willing to buy 25 rounds. So, to maximize its profit, the golf club should charge a fixed fee of

$$\text{Area } A = 0.5 \times (\$110 - \$60) \times 25 = \$625 \text{ per year}$$

in addition to the per-unit price of $60 per round. By using this two-part tariff, the golf club will be able to capture the entire surplus in the market.

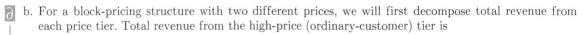

b. For a block-pricing structure with two different prices, we will first decompose total revenue from each price tier. Total revenue from the high-price (ordinary-customer) tier is

$$TR_1 = TR(P_1) = P_1 \times Q(P_1) = P_1(55 - 0.5P_1) = 55P_1 - 0.5P_1^2$$

Excess demand for output at the lower-price tier is

$$Q_2 = 55 - 0.5P_2 - Q_1(P_1)$$
$$Q_2 = 55 - 0.5P_2 - (55 - 0.5P_1)$$
$$Q_2 = 0.5P_1 - 0.5P_2$$

Total revenue from this lower-price tier is

$$TR_2 = P_2 \times Q(P_2) = P_2(0.5P_1 - 0.5P_2) = 0.5P_1P_2 - 0.5P_2^2$$

The golf course's combined total revenue function is

$$TR = 55P_1 - 0.5P_1^2 + 0.5P_1P_2 - 0.5P_2^2$$

The golf course's total production cost for output associated with tier-one pricing is

$$TC_1 = \int_0^{55-0.5P_1} 60dQ = [60Q]_0^{55-0.5P_1}$$
$$= 60(55 - 0.5P_1) - 60(0) = 3{,}300 - 30P_1$$

The golf course's total production cost for output associated with tier-two pricing is

$$TC_2 = \int_{55-0.5P_1}^{55-0.5P_1+0.5P_1-0.5P_2} 60dQ = \int_{55-0.5P_1}^{55-0.5P_2} 60dQ = [60Q]_{55-0.5P_1}^{55-0.5P_2}$$
$$= 60(55 - 0.5P_2) - 60(55 - 0.5P_1)$$
$$= 3{,}300 - 30P_2 - 3{,}300 + 30P_1$$
$$= 30P_1 - 30P_2$$

The golf course's total production cost for producing output across both pricing blocks is

$$TC = 3{,}300 - 30P_1 + 30P_1 - 30P_2$$
$$= 3{,}300 - 30P_2$$

The block-pricing monopoly producer surplus is

$$PS = TR - TC = 55P_1 - 0.5P_1^2 + 0.5P_1P_2 - 0.5P_2^2 - 3{,}300 + 30P_2$$

The golf course's objective is to choose P_1 and P_2, which maximize PS. The relevant system of first-order conditions is

$$0 = \frac{\partial PS}{\partial P_1} = 55 - P_1 + 0.5P_2$$

$$0 = \frac{\partial PS}{\partial P_2} = 0.5P_1 - P_2 + 30$$

Using the first of these first-order conditions, we may solve for P_1. This produces

$$P_1 = 55 + 0.5P_2$$

Inserting the right-hand side of this statement for P_1 into the second of the first-order conditions and solving for P_2, we have

$$0 = 0.5(55 + 0.5P_2) - P_2 + 30$$

$$0 = 27.5 + 0.25P_2 - P_2 + 30$$

$$0.75P_2 = 57.5$$

$$P_2 \approx 76.67$$

Thus,

$$P_1 = 55 + 0.5(76.67) \approx 93.34$$

The corresponding block-one output is $Q_1 = 55 - 0.5P_1 = 55 - 0.5(93.34) = 8.33$. The block-two output is $Q_2 = 55 - 0.5P_2 - Q_1(P_1) = 55 - 0.5(76.67) - 8.33 = 8.34$.

c. Producer surplus is $PS = 55P_1 - 0.5P_1^2 + 0.5P_1P_2 - 0.5P_2^2 - 3,300 + 30P_2 = 55(93.34) - 0.5(93.34)^2 + 0.5(93.34)(76.67) - 0.5(76.67)^2 - 3,300 + 30(76.67) \approx 416.67$.

The inverse demand curve is $P = 110 - 2Q$. Consumer surplus then is

$$CS = \int_0^{8.33}(110 - 2Q - 93.34)dQ + \int_{8.33}^{8.33+8.34}(110 - 2Q - 76.67)dQ$$

$$= \int_0^{8.33}(16.66 - 2Q)dQ + \int_{8.33}^{16.67}(33.33 - 2Q)dQ$$

$$= [16.66Q]_0^{8.33} - \left[\frac{2Q^2}{2}\right]_0^{8.33} + [33.33Q]_{8.33}^{16.67} - \left[\frac{2Q^2}{2}\right]_{8.33}^{16.67}$$

$$= [16.66Q]_0^{8.33} - [Q^2]_0^{8.33} + [33.33Q]_{8.33}^{16.67} - [Q^2]_{8.33}^{16.67}$$

$$= [16.66(8.33) - 16.66(0)] - [(8.33)^2 - (0)^2] + [33.33(16.67) - 33.33(8.33)]$$

$$- [(16.67)^2 - (8.33)^2]$$

$$= (138.78 - 0) - (69.39 - 0) + (555.61 - 277.64) - (277.89 - 69.39)$$

$$= 129.86$$

Total surplus in the market with a block pricing structure (with two-pricing tiers) is $416.67 + 129.86 = \$546.53$.

Problem 10

a. First, we need to find the market demand curve faced by Amazon, which can be calculated as the horizontal sum of all customers' demand curves. Since the numbers of customers in each group are the same, we can simplify our calculations by assuming that there is one customer of each type in the market. Then, we sum the Type A customer's and Type B customer's individual demand curves to get the market demand curve:

$$Q_M = Q_A + Q_B$$
$$Q_M = (200 - 200P) + (90 - 50P)$$
$$Q_M = 290 - 250P$$

To derive the market demand curve correctly, we also need to find the demand choke prices for each group of customers. We do this by setting $Q = 0$ and solving each group's demand curve for P. For Type A customers,

$$Q_A = 200 - 200P$$
$$0 = 200 - 200P$$
$$200P = 200$$
$$P = 1$$

And for Type B customers,

$$Q_B = 90 - 50P$$
$$0 = 90 - 50P$$
$$50P = 90$$
$$P = 1.8$$

This means in the price range between $1 and $1.80, Type A customers' quantity demanded is zero, so the market demand curve is

$$Q_M = Q_B$$
$$Q_M = 90 - 50P$$

And at $1 and below, the market demand curve is the horizontal sum of the two demand curves as calculated in the preceding. That is, the market demand curve is kinked, as shown on the following graph.

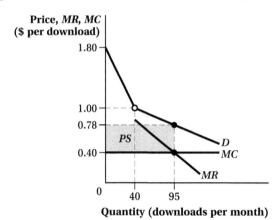

To find Amazon's profit-maximizing price, we need to know the marginal revenue curve, which can be derived from the inverse demand curve. For the part of the market demand curve below the kink, the inverse demand curve can be found as follows:

$$Q_M = 290 - 250P$$
$$250P = 290 - Q_M$$
$$P = 1.16 - 0.004Q$$

We know that the marginal revenue curve is the inverse demand curve, with the coefficient on quantity twice as large. Thus, Amazon's marginal revenue curve is

$$MR = 1.16 - 0.008Q$$

To find the profit-maximizing number of downloads, we set $MR = MC$ and solve this equation for Q:

$$1.16 - 0.008Q = 0.4$$
$$0.008Q = 0.76$$
$$Q = 95$$

And from the inverse demand curve, we can calculate the maximum price at which Amazon can sell this quantity of downloads:

$$P = 1.16 - 0.004 \times 95$$
$$P = 0.78$$

This price is on the part of the demand curve that is below the kink, so the demand and marginal revenue curves that we've used to find the profit-maximizing quantity are the ones that are relevant. Thus, when Amazon charges the same price to all customers, its profit- maximizing price is $0.78.

Amazon's producer surplus from selling downloads to two customers is the area below the price and above the marginal cost up to the quantity sold (see the preceding graph), which is

$$PS = (\$0.78 - \$0.40) \times 95 = \$36.10$$

or $\dfrac{\$36.10}{2} = \$18.05$ per customer.

b. Type A customers will certainly not accept the $1.10 per download option because, as shown in (a), their quantity demanded is zero at this price. But will they accept the quantity discount option? To answer this question, we need to calculate the consumer surplus that Type A customers receive if they accept this plan. From their demand curve, we can calculate that at $0.70, a Type A customer's quantity of downloads demanded is

$$Q_A = 200 - 200 \times 0.7 = 60$$

Thus, she will receive consumer surplus only for the first 60 downloads purchased and lose consumer surplus when buying the remaining 40 downloads that she has to buy to meet the minimum quantity discount requirement. The left panel on the following graph illustrates this situation. The consumer surplus gain from the first 60 downloads is the area below the demand curve and above $P = \$0.70$ up to $Q = 60$ (area A), which is

$$\text{Area } A = 0.5 \times (\$1.00 - \$0.70) \times 60 = \$9$$

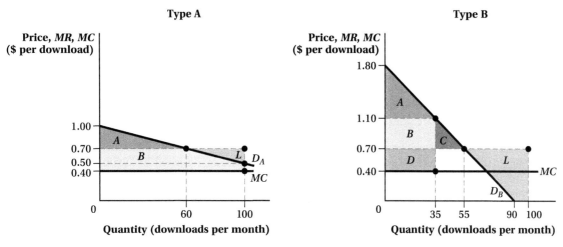

The consumer surplus loss from the 40 more downloads purchased to meet the quantity discount requirement is the area below the price ($0.70) and above the demand curve between $Q = 60$ and $Q = 100$ (area L). To calculate this area, we need to know the point on the demand curve that corresponds to the price at which a Type A consumer will want to buy 100 downloads. This price can be calculated by substituting $Q = 100$ into the Type A customer's demand curve and solving the equation for P:

$$Q_A = 200 - 200P$$
$$100 = 200 - 200P$$
$$200P = 100$$
$$P = 0.50$$

Now we can calculate area L as a triangle with a base of $\$0.70 - \$0.50 = \$0.20$ and a height of $100 - 60 = 40$:

$$\text{Area } L = 0.5 \times \$0.20 \times 40 = \$4$$

Since the gain in consumer surplus ($9) is greater than the loss ($4), Type A consumers will accept the quantity discount offer and buy 100 downloads each. Since Amazon's Type A customers will take the offer designed for them, the pricing scheme is incentive compatible for Type A consumers.

To see whether Amazon's pricing strategy is also incentive compatible for Type B customers, we need to compare the consumer surpluses these customers receive under each option. If a Type B customer chooses to pay the regular price ($1.10 per download), his quantity demanded will be

$$Q_B = 90 - 50P$$
$$Q_B = 90 - 50 \times 1.10$$
$$Q_B = 35$$

so his consumer surplus will be the area below the demand curve and above the price up to this quantity (area A on the right-hand part of the preceding graph):

$$CS = 0.5 \times (\$1.80 - \$1.10) \times 35 = \$12.25$$

If a Type B consumer chooses the quantity discount plan, he will have to purchase at least 100 downloads per month. This is more than his quantity demanded at the discount price, which is

$$Q_B = 90 - 50 \times 0.70$$
$$Q_B = 55$$

This means a Type B consumer's demand curve will be above the price only up to this quantity, that is, he will receive consumer surplus only from the first 55 downloads. This consumer surplus is the area below the demand curve and above $P = \$0.70$ up to $Q = 55$ (area $A + B + C$), which is

$$(\text{Area } A + B + C) = 0.5 \times (\$1.80 - \$0.70) \times 55 = \$30.25$$

To get the quantity discount, however, a Type B customer has to buy 45 more downloads, and for these downloads, the price he pays is above his demand curve. This means he values these downloads less than he has to pay for them. So when he buys these downloads, he incurs a loss of consumer surplus. As follows from the Type B consumer's demand curve, if the price was zero, he would want to buy 90 downloads ($Q_B = 90 - 50 \times 0 = 90$). So the loss in consumer surplus is area L, which is a trapezoid whose longer base is $100 - 55 = 45$, while shorter base is $100 - 90 = 10$, and the height is \$0.70, so

$$\text{Area } L = 0.5 \times (45 + 10) \times \$0.70 = \$19.25$$

Thus, with the quantity discount price, a Type B consumer's surplus is

$$CS = (\text{Area } A + B + C) - \text{Area } L = \$30.25 - \$19.25 = \$11$$

Since this is less than the consumer surplus a Type B customer receives in choosing the \$1.10 per-user option (\$12.25), he will take the latter option, which is the one designed for Type B customers. That is, Amazon's pricing plan is incentive compatible for Type B customers. We can also see this if we compare a Type B customer's consumer surplus gain from the quantity discount option (area $B + C$) with his consumer surplus loss (area L). Area $(B + C)$ is a trapezoid whose longer base is 55, while the shorter base is 35, and the height is $\$1.10 - \$0.70 = \$0.40$. Thus:

$$(\text{Area } B + C) = 0.5 \times (55 + 35) \times \$0.40 = \$18$$

Since this gain in consumer surplus is smaller than the loss in consumer surplus calculated in the preceding (\$19.25), Type B consumers will not opt for the quantity discount. They will choose the \$1.10 per download option, which is intended for them. Thus, Amazon's pricing plan is incentive compatible for both Type A and Type B customers.

c. As shown in the preceding, under the price scheme in (b), Type A customers will choose the discounted price (\$0.70) and buy 100 downloads per month. Since Amazon's marginal cost is \$0.40 per download, the company's producer surplus received from a Type A customer will be ($\$0.70 - \$0.40) \times 100 = \$30$ (area $B + L$ on the left-hand part of the preceding graph). A Type B customer will choose the regular price (\$1.10) and buy 35 downloads per month, so Amazon's producer surplus received from a Type B customer will be ($\$1.10 - \$0.40) \times 35 = \$24.50$ (area $B + D$ on the right-hand part). Thus, Amazon's producer surplus per customer will be $\dfrac{(\$30 + \$24.50)}{2} = \$27.25$. As we calculated in (a), the producer surplus that the company receives when charging a single profit-maximizing price is \$18.05 per customer. As we can see, using the pricing scheme in (b) allows Amazon to increase its producer surplus. Therefore, Amazon should use the pricing scheme in (b).

∂ Problem 11

a. To identify the single price per pound that maximizes revenue, we first identify the inverse demand function for olives. That is, $P = 1{,}350 - 2.5Q$. Total revenue is $TR(Q) = 1{,}350Q - 2.5Q^2$. The first-order condition to maximize total revenue is $0 = \dfrac{dTR}{dQ} = 1{,}350 - 5Q$. Solving for Q, we have $Q = 270$. The grocer's price is $P = 1{,}350 - 2.5(270) = 675$, or \$6.75 per pound.

b. To identify the grocer's revenue maximizing two-tier block pricing structure, we must first identify the grocer's revenue function across two tiers. To derive this two-tier revenue function, we first note that the grocer's customers will purchase $Q_1 = 540 - 0.4P_1$ olives at the first-tier price of P_1. This implies the excess demand for olives at tier-two prices is: $Q_2 = 540 - 0.4P_2 - (540 - 0.4P_1) = 0.4P_1 - 0.4P_2$. The two-tier revenue function for the grocer is $TR = 540P_1 - 0.4P_1^2 + 0.4P_1P_2 - 0.4P_2^2$. The grocer's revenue maximization problem with choice variables P_1 and P_2 implies a two-equation system of first-order conditions. The first-order condition relative to P_1 is $0 = \dfrac{\partial TR}{\partial P_1} = 540 - 0.8P_1 + 0.4P_2$. Solving this first-order condition for P_1, we identify $P_1 = 675 + 0.5P_2$. The first-order condition relative to P_2 is $0 = \dfrac{\partial TR}{\partial P_2} = 0.4P_1 - 0.8P_2$. Solving for P_2, we have $P_2 = 0.5P_1$. Combining these equations, we have $P_1 = 675 + 0.5(0.5P_1)$, or $0.75P_1 = 675$ or $P_1 = 900$. Therefore, the optimal tier-one price is \$9 per pound. A customer will purchase $Q_1 = 540 - 0.4(900) = 180$. The optimal tier-two price is $P_2 = 0.5(900) = 450$. At the tier-two price of \$4.50 per pound of olives, a customer will purchase $Q_2 = 0.4(900) - 0.4(450) = 0.4(450) = 180$.

Imperfect Competition

11

Solutions for Practice Problems

Problem 1

a. Since the gas stations sell identical products and consumers don't view them differently, consumers will only compare prices. Therefore, the gas station charging the lowest price will get all the demand. Thus, the gas stations have a strong incentive to undercut each other and will continue to try and do so until each gas station charges the price equal to its marginal cost, $2 per gallon, so its economic profit is zero. The undercutting will stop at this level because dropping prices below marginal cost will cause the gas stations to suffer losses. This is a Nash equilibrium in the Bertrand model of oligopoly with identical products, which is the same as the market outcome would be under perfect competition. We can find the quantity of gas sold by all gas stations at $2 per gallon by substituting $P = 2$ into the inverse demand curve and solving this equation for Q:

$$2 = 6 - 0.5Q$$
$$0.5Q = 4$$
$$Q = 8$$

Since all gas stations charge the same price, consumers will choose randomly from which station to buy. Therefore, the demand is likely to be divided evenly among the stations. Thus, each gas station will sell $\frac{8,000}{4} = 2,000$ gallons of gas at $2 per gallon and earn zero economic profit.

b. If the gas stations collude, they act as a monopoly and choose to supply the quantity of gas that maximizes their combined profits by equating the cartel's marginal revenue to the marginal cost. The monopoly's marginal revenue curve will be the inverse market demand curve with the coefficient on quantity twice as large:

$$MR = 6 - 2 \times 0.5Q$$
$$MR = 6 - Q$$

Now we set $MR = MC$ to solve for the profit-maximizing output:

$$6 - Q = 2$$
$$Q = 4$$

This means each gas station will supply $\frac{4,000}{4} = 1,000$ gallons of gas. To find the price that the gas stations will charge, we substitute the market quantity ($Q = 4$) into the inverse demand curve:

$$P = 6 - 0.5 \times 4 = 4$$

Thus, if the gas stations follow their agreement, they will charge $4 per gallon and make a profit of $4 – $2 = $2 per gallon and a total profit of $2 \times 1,000 = $2,000 each.

c. If one of the stations sells an additional thousand gallons of gas, that is, 2,000 gallons instead of 1,000 gallons, the market quantity will increase to $4,000 + 1,000 = 5,000$ gallons. Therefore, the price of gas will be

$$P = 6 - 0.5 \times 5 = 3.5 \text{ (dollars per gallon)}$$

The cheater's profit then will be ($3.50 – $2) \times 2,000 = $3,000. Since selling an additional thousand gallons increases the cheater's profit (from $2,000 to $3,000), the gas stations have an incentive to cheat. Therefore, their cartel agreement is unstable.

d. The collusion's total revenue function is $R(Q) = P(Q) \times Q = (6 - 0.5Q)Q = 6Q - 0.5Q^2$. Marginal revenue is $\frac{dR}{dQ} = 6 - Q$. Notice that this is the same marginal revenue as noted in (b) and that the rest of the calculations are the same, so $Q = 4$ and $P = $4 per gallon. Alternately, we could set up the profit function by noting that marginal cost is constant and there are no fixed costs, and therefore

$TC = 2Q$. With this information, the profit function is $\pi = R(Q) - TC = 6Q - 0.5Q^2 - 2Q = 4Q - 0.5Q^2$. We can maximize this with respect to quantity by taking the derivative with respect to Q and setting it equal to zero to form the collusion's first-order condition. Here, $\dfrac{d\pi}{dQ} = 4 - Q = 0$, so $Q = 4$, as noted in the preceding.

Problem 2

a. Since both companies face capacity constraints, they can only undercut the competitor's price to a certain limit, after which they won't be able to satisfy the demand they face. Therefore, the firms will first decide how much output to produce, and then the market demand will determine the price at which they will sell this output. Thus, we should use the Cournot model to analyze the firms' decision.

Let q_B be the quantity of electricity produced by Blue Line and q_R be the quantity of electricity produced by Red Power. Then, $Q = q_B + q_R$. Substituting this expression into the market inverse demand curve, we get:

$$P = 8 - 0.05(q_B + q_R)$$
$$P = 8 - 0.05q_B - 0.05q_R$$

Because the slope of the marginal revenue curve is twice the slope of the inverse demand curve faced by each company, Blue Line's marginal revenue curve is

$$MR_B = 8 - 0.1q_B - 0.05q_R$$

And Red Power's marginal revenue curve is

$$MR_R = 8 - 0.05q_B - 0.1q_R$$

Each firm will maximize its profit by setting $MR = MC$, so for Blue Line we can write:

$$MR_B = MC_B$$
$$8 - 0.1q_B - 0.05q_R = 4$$

Solving this equation for q_B, we get Blue Line's reaction curve:

$$0.1q_B = 4 - 0.05q_R$$
$$q_B = 40 - 0.5q_R$$

And for Red Power:

$$MR_R = MC_R$$
$$8 - 0.05q_B - 0.1q_R = 5$$
$$0.1q_R = 3 - 0.05q_B$$
$$q_R = 30 - 0.5q_B$$

These reaction curves are shown on the following graph.

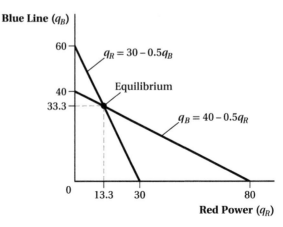

Reaction curves: quantities of electricity in millions of kilowatt-hours

b. The Cournot equilibrium is where both competitors are simultaneously producing optimally given the other's actions, that is, where the two firms' reaction curves intersect. To solve for this equilibrium, we substitute Red Power's reaction curve into Blue Line's reaction curve and solve the equation for q_B:

$$q_B = 40 - 0.5q_R$$
$$q_B = 40 - 0.5(30 - 0.5q_B)$$
$$q_B = 40 - 15 + 0.25q_B$$
$$0.75q_B = 25$$
$$q_B = 33\frac{1}{3}$$

Then,

$$q_R = 30 - 0.5 \times 33\frac{1}{3} = 13\frac{1}{3}$$

Thus, in equilibrium, Blue Line produces about 33.3 million kWh of electricity, and Red Power produces about 13.3 million kWh.

c. To find the market price, we substitute the quantities of electricity produced by both companies into the inverse market demand curve:

$$P = 8 - 0.05\left(33\frac{1}{3} + 13\frac{1}{3}\right)$$
$$P = 5\frac{2}{3}$$

That is, the market price is about 5.67 cents per kWh.

d. Blue Line produces about 33.3 million kWh of electricity and earns about $5.67 - 4 = 1.67$ cents per kWh. So the company's total profit is about $\$0.0167 \times 33.3$ million $= \$556,000$. Red Power produces about 13.3 million kWh of electricity and earns about $5.67 - 5 = 0.67$ cents per kWh. So the company's total profit is about $\$0.0067 \times 13.3$ million $= \$89,000$. Note that the firm with the lower marginal cost produces more output and earns a greater profit.

e. Blue Line's profit function can be written:

$$\pi_B = \big(8 - 0.05(q_B + q_R)\big)q_B - 4q_B$$
$$= 8q_B - 0.05q_B^2 - 0.05q_Bq_R - 4q_B$$
$$= 4q_B - 0.05q_B^2 - 0.05q_Bq_R$$

Blue Line's objective is to maximize π_B by choosing q_B. Its first-order condition is

$$0 = \frac{\partial \pi_B}{\partial q_B} = 4 - 0.1q_B - 0.05q_R$$

Blue Line's reaction function then is derived as:

$$0.1q_B = 4 - 0.05q_R$$
$$q_B = 40 - 0.5q_R$$

Red Power's profit function can be written:

$$\pi_R = \big(8 - 0.05(q_B + q_R)\big)q_R - 5q_R$$
$$= 8q_R - 0.05q_R^2 - 0.05q_Bq_R - 5q_R$$
$$= 3q_R - 0.05q_R^2 - 0.05q_Bq_R$$

Red Power's objective is to maximize π_R by choosing q_R. Its first-order condition is

$$0 = \frac{\partial \pi_R}{\partial q_R} = 3 - 0.1q_R - 0.05q_B$$

Red Power's reaction function then is derived as:

$$0.1q_R = 3 - 0.05q_B$$
$$q_R = 30 - 0.5q_B$$

Since these reaction curves are the same as in (a) of the problem, all subsequent analysis is the same and the final solution is using calculus as using algebraic methods as in (a–d).

Problem 3

a. Given that Blue Line is going to move first and it knows from previous experience that Red Power's output is a function of Blue Line's output, we can find the demand curve faced by Blue Line by substituting Red Power's reaction curve directly into the market inverse demand curve. As we've found in Problem 2, Red Power's reaction curve is

$$q_R = 30 - 0.5q_B$$

and the market demand curve can be expressed as

$$P = 8 - 0.05(q_B + q_R)$$
$$P = 8 - 0.05q_B - 0.05q_R$$

So we can write:

$$P = 8 - 0.05q_B - 0.05(30 - 0.5q_B)$$
$$P = 8 - 0.05q_B - 1.5 + 0.025q_B$$
$$P = 6.5 - 0.025q_B$$

Because the slope of Blue Line's marginal revenue curve is twice the slope of the inverse demand curve it faces, the company's marginal revenue curve is

$$MR_B = 6.5 - 0.05q_B$$

Blue Line maximizes its profit by setting $MR_B = MC_B$, so we can write:

$$6.5 - 0.05q_B = 4$$

Solving this equation for q_B, we get:

$$0.05q_B = 2.5$$
$$q_B = 50$$

Now we can find Red Power's output by plugging $q_B = 50$ into Red Power's reaction curve:

$$q_R = 30 - 0.5 \times 50 = 5$$

Thus, Blue Line produces 50 million kWh of electricity and Red Power produces 5 million kWh.

We can find the market price by substituting these quantities into the market inverse demand curve:

$$P = 8 - 0.05(50 + 5)$$
$$P = 5.25$$

That is, the market price is 5.25 cents per kWh.

Since Blue Line produces 50 million kWh and earns $5.25 - 4 = 1.25$ cents per kWh, its profit is $\$0.0125 \times 50$ million $= \$625,000$. Red Power produces 5 million kWh and earns $5.25 - 5 = 0.25$ cents per kWh, so its profit is $\$0.0025 \times 5$ million $= \$12,500$. Note that the advantage of being the first-mover allows Blue Line to increase its profit from $556,000 (see Problem 2) to $625,000, while Red Power's profit falls from $89,000 to $12,500.

b. Now Red Power is moving first, knowing from previous experience that Blue Line's output is a function of Red Power's. Therefore, we can find the demand curve faced by Red Power by substituting Blue Line's reaction curve into the market inverse demand curve. As we've found in Problem 2, Blue Line's reaction curve is

$$q_B = 40 - 0.5q_R$$

So we can write:

$$P = 8 - 0.05(40 - 0.5q_R) - 0.05q_R$$
$$P = 8 - 2 + 0.025q_R - 0.05q_R$$
$$P = 6 - 0.025q_R$$

Because the slope of Red Power's marginal revenue curve is twice the slope of the inverse demand curve it faces, the company's marginal revenue curve is

$$MR_R = 6 - 0.05q_R$$

Red Power maximizes its profit by setting $MR_R = MC_R$, so we can write:

$$6 - 0.05q_R = 5$$

Solving this equation for q_R, we get:

$$0.05q_R = 1$$
$$q_R = 20$$

Now we can find Blue Line's output by plugging $q_R = 20$ into Blue Line's reaction curve:

$$q_B = 40 - 0.5 \times 20 = 30$$

Thus, Red Power produces 20 million kWh of electricity and Blue Line produces 30 million kWh.

We can find the market price by substituting these quantities into the market inverse demand curve:

$$P = 8 - 0.05(30 + 20)$$
$$P = 5.5$$

That is, the market price is 5.5 cents per kWh.

Since Red Power produces 20 million kWh and earns $5.5 - 5 = 0.5$ cents per kWh, its profit is $\$0.005 \times 20$ million $= \$100,000$. Blue Line produces 30 million kWh and earns $5.5 - 4 = 1.5$ cents per kWh, so its profit is $\$0.015 \times 30$ million $= \$450,000$. Note that the advantage of being the first-mover allows Red Power to increase its profit from $\$89,000$ to $\$100,000$, while Blue Line's profit falls from $\$556,000$ to $\$450,000$.

Problem 4

a. To derive the reaction curves we need to know each firm's marginal revenue curve expressed as a function of price. We can find these marginal revenue curves from the demand curves using the following rule: if the demand curve is

$$Q = a - bP$$

then the marginal revenue curve is

$$MR = a - 2bP$$

In the demand curve faced by Roland, $a = 200 + 0.2p_Y$ and $b = 0.4$. Thus, Roland's marginal revenue curve is

$$MR_R = (200 + 0.2p_Y) - 2 \times 0.4p_R$$
$$MR_R = 200 - 0.8p_R + 0.2p_Y$$

Now we can derive Roland's reaction curve by setting $MR_R = MC_R = 0$ and solving this equation for p_R:

$$200 - 0.8p_R + 0.2p_Y = 0$$
$$0.8p_R = 200 + 0.2p_Y$$
$$p_R = 250 + 0.25p_Y$$

Similarly, given the demand curve faced by Yamaha, its marginal revenue curve is

$$MR_Y = 240 - p_Y + 0.1p_R$$

And we can derive Yamaha's reaction curve by setting $MR_Y = MC_Y = 0$ and solving this equation for p_Y:

$$240 - p_Y + 0.1p_R = 0$$
$$p_Y = 240 + 0.1p_R$$

These reaction curves are shown on the graph on the next page.

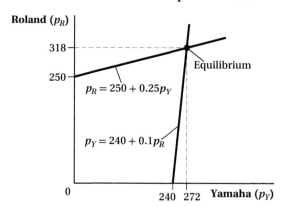

Reaction curves: prices in dollars

b. We can solve for Roland's equilibrium price by substituting Yamaha's reaction curve into Roland's reaction curve:

$$p_R = 250 + 0.25p_Y$$
$$p_R = 250 + 0.25(240 + 0.1p_R)$$
$$p_R = 250 + 60 + 0.025p_R$$
$$0.975p_R = 310$$
$$p_R = 317.95$$

And to find Yamaha's equilibrium price we substitute $p_R = 317.95$ into Yamaha's reaction curve:

$$p_Y = 240 + 0.1 \times 317.95 = 271.80$$

Thus, Roland's optimal price is $317.95 and Yamaha's optimal price is $271.80.

c. We can find each firm's profit-maximizing output by plugging the prices found in the preceding into the demand curves faced by each firm. For Roland:

$$q_R = 200 - 0.4p_R + 0.2p_Y$$
$$q_R = 200 - 0.4 \times 317.95 + 0.2 \times 271.80$$
$$q_R = 127.18$$

And for Yamaha:

$$q_Y = 240 - 0.5p_Y + 0.1p_R$$
$$q_Y = 240 - 0.5 \times 271.80 + 0.1 \times 317.95$$
$$q_R = 135.90$$

Thus, Roland's optimal output is 127,180 keyboards, and Yamaha's optimal output is 135,900 keyboards.

d. Roland's profit function can be written (which is equivalent to its revenue function since marginal cost is assumed to be zero):

$$\pi_R = (200 - 0.4p_R + 0.2p_Y)p_R$$
$$= 200p_R - 0.4p_R^2 + 0.2p_Rp_Y$$

Roland's objective is to maximize π_R by choosing p_R. The firm's first-order condition is

$$0 = \frac{\partial \pi_R}{\partial p_R} = 200 - 0.8p_R + 0.2p_Y$$

Roland's reaction function then is derived as:

$$0.8p_R = 200 + 0.2p_Y$$
$$p_R = 250 + 0.25p_Y$$

Yamaha's profit function can be written (which also is equivalent to its revenue function, since marginal cost is assumed to be zero):

$$\pi_Y = (240 - 0.5p_Y + 0.1p_R)p_Y$$
$$= 240p_Y - 0.5p_Y^2 + 0.1p_Rp_Y$$

Yamaha's objective is to maximize π_Y by choosing p_Y. The firm's first-order condition is

$$0 = \frac{\partial \pi_Y}{\partial p_Y} = 240 - p_Y + 0.1 p_R$$

Yamaha's reaction function then is:

$$p_Y = 240 + 0.1 p_R$$

Since these reaction curves are the same as in (a), all subsequent analysis is the same and the final solution is using calculus as using algebraic methods as in the text.

Problem 5

a. Given that the market for smartphone cases is in equilibrium, we know that Strelkin is maximizing its profit. This means the firm's marginal revenue equals its marginal cost. Thus, to find how many cases Strelkin is producing, we should set $MR = MC$ and solve this equation for Q. To find the firm's MR curve, we first derive its inverse demand curve by solving the demand equation for P:

$$Q = 200 - 10P$$
$$10P = 200 - Q$$
$$P = 20 - 0.1Q$$

We know that the marginal revenue curve is the inverse demand curve with the coefficient on quantity twice as large, so the firm's marginal revenue curve is

$$MR = 20 - 0.2Q$$

Thus, we can write:

$$MR = MC$$
$$20 - 0.2Q = 10$$

And solving this equation for Q, we get:

$$0.2Q = 10$$
$$Q = 50$$

Thus, Strelkin is producing 50,000 smartphone cases per year.

b. We can find the price that the firm charges by substituting the quantity of smartphone cases produced into the inverse demand curve:

$$P = 20 - 0.1 \times 50 = 15$$

Thus, Strelkin charges $15 per case.

c. When a monopolistically competitive market is in long-run equilibrium, the firms in the market are making zero economic profits. This means Strelkin's price must be equal to its average total cost. Thus, the firm's average total cost is $15 per case.

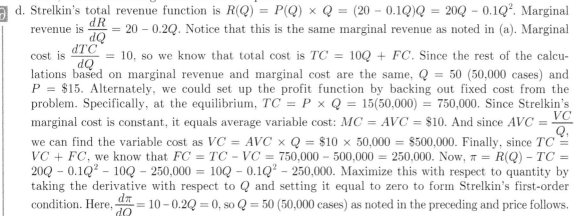

d. Strelkin's total revenue function is $R(Q) = P(Q) \times Q = (20 - 0.1Q)Q = 20Q - 0.1Q^2$. Marginal revenue is $\frac{dR}{dQ} = 20 - 0.2Q$. Notice that this is the same marginal revenue as noted in (a). Marginal cost is $\frac{dTC}{dQ} = 10$, so we know that total cost is $TC = 10Q + FC$. Since the rest of the calculations based on marginal revenue and marginal cost are the same, $Q = 50$ (50,000 cases) and $P = \$15$. Alternately, we could set up the profit function by backing out fixed cost from the problem. Specifically, at the equilibrium, $TC = P \times Q = 15(50,000) = 750,000$. Since Strelkin's marginal cost is constant, it equals average variable cost: $MC = AVC = \$10$. And since $AVC = \frac{VC}{Q}$, we can find the variable cost as $VC = AVC \times Q = \$10 \times 50,000 = \$500,000$. Finally, since $TC = VC + FC$, we know that $FC = TC - VC = 750,000 - 500,000 = 250,000$. Now, $\pi = R(Q) - TC = 20Q - 0.1Q^2 - 10Q - 250,000 = 10Q - 0.1Q^2 - 250,000$. Maximize this with respect to quantity by taking the derivative with respect to Q and setting it equal to zero to form Strelkin's first-order condition. Here, $\frac{d\pi}{dQ} = 10 - 0.2Q = 0$, so $Q = 50$ (50,000 cases) as noted in the preceding and price follows.

Problem 6

a. According to the agreement, the two countries will produce $12 \times 2 = 24$ million barrels of oil per day. Given the inverse demand curve they face, the market price of oil will be

$$P = 200 - 4 \times 24 = 104 \text{ (dollars per barrel)}$$

Then, Saudi Arabia's profit will be ($104 – $4) $\times$ 12 million = $1,200 million, and Iran's profit will be ($104 – $12) $\times$ 12 million = $1,104 million.

b. If Iran produces an additional million barrels, the total oil production will increase to 25 barrels per day. Then, the price of oil will be

$$P = 200 - 4 \times 25 = 100 \text{ (dollars per barrel)}$$

Iran's profit will be ($100 – $12) $\times$ 13 million = $1,144 million, and Saudi Arabia's profit will be ($100 – $4) $\times$ 12 million = $1,152 million. That is, Iran's profit will increase from $1,104 million to $1,144 million, while Saudi Arabia's profit will fall from $1,200 million to $1,152 million. Since Iran can increase its profit by cheating on the agreement, it has an incentive to cheat. Therefore, the cartel is unlikely to be stable.

c. To maximize its profit, Saudi Arabia will produce the quantity of oil for which its marginal revenue equals its marginal cost. Saudi Arabia's marginal revenue curve will be the inverse market demand curve with the coefficient on quantity twice as large:

$$MR = 200 - 2 \times 4Q$$
$$MR = 200 - 8Q$$

Setting $MR = MC$ and solving for Q, we get:

$$200 - 8Q = 4$$
$$8Q = 196$$
$$Q = 24.5$$

That is, Saudi Arabia will produce 24.5 million barrels per day. Given the inverse demand curve, to sell this quantity of oil, Saudi Arabia will charge

$$P = 200 - 4 \times 24.5 = 102 \text{ (dollars per barrel)}$$

so its profit will be ($102 – $4) $\times$ 24.5 million = $2,401 million. Thus, the cartel's profit will increase from $1,200 million + $1,104 million = $2,304 million to $2,401 million.

d. Iran will accept the deal, since the amount Saudi Arabia offers ($1,150 million) is greater than Iran's profit received under the agreement in (a) ($1,104 million). Note that Saudi Arabia is willing to offer Iran $1,150 million because, after paying this amount out of its profit, Saudi Arabia is still left with $2,401 million – $1,150 million = $1,251 million, which is more than the profit it receives under the agreement in (a) ($1,200 million). In fact, Saudi Arabia offers Iran to split the gains from more cost-efficient production of oil ($2,401 million – $2,304 million = $97 million) about equally, giving $1,150 million – $1,104 million = 46 million out of this gain to Iran and leaving $1,251 million – $1,150 million = 51 million to itself.

e. If Iran produces 1 million barrel in addition to Saudi Arabia's 24.5 million, the total oil production will increase to 25.5 barrels per day. Then, the price of oil will be

$$P = 200 - 4 \times 25.5 = 98 \text{ (dollars per barrel)}$$

Iran's profit from oil production will be ($98 – $12) $\times$ 1 million = $86 million, so together with the payment from Saudi Arabia, Iran will end up receiving $1,150 million + $86 million = $1,236 million. Saudi Arabia's profit will be ($98 – $4) $\times$ 24.5 million = $2,303 million. And after paying $1,150 million to Iran, Saudi Arabia will be left with $2,303 million – $1,150 million = $1,153 million. That is, Iran has an even stronger incentive to cheat on the agreement in (d) than on the agreement in (a).

Problem 7

a. Since the countries face capacity constraints, they will choose quantities to produce rather than prices to charge, so we should use the Cournot model to analyze their decision. Let q_I be the quantity of oil produced by Iran and q_S be the quantity of oil produced by Saudi Arabia. Then, $Q = q_I + q_S$. Substituting this expression into the market inverse demand curve, we get:

$$P = 200 - 4(q_I + q_S)$$
$$P = 200 - 4q_I - 4q_S$$

Because the slope of the marginal revenue curve is twice the slope of the inverse demand curve faced by each country, Iran's marginal revenue curve is

$$MR_I = 200 - 8q_I - 4q_S$$

And Saudi Arabia's marginal revenue curve is

$$MR_S = 200 - 4q_I - 8q_S$$

Each country will maximize its profit by setting $MR = MC$, so for Iran we can write:

$$MR_I = MC_I$$
$$200 - 8q_I - 4q_S = 12$$

Solving this equation for q_I, we get Iran's reaction curve:

$$8q_I = 188 - 4q_S$$
$$q_I = 23.5 - 0.5q_S$$

And for Saudi Arabia:

$$MR_S = MC_S$$
$$200 - 4q_I - 8q_S = 4$$
$$8q_S = 196 - 0.5q_I$$
$$q_S = 24.5 - 0.5q_I$$

These reaction curves are shown on the following graph.

**Reaction curves: quantities of oil
in millions of barrels per day**

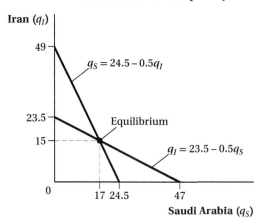

b. The Cournot equilibrium is where both competitors are simultaneously producing optimally given the other's actions, that is, where the two firms' reaction curves intersect. To solve for this equilibrium, we substitute Saudi Arabia's reaction curve into Iran's reaction curve and solve the equation for q_I:

$$q_I = 23.5 - 0.5q_S$$
$$q_I = 23.5 - 0.5(24.5 - 0.5q_I)$$
$$q_I = 23.5 - 12.25 + 0.25q_I$$
$$0.75q_I = 11.25$$
$$q_I = 15$$

Then,

$$q_S = 24.5 - 0.5 \times 15 = 17$$

Thus, in equilibrium, Iran produces 15 million barrels of oil per day and Saudi Arabia produces 17 million barrels per day.

c. To find the market price, we substitute the quantities of oil produced by both countries into the inverse market demand curve:

$$P = 200 - 4 \times (15 + 17)$$
$$P = 72$$

That is, the market price of oil is $72 per barrel.

d. Iran produces 15 million barrels of oil and earns $72 − $12 = $60 per barrel. So Iran's total profit is $60 × 15 million = $900 million. Saudi Arabia produces 17 million barrels and earns $72 − $4 = $68 per barrel. So Saudi Arabia's total profit is $68 × 17 million = $1,156 million.

e. The following table compares the Cournot equilibrium outcome in this scenario with the most profitable cartel outcome (i.e., when the lower-cost country, Saudi Arabia, produces all the oil). As we can see, competition leads to a greater industry output, which results in a lower market price and a lower industry profit.

	Total output (millions of barrels per day)	Price ($ per barrel)	Industry profit ($ millions per day)
Cartel	24.5	102	2,401
Cournot competition	32	72	2,056

Problem 8

a. Since Saudi Arabia moves first and knows from previous experience that Iran's output is a function of Saudi Arabia's output, we can find the demand curve Saudi Arabia faces by substituting Iran's reaction curve directly into the market inverse demand curve. As we've found in Problem 7, Iran's reaction curve is

$$q_I = 23.5 - 0.5q_S$$

And the market demand curve is

$$P = 200 - 4q_I - 4q_S$$

So we can write:

$$P = 200 - 4(23.5 - 0.5q_S) - 4q_S$$
$$P = 200 - 94 + 2q_S - 4q_S$$
$$P = 106 - 2q_S$$

Because the slope of Saudi Arabia's marginal revenue curve is twice the slope of the inverse demand curve it faces, Saudi Arabia's marginal revenue curve is

$$MR_S = 106 - 4q_S$$

Saudi Arabia maximizes its profit by setting $MR_S = MC_S$, so we can write:

$$MR_S = 106 - 4q_S = 4$$

Solving this equation for q_S, we get:

$$4q_S = 102$$
$$q_S = 25.5$$

Now we can find Iran's output by plugging $q_S = 25.5$ into Iran's reaction curve:

$$q_I = 23.5 - 0.5 \times 25.5 = 10.75$$

Thus, Saudi Arabia produces 25.5 million barrels of oil per day and Iran produces 10.75 million barrels. We can find the market price by substituting these quantities into the world's inverse demand curve:

$$P = 200 - 4(25.5 + 10.75)$$
$$P = 55$$

That is, the market price of oil is $55 per barrel.

Saudi Arabia produces 25.5 million barrels of oil and earns $55 − $4 = $51 per barrel. So Saudi Arabia's profit is $51 × 25.5 million = $1,300.5 million. Iran produces 10.75 million barrels and earns $55 − $12 = $43 per barrel. So Iran's profit is $43 × 10.75 million = $462.25 million.

Comparing these outcomes with those in Problem 7, we can see that moving first allows Saudi Arabia to increase its profit from $1,156 million to $1,300.5 million, while Iran's profit falls from $900 million to $462.25 million. The total industry output increases from 32 million barrels per day to 25.5 + 10.75 = 36.25 million barrels per day, and as a result of a greater quantity of oil supplied, the market price falls from $72 per barrel to $55 per barrel.

b. Now Iran moves first and knows that Saudi Arabia's output is a function of Iran's output. Therefore, we can find the demand curve Iran faces by substituting Saudi Arabia's reaction curve directly into the market inverse demand curve. As we've found in Problem 7, Saudi Arabia's reaction curve is

$$q_S = 24.5 - 0.5q_I$$

And the market demand curve is

$$P = 200 - 4q_I - 4q_S$$

So we can write:

$$P = 200 - 4q_I - 4(24.5 - 0.5q_I)$$
$$P = 200 - 4q_I - 98 + 2q_I$$
$$P = 102 - 2q_I$$

Because the slope of Iran's marginal revenue curve is twice the slope of the inverse demand curve it faces, Iran's marginal revenue curve is

$$MR_I = 102 - 4q_I$$

Iran maximizes its profit by setting $MR_I = MC_I$, so we can write:

$$MR_I = 102 - 4q_I = 12$$

Solving this equation for q_I, we get:

$$4q_I = 90$$
$$q_I = 22.5$$

That is, Iran would maximize its profit if it produced 22.5 million barrels of oil per day. Recall, however, from Problem 6 that Iran's oil production capacity is limited to 16 million barrels per day. Thus, the best Iran can do is to use its full capacity and produce 16 million barrels per day. Now we can find Saudi Arabia's output by plugging $q_I = 16$ into Saudi Arabia's reaction curve:

$$q_S = 24.5 - 0.5 \times 16 = 16.5$$

Thus, Iran produces 16 million barrels of oil per day and Saudi Arabia produces 16.5 million barrels. We can find the market price by substituting these quantities into the world's inverse demand curve:

$$P = 200 - 4(16 + 16.5)$$
$$P = 70$$

That is, the market price of oil is $70 per barrel.

Iran produces 16 million barrels and earns $70 − $12 = $58 per barrel. So Iran's profit is $58 × 16 million = $928 million. Saudi Arabia produces 16.5 million barrels of oil and earns $70 − $4 = $66 per barrel. So Saudi Arabia's profit is $66 × 16.5 million = $1,089 million.

Problem 9

a. Nature's Path is maximizing its profit when it produces the quantity for which the firm's marginal revenue equals its marginal cost. To calculate this quantity, we set $MR = MC$ and solve this equation for Q. To find the firm's MR curve, we derive its inverse demand curve by solving the demand equation for P:

$$Q = 12.5 - 2.5P$$
$$2.5P = 12.5 - Q$$
$$P = 5 - 0.4Q$$

We know that the marginal revenue curve is the inverse demand curve with the coefficient on quantity twice as large, so the firm's marginal revenue curve is

$$MR = 5 - 0.8Q$$

Thus, we can write:

$$MR = MC$$
$$5 - 0.8Q = 2$$

And solving this equation for Q, we get:

$$0.8Q = 3$$
$$Q = 3.75$$

Thus, Nature's Path is producing 3.75 million boxes of cereal per year.

We can find the price that the firm charges by substituting the quantity of cereal produced into the inverse demand curve:

$$P = 5 - 0.4 \times 3.75 = 3.5$$

Thus, Nature's Path charges $3.50 per box of its cereal.

b. Nature's Path profit is

$$\pi = TR - TC$$

The firm's total revenue is $TR = P \times Q = \$3.50 \times 3.75$ million $= \$13.125$ million. And its total cost is

$$TC = FC + VC$$

We know that $FC = \$5$ million. And since the firm's marginal cost is constant, $MC = AVC = \$2$. This means $VC = AVC \times Q = \$2 \times 3.75$ million $= \$7.5$ million. Thus, the firm's total cost is

$$TC = \$5 \text{ million} + \$7.5 \text{ million} = \$12.5 \text{ million}$$

And its economic profit is

$$\pi = \$13.125 \text{ million} - \$12.5 \text{ million} = 0.625 \text{ million}$$

Since Nature's Path's economic profit is greater than zero, the monopolistically competitive market for organic cereals is not in long-run equilibrium. Attracted by the opportunity of economic profit, other firms will enter the market, changing the demand curve faced by Nature's Path and altering the firm's output and price decisions.

c. We find the inverse demand curve that corresponds to the new demand curve faced by Nature's Path as follows:

$$Q = 20 - 5P$$
$$5P = 20 - Q$$
$$P = 4 - 0.2Q$$

The firm's marginal revenue curve is the inverse demand curve with the coefficient on quantity twice as large:

$$MR = 4 - 0.4Q$$

To find the firm's profit-maximizing output, we solve the following equation for Q:

$$MR = MC$$
$$4 - 0.4Q = 2$$
$$0.4Q = 2$$
$$Q = 5$$

Thus, to maximize its profit under new market conditions, Nature's Path has to increase its output from 3.75 million boxes to 5 million boxes of cereal per year. Given the new (inverse) demand curve, the price that the firm needs to charge to sell this quantity is:

$$P = 4 - 0.2 \times 5 = 3$$

That is, Nature's Path has to lower its price from $3.50 per box to $3 per box. The firm's total revenue is now $TR = P \times Q = \$3 \times 5$ million $= \$15$ million. And its variable cost is $VC = AVC \times Q = \$2 \times 5$ million $= \$10$ million, so its total cost is $TC = FC + VC = \$5$ million $+ \$10$ million $=$

$15 million. Since $TR = TC$, the firm's economic profit is zero. Since Nature's Path and other firms in the industry are no longer making any economic profit, there will be no more entry, which means the market is in long-run equilibrium.

Problem 10

a. To derive the reaction curves we first need to know each firm's marginal revenue curve expressed as a function of price. We can find these marginal revenue curves from the demand curves using the following rule: If the demand curve is

$$Q = a - bP$$

then the marginal revenue curve is

$$MR = a - 2bP$$

In the demand curve faced by Asus, $a = 100 + 0.05p_T$ and $b = 0.1$. Thus, Asus's marginal revenue curve is

$$MR_A = (100 + 0.05p_T) - 2 \times 0.1p_A$$
$$MR_A = 100 - 0.2p_A + 0.05p_T$$

Now, since marginal revenue here is expressed as a function of price, to derive Asus's reaction curve, we need to express its marginal cost as the change in total cost in response to a unit change in price, that is, as $\dfrac{\Delta TC}{\Delta p_A}$. First, note that since there is no fixed cost and the marginal cost is constant, Asus's total cost (in thousands of dollars) can be expressed as

$$TC_A = MC_A \times q_A = 100q_A$$

Now, we substitute the demand curve faced by Asus into the total cost function above to express total cost in price terms:

$$TC_A = 100(100 - 0.1p_A + 0.05p_T)$$
$$TC_A = 10{,}000 - 10p_A + 5p_T$$

The coefficient of p_A in this equation (–10) shows that for each dollar drop in price, the firm's total cost increases by 10 thousand dollars (since the quantity is in thousands). Thus, Asus's marginal cost expressed in price terms is $MC_A^P = -10$. (The MC_A^P is negative because raising the price results in less output produced and therefore in a lower total cost.)

Now we can derive Asus's reaction curve by setting $MR_A = MC_A^P = -10$ and solving this equation for p_A:

$$100 - 0.2p_A + 0.05p_T = -10$$
$$0.2p_A = 110 + 0.05p_T$$
$$p_A = 550 + 0.25p_T$$

Similarly, given the demand curve faced by Toshiba, its marginal revenue curve is

$$MR_T = 90 - 0.16p_T + 0.04p_A$$

And to derive Toshiba's reaction curve, we need to express its marginal cost in price terms. Toshiba's total cost is

$$TC_T = MC_T \times q_T = 80q_T$$

Substituting the demand curve faced by Toshiba into the total cost function above, we get:

$$TC_T = 80(90 - 0.08p_T + 0.04p_A)$$
$$TC_T = 7{,}200 - 6.4p_T + 3.2p_A$$

The coefficient of p_T in this equation (–6.4) shows that for each dollar drop in price, the firm's total cost increases by 6.4 thousand dollars. Thus, Toshiba's marginal cost expressed in price terms is $MC_T^P = -6.4$.

Now we can derive Toshiba's reaction curve by setting $MR_T = MC_T^P = -6.4$ and solving this equation for p_T:

$$90 - 0.16p_T + 0.04p_A = -6.4$$
$$0.16p_T = 96.4 + 0.04p_A$$
$$p_T = 602.5 + 0.25p_A$$

The firms' reaction curves are shown on the following graph.

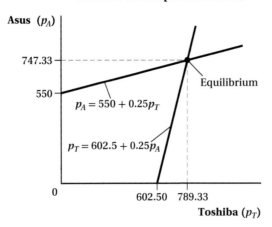

Reaction curves: prices in dollars

b. We can solve for Asus's equilibrium price by substituting Toshiba's reaction curve into Asus's reaction curve:

$$p_A = 550 + 0.25p_T$$
$$p_A = 550 + 0.25(602.5 + 0.25p_A)$$
$$p_A = 550 + 150.625 + 0.0625p_A$$
$$0.9375p_A = 700.625$$
$$p_A = 747.33$$

And to find Toshiba's equilibrium price, we substitute $p_A = 747.33$ into Toshiba's reaction curve:

$$p_T = 602.5 + 0.25 \times 747.33 = 789.33$$

Thus, Asus's optimal price is $747.33 and Toshiba's optimal price is $789.33.

c. We can find each firm's profit-maximizing output by plugging the prices found in the preceding into the demand curves faced by each firm. For Asus:

$$q_A = 100 - 0.1p_A + 0.05p_T$$
$$q_A = 100 - 0.1 \times 747.33 + 0.05 \times 789.33$$
$$q_A = 64.73$$

And for Toshiba:

$$q_T = 90 - 0.08p_T + 0.04p_A$$
$$q_T = 90 - 0.08 \times 789.33 + 0.04 \times 747.33$$
$$q_T = 56.75$$

Thus, Asus's optimal output is 64,730 laptops, and Toshiba's optimal output is 56,750 laptops.

∂ Problem 11

a. Paradise Plaza's profit is: $\pi_P = (900 - p_P + 0.5p_T)p_P - 15(900 - p_P + 0.5p_T)$. Paradise Plaza's profit-maximizing first-order condition is: $0 = \dfrac{d\pi_P}{dp_P} = 900 - 2p_P + 0.5p_T + 15$. Solving for p_P, we identify: $p_P = 442.5 + 0.25p_T$. This is Paradise Plaza's profit-maximizing reaction to Turtle Terrace's apartment price.

b. Turtle Terrace's profit function is $\pi_T = (1,000 - 0.5p_T + p_P)p_T - 20(1,000 - 0.5p_T + p_P)$. The profit-maximizing first-order condition is: $0 = \dfrac{d\pi_T}{dp_T} = 1,000 - p_T + p_P + 10$. Solving for p_T, we find: $p_T = 990 + p_P$. This is Turtle Terrace's profit-maximizing response to Paradise Plaza's apartment price.

c. By substituting Turtle Terrace's reaction function into Paradise Plaza's reaction function, we find: $p_P = 442.5 + 0.25(990 + p_P) = 690 + 0.25p_P$. Solving for p_P, we determine: $p_P = \$920$ per month. This implies that Turtle Terrace's optimal apartment price is $p_T = 990 + 920 = \$1,910$ per month.

Game Theory

12

Solutions for Practice Problems

Problem 1

a. The payoff matrix for this game (with payoffs in millions of dollars) follows.

		DirecTV	
		Advertise	Don't advertise
Dish Network	Advertise	✓11 , 12✓	✓27 , 8
	Don't advertise	7 , 25✓	24 , 22 ✗
		✗	

b. A dominant strategy is a strategy that is best for a player whatever strategy its opponent follows. To see whether Dish Network has a dominant strategy, we consider its choices given each of the possible actions by DirecTV. As we can see from the payoff matrix, if DirecTV chooses to advertise, Dish Network's best option is to advertise too, since its payoff in this case ($11 million) is greater than its payoffs when it does not advertise ($7 million). If DirecTV decides not to advertise, then Dish Network's best option is, again, to advertise, since $27 million > $24 million. The two check marks next to Dish Network's payoffs in the "Advertise" row indicate that whatever DirecTV's decision is, Dish Network's preferred option is always to advertise. Therefore, to advertise is the dominant strategy for Dish Network.

Now let's consider DirecTV's choices given each of the possible actions by Dish Network. If Dish Network chooses to advertise, DirecTV's best option is also to advertise, since its payoff in this case ($12 million) is greater than its payoffs when it does not advertise ($8 million). If Dish Network decides not to advertise, then DirecTV's preferred option is, again, to advertise, since $25 million > $22 million. The two check marks next to DirecTV's payoffs in the "Advertise" column indicate that whatever Dish Network's decision is, DirecTV's preferred option is always to advertise. Therefore, to advertise is the dominant strategy for DirecTV as well.

c. A dominated strategy is a losing strategy for a player, regardless of what its opponent does. Dish Network's dominated strategy is indicated by the row of the payoff matrix with no check marks next to Dish Network's payoffs. That is, no check marks in the "Don't advertise" row means that under no circumstances is it best for Dish Network to choose this option. Therefore, not to advertise is Dish Network's dominated strategy, and we can cross out this row.

DirecTV's dominated strategy is indicated in the column of the payoff matrix with no check marks next to DirecTV's payoffs. This is the "Don't advertise" column, which means under no circumstances is it the best choice for DirecTV. Therefore, not to advertise is DirecTV's dominated strategy, and we can cross out this column.

d. There is a box in the payoff matrix in which two check marks appear. It is where both companies advertise. This is the Nash equilibrium of the game because to advertise is the dominant strategy for both Dish Network and DirecTV, and not to advertise is the dominated strategy for both companies. This is a prisoner's dilemma because the Nash equilibrium is an outcome that for both companies is worse than another (unstable) outcome. In the Nash equilibrium, that is, when both companies advertise, both of them receive lower profits than in the situation when neither company advertises.

e. In the Nash equilibrium, neither of the companies wants to unilaterally change its strategy whatever strategy the other company is choosing. Therefore, the Nash equilibrium—that is, when both companies advertise—is the likely outcome of this game.

Problem 2

a. First, let's consider Noble's choices, given each Malty's action. As we can see from the payoff matrix, if Malty chooses to produce cheap beer, Noble's preferred choice is to produce high-quality beer (since $40 million > $18 million). If Malty chooses to produce high-quality beer, Noble's preferred option is to produce cheap beer (since $30 million > $15 million). The check marks on the following playoff matrix indicate these Noble's choices. Now, let's consider Malty's choices given each Noble's action. If Noble chooses the cheap beer option, Malty's preferred choice is also cheap beer (as $25 million > $10 million). And if Noble goes with high-quality beer, Malty's preferred option is to produce cheap beer, since this allows Malty to earn $20 million rather than lose $5 million.

Malty

		Cheap	High quality
Noble	Cheap	18 , 25✓	✓30 , 10
	High quality	✓40 , 20✓	12 , –5

The box in the payoff matrix in which two check marks appear indicates that a Nash equilibrium occurs where Noble produces high-quality beer and Malty produces cheap beer. Since this is the only Nash equilibrium, it is the predicted outcome of the game when both breweries act rationally to maximize their profits.

b. If Noble is not sure that Malty will choose its highest payoff options, it makes sense for Noble to use a maximin strategy. This means Noble should choose to produce cheap beer. The lowest profit it could expect in this case is $18 million. If Noble decided to produce high-quality beer, its profit could fall as low as $12 million, if Malty in fact decides to go with high-quality beer.

c. The check method leads us to find no pure strategy Nash equilibria because there are no boxes with two checks in them.

Malty

		Cheap	High quality
Noble	Cheap	18 , 25✓	✓30 , 10
	High quality	✓40 , 20	12 , 30✓

d.

Malty

		q Cheap	$1-q$ High quality
Noble	p Cheap	18 , 25	30 , 10
	$1-p$ High quality	40 , 20	12 , 30

Now, we can set up the equilibrium conditions.
For Noble Hops:

$$18q + 30(1 - q) = 40q + 12(1 - q)$$
$$22q = 18(1 - q)$$
$$22q = 18 - 18q$$
$$q = \frac{9}{20}$$

For Malty Twist:

$$25p + 20(1 - p) = 10p + 30(1 - p)$$
$$15p = 10(1 - p)$$
$$15p = 10 - 10p$$
$$p = \frac{2}{5}$$

Since neither producer knows exactly what the other will do, both find it optimal to mix their strategies (randomize) over their possible actions until the point that each is exactly indifferent between the pure strategies available to him or her. The optimal degree of randomization then depends on the possible payoffs at stake. The mixed strategy Nash equilibrium therefore is for Noble Hops to produce cheap beer, with probability $\frac{2}{5}$, and high-quality beer, with probability $\frac{3}{5}$, and for Malty Twist to produce cheap beer, with probability $\frac{9}{20}$, and high quality, with probability $\frac{11}{20}$. (Note that q corresponds to the probability that Malty Twist will produce cheap beer and p corresponds to the probability that Noble Hops will do so.)

Problem 3

a. The following shows the extensive form (decision tree) for the game.

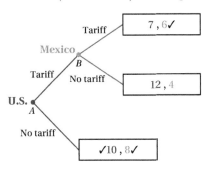

b. We use backward induction to look for a Nash equilibrium in this game. Suppose the United States decides to impose the tariff. This takes us to node B in the game tree, where Mexico makes its decision. If Mexico chooses to retaliate, its surplus will be $6 billion; with no retaliation, its surplus will be only $4 billion. That is, Mexico's best response is to impose the retaliatory tariff. Now that we know how Mexico will respond, we can work backward to figure out what choice the United States should make at node A. The United States knows that if it imposes the tariff, then Mexico will retaliate, so the United States' surplus will be $7 billion. And if the United States remains committed to free trade with Mexico, its surplus will be $10 billion. Since $10 billion > $7 billion, the United States will choose not to impose the tariff. Thus, the Nash equilibrium in this game is free trade between the United States and Mexico.

Problem 4

a. On the following payoff matrix, we place check marks next to each restaurant's preferred choices, given the competitor's actions. First, we consider Art's choices, given each possible Bob's action. As we can see from the payoff matrix, if Bob chooses to expand, Art's best option is to expand too, since Art's payoff in this case ($30,000) is greater than his payoffs when he does not expand ($25,000). If Bob chooses not to expand, Art's preferred option is, again, to expand, since $47,000 > $35,000.

		Bob's	
		Expand	Don't expand
Art's	Expand	✓30 , 38✓	✓47 , 28
	Don't expand	25 , 49✓	35 , 41

Now consider Bob's choices, given Art's actions. If Art chooses to expand, Bob's preferred option is to expand too, since Bob's payoff in this case ($38,000) is greater than his payoffs when he does not expand ($28,000). And if Art chooses not to expand, Bob's best option is to expand, since $49,000 > $41,000.

As we can see, two check marks appear in one box, which is where both restaurants decide to expand. This is not the best cooperative outcome for the game, but it is the only stable equilibrium.

b. If the game is played twice, the outcome will not change because there will be no change in the players' strategies. In the second period, both restaurants will expand because that is the Nash equilibrium in a one-period game. Knowing this and using backward induction, Art and Bob will opt to expand in the first period as well.

c. Art's payoff from cheating on the agreement and expanding is the $47,000 for the first period, when Bob does not expand and Art cheats, and $30,000 for each period after that, when Bob also expands. Thus, in an infinitely repeated game, Art's total expected payoff when cheating is

$$47 + d \times 30 + d^2 \times 30 + d^3 \times 30 + \ldots$$

Art's payoff from following the agreement (when neither of the restaurants expands) is $35,000 in each period. So, in an infinitely repeated game, Art's total expected payoff when following the agreement is

$$35 + d \times 35 + d^2 \times 35 + d^3 \times 35 + \ldots$$

Art will be indifferent between these two options when his payoff streams from cheating and following the agreement are equal:

$$47 + d \times 30 + d^2 \times 30 + d^3 \times 30 + \ldots = 35 + d \times 35 + d^2 \times 35 + d^3 \times 35 + \ldots$$

Solving this equation for d, we get:

$$47 + 30 \times (d + d^2 + d^3 + \ldots) = 35 + 35 \times (d + d^2 + d^3 + \ldots)$$
$$5 \times (d + d^2 + d^3 + \ldots) = 12$$
$$d + d^2 + d^3 + \ldots = 2.4$$

Since $d + d^2 + d^3 + \ldots = \dfrac{d}{1-d}$ for any d between zero and one ($0 \le d < 1$), we can write:

$$\frac{d}{1-d} = 2.4$$
$$d = 2.4(1-d)$$
$$d = 2.4 - 2.4d$$
$$3.4d = 2.4$$
$$d = 0.706$$

Thus, Art is indifferent between keeping the agreement and cheating on it if his discounting of the future factor is 0.706. This means if Art's discounting factor is higher than this ($d > 0.706$), he will follow the agreement and won't expand.

Bob's payoff from cheating on the agreement is the $49,000 from the first period and $38,000 from each period after that. Thus, in an infinitely repeated game, Bob's total expected payoff when cheating is

$$49 + d \times 38 + d^2 \times 38 + d^3 \times 38 + \ldots$$

Bob's payoff from following the agreement is $41,000 in each period, so in an infinitely repeated game, Bob's total expected payoff when following the agreement is

$$41 + d \times 41 + d^2 \times 41 + d^3 \times 41 + \ldots$$

Bob will be indifferent between the two options when these payoff streams are equal:

$$49 + d \times 38 + d^2 \times 38 + d^3 \times 38 + \ldots = 41 + d \times 41 + d^2 \times 41 + d^3 \times 41 + \ldots$$

Solving this equation for d, we get:

$$49 + 38 \times (d + d^2 + d^3 + \ldots) = 41 + 41 \times (d + d^2 + d^3 + \ldots)$$
$$3 \times (d + d^2 + d^3 + \ldots) = 8$$
$$d + d^2 + d^3 + \ldots = \frac{8}{3}$$
$$\frac{d}{1-d} = \frac{8}{3}$$
$$3d = 8(1-d)$$
$$3d = 8 - 8d$$
$$11d = 8$$
$$d = 0.727$$

Thus, Bob is indifferent between keeping the agreement and cheating on it if his discounting of the future factor is 0.727. This means if Bob's discounting factor is higher than this ($d > 0.727$), he will follow the agreement and won't expand.

Problem 5

a. The following is the payoff matrix for this problem (the payoffs are in millions of dollars).

		Saudi Arabia	
		Follow agreement	Cheat
Iran	Follow agreement	1104 , 1200	1056 , 1248✓ ✗
	Cheat	✓1144 , 1152 ✗	✓1092 , 1196✓

b. A dominant strategy is a strategy that is best for a player whatever strategy its opponent follows. To see whether Iran has a dominant strategy, we consider its choices, given each of the possible actions by Saudi Arabia. As we can see from the payoff matrix, if Saudi Arabia chooses to follow the agreement, Iran's best option is to cheat, since its payoff in this case ($1,144 million) is greater than its payoffs from following the agreement ($1,104 million). If Saudi Arabia decides to cheat, Iran's best option is, again, to cheat, since $1,092 million > $1,056 million. Our two check marks next to Iran's payoffs in the "Cheat" row indicate that no matter what Saudi Arabia's decision is, Iran's best option is always to cheat. This is the dominant strategy for Iran.

To see whether Saudi Arabia has a dominant strategy, we consider its choices, given each of the possible actions by Iran. If Iran chooses to follow the agreement, Saudi Arabia's best option is to cheat, since its payoff in this case ($1,248 million) is greater than its payoffs from following the agreement ($1,200 million). If Iran decides to cheat, Saudi Arabia's best option is, again, to cheat, since $1,196 million > $1,152 million. The two check marks next to Saudi Arabia's payoffs in the "Cheat" column indicate that, whatever Iran's decision is, Saudi Arabia's best option is always to cheat. This is the dominant strategy for Saudi Arabia.

c. A dominated strategy is a losing strategy for a player, regardless of what its opponent does. Iran's dominated strategy is indicated by the row of the payoff matrix with no check marks next to Iran's payoffs. That is, no check marks in the "Follow agreement" row means that under no circumstances is it best for Iran to choose this option. This is Iran's dominated strategy, and we can cross out this row.

Saudi Arabia's dominated strategy is indicated by the column of the payoff matrix with no check marks next to Saudi Arabia's payoffs. This is the "Follow agreement" column, which means under no circumstances is it the best choice for Saudi Arabia. This is Saudi Arabia's dominated strategy, and we can cross out this column.

d. There is a box in the payoff matrix in which two check marks appear. It is where both countries choose to cheat. This is the Nash equilibrium of the game. This is because cheating is the dominant strategy for both Iran and Saudi Arabia and following the agreement is the dominated strategy for both countries.

Problem 6

a. If the game is played for four periods, there would be no change in the countries' behavior. In the last period, both countries would cheat because that is the Nash equilibrium in a one-period game. Knowing this and using backward induction, Iran and Saudi Arabia will choose to cheat in all previous periods.

b. The following shows the payoff matrix from Problem 5.

Saudi Arabia

	Follow agreement	Cheat
Iran Follow agreement	1104 , 1200	1056 , 1248
Iran Cheat	1144 , 1152	1092 , 1196

Iran's payoff from cheating is $1,144 million for the first period (when Saudi Arabia follows the cartel agreement and Iran cheats) and $1,092 million for each period after that (when Saudi Arabia also starts cheating). Thus, in an infinitely repeated game, Iran's total expected payoff when cheating is

$$1{,}144 + d \times 1{,}092 + d^2 \times 1{,}092 + d^3 \times 1{,}092 + \ldots$$

$$= 1{,}144 + 1{,}092 \times (d + d^2 + d^3 + \ldots)$$

Since $d + d^2 + d^3 + \ldots = \dfrac{d}{1-d}$ for any d between zero and one ($0 \le d < 1$), we can calculate this payoff as follows:

$$1{,}144 + 1{,}092 \times \frac{d}{1-d}$$

$$= 1{,}144 + 1{,}092 \times \frac{0.85}{1 - 0.85} = 7{,}332$$

Iran's payoff from following the agreement (when neither of the countries cheats) is $1,104 million in each period. So, in an infinitely repeated game, Iran's total expected payoff when following the agreement is

$$1{,}104 + d \times 1{,}104 + d^2 \times 1{,}104 + d^3 \times 1{,}104 + \ldots$$

$$= 1{,}104 + 1{,}104 \times \frac{d}{1-d}$$

$$= 1{,}104 + 1{,}104 \times \frac{0.85}{1 - 0.85} = 7{,}360$$

Since Iran's payoff from following the agreement ($7,360 million) is greater than its payoff from cheating ($7,332 million), Iran's preferred strategy is to follow the agreement.

Saudi Arabia's payoff from cheating is $1,248 million for the first period (when Iran follows the cartel agreement and Saudi Arabia cheats) and $1,196 million for each period after that (when Iran also starts cheating). Thus, in an infinitely repeated game, Saudi Arabia's total expected payoff when cheating is

$$1{,}248 + d \times 1{,}196 + d^2 \times 1{,}196 + d^3 \times 1{,}196 + \ldots$$
$$= 1{,}248 + 1{,}196 \times (d + d^2 + d^3 + \ldots)$$
$$= 1{,}248 + 1{,}196 \times \frac{d}{1-d}$$
$$= 1{,}248 + 1{,}196 \times \frac{0.93}{1-0.93} = 17{,}138$$

Saudi Arabia's payoff from following the agreement (when neither of the countries cheats) is $1,200 million in each period. So in an infinitely repeated game, Saudi Arabia's total expected payoff when following the agreement is

$$1{,}200 + d \times 1{,}200 + d^2 \times 1{,}200 + d^3 \times 1{,}200 + \ldots$$
$$= 1{,}200 + 1{,}200 \times \frac{d}{1-d}$$
$$= 1{,}200 + 1{,}200 \times \frac{0.93}{1-0.93} = 17{,}143$$

Since Saudi Arabia's payoff from following the agreement ($17,143 million) is greater than its payoff from cheating ($17,138 million), Saudi Arabia's preferred strategy is to follow the agreement.

Thus, in the infinitely repeated game, both countries will follow the agreement. That is, the outcome will be different from that in the one-period game in Problem 5, where the Nash equilibrium occurs when both countries cheat.

Problem 7

a. A dominant strategy is a strategy that is best for a player whatever strategy its opponent follows. To see whether Sony has a dominant strategy, we consider its choices, given each of the possible actions by Panasonic. On the following payoff matrix, we place check marks next to the payoffs from the companies' best options. If Panasonic chooses to develop a new model of its camcorder, Sony's best option is to develop a new model of its camcorder too, as its payoff in this case (120) is greater than its payoffs from upgrading its existing model (110) or from leaving its camcorder, since it is (95). If Panasonic chooses to upgrade its camcorder, Sony's best option is also to upgrade, since 130 > 125 and 130 > 100. And if Panasonic chooses to leave its camcorder as it is, Sony's best option is to develop a new model, since 140 > 125 and 140 > 90. As you can see, our three check marks indicating Sony's best options are not in the same row. That is, Sony's preferred options depend on Panasonic's choices. This means Sony does not have a dominant strategy.

		Panasonic		
		New model	Upgrade	Leave as is
	New model	✓120 , 110✓	125 , 100	✓140 , 80
Sony	Upgrade	110 , 115	✓130 , 140✓	125 , 85
	Leave as is	95 , 130✓	100 , 120	90 , 95 ✗

To see whether Panasonic has a dominant strategy, we consider its choices, given each of the possible actions by Sony. If Sony chooses to develop a new model of its camcorder, Panasonic's best option is to also develop a new model, as its payoff in this case (110) is greater than its payoffs from upgrading (100) or leaving its camcorder as it is (80). If Sony chooses to upgrade its camcorder, Panasonic's best option is to upgrade too, since 140 > 115 and 140 > 85. And if Sony chooses to leave its camcorder as it is, Panasonic's best option is to develop a new model, since 130 > 120 and 130 > 95. As you can see, our three check marks next to Panasonic's payoffs are not in the same column. That is, Panasonic's best option depends on Sony's choice. This means Panasonic does not have a dominant strategy.

b. A dominated strategy is a losing strategy for a player, regardless of what its opponent does. Sony's dominated strategies are indicated by the rows of the payoff matrix with no check marks next to its payoffs. That is, no check marks in the "Leave as is" row means that under no circumstances is it best for Sony to choose this option. This is Sony's dominated strategy (so we can cross out this row).

Panasonic's dominated strategies are indicated by the columns of the payoff matrix with no check marks next to its payoffs. That is, no check marks in the "Leave as is" column means that under no circumstances is this the best choice for Panasonic. This is Panasonic's dominated strategy (so we can cross out this column).

c. To find a Nash equilibrium, we look at the companies' mutual best responses, where there are two checks in the same box. There are two of them. Either both companies decide to develop a new model of their camcorders or both decide to upgrade their existing model. Both outcomes are Nash equilibria of the game. Therefore, we cannot predict the exact outcome of this game. We can narrow down the possibilities—neither of the companies will choose to leave its camcorder as it is, and both will choose either to develop a new model or to upgrade if the opponent makes the same choice—but we cannot tell whether the companies will choose to develop a new model or to upgrade.

Problem 8

a. Before we construct the decision tree, let's recall from Problem 7 that leaving their camcorders unchanged is a dominated strategy for both companies. That is, this strategy is never optimal regardless of what the competitor might do. Therefore, in Problem 7, we crossed out the outcomes with either company leaving its camcorder as it is. This simplifies the normal form of the game to a payoff matrix with only two rows and two columns, as in the following payoff.

Panasonic

	New model	Upgrade
New model	✓120 , 110✓	125 , 100
Upgrade	110 , 115	✓130 , 140✓

Sony

We can construct the extensive-form game based on the preceding simplified payoff matrix as follows:

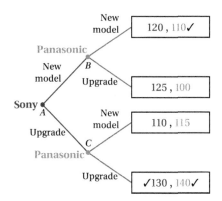

b. We use backward induction to look for a Nash equilibrium. Suppose Sony decides to develop a new model of its camcorder. That puts us at node B in the game tree, where Panasonic makes its decision. If Panasonic also chooses to develop a new model, it will make $110 million, and if it chooses to upgrade, its profit will be $100 million. That is, Panasonic's preferred response is to develop a new model. Now suppose Sony chooses to upgrade its camcorder, putting the game at node C. Here, if Panasonic chooses to develop a new model, it earns $115 million, and if it chooses to upgrade, it earns $140 million. So, Panasonic's best response is to upgrade.

Now that we know how Panasonic will respond to all possible first moves by Sony, we can work backward to figure out what choice Sony will make at node A. Sony knows that if it chooses to develop a new model, Panasonic will also choose to develop a new model, so Sony will earn $120 million. And if Sony decides to upgrade its camcorder, Panasonic will respond by upgrading its camcorder too, so Sony will earn $130 million. As we can see, Sony's payoff is higher when it chooses to upgrade (130 > 120). Thus, the (only) Nash equilibrium in this game is when both companies upgrade, with Sony earning $130 million and Panasonic earning $140 million. This outcome is different from that in the simultaneous-move game in Problem 7, where there were two equilibria, one with both companies developing a new model of their camcorders and the other with both companies upgrading their existing models.

Problem 9

a. To find a Nash equilibrium, we first consider GM's choices, given each of the possible actions by Toyota. If Toyota chooses to produce the new car, GM's best option is not to produce its car as its payoff in this case is zero, rather than a loss of $2 billion. If Toyota chooses not to produce its car, GM's best option is to produce, since choosing this option allows GM to earn $12 billion as opposed to nothing. Now let's consider Toyota's choices, given each of the possible actions by GM. If GM chooses to launch the new car, Toyota's best option is not to produce its car, since the result is a zero profit rather than a loss of $1 billion. But if GM chooses not to produce its car, Toyota's best option is to produce, since this allows it to earn $15 billion instead of nothing, as shown in the following payoff matrix.

		Toyota	
		Produce	Don't produce
GM	**Produce**	−2 , −1	✓12 , 0✓
	Don't produce	✓0 , 15✓	0 , 0

To find a Nash equilibrium, we look at the companies' mutual best responses, where there are two checks in the same box. As we can see, there are two Nash equilibria: (1) GM launches its new car and Toyota does not and (2) Toyota launches its car and GM does not. This means we cannot predict the exact outcome of the game. We can only tell that one of the companies will produce its new electric car, but we cannot tell with certainty whether this will be GM or Toyota.

b. The following shows the extensive-form game, given that Toyota makes its decision first.

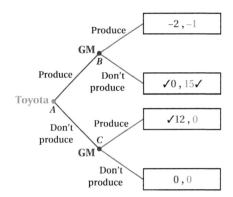

Let's use backward induction to find Nash equilibria in this sequential game. First, suppose that Toyota decides to produce its new car. This decision puts us at node B in the game tree, where GM makes its decision. If GM also chooses to produce, it will lose $2 billion. If it chooses not to produce, its profit will be zero. That is, GM's preferred response here is not to produce. Now suppose Toyota chooses not to launch its car, putting the game at node C. Here, if GM chooses to produce, it will earn $12 billion, and if it chooses not to produce, its profit will be zero. So, GM's best option is to produce.

Now that we know how GM will respond to all possible first moves by Toyota, we can work backward to figure out what choice Toyota will make at node A. Toyota knows that if it chooses to produce its car, GM will not launch its car, so Toyota will earn $15 billion. And if Toyota decides not to produce, GM will respond by launching its car and Toyota's profit will be zero. Clearly, Toyota's preferred option is to launch its new car. Thus, the (only) Nash equilibrium in this game is when Toyota launches its car and GM does not.

In the simultaneous-move game in (a), we had two equilibria and were uncertain about which company's car will be on the market. But when Toyota moves first, there is only one Nash equilibrium, with only Toyota making a positive profit from its new car and GM not producing its new car. Thus, Toyota has a first-mover advantage.

c. The government subsidy adds $3 billion to GM's payoffs if the company produces its new car. The following shows the decision tree with the subsidy. Let's use backward induction again to find the Nash equilibria. If Toyota decides to produce its new car, GM's decision at node B is now to produce its car too, since the subsidy allows GM to earn −$2 billion + $3 billion = $1 billion when producing the car instead of nothing when not producing it. And if Toyota chooses not to produce its car, then GM's best response is, again, to produce, since it earns $3 billion + $12 billion = $15 billion if it chooses to produce and nothing if it does not.

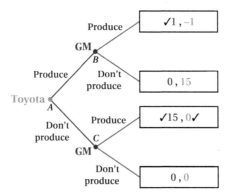

Now we can work backward to figure out what choice Toyota will make at node A. Toyota knows that if it chooses to produce its car, GM will also launch its car, so Toyota will incur a loss of $1 billion. But if Toyota decides not to produce, it will incur no loss. Thus, Toyota's preferred option is not to launch its car. That is, with the government subsidy to GM, the Nash equilibrium in this game is when GM produces its new car and Toyota does not. Thus, the subsidy changes the outcome of the game to GM's advantage despite the fact that Toyota could move first.

Problem 10

a. The following shows the extensive form of the game (with payoffs in millions of dollars).

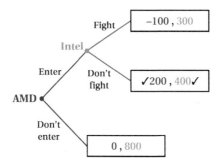

b. This is a sequential game. First, AMD decides whether to enter the market. If it doesn't enter, the game is over. AMD earns a profit of zero and Intel earns the monopoly profit of $800 million. If AMD enters the market, however, then Intel must decide how to react. If Intel fights, it earns $300 million. If it doesn't, it earns $400 million. Thus, Intel's preferred choice is not to fight. By using backward induction, then, AMD realizes that it has to choose between entering and earning $200 million (since Intel won't fight) and not entering and earning nothing. So, AMD will enter and earn $200 million. Intel then won't fight AMD's entry and will earn $400 million.

c. The outcome of the game won't change, because Intel's threat is not credible. AMD knows that if it enters, Intel will earn only $300 million if it fights and $400 million if it goes along. AMD will, therefore, call Intel's bluff and enter, so the outcome of the game will be the same as in (b).

d. Intel's investment in the extra capacity makes its threat to fight credible, changing the game tree as the following shows. Now, if AMD enters, Intel makes more profit when it fights ($300 billion) than when it does not ($290 billion). AMD realizes that Intel will fight and chooses not to enter, because zero profit is better than a $100 million loss. Intel remains a monopolist in the market, earning $580 billion, which is $180 million more than the $400 billion the company would have made as a duopolist in (b) or (c). Thus, building the excess capacity to create a credible threat is a good strategic move for Intel, even though it will not use that extra capacity.

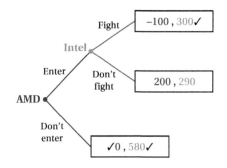

Problem 11

a. The check method leads us to find two pure strategy Nash equilibria. These correspond to the mismatch cases where one specializes in espresso and the other specializes in regular coffee.

		Mike	
		Espresso	**Coffee**
John	**Espresso**	100 , 100	✓120 , 110✓
	Coffee	✓110 , 120✓	90 , 90

b.

		Mike	
		q	$1-q$
		Espresso	**Coffee**
John	p **Espresso**	100 , 100	120 , 110
	$1-p$ **Coffee**	110 , 120	90 , 90

Now, we can set up the equilibrium conditions.

For John:

$$100q + 120(1 - q) = 110q + 90(1 - q)$$
$$10q = 30(1 - q)$$
$$10q = 30 - 30q$$
$$q = \frac{3}{4}$$

For Mike:

$$100p + 120(1 - p) = 110p + 90(1 - p)$$
$$10p = 30(1 - p)$$
$$10p = 30 - 30p$$
$$q = \frac{3}{4}$$

Since neither owner knows exactly what the other will do, both find it optimal to mix their strategies (randomize) over their possible actions until the point that each is exactly indifferent between the pure strategies available to him or her. The optimal degree of randomization then depends on the possible payoffs at stake. The mixed strategy Nash equilibrium therefore is for each owner to specialize in espresso, with probability $\frac{3}{4}$, and regular coffee, with probability $\frac{1}{4}$.

13

Investment, Time, and Insurance

Solutions for Practice Problems

Problem 1

a. Since the store is expected to earn a regular annual profit forever, its present discounted value can be calculated, using the perpetuity formula:

$$PDV = \frac{M}{r}$$

where M is the annual payment, and r is the real interest rate (expressed as a fraction), which is the nominal interest rate minus the rate of inflation. For the investment in question, $M = \$80,000$ and $r = 0.07 - 0.02 = 0.05$. Substituting these values into the preceding formula, we get:

$$PDV = \frac{\$80,000}{0.05} = \$1,600,000$$

b. The net present value of Robert's investment will be the negative of the amount he pays for it plus the PDV of the store:

$$NPV = -\$1.1 \text{ million} + \$1.6 \text{ million} = \$0.5 \text{ million}$$

Since the NPV is positive, that is, the PDV of the investment's benefits outweighs its cost, it is worthwhile to purchase the store.

c. When the nominal interest rate is 10%, the real interest rate is $r = 0.10 - 0.02 = 0.08$, so the PDV of the store is

$$PDV = \frac{\$80,000}{0.08} = \$1,000,000$$

and

$$NPV = -\$1.1 \text{ million} + \$1.0 \text{ million} = -\$0.1 \text{ million}$$

Since the NPV is negative, purchasing the store is not a good investment.

Problem 2

a. First, we find the amount of each coupon payment by multiplying the face value of the bond by the coupon rate: $\$1,000 \times 0.04 = \$40$. This means Alicia expects to receive $\$40$ in each of the four years plus the face value of the bond ($\$1,000$) at maturity, that is, four years from now. Thus, the present discounted value of the bond is

$$PDV = \frac{\$40}{1 + 0.02} + \frac{\$40}{(1 + 0.02)^2} + \frac{\$40}{(1 + 0.02)^3} + \frac{\$40}{(1 + 0.02)^4} + \frac{\$1,000}{(1 + 0.02)^4} = \$1,076.15$$

b. After one year, there will be three coupon payments left, so the present discounted value of the bond will be

$$PDV = \frac{\$40}{1 + 0.02} + \frac{\$40}{(1 + 0.02)^2} + \frac{\$40}{(1 + 0.02)^3} + \frac{\$1,000}{(1 + 0.02)^3} = \$1,057.68$$

Since the amount Alicia's friend offers is greater than the bond's PDV, Alicia is better off if she sells the bond.

Problem 3

a. An equilibrium interest rate is the one at which the quantity of capital demanded equals the quantity of capital supplied. Thus, we set $Q^D = Q^S$ and solve this equation for r:

$$Q^D = Q^S$$
$$80 - 800r = 800r$$
$$1{,}600r = 80$$
$$r = 0.05$$

Now we can find the quantity of capital invested by substituting the interest rate into either the demand or the supply equation:

$$Q^D = 80 - 800 \times 0.05 = 40$$
$$Q^S = 800 \times 0.05 = 40$$

Thus, the market interest rate is 5%, and $40 billion is invested at this rate.

b. The fact that households are willing to save $16 billion more at each given interest rate means the supply of capital curve shifts rightward by $16 billion (see the following graph). To derive the new supply curve algebraically, we add 16 to the original supply curve:

$$Q_2^S = 800r + 16$$
$$Q_2^S = 16 + 800r$$

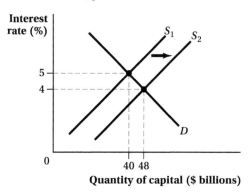

To find the new market equilibrium, we set $Q^D = Q_2^S$ and solve this equation for r:

$$Q^D = Q_2^S$$
$$80 - 800r = 16 + 800r$$
$$1{,}600r = 64$$
$$r = 0.04$$

Now we can find the quantity of capital invested by substituting the interest rate into either the demand or the supply equation:

$$Q^D = 80 - 800 \times 0.04 = 48$$
$$Q_2^S = 16 + 800 \times 0.04 = 48$$

Thus, the market interest rate falls from 5% to 4%, and the quantity of capital invested increases from $40 billion to $48 billion.

Problem 4

a. To make your choice, you should compare the present discounted values of the three options. The PDV of option (1) is

$$PDV = \$200{,}000 + \frac{\$200{,}000}{1 + 0.05} + \frac{\$200{,}000}{(1 + 0.05)^2} + \frac{\$200{,}000}{(1 + 0.05)^3} + \frac{\$200{,}000}{(1 + 0.05)^4} = \$909{,}190$$

The PDV of option (2) is $900,000, since you receive this payment in the present. And option (3) is a perpetuity, so its PDV is

$$PDV = \frac{\$50{,}000}{0.05} = \$1{,}000{,}000$$

Since option (3) has the highest PDV, you should choose this option.

b. When the interest rate is 6%, the PDV of option (1) is

$$PDV = \$200{,}000 + \frac{\$200{,}000}{1 + 0.06} + \frac{\$200{,}000}{(1 + 0.06)^2} + \frac{\$200{,}000}{(1 + 0.06)^3} + \frac{\$200{,}000}{(1 + 0.06)^4} = \$893{,}021$$

The PDV of option (2) is still $900,000. Since you receive this payment in the present, it is not affected by changes in the interest rate. And for option (3), the PDV is

$$PDV = \frac{\$50{,}000}{0.06} = \$833{,}333$$

Since option (2) has now the highest PDV, you should choose this option.

Problem 5

a. The partnership's cost is $1,600 today ($C_0 = \$1{,}600$), and its benefits are $B_1 = B_2 = B_3 = \$450$ (additional profit) plus $S_3 = \$500$ from reselling the computer at the end of the third year. Thus, the net present value of the investment is

$$NPV = -C_0 + \frac{B_1}{1 + r} + \frac{B_2}{(1 + r)^2} + \frac{B_3 + S_3}{(1 + r)^3}$$

The r in this formula is the real interest rate, which is the market interest rate minus the rate of inflation, so $r = 0.10 - 0.02 = 0.08$. Thus,

$$NPV = -\$1{,}600 + \frac{\$450}{1 + 0.08} + \frac{\$450}{(1 + 0.08)^2} + \frac{\$450 + \$500}{(1 + 0.08)^3}$$

$$NPV = -\$43.39$$

b. George does not take into account the fact that the value of a future benefit is not the same as that of a present cost. He treats future payments as equivalent to current payments in dollar terms, which is actually not the case. Discounting the future payments when assessing the net present value of the investment in (a) allows us to calculate future benefits in terms of equivalent present-period dollars, so they can be correctly compared with the investment's cost. The negative NPV calculated in (a) means that the present value of the investment's cost outweighs the PDV of its benefits. Therefore, purchasing the computer is not worthwhile.

c. With the market interest rate of 7% and the expected inflation rate of 3%, the real interest rate is $r = 0.07 - 0.03 = 0.04$. Thus,

$$NPV = -\$1{,}600 + \frac{\$450}{1 + 0.04} + \frac{\$450}{(1 + 0.04)^2} + \frac{\$450 + \$500}{(1 + 0.04)^3}$$

$$NPV = \$93.29$$

Since the lower real interest rate makes the NPV of the investment positive, purchasing the computer is now worthwhile.

Problem 6

a. Bob's cost is $85,000 in the present period ($C_0 = \$85{,}000$), and his benefits are $B_1 = B_2 = B_3 = B_4 = B_5 = \$20{,}000$. Thus, the net present value of his investment is

$$NPV = -C_0 + \frac{B_1}{1 + r} + \frac{B_2}{(1 + r)^2} + \frac{B_3}{(1 + r)^3} + \frac{B_4}{(1 + r)^4} + \frac{B_5}{(1 + r)^5}$$

$$NPV = -\$85{,}000 + \frac{\$20{,}000}{1 + 0.04} + \frac{\$20{,}000}{(1 + 0.04)^2} + \frac{\$20{,}000}{(1 + 0.04)^3} + \frac{\$20{,}000}{(1 + 0.04)^4} + \frac{\$20{,}000}{(1 + 0.04)^5}$$

$$NPV = \$4{,}036.45$$

Since the project's NPV is positive (even with our conservative assumption of no additional profit after five years), Bob should definitely expand.

b. Now Bob's cost is $30,000 in the present period (the down payment) and $30,000 at the end of each of the first two years ($C_0 = C_1 = C_2 = \$30{,}000$). And his benefits are $B_1 = B_2 = B_3 = B_4 = B_5 = \$20{,}000$. Thus, the net present value of his investment is

$$NPV = -\$30{,}000 + \frac{-\$30{,}000 + \$20{,}000}{1 + 0.04} + \frac{-\$30{,}000 + \$20{,}000}{(1 + 0.04)^2} + \frac{\$20{,}000}{(1 + 0.04)^3} + \frac{\$20{,}000}{(1 + 0.04)^4} + \frac{\$20{,}000}{(1 + 0.04)^5}$$

$$NPV = \$2{,}453.61$$

Since the project's NPV is positive, Bob should expand.

Problem 7

a. The expected value of Bob's additional profit is the probability-weighted average of the three possible outcomes:

$$\text{Expected value} = (p_1 \times M_1) + (p_2 \times M_2) + (p_3 \times M_3)$$
$$= (0.7 \times \$20{,}000) + (0.2 \times \$30{,}000) + (0.1 \times \$5{,}000)$$
$$= \$20{,}500$$

b. To calculate the net present value of Bob's investment, we substitute the expected value of his additional profit into the NPV formula:

$$NPV = -\$85{,}000 + \frac{\$20{,}500}{1 + 0.04} + \frac{\$20{,}500}{(1 + 0.04)^2} + \frac{\$20{,}500}{(1 + 0.04)^3} + \frac{\$20{,}500}{(1 + 0.04)^4} + \frac{\$20{,}500}{(1 + 0.04)^5}$$

$$NPV = \$6{,}262.36$$

Since the NPV of the investment is positive, Bob should implement the project.

Problem 8

a. If Agatha's house suffers a fire, her wealth will be reduced to $\$196{,}000 - \$160{,}000 = \$36{,}000$. The probability of this event is 0.03, so the probability that Agatha's wealth will remain at \$196,000 is $1 - 0.03 = 0.97$. Therefore, Agatha's expected wealth is

$$0.97 \times \$196{,}000 + 0.03 \times \$36{,}000 = \$191{,}200$$

b. If there is no fire, Agatha's utility is

$$U = 10 \times 196^{0.5} = 140$$

And if there is a fire, her utility is

$$U = 10 \times 36^{0.5} = 60$$

Since the probability of a fire is 0.03, and the probability of no fire is 0.97, Agatha's expected utility is

$$0.97 \times 140 + 0.03 \times 60 = 137.6$$

c. Agatha's risk premium is the extra amount of expected wealth she must receive to make her as well off when her wealth is uncertain as when it is guaranteed. To calculate Agatha's risk premium, we first need to determine the guaranteed wealth that would offer her the same utility level as her uncertain wealth (137.6). To find this certainty equivalent, we substitute $U = 137.6$ into Agatha's utility function and solve this equation for W:

$$137.6 = 10W^{0.5}$$
$$W^{0.5} = 13.76$$
$$W = 189.338$$

Thus, Agatha derives the same expected utility from a guaranteed wealth of \$189,338 as she does from her expected uncertain wealth of \$191,200. This means Agatha is willing to give up $\$191{,}200 - \$189{,}338 = \$1{,}862$ in exchange for eliminating her wealth uncertainty. This difference is Agatha's risk premium.

d. With the insurance, Agatha's wealth is \$190,000, regardless of whether a fire occurs. If there is no fire, her wealth will be $\$196{,}000 - \$6{,}000 = \$190{,}000$, and in the case of a fire she will end up with $\$196{,}000 - \$160{,}000 + \$154{,}000 = \$190{,}000$. Thus, Agatha's guaranteed utility is

$$U = 10 \times 190^{0.5} = 137.84.$$

And since her expected utility is greater with the insurance policy than with no insurance ($137.84 > 137.6$), she is better off with the insurance. Note that with the insurance, Agatha's expected wealth (\$190,000) is less than that with no insurance (\$191,200), but since the insurance eliminates her risk, she derives more utility from the lower expected wealth and therefore is happy to give up \$1,200 (which goes to the insurance company) in exchange for more certainty.

Problem 9

a. To see which option is preferable, we calculate the net present value of the first option compared with that of the second option. In the current period, the airline has to pay for the new plane, but saves on the refurbishing costs, so $B_0 - C_0 = \$5$ million $-$ $\$40$ million $= -\$35$ million. In years 1–4, buying a new plane allows the airline to save $\$1.2$ million on its operating costs, so $B_1 = B_2 = B_3 = B_4 = \$1.2$ million. And in year 5, the airline still saves on the operating costs but also on that it does not have to buy new planes in this period (which it would have to if it chose the second option), so $B_5 = \$1.2$ million $+ \$40$ million $= \$41.2$ million. Therefore, we can calculate the net present value of choosing the first option (in millions of dollars) as follows:

$$NPV = -35 + \frac{1.2}{1 + 0.05} + \frac{1.2}{(1 + 0.05)^2} + \frac{1.2}{(1 + 0.05)^3} + \frac{1.2}{(1 + 0.05)^4} + \frac{1.2 + 40}{(1 + 0.05)^5} = 1.54$$

Since the net present value of the first option is positive ($\$1.54$ million), the airline should choose this option.

b. If the interest rate rises to 7%, the NPV will be

$$NPV = -35 + \frac{1.2}{1 + 0.07} + \frac{1.2}{(1 + 0.07)^2} + \frac{1.2}{(1 + 0.07)^3} + \frac{1.2}{(1 + 0.07)^4} + \frac{1.2 + 40}{(1 + 0.07)^5} = -1.56$$

Since the net present value of the first option is negative ($-\$1.56$ million), the airline should choose the second option. A higher interest rate means that the future cost savings are discounted more, and so are the savings from not having to purchase new planes five years from now. Both these factors lower the value of buying new planes now as opposed to renovating the old planes and postponing the purchase of replacement planes for five years.

Problem 10

a. If Monica purchases the building, her current cost is $\$250,000$. And starting from the next year, her benefits will be $\$40,000$ per year forever. Using the perpetuity formula, we can calculate the PDV of this infinite stream of payments as follows:

$$B_1 = \frac{M}{r} = \frac{\$40,000}{0.05} = \$800,000$$

But since there is a 25% chance that the city council will rezone the district next year and Monica's profit will be zero, there is only a 75% chance that Monica will receive this stream of benefits, and a 25% chance that she will receive her profit only for the first year. Therefore, the net present value of the project is

$$NPV = -\$250,000 + \left(0.75 \times \frac{\$800,000}{1 + 0.05} + 0.25 \times \frac{\$40,000}{1 + 0.05} \right) = \$330,952$$

b. If Monica decides to wait, her investment in the store will occur one year in the future, and the stream of benefits will start in two years. Therefore, we should discount these payments accordingly. Note also that if the city council rezones the district, Monica will not buy the building. That is, there is only a 75% chance that any payment will occur. Therefore, the net present value of the project is

$$NPV = 0.75 \times \frac{-\$250,000}{1.05} + 0.75 \times \frac{\$800,000}{(1 + 0.05)^2} = \$365,646$$

c. While the NPV of opening the store today is positive ($\$330,952$), waiting one year before buying the building has an even higher NPV ($\$365,646$). Therefore, Monica should wait. The option value of waiting is the difference between the NPV of the project if Monica waits and the NPV of buying the building now: $\$365,646 - \$330,952 = \$34,694$.

General Equilibrium

14

Solutions for Practice Problems

Problem 1

a. Since corn chips and salsa are complements, the quantity demanded of one good is negatively related with the price of the other good. This is reflected by the demand equation for each good, where the price of the complementary good appears with a negative coefficient. In the supply equations, the quantity supplied of each good is a function of only its own price, with no relation with the other good. Thus, the markets are linked on the demand side and not on the supply side.

b. We first solve for the price of corn chips as a function of the price of salsa by setting quantity demanded and quantity supplied equal in the market for corn chips:

$$Q_c^d = Q_c^s$$
$$10 - P_c - 0.5P_s = 1 + P_c$$
$$-2P_c = -9 + 0.5P_s$$
$$2P_c = 9 - 0.5P_s$$
$$P_c = 4.5 - 0.25P_s$$

Similarly, we solve for the equilibrium in the salsa market, expressing the price of salsa as a function of the price of corn chips:

$$Q_s^d = Q_s^s$$
$$10 - P_s - 0.5P_c = 1 + P_s$$
$$-2P_s = -9 + 0.5P_c$$
$$2P_s = 9 - 0.5P_c$$
$$P_s = 4.5 - 0.25P_c$$

Now, to find the general equilibrium price of corn chips, we insert the preceding equation into the equation for the price of corn chips and solve it for P_c:

$$P_c = 4.5 - 0.25(4.5 - 0.25P_c)$$
$$P_c = 4.5 - 1.125 + 0.0625P_c$$
$$0.9375P_c = 3.375$$
$$P_c = 3.6$$

And to find the price of salsa in general equilibrium, we insert $P_c = 3.60$ into the equation for the price of salsa:

$$P_s = 4.5 - 0.25 \times 3.6$$
$$P_s = 3.6$$

We can calculate the general equilibrium quantities of corn chips and salsa by substituting the equilibrium prices found in the preceding into the supply or demand equations for corn chips and salsa. For corn chips:

$$Q_c^d = 10 - 3.6 - 0.5 \times 3.6 = 4.6$$
$$Q_c^s = 1 + 3.6 = 4.6$$

And for salsa:

$$Q_s^d = 10 - 3.6 - 0.5 \times 3.6 = 4.6$$
$$Q_s^s = 1 + 3.6 = 4.6$$

Thus, the general equilibrium price of corn chips is \$3.60 per pound, and the quantity of corn chips produced is 4.6 million pounds. The general equilibrium price and quantity of salsa are the same as those of corn chips.

c. When the demand for corn chips decreases, both markets are affected. We follow the same steps as in (b) to solve for the new equilibrium prices and quantities. First, we find the new demand equation for corn chips. Since consumers are willing to buy 3 million pounds less at any given P_c and P_s, we derive the new equation by subtracting 3 from the right-hand side of the original equation:

$$Q_c^{d*} = (10 - P_c - 0.5P_s) - 3$$
$$= 7 - P_c - 0.5P_s$$

Now we solve for the price of corn chips as a function of the price of salsa as follows:

$$Q_c^{d*} = Q_c^s$$
$$7 - P_c - 0.5P_s = 1 + P_c$$
$$2P_c = 6 - 0.5P_s$$
$$P_c = 3 - 0.25P_s$$

As explained in (a), the demand for salsa is not directly affected. Therefore, the equation for the price of salsa as a function of the price of corn chips remains the same:

$$P_s = 4.5 - 0.25P_c$$

Thus, we find the general equilibrium price of corn chips by inserting the preceding equation into the new equation for the price of corn chips and solve it for P_c:

$$P_c = 3 - 0.25(4.5 - 0.25P_c)$$
$$P_c = 3 - 1.125 + 0.0625P_c$$
$$0.9375P_c = 1.875$$
$$P_c = 2$$

And to find the price of salsa in general equilibrium, we insert $P_c = 2$ into the equation for the price of salsa:

$$P_s = 4.5 - 0.25 \times 2$$
$$P_s = 4$$

We can calculate the general equilibrium quantities of corn chips and salsa by inserting the equilibrium prices found in the preceding into the supply or demand curve equations for corn chips and salsa. For corn chips:

$$Q_c^{d*} = 7 - 2 - (0.5 \times 4) = 3$$
$$Q_c^s = 1 + 2 = 3$$

And for salsa:

$$Q_s^d = 10 - 4 - 0.5 \times 2 = 5$$
$$Q_s^s = 1 + 4 = 5$$

Thus, as a result of the decreased demand for corn chips, the general equilibrium price of corn chips falls from $3.60 per pound to $2 per pound, and the quantity of corn chips produced falls from 4.6 million pounds to 3 million pounds. The general equilibrium price of salsa rises from $3.60 per pound to $4 per pound, and the quantity of salsa increases from 4.6 million pounds to 5 million pounds. Since the demand for salsa is affected by the price of corn chips, the decreased demand for corn chips affects not only the equilibrium price and quantity of corn chips but also those of salsa.

Problem 2

a. As the demand curves show, only a good's own price affects its quantity demanded. Thus, the markets are not linked on the demand side. The supply equations, however, show connections between the two markets. The quantity supplied of each good increases as its own price increases and decreases as the other good's price increases. This is because when one good's price increases, production shifts toward that good, which allocates resources away from production of the other good (e.g., replanting corn fields as soybean fields). That is, the markets are linked on the supply side.

b. We first solve for the price of corn as a function of the price of soybeans by setting quantity demanded and quantity supplied equal in the market for corn:

$$Q_c^d = Q_c^s$$
$$10 - P_c = 1 + P_c - 0.5P_s$$
$$-2P_c = -9 - 0.5P_s$$
$$2P_c = 9 + 0.5P_s$$
$$P_c = 4.5 + 0.25P_s$$

Similarly, we solve for the equilibrium in the soybean market, expressing the price of soybeans as a function of the price of corn:

$$Q_s^d = Q_s^s$$
$$10 - P_s = 1 + P_s - 0.5P_c$$
$$-2P_s = -9 - 0.5P_c$$
$$2P_s = 9 + 0.5P_c$$
$$P_s = 4.5 + 0.25P_c$$

To find the general equilibrium price of corn, we insert the preceding equation into the equation for the price of corn and solve it for P_c:

$$P_c = 4.5 + 0.25(4.5 + 0.25P_c)$$
$$P_c = 4.5 + 1.125 + 0.0625P_c$$
$$0.9375P_c = 9 + 5.625$$
$$P_c = 6$$

And to find the price of soybeans in general equilibrium, we insert $P_c = 6$ into the equation for the price of soybeans:

$$P_s = 4.5 + (0.25 \times 6)$$
$$P_s = 6$$

We can calculate the general equilibrium quantities of corn and soybeans by inserting the equilibrium prices found in the preceding into the supply or demand equations for corn and soybeans. For corn:

$$Q_c^d = 10 - 6 = 4$$
$$Q_c^s = 1 + 6 - (0.5 \times 6) = 4$$

And for soybeans:

$$Q_s^d = 10 - 6 = 4$$
$$Q_s^s = 1 + 6 - 0.5 \times 6 = 4$$

Thus, the general equilibrium price of corn is $6 per bushel, and the quantity of corn produced is 4 million bushels. The general equilibrium price and quantity of soybeans are the same as those of corn.

c. When the demand for corn increases, both markets are affected. We follow the same steps as in (b) to solve for the new equilibrium prices and quantities. First, we find the new demand equation for corn. Since consumers are willing to buy 3 million bushels more at any given price, we derive the new equation by adding 3 to the right-hand side of the original demand equation:

$$Q_c^{d*} = (10 - P_c) + 3$$
$$= 13 - P_c$$

So we solve for the price of corn as a function of the price of soybeans as follows:

$$Q_c^{d*} = Q_c^s$$
$$13 - P_c = 1 + P_c - 0.5P_s$$
$$2P_c = 12 + 0.5P_s$$
$$P_c = 6 + 0.25P_s$$

Since the demand for soybeans is not directly affected, the equation for the price of soybeans as a function of the price of corn remains the same:

$$P_s = 4.5 + 0.25P_c$$

To find the general equilibrium price of corn, we insert the preceding equation into the equation for the price of corn and solve it for P_c:

$$P_c = 6 + 0.25(4.5 + 0.25P_c)$$
$$P_c = 6 + 1.125 + 0.0625P_c$$
$$0.9375P_c = 7.125$$
$$P_c = 7.6$$

And to find the price of soybeans in general equilibrium, we insert $P_c = 7.6$ into the equation for the price of soybeans:

$$P_s = 4.5 + 0.25 \times 7.6$$
$$P_s = 6.4$$

We can calculate the general equilibrium quantities of corn and soybeans by inserting the equilibrium prices found in the preceding into the supply or demand equations for corn and soybeans. For corn:

$$Q_c^{d*} = 13 - 7.6 = 5.4$$
$$Q_c^s = 1 + 7.6 - 0.5 \times 6.4 = 5.4$$

And for soybeans:

$$Q_s^d = 10 - 6.4 = 3.6$$
$$Q_s^s = 1 + 6.4 - 0.5 \times 7.6 = 3.6$$

Thus, as a result of the increased demand for corn, the general equilibrium price of corn rises from \$6 per bushel to \$7.60 per bushel, and the quantity of corn produced increases from 4 million bushels to 5.4 million bushels. The general equilibrium price of soybeans rises from \$6 per bushel to \$6.40 per bushel, and the quantity of soybeans produced decreases from 4 million bushels to 3.6 million bushels. Since the supply of soybeans is affected by the price of corn, the increased demand for corn affects not only the equilibrium price and quantity of corn but also those of soybeans.

Problem 3

a. Given the individual utility function, we can calculate the levels of utility for each individual. It is $225^{0.5} = 15$ for Archibald, $25^{0.5} = 5$ for Benedict, and $1{,}600^{0.5} = 40$ for Carole. The Rawlsian social welfare function used in this problem computes society's welfare as the welfare of the worst-off individual. Therefore, the commune's level of social welfare is equal to Benedict's level of utility: $W = \min[15, 5, 25] = 5$.

b. Any wealth transfer that increases Benedict's utility will increase the commune's level of social welfare. For example, if \$75,000 is transferred to Benedict either from Archibald or from Carole (or both), Benedict's wealth will be \$25,000 + \$75,000 = \$100,000, so his utility level will be $100^{0.5} = 10$. Since this is still the lowest level of utility in the commune, it is also the commune's value of social welfare, so the transfer raises the commune's level of social welfare from 5 to 10.

c. The highest level of social welfare is achieved if wealth is distributed equally among the three individuals. In this case, each individual's wealth is $\dfrac{(\$225{,}000 + \$25{,}000 + \$1{,}600{,}000)}{3} = \$616{,}667$, so $u_A = u_B = u_C = 616.667^{0.5} = 24.8$. Since this is the lowest level of utility in the commune, it is also the commune's level of social welfare. It is the commune's maximum possible level of welfare because any further wealth transfer will necessarily lower at least one individual's wealth, decreasing the value of $W = \min[u_A, u_B, u_C]$.

Problem 4

a. As in Problem 3, given the individual utility function, the individual levels of utility are $225^{0.5} = 15$ for Archibald, $25^{0.5} = 5$ for Benedict, and $1{,}600^{0.5} = 40$ for Carole. The utilitarian social welfare function (which is social welfare function in this problem) computes society's welfare as the sum of every individual's welfare. Therefore, the commune's level of social welfare is $W = 15 + 5 + 40 = 60$.

b. Since the individual utility function exhibits diminishing marginal utility, a certain amount of wealth taken from a wealthier person lowers her utility level by less than the same amount given to a poorer person increases his level of utility. For example, reducing Archibald's wealth by \$10,000 lowers his utility by only 0.3 units ($225^{0.5} - 215^{0.5} = 15 - 14.7 = 0.3$), but increasing Benedict's wealth by the same amount raises his utility level by 0.9 units ($35^{0.5} - 25^{0.5} = 5.9 - 5 = 0.9$). Therefore, any wealth transfer from a wealthier individual to a poorer individual will increase the commune's level of social welfare. As an example, let's transfer \$75,000 to Benedict from Carole. After the transfer, Benedict's wealth is \$25,000 + \$75,000 = \$100,000, so his utility level is $100^{0.5} = 10$. And Carole's wealth is \$1,600,000 – \$75,000 = \$1,525,000, so her utility level is $1,525^{0.5} = 39.1$. The commune's level of social welfare is now $W = 15 + 10 + 39.1 = 64.1$. That is, the transfer raises the level of social welfare from 60 to 64.1.

c. The highest level of social welfare is achieved if wealth is distributed equally among the three individuals. In this case, each individual's wealth is (\$225,000 + \$25,000 + \$1,600,000)/3 = \$616,667, and each individual's level of utility is $616.667^{0.5} = 24.83$. Thus, the commune's level of social welfare is $W = 3 \times 24.83 = 74.5$. This is the commune's maximum possible level of welfare because when wealth is distributed equally, transferring any amount from one individual to another will necessarily make the donor poorer than the recipient. As explained in (b), this means that after the transfer, we can increase the level of social welfare by transferring wealth back from the wealthier to the poorer individual, that is, by returning to the equal distribution of wealth.

Problem 5

a. At point A, Harry has 8 cauldron cakes and 2 chocolate frogs. And Ron has 2 cauldron cakes and 6 chocolate frogs. At point A, Ron's indifference curve (U_R) is steeper than Harry's indifference curve (U_H). This means Ron's marginal rate of substitution of cauldron cakes for chocolate frogs (MRS_{CF}) is greater than Harry's MRS_{CF}. In other words, Ron is willing to give up more chocolate frogs to get an additional cauldron cake than is Harry. That is, Ron values cauldron cakes higher than Harry does.

b. If Ron gives Harry one chocolate frog in exchange for two cauldron cakes, Harry will end up with $8 - 2 = 6$ cauldron cakes and $2 + 1 = 3$ chocolate frogs. And Ron will end up with $2 + 2 = 4$ cauldron cakes and $6 - 1 = 5$ chocolate frogs. This allocation is represented by point B on the following diagram. A Pareto improvement occurs if one of the individuals is made better off without making the other worse off. At point B, Harry is on the same indifference curve as he was at point A, but Ron is on a higher indifference curve (U_{R2}), which means the exchange makes Ron better off while leaving Harry as well off as before. Therefore, it is a Pareto improvement.

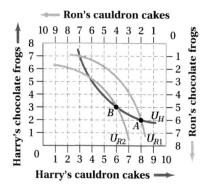

c. If Harry accepts Ron's offer, he'll end up with $8 - 3 = 5$ cauldron cakes and $2 + 3 = 5$ chocolate frogs (point C on the following graph), which takes him to a higher indifference curve (U_{H2}). Therefore, Harry should accept the offer. If the exchange takes place, Ron will end up with $2 + 3 = 5$ cauldron cakes and $6 - 3 = 3$ chocolate frogs. This will take him to a higher indifference curve (U_{R2}). Since the exchange make both individuals better off, it results in a Pareto improvement.

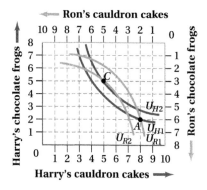

Problem 6

a. Robin and Quinn use 12 hours of labor and 5 units of capital in fishing. They use 28 hours of labor and 3 units of capital in picking berries.

b. Robin and Quinn should reallocate labor from picking berries to fishing and reallocate capital from fishing to picking berries. For example, if they reallocate 8 hours of labor from picking berries to fishing and 2 units of capital from fishing to picking berries, they will end up at point B (see the following graph). As the graph shows, this reallocation of resources allows Robin and Quinn to get on a higher isoquant for both fishing (Q_{F2}) and picking berries (Q_{B2}). That is, by reallocating inputs this way, they can increase production of both goods.

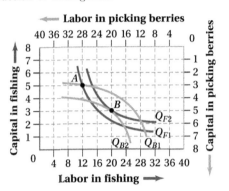

Problem 7

a. See the following graph. The current allocation of the goods is at point A. Given that Billy has 6 movie tickets, we know that Jean has $20 - 6 = 14$ movie tickets. And since Billy has 5 concert tickets, Jean has $8 - 5 = 3$ concert tickets. Pareto efficiency is achieved when the marginal rates of substitution are equal between the two consumers. Since Billy's $MRS_{MC} = 1$ is not equal to Jean's $MRS_{MC} = 0.1$, the current allocation of goods is not Pareto-efficient. The following graph illustrates this situation. At point A, Billy's indifference curve (U_B) is steeper than Jean's indifference curve (U_J), reflecting the fact that Billy's MRS_{MC} is greater than Jean's MRS_{MC}.

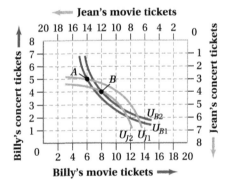

b. Since with the current allocation of goods Billy is willing to give up one concert ticket to get one more movie ticket (i.e., his $MRS_{MC} = 1$) and Jean would accept as little as 0.1 concert tickets per each movie ticket she gives to Billy (since her $MRS_{MC} = 0.1$), movie tickets should be reallocated from Jean to Billy, and concert tickets should be reallocated from Billy to Jean. For example, suppose that Billy gives Jean one concert ticket in exchange for two movie tickets. Then the allocation of the goods will be at point B (see the preceding graph). At this point, both consumers are on a higher indifference curve than they were at point A. That is, both Billy and Jean are better off, which means the exchange has resulted in a Pareto improvement.

Problem 8

a. See the following diagram. The production contract curve (PCC) connects the points of tangency between cotton isoquants and wheat isoquants. Each of these points represents a Pareto-efficient allocation of labor and capital.

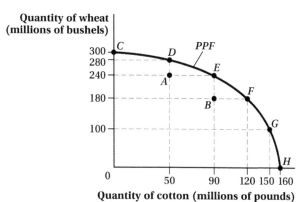

b. The production possibilities frontier (PPF) is shown on the following diagram. It connects all efficient output combinations of the two goods. To draw the PPF, we start from the lower-left corner of the Edgeworth box, where all inputs are used to produce wheat, so cotton production is zero and wheat production is 300 million bushels (point C). Next, we move up and to the right along the production contract curve on the preceding diagram to the input allocation at point D. As the isoquants indicate, cotton output, at this point, is 50 million pounds ($Q_C = 50$) and wheat output is 280 million ($Q_W = 280$). We plot the corresponding point on the PPF graph. Similarly, we plot point E ($Q_C = 90$, $Q_W = 240$), point F ($Q_C = 120$, $Q_W = 180$), and point G ($Q_C = 150$, $Q_W = 100$). Finally, we plot point H, where all inputs are used to produce cotton, so wheat production is zero and cotton production is 160 million pounds. We draw the economy's PPF by connecting points C, D, E, F, G, and H.

c. As the isoquants indicate, at point A, $Q_C = 50$ and $Q_W = 240$, that is, cotton output is 50 million pounds and wheat output is 240 million bushels. So we plot the corresponding point on the PPF graph. As both the Edgeworth box and the PPF graph show, when the economy is at point A, labor and capital can be reallocated to increase the production of one good without reducing the production of the other good. For example, cotton output can be increased to 90 million pounds while keeping wheat output at 240 million bushels. Therefore, this point is not input-efficient. Similarly, at point B, $Q_C = 90$ and $Q_W = 180$. And when the economy is at this point, the production of one good can be increased without reducing the production of the other good. For example, wheat output can be increased to 240 million pounds while keeping cotton output at 90 million bushels. Therefore, point B is not input-efficient either.

Problem 9

a. The marginal rate of transformation from textiles to corn (MRT_{TC}) shows how much textiles firms are willing to give up to produce one more bushel of corn. Given that the marginal cost of a bushel of corn is $6 and the marginal cost of a square yard of textiles is $4, we know that to produce an additional bushel of corn firms must give up $\frac{\$6}{\$4} = 1.5$ square yards of textiles. That is, $MRT_{TC} = \frac{MC_C}{MC_T} = \frac{\$6}{\$4} = 1.5$.

b. Output efficiency is achieved when the marginal rates of transformation equals the marginal rate of substitution: $MRT_{TC} = MRS_{CT}$. Since the $MRT_{TC} = 1.5$ is not equal to the $MRS_{CT} = 1$, the economy is not output-efficient. The following graph illustrates this situation. The economy is currently at point A. Since we've assumed the economy is input-efficient, the combination of the two goods produced is on the PPF. However, since at this point $MRT_{TC} > MRS_{CT}$, the PPF is steeper than the consumers' indifference curve (U_1).

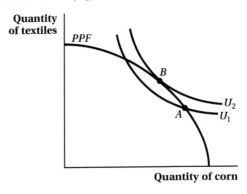

c. The fact that $MRS_{CT} < MRT_{TC}$ means that consumers are willing to pay a lower price of corn in terms of textiles (1 square yard of textiles per bushel of corn) than the firms' opportunity cost of corn in terms of textiles (1.5 square yard per bushel). Therefore, firms will decrease the production of corn and increase the production of textiles, moving to the left and upward along the PPF. And as less corn and more textiles are produced, the MRT_{TC} falls (i.e. the PPF becomes less steep). At the same time, with less corn and more textiles available to consumers, the marginal utility of corn (MU_C) increases while the marginal utility of textiles (MU_T) decreases, so $MRS_{CT} = \dfrac{MU_C}{MU_T}$ rises. The production of corn will continue to decrease and the production of textiles will continue to increase until MRS_{CT} and MRT_{TC} are equalized (point B on the graph). Note that, at this point, the PPF is tangent to a higher indifference curve (U_2), which means consumers are better off. Also, since at point B the slopes of the PPF and the indifference curve are equal, that is, $MRS_{CT} = MRT_{TC}$, the economy is output-efficient.

Problem 10

a. On the demand side, since corn and soybeans are substitutes in consumption, the quantity demanded of one good is positively related with the price of the other good. This is reflected by the demand equation for each good, where the price of the substitute good appears with a positive coefficient. On the supply side, since common inputs are used in corn production and soybean production, when one good's price increases, production shifts toward that good, allocating resources away from production of the other good (e.g., replanting soybean fields as corn fields). Therefore, the quantity supplied of each good increases as its own price increases and decreases as the other good's price increases. This link is reflected by the supply equation for each good, where the price of the other good appears with a negative coefficient. Thus, the markets are linked on both the demand side and the supply side.

b. We first solve for the price of corn as a function of the price of soybeans by setting quantity demanded and quantity supplied equal in the market for corn:

$$Q_c^d = Q_c^s$$
$$10 - P_c + 0.5P_s = 1 + P_c - 0.25P_s$$
$$-2P_c = -9 - 0.75P_s$$
$$2P_c = 9 + 0.75P_s$$
$$P_c = 4.5 + 0.375P_s$$

Similarly, we solve for the equilibrium in the soybean market, expressing the price of soybeans as a function of the price of corn:

$$Q_s^d = Q_s^s$$
$$10 - P_s + 0.5P_c = 1 + P_s - 0.25P_c$$
$$2P_s = 9 + 0.75P_c$$
$$P_s = 4.5 + 0.375P_c$$

To find the general equilibrium price of corn, we insert the preceding equation into the equation for the price of corn and solve it for P_c:

$$P_c = 4.5 + 0.375(4.5 + 0.375P_c)$$
$$P_c = 4.5 + 1.6875 + 0.140625P_c$$
$$0.859375P_c = 6.1875$$
$$P_c = 7.2$$

And to find the price of soybeans in general equilibrium, we insert $P_c = 7.2$ into the equation for the price of soybeans:

$$P_s = 4.5 + (0.375 \times 7.2)$$
$$P_s = 7.2$$

We can calculate the general equilibrium quantities of corn and soybeans by inserting the equilibrium prices in the preceding into the supply or demand equations for corn and soybeans. For corn:

$$Q_c^d = 10 - 7.2 + 0.5 \times 7.2 = 6.4$$
$$Q_c^s = 1 + 7.2 - 0.25 \times 7.2 = 6.4$$

And for soybeans:

$$Q_s^d = 10 - 7.2 + 0.5 \times 7.2 = 6.4$$
$$Q_s^s = 1 + 7.2 - 0.25 \times 7.2 = 6.4$$

Thus, the general equilibrium price of corn is $7.20 per bushel, and the quantity of corn produced is 6.4 million bushels. The general equilibrium price and quantity of soybeans are the same as those of corn.

c. When the demand for corn increases, both markets are affected. We follow the same steps as in (b) to solve for the new equilibrium prices and quantities. First, we find the new demand equation for corn. Since consumers are willing to buy 3 million bushels more at any given price, we derive the new equation by adding 3 to the right-hand side of the original demand equation:

$$Q_c^{d*} = 10 - P_c + 0.5P_s + 3$$
$$= 13 - P_c + 0.5P_s$$

Now we solve for the price of corn as a function of the price of soybeans as follows:

$$Q_c^{d*} = Q_c^s$$
$$13 - P_c + 0.5P_s = 1 + P_c - 0.25P_s$$
$$2P_c = 12 + 0.75P_s$$
$$P_c = 6 + 0.375P_s$$

Since the demand for soybeans is not directly affected, the equation for the price of soybeans as a function of the price of corn remains the same:

$$P_s = 4.5 + 0.375P_c$$

Now, to find the general equilibrium price of corn, we insert the preceding equation into the equation for the price of corn and solve it for P_c:

$$P_c = 6 + 0.375(4.5 + 0.375P_c)$$
$$P_c = 6 + 1.6875 + 0.140625P_c$$
$$0.859375P_c = 7.6875$$
$$P_c = 8.94545 \approx 8.95$$

And to find the price of soybeans in general equilibrium, we insert $P_c = 8.94545$ into the equation for the price of soybeans:

$$P_s = 4.5 + 0.375 \times 8.94545$$
$$P_s = 7.8545 \approx 7.85$$

We can now calculate the general equilibrium quantities of corn and soybeans by substituting the equilibrium prices found above into the supply or demand equations for corn and soybeans. For corn:

$$Q_s^d = 13 - 8.95 + 0.5 \times 7.85 = 8.0$$
$$Q_c^s = 1 + 8.95 - 0.25 \times 7.85 = 8.0$$

And for soybeans:

$$Q_s^d = 10 - 7.85 + 0.5 \times 8.95 = 6.6$$
$$Q_s^s = 1 + 7.85 - 0.25 \times 8.95 = 6.6$$

Thus, as a result of the increased demand for corn, the general equilibrium price of corn rises from $7.20 per bushel to $8.95 per bushel, and the quantity of corn produced increases from 6.4 million bushels to 8.0 million bushels. The general equilibrium price of soybeans rises from $7.2 per bushel to $7.85 per bushel, and the quantity of soybeans produced increases from 6.4 million bushels to 6.6 million bushels. Since the two markets are linked (on both demand and supply sides), the increased demand for corn affects not only the equilibrium price and quantity of corn but also those of soybeans.

Asymmetric Information

Solutions for Practice Problems

Problem 1

a. If buyers expect that 50% of the contractors are high-quality and the other 50% are incompetent, the expected value to buyers of a typical remodeling is

$$(0.5 \times \$25,000) + (0.5 \times \$0) = \$12,500$$

Therefore, the price that buyers are willing to pay for a remodeling is $12,500.

b. A high-quality contractor values his work at $20,000, but because buyers don't know for sure whether the quality of his service is high, they are not willing to pay more than $12,500. Therefore, no transaction will take place. An incompetent contractor values his service at only $10,000, so he will be happy to offer it for $12,500. As a result, all home remodeling services will be offered by incompetent contractors. As homeowners start to recognize this, they will not be willing to buy home remodeling services at any price (since remodeling done by an incompetent contractor has no value to them). As a result, no sales will take place; that is, there will be no market for home remodeling services.

Problem 2

a. If buyers expect that 60% of the used cars available are of low quality and the other 40% are of high quality, then their expected value of a used car is

$$(0.4 \times \$9,000) + (0.6 \times \$4,000) = \$6,000$$

Therefore, the price that buyers are willing to pay for a used car is $6,000.

b. If buyers offer $6,000 for a used car, the quantity of high-quality cars supplied is

$$Q_H = -1,250 + 0.25 \times 6,000 = 250$$

and the quantity of low-quality cars supplied is

$$Q_L = -1,250 + 0.5 \times 6,000 = 1,750$$

This means the assumption that the chance of buying a low-quality used car is 60% is incorrect. The probability that a used car on the market is of low quality is actually $\dfrac{1,750}{(1,750 + 250)} = 0.875$, or 87.5%.

c. If buyers expect that 87.5% of the used cars available are of low quality (which means they expect only 12.5% of used cars to be of high quality), then the expected value of a used car is

$$(0.125 \times \$9,000) + (0.875 \times \$4,000) = \$4,625$$

That is, the price that buyers are willing to pay for a used car falls from $6,000 to $4,625. This is below the lowest price that owners of high-quality cars are willing to accept, which is $5,000 (since at $P_H = \$5,000$, $Q_H = -1,250 + 0.25 \times 5,000 = 0$). This means all cars available in the market will be of low quality.

Problem 3

a. Caroline's cost of switching from junk food to healthy food is the monetary equivalent of the utility she gives up, $700. Her benefit is the $2,000 she saves on medical expenses. Since Caroline's benefit from eating healthier food exceeds her cost, she should stop eating junk food.

b. With the insurance policy, Caroline pays 20% of her medical expenses. Thus, if she eats junk food, she pays $0.2 \times \$4,000 = \$800$ per year. If she switches to healthy food, she pays $0.2 \times \$2,000 = \$400$ per year. This means that Caroline saves $800 – $400 = $400 on medical expenses by switching to healthy food. Since this is less than the monetary equivalent of the utility she gives up if she stops eating junk food ($700), Caroline will continue to eat junk food. (Note that since Caroline pays the same insurance premium regardless of whether she eats junk food, the amount of insurance premium is irrelevant to her decision.)

c. After purchasing the insurance policy, Caroline changes her behavior, making less effort to reduce her medical expenses because they are mostly covered by the insurer. This means the insurance company faces a moral hazard problem. If Caroline eats junk food, the insurance company pays $4,000 \times 0.8 = $3,200$ to cover her medical expenses. Since this is less than the insurance premium it receives from Caroline ($1,800), the company incurs a loss. But if Caroline switched to healthy food (i.e., made the same effort to reduce her medical expenses as she would without insurance), then the insurance company would pay only $2,000 \times 0.8 = $1,600$ to cover her medical expenses, which is less than the insurance premium the company receives from Caroline.

Now suppose the insurance company covers only 60% of Caroline's medical expenses. Then, Caroline has to pay $0.4 \times $4,000 = $1,600$ per year if she eats junk and $0.4 \times $2,000 = 800 per year if she switches to healthy food. That is, Caroline now saves $800 on medical expenses by switching to healthy food. Since this is more than the monetary equivalent of the utility she gives up if she stops eating junk food ($700), Caroline is better off by switching to healthy food. And when she does, the insurance company pays $2,000 \times 0.6 = $1,200$ to cover Caroline's medical expenses, which is less than the insurance premium the company receives from Caroline. Thus, the insurance company will avoid the moral hazard problem in (b) if it pays only 60% of Caroline's medical expenses.

Problem 4

a. Simona's optimal number of hours to exercise is where her marginal benefit of saving on medical expenses equals the marginal cost of exercise. As explained in 15.2 figure it out 2, if the benefit function has the form

$$B = aH - bH^2$$

then the marginal benefit curve is given by

$$MB = a - 2bH$$

So, given Simona's benefit function, her marginal benefit curve is

$$MB = 100 - 2 \times 5H$$
$$MB = 100 - 10H$$

Now we set $MB = MC$ and solve this equation for H:

$$100 - 10H = 1 + H$$
$$11H = 99$$
$$H = 9$$

Thus, Simona's optimal number of hours to exercise is 9 hours per week.

b. Since the insurance plan pays 90% of Simona's medical expenses, she pays only 10%. Therefore, with insurance, her medical expenses function is

$$X_I = 0.1X$$
$$X_I = 0.1 \times [4,000 - (100H - 5H^2)]$$
$$X_I = 400 - (10H - 0.5H^2)$$

This means Simona's benefit from exercise is now

$$B_I = 10H - 0.5H^2$$

In this function, $a = 10$ and $b = 0.5$, so the corresponding marginal benefit curve is

$$MB_I = 10 - H$$

Now we can set $MB_I = MC$ and solve this equation for H:

$$10 - H = 1 + H$$
$$2H = 9$$
$$H = 4.5$$

Thus, the insurance coverage reduces Simona's optimal time to devote to exercise from 9 hours per week to 4.5 hours per week.

Problem 5

a. If consumers know what type of computers they are purchasing, in a perfectly competitive market they will pay $800 for a high-quality computer and $300 for a low-quality computer. At these prices, the quantity of high-quality computers supplied will be

$$Q_H = -55 + 0.1 \times 800 = 25$$

and the quantity of low-quality computers supplied will be

$$Q_L = -50 + 0.25 \times 300 = 25$$

Thus, in equilibrium, 25,000 high-quality computers and 25,000 low-quality computers will be sold.

b. If buyers expect 50% of the computers to be of low quality (which means they expect the other 50% to be high quality), then the expected value of a computer on the market is

$$(0.5 \times \$800) + (0.5 \times \$300) = \$550$$

Therefore, the price that buyers are willing to pay for a computer is $550. And if buyers offer $550 for a computer, the quantity of high-quality computers supplied will be

$$Q_H = -55 + 0.1 \times 550 = 0$$

and the quantity of low-quality computers supplied will be

$$Q_L = -50 + 0.25 \times 550 = 87.5$$

This means no high-quality computers will be offered for sale, and all 87,500 computers sold will be of low quality.

c. See the following graph. In the market for high-quality computers, when full information is available to buyers, the demand curve is D_H, the supply curve is S_H, and the market is in equilibrium at point E_H. Since all buyers are willing to pay the same price, there is no consumer surplus. That is, the market surplus equals the producer surplus, which is the area below the price and above the supply curve (area A). The value represented by this area is $0.5 \times (\$800 - \$550) \times 25,000 = \$3,125,000$. In the market with asymmetric information, the demand curve is D_{HA}, and the market is in equilibrium at point E_{HA}, where no computers are sold. Therefore, the market surplus (area A) is completely lost.

High-quality Computers 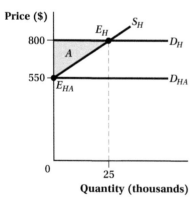 **Low-quality Computers**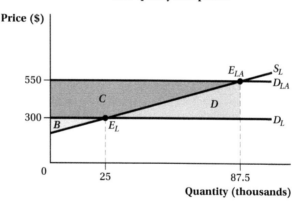

In the market for low-quality computers, with full information available to buyers the demand curve is D_L, the supply curve is S_L, and the market is in equilibrium at point E_L. Again, since all buyers are willing to pay the same price, there is no consumer surplus, so the market surplus equals the producer surplus, the area below the price and above the supply curve (area B). In the market with asymmetric information, the demand curve is D_{LA}, and the market is in equilibrium at point E_{LA}. Now the producer surplus is area $B + C$. And since consumers actually pay a higher price ($550) than they are willing to pay ($300), there is a loss in consumer surplus equal to this price difference times the number of computers bought (area $C + D$). This loss of consumer surplus is partly offset by the gain in producer surplus (area C), but the rest of it (area D) is the deadweight loss. That is, the deadweight loss in the market for low-quality computers is: Area $D = 0.5 \times (\$550 - \$300) \times (87,500 - 25,000) = \$7,812,500$.

Thus, the loss of market surplus resulting from asymmetric information is $3,125,000 in the market for high-quality computers and $7,812,500 in the market for low-quality computers; that is, the total deadweight loss in the online market for desktop computers caused by asymmetric information is $3,125,000 + \$7,812,500 = \$10,937,500$.

Problem 6

a. Given the risk premium that a risk-averse individual agrees to pay, Type A individuals are willing to pay an insurance premium of $1,000 + 0.1 × 1,000 = $1,100 per year. The lowest price that insurance companies are willing to accept is their expected insurance payment plus the cost of providing insurance, including screening: (0.8 × 1,000) + 200 + 150 = $1,150. Since the lowest price sellers are willing to accept is higher than the price buyers are willing to pay, insurance policies won't be sold to Type A individuals.

Type B individuals are willing to pay $5,000 + (0.1 × 5,000) = $5,500 per year. The lowest premium that insurance companies are willing to accept when selling policies to these individuals is 0.8 × 5,000 + 200 + 150 = $4,350. Since Type B individuals are willing to pay more than the lowest price sellers are willing to accept, insurance companies will be able to sell their policies to Type B individuals.

b. When 40% of the potential customers are Type A and 60% are Type B, the insurance companies' expected cost of coverage is 0.4 × (0.8 × 1,000) + 0.6 × (0.8 × 5,000) + 200 = $2,920 per customer. This is the lowest premium the insurance companies are willing to accept when selling their insurance policies. Since this is above the price that Type A individuals are willing to pay, no insurance policy will be sold to these individuals. Realizing that all their potential customers are Type B individuals, insurance companies will raise their premiums to be able to cover the higher expected cost of providing coverage to these individuals, which is (0.8 × 5,000) + 200 = $4,200. This is still less than the price that Type B individuals are willing to pay ($5,500), so Type B individuals will be insured.

c. With no government mandate, only Type B individuals will buy health insurance. In the competitive market, the price will be equal to the insurance companies' average cost, $4,200, so there will be no producer surplus. Given Type B individuals' willingness to pay for the insurance policy ($5,500), which shows how they value the insurance, the consumer surplus realized in the market will be ($5,500 − $4,200) × 60 million = $78,000 million or $78 billion.

With the mandate, since everyone buys an insurance policy, the insurance companies' expected cost of coverage is 0.4 × (0.8 × 1,000) + 0.6 × (0.8 × 5,000) + 200 = $2,920 per customer. This is the premium the insurers will charge in the competitive market. Since Type A individuals are willing to pay $1,100 for an insurance policy but will actually have to buy it for $2,920, their loss of consumer surplus will be ($2,920 − $1,100) × 40 million = $72,800 million, or $72.8 billion. Type B individuals, however, are willing to pay $5,500 for an insurance policy but will actually pay only $2,920, so their consumer surplus will be ($5,500 − $2,920) × 60 million = $154,800 million, or $154.8 billion. That is, the total surplus (gains from trade) realized in the market will be −$72.8 billion + $154.8 billion = $82 billion. Thus, the mandate increases gains from trade in the health insurance market from $78 billion to $82 billion.

Problem 7

a. Let's calculate each player's expected payoffs for each option. The hotel's expected profit is (0.75 × $500,000) + (0.25 × $100,000) = $400,000 if the manager works hard and (0.25 × $500,000) + (0.75 × $100,000) = $200,000 if she exerts only modest effort. With the flat salary option, if the manager puts a lot of effort into the job, the hotel's expected payoff is $400,000 − $70,000 = $330,000, while the manager's payoff is $70,000 − $50,000 = $20,000. If the manager does not work hard, the hotel's payoff is $200,000 − $70,000 = $130,000, while the manager's payoff is $70,000 − $25,000 = $45,000.

With the profit-sharing option, if the manager works hard, she earns $30,000 + (0.15 × $400,000) = $90,000. In this case, the hotel's payoff is $400,000 − $90,000 = $310,000, while the manager's payoff is $90,000 − $50,000 = $40,000. If the manager works with modest effort, her compensation is $30,000 + (0.15 × $200,000) = $60,000. Thus, the hotel's payoff will be $200,000 − $60,000 = $140,000, while the manager's payoff will be $60,000 − $25,000 = $35,000. The following game tree shows each player's payoffs (in thousands of dollars) associated with each of the two options.

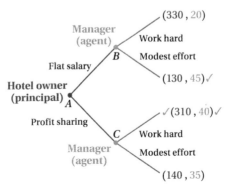

b. We can find the equilibrium, using backward induction. Suppose the hotel owner chooses the flat salary option. This takes the game to node B, where the manager decides whether to work hard or put only modest effort into the job. Since the manager's payoff from choosing modest effort is greater $(45 > 20)$, she will choose not to work hard. Now suppose the hotel owner chooses to offer the profit-sharing plan. This takes us to node C, where the manager makes her decision. Here, since the manager's expected payoff is greater when she works hard $(40 > 35)$, she will prefer this choice. Now we can figure out the hotel owner's choice in the first stage. If he chooses the flat salary option, the manager will not work hard and the hotel's expected payoff will be $130,000. But if the hotel owner chooses to link the manager's pay to the hotel's profit, the manager will work hard and the hotel's expected payoff will be $310,000. Therefore, the hotel owner's preferred option is the compensation structure linked to the hotel's profit. Thus, the equilibrium of this principal–agent game is where the hotel owner offers the manager the profit-sharing compensation plan and the manager works hard.

Problem 8

For a hard worker, the cost of completing college is

$$C_H = \$25,000 \times 4 = \$100,000$$

and for a slacker, it is

$$C_S = \$35,000 \times 6 = \$210,000$$

Employers will be able to separate the two categories of workers if they offer a wage premium that is higher than a hard worker's cost of completing college but lower than a slacker's cost of college. If firms offer $300,000 to job applicants without a college degree and $450,000 to those with a college degree, the wage premium paid to an applicant with higher education will be $150,000. Then, the net benefit of completing college for a hard worker will be

$$NB_H = \$150,000 - \$100,000 = \$50,000$$

and for a slacker, it will be

$$NB_S = \$150,000 - \$210,000 = -\$60,000$$

This means hard workers are $50,000 better off if they finish college, and so they will. And slackers are worse off (since their net benefit of completing college is negative), so they won't go to college. As a result, all job applicants with a college degree will be hard workers, and all those without higher education will be slackers. That is, firms will be able to hire a hard worker for $450,000 and a slacker for $300,000.

Problem 9

For a hard worker, the cost of completing college is still

$$C_H = \$25,000 \times 4 = \$100,000$$

but for a slacker, it is now

$$C_S = \$28,000 \times 5 = \$140,000$$

If firms offer $300,000 to job applicants without a college degree and $450,000 to those with a college degree (the lowest wage a hard worker is willing to accept), the wage premium paid to an applicant with higher education is $150,000. Then, the net benefit of completing college for a hard worker is still

$$NB_H = \$150,000 - \$100,000 = \$50,000$$

but for a slacker, it is now

$$NB_S = \$150,000 - \$140,000 = \$10,000$$

This means both hard workers and slackers are better off if they finish college, and so they will. Therefore, there will be both hard workers and slackers among job applicants with a college degree, and employers won't be able to separate them. In this situation, as firms expect half of the job applicants to be slackers and the other half to be hard workers, the wage that they are willing to offer is $0.5 \times \$450,000 + 0.5 \times \$300,000 = \$375,000$. But since hard workers won't accept a wage below $450,000, only slackers will apply for a job. As employers realize that, they will lower the wage they offer to $300,000 (given the value a slacker produces for them). In this situation, neither hard workers nor slackers benefit from going to college. Thus, grade inflation actually hurts students, since it makes a college degree useless as a signal of a job applicant's productivity.

Problem 10

a. Principal–agent relationships occur when one party (the principal) hires another (the agent) to perform some task, and the principal has an asymmetric information problem because he cannot fully observe the agent's actions. So, clearly, Mr. Fairfield is the principal and his lawyer is the agent.

To draw the game tree, we first calculate each player's expected payoffs for each option. With the flat fee, if the lawyer hires a detective, Mrs. Fairfield's infidelity will be proved, so Mr. Fairfield's payoff will be $2,000,000 – $100,000 = $1,900,000. And the lawyer's payoff will be $100,000 – $30,000 = $70,000. If, however, the lawyer does not hire a detective and there is only a 10% chance that Mrs. Fairfield's adultery will be proved, the expected settlement is $0.1 \times \$2,000,000 + 0.9 \times \$1,000,000 = \$1,100,000$. Then, Mr. Fairfield's payoff will be $1,100,000 – $100,000 = $1,000,000, and the lawyer's payoff will be $100,000.

If Mr. Fairfield chooses the 10% of the settlement option, and the lawyer hires a detective, Mr. Fairfield's payoff will be $2,000,000 – 0.1 \times \$2,000,000 = 0.9 \times \$2,000,000 = \$1,800,000$. And the lawyer's payoff will be $0.1 \times \$2,000,000 - \$30,000 = \$170,000$. If the lawyer does not hire a detective, Mr. Fairfield's payoff will be $0.9 \times \$1,100,000 = \$990,000$, while the lawyer's payoff will be $0.1 \times \$1,100,000 = \$110,000$. The following game tree shows each player's payoffs (in thousands of dollars) associated with each of the two options.

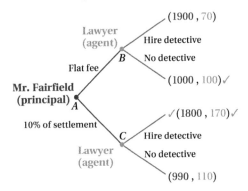

b. We find the equilibrium using backward induction. Suppose Mr. Fairfield chooses the flat fee option. This takes the game to node B, where the lawyer decides whether to hire a detective. Since the lawyer's payoff is greater when he does not hire a detective ($100 > 70$), he will choose not to hire a detective. Now suppose Mr. Fairfield chooses the 10% of the settlement option. This takes us to node C, where the lawyer makes his decision. Here, since the lawyer's expected payoff is greater when he hires a detective ($170 > 110$), he will decide to hire a detective. Now we can figure out Mr. Fairfield's choice in the first stage. If he chooses the flat fee option, the lawyer will not hire a detective and Fairfield's expected payoff will be $1,000,000. But if Fairfield chooses the 10% of the settlement option, the lawyer will hire a detective, and Fairfield's expected payoff will be $1,800,000. Therefore, Fairfield's preferred option is to pay the lawyer 10% of the settlement. Thus, the equilibrium of this principal–agent game is where Mr. Fairfield pays the lawyer 10% of the settlement, the lawyer hires a private detective to prove Mrs. Fairfield's adultery, and Mr. Fairfield receives a payoff of $1.8 million.

Externalities and Public Goods | 16

Solutions for Practice Problems

Problem 1

a. The neighborhood watch program is efficient to implement if the benefits from it exceed its cost. Since the program is a non-rival good, its total marginal benefit equals the sum of the marginal benefits received by each of the ten households, which are reflected by each household's willingness to pay for the program. That is,

$$MB_T = \$300 + \$450 + \$200 + \$350 + \$400 + \$425 + \$340 + \$270 + \$340 + \$285 = \$3{,}360$$

Since the total marginal benefit exceeds the cost of the program ($3,360 > $3,300), it is efficient for the community to implement the program.

b. Each household's willingness to pay is far below the cost of the program. Therefore, none of the households will implement the program privately.

c. If the cost of the program is split evenly among the homeowners, each will have to pay $\dfrac{\$3{,}300}{10} = \$330$.

Six homeowners out of 10 (Betty, Don, Elliot, Frank, George, and Ivan) are willing to pay more than that. Thus, the program will pass by majority vote.

Problem 2

a. The socially optimal outcome will be for the farm to use the alternative production process. Because the resort loses $20,000 per year as a result of the pollution, it will require that the farm pays the resort at least this amount if it continues to pollute the river. Since altering the production process will cost the farm less ($18,000 < $20,000), the farm will have the incentive to use the alternative technology than to purchase the right to pollute the river from the resort.

b. The socially optimal outcome still is for the farm to use the alternative production process. Since the resort loses $20,000 per year as a result of the pollution, it will be willing to pay the farm up to $20,000 per year to reduce the pollution to a level that does not affect the resort's profit. The lowest amount the farm is willing to accept from the resort to reduce the pollution is $18,000, since this is what it costs the farm to switch to the alternative production process. Thus, the resort will pay the farm between $18,000 and $20,000, and the farm will use the alternative production process to reduce the pollution.

Problem 3

a. In an unregulated competitive market, individuals don't take into account external benefits of education when deciding whether to pursue a college degree. Therefore, the market equilibrium is at the point where the private marginal benefit of higher education, which is represented by the (inverse) demand curve, equals the marginal cost of producing a college degree, which is represented by the (inverse) supply curve. Thus, we can find the market equilibrium price by setting $Q^S = Q^D$ and solving this equation for P:

$$Q^S = Q^D$$
$$-25 + 0.5P = 45 - 0.5P$$
$$P = 70$$

Now we can find the equilibrium quantity by substituting $P = 70$ into either the demand or the supply equation:

$$Q^D = 45 - (0.5 \times 70) = 10$$
$$Q^S = -25 + (0.5 \times 70) = 10$$

Thus, the market equilibrium price is $70,000 per college degree, and the equilibrium quantity is 10 million college graduates per year.

b. The socially optimal level of output is where the social marginal benefit of higher education equals the marginal cost of producing it. The social marginal benefit (SMB) equals the sum of the private marginal benefit (MC_P) and the external marginal benefit (EMB). The private marginal benefit received by individuals is reflected by the price they are willing to pay, so the inverse demand curve is also the marginal benefit curve. To derive this curve, we solve the demand equation for P:

$$Q^D = 45 - 0.5P$$
$$0.5P = 45 - Q$$
$$P^D = 90 - 2Q$$
$$MB_P = 90 - 2Q$$

Since $SMB = MB_P + EMB$, we can calculate the SMB of a college degree as follows:

$$SMB = 90 - 2Q + 20$$
$$SMB = 110 - 2Q$$

The marginal cost of producing a college degree is represented by the inverse supply curve, which can be derived by solving the supply equation for P:

$$Q^S = -25 + 0.5P$$
$$0.5P = 25 + Q$$
$$P^S = 50 + 2Q$$
$$MC = 50 + 2Q$$

Now we can solve for the socially optimal number of college degrees by setting $SMB = MC$:

$$110 - 2Q = 50 + 2Q$$
$$-4Q = -60$$
$$4Q = 60$$
$$Q = 15$$

Thus, the socially optimal number of college graduates is 15 million per year. And at this socially optimal level of output. $SMB = 110 - (2 \times 15) = \$80,000$, which is the same as $MC = 50 + (2 \times 15) = \$80,000$. The diagram on the right illustrates this solution.

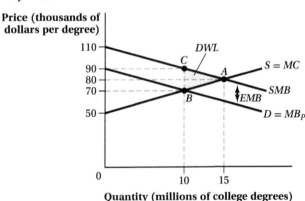

c. The deadweight loss arises because individuals decide whether to obtain a college degree without taking into account external benefits of higher education, so fewer people complete college than it is socially optimal. At the socially optimal level of output (point A on the preceding diagram), the marginal benefit of higher education to society, including the external benefits, equals the marginal cost of producing a college degree. The unregulated market produces at point B, however, and the college degrees between points B and A are valued by society higher than they would cost to produce. Therefore, the deadweight loss is the triangular area below the social marginal benefit curve (SMB) and above the supply (marginal cost) curve ($S = MC$), between the level of output produced by the market (10 million) and the socially optimal level of output (15 million tons). This triangle is the sum of the losses from not producing each college degree for which society's benefits would be greater than its costs. When 10 million college degrees are produced, the social marginal benefit is $SMB = 110 - 2 \times 10 = \$90,000$ (point C), and the marginal cost is $MC = 50 + (2 \times 10) = \$70,000$ (point B). Thus, the deadweight loss in the unregulated market for higher education is the area of a triangle whose base is $\$90,000 - \$70,000 = \$20,000$ and whose height is 15 million - 10 million = 5 million, so we can calculate this area as

$$DWL = 0.5 \times \$20,000 \times 5 \text{ million} = \$50,000 \text{ million, or } \$50 \text{ billion.}$$

Problem 4

a. See the following graph. The subsidy increases the private marginal benefit of a college degree, that is, it shifts the private marginal benefit curve (MB_P) up by the amount of the subsidy ($Sub = 20$). That is, the inverse demand curve with the subsidy is

$$P^D_{Sub} = MB_P + Sub$$
$$P^D_{Sub} = (90 - 2Q) + 20$$
$$P^D_{Sub} = 110 - 2Q$$

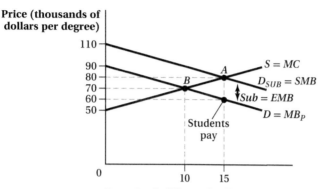

We can solve for the market equilibrium quantity by equating this inverse demand curve and the inverse supply (marginal cost) curve derived in Problem 3:

$$P^D_{Sub} = P^S$$
$$110 - 2Q = 50 + 2Q$$
$$-4Q = -60$$
$$4Q = 60$$
$$Q = 15$$

That is, 15 million college degrees are produced. Now we can find the equilibrium price of a college degree by substituting $Q = 15$ into either the demand or the supply equation:

$$P^D_{Sub} = 110 - 2 \times 15 = 80$$
$$P^S = 50 + 2 \times 15 = 80$$

Thus, the market equilibrium price is $80,000 per college degree. However, since the subsidy pays $20,000 to each student who completes college, a student pays only $80,000 - $20,000 = $60,000 to obtain a college degree.

b. Because the subsidy equals the external marginal benefit of a college degree, the demand curve for higher education is the same as the social marginal benefit curve (SMB):

$$D_{SUB} = MB_P + Sub = SMB$$

Therefore, with the subsidy, when the market is in equilibrium, the social marginal benefit of higher education equals its marginal cost. This means the efficient level of output is achieved, so there is no deadweight loss.

Problem 5

a. In an unregulated perfectly competitive market, firms choose their optimal level of output at the point where the price that consumers are willing to pay (as reflected by the demand curve) equals the firms' private marginal cost (as reflected by the supply curve). Thus, we can find the market equilibrium price by setting $Q^S = Q^D$ and solving this equation for P:

$$Q^S = Q^D$$
$$-100 + 100P = 200 - 25P$$
$$125P = 300$$
$$P = 2.4$$

Now we can find the equilibrium quantity of gasoline by substituting $P = 2.4$ into either the demand or the supply equation:

$$Q^D = 200 - (25 \times 2.4) = 140$$
$$Q^S = -100 + (100 \times 2.4) = 140$$

Thus, the market equilibrium price of gasoline is $2.40 per gallon, and the equilibrium quantity is 140 billion gallons per year.

b. The socially optimal level of output is where consumers' marginal benefit equals social marginal cost. The marginal benefit received by consumers is reflected by the price they are willing to pay, so the inverse demand curve—which shows the prices that consumers are willing to pay at each given level of output—is also the marginal benefit curve. To derive this curve, we solve the demand equation for P:

$$Q^D = 200 - 25P$$
$$25P = 200 - Q$$
$$P^D = 8 - 0.04Q$$
$$MB = 8 - 0.04Q$$

The social marginal cost of gasoline (SMC) equals the sum of the industry's private marginal cost (MC_I) and the external marginal cost (EMC). The industry's marginal cost is represented by its inverse supply curve, which can be derived by solving the supply equation for P:

$$Q^S = -100 + 100P$$
$$100 + Q = 100P$$
$$100P = 100 + Q$$
$$P^S = 1 + 0.01Q$$
$$MC_I = 1 + 0.01Q$$

Since $SMC = MC_I + EMC$, we can calculate the SMC of gasoline as follows:

$$SMC = 1 + 0.01Q + 0.01Q$$
$$SMC = 1 + 0.02Q$$

Now we can solve for the socially optimal output of gasoline by setting $MB = SMC$:

$$8 - 0.04Q = 1 + 0.02Q$$
$$-0.06Q = -7$$
$$0.06Q = 7$$
$$Q = 116.7$$

Substituting $Q = 116.7$ into either the SMC or the MB equation, we find the socially optimal price of gasoline:

$$SMC = 1 + (0.02 \times 116.7) = 3.33$$
$$MB = 8 - 0.04 \times 116.7 = 3.33$$

Thus, the socially optimal output of gasoline production is 116.7 billion gallons per year, and the socially optimal price is $3.33 per gallon. The following diagram illustrates this solution.

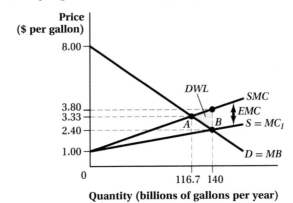

Quantity (billions of gallons per year)

c. The deadweight loss arises because the unregulated market does not take the external costs of gasoline into account. Therefore, it produces more gasoline than the efficient level of output. At the socially optimal level of output (point A on the preceding diagram), every buyer of gasoline values it at least as much as it costs society, including the external costs. The industry produces at point B, however, and the portion of the demand curve between points A and B represents buyers who value gasoline less than it costs society. If the price reflected the true cost of gasoline, the output between 116.7 billion gallons and 140 billion gallons would not be bought. Therefore, the deadweight loss is the triangular area below the social marginal cost curve (SMC) and above the demand (marginal benefit) curve ($D = MB$), between the socially optimal level of output (116.7 billion gallons) and the market equilibrium output (140 billion gallons). Since at $Q = 140$, $SMC = 1 + (0.02 \times 140) = 3.80$, we can calculate the deadweight loss as the area of a triangle whose base is $\$3.80 - \$2.40 = \$1.40$ and whose height is 140 billion − 116.7 billion = 23.3 billion. Thus:

$$DWL = 0.5 \times \$1.40 \times 23.3 \text{ billion} = \$16.3 \text{ billion}$$

Problem 6

a. See the following graph. The tax increases the private marginal cost of gasoline; that is, it shifts the industry's private marginal cost curve (MC_I) up by the amount of the per gallon tax ($T = \$0.50$). That is, the industry's inverse supply curve with the tax is

$$P^{ST} = MC_I + T$$
$$P^{ST} = 1 + 0.01Q + 0.5$$
$$P^{ST} = 1.5 + 0.01Q$$

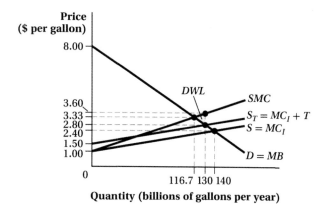

We can solve for the market equilibrium quantity by equating this inverse supply curve and the inverse demand curve derived in Problem 5:

$$P^{ST} = P^D$$
$$1.5 + 0.01Q = 8 - 0.04Q$$
$$0.05Q = 6.5$$
$$Q = 130$$

Now we can find the equilibrium price by substituting $Q = 130$ into either the demand or the supply equation:

$$P^D = 8 - (0.04 \times 130) = 2.80$$
$$P^{ST} = 1.5 + 0.01 \times 130 = 2.80$$

Thus, with the tax, the market equilibrium price of gasoline is $2.80 per gallon, and the equilibrium quantity of gasoline is 130 billion gallons per year.

b. Although the tax reduces the output of gasoline, it is still above the socially optimal level. Therefore, for the output between 116.7 billion gallons and 130 billion gallons, the value of gasoline to buyers is still below its cost to society. So, the deadweight loss is the triangular area below the social marginal cost curve (SMC) and above the demand (marginal benefit) curve ($D = MB$), between the socially optimal level of output (116.7 billion gallons) and the market equilibrium output (130 billion gallons). Since at $Q = 130$, $SMC = 1 + (0.02 \times 130) = 3.60$, we calculate the deadweight loss as follows:

$$DWL = 0.5 \times (\$3.60 - \$2.80) \times (130 \text{ billion} - 116.7 \text{ billion}) = \$5.3 \text{ billion}$$

Thus, the $0.50 per gallon tax decreases the deadweight loss in the market for gasoline from $16.3 billion to $5.3 billion. The tax, however, is not high enough to completely eliminate the deadweight loss.

Problem 7

a. ABC will have to cut $30 - 15 = 15$ tons of pollution, so its total abatement cost is

$$TAC_A = 15 + (1.5 \times 15^2) = 352.5 \text{ (thousand dollars)}$$

DEF will have to cut $20 - 15 = 5$ tons of pollution, so its cost will be

$$TAC_D = (2 \times 5) + 5^2 = 35 \text{ (thousand dollars)}$$

Thus, the total cost of reducing the pollution to its optimal level will be

$$\$352,500 + \$35,000 = \$387,500$$

b. The firms will trade the permits until their marginal abatement costs are equalized, that is,

$$MAC_A = MAC_D$$
$$1 + 3e_A = 2 + 2e_D$$

We also know that, since the number of permits is 300, the industry must reduce the pollution by $(30 + 20) - (300 \times 0.1) = 20$ tons. That is,

$$e_A + e_D = 20$$

from which

$$e_D = 20 - e_A$$

We can substitute this expression into the marginal abatement cost equality condition and solve it for e_A:

$$1 + 3e_A = 2 + 2(20 - e_A)$$
$$1 + 3e_A = 2 + 40 - 2e_A$$
$$5e_A = 41$$
$$e_A = 8.2$$

This means

$$e_D = 20 - 8.2 = 11.8$$

That is, ABC will emit $30 - 8.2 = 21.8$ tons of pollution, and DEF will emit $20 - 11.8 = 8.2$ tons.

When the market for tradable permits is in equilibrium, the price of the permission to release a ton of pollution is equal to each firm's marginal cost of abatement:

$$P_{per} = MAC_A = MAC_D$$
$$P_{per} = 1 + 3e_A = 1 + (3 \times 8.2) = 25.6$$
$$P_{per} = 2 + 2e_B = 2 + (2 \times 11.8) = 25.6$$

So, the price of a permit to release 0.1 tons of pollution will be $2,560.

Since ABC has to cut 8.2 tons of pollution, its total abatement cost is

$$TAC_A = 8.2 + (1.5 \times 8.2^2) = 109.06 \text{ (thousand dollars)}$$

And since DEF must cut 11.8 tons of pollution, its total abatement cost is

$$TAC_D = (2 \times 11.8) + 11.8^2 = 162.84 \text{ (thousand dollars)}$$

Thus, the total cost of reducing the pollution to its optimal level is $109,060 + $162,840 = $271,900, which is $115,600 less than the abatement cost of the quantity regulation in part (a).

Problem 8

a. If the resort owns the lake, it charges the pulp mill the cost of the pollution, so it becomes part of the mill's private marginal cost. That is, the private marginal cost of producing pulp is

$$MC_P = MC + EMC$$
$$MC_P = 4 + 0.6Q + 0.4Q$$
$$MC_P = 4 + Q$$

In a perfectly competitive market, this is also the pulp mill's inverse supply curve. Therefore, we can solve for the equilibrium quantity of pulp by equating this inverse supply curve with the inverse demand (MB) curve:

$$MC_P = MB$$
$$4 + Q = 40 - Q$$
$$2Q = 36$$
$$Q = 18$$

Thus, 18 tons of pulp per week will be produced, and the resort will charge the mill $0.4 \times 18 = 7.20$ dollars per ton or $\$7.20 \times 18 = \$129.60$ per week for polluting the lake.

Since the transacting parties take the external costs of producing pulp (i.e., the cost of the pollution to the resort) into account, in equilibrium, the social marginal cost of producing pulp equals the marginal benefit. Therefore, the market outcome is socially optimal.

b. Since the pollution reduces the market value of the lake, the rent that the resort is willing to pay is lower than it would pay if the lake were pollution free. The rent is reduced by the amount of $EMC = 0.4Q$ per ton of pulp produced. This is the pulp mill's opportunity cost of polluting the lake, that is, it is essentially an increase in the mill's private marginal cost. Therefore, the mill's private marginal cost is, again,

$$MC_P = MC + EMC$$
$$MC_P = 4 + Q$$

Thus, the equilibrium quantity of pulp produced will be the same as in (a), 18 tons per week. But the cost of pollution is now borne by the mill in the form of a lower rent paid for the lake it owns. The rent is reduced by $0.4 \times 18 = 7.20$ dollars per ton of pulp produced, or by $\$7.20 \times 18 = \$129.60$ per week. That is, instead of $\$800$ that the mill would receive for its lake if it were pollution free, it receives only $\$800 - \$129.60 = \$670.40$ per week.

Again, since the transacting parties take the external costs of producing pulp into account, the market equilibrium occurs where the social marginal cost of producing pulp equals the marginal benefit. Therefore, the market outcome is socially optimal.

Problem 9

a. The socially optimal length of the fireworks is the one for which the households' marginal benefit equals the marginal cost of the show. Since a fireworks display is a nonrival good, the total marginal benefit curve is the vertical sum of the individual marginal benefit curves. And since the households have the same MB curves, we can find the total marginal benefit curve simply by multiplying the individual MB curve by four:

$$MB_T = 4 \times MB = 4(100 - 2Q)$$
$$MB_T = 400 - 8Q$$

Now we can find the equilibrium length of the fireworks show by setting $MB_T = MC$ and solving this equation for Q:

$$MB_T = MC$$
$$400 - 8Q = 60 + 0.5Q$$
$$-8.5Q = -340$$
$$8.5Q = 340$$
$$Q = 40$$

Thus, the socially optimal length of the fireworks show is 40 minutes.

b. If each household put on its own fireworks display, it would choose the length of the show for which the household's individual marginal benefit equals the marginal cost. So we can find the equilibrium length of the show by setting $MB = MC$ and solving this equation for Q:

$$MB = MC$$
$$100 - 2Q = 60 + 0.5Q$$
$$2.5Q = 40$$
$$Q = 16$$

Thus, each household would put on a fireworks display for 16 minutes, which is much shorter than the socially optimal length of the show.

Problem 10

a. The payoff matrix for the game follows. The payoffs are each farmer's revenues (in dollars) from selling milk. If each farmer keeps 1 cow on the common pasture, each gets a revenue of $2 × 2,500 = $5,000. If one of the farmers keeps 1 cow while the other keeps 2 cows, there are 3 cows in the pasture, each producing 1,900 gallons of milk. Therefore, the farmer who keeps 1 cow gets $2 × 1,900 = $3,800, and the one who keeps 2 cows gets $3,800 × 2 = $7,600. Finally, if each farmer grazes 2 cows, there are 4 cows on the pasture, each giving 1,000 gallons of milk, so each farmer gets $2 × 1,000 × 2 = $4,000.

Brandon

		1 cow	2 cows
	1 cow	5000 , 5000	3800 , 7600✓
Albert	2 cows	✓7600 , 3800	✓4000 , 4000✓

First, let's consider Albert's choices given each Brandon's action. As we can see from the payoff matrix, if Brandon chooses to graze 1 cow, Albert's preferred choice is to graze 2 cows (since $7,600 > $5,000). If Brandon chooses to graze 2 cows, Albert's preferred option is, again, to graze 2 cows (since $4,000 > $3,800). Now, let's consider Brandon's choices given each Albert's action. If Albert chooses to graze 1 cow, Brandon's preferred choice is 2 cows (as $7,600 > $5,000). And if Albert grazes 2 cows, Brandon's preferred option is, again, to graze 2 cows (as $4,000 > $3,800). The box in the payoff matrix in which two check marks appear indicates that the Nash equilibrium occurs where each farmer chooses to keep 2 cows in the common pasture. Since this is the only Nash equilibrium in this game, it is the predicted outcome of the game. That is, when both farmers act rationally to maximize their revenues, each will keep 2 cows in the common pasture.

b. The optimal number of cows is the one that maximizes the farmers' joint revenue from the pasture. As we can see from the calculations in (a), with 2 cows kept in the pasture, the farmers' total revenue is $5,000 × 2 = $10,000, with 3 cows it rises to $3,800 × 3 = $11,400, and with 4 cows it falls to $2,000 × 4 = $8,000. Thus, the optimal number of cows to keep on the pasture is 3.

Behavioral and Experimental Economics   17

Solutions for Practice Problems

Problem 1

BDigit's customers fall prey to anchoring, a type of framing bias in which a person's decision is influenced by specific pieces of information that are given. By anchoring in the consumer's mind the idea that the good is worth the "regular" price, BDigit makes its price look like a bargain, even though this "50% off" price is what the camera is normally sold for.

Problem 2

Antonio has fallen victim to the sunk cost fallacy. The money he has paid for the ticket is already spent and cannot be recovered. That is, Antonio cannot get his money's worth, no matter whether he stays or leaves. The $40 he has spent is a sunk cost, and therefore it should not affect his decision. Note, however, that the sunk cost fallacy illustrated in this problem is very common. Studies show that people, companies, and even governments often fail to ignore sunk costs, even though they rationally should ignore them.

Problem 3

a. The expected payoffs of two plans are identical. In either case, a sales person receives a $1,000 bonus if she increases her sales by 15% or more and does not receive it otherwise. Therefore, if the sales people are completely rational, the two plans will motivate them equally.
b. The endowment effect occurs when the perceived loss a person suffers when giving up something he already has is greater than the perceived gain from acquiring that same thing. Thus, sales people influenced by the endowment effect will exert more effort not to lose the bonus they already have than they will exert to get the bonus they are yet to earn. Therefore, Plan A is likely to motivate them more effectively.

Problem 4

a. If Yolanda is a rational consumer, she should choose the pay per visit option. If Yolanda attended the gym three times a week, paying per visit would cost her $5 \times 3 \times 52$ (weeks) = $780 for the year, which is more than $700 that she must pay up-front for the annual gym membership. However, judging by her experience last year, it is hard to believe that Yolanda will stick to her resolution this year. Even if she attends the gym three times a week for the first five weeks and two times a week for the rest of the year, paying per visit will cost her only $545 ($5 \times 3 \times 5 + $5 \times 2 \times 47 = $545). Thus, she will be better off paying per visit. (To be exact, we should compare the membership fee paid up front with the present value of the per visit payments made over the course of the year, which is less than the same amount paid up-front. This makes the argument for choosing the pay per visit option even more convincing.)
b. The behavioral bias that Yolanda is likely to fall victim to is known as overconfidence. She overconfidently believes that she will be using the gym heavily, so she is willing to make a big up-front membership fee even though she would have been better off paying per visit because of how infrequently she is likely to end up going to the gym. As a result, Yolanda's annual membership contract extracts more revenue for the gym than charging her per visit would. According to behavioral economics research, this strategy is typical in the health club business.

Problem 5

a. If the managers are rational, they should discontinue the project. The $15 billion already invested is a sunk cost that should not affect the company's decision, since the company incurs that cost whether or not it continues the project. Rational decision makers think at the margin and only consider opportunity costs. Thus, what matters here is that the additional costs of completing the project

($40 billion − $15 billion = $25 billion) exceed the expected revenue from launching the new aircraft ($23 billion). That is, the company will lose $15 billion anyway, but this is all it will lose if it stops the project, while if it continues developing the aircraft, it will lose $2 billion more (i.e., it will lose $40 billion − $23 billion = $17 billion).

b. The managers are falling prey to the sunk cost fallacy; that is, they allow sunk costs to influence their decision. Again, no matter how much the company has already invested, this money has already been spent and cannot be recovered, so it shouldn't be a factor in the managers' decision.

Problem 6

a. As a rational consumer, Alex would compare the present value of the quarterly payments with the amount paid up-front. Given the interest rate that Alex would earn from his best alternative use of money ($r = 0.025$), the present discounted value of the quarterly payments is

$$PDV = \frac{\$1,000}{1 + 0.025} + \frac{\$1,000}{(1 + 0.025)^2} + \frac{\$1,000}{(1 + 0.025)^3} = \$2,856.02$$

Since the present value of the three payments ($2,856) is greater than the amount of the up-front payment ($2,500), Alex should pay for the TV up-front.

b. The behavioral bias that Alex could fall victim to is known as hyperbolic discounting. It is the tendency of people to place much greater importance on the immediate present than even the near future when making economic decisions. If Alex is a hyperbolic discounter, he really wants things now. Therefore, he will opt for the installment plan because it allows him to have the TV and keep more of his money today, so he can buy other things that he also wants now. The seller's advantage then would be the additional $356 (in present value terms, assuming that the seller's discount rate is also 2.5%) that it receives for the TV if Alex chooses the quarterly payment plan.

Problem 7

a. If Larry is a rational consumer, he should sell his ticket. As a rational decision maker, he would consider his opportunity costs. Larry's willingness to pay $60 for the ticket means that he values it at $60. This is his opportunity cost of selling the ticket. If Larry sells his ticket for $90, his benefit will exceed this cost ($90 > $60), so Larry will be better off by $30.

b. Larry could be falling victim to a combination of behavioral biases. First, he cannot really take advantage of the "good deal" he got when purchasing the ticket. The $40 he paid for it is already spent, no matter whether or not Larry attends the game. That is, it is a sunk cost and therefore should not influence Larry's decision. Second, Larry could be influenced by the endowment effect; that is, the fact that he possesses the ticket could make him more reluctant to sell it because his perceived value of the ticket has increased after his taking ownership of it. Finally, the anchoring bias could enter the picture. When Larry sees the tickets selling for $90, he might view this price as the "true value" of attending the game and be even more inclined to keep it for a price as low as $40.

Problem 8

To your hyperbolic discounting customers, the present discounted value of the three monthly payments is

$$PDV = \frac{\$20}{1 + 0.25} + \frac{\$20}{(1 + 0.1)^2} + \frac{\$20}{(1 + 0.05)^3} = \$49.81$$

Since this is less than $51, they will choose the three payments option. Your present value of the three payments is

$$PDV = \frac{\$20}{1 + 0.005} + \frac{\$20}{(1 + 0.005)^2} + \frac{\$20}{(1 + 0.005)^3} = \$59.41$$

Thus, by offering this payment plan to hyperbolic discounters, you increase the present value of your revenue by $59.41 − $49.81 = $9.60 per video game sold.

Problem 9

a. David falls prey to both the loss aversion bias and the sunk cost fallacy. As a loss averse person, David has a reference point, the price he paid for his house, that is of special significance to him. If David sells his house below this price, his perceived loss would hurt him more than it would hurt a rational homeowner. In addition, David chooses this reference point incorrectly due to his sunk cost fallacy. The price he paid for the house is a sunk cost and therefore is irrelevant to the price for which he should sell it. What matters is how the price offered by a buyer compares to the value that David places on his house ($200,000). If David sells the house for any price above $200,000, he will receive a seller surplus.

b. Laura's statement is false. Like David, she falls victim to the sunk cost fallacy. Thinking rationally, if David had sold his house for $230,000, he would have received a seller surplus of $230,000 − $200,000 = $30,000. (For the sake of simplicity, we ignore the transaction costs (which are likely to be much less than $30,000). We also ignore David's carrying costs of the house if it stays on the market. Accounting for these costs would make David's gain from selling the house even greater.)

Problem 10

First, the behavioral anomalies do not invalidate the economic models you've learned. They only show that some people, under certain circumstances, act in a way that the basic models might miss. Those basic models still accurately describe how the economic world works most of the time.

Second, in many cases when behavioral economics seems to give a different answer, simple adjustments to the basic economic model provide good alternative explanations. For example, a conventional economic model has been developed to explain the seemingly irrational behavior of individuals addicted to things that are bad for them, such as smoking of cigarettes.

Third, people and firms that have systematic behavioral biases tend to lose out to people in the marketplace who are rational. Markets can weed out systematic biases, and economic actors that participate repeatedly in markets often recognize and adjust for their behavioral biases or just exit the marketplace.